THE INDUSTRIAL REVOLUTION IN THE EIGHTEENTH CENTURY

PAUL MANTOUX

THE INDUSTRIAL REVOLUTION IN THE EIGHTEENTH CENTURY

an outline of the beginnings of the modern factory system in England

PREFACE BY T. S. ASHTON

HARPER TORCHBOOKS
The Academy Library

HARPER & ROW PUBLISHERS
New York and Evanston

THE INDUSTRIAL REVOLUTION IN THE
EIGHTEENTH CENTURY

Revised edition, reset, 1961
© 1961 by Jonathan Cape Ltd.

Printed in the United States of America

The first edition of this book was translated from the French by
Marjorie Vernon and published in Great Britain in 1928. The
revised edition was published in 1961 by Jonathan Cape Ltd.,
London, and The Macmillan Company, New York, and is here
reprinted by arrangement.

First HARPER TORCHBOOK edition published 1962 by Harper & Row,
Publishers, Incorporated, New York and Evanston.

CONTENTS

PREFACE BY PROFESSOR T. S. ASHTON   19

PUBLISHER'S NOTE   22

AUTHOR'S PREFACE TO THE SECOND EDITION   23

Introduction

I   The modern factory system: its present characteristics and its economic and social consequences   25

II   The need for and the difficulty of a definition. Large-scale industry in the seventeenth century: how it differed from the modern factory system   28

III   Industrial capitalism before the factory system. The English cloth merchants of the Renaissance. Steps taken to protect the small producers   33

IV   The 'manufacture': centralization and division of labour. Distinction between 'manufacture' and the factory system: machine industry. Why this term cannot be substituted for factory system   35

V   The correlative development of exchange and the division of labour: technical improvements are more the cause than the result. The industrial revolution was no accident. The limits of the subject defined   41

Part I   Preparatory Changes

CHAPTER ONE

THE OLD TYPE OF INDUSTRY AND ITS EVOLUTION

I   The woollen trade — type of the old form of industry. Its ancient origin, importance and privileged position. The abundance of the documents dealing with it   47

II   The dispersion of the industry: in England generally,
     according to Daniel Defoe's *Tour through the Whole
     Island of Great Britain* (1724-7); within a district —
     examples of Norfolk, Devonshire and Yorkshire; in a
     locality — the parish of Halifax   49

III Its organization: this varied with the degree of centraliza-
     tion. The domestic system in the West Riding: indepen-
     dence of the master craftsman, alliance of small-scale
     industry with small holdings   56

IV   Part played by commercial capital: its gradual influence
     on industry. The *merchant manufacturers* of the south-west,
     in possession first of the raw material and later of the
     instruments of production. Home work often combined
     with agriculture. Development of capitalist undertakings
     in the wool-combing industry. Small number of manu-
     factures: the manufacturer above all a merchant   62

V   Condition of the industrial classes. The master craftsman;
     his comparative comfort. The workers: their wages fall
     as their independence disappears. The difference in con-
     ditions recalls the successive stages of the economic
     evolution   68

VI   Conflicts between capital and labour. The cleavage be-
     tween the producer and the instruments of production
     creates a separation and an opposition between the
     industrial classes. Permanent combinations of the wool-
     combers and of the weavers in the south-west. Origins
     of trade unionism. Examples from other industries; the
     journeyman tailors, the frame-work knitters, the silk
     weavers and the Newcastle colliers   74

VII Conservative tendencies. Economic legislation: its twofold
     object, regulation and protection. Trade regulations an
     obstacle to technical improvements. Privileges of the
     woollen industry: acts against Irish competition; quarrel
     between the manufacturers and breeders over the export
     of raw wool. Monopoly and objection to change   83

VIII Gradual transformation of the old industry: this was due
     more to economic than to technical causes. Predominance
     of the commercial factor, bound up with the develop-
     ment of trade   89

CHAPTER TWO
COMMERCIAL EXPANSION

I   Interdependence of exchange and production. Commercial expansion often precedes and determines industrial progress   91

II   Outlines of the history of British trade. Maritime expansion under Elizabeth. Navigation Act of 1651. Part played in the 1688 revolution by the middle-class merchants. The foundation of the Bank of England and the final establishment of the East India Company. Colonial conquests and the 'mercantile system'   92

III   Development of foreign trade. Growth of maritime trade; imports and exports from 1700 to 1800. Stimulating influence of export on industry   99

IV   Examples of this influence: the growth of the port of Liverpool began before the industrial development of Lancashire, which it aided, even if it did not actually give rise to it   105

V   Organization of home trade. Fairs, special markets as distributing centres of goods. Middlemen, pedlars, hawkers and town shopkeepers   108

VI   Communications: bad state of the roads. Early efforts to improve them: the turnpikes. Road builders: John Metcalf. In spite of the incompleteness of the new system of roads, communication became easier and more regular. But the dearness of mails and transport still remained an obstacle to trade   112

VII   The creation of canals retarded by the development of the coasting trade. Andrew Yarranton's schemes (1677). The first canals were connected with coal deposits. The Duke of Bridgewater builds the Worsley Canal (1759). James Brindley and his work. The system completed in a few years: the canal fever of 1793. The promoters: great landowners and manufacturers. Wedgwood and the Grand Trunk Canal. The immediate effect on local industries   120

VIII   Results of commercial expansion. Division of labour varies with the size of the market. The author of *Considerations upon the East-India Trade* (1701) anticipates the advent of machinery. The commercial class becomes wealthy: its position in society   132

CHAPTER THREE

THE REDISTRIBUTION OF THE LAND

I   Decline and extinction of the yeomanry: when did they actually begin? 136

II   The Acts of Enclosure in the eighteenth century. The open field and its distribution in small plots. Problem of its origins 141

III   The open-field system: individual ownership and common rules for cultivation 146

IV   Common lands and rights of common. Unequal distribution of such rights. Their customary extension to cottagers and squatters 148

V   The process of enclosure. Redistribution of the open fields and division of the common lands. History of the sixteenth- and seventeenth-century enclosures 151

VI   Agricultural reform. The condition of the country before 1730. Theory and experiments: Jethro Tull. Part played by the nobility: Lord Townshend. The first generation of great farmers: Coke of Holkham; Bakewell and systematic breeding. Arthur Young and the 'Board of Agriculture' 156

VII   The open field an obstacle to improvements: hence the eighteenth-century enclosures. How Acts of Enclosure were made and applied. Their operation favours the interests of great landowners 163

VIII   Economic and social results. Disappearance of common lands; small holdings sold to great landowners after the enclosures; the 'engrossing of farms'. The prosperity of agriculture in the latter part of the eighteenth century stops the extension of pasture land without retaining all the labour employed previously. Arguments for and against the enclosures. Sufferings in the rural population 169

IX   The townward movement begins. Yeomen after selling their land and unemployed labourers ready to leave their villages. Attraction of industry. Connection between the land movement and the industrial revolution 180

Part II Inventions and Factories

CHAPTER ONE

THE BEGINNINGS OF MACHINERY IN THE TEXTILE INDUSTRY

I   Distinction between a machine and a tool, and between the use of machines and an industrial system based on machinery. The knitting frame, the silk-throwing mill. Results of these inventions: capitalist undertakings; the factory of the brothers Lombe (1718). Foreshadowing of the factory system: why it could be only outlined   189

II   The cotton industry in England: its beginnings. The prohibitions of 1700 and 1719 against Indian printed calicoes: success of the new industry in spite of the jealousy of the woollen trade. Advantages offered by Lancashire for the growth of the industry   197

III   The cotton industry before the introduction of machinery. The first inventions entirely of an empirical and practical character. John Kay's fly shuttle (1733). By speeding up weaving it upset the equilibrium between the two complementary operations of the industry, and opened the way for mechanical spinning   204

IV   The first spinning machine. John Wyatt: his invention (1733). His association with Lewis Paul. The patent of 1738. Wyatt and Paul's industrial undertakings: their failure   209

V   Hargreaves's invention of the jenny (1765). His difficulties. But the use of his machine spread rapidly throughout the north of England. Transition from small- to large-scale production   216

CHAPTER TWO

THE FACTORIES

I   Arkwright. His beginnings: doubtful origin of his inventions. The water frame (1768) and the first patent. Arkwright settles at Nottingham (1771)   220

II   Arkwright's success. The Cromford spinning mill: mechanical automatic equipment run by water-wheels.

The cotton industry freed from prohibitions raised against it. The second patent (1775). Arkwright's undertakings become manifold. His competitors. Action for infringement of patent: case brought before Court of King's Bench in 1785 — 223

III The trial of 1785. Evidence of Thomas Highs and John Kay. Highs was probably the real inventor of the water frame. Arkwright accused of other piracies. Cancellation of his patents. His career unaffected: he is knighted (1787); he dies a millionaire (1792). His actual position in industrial history: his gifts as an organizer and businessman — 228

IV Samuel Crompton's mule (1779). How the manufacturers got hold of it and deprived the inventor of his profits. Successive improvements of the mule: its use at the beginning of the nineteenth century. The muslin industry of Bolton, Paisley and Glasgow — 234

V The introduction of spinning machinery again destroys the equilibrium between spinning and weaving. Cartwright's power loom (1785). His unlucky enterprises. The success of his invention retarded by the fall in wages. Minor inventions: printing by machinery, chemical processes for bleaching and dyeing. Complete transformation of the industry — 238

VI Stages in this transformation: 1. Period of the jenny: cottage industry. 2. Period of the water frame. The spinning mills: their situation on rivers, outside the towns. Concentration of the industry round the Pennine range. Great undertakings: their individual character. 3. Intermediary stages: temporary combination of the factory system with the domestic system of manufacture — 246

VII Material consequences. Increase in production. Periodical crises: are they to be attributed solely to over-production? The crisis of 1793, due not to causes affecting solely the cotton industry, but to the surrounding economic conditions — 251

VIII Economic liberty. It is not true to say that the cotton industry grew up without any official protection: frequent appeals to State intervention. Indecisive fiscal policy: the fustian tax affair (1784). The cotton industry freed from regulations of apprenticeship and manufacture: liberty of production — 256

IX Machinery in the woollen trade. Concentration of the industry: detrimental to the eastern and south-western counties. Introduction of machinery into Yorkshire. Cloth merchants turned manufacturers. Alarm amongst the small master manufacturers: but the domestic system disappears only gradually. The worsted industry: invention of the wool-combing machine (1790). Bradford spinning mills. The progress of the woollen trade still behind that of the cotton industry   261

CHAPTER THREE

COAL AND IRON

I Transformation of the metal-working industries parallel to that of the textile trades. The iron industry at the beginning of the eighteenth century. Smallness of the production. Decline of such old centres as Sussex and the Forest of Dean. Subsidiary industries: their relative prosperity; Sheffield cutlery and Birmingham ironmongery. Organization of undertakings: mining companies, ironmasters and small manufacturers. Specialized workshops and an advanced division of labour. But the industry does not develop owing to a lack of raw material   271

II The question of fuel. Smelting with charcoal: the vanishing of the forests results in blast furnaces being shut down. Coal: obstacles to its use. Researches and experiments of Sturtevant, Dudley and Wood. The Darbys: the first Abraham Darby succeeds in smelting ore in a coke furnace (1709?). Vital importance of this invention   280

III Conversion of pig iron into bar iron. Invention of puddling by Cort (1784). Cast steel, Huntsman's invention. The mechanical equipment of the iron industry: hammers, blowing machines, metal lathes   292

IV The great ironworks. The Darbys at Coalbrookdale, Wilkinson at Bersham, Bradley and Broseley. The Welsh ironworks: Crawshay the 'iron king'. The Carron ironworks founded by Roebuck. Samuel Walker's steelworks at Rotherham. All individual enterprises as in the textile industry   299

v   The iron industry in England at the end of the eighteenth century. Svedenstjerna's and Faujas de Saint-Fond's descriptions. The future of the metal industry. Wilkinson's far-sighted views. The first iron bridge (1779); the first iron ship (1787). Interdependence of the development of the metal trades and of machine industry   305

CHAPTER FOUR

THE STEAM ENGINE

Power and motor machinery. Machinery run by water power. Savery's engine (1698) and Newcomen's engine (1705) used to pump water out of mines, and later as aids to hydraulic machinery   311

ii   James Watt. With him, science first makes its appearance in the industrial revolution. His early years: his speculative genius. Origin of his invention: his study of the Newcomen engine. Invention of the condenser: pressure of steam utilized instead of atmospheric pressure. The patent of 1769. Subsidiary inventions: circular motion   318

iii   Industrial application of the invention. Association with Roebuck: it enabled Watt to continue his researches. Bankruptcy of Roebuck (1773): his rights bought up by Matthew Boulton   322

iv   The Soho factory: Boulton's activity and ambition: completion of the steam engine. Extension of the patent. The first orders: for Wilkinson's ironworks (1775); for Cornish mines (1777); for the Paris water supply (1778). Commercial difficulties: debtors and competitors. Industrial difficulties: Watt's collaborators. William Murdock   325

v   The use of the steam engine: for metal works; for mills; the Albion Mills (1786); for spinning mills. Steam in the Soho factory: the automatic coining of money   332

vi   The invention of the steam engine completes industrial centralization. It binds industries more closely together and unifies their evolution   337

Part III The Immediate Consequences

CHAPTER ONE

THE FACTORY SYSTEM AND POPULATION

I Growth of the English population: its slowness before the industrial revolution. Gregory King's forecasts (1696). The fear of depopulation. Discussions on the subject: Richard Price's *Essay on the Population of England* (1780). Young's theory: growth of population necessarily bound up with economic progress. Malthus's book (1798): overpopulation the cause of poverty. The census of 1801   341

II Change in distribution of population. Its present distribution: comparison with that of 1700, 1750 and 1801. Movement towards the north and west   349

III The great industrial towns. Centres of the textile industry. Manchester: its growth during the first half of the eighteenth century: the local census of 1773. Between 1773 and 1801 its population trebles. The new quarters. The spinning towns round Manchester. Slower growth of the woollen towns: Leeds, Halifax. Decay of the southern towns   355

IV The centres of the iron industry. Birmingham and the Black Country. Sheffield. Aspect of the manufacturing towns   362

CHAPTER TWO

INDUSTRIAL CAPITALISM

I The class of great manufacturers. Barrier erected by large-scale industry between employer and employed   365

II Formation of this class. Its diverse origins. Inventors: their commercial incompetence. Merchants and contractors: their unwillingness to undertake the management of the technical side of industry. The first generation of manufacturers partly recruited from the country: the Peels, Radcliffes, Fieldens, Wilkinsons, Darbys and Boultons,

etc. The yeomen, driven from the land by the growth of
large estates, supplied much of the raw material for the
new society which sprang from the industrial revolution   367

III   The qualities needed. The question of capital; organization
of work; factory discipline. The question of markets;
commercial correspondence of a great firm (Soho
factory)   373

IV   The higher type of manufacturer. Matthew Boulton: his
intellectual culture; his relations; his professional
conscience; his leanings to philanthropy; his aristocratic
demeanour. Wedgwood: artistic value of his work; his
scientific researches; his humanitarian and democratic
opinions. The development of the potting industry and
the prosperity of the Potteries due to his efforts. Wedgwood and Boulton both exceptional men: narrow-
mindedness and selfishness of their class   378

V   Consciousness of common interests. Understanding between the great manufacturers and collective action:
against taxation of metal (1784); against the Anglo-
Irish commercial treaty (1785). The General Chamber of
Manufacturers: difference of opinion with regard to
the French Treaty (1786). Solidarity of the employers
against the men: opposition to the maintenance of the
old regulations asked for by the men. Instinctive leaning
towards laissez-faire   388

VI   The manufacturers' position in society. Their local power;
their part in works of public utility. Relations with the
nobility. Wedgwood's friends and patrons. Boulton
received by George III; Catherine II his guest at Soho;
he is invited with Watt to the French Court. The road
to political power: the two Peels, father and son   394

CHAPTER THREE

THE INDUSTRIAL REVOLUTION
AND LABOUR

I   Hostility of the workers to machinery. Riots in Lancashire
in 1779. Troubles in Yorkshire (1796), in the south-
west (1802); the Luddite movement (1811-12).
Applications to Parliament to prohibit the use of
machinery; petitions from the cotton-spinners and
wool-combers. Their rejection   399

II   Labour in the factories. Dislike of the workers for factory work. Employment of women and children. Children's work before the factory system. Poor-law apprentices in the spinning mills; their sufferings: Robert Blincoe. Unhealthiness of the workshops; factory fever. Unrestricted power of the manufacturers   408

III   Conditions of life of the workers: their income. Insufficiency and difficulty of interpretation of statistics: our conclusions can be only approximate. Wages in 1770 and in 1795: general rise, but growing difference between agricultural and industrial wages: attraction of industry. Rise followed by steady fall, due to excessive supply of labour: example of the weavers. Low wages of women and children   418

IV   Conditions of life of the workers: their expenses. Rise in prices caused by the war: the famines of 1795 and 1802. Food of labourers and workmen. Housing: the working-class districts of industrial towns. Chronic deficit in working-class budgets   426

V   Public relief. The Elizabethan Poor Law: alternating slackness and rigour in its application. Influence of philanthropic ideas at the end of the eighteenth century. The Act of Settlement and forced residence: abuses to which this gave rise. Its repeal (1795). Out-relief: Gilbert's Act (1782). Exceptional measures occasioned by public distress and the fear of a popular revolt: the 'Speenhamland Law' (1795). A minimum income guaranteed by parish relief. This causes a further fall in wages and an increase in pauperism   431

CHAPTER FOUR

INTERVENTION AND *LAISSEZ-FAIRE*

I   The modern social problem the outcome of the divorce of capital and labour. Workmen's combinations. Combinations in the textile industry in Glasgow and Lancashire. Their common action. The Society of Cotton Weavers (1799); the Institution of Woollen Workers (1796). Combinations of Sheffield cutlers and of Kent paper-makers. Movement of the agricultural labourers. Fears of the ruling classes. Combination Act of 1799. Heroic

period in the history of trade unions; how they survived persecution   441

II   Appeal to State intervention. The workers ask for the
maintenance of the old industrial legislation. Apprenticeship regulations: their disuse. Complaints of the calico-
printers as to the number of apprentices, and of the
weavers as to the length of apprenticeship. Employers
demand and obtain repeal of regulations (1803-14)   451

III   The legal fixing of wages. Powers of Justices of the Peace
under the Statute of Artificers; special regulations in
certain industries. Idea of a minimum wage guaranteed
by law: Whitbread's Bill rejected by the House of
Commons (1796). Arbitration in the cotton industry
(1800). Opposition of the employers, who succeed in
practically defeating the Act. Further efforts made by
the cotton-weavers to secure a regulation of wages:
their failure and the triumph of *laissez-faire*   456

IV   The humanitarian movement. Its origins entirely outside
the economic movement: moral and religious influences.
Philanthropic manufacturers. David Dale founds New
Lanark (1784): his efforts to improve the conditions of
the workmen and apprentices. Robert Owen improves
and continues Dale's work: his socialism, developed
out of the philanthropy of the employer   464

V   The first Factory Act. Children's work in the spinning
mills. Dr Percival's report (1796). Sir Robert Peel
obtains the passing of the Act of 1802 for the physical and
moral protection of apprentices. Terms of the Act; their
limited practical effects. Their historic importance:
although regarded by Peel himself — a great manufacturer and an advocate of the *laissez-faire* policy — as a
merely exceptional measure without ulterior significance,
the Act of 1802 is the beginning of the social legislation
of the nineteenth century   468

CONCLUSION: General characteristics of the industrial revolution   474

BIBLIOGRAPHY   478

SUPPLEMENT TO THE BIBLIOGRAPHY   507

INDEX   517

MAPS AND CHARTS

PAGE

Centres of the English woollen trade at the beginning of the
eighteenth century   53

Movements of English foreign trade between 1700 and 1800   102

Navigable waterways in the centre and north of England at the
end of the eighteenth century   127

Canals around Birmingham and Manchester   131

Savery's engine (diagram)   314

Newcomen's engine (diagram)   316

Distribution of population in England, in 1700, 1750, 1801 and
1901   350-3

PREFACE TO THE PRESENT EDITION

AUL MANTOUX is one of a long line of French men of letters – the names of Voltaire, Taine and Halévy spring to one's mind – who, in interpreting England to their own countrymen, have also made her more understandable to Englishmen. The very phrase 'industrial revolution' was coined by a French writer in the eighteenth century, and it is fitting that the first comprehensive work on the subject should have come from across the Channel. More than fifty years have passed since M. Mantoux's book saw the light, and more than thirty since the revised edition was published in England. But it is one of those books that age cannot stale, and this new edition, which makes it more accessible to the growing body of students of economic history, is unlikely to be the last.

At the beginning of the century the chief foreign influence on English historical scholarship was from Germany. No doubt it was salutary that something of the system and discipline inculcated at Berlin should have been brought to bear on a subject still young and uncertain of itself. But elaborate classification and metaphysical interpretations have never made much appeal to English minds; and it was a relief to a young student in 1909 or 1910 to be introduced to a work by a French scholar who said that all classifications must be more or less artificial, and was content to 'distinguish certain facts which belong together and which ... give their character to the great periods of economic history'. The industrial revolution was treated simply as a movement arising from a growing division of labour, a widening of markets and the adoption of new devices by ordinary people. Due attention was paid to changes in speculative thought and in the attitude of the State to economic life. But these were minor considerations; and even the growth of individual freedom, on which stress had been laid by some of his predecessors, was considered by M. Mantoux as a consequence rather than a cause of the upsurge of industry and trade. The treatment was at once logical and chronological. Generally the facts were so deployed as to tell their own story. But the author's comments were always apposite, and the presentation was superbly lucid.

There was nothing pontifical about Mantoux. Unlike the Frenchman of English legend, who asserted that the sun revolved round the earth and offered his *parole d'honneur* that this was true, he never asked his readers to take anything on trust. He was well versed in the economic literature, especially the pamphlets, of the eighteenth century, and had made use also of many manuscript sources. Yet he spoke of his work as a *provisional* synthesis. In contrast to the celebrated historian of the siege of Rhodes, he was ready to revise his findings in the light of the discoveries of later investigators — how ready can be seen by comparing the English edition of 1928 with the original version in French. It is this open-mindedness that emboldens one, in paying this brief tribute, to call attention to a few points on which modern scholars have given verdicts differing from his. They are all, let it be said, of secondary importance.

One of the most illuminating chapters is that dealing with the changes in agriculture. There is a myth in England about the yeoman, just as there is — dare one say it? — a myth in France about the peasant. It may be true that outright ownership of small plots of land breeds independence and other manly virtues. But, as M. Mantoux's discussion makes plain, the lament for the 'decline of the yeomanry' was overdone, and the part played by the enclosures exaggerated. Most of the freeholders had left the soil or become leaseholders — generally with larger holdings — before the beginning of what is sometimes unfortunately termed the agrarian revolution. It was otherwise, however, with the squatters and cottagers, and possibly also with the small tenant farmers. The enclosures bore heavily on them. It must be pointed out, however, that historians now take a more favourable view of the work of the parliamentary committees and enclosure commissioners than was common a generation ago: they seem to have been scrupulous about legal, if not always about equitable, claims to the soil.

The account given in this book of the improvements in agricultural techniques could hardly be bettered. All one would add is that Jethro Tull now appears, in some respects, as a reactionary rather than a reformer, and that other names now appear in the list of the pioneers alongside those of Townshend, Coke and Arthur Young. It is realized that only parts of the land were suitable for the new methods of Norfolk husbandry, and that the pace of advance varied greatly between regions. But both the area under cultivation and the output per acre in the country as a whole were enlarged. M. Mantoux's conclusion that the initiative was both self-seeking and beneficial to the community met with some opposition years ago, but is now generally approved.

Several accounts have been given of the innovations in manufacture and transport. But though some of these are more detailed, none has greater clarity than the exposition offered here. It must be said, however, that English writers, supported by fresh evidence, still incline to the view that it was Lewis Paul, and not John Wyatt, who was chiefly responsible for the first advance in mechanical spinning. Doubts have also been expressed about the story of the stratagem employed by Samuel Walker to obtain knowledge of Huntsman's crucible process: it is out of keeping with everything else we know of Walker. Modern scholars would lay more stress on inventions made outside Britain, of which the cotton gin is an outstanding example. And recent investigations into the history of industries about which little was known when M. Mantoux wrote suggest that the part played by scientists, and especially by chemists, was greater than had been imagined. Controlled experiment, as well as discovery by simple trial and error, had much to do with the advance of technology.

Almost everything that can usefully be said of the effects of the inventions on the workers is said in the penultimate chapter of this book. The fuller detail we now have of the water-driven mills leads to the conclusion that the use of pauper child labour was less extensive and declined earlier than had been thought. The ill-treatment of the children was at its worst, not when a rigid discipline was enforced by the employer but when, as often happened, supervision was left to ignorant and callous subordinates: under humane masters like David Dale, Robert Peel and Samuel Greg, factory life was not incompatible with health and, it would appear, some measure of happiness. M. Mantoux's discussion of the subject is judicious; and he rendered a service by destroying the legend, given currency by Michelet, of the 'terrible answer' of Pitt to the manufacturers ('Take the children').

More is now known of the processes by which adult workers were drawn into the factories, and of the inducements, as well as the compulsions, by which their reluctance to work for regular hours under strict supervision was gradually overcome. That the earnings of the factory workers increased while those of the domestic workers declined is generally recognized. As M. Mantoux pointed out, the low wages of hand-loom weavers after 1792 was not due to the power loom (for this came later) but to the excessive number of those who sought to earn a living in their own homes. It is a problem that still exists in many countries today; but it was intensified at this time by circumstances to which insufficient attention has been paid. For centuries spinning had been women's work, weaving men's work. After the introduction of the mule the demand for home-spun yarn declined, and many women put aside their spinning wheels and learnt to work the loom. They were not necessarily themselves worse off for the change (spinning had always been a low-paid occupation) but the effect of their competition with the men was to force down rates of wages of weavers generally. While, therefore, M. Mantoux was right in saying that the fall of earnings was not due to the competition of the power loom, it was due to the introduction of machinery – though in the spinning branch of the industry.

On two other matters of fact some restatement is called for. The account given of the Poor Law is admirable, but it is not true that the Speenhamland system was applied to the whole of England. It was a remedy for agrarian distress, and — for good or ill — there was little trace of it in the industrial north. Again, all that M. Mantoux says of the Combination Act of 1799 is true. He rightly points out that it is only one of a long series of similar measures. But it is important to add that the penalties it imposed were much lighter than those under earlier Acts, and — perhaps for this reason — it was rarely invoked. Most of the prosecutions of workers for forming trade unions were made, as before, under the Common Law of conspiracy, but there is evidence that a good many unions were left undisturbed.

A word of warning. Again and again in these pages comparisons or contrasts are drawn between conditions in the period of the industrial revolution and those of today. It must be remembered, however, that 'today' means the third and not the seventh decade of the twentieth century. Since M. Mantoux wrote, great changes have taken place in English society. Large areas of the land are again owned by those who cultivate them. The visitor to Manchester would be hard put to it to find a single cotton factory. Industry is again widely dispersed; the south is no longer stunted and sleepy. And Englishmen's dreams of Empire are not what they were.

'Expect poison from the standing water.' There is no finality in history. As time goes on, further modifications will be called for in our views of the industrial revolution. But, let it be repeated, in both its architecture and detail this volume is by far the best introduction to the subject in any language. It is, moreover, a permanent work of reference. Rereading it recently from cover to cover has been an experience one would not have missed. It is astonishingly fresh. And not a few of the findings of modern writers that one had thought of as new are now seen to have been anticipated by M. Mantoux. His book is one of a few works on economic history that can justly be spoken of as classics.

June 1961

T. S. ASHTON
Emeritus Professor of Economic History,
University of London

PUBLISHER'S NOTE

For this new edition the type has been entirely reset. In the course of preparation for the printer the whole apparatus of references has been checked and verified; and a new supplement has been added to the bibliography. The publishers are indebted to Madame Mantoux, the author's widow, for her patient assistance with this work after supervising the preparation of a revised French edition.

PREFACE TO THE SECOND EDITION

WHEN this book was first published, more than twenty years ago, its intended object was a double one. It was an attempt to lay before the public a comprehensive survey of one of the most important movements in modern history – the consequences of which have affected the whole civilized world, and are still transforming and shaping it under our own eyes. It was also meant to call the attention of students, especially in my own country, to a field in which research had hardly begun. How far the first of these aims has been attained it is for readers to decide. As for the second, the realities as well as the spirit of our times have done more than any individual effort to give its proper value to the economic side of history, and to encourage investigation into the origins and development of that tremendous event, the industrial revolution.

On the various aspects of the facts described in this book, much excellent work has now been done. Special subjects have been studied with much application and success. Original sources have been sought for and scientifically explored. It was not my purpose, had even the time and means at my disposal made it possible, to write another book on the basis of such new information, but only to improve the old one, by giving full consideration to any criticism it may have deserved, as well as to all the valuable results of research in the last twenty years. I have tried to correct and complete a picture, the main lines of which, I believe, should remain unaltered. It would be very gratifying to me if this book in its present form could still serve as an introduction to studies of a more limited scope and a more thorough character. As it was when first written, so it has to remain at present – a provisional *synthesis*, open to further improvements. Whoever wishes to retain the confidence of students must regard himself as a student all his life.

PAUL MANTOUX

January 7, 1927

23

INTRODUCTION

THE modern factory system originated in England in the last third of the eighteenth century. From the beginning its effects were so quickly felt and gave rise to such important results that it has been aptly compared to a revolution,[1] though it may be confidently asserted that few political revolutions have ever had such far-reaching consequences. Today the factory system surrounds us on all sides. The words evoke such familiar and striking images that it hardly seems necessary to define them. The great factories on the outskirts of our cities, the tall chimneys smoking by day and glowing by night, the incessant hum of machinery, the bustle of crowds of workmen, all these are familiar enough. Nevertheless, and in spite of the apparent rapidity of its development, the industrial revolution sprang from far-distant causes, and was destined to produce consequences whose process of development, after more than a century, is still incomplete. The distinctive characteristics of the factory system did not reveal themselves at once. In order to enable us to recognize them more easily in the half-light of their beginning we shall start by describing them as they present themselves to us today.

I

The object of all industry is the production of goods, or to be more explicit, of articles of consumption which are not directly provided by nature. By 'factory system' we therefore primarily mean a particular organization, a particular system of production. But this organization affects the whole economic system and consequently the whole social system, which is controlled by the growth and distribution of wealth.

The factory system concentrates and multiplies the means of production so that the output is both accelerated and increased. Machinery is

---

[1] The credit for originating this comparison is generally ascribed to Arnold Toynbee, whose book, unfinished through his early death, was published in 1884 under the title of *Lectures on the Industrial Revolution in England*. But William Rappard (*La Révolution industrielle et les origines de la protection légale du travail en Suisse*, p. 4) observes that Karl Marx, in the first volume of *Das Kapital* (1867), gives a systematic description of what he called 'die industrielle Revolution', an expression used before by Karl Marlo in 1850, by John Stuart Mill in 1848 (*Principles of Political Economy*, original edition, p. 581), and as early as 1845 by Friedrich Engels (*Die Lage der arbeitenden Klasse in England*, pp. 11 and 355).

employed which accomplishes with infallible precision and prodigious rapidity the heaviest and most complicated tasks. Its motive power is not the limited and irregular effort of human muscles, but either natural forces such as wind and running water, or artificial forces such as steam or electricity; these are tractable, regular and indefatigable, and can be increased indefinitely and at will. A vast number of persons, men, women and children, are brought together to tend the machines, all with specialized tasks – mere wheels within wheels. Implements more and more complicated, workmen more and more numerous and highly organized, these make up great undertakings, which are indeed industrial commonwealths. And, as the mainspring of this terrific activity, as a cause and as an end, behind this use of human labour and of mechanical force, capital is at work, swept forward by its own law – the law of profit – which urges it ceaselessly to produce, in order ceaselessly to grow.

The characteristic monument containing within its walls the raw material of modern production, and embodying in a visible form its very principle, is the factory. Within are vast workshops through which run belts or transmission wires by which power is distributed. Each workshop is fitted with powerful and delicate machinery, which fills the place with its clatter, aided by the frenzied labour of its disciplined population which the machines seem to sweep along with them in their panting rhythm. The one object of all this is the production of commodities as quickly as possible in unlimited quantities. Here are woven goods unrolling themselves in yards and yards of cloth, or piling up in mountains of cylindrical bales; there steel is boiling in gigantic retorts and flinging up showers of dazzling sparks. Continuous production has become the rule for all industrial undertakings, unless it is limited in consequence of a definite agreement between producers. Left entirely to itself, production would rush on to excess, until it became ruinous over-production: a paradoxical result of the instinctive tendency of capital, which ends in self-destruction.

Once manufactured, these quantities of goods must be sold. Sale, resulting in profit, is the final goal of all industrial production. The immense stimulus given to production by the factory system immediately affects the distribution of commodities. The increased amount of goods on the market lowers prices, lower prices mean increased demand, and more business. Competition becomes more intense. As improvements in transport open an ever wider field to its activities it extends from individuals to regions and to nations, more eager than ever in the pursuit of their material interests. Conflicts and economic wars are let loose, and the winner is he who succeeds in spite of his competitors in enlarging his sphere of operations, and in finding more and ever more new markets. The ambition of producers makes them daring, and the most distant countries, continents hardly yet explored, become their prey. The whole world henceforward is nothing but one immense market, where the great industries of all countries contend as on a battlefield.

A special method of distributing wealth goes with this great productivity, with its enlarged circulation reaching to the confines of the inhabited world. Obviously the consumer is now in a much more favourable position than he was before the industrial revolution took place. Goods have greatly increased in quantity, while prices have been, on the whole, considerably reduced. Many things, formerly expensive and hard to come by, are obtainable in localities and in circles where previously they were unknown. Nevertheless the optimistic view with which such a spectacle inspired the classical economist is profoundly changed when the condition of the producers is examined. The whole structure of the factory system is built up on the power furnished by machinery, together with an immense accumulation of human labour, supporting, at the top, the towering and ever-growing force of capital. Producers are divided into two classes. The first gives its labour and possesses nothing else, selling the strength of its arms and the hours of its life for a wage. The second commands capital, owns the factories, the raw materials, the machinery, and reaps the profits and dividends. At its head are the great leaders, the captains of industry, as Carlyle called them, organizers, rulers and conquerors.

From this has grown up the social system characteristic of our modern civilization, which forms a whole as complete and as coherent as the feudal system of the tenth century can have been. But whilst the latter was the consequence of military necessity and of the dangers which threatened human life in a Europe given over to anarchical barbarism, the former has been produced by a concatenation of purely economic forces, grouped round the central fact of the factory system. It is to the factory system that we owe the recent growth of our manufacturing towns, into which are crowded competing, though independent, undertakings. It is in these districts that we see that extraordinary growth of population, in its most extreme form, which has become the rule in most industrial countries. In 1773, Manchester had a population of barely thirty thousand.[1] Today (1927) its population is nearly a million. In 1801 the population of Great Britain and Ireland was fourteen and a half million, it is now (1927) forty-eight million. This development, which could not have been foreseen by preceding generations, has had incalculable consequences. For instance, to take only one example, emigration, with the resulting flow of capital and labour to distant countries, has caused the rapid growth of similar communities across the seas which display, in an even more extreme degree, all the characteristics of our economic system.

[1] Census of Manchester and Salford (1773), Chetham's Library, Manchester.

The social problem, in the particular form it now assumes in every country with a European civilization, arose as a consequence of the factory system. The simultaneous growth of population and wealth, without this increased wealth appearing to benefit the bulk of the population in proportion to the effort it has supplied for its production; the opposition of two classes, of which the one increases in numbers and the other in wealth; of which the one earns, by increasing labour, only a precarious subsistence wage, whilst the other enjoys all the benefits of a refined civilization; these conditions are everywhere manifest, and are everywhere followed by the same movements of thought and feeling. It is the sight of this industrial activity, of the vast organization on which it is built and of the power of capital which unites and directs its collective force, that has given birth to modern socialism. One of the most striking features of our times is the general expectation of far-reaching changes, hoped for by some and feared by others, which, if they actually did take place, might be regarded as closing the period which opened with the birth of the factory system.

All these facts, covering so wide a field, cannot be contained in a narrow definition, which would only take into account the material conditions of production. To give them their true value one must regard them as a living and complex whole, which will then appear as one of those illuminating facts which, rightly understood, light up a whole period. The factory system, science and democracy are the forces which, from the economic, intellectual and political points of view, control the evolution of modern societies. The beginnings of modern industry are like those of democracy or science. It would be absurd to affirm that science began with Galileo or Descartes, or that democracy did not exist anywhere before the American and the French revolutions. Nevertheless, the scientists of the seventeenth century and the revolutionaries of the eighteenth are justly regarded as the real founders of modern science and modern democracy. In the same way, in the forms of production which immediately preceded, some of the features of the factory system can already be distinguished. But it is only with the age of the great technical inventions, the age of Hargreaves, Crompton and Watt, that the modern factory system truly comes into its own, and with it those consequences from which it cannot be detached, and which make its development one of the main events of history.

II

It may appear to the reader that we have laid almost too much stress on ideas which seem, and which ought to be, commonplaces. This has been done in order that there may be no doubt as to what we mean by the factory system. It is not an altogether unnecessary precaution, as the use of the term in common parlance is confused and loose, and the efforts which have been made to find a suitable formula have so far resulted in nothing satisfactory. The suggestion has been made that the distinction between small-scale industry and the factory system should depend on the size of the markets served: thus small-scale industry would be that which supplied a district or a limited area, whilst the factory system would be that which produced for a national or an international market.[1] In itself this is not an impossible definition, and it has the advantage of accentuating the importance of the commercial element in economic evolution. Nevertheless it departs from the current use of the phrase which, though no doubt loose, does not lend itself to such an arbitrary interpretation. No one would think of including in the factory system the carpet manufacture as it exists today in Turkey and Persia. Nevertheless oriental carpets are sold throughout the world. Can the factory system be said to have existed in Corinth in the days when the pottery of the isthmus was sold in all the countries of the Mediterranean? To us handwork in small workshops, by workmen whose individual skill makes up for the deficiencies of their primitive tools, is the exact opposite of the factory system. External expansion therefore is not the essential characteristic. This must be sought rather in the internal organization and the technical equipment. For, as we have said, the factory system is above all a system of production.

But here we are confronted with fresh difficulties, for industrial evolution has many stages, which follow one another in a continuous series to which precise limits can only be set in theory. The factory system can be said to have begun one, or even several, centuries earlier, if one development is selected instead of another as marking the initial stage. We have fixed the time in England between 1760 and 1800. But if one can credit certain works, or at least their titles,[2] the factory system existed in France at least a hundred years before, as early as the reign of Louis XIV. Is this a contradiction or a misunderstanding?

The large-scale industry which has been studied by M. Germain Martin was not, as he points out at the beginning of his book, the result of a natural evolution.[3] It was almost exclusively artificial and only survived through the support and patronage of the French Crown. Colbert, who may rightly be considered its founder, 'was of opinion

[1] A. Milhaud, 'De la vie industrielle en France depuis le XVIIᵉ siècle', *Revue de synthèse historique*, III, 335.

[2] Germain Martin, *La grande industrie en France sous le règne de Louis XIV* (1899); A. des Cilleuls, *Histoire et régime de la grande industrie aux XVIIᵉ et XVIIIᵉ siècles* (1898).

[3] 'The object of this book is to show the part played by the Crown in the development of the factory system in France between 1660 and 1715, by describing the industrial legislation, the system of supervision and inspection of trades, and all the methods of administrative intervention in the field of industry.' *La grande industrie en France sous le règne de Louis XIV*, Preface, p. i.

that no large-scale industry could exist unless created and supported by the State'.[1] He thought of it only as an annex to the big royal workshops which, in all ages and in civilizations of the most varied development, have always worked for and at the command of the sovereign. The documents which M. Germain Martin has collected on the manufactures of the seventeenth century give us a picture which at first sight reminds us of that of modern factories. The importance of the undertakings, the number of workmen employed, their division into specialized gangs, the severity of the discipline to which they were subjected, are all characteristics which can be found in the modern factory system. But this genuine analogy loses much of its significance when its origin is disclosed.

Industrial establishments, in the classifications drawn up by the Inspectors of Manufactures, were divided into three classes.[2] In the first class were State factories which belonged to the King, whose capital came from the royal treasury, and the products of which were mainly luxuries destined for the King himself. The best example of this class is the Gobelins works, of which the official title, when first founded, was: *Manufacture royale des meubles de la Couronne.* The legions of artists and of artisans who were employed there under Lebrun, and later under Mignard, only worked at the King's pleasure, to decorate his palaces and to add to the splendour of his court. Their work went to embellish Versailles, Saint-Germain and Marly: tapestries, carvings, sculptures, bronzes, trophies and that wonderful chased silverwork which was sent to the Mint in the dark days of the reign. Everything here was connected with the person of the King: from him everything came and to him everything returned. Such an industry was outside the necessities of economic life: it sought no profit and it knew no competition. It is not to the modern factory system that it should be compared, but rather to the home industry of antiquity, to the work of slaves attached to a household, who actually made in that house the objects required for the needs or the pleasures of their master.

The second class is that of *manufactures royales*. These belonged to private individuals and produced for public consumption. But their very name indicates clearly enough the complete control of the Crown. Official protection was not enough; more than once, manufacturers established themselves in specially designated districts on the formal invitation of the King and his ministers, who if necessary sought them out abroad.[3] No help was refused them: direct Treasury subsidies, loans

---

[1] *La grande industrie en France sous le règne de Louis XIV*, p. 94.   [2] Ibid., p. 8.

[3] On the steps taken by Colbert to attract workmen and foreign manufacturers to France, cf. ibid., chap. V, pp. 60 ff. He brought clothiers from Holland (pp. 68-71), tinsmiths from Germany (pp. 71-5), mining engineers from Sweden (p. 75), glassworkers and lace-makers from Venice and Milan (pp. 76-9).

free of interest voted by towns or provincial councils, exemption from the heaviest taxes, such as tallage, the salt tax, and the billeting of soldiers.[1] Dispensation was even given from obedience to the narrow, tyrannical industrial regulations to which small manufacturers were subject. They were practically placed outside the laws of the State. Thus we find the Van Robais, of Abbeville, freely professing Protestantism after the revocation of the Edict of Nantes and during the whole of the *ancien régime*.[2]

Lastly, the *manufactures privilégiées* received perhaps even more favoured treatment than the royal manufactures. They had the sole right of making and selling certain articles. They enjoyed an absolute monopoly with which fraud alone could interfere, and it is well known with what severity fraud of all kinds was dealt with under the *ancien régime*. It would seem that Colbert wanted to vest some of the royal prerogative in the manufacturers themselves, so that in the control of their undertakings they should only be delegates for the Crown.[3]

If the hand which built and upheld this structure was withdrawn everything broke down and ruin was imminent. These undertakings only lived on protection and privilege. Left to themselves many would have disappeared at once, and so when, under Louis XV, the government paid them less attention, they began to decline. The royal and the privileged factories, which had at one time produced nearly two-thirds of all the cloth in France, produced only about one-third. In those days small-scale production, which has so quickly retreated with the advance of the modern factory system, was still full of life. It had withstood the acute competition originated by Colbert, in spite of the difficulties and limitations which hampered it. This was because it depended on a number of social and economic conditions which nothing had as yet disturbed. For instance, in Languedoc it not only continued to exist but it prospered and grew, whilst still preserving its domestic and rural character: 'Every industrious person, who finds a spot between two mountains where there is water, regulates it, stores it, or lets it flow according as it is plentiful or scarce. There he creates a natural pasture, sometimes not more than twelve feet wide, and a quarter or half a league long. He buys sheep which he pastures there. His wife and children spin the wool he has shorn and carded. He weaves it and sells his cloth in the nearest market. His neighbour, if he can properly be called neighbour, since he is sometimes at least a quarter of a league away, does the same, and imperceptibly all this results in the formation of a

---

[1] *La grande industrie en France sous le règne de Louis XIV*, pp. 10, 11.
[2] Ibid., pp. 67-9.
[3] G. Martin gives a certain number of examples, amongst others that of the factories of Clermont, Sapte and Conques, which had the monopoly of fine cloth in Languedoc, p. 12.

community which it would take perhaps more than a day to visit.'[1]

The creation of royal manufactures in the seventeenth century must not therefore be confused with the spontaneous growth of the factory system in the following century. It is indeed a fact of very limited significance, though no doubt it contributed to the prosperity which Colbert sought to give France. It produced no general consequences, and no relationship can be traced between it and the economic system of our times.[2]

The same observations would apply to the monopolized industries in England in the seventeenth century, which have been studied by Hermann Levy.[3] In the trades the development of which he describes — mining, glass manufacture, salt, soap, wire industries, etc. — the creation of important capitalistic organizations was made possible only by active and continued government support. 'Privileges from the Crown, suppression of internal competition by law, and a protective trade policy',[4] were the means by which that artificial growth was fostered. The very support they received accounts for the unpopularity of such organizations, for the attacks made against their privileges as early as during the Commonwealth, and for their collapse as soon as those privileges had been removed. Would it be possible to maintain that their temporary existence 'contradicts the frequently repeated contention that industrial capitalism started in England about 1760'?[5] They clearly belong to a class of facts which differs essentially from the modern factory system and does not in any way explain its appearance at a later period. What has been, however, clearly shown by the authors of the books to which we refer is that before the era of the factory system it was possible, under particularly favourable circumstances, to develop big industrial undertakings in which considerable capital was sunk and a large amount of labour was employed. But we need not look particularly for this to

---

[1] Report of the Inspector-General of Manufactures in Languedoc (Archives de l'Hérault, C. 2561, quoted by G. Martin, p. 17). Compare with Defoe's famous description of the valley of Halifax, quoted below (Part I, chap. I).

[2] According to H. Pirenne, the eminent Belgian historian, the progress of economic organization does not show a continuous movement, but a succession of leaps forward: 'I believe that, for each period into which our economic history may be divided, there is a distinct and separate class of capitalists. In other words, the group of capitalists of a given epoch does not spring from the capitalist group of the preceding epoch. At every change in economic organization we find a breach of continuity.' — 'The Stages in the Social History of Capitalism', *American Historical Review*, XIX, 494 (1914). This view is supported by our own observations on the transition between manufacture and the factory system.

[3] *Monopoly and Competition, a Study in English Industrial Organisation* (1911); *Die Grundlagen des ökonomischen Liberalismus in der Geschichte der englischen Volkswirtschaft* (1914).

[4] H. Levy, *Monopoly and Competition*, p. 43.

[5] Ibid., p. 15.

France or to the seventeenth century. There are plenty of instances of the same development at the time of the Renaissance or towards the end of the Middle Ages as well as in the age of Louis XIV. Most of them are due not to a policy like that of Colbert but to the presence of more deeply seated causes.[1]

III

Such works as those of Sir William Ashley[2] and Professor Unwin[3] on English economic history, and of Herr Doren on that of Florence,[4] tell us of the existence of capitalist undertakings, particularly in the woollen industry, at the beginning of the sixteenth century and even in the fifteenth and fourteenth. If we confine ourselves to England it is certain that from the reign of Henry VII onwards a number of rich cloth merchants in the north and west played the same part then, though on a smaller scale, as our great manufacturers play today. Tradition has preserved the names of Cuthbert of Kendal, Hodgkins of Halifax, Stump of Malmesbury, Bryan of Manchester, John Winchcombe of Newbury. Instead of being mere merchants, buying cloth from the weavers and selling it in markets or at fairs, they set up workshops which they supervised themselves. They were manufacturers in the modern sense. Their wealth and their power appear to have made a great impression on their contemporaries. Their semi-legendary names have been handed down to us, together with a picture, no doubt excessively embellished and exaggerated, but still recognizable, of this early attempt at industrial capitalism. John Winchcombe, or as he was commonly called, Jack of Newbury, is the figure round which history and legend have collected most memories. Over two hundred years after his death stories were still told in his native town of how he had the parish church built at his expense, of how he entertained King Henry VIII and Queen Catherine of Aragon, and of how in the war against Scotland, in 1513, he equipped a hundred men out of his own purse and led them in person at the battle of Flodden Field.[5] One day, so the story goes, the King, meeting on a road near London a string of carts all laden with

---

[1] On the causes of the early developments of the capitalist system of industry, chiefly in France, see the illuminating observations of H. Hauser ('Les Origines du Capitalisme moderne en France', *Revue d'économie politique*, 1902, pp. 193 ff. and 313 ff.).

[2] *An Introduction to English Economic History and Theory*, Part II, 516.

[3] G. Unwin, *Industrial Organization in the Sixteenth and Seventeenth Centuries*.

[4] *Studien aus der Florentiner Wirthschaftsgeschichte: die Florentiner Wollentuchindustrie vom 14ten bis zum 16ten Jahrhundert*.

[5] Daniel Defoe, *A Tour Through the Whole Island of Great Britain*, II, 56-8. The only one of these facts which it has been possible to verify is the donation for the building of the parish church. This is recorded in the authentic will of John Winchcombe, dated 1519.

cloth and learning that they belonged to Winchcombe, exclaimed: 'This Jack of Newbury is richer than I.'

Winchcombe owed his fortune to his large and busy workshops, where great numbers of workmen were employed in carding, spinning and weaving wool. There still exists a curious if not very reliable description of them in a little book, which tells in rather poor verse the story of the great cloth merchant.[1] Two hundred weavers all together in a large room managed two hundred looms, and were helped by as many apprentices. A hundred women were employed in carding. Two hundred girls 'in petticoats of stammel red – and milke white kerchers on their head' plied the distaff and the spinning wheel. The sorting of wools was done by a hundred and fifty boys and girls, 'the children of poor silly men'. Once woven, the cloth went on to fifty clippers and to eighty dressers. This factory also comprised a fulling mill and dye works which employed twenty and forty men respectively.[2] These figures are probably exaggerated. What is certain is that John Winchcombe's factory differed both in organization and in importance from the usual forms of industry. To this he owed his fame, the echo of which, no doubt magnified by distance, has come down to us from the following generation.

The class of manufacturers which Jack of Newbury represents developed rapidly during the first half of the sixteenth century. And this development was not an artificial one, for the tendency of the woollen industry towards concentration in the hands of a few rich clothiers was not promoted by any outside influence. Far from giving it any encouragement, as the French Crown did later on, the Tudor Government were seriously alarmed by this development. They felt that it was a menace to the traditional organization of trade, and an overwhelming competitor to the numerous small artisans. Steps were taken to protect at any rate the country weavers:[3] 'Forasmuch as the weavers of this realm have, as well at the present Parliament as at divers other times, complained that the rich and wealthy clothiers do in many ways oppress them, some by setting up and keeping in their houses divers looms, and keeping and maintaining them by journeymen and

---

[1] Thomas Deloney, *The Story of John Winchcombe, commonly called Jack of Newbury*, London, 1597. This book ran through many editions under the slightly altered title of *The Pleasant History of John Winchcombe, in his Younger Years called Jack of Newbury*. It should be noted that its publication took place nearly eighty years after the death of that worthy.

[2] Ibid., p. 37.

[3] One of the most usual proceedings of ancient economic legislation was to limit the expansion of one particular industry to certain specified localities. See 14-15 Henry VIII, c. 1 (the inhabitants of Norfolk are forbidden to dye, shear or prepare cloth save in the town of Norwich); 33-4 Henry VIII, c. 10 (prohibition to manufacture blankets outside the town of York).

persons unskilful, to the decay of a great number of artificers who were brought up in the said art of weaving ... and letting them out at such unreasonable rents as the poor artificers are not able to maintain themselves, much less to maintain their wives, families, and children; some also by giving much less wages and hire for weaving and workmanship than in times past they did, whereby they are forced utterly to forsake their art and occupation wherein they have been brought up, it is, therefore, for remedy of the premises, and for the averting of a great number of inconveniencies which may grow if in time it be not foreseen, ordained and enacted by authority of this present Parliament, that no person using the mystery of cloth-making, and dwelling out of a city, borough, market town, or incorporate town, shall keep, or retain, or have in his or their houses or possession more than one woollen loom at a time, nor shall by any means, directly or indirectly, receive or take any manner of profit, gain, or commodity by letting or selling any loom, or any house wherein any loom is or shall be used or occupied ... upon pain or forfeiture for every week that any person shall do the contrary ... of twenty shillings.'[1]

In England then, with the Tudors, began a spontaneous development of industrial capitalism,[2] of sufficient importance to cause anxiety for the safety of the small industries. Can we therefore say that the modern factory system dates at least from the sixteenth century? Would it not be nearer the truth to say that a long succession of events, in which Colbert's attempt is only an episode, has from afar off signalized and prepared the way for the industrial revolution?

IV

One word brings together and characterizes these facts, the word *manufacture*. We owe it to Karl Marx, whose great dogmatic treatise contains pages of historical value. According to Marx the evolution of modern capitalism began at the time of the Renaissance and with the discovery of the New World. For the sudden growth of trade, together with the increase of currency and of wealth, completely changed the economic life of the western nations.[3] This evolution may be divided

---

[1] 3 & 4 Philip and Mary, c. 11. At the same period it was forbidden to weavers to own a fulling mill; to fullers to own a weaving loom; to have (save in towns) more than two apprentices, etc., etc.

[2] A. Held, *Zwei Bücher zur socialen Geschichte Englands*, p. 498. 'Already under the Tudors, the cloth industry was in many respects a capitalistic one: that is to say, an industry whose markets were dependent on the world's commerce and were in the hands of wholesale traders.' Laurent Dechesne in *L'évolution économique et sociale de l'industrie de la laine en Angleterre*, pp. 35-7, shows clearly how premature this tendency was in many respects.

[3] This date should really be put earlier. According to Doren, pp. 22 ff., the element

into two periods. Until the middle of the eighteenth century production was in the stage of 'manufacture'. About 1760 the modern factory system really set in.[1] On what do we base this distinction, and what does it mean?

'Manufacture' itself implies the separation of labour and capital. We have already noted, in the preamble to the law of 1557, how this was effected. The artisan who previously worked for himself in his own house and with his own tools had become nothing more than a tenant, paying rent for the use of tools which no longer belonged to him. The manufacturer then went still further. He kept the tools, and organized workshops under his direct supervision, whilst the artisan sold him only his labour, for which he received a wage: this is what happened alike with John Winchcombe at Newbury and with the Van Robais at Abbeville.

The main principle, and the whole *raison d'être* of manufacture, is the division of labour.[2] In the artisan's little room, where he is helped by two or three companions, or in the cottage of the village workman, surrounded by his wife and children, division of labour is rudimentary. It is quite enough if a minimum number of indispensable operations take place simultaneously. One man, for instance, blows the bellows, while another uses the hammer. Let us set beside this Adam Smith's famous description of a pin factory in the eighteenth century:

'A workman not educated to this business (which the division of labour has rendered a distinct trade), nor acquainted with the use of the machinery employed in it (to the invention of which the same division of labour has probably given occasion), should scarce, perhaps, with his utmost industry, make one pin in a day, and certainly could not make twenty. But in the way in which this business is now carried on, not only the whole work is a peculiar trade, but it is divided into a number of branches, of which the greater part are likewise peculiar trades. One man draws out the wire; another straights it; a third cuts it; a fourth points it; a fifth grinds it at the top for receiving the head; to make the

[1] *Das Kapital*, I, 335 (third edition).

[2] 'The basis of capitalistic production is co-operation, whose early form, whilst containing the germ of more complex forms, not only reappears as a factor in them, but also exists alongside them as a special form of capitalism. This kind of co-operation, whose basis is division of labour, takes on in manufacture its classic form and predominates during the real manufacturing period, which begins in the middle of the sixteenth century and ends about the last third of the eighteenth.' Ibid. Sombart's definition of 'manufacture' does not differ from that given by Marx. But he admits that if it represents in most cases a transitional stage, sometimes it becomes a lasting organization of industry — for instance in the pottery and in the high-class furnishing trades. See Sombart, *Der Moderne Kapitalismus*, I, 38, 41, 42.

of capitalism appears in Florentine industry as early as the end of the thirteenth century. See also Lujo Brentano, *Die Anfänge des modernen Kapitalismus* (1916), p. 199.

head requires two or three distinct operations; to put it on is a peculiar business; to whiten the pin is another; it is even a trade by itself to put them into the paper; and the important business of making a pin is in this manner divided into about eighteen distinct operations, which, in some manufactories, are all performed by distinct hands, though in others the same man will sometimes perform two or three of them. I have seen a small manufactory of this kind, where ten men only were employed, and where some of them, consequently, performed two or three distinct operations. But though they were very poor, and, therefore, but indifferently accommodated with the necessary machinery, they could, when they exerted themselves, make among them about twelve pounds of pins in a day. There are in a pound upwards of four thousand pins of a middling size. Ten persons, therefore, could make among them upwards of forty-eight thousand pins in a day ... '[1]

Division of labour has so often been the theme for the disquisitions of economists that it is hardly necessary to add anything more. Moreover the founders of the first factories very quickly observed the accuracy and quickness attained by specialized workmen, and the effect this had on production. Before Adam Smith, before even the author of *Considerations upon the East-India Trade*, they had observed that 'the greater the Order and Regularity of every Work, the same must needs be done in less time, the Labour must be less, and consequently the price of Labour less, tho' Wages shou'd not be abated'.[2]

How then can we distinguish 'manufacture', which does belong to a degree of high development in economic evolution, from the modern

---

[1] Adam Smith, *Inquiry into the Nature and Causes of the Wealth of Nations*, Book I, chap. I. – Another text, written three-quarters of a century earlier, may be compared with Adam Smith's famous page: 'A watch is a work of great variety, and 'tis possible for one artist to make all the several parts, and at last to join them all together. But if the demand of watches should become so very great as to find constant employment for as many persons as there are parts in a watch, if to every one shall be assigned his proper and constant work, if one shall have nothing else to make but cases, another wheels, another pins, another screws, and several others their proper parts; and lastly if it shall be the constant and only employment of one to join these several parts together, this man must needs be more skilful and expeditious in the composition of these several parts than the same man could be if he were also to be employed in the manufacture of all these parts. And so the maker of the pins, or wheels, or screws, or other parts, must needs be more perfect and expeditious at his proper work ... ' (*Considerations upon the East-India Trade* (1701), p. 70.) This illustrates what Marx calls 'heterogeneous' division of labour, as opposed to the 'organic' type described by Adam Smith. The difference is that in the first system each worker produces a complete part which has only to be fitted to other parts, while in the second system one and the same thing is gradually transformed through a succession of distinct operations. A thorough study of the division of labour with a systematic classification of all the facts connected with it is to be found in Karl Bücher's *Entstehung der Volkswirtschaft* (second edition, 1898).

[2] *Considerations upon the East-India Trade*, p. 68.

factory system? For Marx, as for most of those who have gone into this question, the distinctive characteristic of the factory system is the use of machinery. Following on his chapter on 'The Division of Labour and Manufacture' is one called 'Machinery and the Factory System'. He indulges in a long discussion on machinery and the part it plays in economics. He defines a factory as 'a workshop in which machinery is employed', and where one can still distinguish that division of labour which reigned in 'manufacture', though here carried to an extreme by automatic aids, each one as strong as an army of workers and performing its task with infallible accuracy. According to Hobson[1] it is machinery which, by replacing relatively simple tools, has considerably increased the fixed capital necessary to an undertaking, and which, by the great speeding up of production, has more and more increased the circulation of capital, thus rendering the management of industry increasingly inaccessible to the workman without capital, and in this way creating our present social system.[2]

Another writer affirms that an organization of labour analogous to that of 'manufacture' can develop, and in fact has developed, in all societies, ancient and modern, which have reached a certain degree of civilization and material prosperity.[3] But at the close of the eighteenth century a new factor is introduced, and the appearance of power machinery opens a new chapter in the economic history of the world.

The words themselves seem to bring out the fundamental identity of machine industry and the factory system. For 'factory system' is the best translation of the French expression 'la grande industrie'. In the middle of the eighteenth century the word 'factory' was still only used in the same sense as the French word to which it is related: 'factorerie', which means shop, warehouse or depot.[4] The first factories were not called factories, but mills. For that which first caught the eye was the great water-wheel, similar to that of a flour mill. Ultimately the word, used in an ever wider sense, came to be almost synonymous with machinery: thus factory, mill and machine were one and the same thing.[5] During the last years of the eighteenth century the words mill and factory were constantly used for one another.[6] Both words appear

[1] J. A. Hobson, *The Evolution of Modern Capitalism*, p. 40.

[2] 'The chief material factor in the evolution of Capitalism is machinery. The growing quantity and complexity of machinery applied to purposes of manufacture and conveyance, and to the extractive industries, is the great special fact in the narrative of the expansion of modern industry.' Ibid., pp. 5-6.

[3] R. W. Cooke Taylor, *The Factory System and the Factory Acts*, p. 29.

[4] Such is still the meaning attached to it in Johnson's dictionary. It is possible that 'factory' owes its modern meaning to the word 'manufactory'.

[5] E.g. the expressions paper mill, silk mill, etc.

[6] For instance, in Aikin's book (*A Description of the Country from thirty to forty miles round Manchester*), 1795, the place where cotton-spinning takes place is almost always referred to as a cotton mill. Cf. F. M. Eden, *State of the Poor* (1797), II, 129-30.

in the text of the earliest Act for regulating the conditions of labour in factories.[1] As early as 1806 we find the expression 'factory system' used in the report of a Parliamentary Committee on the woollen industry, although the idea of machinery does not appear in this case to have been implied in the definition.[2] When 'factory system' had become a current expression it was defined as follows in Ure's *Philosophy of Manufactures*: 'The factory system designates the combined operations of many orders of workpeople, adult and young, in tending with assiduous skill a series of productive machines, continuously impelled by a central power.'[3] The legal definition of a factory dates from 1844: 'The word factory ... shall be taken to mean all buildings and premises ... wherein or within the close or curtilage of which steam or any other mechanical power shall be used to move or work any machinery employed in preparing, manufacturing, or finishing, or in any process incident to the manufacture of cotton, wool, hair, silk, flax, hemp, jute, or tow ... '[4]

If, then, the use of machines distinguishes the factory from 'manufacture', and gives its special character to the new system as against all preceding ones, would it not be better, instead of using the term 'factory system', to use that of 'machine industry'? It would have the advantage of being short and distinctive, and of avoiding confusion, which so often is more due to words than to things. It may be, however, that this new term would give an unreal simplicity to facts which are really both complicated and confusing. To begin with, the introduction of machinery was not accomplished all at once. At what point do machines begin and tools end? The hammers and the bellows in the ironworks and foundries of the sixteenth century were worked by a water-wheel;[5] and whoever looks through the volumes of engravings in Diderot and d'Alembert's Encyclopaedia, which was published a few years before the first cotton mills appeared in England, will be impressed by finding there a large number of designs of quite ingenious and often quite powerful machines.[6] It is doubtful whether the origin of machinery is easier to discover than that of the factory system. Moreover, the word

---

[1] 42 Geo. III, c. 73 (1802). *An Act for the Preservation of the Health and Morals of Apprentices Employed in Cotton and other Mills and in Cotton and other Factories.*

[2] *Report from the Select Committee appointed to consider the State of the Woollen Manufacture in England* (1806), p. 8: 'In the *factory system*, the master manufacturers, who sometimes possess a very great capital, employ in one or more buildings or factories, under their own or their superintendent's inspection, a number of workmen, more or fewer, according to their trade.'

[3] A. Ure, *Philosophy of Manufactures*, p. 14.

[4] 8 Victoria, c. 15 (*An Act to amend the Laws relating to Labour in Factories*, June 6th, 1844). It should be noticed that this legal definition applied only to textile factories.

[5] See Ludwig Beck, *Die Geschichte des Eisens in technischer und kulturgeschichtlicher Beziehung*, II, 130-42.

[6] Cf. specially vol. IV (*Hydraulique*), and also articles on Cloth, Ironworks, Wool, Mines, Powder, etc.

is perhaps a narrow one for all it has to express. In the textile industry the cause of the capital changes and developments was indisputably the invention of the spinning machine. But in the metal industries the turning-point was the use of coal in the smelting of iron ore. Is this a fact which would be covered by the phrase 'machine industry'? Moreover, it was only by imperceptible changes that the system of 'manufacture' developed into the factory system, as for instance in the Potteries in the time of Josiah Wedgwood. We should therefore have to substitute for the words 'machine industry' a much broader term which would cover every form of technical improvement. The use of machinery was only one of the principal factors, and probably the most fundamental one, in the modern factory system. If, then, a choice must be made between the two expressions, is it not better to choose the most inclusive one, the one which not only indicates the origin or one of the origins of the phenomena it describes, but which comprises those phenomena in their entirety and thus makes use of their actual inter-relation to define them?[1]

It may well be argued that there is no clearly marked division between 'manufacture' and the factory system, and that one should stress their common characteristics rather than those in which they differ. 'In "manufacture",' writes Held, 'the independence of the workman is already gone. Labour in each building is already specialized, and this makes it impossible for a workman ever again to recover his general technical knowledge.' But can we go so far as to affirm 'that the distinction between "manufacture" and the factory system is not of essential importance'?[2] Nowhere do phenomena succeed one

---

[1] Sombart tries to define the factory both by technical and economic characteristics (*Betriebsform* and *Wirtschaftsform*). From the technical point of view its main feature is the concentration of industry in one establishment, with machinery moved by some central force. From the economic point of view the commanding factor is the power of the capitalist, who, owning the factory with the plant and the raw material, organizes the production and finds the market. Sombart, *Der Moderne Kapitalismus*, p. 46.

[2] A. Held, *Zwei Bücher zur socialen Geschichte Englands*, pp. 544-5. Held goes almost as far as to confuse the two. After *domestic industry* (*Familienindustrie*) which produces directly for its own use, *handwork* (*Handwerk*) the sphere of the small free artisan, and *home industry* (*Hausindustrie*) where the worker works at home for an employer, he brings together under the name of the *factory industry* (*Fabrikindustrie*) all the forms of exploitation where the buildings, the tools and the management are in the hands of the capitalist (pp. 541-3). This classification is defective in several ways. If we consider the question of tools and production, the term *factory industry* is not enough. If we only consider the relation of capital and labour *home industry* should not be classed separately, it is already a capitalist industry. What Held calls *Hausindustrie* is often termed *collective workshops*. Instead of this rather equivocal expression G. Renard has suggested the more accurate expression *scattered workshops* ('Coup d'œil sur l'évolution du travail dans les quatre derniers siècles', *Revue politique et parlementaire*, Dec. 10th, 1904, p. 516).

another so gradually or so imperceptibly as in the sphere of economics, that domain of necessities and instincts, where every classification and every distinction of kind or time become more or less artificial. Nothing can be further removed from deductive sociology with its clear, elegant and arbitrary categories. Nevertheless differences do exist, and in spite of the vagueness of their outline one can easily distinguish certain groups of facts which belong together and which, by the relative position they occupy, give their character to the great periods of economic history. In order to define each period it is enough to indicate the tendency which is predominant, 'tonangebend', to use Held's expression. Moreover, while we try to distinguish and to describe these successive phases we must bear in mind that, after all, they are only different moments in the course of one and the same evolution.[1]

V

Two fundamental facts, closely interwoven, transforming one another, infinitely varied in their consequences and always the same in principle, govern this whole evolution: the exchange of commodities and the division of labour. As old as the desires and the work of mankind, they pursue their way together through the changes in all civilizations, which they accompany or direct. Every extension or multiplication of exchanges, by throwing open more channels to production, gives rise to an ever more elaborate and effective division of labour, a more and more narrow distribution of functions between producing areas, between trades and between different parts of the same trade. Conversely, division of labour, aided by technical improvement, which is its most active manifestation, implies a co-operation between all these mutually interdependent specialized activities, which becomes ever more extensive and in which the whole world ultimately takes part.[2]

The periods which are marked in the history of economics correspond to the more or less clearly defined stages of this double development. From this point of view the use of machinery itself, important as are its consequences, is only a secondary phenomenon. Before it became one of the most powerful causes in influencing modern societies it began by being the resultant, and as it were the expression of these two phenomena, at one of the decisive moments in their evolution.

---

[1] A. Held, *Zwei Bücher zur socialen Geschichte Englands*, p. 414. One could nevertheless maintain that manufacture has never been *tonangebend*.

[2] See Adam Smith, Book I, chap. II, 'Of the Principle which gives Occasion to the Division of Labour', and chap. III, 'That the Division of Labour is limited by the Extent of the Market'.

This crisis, distinguished by the appearance of machinery, best defines the industrial revolution.

If these remarks still leave the subject in some obscurity, only a close study of the facts will dissipate it. The beginnings of intellectual, religious and political movements are always difficult to discover. But the part played in that field by individual thought and action is always large and often predominant. Here and there events, men and books act as landmarks in the continuous stream of events. Economic movements are more confused. Their progress is like the slow growth of seeds scattered over a vast area. Endless obscure facts, in themselves almost insignificant, form great, confused wholes and mutually modify one another indefinitely. No one can hope to grasp them all, and when we pick out a few for description it is obvious that we must give up, together with some of the truth, the rather vain ambition of arriving at rigorous definitions and final explanations.

The industrial revolution opens a large and still partly unexplored field for historical investigation. We had to fix definite limits for this work, even though we were at times sorely tempted to overstep them. Thus, to mention the geographical limits, we have confined ourselves to England. The economic history of Scotland has been given a secondary place where it has not been completely disregarded, and in England our attention has been almost exclusively confined to the midland and northern counties, the chief home of the events which are the objects of our study. There are also chronological limits: Arnold Toynbee, who had begun to write this history before he was carried off by premature death, wanted to begin it in 1760 and carry it on until 1820 or 1830. We have preferred, for reasons which seem to us conclusive, to close with the first years of the nineteenth century. By then the great technical inventions, including the most important invention of all, the steam engine, had all become practical realities. Many factories were already at work which, apart from certain details as to tools, were identical with those of today (1927). Great centres of industry had begun to grow up, a factory proletariat made its appearance, the old trade regulations, already more than half destroyed, made way for the system of *laissez-faire*, itself even then doomed through the pressure of already half-perceived necessities. The law which inaugurated factory legislation was passed in 1802. The stage was ready set; there was nothing left but to follow the working out of the drama. Moreover, during the following period economic phenomena were submitted to perturbation which greatly affected their natural progress. The period of the continental blockade and that of the Corn Laws undoubtedly require special investigation and treatment.

These were not the only limits we felt bound to set to our work. In the plan outlined by Toynbee there was room both for the evolution of facts and for that of economic doctrines. We set aside the doctrines, save where they were intimately connected with the facts themselves. Many writers on economic history had made a special study of institutions and legislation: we thought we ought to pay less attention to the Acts regulating industry than to industry itself.[1] As it was impossible to describe the changes in all industries, even over a very short period, we picked out a few of those whose development appeared to us to be at the same time most important and most typical. The wool industry gave us the most complete example of the old system of production, showing at the same time the influences which made for its gradual transformation. The cotton industry supplied us with the most striking pictures of the advent of machinery. In the story of the iron industry we found the beginnings of the great part played today by the metal trades, with which is bound up a no less important fact, the entry of coal into the sphere of production. The development of mines is inseparable from that of ironworks, and both furnish the explanation of the steam engine.

Even within these limits the field which lay open before us was very wide, and could only be covered rapidly and without stopping. We wished nevertheless to give a general view of the whole, rather than to take up again the detailed study of special points, which had already long ago been begun by English students. No doubt that study was still very incomplete. But we thought that it could be better pursued or renewed after such general ideas had been collected as will give direction to fresh research. As the industrial revolution in England was the preface to the industrial revolution in the whole world, these general ideas may be of use to those who, in other countries, may desire to contribute to the history of this great transformation.

*   *   *

In reaching the conclusion of this long work our thanks are due to those who have helped in its completion: to the London School of Economics; to our friend F. W. Galton, secretary of the London Reform Union and one of Mr Sidney Webb's most active collaborators, to Professor Foxwell, of the University of Cambridge, who threw open to us his library, rich in economic literature; to Sir William Forwood and to the trustees of the Liverpool Museum, who have allowed

---

[1] Charles Beard, author of the interesting little book which bears the same title as the one we have adopted (*The Industrial Revolution*, London, first edition 1901, second edition 1902, compare p. 22), goes further than Toynbee. He shows — with reason — how the industrial revolution continued through the nineteenth century right into our own times.

us to examine Wedgwood's unpublished papers, now the property of the Museum, and also the ceramic collection belonging to Mr Mayer; to Mr George Tangye of Birmingham, thanks to whom we were able to gain access to the commercial correspondence of Boulton and Watt and the collection of registers, contracts, estimates, etc., of the Soho factory; to M. Ferdinand Dreyfus, who kindly lent us two interesting accounts of journeys in England, written in 1784 and 1786 by the sons of the duc de La Rochefoucauld-Liancourt; finally, to Dr Cunningham, whose kindness encouraged us to persevere in an arduous task, and whose classic work was our guide whenever we had to deal with matters outside our own subject.[1]

[1] For the whereabouts in 1961 of the documents referred to in this paragraph, see Bibliography.

PART I

Preparatory Changes

CHAPTER ONE

THE OLD TYPE OF INDUSTRY AND ITS EVOLUTION

Nowhere is the contrast more striking than it is in England between the great industrial towns of the present time, humming with factories and black with smoke, and the quiet small towns of the past, where artisans and merchants went leisurely about their business. For today it is still possible to compare them, without crossing that imaginary line which, as has been aptly remarked, seems to divide England into halves, one being pastoral and the other industrial.[1] Not far from Manchester and only a few miles from Liverpool, Chester still stands, with its massive walls whose foundations were built by the Romans, its quaint old streets lined with over-hanging lath-and-plaster houses, its shops sheltered under two 'rows' of superimposed arcades. But these towns of other days bear, like fossils, only the stamp of the activities of which they were a living part. The activities themselves, the old forms of industry, have vanished, save here and there in remote and poor localities or in some backward industries. We must nevertheless know what they were, in order to compare them with the conditions of economic life in the following period, and to appreciate the importance of the changes which, towards the end of the eighteenth century, marked the coming of the modern factory system.

I

The woollen industry in England was the most characteristic and the most complete example of the early system of manufacture. Because of its existence in nearly all parts of the country, of its intimate connection with agriculture and of the age and strength of its traditions, the records of this ancient trade throw light into the general condition of industry before the industrial revolution.

From time immemorial, long before its industrial awakening, England, a country of pasture, has bred sheep and sold their wool. A large part of it was sold abroad, either in exchange for the wines of southern France, or to provide the raw material for the looms of busy Flemish towns. After the Norman conquest, Flemish artisans crossed the Channel and taught the English how to use some of this wealth themselves. Their immigration was encouraged by the Crown, which

[1] A. Chevrillon, *Sydney Smith*, Preface.

several times, and notably at the beginning of the fourteenth century, tried, with the help of these foreign pioneers, to lay the foundations of a national industry. It developed and prospered from the reign of Edward III onwards, spread to the towns and villages and became the main source of wealth to whole populations. Nay more: if it be true, as the theorists of the mercantile system argued in the seventeenth century, that a nation is rich only in proportion to the quantity of gold and silver in its possession, and that it can grow rich only by exporting goods in exchange for specie, then the woollen industry has made England's fortune. Wholly English, in raw material as in labour, it asked nothing from the outside world, and the stream of gold and silver all went to swell the common treasury, that indispensable adjunct to national greatness.

The prestige with which the woollen trade was surrounded until towards the end of the eighteenth century, and the kind of precedence it enjoyed over all others, are attested by the standard phrase used in describing it. It is 'the staple trade, the great staple trade of the kingdom'. All other interests come only second to it. According to Arthur Young 'wool has been so long supposed the sacred staple and foundation of all our wealth, that it is somewhat dangerous to hazard an opinion not consonant to its single advancement'.[1] The sole object of a whole series of laws and regulations was only to safeguard, to support and to guarantee the quality of its products and the high rate of its profits.[2] Parliament was besieged by its complaints, requests and constant demands for intervention, which gave rise to no astonishment, for its right to claim and to obtain was recognized by everyone.

The best proof which we still have of this self-asserting supremacy is the mass of publications relating to the woollen industry and the woollen trade. It is common knowledge that English economic literature in the seventeenth and eighteenth centuries abounds in polemics written from day to day on current events: pamphlets, tracts, sometimes one-page leaflets. In an age when the press was still in its infancy it was in this way that people, or groups of people wishing to make generally known any particular fact, or to win support for their cause, reached the ear of the public or of Parliament. There was no question of any importance that was not in this way forced upon public attention and discussed with a view to a practical solution. In this immense collection of pamphlets, the woollen industry can lay claim to a very

[1] A. Young, *The Farmer's Letters to the People of England*, p. 22. Specimens of lyrical expressions used by English writers of the seventeenth and eighteenth centuries about the woollen industry are collected in Hasbach's article, 'Zur Charakteristik der englischen Industrie', *Jahrbuch für Gesetzgebung*, XXVI, 462, 1902.

[2] On the legislation regulating the woollen trade, see H. Heaton, *The Yorkshire Woollen and Worsted Industries*, chap. XII ('The State and Industrial Morality in the Eighteenth Century').

long shelf. Nothing which concerns it is forgotten; its progress is vaunted, its decadence is deplored, a thousand contradictory pleadings are to be found, mixing authentic facts with interested allegations. Now it may be a question of permitting or prohibiting the export of wool, or of encouraging or discouraging its manufacture in Ireland, or of reinforcing or abolishing the ancient regulations of manufacture, or of imposing fresh penalties on practices considered damaging to this privileged and all but sacred industry. No one will realize the aggregate bulk of petitions presented to Parliament by employers, workmen and merchants, interested in the woollen trade, unless he has perused page after page many volumes of the *Journals* of the House of Commons and of the House of Lords. The woollen industry before the industrial revolution had its historians,[1] and even its poets, for 'The Fleece', sung by Dyer,[2] is not the legendary Golden Fleece but that of English sheep, from which the cloth of Leeds and the serges of Exeter are made. The Woolsack which, in front of the royal dais and beneath the gilded ceiling of the House of Lords, serves as a seat to the Lord Chancellor of England, is not an empty symbol.

In English eyes — until the day when a new system of production altered everything, including ideas — the prosperity of the country was chiefly maintained by the woollen industry. Proud as it was of its ancient traditions, and already flourishing when the maritime trade of England hardly existed, it represented the work and acquisitions of a long past. The main features of the old industry which in 1760 were almost intact, and which in 1800 still partly survived, were those handed down from the past: its evolution had, so to speak, taken place by their side and without destroying them. To define these characteristics and to explain this evolution is to describe the main features of the old economic system.

II

To begin with, let us look at the industry from the outside, as a traveller on his journey might make inquiries as to the products of each district and the occupations of its inhabitants. One thing strikes us at once — namely, the great number of industrial centres and their dispersion, or rather their diffusion, over the whole country. The fact is the more striking for us as nowadays, under the factory system, the opposite is the case. Each industry is highly centralized and controls

---

[1] John Smith, *Chronicon rusticum-commerciale; or Memoirs of Wool, Woollen Manufacture and Trade* (1747). This book contains the reprints of a number of rare pamphlets.

[2] J. Dyer, '*The Fleece*', a Poem (1757). This title has been aptly borrowed by G. W. Morris and L. S. Wood: *The Golden Fleece, An Introduction to the Industrial History of England* (1922).

a limited area in which its productive power is concentrated. Cotton spinning and weaving occupy, in the Great Britain of today, two districts, narrowly concentrated round two centres. The first is Manchester, surrounded by a belt of growing towns all with the same functions and the same needs, and forming together as it were but one factory and one market. The second is Glasgow, which stretches along the Clyde Valley from Lanark to Paisley and Greenock. Outside these two districts there is nothing comparable to them or which deserves to be mentioned in the same breath.

Let us now follow Daniel Defoe in his 'Tour through the whole island of Great Britain',[1] and let us visit with him the counties of England proper. In the villages of Kent the yeoman, while still owning and cultivating land, weaved that fine cloth known as Kentish broadcloth, which in spite of its name was also made in Surrey.[2] In Essex, today a purely agricultural county, the old town of Colchester was famous for its druggets, 'those stuffs which we see the nuns and friars clothed with abroad';[3] several neighbouring villages, fallen now into complete obscurity, were then busy hives of industry.[4] In Suffolk, at Sudbury and Lavenham, coarse woollen goods were made, called says and calimancoes.[5] As soon as Norfolk is reached 'we see a face of diligence spread over the whole country'.[6] There lies the town of Norwich surrounded by a dozen market towns,[7] and a throng of villages 'so large and so full of people, that they are equal to market towns in other countries'. There long staple wool was used, and it was combed instead of being carded.[8] In the counties of Lincoln, Nottingham and Leicester the making of woollen stockings, either by hand or on frames, created a fairly extensive trade.[9]

[1] Daniel Defoe, A Tour through the Whole Island of Great Britain, 1724-7, 3 vols. (second edition in 1738, third in 1742). Compare with the geographical distribution of the woollen industry at different periods as given by E. Lipson, History of the Woollen and Worsted Industries, pp. 220-55 (with map).

[2] Defoe, Giving Alms no Charity, p. 18. By the end of the eighteenth century these yeomen and their industry had almost completely disappeared. Cf. F. M. Eden, State of the Poor, II, 283 (1797).

[3] Defoe, Tour, I, 20, 43, 53; J. Brome, Travels over England, Scotland and Wales, p. 119; A Journey through England, I, 17.

[4] Dunmow, Braintree, Thaxted, Coggeshall.

[5] Defoe, Tour, I, 70; A. Young, A Six Weeks Tour through the Southern Counties of England and Wales, p. 55 (1768).   [6] Defoe, Tour, I, 91.

[7] Thetford, Diss, Harling, Bucknam, Hingham, West Dereham, Attleborough, Windham, Harleston, East Dereham, Walton, Loddon, etc., ibid., I, 92.

[8] The worsted industry flourished in the neighbourhood of Norwich long before it made its appearance in Bradford, which has since become the principal centre. See J. James, History of Bradford, p. 195.

[9] Defoe, Tour, II, 133, and III, 18. The town of Nottingham, then still unimportant, was already the centre of frame-work knitting. Cf. W. Felkin, A History of the Machine-wrought Hosiery and Lace Manufactures, pp. 42 ff.

We are now reaching the district where in modern times the woollen trade has concentrated more and more. The West Riding of Yorkshire, all along the Pennine range, was already peopled with spinners and weavers, all grouped round certain towns: Wakefield, 'a large, handsome, rich clothing town, full of people and full of trade';[1] Halifax, where coarse materials called kerseys and shalloons are made;[2] Leeds, the market town for the whole district;[3] Huddersfield and Bradford,[4] whose products had not yet become famous.[5] Further north lay Richmond and Darlington, in the county of Durham;[6] further east, York, the ancient seat of the Primate, of which a fallacious popular verse prophesied that it should one day throw even London into the shade.[7] Crossing the watershed, and entering Lancashire whence later cotton practically drove out wool, we find in Kendal and right up in the hills of Westmorland, the manufacture of druggets and ratteens,[8] whilst in Rochdale they imitated the bays made in Colchester.[9] Further south, round Manchester, Oldham and Bury,[10] wool had been spun and woven long before cotton had ever made its appearance in England.

The industry was less developed in the Midlands. Nevertheless Defoe quotes Stafford as 'an old and indeed ancient town ... grown rich by the clothing trade'.[11] Towards Wales, there were Shrewsbury,[12] Leominster, Kidderminster, Stourbridge,[13] and Worcester, where 'the number of hands which [the woollen trade] employs in this town and

---

[1] Defoe, *Tour*, III, 86; J. Aikin, *A Description of the Country from thirty to forty miles round Manchester*, pp. 579-80.

[2] Defoe, *Tour*, III, 105-6. Shalloons = serges of Châlons.

[3] Ibid., 115-21.

[4] Ibid., 87.

[5] J. James, *History of Bradford*, p. 278, quotes a text of Fuller (*Worthies of England*): 'Bradford cloth is a giant to the eye, and a dwarf to the use thereof.'

[6] Defoe, III, 144 ff., and A. Young, *A Six Months Tour through the North of England*, II, 247.

[7] Lincoln was – and London is – and York shall be –
    The Fairest city of the three.
See W. Stukeley, *Itinerarium Curiosum*, Iter V, p. 90 (1722); also J. Brome, *Travels over England*, p. 148 (1704).

[8] Some of those woollen fabrics were known as Kendal cottons. On the use of the word cotton before the birth of the cotton industry in England, see below, Part II, chap. I.

[9] Cf. *Journals of the House of Commons*, XIX, 618. 'This trade is very considerable, and employs the inhabitants of twelve or thirteen miles square ... '

[10] Defoe, *Tour*, III, 221; J. Beeverell, *Les Délices de la Grand' Bretagne*, II, 301-2; J. Aikin, *A Description of the Country round Manchester*, p. 157; Edwin Butterworth, *History of Oldham*, pp. 79, 80, 88.

[11] Defoe, *Tour*, II, 119.

[12] Ibid., II, 114; A. Anderson, *An Historical and Chronological Deduction of the Origin of Commerce*, III, 457.

[13] Defoe, *Tour*, III, 301.

adjoining villages is almost incredible'.[1] In the county of Warwick, picturesque Coventry, the town of three spires, wove not only ribbons but woollen materials.[2] In the counties of Gloucester and Oxford, between the Severn estuary and the upper reaches of the Thames, the valley of Stroudwater was famous for its fine scarlet woollens, which were manufactured at Stroud and Cirencester,[3] while Witney blankets were sent as far as America.[4]

We now reach the south-western counties, and here we must stop at almost every step. On Salisbury Plain and along the course of the Avon the numerous cloth-making towns followed one another thick and fast: Malmesbury, Chippenham, Calne, Trowbridge, Devizes, Salisbury:[5] the land of flannels and fine cloths. In Somerset — apart from Taunton and the great port of Bristol[6] — the industrial centres were closely packed together towards the south and east: Glastonbury, Bruton, Shepton Mallet and Frome, which was destined, they said, to become 'one of the greatest and wealthiest inland towns in England'.[7] This district extended, with Shaftesbury and Blandford, across Dorset,[8] and with Andover and Winchester, right into the heart of Hampshire.[9] Lastly, in Devonshire the serge industry was vigorous and thriving. At Barnstaple, Irish wool was imported to provide for the activity of the weavers,[10] and manufacture took place in such small towns as Crediton, Honiton, Tiverton,[11] which between 1700 and 1740 were as famous and flourishing as today they are, from the industrial point of view, unknown and forsaken. Exeter was the market where the finished goods were collected for sale.[12] Defoe closes his description of Devonshire by declaring that 'not only it cannot be equalled in England, but perhaps not in Europe.'

From this it will be seen that the woollen industry was far from being localized. It was impossible to move any distance without meeting

[1] Defoe, *Tour*, III, 293 (edition of 1742).

[2] Anderson, loc. cit. The ribbon industry is of more recent date.

[3] Defoe, *Tour*, III, 64, and Anderson, loc. cit.

[4] A. Young, *Southern Counties*, p. 99.

[5] Defoe, *Tour*, II, 41, 42; III, 29 (edition of 1742). Wilton, near Salisbury, already manufactured carpets.

[6] Ibid., II, 27-8.

[7] Ibid., II, 42. The industrial importance of this district was chiefly due to the quality of the wool of the Cotswold sheep.

[8] Ibid., I, 77, and II, 36.

[9] J. Beeverell, *Les Délices de la Grand' Bretagne*, III, 699, and A. Anderson, *An Historical and Chronological Deduction of the Origin of Commerce*, III, 456.

[10] Defoe, *Tour*, II, 14.

[11] Ibid., I, 87, and II, 17. Cf. Harding, *History of Tiverton*, and Martin Dunsford, *Historical Memoirs of the Town of Tiverton*.

[12] Defoe, *Tour*, I, 83. Compare this description as a whole with that given, fifty years later, in the *Encyclopédie Méthodique*, Arts et Manufactures, II, 256-7 (article 'Draperie', by Roland de la Platière).

Centres of the English Woollen Trade at the Beginning of the Eighteenth Century

it, spreading as it did over the whole of England. Nevertheless three main industrial districts could be recognized: Yorkshire, with Leeds and Halifax; Norfolk, with Norwich; and the south-west, between the English and the Bristol Channels.[1] But even there, industry was far from concentrated, and the larger centres were linked together by smaller ones. They were nothing like industrial islands, each of them showing only a local strengthening of the general activity spread over the whole Kingdom.

If, instead of considering the country as a whole, we were to examine separately each of the districts we have just surveyed, we should find within each particular centre the same characteristic diffusion. For instance, take Norfolk: Norwich, the capital, was in the eighteenth century a very important town. From the time of the Revolution it had been the third town in the country and the rival of Bristol. Contemporary writers described it pompously, with its three-mile circumference and its six bridges. They marvelled at the silence of its streets, whilst the hum of looms issued from its industrious houses.[2] Yet Norwich, at the height of its prosperity, had at the most 30,000 to 40,000 inhabitants.[3] How then is it possible to credit those witnesses who affirmed that the industry of Norwich provided occupation for 70,000 to 80,000 persons?[4] It was because the industry was not limited to Norwich alone. It overflowed into the surrounding country for a considerable distance, and caused the growth of that 'throng of villages'[5] so close together that Defoe wondered at it. The same conditions held in the south-west, save that no centre there had predominance over the others. According to Defoe, 'Devonshire is so full of great towns, and those towns so full of people, and those people so universally employed in trade and manufactures, that not only it cannot be equalled in England, but perhaps not in Europe.'[6] What Defoe really meant was almost the opposite of what he appeared to say. We know quite well that there never were any large towns in Devonshire,[7] except Plymouth, which had nothing to do with the woollen

[1] See Laurent Dechesne, *L'évolution économique et sociale de l'industrie de la laine en Angleterre*, p. 50, and J. A. Hobson, *The Evolution of Modern Capitalism*, pp. 27-8.

[2] Defoe, *Tour*, I, 94.

[3] A. Anderson, *An Historical and Chronological Deduction of the Origin of Commerce*, III, 324, gives 50,000 to 60,000 (1761), but this figure is undoubtedly exaggerated. F. M. Eden, *State of the Poor*, II, 477, gives 29,000 in 1693, 36,000 in 1752, and 40,000 in 1796. There was no official census before 1801 and then the population was only 36,832. Vide *Abstract of returns to the Population Act*, 41 Geo. III, I, XXIII.

[4] *Journals of the House of Commons*, XXXV, 77. According to A. Young, *The Farmer's Tour through the Eastern Counties of England*, II, 79, 12,000 looms and 72,000 workers (1771).

[5] Defoe, *Tour*, I, 93, 108.   [6] Ibid., I, 81.

[7] Tiverton, one of the biggest, never had more than 10,000 inhabitants. See F. M. Eden, *State of the Poor*, II, 142.

trade. The quite obscure names of most of these 'large towns' are
enough to undeceive us:[1] at most they were small prosperous towns.
Often they were nothing more than average market-towns or large
villages, all the more numerous because people had not left them for
bigger centres.[2] Occasionally smaller places form an almost continuous
chain. 'These towns are interspersed with a very great number of
villages, I had almost said, innumerable villages, hamlets, and
scattered houses, in which ... the spinning work of all this manufacture is performed.'[3]

In Yorkshire the industry seems to have been more narrowly localized, for it lay almost wholly in the area between Leeds and Wakefield,
Huddersfield and Halifax. A few miles north of Leeds the moors
began, barren and almost uninhabited. But this comparative centralization does not alter the general rule, which again holds good within this
restricted area. The West Riding was very densely populated. In 1700
the population numbered about 240,000; in 1750, 360,000; in 1801,
582,000.[4] But only a small percentage lived in the towns. In the middle
of the eighteenth century Leeds had hardly more than 17,000 inhabitants; Halifax had 6,000, Huddersfield less than 5,000, and Bradford
consisted of three streets with meadows on all sides.[5] The countryside,
on the other hand, was thickly populated; not only were strings of
villages and hamlets as frequent as in the south-west,[6] but sometimes
the process of dispersion was carried a stage further, and several
villages merging into one another became one vast and loose agglomera-
tion.

The parish of Halifax was one of the largest in England. It contained,
in 1720, nearly 50,000 souls, and it is the subject of a famous
description: 'After having passed the second hill, and come down into
the valley again, and so still the nearer we came to Halifax, we found
the houses thicker, and the villages greater in every bottom; and not

[1] Bampton, Crediton, Cullompton, Honiton, Ottery Saint Mary, Ashburton, etc.
See Defoe, *Tour*, I, 84.

[2] It was still like this at the beginning of the nineteenth century. See the evidence
collected by the Select Committee of 1806. The weavers of the south-west, when
questioned as to where they lived, often answered, 'It is a large village ... a very
extensive village ... perhaps the largest there is in England.' – *Report from the Select
Committee appointed to consider the state of the Woollen Manufacture in England* (1806).

[3] Defoe, *Tour*, II, 41.

[4] The two first figures are approximate estimates: the third is that of the census
of 1801. See J. Rickman, *Observations on the Returns to the Population Act*, 11 Geo. IV,
p. 11.

[5] J. Aikin, *A Description of the Country round Manchester*, pp. 557 and 571; J. James,
History of the Worsted Manufacture, p. 316, and *Continuation to the History of Bradford*,
p. 89. Today (1927) the population of these towns are: Leeds 470,000, Bradford
290,000, Huddersfield 110,000, Halifax 100,000.

[6] See *Journals of the House of Commons*, XXVIII, 133.

only so, but the sides of the hills, which were very steep every way, were spread with houses, and that very thick, for the land being divided into small enclosures, that is to say, from two acres to six or seven acres each, seldom more, every three or four pieces of land had a house belonging to it ... After we had mounted the third hill, we found the country, in short, one continued village, though mountainous every way, as before; hardly a house standing out at a speaking distance from another, and (which soon told us their business) the day clearing up and the sun shining, we could see that almost at every house there was a tenter and almost on every tenter a piece of cloth, or kersie, or shalloon,[1] for they are the three articles of that country's labour; from which the sun glancing, and as I may say, shining (the white reflecting its rays) to us, I thought it was the most agreeable sight that I ever saw, for the hills, as I say, rising and falling so thick and the valleys opening sometimes one way, sometimes another, so that sometimes we could see two or three miles this way, sometimes as far another; sometimes like the streets near St Giles's, called the Seven Dials, we could see through the glades almost every way round us, yet look which way we would, high to the tops, and low to the bottoms, it was all the same innumerable houses and tenters, and a white piece upon every tenter.'[2]

This is an extreme instance of the dispersion which was to be found everywhere, and which it remains for us to explain. A visible sign of the general conditions of production, it can only be accounted for by the organization of the industry.

III

The centralization of modern industries is bound up with certain facts by which alone it can be explained. Foremost among them is the division of labour constantly increased by the use of machinery. Economic factors as varied and complex as machinery itself need to be in constant touch with one another, for if they are not accurately adjusted and in permanent contact, the loss of time and power destroys all the advantages of their combination. Another commanding fact is the stricter and stricter specialization of functions: like men and workshops, districts too become specialized and each tends to become the sole home of a single industry. Intensified output is another factor which tends in the same direction. A few powerful factories within a

[1] See p. 51, n. 2.
[2] Defoe, *Tour*, III, 97-9. This description dates from 1727, but we find a very similar one in the Parliamentary Report of 1806: 'The greater part of the domestic clothiers live in villages and detached houses, covering the whole face of a district of from 20 to 30 miles in length, and from 12 to 15 in breadth ... A great proportion of the manufacturers occupy a little land, from 3 to 12 or 15 acres each.' *Report from the Select Committee on Woollen Manufacture*, p. 9.

limited area can supply the needs of an extensive market, while the development of means of communication enlarges it still further. And lastly, capital goes on piling up and absorbing and uniting small businesses until it gives rise to vast interconnected undertakings, which bring about the disappearance of small local production, the continuance of which becomes gradually useless and finally impossible. These forces, however, now all-powerful, had but little effect in England as it was about the middle of the eighteenth century.

It would be a mistake, however, to think that their effect had not begun to be felt. The distribution and the density of the industrial population varied, as we have seen, in different districts. This variation corresponded to differences in organization. Between 'manufacture' which had more than one point in common with the factory system, and the almost primitive workshop of the master craftsman, a series of intermediate stages mark the ground already covered. The process of evolution, which had started long ago, and which after a long period of hardly perceptible change was to culminate in a decisive crisis, was, so to speak, outlined by the succession of those economic forms, grown one from the other, of which the oldest still existed side by side with the most recent.

Where there is least centralization we must expect to find least interdependence between the means of production, the simplest methods of manufacture and the most elementary division of labour. Let us turn again to those dwellings in the Halifax valley, which from outside seemed to form, each on its own plot of land, so many independent units. Instead of looking at them from the outside, let us now visit one of them — get to know the people and their occupations. No doubt it did not come up to the seductive descriptions given of such houses by the credulous admirers of old times.[1] It was a cottage, often in unhealthy surroundings, with few and narrow windows, very little furniture and even fewer ornaments. The main, and sometimes the only, room did duty both for kitchen and for workshop. There stood the loom of the weaver, who lived and worked there.

That loom — which can still be found in country districts — had changed very little since the days of antiquity. The threads forming the warp of the fabric were fastened parallel on a double frame, of which the two ends rose and fell alternately and were worked by two pedals; to make the woof the weaver threw the shuttle between them, from one hand to the other. As early as 1733 an ingenious device[2] had enabled

---

[1] On the unhealthy conditions of work in 'what poetry calls a cottage, and history a hovel', see R. W. Cooke Taylor, *The Modern Factory System*, p. 423, and H. Heaton, *The Yorkshire Woollen and Worsted Industries*, p. 349.

[2] The flying shuttle of John Kay. On this invention, of capital importance, see Part II, chap. I.

the shuttle to be thrown and brought back with one hand. The use o
this improvement, however, only spread rather slowly.[1] The rest of the
apparatus was still simpler. For carding, hand cards were used, of
which one, immovable, was fixed to a wooden support.[2] For spinning,
the hand or foot spinning wheel in use since the sixteenth century was
employed,[3] often even the distaff and spindle, as old as the textile
industry itself. The small man could easily provide himself with these
cheap implements. At his door was water for removing the grease from
the wool and for washing the cloth. If he wanted to dye the fabric he
had woven, a tub or two were enough. As for the things which could
not be done without special and costly plant, these were the object of
separate undertakings. For instance, for fulling and teaseling wool
there were water mills, to which all the neighbouring manufacturers
brought their cloth. They were called public mills, as they could be
used by everyone for a fixed payment.[4]

To match these simple tools there was an equally simple organization of labour. If the weaver's family was large enough it did everything, its members dividing all the minor operations amongst
themselves — the wife and daughters at the spinning wheel, the boys
carding the wool, while the man worked the shuttle. This is the classic
picture of that patriarchal state of industry. As a matter of fact these
extremely simple conditions were but rarely found. They were altered
by the frequent necessity of getting part of the wool spun outside. One
loom, working regularly, was reckoned to provide work for five or six
spinners.[5] In order to find them, the weaver had sometimes to go far
afield. He went from house to house, until he had distributed all his
wool.[6] It was in this way that specialization first came about. There
were houses where only spinning was done. In others, several weaving
looms were gathered together; and the weaver, while still remaining

[1] In the Manchester district the flying shuttle was only in constant use from 1760.
Cf. Edwin Butterworth, *History of Oldham*, p. 111.

[2] Cf. *Encyclopédie Méthodique*, Manufactures, I, article 'Draperie'. The proceedings
in France and England were almost identical.

[3] J. James, *History of the Worsted Manufacture*, pp. 334-5. A complete description
of the processes of manufacture before the industrial revolution fills a whole chapter
in Heaton's *Yorkshire Woollen and Worsted Industries* (pp. 322-58).

[4] In 1775 there were about a hundred of these public mills in the parish of Halifax. See T. Baines, *Yorkshire, past and present*, IV, 387. The development of the use
of machinery first of all tended to increase their number. *Report from the Select Committee
on Woollen Manufacture*, pp. 5 and 9.

[5] J. Bischoff, *A Comprehensive History of the Woollen and Worsted Manufactures*, I,
185, gives a proportion of only four spinners to one weaver. A text quoted by G.
Townsend Warner (Traill and Mann, *Social England*, V, 149) gives, on the contrary,
a proportion of ten spinners to one weaver. These are extreme figures. Cf. W. Radcliffe, *Origin of the New System of Manufacture, commonly called 'Power Loom Weaving'*,
pp. 59-60.

[6] R. Guest, *A compendious history of the cotton-manufacture*, p. 12.

an artisan working with his hands, had under him a small number of hired hands.[1]

Thus the weaver, in the cottage which was both his dwelling-place and his workshop, controlled production, and did not depend on a capitalist since he owned not only the tools but the raw material. The woven fabric he sold himself in the market of the nearest town. The aspect of that market alone would be enough to show how the means of production were scattered amongst this multitude of small independent producers. At Leeds, before the two Cloth Halls were built,[2] the market was held in the High Street, known as the Briggate. Trestles, running along both sides, made two long counters. 'The clothiers come early in the morning with their cloth ... *few clothiers bring more than one piece.*' At seven o'clock in the morning a bell rang. The street filled, the counters were covered with goods, each clothier standing behind his piece of cloth. The merchants and their clerks walked up and down between the trestle tables, choosing and buying, and by eight o'clock in the morning it was all over.[3] In Halifax, 'the clothiers who work in the surrounding villages come to town every Saturday, each bringing with him the cloth he has made ... The cloth merchant goes to the Hall, and buys from the clothiers the white cloth, which he gets dyed or dressed according to his requirements. As that Hall, although very spacious, is not large enough for the number of clothiers who visit Halifax every Saturday, the whole town on Saturdays becomes one huge white cloth hall. I saw cloth displayed in every street, in every square and every inn, and in the evening, as I was returning to Leeds, I met an incredible number of clothiers going home on horseback or in small carts.'[4]

This class of small manufacturers made up, if not the majority, at

[1] A small manufacturer of Harmley, near Leeds, employs two workmen, one apprentice and one family of spinners 'who spin for him in their own house', supplying yarn for three looms (*Report ... on Woollen Manufacture*, p. 5). He buys the wool and the dye, then sends it to the public mill where it is picked, carded and rolled. Then he has it spun and woven. He returns the material to the mill to be shorn and fulled. Finally he has it dried and sells it himself in the Cloth Hall at Leeds. (Ibid., pp. 6-7.)

[2] The first White Cloth Hall had been built in 1711: it was replaced by a larger building in 1775. The Mixed (or Coloured) Cloth Hall was opened in 1755 or 1756. See Aikin, *A Description of the Country round Manchester*, p. 572. There is some confusion in the account given of these successive constructions by Heaton (p. 360 f.) and Lipson (pp. 80, 81).

[3] Defoe, *Tour*, III, 116-17.

[4] *Tournée faite en* 1788 *dans la Grande Bretagne par un français* ..., p. 198. It is enough to compare this text with the preceding one (published in 1727) to see that in sixty years things had changed very little. It should not be imagined that the advent of the factory system altered them suddenly: as late as 1858 T. Baines wrote about the clothing trade in Leeds: 'The manufacturers of the outlying district bring the cloth made in their looms, twice in the week, to be sold to the merchants in the two great Cloth Halls of this town.' *Yorkshire, past and present*, p. 655.

any rate a considerable part of the population. Around Leeds, in 1806, there were still more than 3,500 of them.[1] They were all approximately equal amongst themselves. The case of a man who owned four or five looms was regarded as exceptional.[2] There was little difference between them and their workmen. The workman, eating and often sleeping in his master's house and working beside him, did not regard his master as belonging to a different social class. In some places there were more masters than workmen.[3] As a matter of fact the latter only served as a sort of reserve from which the class of small manufacturers was recruited. 'A young man of good character can always obtain credit for as much wool as will enable him to set up as a little master manufacturer.'[4] This conjunction of words is almost a definition. The 'manufacturer' at that time was not a captain of industry but, on the contrary, an artisan, a man working with his own hands.[5] The Yorkshire manufacturer represented at the same time capital and labour, allied and almost blended together.

He was also – last but not least – a landed proprietor. His house stood in an enclosure of a few acres. Defoe wrote that a manufacturer must have one or two horses, to fetch wool and foodstuffs in town, to bring the wool to the spinner, and the cloth, once woven, to the fulling mill, and finally to take the pieces to the market: he noticed, moreover, that most clothiers kept a cow or two to supply their family with milk, and fed them on the plots of land surrounding their houses.[6] The witnesses who gave evidence before the Parliamentary Committee of 1806 expressed themselves in similar terms.[7] This small property increased the means of the working manufacturer. He could hardly cultivate; when he tried ploughing he ran the risk of losing all he made on the sale of his cloth.[8] But he could raise poultry, a few head of

---

[1] *Report ... on Woollen Manufacture*, p. 8.

[2] Ibid., pp. 59 and 339.

[3] In the two villages of Uley and Owlpen there were in 1806 seventy master weavers and only thirty or forty apprentices. Cf. *Report ... on Woollen Manufacture*, p. 337.

[4] Ibid., p. 10.

[5] Ibid., pp. 9, 447, etc. Arnold Toynbee, noticing that before 1800 the word 'capitalist' was very seldom used, while the word 'manufacturer', which now applies to the employer, meant a man working with his own hands, observed that this change in the meaning of the word was a significant illustration of the change in industrial life and organization. – *Lectures on the Industrial Revolution in England*, p. 183. Cf. the word 'manufacturer' in Johnson's *Dictionary*.

[6] Defoe, *Tour*, III, 100.

[7] *Report ... on Woollen Manufacture*, p. 13, evidence of James Ellis: 'Some of them have only half a rood, to hold tenters or something of that sort, and others two or three acres, those that can keep a cow or a galloway.'

[8] Ibid. There were, however, some weavers who were at the same time farmers. Ibid., p. 8: 'Is this manufactory principally carried on in villages or market

cattle, the horse which took his goods to market or on which he rode to neighbouring villages in search of spinners. Although agriculture was not his main occupation, part of his living was derived from the land, this being a further element of his independence.

To this system of production the term domestic system has been applied, and the report of 1806 gives a definition which sums up fairly well what has just been read: 'In the domestic system, which is that of Yorkshire, the manufacture is conducted by a multitude of master manufacturers, generally possessing a very small and scarcely ever any amount of capital. They buy the wool of the dealer and, in their own houses, assisted by their wives and children, and from two or three to six or seven journeymen, they dye it, when dyeing is necessary, and through all the different stages work it up into undressed cloth.'[1] This is the industry of the Middle Ages, still almost unchanged, on the threshold of the nineteenth century.[2]

And it did not seem to be at its last gasp. Its production, broken up though it was among many small workshops, was nevertheless, taken altogether, pretty considerable. In 1740 the West Riding of Yorkshire, where the domestic industry flourished, produced nearly 100,000 pieces of cloth; in 1750 nearly 140,000; in 1760 the French war and its commercial consequences reduced the figure to 120,000. But in 1770 it went up again to 178,000. A relatively slow growth, if compared to that of the following period, but well marked and continuous, corresponding to the gradual extension of its markets.[3] For it would be a mistake to think that this small-scale industry was a purely local one, without foreign outlets. From the cloth halls of Leeds and Halifax, where the weaver himself came to sell the piece he had made with his

---

[1] *Report ... on Woollen Manufacture*, p. 1. A. Held, *Zwei Bücher zur socialen Geschichte Englands*, pp. 541 ff., gives rather a different definition to the word *Hausindustrie*. By it he means an industry managed by a capitalist who employs workmen in their own homes; and he classifies the small industry of Yorkshire as *Handwerk*, which applies equally to the trades of the Middle Ages. J. A. Hobson, *The Evolution of Modern Capitalism*, p. 35, uses the more precise term of *domestic manufacture*.

[2] L. W. Moffit (*England on the Eve of the Industrial Revolution*, p. xvii) shows how in Canada the old system of industry survived far into the nineteenth century.

[3] J. Bischoff, *A Comprehensive History of the Woollen and Worsted Manufactures*, II, Table IV; A. Anderson, *An Historical and Chronological Deduction of the Origin of Commerce*, IV, 146-7; F. M. Eden, *State of the Poor*, III, cclxiii. The exact figures are as follows:

In 1740, 41,441 broad pieces and 58,620 narrow pieces
„ 1750, 60,447 „ „ „ 78,115 „ „
„ 1760, 49,362 „ „ „ 69,573 „ „
„ 1770, 93,074 „ „ „ 85,376 „ „

---

towns? — In villages a good deal; many persons who have small farms also carry on the business in the way I have mentioned, employing their wives, children and servants. — They send them out to harvest work, of course, in harvest time? — Yes.'

own hands, Yorkshire cloth spread all over England.[1] It was exported to Dutch ports, to the Baltic countries, and beyond Europe to the commercial ports of the Levant and the American Colonies. It was just this commercial growth which made the transformation of the industry inevitable.

IV

Domestic industry, as soon as its production becomes larger than local consumption can absorb, can only continue to exist on one condition: the manufacturer, unable to dispose of his goods himself, must come to an arrangement with a trader, who buys them and undertakes to sell them again, either in the home market or abroad. This trader, this indispensable ally, holds in the hollow of his hand the fate of the industry itself. With him a new element comes into play, which very soon reacts on production. The merchant clothier is a capitalist. Often he only acts as middleman between the small producer on the one hand and the small shopkeeper on the other, and his capital, therefore, is still used for purely commercial purposes. Nevertheless, from the first it was customary to leave the merchant to take charge and meet the expenses of certain minor details of manufacture. The piece of cloth as delivered by the weaver was usually neither dressed nor dyed, and the merchant was responsible for the process of finishing which preceded the actual sale.[2] To do this he had to engage workmen, and he had one way or another to become an employer. This was the first stage in the gradual transformation of commercial capital to industrial capital.

In the south-western counties the action of the merchant clothier, or as he was sometimes significantly called the merchant manufacturer,[3] was felt from the very beginning of the process of manufacture. He bought the raw wool and had it carded, spun, woven, fulled and dressed at his own expense.[4] He owned the raw material and consequently the product, in its successive forms; those through whose hands this product passed in the processes which it underwent were no more, in spite of their apparent independence, than workmen in the service of an employer.

[1] On the importance of Halifax in the middle of the eighteenth century, see H. Heaton, *The Yorkshire Woollen and Worsted Industries*, pp. 269 ff.

[2] See F. M. Eden, *State of the Poor*, II, 821.

[3] The merchant manufacturer corresponds to the French *fabricant*, with the special meaning that word preserved for a long time and in a number of trades, particularly in the silk trade. The Lyons *fabricant* until a comparatively recent date had no factory, but simply delivered out-work to silk-weavers working in their own homes: that system, even now (1927), has not entirely disappeared.

[4] *Report on the State of the Woollen Manufacture*, p. 8; *Parliamentary Debates*, II, 668.

These workmen, however, were still very different from those employed in 'manufacture' or in a modern factory. Most of them lived in the country and, even more than the small craftsmen in Yorkshire, earned part of their living on the land. For them, industry was often no more than an additional occupation. The man worked in the fields whilst his wife spun wool, brought her by the merchant from the neighbouring town.[1] William Radcliffe describes how in the village of Mellor, near Stockport, about 1770, not more than six or seven farmers out of fifty or sixty derived their whole income from their farms: the rest supplemented their agricultural gains by their earnings as spinners or weavers.[2] In the Leeds district 'there was not a farmer who got his living by farming without the trade besides in the town'.[3]

Agriculture and industry were often so closely interwoven that an increase of activity on the one side meant an equivalent decrease on the other. In winter, when outdoor work was impossible, the busy hum of the spinning wheel was heard at all cottage firesides. At harvest time, on the other hand, the spinning wheels were idle and the looms themselves had to stop work for lack of yarn. 'The custome hath been retained time out of mind and found expedient that there should be a cessation of weaving every yeare, in the time of harvest, in regard the spinners of yarn, which the said weavers doe use, at that time chiefly employed in harvest worke ...' Thus runs the preamble of an Act of Parliament of the year 1662.[4]

If the merchant was wealthy and bought his wool in large quantities he was forced, in order to get it spun cheaply, to send it great distances, often fifteen or twenty miles away.[5] He had to employ agents to distribute the work, sometimes farmers and often village publicans. This system had its drawbacks. The publican dealt with his usual customers, and as he was anxious not to displease them he was not too particular over the quality of the work, and the merchant

[1] 'As far as I have been able to understand the nature of the system in the West, it is all, in some measure, the factory system: there is no such thing as what we in Yorkshire call the domestic system; what I mean by the domestic system is the little clothiers living in villages, or in detached places, with all their comforts, carrying on business with their own capital ... In the West of England it is quite the reverse of that: the manufacturer there is the same as our common workman in a factory in Yorkshire except being in a detached house. In the West the wool is delivered out to them to weave, in Yorkshire the wool is the man's own property, till it is sold in the cloth.' *Report on the State of the Woollen Manufacture*, p. 446.
[2] W. Radcliffe, *Origin of the New System of Manufacture, commonly called 'Power Loom Weaving'*, p. 59; S. Bamford, *Dialect of South Lancashire*, pp. iv and v.
[3] *Report on the State of the Woollen Manufacture*, p. 13.
[4] 14 Chas. II, c. 5.
[5] T. Crosley, of Bradford, used to send distaffs of combed wool to Kirkby Lonsdale (about 50 miles away) and Ormskirk, near Liverpool; J. James, *History of the Worsted Manufacture*, pp. 254 and 325.

clothier sometimes complained about it.[1] Already, as we have seen, the small manufacturer was obliged to employ outside labour. As the influence of capital made itself felt, this early type of industrial organization became more and more general.[2]

After having passed through the hands of the spinners (both men and women) the wool was handed on to the weaver. He still kept all the outward semblance of independence. He worked at home on his own loom. He even sometimes played the part of employer, and took charge of the manufacture. He often had the carding and spinning done at his own expense. He supplied tools and some of the minor raw materials of production.[3] He was moreover not bound to a single master, for he often had work given him by four or five different cloth merchants.[4] In these circumstances he was naturally inclined to consider himself not as a workman, but as a contractor dealing on terms with a rich client.

But he was poor. After deducting from the money he received the wages he had to pay himself, there was very little left.[5] If it was a bad year and the harvest was deficient, he was in difficulties. He had to borrow, and who was the most likely person to lend if not the merchant who employed him? The merchant was generally willing to lend him money, but he needed security, and the readiest pledge was the weaver's loom which, after becoming the means of earning mere wages, now ceased to be the exclusive property of the producer. In this way, following on the raw material, the implement in its turn fell into the capitalist's hands. From the end of the seventeenth and the beginning

[1] James, p. 312 (evidence of H. Hall, President of the Worsted Committee of Leeds). The spinners of both sexes were paid on piece work. A certain specified amount of work was called a penny; twelve times as much was called a shilling; words which, in this use, lost their usual meaning: for the value of the shilling was subject to fluctuation between 10 and 15 pence. See *Annals of Agriculture*, IX, 447-9, and *Norfolk Herald*, Feb. 14th, 1832.

[2] The part played, during the eighteenth century, by 'commercial capitalism, paving the way to industrial capitalism', is very well explained, with illustrations from French economic history, in an article by Henri Sée, 'Les Origines de l'Industrie Capitaliste en France', *Revue historique*, CXLIV (1923), 187-200.

[3] Amongst others, starch for finishing and candles for night work. See Edwin Butterworth, *History of Oldham*, p. 103; R. Guest, *A compendious history of the cotton-manufacture*, p. 10; *Journals of the House of Commons*, LV, 493. These passages refer to the cotton industry, where this practice was more usual than in the wool industry.

[4] *Report from the Select Committee on the Petitions of Persons concerned in the Woollen Manufacture in the Counties of Somerset, Wilts and Gloucester* (1803), Parliamentary Reports, V, 243.

[5] The weaver received 36 shillings for weaving 12 lb. of yarn. The preliminary operations (picking, carding, and roving) cost him 9 shillings; spinning at 9d. a pound, 9 shillings. He had therefore 18 shillings left for work which took a fortnight. (Cotton industry, 1750, see R. Guest, *A compendious history of the cotton-manufacture*, p. 10.)

of the eighteenth century, this process of alienation, slow and unnoticed, took place almost wherever home industry had been at all
impaired. So much so that at last the merchant clothier owned the
wool, the yarn, the loom, the stuff, together with the mill where the
cloth was fulled and the shop where it was sold. In certain branches of
the woollen industry, where the plant was more elaborate and therefore
more expensive, the capitalist gained control more quickly and more
completely. The frame-work stocking-knitters in London and Nottingham paid rent — frame-rent — for the use of their knitting frames.
When they had a grievance against their employer one of their ways of
showing fight was to break the frames.[1] Thus the producer, gradually
deprived of all rights of ownership over the instruments of production,
had in the end only his labour to sell and his wages to live on.

His position was even more precarious when, instead of living in
the country, where the land itself still helped him to make a living,
he lived in the town inhabited by the merchant clothier. Then he
became completely dependent, having none but the clothier to look
to for the work on which he lived. In 1765 a rich Tiverton merchant
died without heirs. There was great anxiety among the weavers,
who already saw themselves deprived of their livelihood. They went
in a body to the Mayor and requested him to try and induce an
Exeter merchant to come to Tiverton, by offering him a seat on the
town council.[2] The man's death was for them what the sudden closing
down of a factory is for the workman of today. Only one thing was
missing to complete the likeness. The man still worked at home,
without being subject to factory discipline, and the employer confined
himself to arranging the order and connection of the various technical
processes, without trying to supervise them. Here and there, however,
'manufacture' on a small scale made its appearance, the merchant
collecting the looms under his own roof, and grouping ten or twelve
men in one workshop, instead of three or four as did the master
craftsman. At the same time he continued to employ workmen in their
own homes.[3] In this way we pass, by hardly perceptible degrees, from
the merchant who came to the cloth hall to buy stuffs woven by the

[1] W. Felkin, *A History of the Machine-wrought Hosiery and Lace Manufactures*, chaps. II
and III; G. Howell, *Conflicts of Capital and Labour*, p. 84 f. The most important text
is the Parliamentary Enquiry of 1753, vol. XXVI of the *Journals of the House of
Commons*.

[2] Martin Dunsford, *Historical Memoirs of the Town of Tiverton*, anno 1765. A good
relation of the incident will be found in E. Lipson, *History of the English Woollen and
Worsted Industries*, pp. 54-6.

[3] Examples quoted in the *Report on the State of the Woollen Manufacture* of 1806: a
clothier employed 21 weavers of whom 11 worked at his house and 10 in their own
homes; the 21 looms belonged to him (p. 175). Another, on a total of 27 looms only
had 13 in his workshop (p. 104).

small man, to the manufacturer, ready to become the industrialist of the coming period.

This form of industry, coming between home industry and the system of 'manufacture', was almost always based upon work done at home. This is the reason why Held frequently calls it 'Hausindustrie'.[1] But the expression is ambiguous: is not the industry of the master craftsman also, and in a much more complete sense, a home industry? Is it not the term which should most appropriately be applied to it? What characterizes this system is not work done at home but the part played by the capitalist, by the merchant, who from being at first only a buyer gradually comes to control the whole of production.[2]

It was mainly in the south-western counties that the economic force of the merchant manufacturer made itself gradually felt. It had its seat in small towns like Frome and Tiverton; from there it spread into the surrounding villages and through the countryside.[3] Not that the south-west was, from this point of view, quite unique. In Yorkshire, very near the parish of Halifax, where the independence of the small craftsman still remained almost untouched, the district of Bradford on the contrary was controlled by wealthy clothiers. A fairly plausible explanation of the existence of these two forms of production side by side is the following.[4] Wools used in Bradford were combed, in Halifax they were carded. Now there was a difference between these, not only in technical details but in the price of the raw materials and the amount of skill demanded of the workers. The industry of combed wools needs long staple wool of better quality and higher price. That of carded wools needs short curly staples, which are cheaper but

---

[1] A. Held, *Zwei Bücher zur socialen Geschichte Englands*, pp. 541-3. That type of industry has somehow maintained its existence in certain branches of production. Hasbach mentions, in England of today (1927), the following examples: cutlery in and round Sheffield, chain- and nail-making in the Black Country, lace-making and hosiery in Nottingham, straw-plaiting in Bedford, glove industry in Worcester and Oxfordshire, small-ware trade in Birmingham and silk-weaving in Macclesfield. W. Hasbach, *Zur Charakteristik der englischen Industrie* (*Jahrbuch für Gesetzgebung*, XXVI, pp. 1032-52). Not to mention the well-known example of the clothing trade in London and other cities.

[2] We have taken the woollen industry as our example. But the same facts are just as much in evidence in other industries. In Nottingham in 1750, 50 hosiers owned together 1,200 knitting frames; cf. W. Felkin, *A History of the Machine-wrought Hosiery and Lace Manufactures*, p. 83. The same in the lace industry, one of those in which the technique changed most slowly. In 1770, James Pilgrim of London employed 2,000 workers, both men and women, of whom the majority worked at home. *Journals of the House of Commons*, XXXII, 127.

[3] Defoe, *Tour*, II, 17, mentions that all the villages round Tiverton 'are full of manufacturers, depending much on the master manufacturers of that town'.

[4] Laurent Dechesne, *L'évolution économique et sociale de l'industrie de la laine en Angleterre*, pp. 69-71. Cf. H. Heaton, *The Yorkshire Woollen and Worsted Industries*, pp. 297 ff.

not so easy to turn to the best account. The first, above all, needed capital, the second skilled and careful labour. The latter could thrive in small free workshops, whilst the former made better progress as part of a more highly commercialized system.

In the east of England — especially in Norfolk — wool-combing was predominant. There it was, therefore, that the best conditions for the beginning of capitalist undertakings were found. Their development does not seem, however, to have been much more rapid or complete there than in the south-west. We note only the existence in Norfolk of a quite special class of middlemen — the master combers — 'rich and efficient men' who lived in the towns, and above all in the city of Norwich. Their name shows their main pursuit, which was to get wool combed, a delicate process to be entrusted only to skilled workmen. Even when the wool was combed, the master comber's work was not done. He had travellers who drove over the country in tilted carts, distributing out the wool to the spinners, taking back the yarn and paying for the work.[1]

The rest of the manufacture, as in the west, was in the hands of the clothiers, and their importance can be judged by the rank they held. In Norwich they were a real aristocracy; they affected the airs of gentlemen and carried a sword. Their commercial connection extended as far as Spanish America, India and China.[2] If they bore some likeness to the industrial magnates of our times, they were even more like the great clothiers of the Middle Ages, those merchants of Ypres and Ghent who ruled their rich and turbulent cities as though they had been huge business houses.

Although they were called manufacturers, they were primarily merchants, occupied not in manufacture but in buying and selling.[3] It should be noted that in the woollen industry, then the most important industry in England, the existence of large workshops under the effective management of the capitalist remained quite an exceptional feature till the end of the eighteenth century. That system was not, as in France, favoured and even organized by the Crown. On the contrary, it was at first denounced as a dangerous novelty.[4] Even if it was not completely stopped by restrictive legislation it was at any rate delayed by various measures, the object of which was the preservation of the threatened traditions and interests. Not only did the small

---

[1] *Norfolk Herald*, Feb. 14th, 1832. The information contained in this article was collected at Norwich itself in 1784.

[2] Ibid.; T. Baines, *Yorkshire, past and present*, I, 677.

[3] The same kind of capitalist entrepreneur, merchant rather than manufacturer, was found in other industries. See F. W. Galton on Merchant Tailors, *Select Documents illustrating the History of Trade Unionism* (I. *The Tailoring Trade*), pp. 46, 54, etc.

[4] Cf. Introduction, p. 34.

industry survive, but even where the producer had lost his independence the old forms of home industry did not disappear and, with almost unaltered technical processes, kept up the illusion that nothing had changed.

V

These different stages of industry, in which we see the effects of a gradual transformation, correspond to an equivalent gradation in the condition of the industrial classes. Nothing could give a falser impression than a uniform picture, even without any deliberate lightening or darkening of the shades.

When we compare the condition of the worker in the past and to-day, we are often tempted to exaggerate the contrast. Idyllic descriptions of old-time industry have been repeatedly given by writers whose intention was to denounce the evils of the present day and to win back the hearts of men to bygone traditions. Then was 'the golden age of industry',[1] in which the craftsman, either in the country or in a small town, lived a simpler and healthier life than in our great modern industrial centres. The preservation of family life protected his morality. He worked at home, at his own time and according to his strength. The cultivation of a few acres, which he either owned or rented, filled his leisure hours. He lived a peaceful life amongst his own people, and was 'a respectable member of society, a good father, a good husband, and a good son'.[2] A funeral oration could not have been delivered in a more moving or edifying manner.

But even supposing that this eulogy were deserved in every way, it could only apply to home industry, properly so called, such as we have described it in the Halifax district. The master manufacturer of Yorkshire, at once a worker and an employer, dividing his time between the workshop and the land, did undoubtedly enjoy comparative prosperity. 'It is ordinary for a clothier that has a large family to come to Halifax on a market day, and buy two or three large bullocks from £8 to £10 a piece: these he carries home and kills for his

---

[1] P. Gaskell, *The Manufacturing Population of England*, pp. 17 ff.

[2] Ibid. All recent students of the conditions of industry in the eighteenth century have on this point arrived at the same conclusions as ourselves. H. Heaton (*The Yorkshire Woollen and Worsted Industries*, p. 351) writes: 'The eighteenth-century worker would be intensely amused if he could realize the glamour which has been cast today over his dreary toil.' W. Bowden (*Industrial Society in England towards the end of the Eighteenth Century*, pp. 250-1) observes that 'the real reason for idealization of the domestic system in contrast with the factory system is not to be found in the advantages or disadvantages accruing to the workers from either system, but rather in the fact that the domestic system afforded an auxiliary income to the farm laborer's family, which enabled employers to reduce farm wages'.

store.'[1] Add to these the cattle he raised on his own holdings, or which he pastured on the common land, and there was enough for him not to lack meat throughout the winter. This was a remarkable sign of prosperity, in times when the roast beef of Old England was still a luxury for many country people, and when the poor peasants in Scotland were reduced to bleeding their cattle and drinking the blood during the winter season.[2] The Yorkshire weaver brewed his own beer.[3] His clothes were made at home, and to buy a suit in town seemed to him a sign of pride and extravagance. Thus his way of life was comfortable although simple and we cannot wonder if he wished for no change.[4] The workmen he employed hardly formed a different class from his own. They often lived in their master's house, where they received free board and lodging, together with an annual wage like farm hands.[5] A man remained almost indefinitely in the employ of the same master,[6] unless in his turn he set up for himself in a neighbouring village. But such a state of affairs was only possible where domestic production, with all its essential features, still existed.

As soon as capital was divorced from labour the situation changed, at the expense of the producer. As he now became only a wage earner, his condition depended entirely on his rate of pay. An idea frequently expressed in economic writings of the eighteenth century is that the worker is always too well paid. 'It is a fact well known to those who are conversant in that matter, that scarcity, to a certain degree, promotes industry, and that the manufacturer who can subsist on three days' work will be idle and drunken the remainder of the week ... The poor in the manufacturing countries will never work any more time in general than is necessary just to live and support their weekly debauches ... Upon the whole we may justly aver that a reduction of wages in the woolen manufactures would be a national blessing and advantage, and no real injury to the poor. By this means we might keep our trade, uphold our rents, and reform the people into the bargain.'[7] Such good advice, often repeated, could hardly fail to be followed.

[1] Defoe, *Tour*, III, 108.

[2] In Brecon in 1787 'the food of the poor people: bread and cheese and milk, or water. Some small beer. Meat never, except on Sundays'. A. Young, *Annals of Agriculture*, VIII, 50. In Hampshire the Justices of the Peace in 1795 expressed the wish that the labourer might have meat once a day, or at least three times in the week. Ibid., XXV, 365. See F. M. Eden, *State of the Poor*, I, 496.

[3] See petition against the duties on malt, *Journals of the House of Commons*, XXXVII, 834.

[4] *Report on the State of the Woollen Manufacture*, p. 10.

[5] £8 to £10 a year. See G. Howell, *Conflicts of Capital and Labour*, p. 74.

[6] See *Report on the Woollen Clothiers' Petition* (1803), p. 4.

[7] J. Smith, *Memoirs of Wool*, II, 308; William Hutton, *History of Birmingham*, p. 97; *An Inquiry into the Connection between the Present Price of Provisions and the Size of Farms,*

Spinning, usually done by women and children, was worst paid of all. According to Arthur Young's figures the wages of a female spinner between 1767 and 1770, varied, with the district and the year, between 4d. and 6d. a day; this being about a third of a day-labourer's wages.[1] It is true that it was only a supplement to the ordinary income of a farmer's family, and the conditions of work were not arduous. In the valley of Bradford 'the women of Allerton, Thornton, Wilsden, and the other villages in the valley, flocked, on sunny days, with their spinning wheels to some favourite pleasant spot to pursue the labours of the day. In Back Lane, to the north of Westgate, rows of wheels might also be seen on summer afternoons.'[2] Only when the spinners of both sexes were reduced to the distaff and the spinning wheel for a living, and when they were thrown back from agriculture on industry, did their situation become really precarious.

As the industry passed from simple to more complicated and delicate processes, to those which demanded concentration and acquired skill, so specialization grew more and more quickly. The weaver, bending hour after hour over his loom, tended more and more to become only a weaver. While he still lived in the country, no doubt he remained a peasant and a farmer: but his agricultural work gradually fell into the background, becoming a supplementary occupation, whose proceeds merely helped to swell the industrial wage. As for the Norwich or Tiverton weaver, he was now no more than a workman who had to rely for subsistence on his weaver's work only. We have already seen how completely he depended on his employer. The closer this dependence became, and the more the employer realized that the worker could not do without the work he gave him, the faster did the rate of wages fall.

In the western villages the weavers, who still combined agricultural

---

[1] Leeds district 2s. 6d. to 3s. a week (*North of England*, I, 139); Lancashire 3s. 3d. a week (ibid., III, 134); Essex 4d. to 5d. a day (*Southern Counties*, p. 65); Suffolk 6d. a day (ibid., p. 58); J. James, *History of the Worsted Manufacture*, p. 325, quotes for the combed-wool industry figures very similar to these: an able spinner, working from Monday morning to Saturday night, would earn 2s. 6d. (6d. a day); a girl of fifteen could spin nine or ten hanks of yarn a day, receiving ½d. for each hank, which meant a daily wage of 4½d. or 5d. To compare these with agricultural wages, see A. Young, *Southern Counties*, pp. 61, 62, 151, 154, 157, 171, 186, 197, 266, and *North of England*, I, 172, 312-13; III, 24-5, 277, 345. General description, ibid., IV, 293-6.

[2] J. James, *Continuation to the History of Bradford*, p. 221.

---

p. 93; cf. the significant title of a pamphlet brought out in 1764: *Considerations on taxes, as they are supposed to affect the price of labour in our manufactures. Also some reflections on the general behaviour and disposition of the manufacturing populace of this kingdom; showing, by arguments drawn from experience, that nothing but necessity will enforce labour, and that no state ever did or ever can make any considerable figure in trade, where the necessaries of life are at a low price.*

with industrial work, earned their living fairly well. In 1757 a Gloucestershire weaver, with his wife to help him, could earn, when work was good, from 13s. to 18s. a week — 2s. to 3s. a day. This was much more than the average weekly wage, which probably approximated to the 11s. or 12s. noted a few years later by Arthur Young.[1] In the Leeds district, where the industrial population had preserved less of its rural character, a good workman earned about 10s. 6d. a week; but frequent unemployment reduced this to an average of 8s.[2] In the Norfolk worsted industry, where the capitalist employer played a greater part, wages were lower still: in Norwich they were only 6s. — hardly 1s. a day.[3] Thus, as we pass from a scattered industry, still connected with agriculture, to an industry which had reached a higher stage of centralization and organization, we find that not only the independence but the resources of the worker grew less — the causes being, on the one hand an excess supply of labour, and on the other the growing difficulty of the worker in earning any livelihood outside his own trade. Only certain workers, whose special occupation needed greater skill, as for instance the wool-combers and shearers, were better paid, and could more easily defend their standard of living.

Most of the troubles of which factory workers complain today were known to the English workers of the early eighteenth century. Let us run through the endless list of grievances presented to Parliament by the journeymen tailors.[4] They complained of the insufficiency of their wage.[5] They complained of unemployment: 'The poor laborious journeymen ... are never called for or employed by the masters above one half, or at most two thirds of the year; whereas it is evident to all impartial judges that such of them as happen to have wives and children cannot possibly subsist the year round upon the wages they so precariously receive; which, for the whole year, very rarely amounts to above fifteen or sixteen pence a day.'[6] They complained of the competition of apprentices brought in in large numbers from the country: 'Many master taylors, in order to have their work done

---

[1] A. Young, *Southern Counties*, p. 270.

[2] Id., *North of England*, I, 137-8.

[3] Id., *Southern Counties*, p. 65; J. James, *History of the Worsted Manufacture*, p. 278.

[4] See the texts collected by F. W. Galton, *Select Documents illustrating the History of Trade Unionism* (I. *The Tailoring Trade*).

[5] In 1720, 1s. 10d. a day (Galton, p. 13). In 1721, from 1s. 8d. to 2s. by Act of Parliament (7 Geo. I. st. I, c. 13). In 1751, 2s. to 2s. 6d. (Galton, p. xxxv). In 1763, 2s. 2d. to 2s. 6d. (a decision given by the City Justices of the Peace in Quarter Sessions, confirmed by the Act, 8 Geo. III, c. 17). In 1775, 3s. (Galton, p. 86).

[6] *The Case of the Journeymen Tailors in and about the Cities of London and Westminster*, 1744. According to a pamphlet dated 1752 'from Midsummer until some time after Michaelmas the journeymen taylors have little or no work and are not employed on the whole more than thirty-two weeks in the year'. *The Case of the Journeymen Tailors and Journeymen Staymakers*, p. 1.

cheap, get a great number of young, raw and unexperienced lads out of the country, who, for better instructions, are glad to work at low prices.'[1] They complained of the excessive length of the working day: 'The hours of work, in most handicraft trades, are from six in the morning till six at night: but the journeymen taylors' and staymakers' hours of work exceed that time by two hours;[2] and in the winter time they work for many hours by candlelight, which is from six till after eight in the morning ... and from four till eight in the afternoon, which is four hours more ... ; and, by sitting so many hours in such a position almost double on the shopboard, with their legs under them, and poring so long over their work by candlelight, their spirits are exhausted, nature is wearied out, and their health and sight are soon impaired ... '[3] And most of them had no more hope of rising above their station in life than has the average worker of today.

It must be admitted that their position was no worse than during the preceding century, and if anything it was rather better. The price of commodities, which for about fifty years remained very low,[4] helped a great deal in this undeniable improvement. Almost everywhere wheat took the place of barley or rye bread which was 'looked upon with a sort of horror'.[5] The eating of meat, though still restricted, was less so than in any other country in Europe.[6] We even find the introduction into cottages of the luxury (or what was considered a luxury in those days) of tea, brought from the Far East by the East India Company.[7] Nevertheless the comparative prosperity, which these facts no doubt indicate, was of a very unstable kind. A few bad harvests, with a consequent rise in prices,[8] was enough to bring

---

[1] *The Case of the Journeymen Tailors and Journeymen Staymakers*, p. 2.

[2] Until the Act of 1768 (8 Geo. III, c. 17) which reduced the number of hours of work to thirteen (from 6 a.m. to 7 p.m.).

[3] *The Case of the Journeymen Tailors and Journeymen Staymakers*, p. 2.

[4] According to Toynbee, *Lectures on the Industrial Revolution in England*, p. 67, the average price of corn in the seventeenth century ranged from about 38s. 2d., and the average wage of a day labourer from 10¾d. From 1700 to 1760 the average price of corn ranged from 32s. and the average wage of a day labourer from 12d.

[5] A. Young, *The Farmer's Letters to the People of England*, I, 207. All the same, in the poorest districts (for example in the Cumberland valleys) white bread remained till the end of the eighteenth century a sought-after delicacy, which was only produced on high days and holidays. Cf. F. M. Eden, *State of the Poor*, I, 564.

[6] A. Young, *Travels in France*, 1793 edition, II, 313. 'Every weaver of any character made a point of having a goose, or some equivalent, for his Sunday dinner.' *Norfolk Herald*, Feb. 7th, 1832.

[7] Imports of tea into England: in 1711, 142,000 lb.; 1760, 2,516,000 lb. Sir George Nicholls, *History of the English Poor Law*, II, 59. The increased consumption of tea seemed to have been linked up with the reduced consumption of milk, which had become too expensive for the land labourer's family. W. Hasbach, *History of the English Agricultural Labourer*, p. 128.

[8] This is what happened in 1765 and 1775.

it to an end. In many districts the enclosure of common lands, which destroyed for ever the traditional alliance of small holdings with small craftsmanship, was enough to make the position of the country workers untenable, and to drive them in crowds to the towns.

Most workers either worked at home or in small workshops. This has given rise to curious mistakes. It is a common and rather natural illusion to think of work at home as being less toilsome, healthier, and above all freer, than factory work under the eye of the foreman and in time with the throb of an engine. As a matter of fact it is in certain home industries that some of the most pitiless forms of exploitation have survived until recently, or still survive to show how a maximum work can be obtained for a minimum salary. The cheap ready-made clothing industry of east London has often been quoted as affording the most typical example of that system of economic oppression, known as the sweating system. Now this industry, where it still exists, is not concentrated in big establishments. Machinery is scarcely used, the absurd rate of wages making it practically unnecessary. These facts are nowadays so well known that they need not be dwelt upon: the descriptions of the ghastly hovels where sweated workers live and work are the best vindication of the factory. It is in home-working trades that old abuses are hardest to eradicate. For instance, payment in kind – or the truck system – forbidden as early as 1701 by Act of Parliament, survived in the lace industry for nearly eighty years. A new Act, imposing severe penalties, was necessary to put an end to this improper practice, which deprived the lace-makers of part of their earnings.[1]

The modern factory system is not responsible for the creation of the industrial proletariat, any more than for the capitalistic organization of production. It only accelerated and completed the working of an evolution long since begun. Between the small craftsman, at once master and artisan, and the wage-earning workman of 'manufacture', can be found all the intermediate stages between independence and economic subjection, between extreme dispersion and highly developed centralization of capital and control. Moreover, side by side with cottage industry, there still survived the remains of an even older order of things, to which it is harder to attach imaginary virtues. Villenage, when it was abolished in France by the Constituent

[1] 1 Anne, c. 18, prohibits the payment of wages to day labourers and workmen otherwise than by legal tender under pain of a fine twice as great as the total amount due. Payment in kind (or truck system) in the lace industry was the subject of 19 Geo. III, c. 49 (1779). The preamble begins in these words: 'Whereas the practice of paying persons employed in the making of bone and thread lace, in the whole or in part, in goods instead of money, is a great injury to the lace makers and tends to the discouragement of the lace manufacture ... ' A first offence was punishable with a fine of £10; any further offence with six months' imprisonment.

Assembly, had only just disappeared in British industry. Till 1775, the workers in the coal mines and the salt pits of Scotland were serfs in the full legal sense of the word. Bound for life to the coal mines or salt pits, they could be sold along with them. They even wore a visible sign of their slavery in the shape of a collar, on which was engraved the owner's name.[1] The Act which put an end to this survival of a barbarous past only took full effect in the last years of the eighteenth century.[2]

VI

An account of the disputes between capital and labour affords the best possible illustration of the economic evolution prior to the coming of the factory system. These struggles were frequent and violent before machinery and factories or even 'manufacture' came into being. As soon as the means of production no longer belong to the producer, and a class of men is formed who buy labour from another class, an opposition of interests must become manifest. The dominant fact, which cannot be too much emphasized, is the divorce of the producer from the means of production. The concentration of labour in factories, and the growth of great industrial centres, later gave this vital fact all its social consequences and all its historical significance. But the fact itself appeared at an earlier date, and its first effects made themselves felt long before it reached maturity as the result of the technical revolution.

It might be asked whether in this matter the original causes can be traced without going back to very remote times. Is not the story of combinations and of strikes as old as the story of industry itself? Mr

[1] David Bremner, *The Industries of Scotland*, p. 5.

[2] 15 Geo. III, c. 28 (1775). In the preamble humanitarian considerations only take second place, the most important thing apparently being to maintain the supply of labour. 'Whereas persons are discouraged and prevented from learning the art or business of colliers and coal bearers, and salters, by their becoming bound to the collieries and salt works for life, where they shall work for the space of one year, by means whereof there are not a sufficient number of colliers, coal bearers, and salters in Scotland, for working the quantities of coal and salt necessarily wanted: and many newly discovered coals remain unwrought, and many are now insufficiently wrought, nor are there a sufficient number of salters for the salt works, to the great detriment of the owners and disadvantage to the public; and whereas the emancipating or setting free the colliers, coal bearers, and salters in Scotland, who are now in a state of servitude, gradually and upon reasonable conditions, and the preventing others from coming into such a state of servitude, would be the means of increasing the number of colliers, coal bearers and salters, to the great benefit of the public, without doing any injury to the present masters, and would remove the reproach of allowing such a state of servitude to exist in a free country ... ' The maximum delay for total emancipation was ten years. But the system was partially maintained in spite of the Act, which made it necessary to pass a further Act in 1799 (39 Geo. III, c. 56). See J. L. and L. B. Hammond, *The Skilled Labourer*, p. 12, n. 1.

and Mrs Sidney Webb have had to solve this difficulty at the beginning of their *History of Trade Unionism*, and their conclusions appear to confirm our preceding observations. To them, the question presented itself rather differently: it was a question of discovering the actual origins of the English trade union movement. According to Mr and Mrs Webb, no authentic example of a trade union can be found prior to the eighteenth century. All the facts brought forward in support of the opposite theory relate either to guilds or corporations — which were something quite different from workers' unions — or to passing combinations formed on the occasion of a particular dispute.[1] As long as the distinction between master and man working side by side in small workshops is almost negligible, as long as the journeyman can cherish the hope of one day becoming a master, grievances and disputes remain unconnected incidents without much significance. It is only when two distinct classes of men are formed, the capitalist employers on the one hand and the wage-earners on the other, with no hope for the vast majority ever to be admitted into the more favoured class, that the opposition of interests becomes a permanent fact, that instead of temporary combinations permanent societies make their appearance, and that strikes follow one another like engagements in a lasting contest.

The power of the merchant manufacturer, especially in the south-west, roused the opposition of the workers at a very early date. One of the documents which show this most clearly is a curious popular song entitled 'The Clothier's Delight',[2] composed apparently in the reign of William III. It makes the employer himself repeat the confession of the things his workmen accused him of:

> Of all sorts of callings that in England be
> There is none that liveth so gallant as we;
> Our trading maintains us as brave as a knight,
> We live at our pleasure, and take our delight;
> We heapeth up riches and treasure great store
> Which we get by griping and grinding the poor.
>   And this is a way for to fill up our purse
>   Although we do get it with many a curse.
>
> Throughout the whole kingdom, in country and town,
> There is no danger of our trade going down,

[1] Sidney and Beatrice Webb, *History of Trade Unionism*, pp. 12-21. The theory of the transformation of guilds into trade unions is maintained by L. Brentano, *On the History and Development of Gilds, and the Origin of Trade-Unions*, and *Die Arbeitergilden der Gegenwart*, vol. I, chaps. I and II. See also G. Howell, *Conflicts of Capital and Labour*.

[2] The complete title is: 'The Clothier's Delight, or, the rich Men's Joy, and the poor Men's Sorrow, wherein is exprest the Craftiness and Subtility of many Clothiers in England, by beating down their Workmen's Wages.' See J. Burnley, *Wool and Woolcombing*, pp. 160-3.

So long as the Comber can work with his comb,
And also the Weaver weave with his lomb;
The Tucker and Spinner that spins all the year,
We will make them to earn their wages full dear.
    And this is a way, etc. ...

And first for the Combers, we will bring them down,
From eight groats a score unto half a crown;
If at all they murmur and say 'tis too small,
We bid them choose whether they will work at all:
We'll make them believe that trading is bad;
We care not a pin, though they are ne'er so sad.
    And this is a way, etc. ...

We'll make the poor Weavers work at a low rate,
We'll find fault where there's no fault, and so we will bate;
If trading grows dead, we will presently show it,
But if it grows good, they shall never know it;
We'll tell them that cloth beyond sea will not go,
We care not whether we keep clothing or no.
    And this is a way, etc. ...

The next for the Spinners we shall ensue,
We'll make them spin three pound instead of two;
When they bring home their work unto us, they complain,
And say that their wages will not them maintain;
But if that an ounce of weight they do lack,
Then for to bate threepence we will not be slack.
    And this is a way, etc. ...

But if it holds weight, then their wages they crave,
We have got no money, and what's that you'd have?
We have bread and bacon and butter that's good,
With oatmeal and salt that is wholesome for food;
We have soap and candles whereby to give light,[1]
That you may work by them so long as you have sight.
    And this is a way, etc. ...

When we go to market our workmen are glad;
But when we come home, then we do look sad:
We sit in the corner as if our hearts did ake;
We tell them 'tis not a penny we can take.

---

[1] Allusion to the truck system.

We plead poverty before we have need;
And thus we do coax them most bravely indeed.
   And this is a way, etc. ...

But if to an alehouse they customers be,
Then presently with the ale wife we agree;
When we come to a reckoning, then we do crave
Twopence on a shilling, and that we will have.
By such cunning ways we our treasure do get,
For it is all fish that doth come to our net.
   And this is a way, etc. ...

And thus we do gain all our wealth and estate,
By many poor men that work early and late;
If it were not for those that do labour full hard,
We might go and hang ourselves without regard;
The Combers, the Weavers, the Tuckers also,
With the Spinners that work for wages full low.
   By these people's labour we fill up our purse,
   Although we do get it with many a curse.

We have thought it worth while to quote the greater part of this effusion, in spite of its long-windedness and its artless style. These, indeed, make it the more characteristic in that they so clearly show its popular origin. We seem to hear the voices of the men who, in a miserable pot-house after their day's work, were the first to think of joining together in order to resist their employers' oppression, and whose meetings became the germ of the trade unions.[1]

[1] 'Adam Smith remarked that "people of the same trade seldom meet together even for merriment and diversion, but the conversation ends in a conspiracy against the public, or in some contrivance to raise prices". And there is actual evidence of the rise of one of the oldest of the existing Trade Unions out of a gathering of the journeymen "to take a social pint of porter together". More often it is a tumultuous strike, out of which grows a permanent organization. Elsewhere, as we shall see, the workers meet to petition the House of Commons, and reassemble from time to time to carry on their agitation for the enactment of some new regulation, or the enforcement of an existing law. In other instances we shall find the journeymen of a particular trade frequenting certain public-houses, at which they hear of situations vacant, and the "house of call" becomes thus the nucleus of an organization. Or we watch the journeymen in a particular trade declaring that "it has been an ancient custom in the kingdom of Great Britain for divers Artists to meet together and unite themselves in societies to promote Amity and true Christian Charity", and establishing a sick and funeral club, which invariably proceeds to discuss the rates of wages offered by the employers, and insensibly passes into a Trade Union with friendly benefits. And if the trade is one in which the journeymen frequently travel in search of work, we note the slow elaboration of systematic arrangements for the relief of these "tramps" by their fellow-workers in each town through which they pass, and the inevitable passage of this far-extending tramping society into a national Trade-Union.' S. and B. Webb, *History of Trade Unionism*, pp. 23-5.

Amongst those who first succeeded in organizing themselves were the wool-combers. It may be noted that organized resistance does not usually begin among the most ill-treated, but on the contrary among those who, being more independent, bear their yoke less patiently and have more strength to cast it off. Wool-combers held a special position in the woollen industry. The peculiar processes of their trade demanded much professional skill.[1] As there were not many of them[2] they were hard to replace, and as they moved from town to town[3] in search of work they were not dependent on one, or even on a group of employers. These circumstances explain both their comparatively high rate of wages[4] and the early beginnings of their organization.

As early as 1700 the wool-combers of Tiverton had formed a friendly society which had every feature of a permanent combination.[5] Shortly afterwards, thanks to the wool-combers' nomadic habits, the movement, no doubt started in several places at once, became general; this 'unchartered corporation' of the wool-combers soon spread all over England and felt itself strong enough to attempt to regulate the industry, to the effect that no man should comb wool under 2s. per dozen; that no master should employ any comber that was not of their club: if he did, they agreed one and all not to work for him; and if he had employed twenty all of them turned out, and oftentimes were not satisfied with that, but would 'abuse the honest man that would labour, and in a riotous manner beat him, break his comb-pots, and destroy his working tools'.[6]

Several of these strikes were comparable to the most violent labour disputes of the nineteenth century. In 1720 the Tiverton clothiers

[1] Wool-combing was, of course, done by hand. A complete description of the processes of wool-combing before the era of machinery is found in H. Heaton, *The Yorkshire Woollen and Worsted Industries*, pp. 332-4. It is interesting to compare that description with the article on 'Peignage' in the French *Encyclopédie Méthodique* ('Manufactures', II, 264*) published in 1785. See also J. James, *History of the Worsted Manufacture*, p. 259.

[2] According to Bischoff, *A Comprehensive History of the Woollen and Worsted Manufactures*, I, 185, there were two wool-combers for every seven weavers. According to J. Haynes, *Provision for the Poor, or A View of the Decayed State of the Woollen Manufacture* (1715), p. 9, the making of 240 lb. of wool into worsted employed for one week 250 spinners, 25 weavers and only 7 combers.

[3] See *Journals of the House of Commons*, XLIX, 323.

[4] Between 1760 and 1770 the wages of a wool-comber varied from 10s. to 12s. a week (which is what the best-paid weavers earned). See A. Young, *North of England*, I, 139; II, 134, and *Southern Counties*, p. 65. It should be said that their work was hard and unhealthy, being done near the charcoal stove – or comb-pot, used to heat the teeth of the comb and to warm the wool – which filled the room with noxious fumes. Heaton, op. cit., p. 334.

[5] Webb MSS., 'General History' (I. Woollen Trade).

[6] *A Short Essay upon Trade in General* (1741) quoted by J. James, *History of the Worsted Manufacture*, p. 232.

wanted to import from Ireland the combed wool needed for the manufacture of serge. The combers, whose interests were directly threatened,
tried forcibly to prevent this importation, which meant ruin for them.
They broke into the clothiers' shops and took possession of the Irish
wool. Some of it they burnt, and the rest they hung on the sign-boards
'as trophies of victory'. Several houses were attacked and defended
with muskets, while constables were unsuccessful in re-establishing
law and order until after a regular pitched battle had taken place.[1]
The same dispute broke out again in 1749, when there was a long and
terrible strike. The wool-combers had vowed to hold out till they had
forced the clothiers, and the weavers who wove the Irish combed wool,
to a total surrender. At first they behaved quietly. Later, however,
having exhausted all their strike funds, their sufferings drove them to
violence and to threats of arson and murder. There were bloody brawls
and the military had to intervene. The merchants then made a few
concessions. They offered to limit the import of wool. But the combers
refused and talked of leaving the town in a body, which many of them
actually did, to the great detriment of the local industry.[2]

The weavers lost no time in following the wool-combers' example.
Although less well equipped for the fight, their associations were soon
strong enough to cause the clothiers serious alarm. Once more it is in
the south-west that we find the earliest signs of their existence and
their action. In 1717 and 1718 several petitions to Parliament denounced the formation, by the weavers of Somerset and Devonshire,
of a permanent association.[3] A royal proclamation solemnly reproved
'lawless clubs and societies which had illegally presumed to use a common seal, and to act as Bodies Corporate, by making and unlawfully
conspiring to execute certain By-laws or Orders, whereby they pretend
to determine who had a right to the Trade, what and how many
Apprentices and Journeymen each man should keep at once, together
with the prices of all their manufactures, and the manner and materials
of which they should be wrought'.[4] The effect of this proclamation,
as we might expect, was absolutely nil. And so a few years later
Parliament, at the clothiers' request, had recourse to more severe
methods of repression. In 1725 an Act was passed forbidding any
combination amongst the weavers for the purpose of regulating the
trade or raising their wages. Strike offences were made punishable

[1] Harding, *History of Tiverton*, I, 95. On the riots of the Wiltshire weavers in 1739
see J. Smith, *Memoirs of Wool*, II, 78-9. On the strikes of the wool-combers in Yorkshire see H. Heaton, *The Yorkshire Woollen and Worsted Industries*, pp. 318 ff.

[2] Harding, I, 113-14. The same circumstances existed in the Norwich district.
In 1752 the wool-combers, threatened with a reduction of wages, left the town and
betook themselves to a kind of Aventine at Rockheath. *Gentleman's Magazine*, XXII, 476.

[3] *Journals of the House of Commons*, XVIII, 715; XX, 268, 598, 602.

[4] S. and B. Webb, *History of Trade Unionism*, p. 34.

with heavy penalties which, in the case of house-breaking, destruction of goods or personal threats, went as far as transportation and death.[1] In spite of the fear engendered by these penalties the weavers' associations remained and persisted.[2] On the other hand in Yorkshire, where cottage industry had survived, they did not come into being until after the introduction of power machinery.

In these matters, as in those we have previously discussed, the woollen industry is only one example among many. Reference has been made above to the complaints of the journeymen tailors, expressed in many pamphlets and petitions. As early as 1720 'to the number of more than seven thousand and upwards', they met in London to obtain an increase of wage and a reduction of the working day.[3] Several times, notably in 1721 and 1768, Parliament intervened. The first time, the fear of hard labour or the press gang did intimidate the men, who did not dare to renew their agitation for a long time. Later it began again and strikes became more and more frequent. In 1767 a comedy produced at the Theatre Royal in the Haymarket represented one of these strikes. It showed the journeymen tailors meeting to make their plans at the 'Hog in Armour' or the 'Goose and Gridiron' tavern. In the next act there was a fight between the strikers and the blacklegs in the middle of the Strand.[4]

The story of the frame-work knitters is equally interesting. The existence of a guild, whose charter had been given in 1663 and which included both employers and workmen,[5] did not prevent antagonism

[1] 12 Geo. I, c. 34. The preamble reproduces more or less the terms of the royal proclamation of 1718. The same year (1725) a decision by the Manchester Justices of the Peace in Quarter Sessions quoted the text of an Act of the sixteenth century (2 & 3 Edward VI, c. 15) which forbade all craftsmen, workmen and journeymen to form alliances against their employers, under penalty of a £10 fine or twenty days of imprisonment for the first offence, £20 fine and the pillory for a second, and for a third a £40 fine or the pillory and one ear cut off. See F. M. Eden, *State of the Poor*, III, cx. Similar provisions to those of the Act of 1725 were passed in 1756 and 1757 by the Acts 29 Geo. II, c. 33, and 30 Geo. II, c. 12.

[2] See Laurent Dechesne, *L'évolution économique et sociale de l'industrie de la laine en Angleterre*, p. 153; S. and B. Webb, *History of Trade Unionism*, p. 35. In Lancashire, the worsted smallware weavers began to organize in 1756, the men employed by the same merchant manufacturers forming what they called 'a shop'. See G. W. Daniels, *The Early English Cotton Industry*, pp. 43 ff., quoting the *Smallware Weavers' Apology* (1756), and T. Percival's *Letter to a Friend: occasioned by the late Disputes betwixt the Check-makers of Manchester and their Weavers* (1759).

[3] S. and B. Webb, *History of Trade Unionism*, p. 31; F. W. Galton, *The Tailoring Trade*, Intro., pp. 13 ff.

[4] *The Tailors: A Tragedy for Warm Weather, in three Acts. As it is performed at the Theatre Royal in the Haymarket*, London, 1778, in 8. The only copy of the original edition is in the British Museum, 643e8 (2). The author is unknown.

[5] For the history of this corporation see W. Felkin, *A History of the Machine-wrought Hosiery and Lace Manufactures*, chap. V, and the more recent book by G. Henson, *History of Framework Knitters*.

from the very beginning. The reason for this state of things has been explained before: the knitting frames belonged not to the workers but to the employers. One of the most frequent subjects of dispute was the question of apprentices. The masters employed a great many, taken from among the workhouse children, a circumstance which reduced *pro tanto* the employment and wages of adult workers. In 1710 the London stocking-knitters after vainly protesting against this abuse of apprenticeship, went on strike and, to get even with the masters, began by breaking their knitting frames.[1] Strikes, accompanied by riots, also broke out more than once amongst the knitters of Leicester and Nottingham. They had not yet thought of organizing themselves, for they were accustomed to appeal in most cases to the authority of the guild. This institution becoming more and more decrepit, the knitters finally, like the wool-combers and weavers of the south-west, formed a real trade union.[2]

Such episodes were very frequent during the period immediately preceding the industrial revolution. From 1763 to 1773 the silk-weavers in east London were engaged in a constantly renewed struggle with their employers. In 1763 they drew up a scale of wages, and upon its being rejected two thousand of them left their workshops after breaking their tools and destroying all materials, and a battalion of Guards had to take possession of Spitalfields.[3] In 1765, when the question arose of allowing French silks to be imported, they marched in force on Westminster, with flags flying and drums beating.[4] In 1768, wages being reduced by 4d. a yard, the weavers rebelled, filled the streets in riotous crowds and pillaged houses. The garrison of the Tower was summoned to the rescue, the workmen resisted, armed with cudgels and cutlasses. Dead and wounded marked the scene of the affray.[5] In 1769 this state of rebellion had become permanent, and revolt, like a smouldering fire, kept flaming up. In March the throwsters held 'tumultuous assemblies'; in August the handkerchief-weavers agreed to pay 6d. a loom towards a strike fund, and forced all their fellow-workmen to subscribe. In September and October the situation became worse. Soldiers were sent to clear 'The Dolphin' public-

---

[1] A. Held, *Zwei Bücher zur socialen Geschichte Englands*, pp. 484-8.

[2] The Stocking Makers' Association for Mutual Protection in the Midland Counties of England. See S. and B. Webb, *History of Trade Unionism*, p. 52, and L. Brentano, *On the History and Development of Gilds and the Origin of Trade-Unions*, pp. 115-21. On the frame-work knitters' early associations in the Midlands, consult also *Victoria History of the County of Derby*, II, 367 ff., and *Victoria History of the County of Nottingham*, II, 353-4.

[3] *Calendar of Home Office Papers*, 1760-1765, Nos. 1029, 1051 (Mil. Entry Book, XXVII, 130, 134, 138).

[4] D. Macpherson, *Annals of Commerce*, III, 415.

[5] *Annual Register*, 1758, p. 57.

house, which was the silk-weavers' usual meeting-place. A regular battle took place and several men were killed on both sides.[1] It was in order to put an end to this continual disorder that, in 1773, Parliament passed the famous Spitalfields Act. This Act set up a standard of rules and rates of pay, under the periodic control of the Justices of the Peace. The weavers were satisfied and only formed a union to ensure the carrying out of the Act.[2]

Let us take one more instance outside the textile industry, which has provided all the above examples. From the seventeenth century onwards the miners and colliers of Newcastle had been engaged in a struggle with the mine-owners and with the powerful corporation of hoastmen, who, by a charter of Queen Elizabeth, had obtained a monopoly of the coal trade.[3] In 1654 the keelmen went on strike for higher wages. In 1709 there was another dispute which for several months held up all traffic on the Tyne.[4] The very serious trouble of 1740 was chiefly due to the high cost of living,[5] and can be compared to the starvation riots in France before the French Revolution. But in 1750, 1761 and 1765 there were real strikes which, for many weeks,[6] stopped the work in the mines and harbour. In 1763 nothing less than a permanent combination was formed by the keelmen to force their employers to use the official measures, fixed by Act of Parliament, for the measurement of loads of coal.[7]

The truth is that the Newcastle colliers, like the Spitalfields silk-weavers, the stocking-knitters and the wool-combers, were, before the introduction of machinery, workmen in the modern sense. The raw materials did not belong to them, and as for tools, they could only own the very simplest and cheapest, while those of any value were in the hands of capitalist traders or employers. Thus the opposition of capital and labour had only to reach its final stage, which coincided

[1] *Annual Register*, 1769, pp. 81, 124, 136 and 138.

[2] 13 Geo. III, c. 68. The Spitalfields Act only applied to London, Westminster, and the County of Middlesex. It was completed by 32 Geo. III, c. 44 (1792), which extended it to include mixed fabrics and 51 Geo. III, c. 7 (1801), which regulated women's work. See J. H. Clapham, 'The Spitalfields Acts, 1773-1824' (*Economic Journal*, XXVI, 459-71). The union dates from 1773 according to S. and B. Webb, *History of Trade Unionism*, p. 37; from 1777 according to Samuel Sholl, *A Short Historical Account of the Silk Manufacture in England*, p. 4.

[3] The text of this document is to be found *in extenso* in Brand, *History of Newcastle upon Tyne*, II, 659-63.

[4] Ibid., II, 293-304.

[5] Ibid., II, 520, and *Gentleman's Magazine*, 1740, p. 355.

[6] *Calendar of Home Office Papers*, 1760-1765, Nos. 107, 1910, 1913. What caused the great strike of 1765 was the suspicion on the part of the men that their employers were planning to bind them to the mines by coming into an agreement that no coal-owner should hire another's men, unless they produced a certificate of leave from their last master. See J. L. and L. B. Hammond, *The Skilled Labourer*, p. 13.

[7] Brand, *History of Newcastle upon Tyne*, II, 309.

with the completion of the gradual conquest by the employer of the means of production. Everything which tended to increase the complication, the importance and the price of tools naturally led to this result, so that the technical revolution was only the logical outcome of economic evolution.

VII

The facts we have just examined bear witness to the gradual change in the early forms of industry. We must now turn to the causes which made for the prevention or the retardation of this change — not only the mass of vested interests and the weight of routine but a whole tradition, a system established by custom and consecrated by law. In the whole economic history of the seventeenth and eighteenth centuries the protection of industry by central or local governments was, for a long time, the subject that attracted most attention.[1] This is not surprising, since it is much easier to study legislation, when all the texts are available, than scattered elusive facts of which it is hard to find even a trace. It may be for this very reason that the importance of this branch of research has long been over-estimated. Toynbee even went so far as to assert that the change from protective regulations to freedom and competition was the main feature of the industrial revolution.[2] This is to mistake effect for cause, and the legal aspect of economic facts for the facts themselves. We shall see how, on the contrary, it was the new organization and the new industrial processes which burst the cramping bonds of obsolete laws by which they were still fettered.

These laws had a double origin. Some went right back to the Middle Ages. What is called Colbertism in France existed long before Colbert. The idea of regulating industry is a medieval one. The State, and earlier the guild (whose activities were intimately associated with local government), regarded itself as having the right of control, in the interests both of producer and consumer. To the one a satisfactory rate of profit, and to the other wares of good quality, had to be guaranteed. From this came the meticulous supervision of manufacture and sales together with elaborate regulations, which became more and more complicated, until the day when they fell into complete disuse.

[1] See A. Held's *Zwei Bücher zur socialen Geschichte Englands*. Some chapters lead to the conclusion that social history is nothing but the history of economic legislation. W. Cunningham, *Growth of English History and Commerce*, vol. II, devotes much space to the study of commercial and industrial policy. The same observation applies to Professor G. Unwin's remarkable book *Industrial Organization in the Sixteenth and Seventeenth Centuries*.

[2] 'The essence of the Industrial Revolution is the substitution of competition for the mediæval regulations which had previously controlled the production.' Arnold Toynbee, *Lectures on the Industrial Revolution in England*, p. 85.

The idea of commercial protection also had its roots in the Middle Ages.[1] But its full force was felt only when the rise of foreign trade made nations become fully conscious of their economic rivalry. Then urban economy, in Karl Bücher's words, made way for national economy,[2] which bound together the interests within each State, in order to oppose them to those of other States. Towards those other nations no economic attitude save that of perpetual antagonism was thought conceivable. In England this change took place in the century of the Tudors. Then it was that the mercantile system came into existence, although it did not find its theoretical expression until much later. As specie was mistaken for wealth the whole commercial policy was limited to two precepts, very similar to the advice given by the elder Cato to the Roman agriculturist: always sell and never buy. Import as little as possible, for this always entails specie leaving the country; on the other hand, export as much as possible, for this causes foreign gold to flow into the country. From this sprang that exaggerated protectionism by which not only were national industries encouraged but efforts were made to secure for them a practical monopoly both at home and abroad.

The woollen industry, being one of the oldest and most important of English industries, was, more than any other, protected and regulated.[3] Innumerable Acts of Parliament contain prescriptions relating to the length, breadth and weight of pieces, the processes of stretching and dyeing, ingredients either prescribed or forbidden for the preparation of raw material, the finishing of the cloth, the methods of folding and packing, the use of gig-mills, etc.[4] Similar regulations existed in France and in other European countries. It was forbidden to weave

[1] It first showed itself in the extreme form of prohibition. See W. J. Ashley, *An Introduction to English Economic History and Theory*, II, 12-15.

[2] Karl Bücher, *Die Entstehung der Volkswirtschaft*, second edition, 1898.

[3] For general study on the regulations of the English woollen industry see F. Lohmann, *Die staatliche Regelung der englischen Wollindustrie vom fünfzehnten bis zum achtzehnten Jahrhundert* (*Staats- und sozialwissenchaftliche Forschungen*, 1900). According to H. Heaton (*The Yorkshire Woollen and Worsted Industries*, p. 124) 'the regulation of the cloth industry by the State was guided by two primary considerations. Firstly, there was a real and genuine desire to keep the English prices at a high and uniform standard of quality, and to maintain the good name of English fabrics both at home and abroad ... Secondly, there were financial considerations, which regarded the cloths from the point of view of revenue. As English wool began to be worked up more at home, the revenue which had formerly been drawn from the export of the raw material must now be obtained from levies imposed upon the manufactured article.'

[4] Teaseling (the operation performed by gig mills) consists in brushing up the cloth after it is woven in order to raise a kind of down on the surface. See manufacturers' petition asking for the abrogation of industrial regulations, *Journals of the House of Commons*, LVIII, 334 (April 7th, 1803). Several of the Acts against which this petition was directed dated from the fourteenth century. See J. Bischoff, *A Comprehensive History of the Woollen and Worsted Manufactures*, I, 173 ff.

cloth unless of legal size and weight, to hang it out to dry in any manner which might tend to stretch it, to dress it by the process known as dry pressing, or to use for dyeing specified substances considered detrimental to the fabric. It need hardly be said that these regulations, originally drawn up to ensure the quality of the material, forbade alike fraudulent practices and needful improvements. In order to enforce these elaborate laws, for ever renewed and broken,[1] England, like France, had set up a regular army of specially appointed officials, measurers, inspectors and checkers, who had to weigh and measure the cloth and count the threads. Each piece had to be stamped by them and had also to bear the mark of the manufacturer. Over them all was the Justice of the Peace, one of whose main duties was to see that the industrial regulations were enforced and that offenders were visited with the prescribed penalties.

The disadvantages of this system have often been pointed out. Manufacturers were impatient of this narrow and tyrannical guardianship and used all their ingenuity in evading a supervision of which they constantly complained, whilst in spite of the terrors of the law fraud cropped up afresh as fast as it was suppressed. Sometimes even the government agents themselves became its accomplices. Cloth, duly weighed in the market, became miraculously lighter as soon as the water with which it was soaked had evaporated. Or again some cloth when unrolled — a thing carefully avoided by the obliging inspector — would disclose a weight of brick or lead.[2] Thus the chief object of all these regulations, the protection of the consumer, was not achieved. But on the other hand, technical improvements were made almost impossible. In 1765, on the eve of those great inventions which were completely to transform the whole system of production, it was forbidden under penalty of a fine to replace the thistles, which were still used in most branches of the textile industry, by cards with metal teeth.[3]

Though during the eighteenth century there was a noticeable breaking-down of these medieval regulations, yet the mercantile system, which was of more recent date, was still in its prime when in

---

[1] 7 Anne, c. 13 (1708); 10 Anne, c. 16 (1711); 1 Geo. I, st. 2, c. 15 & c. 41 (1715); 11 Geo. I, c. 24 (1724); 7 Geo. II, c. 25 (1733); 11 Geo. II, c. 28 (1737); 14 Geo. II, c. 35 (1740); 5 Geo. III, c. 51 (1765); 6 Geo. III, c. 13 (1766); 14 Geo. III, c. 25 (1774); 17 Geo. III, c. 11 (1777). The frequency of these Acts, which all contain very much the same regulations, is the best proof of their increasing inefficacy.

[2] 5 Geo. III, c. 51. On industrial legislation, its drawbacks and violations, see *Journals of the House of Commons*, XVIII, 67; XX, 377, 776; XXI, 246; XXII, 234; XXIII, 52, 75, 89, 481; XXVI, 320, 329, 385; XXX, 91, 143, 155, 158, 167, 207, 262, 529, 623, etc.

[3] On the 'tricks of the trade', see H. Heaton, *The Yorkshire Woollen and Worsted Industries*, pp. 130-1.

1776 Adam Smith dealt it the first blow. This extreme protectionist system was the greatest obstacle to any improvement in the traditional processes of the woollen industry, for privilege has always been fatal to initiative and progress. The fate of England seemed bound up with it, and it was 'watch'd with as much care and jealousie as the Golden Apples of the *Hesperides*'.[1] At home it was assumed that preference should be given it over all other competitive industries. And we shall later on have to refer to the great fight which the manufacturers of woollen stuffs put up, not only against the import of Indian cottons but also against their imitation in England by English labour and for the profit of English capitalists. It was certainly not their fault that this great budding industry did not have its development arrested, and was not destroyed beyond redemption. What they desired was to subject the consumer to a regular monopoly, extending even to the dead, for, by a law of Charles II, all persons dying in English territory had to be buried in a woollen shroud.[2] Abroad, their intentions were similar, though harder to enforce. It was easy enough to suppress competition in countries depending on England. The simplest way was to forbid manufacture. The policy adopted in Ireland affords a typical instance of this method.[3] Towards the end of the seventeenth century the progress of the Irish industry began to alarm English producers. They asked for, and obtained, the establishment of export duties which cut off Ireland from all colonial and foreign markets. A regular blockade of the island was set up and was made effective by the coming and going of a little fleet, consisting of two men-of-war and eight armed sloops.[4]

On the Continent it was obviously impossible to prevent the growth of the woollen industry. The English nevertheless confidently attempted it. Proud as they were of the quality of their raw material they felt convinced that without it only coarse stuffs could be made, that, thrown on their own resources, foreign industries would be condemned to permanent inferiority, and that, unable to purchase English wool, the French, the Dutch and the Germans could not help buying English cloth.[5] To this illusion, dear to national pride, was added an imaginary

---

[1] *Considerations upon the East-India Trade*, p. 79.

[2] 18 Chas. II, c. 4.

[3] W. Cunningham, *Growth of English Industry and Commerce*, II, 374-9. See A. E. Murray, *History of the Commercial and Financial Relations between England and Ireland from the Period of the Restoration* (second edition, 1907).

[4] 10-11 Will. III, c. 10 (1699). The penalties were made more severe by the law of 1732 (5 Geo. II, c. 22).

[5] 'An idea was started, that England alone could grow wool, and that other nations would be obliged, if they were prevented from obtaining it, to buy all their cloths from her, ready manufactured.' Sir Joseph Banks, 'Instructions to Lawyers engaged in fighting the Bill dealing with the Export of Wool', *Annals of Agriculture*, VI, 479.

fear — as if one bale of this wonderful wool, introduced into a neighbouring country, were enough to enable that country to become a formidable rival.[1] The outcome of this double train of thought is obvious, namely, a complete ban on the export of wool in any state but that of finished fabrics. Of course the arguments were stronger still against the export of live sheep, who might have become acclimatized abroad: protection went so far as to make it an offence to shear sheep within five miles of the coast![2]

So jealously protected an industry hardly felt it necessary to introduce innovations. Its one idea, as Parliament's spoilt child, was to keep on asking for additions to the Statute Book in its favour, and to complain whenever a question arose of moderating the rigours of previous Acts. The controversy which raged between 1781 and 1788 over the export of raw wool is an example of this.[3] Sheep-breeding was on the increase, and consequently the breeders, finding the home market too narrow, asked for permission to export. Meanwhile, in spite of all prohibitions, a brisk smuggling trade had sprung up which enabled them to sell at any rate part of their produce abroad. But the manufacturers of woollens trembled at the spectre of foreign competition. Far from lowering the barriers, their one idea was to have them raised even higher and to see smuggling much more firmly suppressed. Both sides defended, or thought they defended, their own interests; but whereas the manufacturers summoned privilege to the help of routine, the sheep-breeders, led by that great school of agriculturists which was then engaged in reforming English agriculture, spoke the language of the new political economy.

Arthur Young on that occasion wrote in his *Annals of Agriculture* that it was in the interest of the woollen industry itself to be refused the excessive protection which was being claimed on its behalf. He compared it with more modern industries, whose rapid progress was calling forth general surprise and admiration: 'Examine the trade,

---

[1] *Annals of Agriculture*, VI, 484.

[2] 13 Geo. III, c. 43.

[3] See the pamphlets at the British Museum, particularly in Vol. B.546, and in the Manchester Library (Nos. 26214 and 26216). In favour of free export we may quote Sir John Dalrymple, *The Question considered, whether Wool should be allowed to be exported* (1781); Josiah Tucker, *Reflections on the present low Price of coarse Wools* (1782). On the opposite side, N. Forster, *An answer to Sir John Dalrymple's pamphlet, entitled: The Question considered*, etc. (1782); *The Contrast, or a Comparison between our Linen, Cotton, and Silk Manufactures* (1783); John Hustler, *Observations on the Wool Bill* (1788); J. Bischoff, *A Comprehensive History of the Woollen and Worsted Manufactures*, I, 207-16; J. James, *History of the Worsted Manufacture*, 301-5. See *Annals of Agriculture* (articles of Arthur Young), VI, 506-16; VII, 73, 94, 134-47, 164-70; VIII, 468, etc.

The mistake had long since been pointed out: see James Anderson, *Observations on the Means of exciting a Spirit of National Industry*, p. 264 (1777).

and you will look in vain for that ardour of enterprise, that activity of pursuit, that spirit of invention, which have so nobly distinguished the efforts of British industry, when exerted on iron, cotton, porcelain, glass, etc. All is sluggish, inactive, dead ... Would you bid a black cloud hang over the rising prosperity of Manchester? Give her monopoly of cotton. Does the unexampled increase of Birmingham offend you? Monopoly would desolate her streets like a pestilence.'[1] The manufacturers beat the breeders: the old regulations were renewed, and the crime of exporting wool was made a felony.[2] The news caused great rejoicings in the Leeds and Norwich districts. Bonfires were lighted and bells were rung as if to celebrate a victory.[3]

Young, however, was right, for the means adopted by the woollen manufacturers to maintain the industry's supremacy, even if they did not stop, at any rate considerably hampered its progress. Anyone listening to the constant complaints with which they supported their requests to Parliament would have thought that the industry was declining. As a matter of fact, its development had never stopped:[4] but was slow and irregular — save in the promised land of the woollen industry, the West Riding of Yorkshire.[5] Though there were many centres of production, they were often small and insignificant. Many, from the beginning of the eighteenth century, only just managed to survive.[6] In spite of their slackness they still lived on. They remained as symbols of the old economic order, which changed slowly, by a gradual internal evolution, while it still retained its ancient forms and was kept going by a time-honoured routine. The woollen industry was too conservative, too weighed down by privilege and prejudice, to reform itself by a complete change in technique. The industrial revolution had to be brought in from outside.

[1] *Annals of Agriculture*, VII, 164-9.

[2] 28 Geo. III, c. 38. Certain dispositions are taken from a law of the Restoration (13-14 Chas. II, c. 18).

[3] 'On Friday morning, on the arrival of the news that the bill for preventing the exportation of wool had passed the House of Lords, all the bells in Leeds and the surrounding villages were set a-ringing, which continued at intervals the whole day; at night there were bonfires, and other demonstrations of joy. Similar rejoicings took place at Norwich ... ' *Letters to the Lincolnshire Graziers, on the subject of the Wool Trade* (1788), p. 1.

[4] This is the judicious conclusion of J. Smith, *Memoirs of Wool*, II, 409, 411.

[5] See statistics of production in F. M. Eden, *State of the Poor*, III, ccclxiii; A. Anderson, *An Historical and Chronological Deduction of the Origin of Commerce*, IV, 146-9; D. Macpherson, *Annals of Commerce*, IV, 525; J. Bischoff, *A Comprehensive History of the Woollen and Worsted Manufactures*, I, 328. Production of the West Riding in 1740: 41,000 wide and 58,000 narrow pieces; in 1750: 60,000 and 78,000; in 1760: 49,000 and 69,000 (period of naval war); 1770: 93,000 and 85,000; 1780: 94,000 and 87,000.

[6] Declining villages in Daniel Defoe's time were Braintree and Bocking (Essex), Needham, Ipswich and Lavenham (Suffolk), Cranbrook (Kent), etc. See *Tour*, I, 32, 34, 40, 118, 192.

VIII

This revolution, however, was only a continuation of the movement which had gradually modified the old economic system, and whose progress we have described. Its successive stages, illustrated by corresponding industrial types and bound together by barely perceptible changes, we have seen exemplified in the history of the woollen industry. First of all industry was in the hands of small independent producers whose classical home we find in the Halifax district. Then followed industry carried on by merchant manufacturers, its organization being looser in the south-west, and more concentrated in and round Norwich. Finally there was 'manufacture', the industry of large workshops, which as a matter of fact had made less progress than its sensational beginnings in the sixteenth century seemed to warrant. To note this diversity is to restore to an economic movement its complex and continuous life. Marx, when he applied to this study all his faculty of abstraction, reduced the movement to much simplified terms and divided it into too sharply defined epochs. Moreover, we must beware of accepting as accurate descriptions of facts what, in Marx's mind, had chiefly an explanatory value. For instance, we should be mistaken if we thought that 'manufacture' was the characteristic and dominant form of industry during the period immediately preceding the advent of the factory system. While, from a logical point of view, it should be considered as the necessary introduction to the factory system, there is no historical truth in the assumption that at any moment 'manufacture' had become a general and commanding feature of industry. Although its appearance at the time of the Renaissance was both important and significant, it remained during the succeeding centuries — at any rate in England — a secondary factor.[1] It may be useful to refer to the system of 'manufacture' for purposes of comparison with the modern factory system, but it should always be borne in mind that 'manufacture' was never predominant, and that side by side with it the vitality of previous industrial systems, although declining, never ceased to manifest itself until the very last.

The continuity of the movement is due to the fact that, until the period we propose to study, it remained of a purely economic and not of a technical nature. It was a change in organization and not in the apparatus of production. It was not determined or modified by new inventions, sprung suddenly from individual minds, but by the

---

[1] It cannot even be said that division of labour implied the existence of 'manufacture'. In 1739 the worsted industry, although carried on at home or in small workshops, comprised about forty different processes, each of which constituted a separate trade. See *Observations on Wool and Woollen Manufacture*, by a Manufacturer of Northamptonshire (1739).

slow progress of commercial relations. One fact is specially worthy of note. Those capitalists who gained so much from the gradual concentration of the means of production were hardly industrialists. They gladly left to the small producer, gradually bereft of his independence, all the care of manufacture. They did not undertake either to improve or to direct it. They were solely merchants, and industry for them was only a form of trade. They cared for one thing only, commercial profit: the gain which resulted from the difference between the buying and the selling prices. And it was only in order to increase this difference, to economize on the buying price, that they became owners first of the material, then of the implements, then of the work-places. And it was as merchants that they were finally brought to take entire charge of production.

It was also the development of British trade which urged them more and more along those lines. Moreover, that law, formulated a few years later by Adam Smith, which connects the division of industrial labour with the size of the commercial market, tended in the same direction. To a superficial observer the growth of the carrying trade, whose interests were outside the country, seemed to be prejudicial to the laborious and patient building up of home industry: 'Is England willing to become like Holland, henceforward founding all its wealth on banking and shipping interests? ... There is small likelihood that England will succeed better than Holland in maintaining industries after they have begun to decay.'[1] A false prophecy indeed! For it was, on the contrary, from trade and the trading spirit that the new industry was about to spring.

[1] *La Richesse de l'Angleterre* by J. Accarias de Sérionne (Vienna, 1771), p. 121.

CHAPTER TWO

COMMERCIAL EXPANSION

THE progress of industry and the development of commerce are so closely interwoven, and mutually influence each other in so many ways, that it is often difficult to discover on which side a new development has been started. Sometimes the advancement of industry, by forcing trade to find new outlets, enlarges and multiplies commercial relations. Sometimes, on the other hand, fresh wants, created by the extension of a commercial market, stimulate industrial enterprise. Nowadays the first case is the more usual. Modern industry, driven forward by the internal force of technical progress, urges on trade and credit, which in the interests of production have undertaken the conquest of the world. Moreover it appears only natural for production to govern the other phenomena of economic life, when their very origin seems to lie in production itself.

I

But is not this as a matter of fact one of the newest and most original features in the modern factory system? The fact that it is able to anticipate demand, to modify, or even sometimes to create it, is due to its extraordinary adaptability and to the rapid and incessant improvements in its technical equipment. Development in transport enables the producer to increase the extent of his market at will, without other limits than those of the inhabited world. This was not the case with the old industry. Limited both by the slowness of technical improvement and by the difficulty of communication, production was forcibly confined to the known wants of its habitual market. To manufacture for a clientele of unknown and distant possible consumers would have been considered an act of madness. In short, industry had to be regulated by the condition of trade connections. On the other hand, failing technical inventions, there remained only one way of improving the processes of manufacture and of varying the goods, and that was by borrowing from foreign industries. Here again it was trade which, by bringing in goods from different places, by setting up intercourse between various countries, created competition and brought to light examples which stimulated industrial initiative.

In those days progress in industry was almost impossible unless it was preceded by some commercial development. It would be worth while to study from this point of view the history of certain areas and of certain towns in Europe: to discover, for instance, how far the growth of the Flemish textile industry was bound up with that of the port of Bruges, whose commercial importance dates from the beginning of the thirteenth century, or how the maritime trade of Venice and Genoa assisted in the establishment in Northern Italy of foreign industries which for many years served as models for the rest of Europe.[1]

Such questions cannot be dealt with in a few lines. What, however, we can say is that, before the era of the factory system, a country's commercial strength bore no relation to its industrial importance. We can see this in the history of Holland. In the seventeenth century, Holland was the leading commercial country of the world. But Dutch ships did not carry Dutch goods. They carried indifferently, to all destinations, produce from the East and the West Indies, metal from the Baltic countries, or precious stuffs from the East. They were only agents, and their ports only bonded warehouses. In the midst of this vortex of capital, of men and of ideas, of which little Holland was the centre, industry could not help growing: woollen, linen, and velvet manufactures were created in the United Provinces, as well as cut-glass and diamond-cutting works, not to mention shipyards in or near the ports. But though these were all flourishing industries, yet they contributed only a very small amount to the wealth of Holland. The most important one, that of shipbuilding, had its origin in the progress of the maritime trade and found there the source of its prosperity, and probably of its very existence.

This instance is of direct interest to us, for it was Holland on which England long wished to model herself. For many years her enemy, then her rival, England fought Holland for that commercial supremacy which was so much admired and coveted by neighbouring countries; and in the end she won. Half a century before she became the land of industry *par excellence*, the land of mines, of ironworks and of spinning mills, England was a great commercial country – 'a nation of shopkeepers', as went the famous phrase. The commercial expansion there preceded – and perhaps determined – the changes in industry.

II

Until the end of the seventeenth century, England's economic position was only of secondary importance. The discovery of the New World put her geographically in a much more favourable position, but she did not at once derive much benefit from it.[2] For many years she

[1] For instance, the silk industry, later imported from Italy into France and England.
[2] Mackinder, *Britain and the British Seas*, pp. 1-13, aptly shows how Great Britain, situated at one of the extremities of the Ancient World, suddenly found herself, through the discovery and settlement of America, in the centre of the modern world.

claimed the empire of the seas. John Selden, in his famous *Mare Clausum*,[1] written in reply to Grotius's *Mare Liberum*, demonstrates, by dint of classical and biblical quotations, the following double proposition: first, that the sea may be owned; second, that its owner by right is the King of England. But neither James I, for whom this work was written, nor Charles I, to whom it was dedicated, was in a position to stand up for such bold claims. As a matter of fact the seas belonged to the Spanish, the French, and above all to the Dutch, quite as much as if not more than to the English.

These premature ambitions may be explained when we remember the extraordinary outburst of vitality which, under Elizabeth I, stimulated the life, the strength and the genius of England to such an exuberant flowering. The progress of commerce and shipping had been rapid and triumphant. The world had been amazed at the daring of English sailors, traders and privateers. Whilst Drake, with his buccaneers, threatened the West Indies, peaceful navigators were paving the way for British triumphs of a more lasting kind. Sir Walter Raleigh founded Virginia, Chancellor and Willoughby sailed round the Scandinavian peninsula, landed at Archangel and put the West in touch with Moscow and Novgorod. Trading companies were started, first only as temporary associations of merchants who shared the expenses of fitting out a ship for a long-distance voyage. Later they became societies invested by charter with privileges and monopolies, and even with official power as representatives of the Crown. Such were the Muscovy Company founded in 1554, the Baltic Company (1579), the Levant Company (1581) and the East India Company (1600).[2]

During the succeeding century, national energy was employed in other directions. It spent itself in that struggle, at once political and religious, which twice led to revolution. Nevertheless it continued sometimes to manifest itself abroad. We can see it in the Puritan emigrants who colonized New England. For an instant it showed itself again, in all its old vigour and prestige, under Cromwell's powerful direction. That famous Navigation Act,[3] not unreasonably considered

---

[1] *Mare Clausum, seu De Dominio Maris, libri duo* (1635).

[2] The oldest of all seems to have been the Company of Merchant Adventurers, erected into a corporation by royal charter in 1564. See W. E. Lingelbach, *Internal Organization of the Merchant Adventurers of England*, Philadelphia, 1903.

[3] 1651, c. 22. This Act, amended and completed in 1660, forbade the import into England by foreign ship of any goods other than those produced in the country of origin. Trade with Asia, Africa and America was reserved for vessels built in England, owned by English shippers and manned by English crews. We must not forget either that this Navigation Act was not the first to figure on the Statute Book. Similar steps had been taken in 1381 (5 Richard II, c. 3), in 1382 (6 Richard II, c. 8), 1390 (14 Richard II, c. 6), 1489 (4 Henry VII, c. 10), 1540 (32 Henry VIII, c. 14), 1552 (5-6 Edward VI, c. 18), 1558 (1 Eliz. I, c. 13), 1562 (5 Eliz. I, c. 5), and 1593 (35 Eliz. I, c. 7).

the origin of the maritime greatness of England, dates from the Commonwealth. By forcing the English to do without Dutch brokers, in their dealings with the rest of the world, the Act obliged them to build a mercantile marine for themselves. Material was not lacking. Although there were not many ships on the high seas there was an active coastal trade, largely because land transport for merchandise was slow, difficult and expensive. The coal trade alone, between Newcastle and London, gave employment to a regular fleet, manned by several thousand men, and was known as 'the great nursery of seamen'.[1] Nevertheless the Navigation Act did not produce immediate results.

The era of internal struggle was not yet over. After a few years of peace it broke out again under the Restoration. But these few years were enough for the spirit of adventure to reassert its vigorous existence. New chartered companies sprang up: the Royal African Company, which traded mainly along the coast of Guinea;[2] the Hudson Bay Company, founded with a view to the lucrative fur trade by the brilliant and adventurous Prince Rupert.[3] At last, after a final period of conflicts and troubles, we reach that great date of 1688 which deserves no less a place in economic than in political history.

1688 saw the end of that long struggle waged for sixty years by the English people. It was a beneficial struggle, for through it England won that which no other great European nation then possessed − a free Government. This dearly bought liberty, strengthened by the efforts it had cost, was the best possible guarantee of public prosperity, and the English, after they had once weathered the difficulties inseparable from a new political system, very soon found it out. The author of a famous description of Great Britain[4] wrote in 1708: 'Our trade is the most considerable of the whole world, and indeed Great Britain is of all countries the most proper for trade, as well from its situation as an island as from the freedom and excellency of its constitution ... '

The Revolution of 1688 was brought about by political and religious forces. The work of the bodies politic and corporate and of the whole Protestant nation, it cannot be attributed to the interested

---

[1] See Charles Povey, *A Discovery of indirect Practices in the Coal Trade*, p. 43.

[2] On the Royal African Company see W. Cunningham, *Growth of English Industry and Commerce*, II, 272-9.

[3] Prince Rupert, son of the Elector-Palatine Frederick V, who became King of Bohemia in 1619, and of Elizabeth Stuart, sister to Charles I, spent most of his life in England. He commanded the royal armies during the great Civil War. Under the Restoration he received the title of Duke of Cumberland and of Grand Admiral. It was then that he was put at the head of the Hudson Bay Company and of a host of other undertakings. He was also interested in science and mechanical inventions. To him is attributed, if not the invention at any rate the introduction into England of mezzotint engraving. See *Dictionary of National Biography*, article 'Rupert'.

[4] Chamberlayne, *Magnae Britanniae Notitia*, I, 42.

motives of any one class of society. We may, however, note the part played by the commercial middle class in these decisive events, which were to have such advantageous consequences for them. It was in the Guildhall, the common home of the merchant companies, that the Lords met, after the flight of the King, to summon the Prince of Orange to London. When James II, who had returned for a short moment to his capital, asked the City Magistrates to take him in and to swear to defend him, they refused. On the contrary, two days later they were the first to visit William at St James's and to thank him for saving English liberty. When the Prince, while waiting for the opening of the Convention which was to proclaim him King, summoned a Provisional Parliament to share his power, the Mayor and Aldermen of the City of London were given seats next to the members of the old House of Commons. Finally, in order to meet immediate necessities and especially in order to pay the Army, the City lent the Treasury two hundred thousand pounds.[1] It was the token of the alliance of the new monarchy with the class of merchants and moneyed men. From that moment began that great movement which ended, a hundred and fifty years later, in the definite triumph of the middle class and their seizure of the reins of government. They reaped, almost at once, the benefit of the attitude they had taken up. Very soon after the Revolution two economic events of first-rate importance took place: the foundation of the Bank of England, and the definite constitution of the East India Company.

It is surprising to note how late credit institutions developed in England. In the City of London, in that small area where today the most powerful financial associations in Europe are crowded together and where capital collects from the ends of the earth, there was not a single banking house until the middle of the seventeenth century. It was during the Civil War that merchants first began to entrust their capital to the goldsmiths of Lombard Street. These men, from mere treasurers, soon came to fill the place of bankers, and their notes took the place of cash in ordinary City transactions.[2] As soon as credit had become usual, public attention turned to instances supplied by other countries which had long had a more developed financial system. It is to Italy and Holland that England owes the idea of a national bank.

Schmoller was the first to call our attention to the influence of public loans on the origin of joint stock companies.[3] This influence is noticeable

---

[1] See Macaulay's *History of England from the Accession of James II.*

[2] Id., *History of England* (ed. Longmans, Green & Co., 1919, vol. V, pp. 516 ff.). A more elaborate study is furnished by W. Cunningham, *Growth of English Industry and Commerce*, II, 142-64, who moreover acknowledges that the subject requires further investigation.

[3] See Gustav Schmoller, 'Die Geschichtliche Entwicklung der Unternehmung', *Jahrbuch für Gesetzgebung, Verwaltung und Volkswirtschaft im Deutschen Reich*, 1893, p. 963.

in the founding of the Bank of England. William III's government was in need of money. While viewing with favour the setting up of a credit establishment on the lines of the Bank of Saint George at Genoa or the Bank of Amsterdam, yet it was chiefly concerned with assuring for itself new resources, both for the moment and for the future. At the beginning the Bank was nothing more than a body of capitalists who pledged themselves to lend the Crown twelve hundred thousand pounds at eight per cent. In return it was granted the title of corporation,[1] together with the right of receiving deposits, of discounting commercial bills, and in a word of performing all the duties of a Bank. There is no doubt that the scheme was successful, and that Parliament passed it in the teeth of very strong opposition, only because of its immediate advantages and of the money which could be raised by it for the war in Flanders. This great institution, on whose importance it is unnecessary to insist, therefore only came into being in the first instance as a kind of budget expedient.[2] Few people were foresighted enough to realize then that the rights given to the Bank were infinitely more important to the nation than the sums advanced by it. The help it gave the Treasury, considerable though it may have been,[3] cannot be compared with the service its daily work rendered to the public.

Thanks to the Bank, London was able to become a centre of trade and enterprise comparable even to Amsterdam. Circulation of capital increased, and the rate of interest fell rapidly. In less than twenty years it fell from seven or eight per cent to four per cent and even lower.[4] The epidemic of speculation which raged in England about the same time as in France, the crazy plans and the endless frauds which swarmed round that castle in the air the South Sea Company, only caused a temporary disturbance. The Bank stood fast without a tremor,

[1] On the origins of the Bank of England, see A. Andreades, *Essai sur la fondation et l'histoire de la Banque d'Angleterre* (1694-1844), and Thorold Rogers, *The First Nine Years of the Bank of England*.

[2] It was the Committee of Ways and Means – in other words the Budget Commission – which drew up the Bill for the creation of the Bank. Its title shows clearly what were the real preoccupations of its authors: 'An Act for granting to their Majesties several rates and duties upon the tonnage of ships and vessels, and upon beer, ale, and other liquors, for securing certain recompenses and advantages in the said Act mentioned to such persons as shall voluntarily advance the sum of twelve hundred thousand pounds towards the carrying on the war with France' (5 & 6 William and Mary, c. 20).

[3] From 1694 to 1731 the sums lent to the State by the Bank amounted to a total of £11,900,000; see G. Schmoller, already quoted, p. 964.

[4] Bank of England shares at the time of the Peace of Utrecht (1713) carried 4 per cent interest and stood at £118 to £130. See Thorold Rogers, *History of Agriculture and Prices in England*, VII, 715-16. The Government, which in 1694 had borrowed at 8 per cent, had become able to issue loans at 3 per cent which by 1732 rose above par. Ibid., p. 884. The fall which began in 1755 was very probably due to the greater number of possible investments following on the development of trade.

and its shares, after having been carried away for a moment in the giddy rise which preceded the crash, reverted almost at once to their normal level.[1] From that moment the confidence it inspired was unshakeable. That which made the part it played so important was the fact that, for a long time, there were very few credit houses. About 1750 there were only, outside the capital, about a dozen banking firms.[2] By one of those reciprocal actions so frequent in economic evolution, credit, after having rendered the development of trade and the changes in industry possible, was to receive in its turn an immense stimulus, which is renewed every day before our eyes.

At the time of the foundation of the Bank of England, the East India Company, already nearly a hundred years old, seemed to be on the verge of collapse. It had just lived through a time of unprecedented prosperity. Its wealth, then in the hands of very few shareholders, had roused jealousy and covetousness. Interlopers tried, in defiance of the Company's exclusive rights embodied in the Royal Charter of 1600, to compete with it and to obtain for themselves some of its immense profits. After the Revolution they attacked the Company, by denouncing the political opinions of its governor, Sir Josiah Child,[3] who had sought the support of the Court and the Tories, and they called on Parliament to put an end to a monopoly which they wished to secure for themselves. An obstinate struggle ensued. The Company's opponents first succeeded in obtaining from the House of Commons a declaration that the Crown had no power to grant commercial privileges, and a permission to all English subjects to trade without restrictions with the East, as long as no law was passed to the contrary.[4] They then formed a new Company which was officially recognized in 1698.[5] For a few years there were two East India Companies, divided by furious rivalry.[6] Finally, in 1702, an arrangement was come to, which in 1708

[1] The average price, during the first four months of 1720, was about £150. On May 7th it rose to £160, the 16th to £180, the 20th to £200, June 2nd to £220, the 3rd to £250, the 24th to £265. This was the highest price ever reached, at a time when the shares of the South Sea Company, quoted at £130 in January, rose to £1,000. In July and August the price fell to £220, in September to £200, and after October 12th it again ranged between £140 and £150. Thorold Rogers, VII, 724-5.

[2] Edmund Burke, *Letters on the Proposals for Peace with the Regicide Directory of France*, Letter I, p. 59 (ed. E. J. Payne, Oxford, 1878).

[3] The economist, author of the *New Discourse of Trade* (1693).

[4] *Parliamentary History*, V, 828.

[5] 9 & 10 Will. III, c. 44.

[6] During this dispute many pamphlets were brought out by both sides. We may quote: *Some Remarks upon the present state of the India Company's Affairs* (1690); *Modest and just Apology for the East India Company* (1690); G. White, *An Account of the Trade to the East Indies* (1691), etc. Some of these pamphlets are very interesting for the history of economic doctrines: see for instance *Reasons for establishing an East Indies Company with a Joint Stock, exclusive to all others* (1691), in which the doctrine of free trade is put forward, and *An Essay on the East India Trade*, by Charles Davenant (1696).

led to an amalgamation.[1] In 1708, the same year which witnessed the break-up of the Grand Mogul's empire after the death of Aureng Zeb, the great East India Company was formed which, with Clive, Warren Hastings and Wellesley, conquered Hindustan, and which, during a century and a half, exploited and administered that vast territory.

The violence of the quarrel to which this union put an end shows how important trade with India had become before the end of the seventeenth century. It was further stimulated by the temporary competition of the two rival companies. Then it was that tea, introduced into England at the beginning of the Restoration, became an article of regular importation; that Chinese porcelain, already for many years appreciated by the Dutch and made fashionable by Queen Mary,[2] became the craze of the Court and of English society; and that the use of cotton materials, chintzes, calicoes and muslins, whose very names betray their Eastern origin, spread so rapidly that manufacturers of woollen materials became seriously alarmed.[3] Trade with India included the most varied articles, took every shape, and became more and more one of the most indispensable factors in the wealth of England.

The Bank of England and the East India Company were the two pivots, at home and abroad, upon which English policy turned. And this policy could now at length be directed towards the goal of which a glimpse had been caught during the reign of Elizabeth and under Cromwell's government: the conquest of the seas and of sea-borne trade. We need hardly remind the reader that the foundations of Great Britain's Colonial Empire were laid in the first sixty years of the eighteenth century. Before 1700 England already owned in North America the territory of the thirteen colonies. Beyond this extensive tract of uncultivated country, to which less importance was attached than to the most diminutive spice island,[4] England's possessions were very few. There was only Jamaica in the West Indies, and three or four commercial 'factories' in India. By her leadership of the coalitions against Louis XIV England, in 1713, was in a position to retain

---

[1] It was only in the following year (1709) that the Company took the name of United Company. Thorold Rogers, VII, 2nd Part (Documents), p. 803.

[2] 'The Queen brought in the custom or humour of furnishing houses with China wares, which increased to a strange degree afterwards.' Defoe, *Tour through the Whole Island of Great Britain*, I, 122.

[3] In a later chapter we shall see how the prohibitions demanded by manufacturers against Indian cotton goods resulted in the establishment of the cotton industry in England itself.

[4] In 1804 G. Chalmers still referred to Canada as 'wilderness across the Atlantic' (*Estimate of the Comparative Strength of Britain*, p. 141). This may well be compared to the phrase 'quelques arpents de neige', for which Voltaire has so often been accused of levity.

Gibraltar, Minorca, St Christopher, Newfoundland with its fisheries, Hudson Bay and Nova Scotia, an outpost of French Canada. Fifty years later the Treaty of Paris, which brought to a triumphant close the great naval and colonial wars directed by Chatham's genius, gave England all Canada, the greater part of the West Indies, and India, that unique prize, coveted in turn by every nation. Thus the spontaneous growth of British trade was further encouraged by war and diplomacy, which opened for it a practically boundless field.

That great achievement of British statesmanship was, at the same time, a triumph for the mercantile system — according to which trade with the colonies, consisting of an export of manufactured goods in exchange for raw materials, was the ideal form of trade. The Treaties of Utrecht and Paris, in addition to their territorial clauses, contain stipulations for commercial privileges to Great Britain; that of *asiento* — the monopoly of the slave trade with Spanish America — and that of the well-known 'permission ship' of Porto Bello, for a long time the inexhaustible base for the British smuggling trade.

This very mercantile system, on which the first British colonial empire was built, became the cause of its partial destruction. The rebellion of the American colonies against the mother country throws light on that period of economic history. The grievances of the Americans were, as we know, mainly economic: they complained of the prohibitions imposed on their industries and favouring those of England,[1] of taxes levied, without their consent, for the benefit of the British Treasury. The American war, much more than the writings of Adam Smith and his disciples, made evident the decay of the old economic policy and precipitated its ruin.

But the fortunes of England were not bound up in an obsolete system: whilst the American Revolution, with all its irreparable consequences, was taking place, the genius of inventors and the happy initiative of manufacturers were creating a new America in the very heart of England.

III

According to the mercantile system the main source of wealth for a nation is its foreign trade. It was for the benefit of foreign trade that

---

[1] In 1732, at the request of the London Hatters, Americans were forbidden to export felt hats (5 Geo. II, c. 22). In 1736 English and American shipbuilders were forbidden to make sails of material manufactured outside the British Isles (9 Geo. II, c. 37). An Act of 1750 (23 Geo. II, c. 29) allowed the colonies to export pig and bar iron (which England needed) but forbade them to work themselves the castings or the iron which they produced. See, on the relations of England with her Colonies, Paul Busching's book, *Die Entwickelung der handelspolitischen Beziehungen zwischen England und seinen Kolonien bis zum Jahre* 1860, pp. 38-46 and 71-6.

chartered companies were formed, that statesmen encouraged navigation and that soldiers and sailors supported the merchant's enterprise.
Authentic documents enable us to follow the progress made, year by
year, and with reasonable accuracy.[1]

Compared with the very intense economic life of our times, the
figures quoted below may seem insignificant: but this will help the
reader to realize the immensity of the change which has taken place.
Moreover, the population of England — another result of the same
causes — was, at the beginning of the eighteenth century, about seven
times smaller than today. Let us first look at the figures connected
with navigation.

According to the Custom House Books, the tonnage of commercial
vessels leaving English ports in 1700 did not amount to more than
317,000 registered tons — a very modest figure, sixty-eight times less than
the traffic today (1927) in the port of Liverpool alone. In 1714, directly
after the Peace of Utrecht, it rose to 448,000 tons. During the following
fifteen or twenty years progress was very slow: 503,000 tons in 1737,
which in 1740, during the war with Spain, fell to 471,000. Favoured
by the general pacification following on the Treaty of Aix-la-Chapelle,
the activity of merchantmen increased again: in 1751 the tonnage of
ships leaving British ports was 661,000. The great war with France
created a fresh depression: 525,000 tons in 1756, 574,000 in 1760.
From 1763 there was a marked revival, continuing with great regularity until the war with America broke out: 658,000 tons in 1764;
746,000 in 1766; 761,000 in 1770; 864,000 in 1774. When rebellion
broke out in the colonies the figures fell at once: 820,000 in 1777;
730,000 in 1779; 711,000 in 1781. But as soon as the crisis was over
the progress was so sudden and so rapid that it could hardly be explained but as the symptom of some powerful new factor: 959,000 tons
in 1783; 1,055,000 in 1785; 1,405,000 in 1787. From 1793 — when a
new period of war began — there was some slackening in the rapidity
of the rise, but in 1800 and 1801 the figures reached 1,924,000 and
1,958,000 respectively. In twenty years the figure of 1781 had been
nearly trebled.[2]

---

[1] The statistics of the Custom House Books have been published by A. Anderson,
An Historical and Chronological Deduction of the Origin of Commerce, III, 59, 82, 103, 115,
124, 134, 142, 154, 162, 170; IV, 322, 692-4; and Chalmers, *Estimate of the Comparative
Strength of Britain*, pp. 231 ff. See also *Journals of the House of Commons*, LVI, 649 and 846.
The figures given by these various authorities do not always coincide, but the difference
is never such as to make serious errors probable.

[2] The tonnage of each individual ship was still very small. In 1789 the number of
outward-bound ships was 14,310 of 1,443,658 tons burden, and in 1800, 18,877 of
1,920,042 tons burden. *Journals of the House of Commons*, LVI, 846. The calculation is
easy and gives an average of hardly more than 100 tons. Nevertheless this was a real
advance from the beginning of the eighteenth century. According to W. Enfield,

Both exports and imports followed curves which, if not parallel to the progress in tonnage, were at any rate similar to it in direction and pace. About 1715, imports rose from 4 to 6 million sterling; towards 1725, to 7. Until about 1750 they varied between 7 and 8 million. In 1760 they rose to 10 million, in 1770 to 12, in 1775 to 15. After the drop from 1776 to 1783, when the figures fell to 11 and even 10 million pounds, a sudden progress in 1785 brought imports to over 16 million, in 1790 to 19 million, in 1795 to nearly 23 million, in 1800 to over 30 million. During seventy or eighty years exports increased rather slowly but steadily and fairly continuously: 6 or 7 million pounds between 1700 and 1710; $7\frac{1}{2}$ in 1715; 11 in 1725; 12 in 1730. From 1730 to 1770 oscillations were frequent. Nevertheless from 1740 onwards the figures never fell below 11 million, or from 1757 below 13 million. The tendency was more and more towards a level round about 15 and 16 million sterling. In 1771 these figures were left far behind (£17,161,000) but only to swing back again to $11\frac{1}{2}$ million. Finally, from 1783 onwards, we find, in an even more marked degree, the same sudden rise as in our previous cases. From 15 million in 1784 the figures rose to 16 in 1785, to 20 in 1790, to 27 in 1795, and finally in 1800 to the then unheard-of sum of £41,877,000.[1]

The conclusions are obvious. The curves which illustrate the figures given above almost explain themselves. The most striking thing is the way they rise almost vertically towards the end. This corresponds precisely to the period when machinery first made itself felt and when the products of the factory system began to spread all over the world: for this reason the exports curve, for a long time uncertain and uneven, shows a more definite progress than the imports curve. The time had not yet come when, the needs of the country keeping pace with its wealth and production becoming more and more specialized, imports greatly exceeded exports.[2]

Let us now look at the first part of the three curves, that which illustrates the development of trade and navigation from 1700 to 1775 or 1780. The general tendency is upwards, and the oscillations,

---

[1] This is the figure given in the *Journals of the House of Commons*, LVI, 649 and 846. Chalmers, *Estimate*, p. 234 (Table), gives £43,152,000: the source of this undoubtedly exaggerated figure is not mentioned.

[2] During the period 1890 to 1900 the exports of the United Kingdom varied between £215,824,000 and £291,192,000; the imports between £404,688,000 and £523,075,000. See *Memorandum on the comparative statistics of population, industry and commerce in the United Kingdom and some leading foreign countries* (Blue Book published by the Board of Trade, 1902), pp. 49 and 51. For the year 1922 the figures were: imports, £1,003,918,214; exports, £824,274,297.

History of Liverpool, p. 67, the average tonnage of vessels using the port of Liverpool in 1703 did not exceed 38 tons.

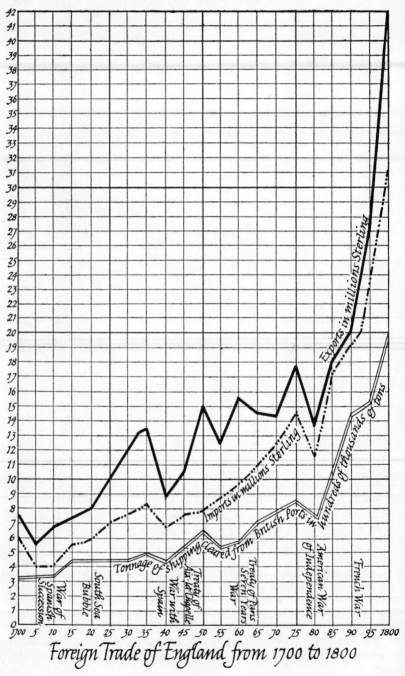

Foreign Trade of England from 1700 to 1800

with their successive drops, are due to purely accidental causes. Each fall in fact corresponds to a war period. Moreover, after each drop, all the curves rise again to a point higher than they had ever previously reached. Finally, if we consider the general trend of the curves, the continuity is immediately apparent. The tendency indicated from the very beginning of the century, although comparatively slow and although sometimes reversed and interrupted, gradually became more definite and already foreshadowed the giddy ascent which was to follow.

The importance of that movement has been disputed. According to J. A. Hobson, the eighteenth-century economists laboured under many delusions in respect of foreign trade. Because nations were then much more cut off from one another than they are today, each lived almost entirely on its own produce. In 1710 England consumed goods to the amount of about sixty million pounds. Imported products were only represented by about a fifteenth of this sum, at the outside by four and a half million.[1] This is true, but if we may borrow an analogy from natural science, only a negligible quantity of ferment is needed to effect a radical change in a considerable volume of matter. The action of foreign trade upon the mechanism of production may be difficult to show, but is not impossible to trace.

In the preceding chapter we have seen how the influence of commercial capital gradually altered the whole organization of early industries. Now the merchant who first, and most easily, played the part of capitalist to the producer was the man who was in touch with foreign countries and who was used to taking the risks of enterprises in distant parts. The most important English export was woollen material,[2] and we already know the chief export centres: some of the towns in the south-west, Norwich where special fabrics for the foreign market[3] were manufactured, and Bradford with the surrounding district.[4] We cannot help noticing that these were all districts in which the worsted industry predominated, and where the economic supremacy of the merchant clothiers had early been established. No doubt their seizure of this branch of the industry was facilitated by the nature of the work and the high price of the raw material. But that which

[1] J. A. Hobson, *The Evolution of Modern Capitalism*, pp. 12-13.

[2] It was not till 1802 that the export of cotton fabrics exceeded that of woollen, as the following table shows:

Export	1797 £	1798 £	1799 £	1800 £	1801 £	1802 £	1803 £
Wool	4,625,000	6,178,000	6,435,000	6,918,000	7,321,000	6,487,000	5,291,000
Cotton	2,446,000	3,544,000	5,556,000	5,323,000	6,465,000	7,130,000	6,467,000

Parliamentary Debates, I, 1147 (*Accounts*).

[3] See J. James, *History of the Worsted Manufacture*, pp. 269, 309.

[4] Ibid., p. 268. The export of worsted from Bradford developed between 1750 and 1760.

enabled them to profit by these favourable circumstances was the continental demand for English worsted. It was maritime trade which gave them wealth and made them ambitious. It was from the ports of Bristol, Yarmouth and Hull that their influence spread inland and finally took possession of the whole country.

After woollens, some of the most important exports were the light metal goods, the hardware and the toys of Birmingham. It was here that, later on, some of the most remarkable and most decisive technical changes in industry took place. However, according to one early historian of the town, the Birmingham manufacturer did not show nearly as much enterprise as he did ingenuity. For when, in his small workshops and with the simplest tools, he had manufactured buttons, shoe-buckles, snuff-boxes, or maybe false coins which had given Birmingham rather a shady reputation,[1] he would often 'keep within the warmth of his own forge'.[2] But alongside this type of producer an active class of merchants had sprung up. These men, who were constantly travelling to the remotest corners of the country, and were in touch with the Continent and America, kept forcing the manufacturers to increase their production and improve their methods.[3] Later, they supervised production themselves. The man who perhaps did most for the industrial greatness of Birmingham, Matthew Boulton of Soho, owed his success quite as much to his commercial gifts as to his genius for organization and as a captain of industry. It was as a bold and clever trader, versed in the needs and possibilities of the market, that he dared to take the responsibility of financing Watt's invention and of converting it to practical use.

Export stimulates existing industries, import leads to the creation of new ones.[4] A closer study of the origin of the cotton industry in England will be found below, showing how that industry arose from the attempt to imitate an Eastern production, so that its seeds were in fact brought to England in the ships of the East India Company. The same holds good of the silk industry, which was borrowed from Italy, and brought to a London suburb by French refugees, after the repeal of the Edict of Nantes.[5] It was precisely in these two industries, silk and cotton, that machinery first made itself felt and that, outside the pale of tradition and legal restraint from which they were emancipated by

---

[1] The word 'Birmingham', or 'Brummagem' wares, was for a long time another word for goods of doubtful quality.

[2] William Hutton, *History of Birmingham*, p. 98.

[3] This is what Hutton describes thus: 'The tradesman stands at the head of the manufacturer.'

[4] See von Guelich, *Geschichtliche Darstellung des Handels, der Gewerbe und des Ackerbaus der bedeutenden handelstreibenden Staaten unserer Zeit*, I, 97 ff.

[5] On industries created in England by foreign refugees, see W. Hasbach, 'Zur Charakteristik der englischen Industrie', *Jahrbuch für Gesetzgebung*, XXVI, 457.

reason of their recent origin and their foreign extraction, the new economic system was born.

IV

Among the facts showing most clearly how the growth of British trade in the eighteenth century reacted on that of industry, none is more significant than the development of certain commercial centres, in the neighbourhood of which groups of factories grew up. The most striking instance is the story of the town and port of Liverpool. We might be tempted to believe that Liverpool was a product of the factory system. Does it not lie on the edge of Lancashire, only a few miles from Manchester, the cotton metropolis? Through the valley where the Weaver and the Trent flow in opposite directions, it communicates with the Pottery district, and beyond that with the Black country of Wolverhampton and Birmingham. To the east it is not far from Leeds and Bradford, the woollen towns, or from Sheffield, the town of iron and steel. Into the broad and deep Mersey estuary, too big for the modest river which runs into it, vast streams of industrial wealth flow from all sides and find there their natural exit, their common outlet towards the sea.

This is the present, but the past was quite different. Until a comparatively recent date Liverpool had little intercourse with the Birmingham district, which faced more towards Bristol and the Severn valley. On the Yorkshire side the Pennine range, crossed only by a few bad roads, was a serious obstacle. Lancashire remained, but the development of her industry can hardly afford a sufficient explanation of the growth of Liverpool in its early stages.

Before the seventeenth century Lancashire was a kind of wilderness, covered with forests and bogs. Liverpool was nothing more than a fishing village, marooned on the edge of its great harbour, then devoid of wharves and almost of ships. Nevertheless the excellent shelter provided by the estuary was already attracting trade. Irish merchants made use of that channel to bring in their woollen yarn which was woven round Manchester.[1] Thus, across several centuries, we can see the relations which still today unite the two cities: the one receiving the raw material which is manufactured by the other. But there is one essential difference: the current then flowed mainly inland from the coast. Manchester, the centre of a modest local industry, had,

---

[1] 'Lyrpole, alias Lyverpole, a paved town, hath but a chapel. Walton, four miles off, not far from the see, is parochial church. The King hath a castelet there, and the Earl of Derby hath a stone house there. Irish merchants come much thither as to a good haven ... At Lyrpole is small custom paid, that causes merchandise to resort thither. Good merchandise at Lyrpole, and much Irish yarn that Manchester men do buy there.' John Leland, *Itinerary of Great Britain*, VII, 37. On the early commercial relations between Liverpool and Ireland, see J. R. B. Muir, *History of Liverpool*, p. 84.

apart from a little cloth bought by the same Irish merchants who provided the yarn,[1] nothing to export. In 1635 Liverpool was still such a small port that Strafford, when he levied the famous 'ship money', only assessed it at £15, whilst Chester paid £100 and Bristol £2,000.[2]

It was during the period of the Revolution, when after a century of political strife maritime expansion had again set in, that the growth of Liverpool began. In 1699 it became an independent parish and built itself a new church.[3] In 1709 its trade began to be important enough for it not to be satisfied any longer with the natural harbour formed by the estuary. It was decided to deepen the basin,[4] which in its turn proved an inducement to the construction of that wonderful series of docks which today extend their wharves over many miles. Men wondered at this rapid prosperity. 'Liverpool', wrote Defoe, 'is one of the wonders of Britain, and that more, in my opinion, than any of the wonders of the Peak:[5] the town was, at my first visiting it, about the year 1680, a large,[6] handsome, well built and increasing or thriving town. At my second visit anno 1690, it was much bigger than at my first seeing it, and, by the report of the inhabitants, more than twice as big as it was twenty years before that; but I think I may safely say at this my third seeing it (for I was surprised at the view) it was more than double what it was at the second, and I am told that it still visibly increases in wealth, people, business, and buildings. What it may grow to in time, I know not.'[7]

The ships which used the port of Liverpool in those days were hardly as large as our sailing trawlers,[8] but their number and their size were

[1] See Lewes Roberts, *The Treasure of Traffike*, p. 17.

[2] *Calendar of State Papers*, Domestic Series, 1634-5, pp. 568, 569 and 581 – £25 in 1636. Ibid., 1636-7, p. 207.

[3] J. Aikin, *A Description of the Country from thirty to forty miles round Manchester*, pp. 334 ff.; A. Anderson, *An Historical and Chronological Deduction of the Origin of Commerce*, III, 143.

[4] 8 Anne, c. 12. See J. R. B. Muir, *History of Liverpool*, p. 176. The second dock was made in 1734.

[5] The Peak of Derbyshire early in the eighteenth century was much visited and admired for its picturesque crags, and still more for its natural caves.

[6] We know what Defoe meant by a large town. According to the figures of baptisms and burials, in 1680 the population of Liverpool cannot be put at more than 4,000 souls. See *Abstracts of the Answers and Returns to the Population Act*, 41 *Geo. III* (1801), II, 149.

[7] Defoe, *A Tour through the Whole Island of Great Britain*, III, 200.

[8] Incoming ships in 1709: 374 with a tonnage of 14,574 tons. Outgoing ships: 334 with a tonnage of 12,636 tons. Average tonnage 38.3. W. Enfield, *History of Liverpool*, p. 67. In 1723 incoming ships: 433 with a tonnage of 18,840 tons. Outgoing ships: 396 with a tonnage of 18,393 tons. Average tonnage 46.4. According to S. Dumbell ('Early Liverpool Cotton Imports', *Economic Journal*, XXXIII, 363), 'in 1709 only 84 ships in all were owned at Liverpool, while by 1752 they numbered 220, of which 106 were engaged in the West Indian and American trade. By 1770 the total number of ships had risen to 309.'

constantly increasing. In 1710 the total number of incoming and out-going ships had a tonnage of not more than 27,000 tons burden. In 1730 it rose to 37,000, in 1750 to 65,000, in 1760 and 1770 it reached 100,000 and 140,000 tons. From the middle of the century Bristol ceased to be the most important port after London, and Liverpool took its place.[1] As to its population, the number rose from 5,000 in 1700 to 10,000 in 1720, to 15,000 in 1740, to 26,000 in 1760: a census taken in 1773 puts the figure at 34,407.[2] The port already had four docks extending over a mile and a half. Arthur Young, although less easily moved to wonder than Defoe, made a special detour in his journey through the rural counties of England, in order to see Liverpool, a town 'too famous in the trading world to allow me to pass it without viewing'.[3]

At the time of this journey of Young's to Liverpool,[4] the factory system in Lancashire had scarcely begun. Manchester was an active and prosperous town, but as yet there were no signs of its marvellous future. English cotton goods were still coarse and of poor quality, and quite incapable of competing with Indian materials. Thus the growth of Liverpool had begun earlier and was progressing faster than that of local industry. It seems to be bound up with the general trade of the country and to run parallel with it in the most marked and most constant manner. It may be said that the history of Liverpool illustrates, during nearly all the eighteenth century, the history of English trade.

Moreover, we not only know when, but how the fortune of Liverpool was made. Above all it was by its connection with the colonies — or plantations as they were then called; by the import of colonial produce such as sugar, coffee and cotton, which were often re-exported to Holland, to Hamburg or to the Baltic ports; and lastly and above all by the slave trade which, since the *asiento* treaty, had become one of the most lucrative sources of revenue to British ship-owners.[5] During the first stage of its development Liverpool very much resembled

[1] In 1766, 803 ships came in and 865 ships went out of Liverpool harbour as compared with 431 coming in and 363 leaving Bristol. (A. Anderson, *An Historical and Chronological Deduction of the Origin of Commerce*, IV, 97).

[2] W. Enfield, *History of Liverpool*, p. 25; J. Aikin, *A Description of the Country round Manchester*, pp. 338-41. This census of 1773 was taken by a group of private persons under the auspices of the Corporation. The figures previous to 1773 are the outcome of approximate valuations, based on the registers of births and deaths. See *Abstracts of the Answers and Returns to the Population Act*, 41 *Geo. III* (1801), II, 149.

[3] A. Young, *North of England*, III, 168.

[4] In 1770.

[5] Defoe, *Tour*, III, 202-3; John Campbell, *Political Survey of Britain*, II, 167; W. Enfield, *History of Liverpool*; Erik Svedenstjerna, *Reise durch einen Theil von England und Schottland in den Jahren* 1802 *und* 1803, p. 181. Re-exported goods accounted for over a third of all exports, see *Journals of the House of Commons*, LVI, 846 ff. An account of the slave trade fills a whole chapter of Muir's *History of Liverpool* (pp. 190 ff.).

some French towns which became wealthy about the same time, through the trade with the West Indies: Nantes, for instance, whose fine stone houses with their frontage on the Loire recall ancient prosperity, when the city grew rich by supplying slaves to the West Indies and receiving in return cargoes of sugar, spices and precious woods.

Liverpool had ceased to be the local market in which the salt of the county of Cheshire and Wigan coal were exchanged for Irish wool. And it had not yet become the huge outlet for the textile and the metal-working large-scale industries. Its function was that of an *emporium*, a warehouse for produce from the countries beyond the seas. The life-blood and wealth of Liverpool flowed in from abroad, from those distant countries where England, mistress of the seas, was already establishing her commercial supremacy.

Outside influences, penetrating into Lancashire, stimulated the growth of a new industry. This was the cotton industry, which borrowed from abroad both its patterns and its raw material. Today the cotton bales, stacked by the thousand in Liverpool warehouses, suggest the neighbourhood of Manchester with its multitude of machines which, like so many ravenous mouths, have constantly to be fed, and the immense mass of manufactured goods which are distributed from the great manufacturing city over the whole world. In this unceasing traffic Liverpool is the place to which goods come and from which they go, but the industrial district of Manchester is the centre and the heart. Nevertheless the force which set all this mechanism in motion came from outside. The growth of Lancashire, of all English counties the one most deserving to be called the cradle of the factory system, depended first of all on the development of Liverpool and of her trade.[1]

v

During the eighteenth century the foreign trade of England grew, but the home trade was completely transformed. Under Queen Anne the different parts of England were still confined to a very narrow local existence. From the economic point of view the country was divided up into a certain number of regional markets, with little connection between them,[2] although England at that time, as compared with

---

[1] This does not mean that the importation of cotton began in Liverpool. According to S. Dumbell, *Economic Journal*, XXXIII, 364, Liverpool became the great cotton port only about 1795, and even at that time Manchester manufacturers bought cotton from other ports as well as from Liverpool.

[2] Prices, between one district and another, differed perceptibly. It is to be regretted that Thorold Rogers's work (*History of Agriculture and Prices in England*) only gives incomplete and insufficient information on this subject. Nevertheless we can find in it

countries like France or Germany, enjoyed the advantage of not having its different parts cut off from one another by customs barriers. Apart from London, there was not a single town which had permanent business connections with the whole country. As for the country districts, their commercial horizon was almost always bounded by the neighbouring town. The means and methods used to establish the minimum and absolutely necessary communications between these various markets had hardly changed during the last four or five hundred years.

The first of these methods were the big fairs which at regular intervals were attended by people who came from great distances either to buy or to sell. The best known was the Stourbridge fair, which Englishmen compared to that of Leipzig. Each year, from the middle of August to the middle of September, a temporary town sprang up on the ground on which it was held, with its own administration, its own police and its own courts.[1] There clothiers from Leeds and Norwich rubbed shoulders with linen merchants from the Lowlands of Scotland, and cutlers from Sheffield with nail-makers from Birmingham. Articles of luxury and colonial produce found their way there from London, Bristol and Liverpool. Thus at this fair all England took part in the exchange of goods. A number of less famous fairs had only regional importance. We may mention Winchester in the West, Boston in the East, and Beverley in the North.[2] Their decline is of much more recent date than is commonly supposed, and a few were still flourishing in a period not very distant from our own.[3]

Apart from fairs, the only markets which were at all extensive were special ones in which the produce of some local industry was sold.

[1] See Defoe, *Tour*, I, 122-30; Thorold Rogers, *Six Centuries of Work and Wages*, pp. 149-52.

[2] Arnold Toynbee, *Lectures on the Industrial Revolution in England*, pp. 54-5; J. A. Hobson, *The Evolution of Modern Capitalism*, p. 32. A complete list of small local fairs will be found in *A New and Accurate Description of the present Great Roads and the Principal Cross Roads of England and Wales* (1756), pp. xlviii-lxiv.

[3] R. W. Cooke Taylor, *Introduction to a History of the Factory System*, p. 218, refers to the Greenwich Fair near London and to Donnybrook Fair near Dublin.

---

some instances which illustrate the difference in prices between the London and some local markets. The following figures are the prices of a quarter of wheat in London, Cambridge and Gloucester at different periods:

Dec. 1703	...	...	...	Cambridge, 40s.	London, 32s.
June 1712	...	...	...	Cambridge, 41s. 4d.	London, 32s.
Mar. 1727	...	...	...	Cambridge, 36s.	London, 24s.
Oct. 1734	...	...	...	Gloucester, 40s.	London, 30s.
June 1741	...	...	...	Cambridge, 50s.	London, 39s.
Dec. 1748	...	...	...	Gloucester, 36s.	London, 28s.
Oct. 1753	...	...	...	Gloucester, 46s.	London, 32s.
Sept. 1760	...	...	...	Gloucester, 37s. 4d.	London, 23s. 6d.

Thorold Rogers, VII, 4, 12, 38, 56, 67, 80, 92, 114, 115.

Such were the markets of the West Riding, patronized by the merchant clothiers from the towns and by the small producers working on the domestic system who lived in the villages. We have given above a description of the Leeds market, which was the biggest and did most business. But there were others fairly close to one another, at Bradford, Huddersfield, Wakefield and Halifax; for the weaver, who attended them every week to sell his piece of stuff, could not go far from his village. The main feature of these local markets was the number of small transactions, and the number of buyers and sellers. A great deal of room was therefore needed, and the cloth halls built or reconstructed during the second half of the eighteenth century[1] were not spacious enough in spite of their large size.[2] Business was also carried on in the streets, in the squares and in public-houses.[3]

The next question is how, from these periodic fairs and permanent markets, goods reached the mass of consumers. Here the medieval condition of commercial relations in England was specially manifest. The class of middlemen[4] in direct contact with the producers would naturally be the richest and most important. This was the class of wholesale or, as they were sometimes called, travelling merchants. They had in fact to travel themselves, partly to buy merchandise and partly to get into touch with retailers. We have a record of the life led by a Manchester merchant, a hundred and fifty years ago, who sold wool and cotton material in the eastern counties and bought up feathers and malt: 'He was from home the greatest part of every year, performing his journeys entirely on horseback. His balances were received in guineas, and were carried with him in his saddle-bags. He was exposed to the vicissitudes of the weather, to great labour and fatigues and to constant danger.' The least of these was to be robbed, which still often happened on the main roads of England and Scotland. Note that this man was a rich merchant, 'who realized a sufficient fortune to keep a carriage when not half a dozen were kept in the town by persons connected with business'.[5]

[1] The Tammy Hall at Wakefield dates from 1766, the Piece Hall at Bradford from 1773, the Manufacturers' Hall at Halifax from 1779. The Mixed Cloth Hall and the White Cloth Hall at Leeds were built in 1756 and 1775 respectively. See J. Aikin, *A Description of the Country from thirty to forty miles round Manchester*, pp. 572 ff.; T. Baines, *Yorkshire, past and present*, I, 678; J. James, *History of Bradford*, p. 280.

[2] At Halifax 'the Cloth Hall is a large square three-storeyed building, in the middle of which is a huge courtyard. No windows are to be seen from the outside, all looking into that central yard. The number of rooms in the Cloth Hall amounts to 370, each of them with a door and a window, opening on an outer gallery which runs round the courtyard along each storey.' *Tournée faite en 1788 dans la Grande Bretagne*, p. 198.

[3] See Defoe's description of Halifax, quoted above.

[4] See R. B. Westerfield's *Middlemen in English Business, particularly between 1660 and 1760* (Yale University Press, 1915).

[5] T. Walker, *The Original*, No. XI (July 29th, 1835).

The goods he thus conveyed from town to town, leaving some of the unsold commodities on deposit in the inns, were almost always carried either on horse or mule back. Pack-horses, selected from a strong and patient breed, each carried two bales or two baskets slung over their backs, which balanced one another. They formed regular caravans moving in single file along the narrow causeways.[1] The leader had a bell round his neck to warn, from a distance, riders or carts coming in the opposite direction. In the same way today, on the stony paths of high Alpine valleys, we may meet mules carrying bundles on their backs destined for some remote villages.

Below the merchant we come across a character who for centuries played a vital part in the lives of country folk, and who still today exists in all isolated and backward countries. The pedlar, his pack on his back or leading a pack-horse, visited all the villages and farms. Not only did he sell scissors and spectacles, coloured handkerchiefs and calendars, but stuffs, fancy leather goods and watches and clocks, in fact everything the village wheelwright and blacksmith could not make. He went everywhere, and in many places he was the only person who brought in goods or ideas from the outer world. Where there was no competition, his hard trade was fairly profitable. But his roving life earned him a bad reputation. Many were the complaints against him, for he was something of a tramp and something of a smuggler as well.[2] He was accused of fraudulently disposing of prohibited merchandise, of selling bad-quality goods, and above all of harming 'fair tradesmen and honest shopkeepers', who denounced him to Parliament, and even went so far as to demand the suppression of peddling altogether.[3] This drastic measure was not granted, and Parliament contented itself with keeping a strict watch on pedlars, who were already subject to a system of taxes and licences.[4]

[1] Francis Place has preserved for us the account of a journey on horseback from Glasgow to London in 1735. As far as Grantham the party 'travelled on a narrow causeway, with an unmade soft road on each side of it. They met from time to time strings of pack horses, from thirty to forty in a gang … The leading horse of the gang carried a bell to give warning to travellers coming in an opposite direction, and, when they met these trains of horses with their packs across their backs, the causeway not affording room, they were obliged to make way for them and plunge into the side road, out of which they found it difficult to get back again to the causeway.' British Museum, Additional MSS. 27828, p. 10. Until the middle of the eighteenth century pack-horses remained the universal means for the conveyance of goods inside the country. S. and B. Webb, *The Story of the King's Highway*, pp. 63–4.

[2] In this connection see S. Smiles's *Lives of the Engineers*, I, 307, on the Derbyshire pedlars, most of whom came from the Flash district, between Macclesfield, Leek and Buxton, a rather backward part of the country: the Flashmen were a rough lot, and reputed to live as much by robbery as by pedlary.

[3] *Parliamentary History*, XIV, 246; XXV, 885 ff.; *Journals of the House of Commons*, XL, 1090, etc.

[4] A law of 1697 decrees that 'every hawker, pedlar and petty chapman or any other

Shops were only found in cities, or in the market-towns frequented on market days by the country people. They were right inside the houses, without windows or any display of wares. Only striking signboards were hung out to catch the attention of their illiterate customers, though often the merchant himself would stand at the door and invite the passers-by to come in. People came in to buy every conceivable thing, for the shops contained an even greater variety than the pedlar's pack. This is why various kinds of shopkeepers were described by equally vague and general names. For instance the word grocer comes from the French 'grossier', meaning wholesale merchant. 'Mercer, haberdasher' meant a trader in stuffs, drugs and ironmongery as well as in haberdashery proper. Such shops still exist in many European villages, but those of the eighteenth century had no knowledge of even this kind of shop. They were only to make their appearance after a complete revolution in all economic conditions.[1]

VI

All these interconnected facts, big periodic fairs, travelling merchants, primitive simplicity in methods of transport, are due to one thing: insufficient means of communication. In this respect England was far behind France. Her position as an island, with a coast well supplied with deep estuaries and sheltered harbours, favoured intercourse by sea. For instance, coal came by sea from Newcastle to London, and Scotch cattle were sent by sea to Norfolk to be fattened.[2] The facilities offered by the coasting trade were, no doubt, largely responsible for the slowness with which a good system of internal communication developed.

If we look at a map showing the road system as it was some time before the era of the great industrial inventions,[3] we shall see roads crossing and recrossing in all directions, joining up not only large towns but all districts of any importance, and forming a close network over the whole country. One main road ran from London towards

[1] 'In my native village the first shop was opened for general trade about sixty years ago, as I have heard, and for many years afterwards the wants of the villagers were supplied by packmen and pedlars.' Thorold Rogers, *Six Centuries of Work and Wages*, p. 147.

[2] Arnold Toynbee, *Lectures on the Industrial Revolution in England*, p. 55.

[3] See the map attached to *A New and Accurate Description of the present Great Roads and the Principal Cross Roads of England and Wales* (1756).

---

trading person going from town to town or to other men's houses, and travelling either on foot or with horse, horses or otherwise within the Kingdom' shall take a licence and pay £4. Moreover he shall pay £4 for every 'horse, ass or mule, or other beast bearing or drawing burden' (8 & 9 Will. III, c. 25).

Land's End, with many branches on the Channel side. Another crossed the Eastern counties, and, after passing through Colchester and Ipswich, forked, one branch going to Norwich and the other to Yarmouth. In the direction of York, Newcastle and Scotland was a much-frequented road which followed pretty closely the old Roman road from Londinium to Eboracum — Ermine Street, as it was called in the Middle Ages. Chester-le-Street marks one of the points on this road and is supposed to be the site of a Roman camp.[1] Its successive stages are marked by a series of ancient cathedral cities, Peterborough, Lincoln, York, Durham, signalized from far off by their towers and steeples. The north-western road, at any rate for some distance, was identical with the old Roman road which the Saxons called Watling Street. It ran from Dover to Chester, the Roman Deva. Several main roads connected London with the towns of the West Country. The Bristol road linked up the North Sea to the Atlantic, whilst the Gloucester road led to Wales. Some transverse roads should also be mentioned: the one from Carlisle to Newcastle, which followed the wall Emperor Hadrian had raised against the Picts, and those which crossed the Pennine range, one from Lancaster through the Aire Valley and the other from Manchester through the Calder Valley. These two met again at York, the ancient metropolis, and finally reached Hull at the mouth of the Humber. Two Roman highways, known as Fosse Way and Icknield Street, linked respectively Bath with Lincoln, and Southampton with Norwich. These communications between West and East were crossed by the long road which, starting at Plymouth and Bristol, served the whole of western England.[2]

Judging from such a map we might infer that England had a first-rate road system, had not the lamentations of contemporary writers thrown light on the state these roads were in. There were undoubtedly plenty of roads, but the majority were almost impassable. No one knew either how to make them or how to keep them up. The best were those which still had some of their original Roman paving left.[3] They were often so narrow that not only two carts but even two pack-horses could hardly pass each other.[4] The soft soil was ploughed into deep ruts, and ultimately the whole road would sink and become a kind of ditch which rains, floods, and tides, if near the sea, soon turned into a

---

[1] Chester, Ceaster = castra, the camp. Street = the road. See W. B. Paley, 'The Roman Roads of Britain', *Nineteenth Century*, XLIV, 840-53 (with map), and C. G. Harper, *The Great North Road*.

[2] On the importance of that road, see Defoe, *Tour*, III, 90.

[3] For instance, Watling Street, which kept its importance until the London to Liverpool railway was built.

[4] Petition relating to the road from Bramcote Old House to Bilper Lane End (Nottinghamshire). *Journals of the House of Commons*, XXIX, 914.

river.[1] The clay soil of the Midlands turned the periodically flooded roads into permanent bogs strewn with big boulders, which were so dangerous to cross that in some places the traveller preferred to leave the road and pick his way across country.[2] With such roads we can realize that communication was difficult. A cart would take five hours to do ten miles, or it would be held up by floods for a whole day.[3] In order to get out of the difficult places which were constantly met with, strong teams were required. Four or six horses were not too many to haul a heavily laden wagon or a bulky travelling carriage out of the quagmire. In really serious cases it was even sometimes necessary to borrow a couple of oxen from a neighbouring farm. Consequently carts were a very slow, a very expensive and a very unpractical means of transport. We can easily realize how it was that merchants usually preferred pack-horses, which could follow in single file along the narrow roads, could ford watercourses, and in case of need could make a track for themselves at the side when the road became impassable. We can understand, too, why districts in England, with no artificial barriers dividing them, as in France or Germany, were nevertheless for a long time almost completely cut off from one another just through the difficulty of communications.

Some progress, however, had been made. It was in the reign of Charles II that the first 'Turnpike Act'[4] was passed by Parliament. These Acts levied a toll on the users of certain roads, the money raised in this way being used exclusively for roadmaking and road repair. The collection of the tolls, and the work on the roads, were placed under the control of special commissions, appointed by the Justices of the Peace for each county.[5] Formerly each parish had been respon-

---

[1] The road from London to Ipswich in the first years of the eighteenth century was 'deep, in time of floods dangerous, and in winter scarce passable'. Defoe, Tour, II, 180. The road from Kingswear to Ladyway Cross (Devon) was at spring tides four feet deep in water. Journals of the House of Commons, XXX, 95. The road from Hull to Leeds 'lies in a low, flat, miry country, and the rains fall upon the same from the neighbouring hills; and, for want of a proper current to carry such waters off, they settle on great part of the road, which is frequently under water'. Ibid., XXIV, 697.

[2] Road from Hatfield to Baldock. Defoe, Tour, II, 185. Roads round Derby, see J. Brome, Travels over England, Scotland and Wales, p. 87, and Defoe, Tour, II, 178 (1727 edition), and III, 66 (1742 edition).

[3] Journals of the House of Commons, XXIII, 105 (road from Grantham to Stamford, Lincolnshire) and XXX, 97 (road from Kingswear to Ladyway Cross, see note 1 above).

[4] 15 Chas. II, c. 1 (1663: road from London to York).

[5] The Surveyors and the Commissioners of Turnpikes. These were chosen from among the landed proprietors of each district. A complete list of their powers and duties may be found in the General Act of 1773 (13 Geo. III, c. 78). Amongst other things they had the right to requisition men, carts and draught animals for compulsory labour. Every landholder was bound to provide a horse and cart and two men for six days. If he had an income of over £50 he contributed more, either in labour or

sible for the upkeep of its roads, and the work was very badly done, especially as all the parishes were not equally interested in the matter. A main road, of use chiefly to the towns at either end, passed through a large number of rural parishes, the inhabitants of which used it very little and cared even less about its upkeep. The principle of the Turnpike Acts was to make those who used the road pay for it.[1]

Wherever this principle was applied the roads improved perceptibly and the ease and safety of communication increased. But for a long time turnpike roads remained exceptions. The earliest one dates from 1663, and it was not until 1690 that anyone thought of making another. Generally, however, the old system was held to, even at the cost of multiplying regulations on the weight of carts, the size of wheels and the number of horses. It was preferred to protect broken-down roads rather than take steps to put them in repair.[2] We must also acknowledge that the toll-gates on the new roads, and tolls levied on travellers, were extremely unpopular. Edicts had to be issued to impose severe penalties on 'ill designing and disorderly persons' who had 'in several parts of this Kingdom associated themselves both by day and night, and cut down, pulled down, burnt, and otherwise destroyed several turnpike gates and houses, which have been erected by the authority of Parliament made for repairing divers roads'.[3] During the eighteenth century turnpike riots kept breaking out – in the south-western counties round 1730, in Herefordshire in 1732, near Bristol in 1749.[4] Perhaps the most serious ones took place in the north of England: in 1753, round Leeds, there was a regular rebellion, a mass

---

[1] This system was much studied and admired in France. See *Notes sur la Législation Anglaise des Chemins, par l'auteur des Notes sur l'Impôt Territorial en Angleterre* (La Rochefoucauld-Liancourt), Paris, 1801. A careful study of the turnpike legislation and of its operation has been made by S. and B. Webb (*The Story of the King's Highway*, chap. VII, pp. 118-64).

[2] *Statutes at Large*, 9 Anne, c. 18 (1710). Analogous steps were taken later on to prevent the deterioration of the turnpike roads. See 30 Geo. II, c. 28 (1757): 'Whereas it hath been found that the use of broad wheels does very much contribute to the improvement and preservation of the turnpike roads of that part of Great Britain called England, and using heavy carriages with narrow wheels is very ruinous and destructive of the same ... ' 14 Geo. II, c. 42 (1741) decreed that weighing machines should be kept at the toll-gates: every cart weighing over 6,000 lb. had to pay twenty shillings for each extra 100 lb.

[3] 1 Geo. II, st. 2, c. 19 (1728). The penalties were, three months' imprisonment for a first offence and seven years' transportation for further offences. 8 Geo. II, c. 20 (1735) makes the destruction of toll-gates a felony.

[4] S. and B. Webb, *The Story of the King's Highway*, p. 123.

---

money. If his income was under £4 he was exempted, save for five days' personal compulsory labour, or he could buy himself off at a moderate rate. 7 Geo. II, c. 42, and 13 Geo. III, c. 78.

rising of the country people against the levies, which had to be put down by force of arms.[1]

It was hardly until 1745, after the landing of the Pretender and his defeat at Culloden, that work on the roads, over the whole kingdom, was taken in hand systematically.[2] Charles Edward and his Highlanders, thanks to the abominable state of the roads which prevented any concentration of the royal army, had been able to advance as far as Derby, into the very heart of England. From that time onwards the Government and the Crown felt a direct interest in the creation of a complete system of well-kept roads 'proper for the passage of troops, horses and carriages, at all times of the year'.[3] Road-making was at once begun all over the country, and long neglect was followed by a period of feverish activity. In less than twenty years the system of turnpike roads had spread over the whole Kingdom.[4] The change seemed miraculous, and became with Englishmen the subject of complacent admiration: 'There never was a more astonishing revolution accomplished in the internal system of any country, than has been within the compass of a few years in that of England. The carriage of grain, coals, merchandise, etc., is in general conducted with little more than half the number of horses with which it formerly was. Journies of business are performed with more than double expedition. Improvements in agriculture keep pace with those of trade. Everything wears the face of dispatch; every article of our produce becomes more valuable; and the hinge upon which all these movements turn is the reformation which has been made in our publick roads.'[5] Between 1760 and 1774 Parliament passed no fewer than four hundred and fifty-two Acts in connection with the construction and upkeep of roads.[6]

Then appeared the first generation of those men who, engineers without knowing it, planned and carried out extensive undertakings, and were the incarnation of the practical empiricism of the English

---

[1] J. James, *Continuation to the History of Bradford*, p. 87.

[2] We must beware of attaching too much importance to this accidental fact in connection with a development which was bound up with so many general causes. It was an event which merely attracted the attention of the authorities to this question of roads. It is nevertheless a fact that, between 1748 and 1760, the number of Turnpike Trusts rose from 160 to 530.

[3] 24 Geo. II, c. 25 (1751: road from Carlisle to Newcastle).

[4] The redistribution of real property, which was taking place about this time in many parishes, often facilitated the opening of new roads. More than one Enclosure Act stipulated that on the ground to be redivided sufficient room for a public highway should be left. (See chap. III, below.)

[5] H. Homer, *An Enquiry into the Means of preserving and improving the Publick Roads of this Kingdom*, p. 8.

[6] See the General Act of 1773 (13 Geo. III, c. 78) and the Standing Orders of the House of Commons. *Journals of the House of Commons*, XXXIII, 949-52.

people. From among this curious group of men, all bearing the same rural stamp, one stands pre-eminent – John Metcalf, the blind man of Knaresborough.[1] This extraordinary character, born in 1717 in a small Yorkshire town, showed such intelligence and boldness as to make everyone almost forget his blindness. In 1745 he joined the volunteers of his county and took part in the Scottish campaign, under the Duke of Cumberland. First a horse-dealer and then a carrier, for many years he scoured the country between the Humber and the Mersey. This was a district where the problem of communications was extremely urgent. The roads which crossed the high and marshy moors of the Pennine range did not suffice for the ever-growing traffic on both sides of the watershed. John Metcalf became a constructor of roads. Alone, with his staff in his hand, he went over all the ground himself, 'the plans which he designs, and the estimates he makes, are done in a method peculiar to himself, and which he cannot well convey the meaning of to others'.[2] Being very ingenious he invented a cheap and quick way of giving a firm surface to bogs, which could then easily be crossed. Among the many roads which he repaired or made we may mention, in the West Riding, those from Wakefield to Doncaster, from Wakefield to Huddersfield, from Huddersfield to Halifax; in Lancashire, from Bury to Blackburn, from Ashton-under-Lyne to Stockport; between Lancashire and Yorkshire the roads from Stockport to Mottram Langley and from Skipton to Burnley; farther south, across the rocks of the Peak district, the roads from Macclesfield to Chapel-en-le-Frith and from Whaley Bridge to Buxton.[3] All this work was done between 1760 and 1790 – some of it just before and some of it just after the birth of the factory system,[4] which thus grew up in a district already prepared for its extension and progress.

But all districts had not a Metcalf. Good roads were not ensured by the setting up of turnpikes. In every one of his journeys Arthur Young kept inveighing against the deplorable condition of the roads, in spite of all tolls and toll-gates. 'What am I to say of the roads

[1] *The Life of John Metcalfe, commonly called Blind Jack of Knaresborough* (York, 1795) – a kind of autobiography dictated to a secretary by Metcalf himself.

[2] Bew, 'Observations on Blindness', *Memoirs of the Literary and Philosophical Society of Manchester*, I, 173-4. 'With the assistance only of a long staff, I have several times met this man traversing the roads, ascending precipices, exploring valleys, and investigating their several extents, forms, and situations, so as to answer his designs in the best manner ... I have met this blind projector of the roads, who was alone as usual, and amongst other conversation, I made some inquiries respecting this new road. It was really astonishing to hear with what accuracy he described the courses and the nature of the different soils through which it was conducted.'

[3] *The Life of John Metcalfe*, pp. 124-41.

[4] At one time Metcalf himself thought of becoming a spinner. In 1781 he bought jennies and a cotton-carding machine. See ibid., p. 148.

of this country? The turnpikes, as they have the assurance to call them, and the hardiness to make one pay for! From Chepstow to the half-way house between Newport and Cardiff they continue mere rocky lanes, full of huge stones as big as one's horse, and abominable holes[1] ... The road from Witney to North Leach is, I think the worst turnpike I ever travelled in: so bad, that it is a scandal to the country[2] ... Of all the cursed roads that ever disgraced this Kingdom, in the very ages of barbarism, none ever equalled that from Billericay to the King's Head at Tilbury. It is for near twelve miles so narrow that a mouse cannot pass by any carriage. I saw a fellow creep under his waggon to assist me to lift, if possible, my chair over a hedge.'[3] In other places he met with ruts four feet deep, bogs which nearly swallowed him up,[4] or was 'racked to dislocation over pieces of rock which they term mending'.[5] On the road from Liverpool to Wigan his indignation could find no adequate expression: 'I know not, in the whole range of language, terms sufficiently expressive to describe this infernal road ... Let me seriously caution all travellers who may accidentally purpose to travel this terrible country to avoid it as they would the devil: for a thousand to one but they break their necks or their limbs by overthrows and breakings down.'[6] It was not until quite the end of the eighteenth century, in the days of Telford and McAdam,[7] that England obtained a network of good roads.[8]

[1] A. Young, *Southern Counties*, p. 120.

[2] Ibid., p. 101.

[3] Ibid., p. 72.

[4] Id., *North of England*, IV, 443.

[5] Ibid., I, 83.

[6] Ibid., I, 430.

[7] The Scotch engineer McAdam was the inventor of the system of making roads with stones which still bears his name. See *Dictionary of National Biography*, articles 'McAdam' and 'Telford'; also S. Smiles, *Lives of the Engineers*, vols. II and III; S. and B. Webb, *The Story of the King's Highway*, chap. VIII. It was only after their time that a regular school of specialist engineers was formed. Up till then the men who planned the roads and carried out the work were nothing more than contractors who had previously been employed in all kinds of trades. The road commissioners consisted of 'a promiscuous mob of peers, squires, farmers and shopkeepers'. See *Edinburgh Review*, XXXII, 480-2 (1819).

[8] Road-builders in the eighteenth century tried various methods, a number of which proved to be mistaken: 'The "road laid wavy", or "trenched road" with a "continuation of little hills and valleys"; the "angular road sloping like a pantile roof from one hand to the other"; the "concave road" or "hollow way" into which a stream was periodically turned to clean its surface; the built-up "horizontal road" flanked by deep ditches, sometimes a "causeway from 20 to 30 feet wide, nearly horizontal on the top, with precipices on each side of four or five feet perpendicular depth", could all be seen within a day's journey of the metropolis.' S. and B. Webb, *The Story of the King's Highway*, p. 133, quoting J. Scott, *Digest of the general Highway and Turnpike Laws*, pp. 320 ff. (1778), and H. Homer, *An Enquiry into the Means of preserving and improving the Publick Roads*, p. 30 (1767).

Nevertheless communication was already becoming easier and more regular. Before 1750, coach services were scarce and slow. It took two days to go from London to Oxford, four to six days to go to Exeter, and a week to go to York.[1] There was no regular service at all between England and Scotland. The hero of one of Smollett's novels leaves Glasgow for London in 1739, on a pack-horse, perched between the two panniers.[2] To this we must add the insecurity of the roads, for robbery was endemic up to the very gates of the capital. In 1757 the Portsmouth Mail was carried off by a gang of thieves on the edge of the suburb of Hammersmith, less than five miles from Charing Cross.[3] Nevertheless the improvement in the roads, even though insufficient and incomplete, produced notable results, particularly in the north. From 1766 the Warrington flying coach, which ran twice a week, brought Liverpool and Manchester to within less than three days of London.[4] About the same time a line of coaches was run between London and Edinburgh, via York and Newcastle, though the journey still took ten to twelve days.[5] Thirty years later, after Palmer's reform of the postal system,[6] it became possible to travel from London to Glasgow in sixty-three hours. With regard to merchandise, pack-horses were superseded by carriers' wagons. Commercial methods changed, and the commercial traveller made his appearance, carrying only samples with him and taking orders. He was a new and curiously modern type when we contrast him with the old-time merchant, who visited periodical fairs, leading a string of pack-horses.[7]

The great obstacle which still interfered with the circulation of produce was the cost of sending letters and goods. The Royal Mail, which from the beginning of the seventeenth century private persons had been allowed to use,[8] had daily services on all the high roads. For

[1] G. R. Porter, *Progress of the Nation*, pp. 296-7.

[2] T. Smollett, *Roderick Random*, chap. VIII.

[3] *Gentleman's Magazine*, 1757, p. 383.

[4] Chas. Hardwick, *History of the Borough of Preston and its Environs*, pp. 382-4; T. Baines and W. Fairbairn, *Lancashire and Cheshire, past and present*, II, 105.

[5] David Bremner, *The Industries of Scotland*, p. 108.

[6] A. Anderson, *An Historical and Chronological Deduction of the Origin of Commerce*, Appendix IV, 710 ff. H. Joyce, *History of the Post Office to 1836*, pp. 208-80. Until 1696, London remained the only centre of distribution for letters sent from one county to another. About the middle of the eighteenth century a regular postal service ran three times a week between all the principal towns of the kingdom. A good summary of this question will be found in Moffit's *England on the Eve of the Industrial Revolution*, pp. 243-6.

[7] J. Aikin, *A Description of the Country from thirty to forty miles round Manchester*, p. 183. Early in the eighteenth century a class of men appeared who were known in the textile trades as *riders out*: they travelled with goods for delivery, while the merchant travelled only with patterns and solicited orders. G. W. Daniels, *The Early English Cotton Industry*, p. 62.

[8] H. Joyce, *History of the Post Office*, pp. 8 ff.

a long time there were complaints as to their slowness and the lack of precautions against robbery.[1] When, finally, a reform of the postal service took place, it was found necessary to raise the rates: in 1711 a letter from London to Chester cost 4d., in 1784 it cost 6d. and from 1796 onwards 8d.[2] The penny post was only operative within a ten-mile radius of the General Post Office. As for the rates for the transport of goods, they were simply exorbitant; £5 a ton from London to Birmingham, £12 from London to Exeter, £13 from London to Leeds. For short distances the rates were even higher. The transport of a ton of merchandise from Liverpool to Manchester, a distance of about thirty miles, cost not less than forty shillings, and from Newcastle-under-Lyme in the Pottery district, to Bridgenorth on the Severn, from 50s. to £3.[3] This is the reason why, in spite of improvements in the roads, a large number of country districts were for a long time left in many respects to their own resources. Even at the end of the century potatoes, sugar and cotton[4] were still unknown in many English villages. In Scotland, not far from the roads, there were tracts of country still untouched by trade and its influences. When Robert Owen was travelling in 1790 between Glasgow and New Lanark, he took half a sovereign out of his purse to pay the toll. The toll man refused to accept it. He had never seen a gold coin.[5]

VII

In every period high rates for transport have brought about the development of internal navigation. In England this development was all the more remarkable in that it took so long to begin. — No country is more suited to a smoothly working and complete system of navigable waterways than England. East and west, on the North Sea coast and on the coast of the Irish Channel, gulfs and estuaries, penetrating far inland, seem to reach out towards each other. The

[1] A. Anderson, op. cit., p. 709: 'The post at present, instead of being the swiftest is almost the slowest conveyance in this country, and though, from the great improvement in our roads, other carriers have proportionably mended their speed, the post is as slow as ever. It is likewise very unsafe, as the frequent robberies of it testify; and to avoid a loss of this nature, people generally cut bank bills, or bills at sight, in two, and send the parts by different posts.'

[2] 9 Anne, c. 10; *Journals of the House of Commons*, LVI, 69 ff. Postage in 1711: under 50 miles, 2d.; 50-80 miles, 3d.; over 80 miles, 4d.; London to Edinburgh, 6d. In 1784: 1 postal stage, 2d.; over one relay and under 50 miles, 3d.; 50-80 miles, 4d.; 80-150 miles, 5d.; over 150, 6d.

[3] These figures relate to 1740-60. See *Journals of the House of Commons*, XXIV, 788, 798, 812 (petitions) and XXVI, 177-82 (Inquiry); J. Aikin, *A Description of the Country round Manchester*, p. 116; Baines and Fairbairn, *Lancashire and Cheshire*, II, 205.

[4] See R. Southey, *The Doctor*, chap. IV.

[5] Robert Owen, *The Life of Robert Owen, written by Himself*, p. 52.

Bristol Channel and the mouth of the Thames, the Humber and the Mersey, the Tyne and the Solway Firth, the Firth of Clyde and the Firth of Forth face one another with ever-narrowing spaces in between.[1] In the broadest part of the island wide plains cause the two sides of the watershed to merge into each other almost imperceptibly. Although rivers may be short and not very deep, their even and regular flow, together with the slightness of the heights between them, render them easy to use. But the same reason which, in England, delayed the building of roads, delayed even more the creation of a system of navigable waterways. The existence of several ports which were both on the sea and at a river mouth, as for instance, London, Hull, Newcastle and Bristol, and, even more important, the short distance from the coast to the inland towns,[2] account for the neglect of means of communication of which other countries would have availed themselves long before. England had not a single canal or a single artificial waterway before 1759, a hundred and fifty years later than the construction in France of the Briare canal and nearly eighty years after the inauguration of the canal which connects the Mediterranean with the Atlantic.

Nevertheless the advantages of communication by water within the country, revealed by foreign examples, had their champions. One of the earliest was Andrew Yarranton.[3] In turn an officer in the army of the Long Parliament, an ironmaster, a linen-cloth manufacturer, an engineer, an agriculturist and an economist, he united the wild schemes of an adventurer with the broad views of a man of genius. In 1677 he published a curious book in which were jumbled together the observations, plans and dreams of his whole life[4] with a

---

[1] From Gravesend on the Thames to Avonmouth on the Severn, about 134 miles; from Runcorn (Mersey) to Goole (Humber), 81 miles; from Tynemouth (Tyne) to Solway Firth, 69 miles; from Dumbarton (Clyde) to Grangemouth (Forth), 34 miles.

[2] Coventry, situated more or less in the centre of England proper, is about 75 miles from the Bristol Channel; 84 miles from the Irish Sea; 77 miles from the North Sea and 100 miles from the English Channel.

[3] See *Dictionary of National Biography*, article 'Yarranton'; S. Smiles, *Industrial Biography*, pp. 60-76; Ludwig Beck, *Die Geschichte des Eisens*, II, 1275-7. On some isolated projects before Yarranton, see MacCulloch, *Literature of Political Economy*, pp. 200-2. As early as the time of the Commonwealth, Francis Mathew, the author of *The Opening of Rivers for Navigation*, had laid before Cromwell a scheme for connecting the Thames with the Avon (see his *Mediterranean Passage from London to Bristol*, 1670).

[4] *England's Improvement by Sea and Land*, First Part published in 1677, Second Part in 1681. The complete title is as follows: *England's Improvement by Sea and Land, to outdo the Dutch without fighting, to pay Debts without Moneys, to set at work all the Poor of England with the Growth of our own Lands; to prevent unnecessary Suits in Law, with the Benefit of a voluntary Register; Directions where vast Quantities of Timber are to be had for the building of Ships, with the Advantage of making the great Rivers of England navigable, Rules to prevent Fires in London and other great Cities, with Directions how the several Companies of Handicraftsmen in London may always have cheap Bread and Drink*, by Andrew Yarranton, gent.

host of new and daring ideas. Yarranton was bold enough to believe that his country could prevail over rival nations without fighting, that a well-used peace was better than a successful war, and that the true glory of a State consisted in the work, wealth and civilization of its inhabitants. Among the sometimes chimerical means he thought would ensure his country's prosperity, the development of an internal system of navigation held first place. He had been to Holland, where he had admired the incomparable activity of the rivers and canals.[1] His first recommendation was for 'making rivers navigable in all places where art could possibly effect it'. He also suggested that the main waterways should be linked up by means of canals, the Thames with the Severn, the Severn with the Trent. This inexhaustible projector, warmly attacked by some of his contemporaries, either because of the wildness of his ideas or simply because they differed from their own prejudices,[2] meant to achieve practical results. Apart from big schemes, the utility of which he realized without having the necessary means to carry them out, he directed and carried out several smaller enterprises, as for instance the deepening of the Stour between Stourport and Kidderminster, of the Avon between Stratford and Tewkesbury.[3] These two rivers afforded communication between the ironworking districts of the centre and the Severn estuary. At the same time he wrote prophetic pages in which, hardly ten years after the Dutch men-of-war sailed triumphantly up the Thames, he announced England's maritime and industrial supremacy.[4]

Yet for a long time people were still content to deepen and to improve certain waterways, without thinking of making a system of artificial ones. These improvements, in themselves of no great importance, deserve to be mentioned by reason of the industries whose interests were involved. The Aire and the Calder were made navigable

---

[1] Andrew Yarranton, *England's Improvement by Sea and Land*, I, 6-7, 181, 191.

[2] See the pamphlet entitled *A Coffeehouse Dialogue, or a Discourse between Captain Y. (Yarranton) and a Young Barrister of the Middle Temple*. Yarranton replied with *The Coffee-house Dialogue Examined and Refuted*. See also *A Word without Doors, A Continuation of the Coffeehouse Dialogue*, etc. (British Museum, T. 3* 17 ff.).

[3] Andrew Yarranton, *England's Improvement by Sea and Land*, I, 193-4.

[4] 'In England there are more things to produce strength, riches and manufacture, and for the life of man and all of the best, as also to make the Prince great and strong, and the people rich, than in any two Kingdoms and any two Commonwealths in the world; and if these riches, growths and manufactures were applied to the best and right ends, England in a very short time would be the glory of nations. For in England there is the great wool, and most of the world, and in England there is the most and best tin in the world, and in England there is the most and best leather in the world, and in England there is the most and best lead in the world, and in England there is the most and best flesh in the world, to feed upon to manufacture these commodities; and in England there is corn sufficient for the life of man, and England has the best and safest harbours in the world ... ' Ibid., I, 4.

at the request of the clothiers of Leeds, Wakefield and Halifax. The work begun in 1701 on the Trent and the Derwent assisted the industrial development of Derby and Nottingham. The canalization of the Mersey, begun in 1720, strengthened the bonds between the twin towns of Liverpool and Manchester.[1] Yet these were only the first symptoms of the great change which was to follow.

Among the immediate causes of this change there is one which cannot be too much emphasized, belonging as it does, more than any other, to the history of the factory system – the use of coal, for a long time mostly employed for domestic purposes, was gradually extended to various industries.[2] Now coal is one of those heavy products, whose low price will be increased in a quite disproportionate degree if the cost of transport is too high. For this reason Newcastle coal, mined on the Tyne and carried by sea – sea coal, as it was commonly called[3] – remained for a long time the only mineral fuel which was procurable at any distance from its source. As the demand for coal increased, and as the coal trade became more important, so the question of transport became more and more urgent. The more we study in detail the history of communication by water in England, the more do we realize how closely it was interwoven with the history of coal. The deepening of the river Douglas between 1719 and 1727 coincided with the development of the collieries round Wigan, to the north-east of Liverpool, and the work on the Sankey in 1755 with the opening of the St Helens mines.[4] The making of the Worsley Canal, the first real canal in England, had no other purpose.

The initiative was taken by a great nobleman, the Duke of Bridgewater. He owned important coal deposits at Worsley, near Manchester, but the exorbitant cost of transport made their exploitation almost impossible. The coal was carried from Worsley to Manchester

[1] 10-11 Will. III, c. 19-20 (Aire, Calder and Trent); 1 Anne, c. 20 (Derwent); 6 Geo. I, c. 27 (Derwent); 7 Geo. I, st. I, c. 15 (Mersey and Irwell). The canalization of the Weaver which crosses the Cheshire saltpans dates from 1720; that of the Don which goes through Sheffield dates from 1725. See John Aikin, *A Description of the Country round Manchester*, pp. 105-11; T. Baines, *History of Liverpool*, pp. 39-40.

[2] On the industrial uses of coal before the invention of the steam engine, see Part II, chap. III. The use of coal in the working of iron began in the first half of the eighteenth century, but it did not become general till 1760.

[3] The name of 'pit coal' was reserved for coal obtained from inland counties and used on the spot.

[4] See the preamble and text of 28 Geo. II, c. 8; 8 Geo. III, c. 38, and petitions summed up in the *Journals of the House of Commons*, XXVI, 905, 969, 977; XXVII, 53, 56, 115, 137, 144, 169, etc. (petitions of the Lancashire mine owners); XXXII, 667 and 771 (petitions of the magistrates and chief merchants of Glasgow); XXXIV, 200 (petitions of ironmasters of Coalbrookdale). On the influence of that work on the growth of industries in the district of St Helens, see *Victoria History of the County of Lancaster*, II, 352.

on horseback at a cost of 9s. to 10s. a ton for a distance of under seven miles.[1] At first the duke thought of using a little stream called the Worsley Brook, which flows into the Irwell not far from its junction with the Mersey. But he gave up the idea on the advice of James Brindley, a man who, in the duke's service, was to stand revealed as a great engineer. Like John Metcalf, and like so many other promoters of the industrial revolution, James Brindley was a remarkable instance of a practical genius formed not by study but by experience and necessity.[2] Without knowledge of the scientific movements of his day, almost illiterate,[3] he succeeded in solving difficult problems, thanks to an exceptional power of imagination and of mental concentration.[4] In 1759 he undertook to cut the Worsley Canal for the Duke of Bridgewater, and achieved the work in two years' time. He laid down two principles to which he was always faithful. He refused to use the beds of the small Lancashire rivers, whose sluggish flow gave no adequate security against silting, and he made a rule of keeping the line of the canal at one level, in order to avoid the necessity of making locks. The Worsley Canal was the most complete embodiment of this somewhat arbitrary and questionable method. It was, throughout its course, a piece of constructional engineering and was kept at one level all the way. It began by underground galleries in the depths of the coal strata and it reached Manchester by crossing the Irwell by an aqueduct forty feet high. Contemporaries regarded it as the eighth wonder of the world.[5]

The success of the undertaking, and especially its immediate results, created a great impression. In Manchester coal fell to half its former price.[6] This was a decisive argument in favour of a system of navigable waterways, and from that moment the work went on uninterruptedly. The Duke of Bridgewater remained the great leader of the movement, into which he did not hesitate to put nearly all his

[1] Petition of the Duke of Bridgewater to the House of Commons (Nov. 25th, 1758). *Journals of the House of Commons*, XXVIII, 321, 322, 335.

[2] On James Brindley, see J. Aikin, *A Description of the Country from thirty to forty miles round Manchester*, pp. 139-45; J. Phillips, *A General History of Inland Navigation*, pp. 87-100; S. Smiles, *Lives of the Engineers*, I, 309-402; J. Ward, *The Borough of Stoke-upon-Trent*, pp. 162 ff.

[3] His spelling was fantastically bad. He never could spell the word 'navigation'. Typical extracts from his note-books may be found in S. Smiles, *Lives of the Engineers*, I, 320-1, and G. Townsend Warner, *Social England*, V, 323.

[4] He very seldom made use of drawings or plans, but relied entirely on his memory, which was extraordinarily sure and accurate. When he had a difficult problem to solve he used to stay in bed for several days to think the whole thing out quietly, until he was able to visualize the last detail of the solution in concrete form. J. Phillips, *General History of Inland Navigation*, p. 97.

[5] J. Aikin, op. cit., pp. 113-14; A. Young, *North of England*, II, 196-241.

[6] J. Phillips, *General History of Inland Navigation*, p. 76.

fortune. First of all the canal from Manchester to the Mersey estuary was made. The route offered by the river, which had been deepened at great expense, was only moderately satisfactory, and the rates of the Mersey Navigation Company, though much lower than those of horse carriage between Liverpool and Manchester, were nevertheless still too high. The canal which, thanks to Brindley's indefatigable activity, was finished in 1761, enabled goods to be transported from one town to the other at six shillings a ton instead of twelve.[1] A much bigger undertaking was already in prospect: the canal from the Trent to the Mersey, which was to establish direct communication between the Irish and the North Sea.[2] The work went on during eleven years, from 1766 to 1777, but Brindley did not live to see it completed. He died in 1772, worn out by his extraordinary labours.[3] He was able, however, to indicate how this trunk line should be extended in all directions, and to sketch out the complete scheme in which the Trent to the Mersey Canal – the Grand Trunk Canal, as it is still called – was, and still remains, the essential feature. One branch, towards the Severn, linked up the ports of Liverpool, Bristol and Hull. Another, via Coventry and Oxford, linked up the Thames, London and the route to the Continent. Brindley, too, planned the Birmingham to Wolverhampton Canal, across an iron district which has since become one of the most active metallurgical areas of the whole world.

Brindley's work took place just before the rise of the factory system. The work of his successors ran parallel with its development, of which it was sometimes the result and sometimes the cause. The maps drawn up during the last years of the eighteenth century enable us to measure the extent of these great undertakings.[4] It was chiefly in the centre and north of England that the navigable waterways increased so rapidly. A complete network was formed in Lancashire, with the Bolton Canal, the Bury Canal, and the Kendal Canal through Preston and Lancaster. Between Lancashire and Yorkshire, through the Pennine range, there were three main arteries: one connected Leeds with Liverpool, running through the transverse depression from north-west to south-east of the

---

[1] J. Aikin, op. cit., pp. 115 ff.; J. Phillips, op. cit., p. 78.

[2] This is the canal often called the Grand Trunk Canal. It is 93 miles long.

[3] In 1767 Wedgwood wrote: 'I am afraid he will do too much, and leave us before his vast designs are executed ... I think Mr Brindley, the great, the fortunate, money-getting Brindley, an object of pity and a real sufferer for the good of the public. He may get a few thousands, but what does he give in exchange? His health, and I fear, his life too.' Wedgwood to Bentley, March 2nd, 1767, John Rylands Library, Manchester.

[4] See the map frontispieces to Aikin's book (1795) and the *History of Birmingham* of the same date by William Hutton. See also L. B. Wells, 'A Sketch of the History of the Canal and River Navigations of England and Wales', *Memoirs of the Literary and Philosophical Society of Manchester*, Fourth Series, VIII, 187-204.

upper Aire valley; the other two linked up Manchester with Hudders-
field and the valley of Halifax. All three converged on the broad
Humber estuary. Round Birmingham, a complicated system of canals
extended its ramifications in all directions.[1] It joined the Grand Trunk
Canal to the north,[2] the Severn and the Thames to the south.[3] The
London market was bound to the northern industrial towns by the
Grand Junction Canal, to the Atlantic by the Thames and Severn
Canal. In South Wales lines of communication, starting from Swansea
and Cardiff, opened up the ironworks and collieries of the interior,
and gave access to still undeveloped mineral wealth. In Scotland the
Forth and Clyde Canal was begun in 1768, and among the engineers
who drew up the plans we find James Watt, who at the same time was
carrying on his researches on the expansion of steam.

Thus in less than thirty years the whole face of England was fur-
rowed with navigable waterways. In this there was a concerted movement, comparable, though on a different scale, with that which in
the following century covered all western Europe with railway lines.
There even came a time, for canals as later for railways, when there
was a kind of over-production. Towards 1793 England was seized
by an attack of canal fever. Endless schemes surged up from all
sides, speculation was rife, and more than one of these early undertakings ended in disaster.[4] This was, however, only one of the consequences of the industrial revolution, and one of the most transient;
one of those incidental effects so common in economic phenomena,
where the rule is action followed by reaction.

The importance of such a transformation was realized from the
start by those interested in its results. It was brought about by their
initiative, and was carried out at their expense and risk. The action of
the Crown and of Parliament was limited to the setting up of inquiries
and to the granting of the necessary powers. Sometimes private
persons, in the interest of their own trade or industry, undertook and
directed a piece of work. Sometimes this was done by joint stock companies formed on purpose to build and exploit these new lines of
communication.[5] In both cases we always find the same men at the

[1] Wyrley and Effington Canal, Stourbridge and Dudley Canal, Netherton Canal,
Fazeley Canal, Birmingham and Worcester Canal, Birmingham and Wolverhampton
Canal, etc. William Hutton, *History of Birmingham* (map of the canals of the district in
1791).
[2] Through the Staffordshire and Worcester Canal.
[3] Through the Coventry and Oxford Canal and the Grand Junction Canal.
[4] The Statute Book contains 9 Acts relating to internal navigation in 1792; 25 in
1793; 17 in 1794. See 32 Geo. III, c. 84 ff., 33 Geo. III, c. 93 ff., 34 Geo. III, c. 24 ff.,
c. 53, c. 77, c. 85, etc.
[5] They were usually known as Companies of Proprietors: see C. Wagner, 'Ueber
die wirtschaftliche Lage der Binnenschifffahrtsunternehmungen in Grossbritannien
und Irland', *Archiv für Eisenbahnwesen*, 1901, pp. 1225 ff.

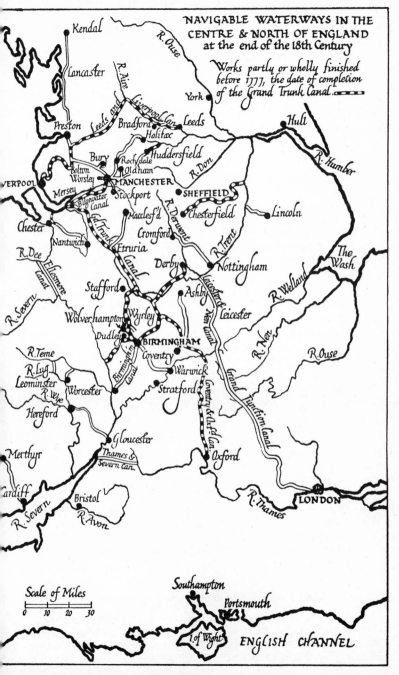

NAVIGABLE WATERWAYS IN THE
CENTRE & NORTH OF ENGLAND
at the end of the 18th Century

Works partly or wholly finished
before 1777, the date of completion
of the Grand Trunk Canal. ═══

head of the movement, raising capital, mobilizing opinion, spending freely both in time and money, and their leadership is a significant fact. First and foremost were great noblemen, who followed the example set by one of their order. The Duke of Bridgewater, even though at the outset he encountered every kind of difficulty, even though at one time his enterprises seemed almost to have ruined him, yet very soon found imitators and rivals. It was at Lord Anson's and the Marquis of Stafford's request that in 1766 Brindley drew up the plans for the Grand Trunk Canal.[1] One of the first meetings held in support of the scheme was presided over by Lord Gower, and was addressed by Lord Grey. Again, we find the Lords Stamford and Moira, together with Viscount Wentworth, supporting a petition for permission to build a canal.[2] As great landowners they were interested in the creation of new means of transport which were to enable them to increase in a considerable proportion the value of the mines, quarries or forests in their lands. They were keenly aware of this, for the English nobility have always known how to make the best of economic as well as political revolutions.

Another class which, at this crisis, gave proof of remarkable intelligence and activity, was the new-born class of captains of industry, the first representatives of another aristocracy which in a not far distant future was to rival the old. Before either the introduction of machinery or the rise of the factory system, these men, almost as though filled with a presentiment of the economic changes which were to make their fortunes, organized in advance the commercial equipment of large-scale industry. Wedgwood, the potter, together with his friend and associate Thomas Bentley, busied themselves with indefatigable zeal over the Mersey to Trent Canal, which was to pass through the Potteries and thus enable Cornish clay to be brought there at a cheap rate. Wedgwood was one of the first subscribers and accepted the post of treasurer.[3] Bentley wrote a pamphlet on 'the Advantages of inland Navigation, with a Plan of a navigable Canal intended for a Communication between the Ports of Liverpool and Hull'.[4] It was not an easy task to overcome all the different opponents who united to defeat the scheme — carriers and innkeepers, who feared that trade would be deflected from the high roads, proprietors who refused to sell land on the line of the canal, and promoters of counter-schemes, who demanded the modification of the plans in favour of a

[1] J. Aikin, A Description of the Country round Manchester, pp. 117-18.

[2] Petition asking for permission to build a canal between Marston Bridge and Ashby-de-la-Zouch. Journals of the House of Commons, XLIX, 238.

[3] Letters from Josiah Wedgwood to Bentley (Jan. 2nd, 1765) and to John Wedgwood (March 11th and July 6th, 1765). Letter from Charles Roe to Wedgwood (Dec. 4th, 1765). John Rylands Library, Manchester.

[4] Published at Newcastle-under-Lyme (1765).

particular district or a particular town.[1] Wedgwood had to head a regular campaign.[2] He went with Brindley to London, to give evidence before the Parliamentary Committee in charge of the preliminary inquiry. While Brindley expounded his plans, Wedgwood pointed out to the Committee the utility of such a canal, showing that not only the Potteries of Staffordshire but also the iron industries of Warwickshire needed water communications, and were condemned to stagnation as long as means of transport were lacking.[3] When at last, on July 26th, 1766, the work was begun, Wedgwood had the honour of turning the first sod. Almost immediately, on the line of the canal, he bought the land on which his great Etruria factory was built shortly after.[4]

Wedgwood and those who helped him, Samuel Garbett of Birmingham, and Matthew Boulton, James Watt's future partner, had a clear vision of the effect which the extension of navigable waterways was to have on the development of their own industries. The home markets, up till then narrow and broken up, could at last communicate without impediment. At the end of the eighteenth century merchandise of every kind, from all parts of the country, could be seen journeying up and down the main waterways, such as the Trent and Mersey Canal: salt from Cheshire, corn from East Anglia, pottery from Staffordshire, coal from Wigan and Newcastle, pig iron from the upper Severn, worked iron and copper from Wolverhampton and Birmingham. The most important item was coal. Everywhere branches from the main lines penetrated right to the heart of the mines.[5] Thus, facilities were offered on the one hand to the producer, who could work new coalfields, and on the other to the consumer, who was enabled by the low price of coal to put it to fresh uses.

Even foreign markets seemed to have been brought nearer. Imports and exports, instead of spreading with great difficulty through the country, circulated everywhere in increased quantities. Industrial centres were now certain to receive a sufficiency of provisions needed by their growing populations. Through the Mersey Canal, Liverpool

[1] See the petitions presented against the bill. *Journals of the House of Commons*, XXX, 613, 708, 713, 720, etc.

[2] Eliza Meteyard, *Life of Josiah Wedgwood*, I, 410-30.

[3] *Journals of the House of Commons*, XXX, 520.

[4] 'One branch of the canal extends right into the factory yard, and the coal barges come right up to the shed into which the coal has to go.' *Tournée faite en 1788 dans la Grande-Bretagne par un Français parlant la langue anglaise*, p. 109.

[5] Most of the Acts anticipate the opening of lines to serve the mines. See for instance 8 Geo. III, c. 38, the title of which runs as follows: 'An Act for making and maintaining a navigable cut or canal from the river Severn, at or near a place called Hawford, in the parish of Claines, in the county of Worcester, to or near a place called Chapel Bridge ... and for making collateral cuts up to several coal mines.' Another typical example may be found in *Journals of the House of Commons*, XLVII, 380.

supplied corn to Manchester, which no longer ran any risk of shortage.[1] Manufactured articles could be sent, without paying an expensive toll to middlemen, straight from the place of manufacture to the most distant destination: 'Until the middle of the century there was not one Birmingham trader who had direct relations with foreign countries: London merchants warehoused and exported Birmingham goods. Now Russian or Spanish firms order what they want direct from Birmingham. The industries for which it is most essential to have exportation made easier by the use of navigable rivers or canals are the metal industries. Since 1768 Birmingham has been sending without difficulty its production to the sea ports, owing to canal traffic.'[2]

In 1776 Adam Smith wrote: 'As by means of water-carriage, a more extensive market is opened to every sort of industry than what land-carriage alone can afford it, so it is upon the sea coast, and along the banks of navigable rivers, that industry of every kind begins to sub-divide and improve itself.'[3] Adam Smith was thinking more of the beginnings of industry than of the changes which were taking place in his own day, and under his own eyes. But he could have found in those changes a confirmation of his principle, for it was along the new navigable waterways and thanks to the growth of trade which they had made possible that the most decisive progress, both techni-cally and economically, was about to take place. And where water-ways formed a network round some privileged spot, marked out either by its geographical position or by natural resources, there a capital of the new industrial world was to grow.

Today the importance of England's system of communications by water within the country is much reduced. Even more than in other countries, railways have dealt it a heavy blow.[4] Railways for the last eighty years (written in 1927) have determined the great currents of commercial life, the branches by which goods reach the most

[1] On the scarcity and the riots of 1750-5, see F. Espinasse, *Lancashire Worthies*, I, 274, and L. W. Clarke, 'History of Birmingham', III, 60-1. In Birmingham in 1766 the mob seized the shops, fixed a maximum price and sold the corn by auction. Mackinder, *Britain and the British Seas*, p. 333, shows how Liverpool became a centre for the distri-bution of foodstuffs in the north-west of England. R. Whitworth, in *The Advantages of Inland Navigation* (1766), pp. 31-2, observed that once the canals were made 'it would then be an uncommon thing to hear of a riot on account of the dearness of corn, and ... that, if corn and provisions are cheap, the manufacturers might be able to work cheaper'.

[2] J. G. A. Forster, *Voyage philosophique et pittoresque en Angleterre et en France*, p. 84.

[3] Adam Smith, *Inquiry into the Nature and Causes of the Wealth of Nations*, Book I, chap. III.

[4] This decadence has been sometimes exaggerated. On their condition about the beginning of the twentieth century, see C. Wagner, 'Ueber die wirtschaftliche Lage des Binnenschifffahrtsunternehmungen in Grossbritannien und Irland', *Archiv für Eisenbahnwesen*, 1901, pp. 1212-68, and 1902, pp. 86-115.

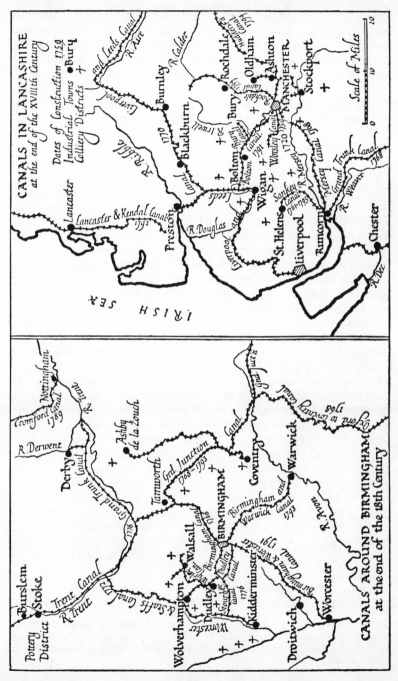

CANALS IN LANCASHIRE *at the end of the XVIIIth Century*

Dates of Construction 1759
Industrial Towns ● Bury
Colliery Districts +

Scale of Miles

R. Aire

Leeds and Leeds Canal

R. Calder

Bury

Burnley

Blackburn

Rochdale

Bury

Oldham

Ashton

Rochdale Canal 1794

Liverpool Canal

Leeds

MANCHESTER

Stockport

R. Irwell

Bolton Canal

Bolton Canal 1791

R. Ribble

1770

Bolton

Worsley Canal 1720 1759

Wigan

Sankey Canal 1761-1793

R. Mersey

Mersey Canal 1708

Grand Trunk Canal

Leeds

R. Douglas

St. Helens

Runcorn

R. Weaver

1768

Lancaster

Lancaster & Kendal Canal 1792

Preston

Liverpool Canal

Liverpool

Chester

R. Dee

IRISH SEA

Scale of Miles
0   5   10   20

CANALS AROUND BIRMINGHAM *at the end of the 18th Century*

Nottingham

Cromford Canal 1789

R. Trent

R. Derwent

Ashby de la Zouch

Oxford & Coventry Canal 1768

Derby

Grand Trunk Canal

Tamworth

Grd. Junction Canal 1768-1793

Coventry Canal

Warwick

1776

Walsall

BIRMINGHAM

Birmingham and Warwick Canal 1793

Wolverhampton

Birmingham Canal 1768

Dudley Canal 1776

R. Avon

Potteries District

Burslem

Stoke

Trent Canal

R. Trent

Staffs Canal

Dudley

Birmingham & Worcester Canal 1791

Kidderminster

Droitwich

Worcester

Worcester

outlying districts, and the junctions where they gather and overflow. But if we compare the two systems we shall realize that the earlier one, stunted and inadequate as it has become, already laid down the main lines followed by the other, so that the railroad often duplicates the canal. If we think of the influence which the railways exert today on the development of industry we shall realize the great part played by canals, after centuries of strictly local economic life.

VIII

We have just quoted Adam Smith. We know that his theory on the influence of navigable waterways is bound up with a more general theory, or rather law, which he has expressed in the famous sentence: The division of labour is limited by the extent of the market.[1] This law holds good whether we look at production and exchange in their most primitive state or in the midst of the most advanced and complex civilization. At one end of the line is the artisan who carries on several trades at once in a village shop; at the other are immense, highly specialized factories, which can only exist if they are able to obtain raw materials from distant countries and to export their production to the whole world. Adam Smith did not carry very far his study of the consequences derived from this principle. He was content to examine a small number of simple cases, which served, however, as examples in support of his theory.[2]

Long before his time an unknown author[3] had propounded the same law in less general terms and a less concise style, but with singular precision. The *Considerations upon the East-India Trade* dates from 1701. Like most economic works prior to the classical period, this was written for a special occasion. Violent polemics had been exchanged over the import of certain foreign products, above all over silk and cotton tissues made in India. The woollen industry, jealous as we know of its monopoly, had complained of this foreign competition and had succeeded in obtaining prohibition, in spite of the habits and tastes of the public. The author of the *Considerations*, taking a purely abstract view of the matter, undertook to prove that the import of goods from India not only benefited the consumer but was also profitable to the national industry itself. For was it not waste of labour to use

---

[1] See *Wealth of Nations*, Book I, chap. III (title).

[2] Ibid., Book I, chaps. II and III.

[3] The authorship of the *Considerations upon the East-India Trade*, which must not be mistaken for the *Essay on the East India Trade* by Charles Davenant (1696), has been attributed, though without decisive proof, to Sir Dudley North (see Halkett and Laing, *Dictionary of Anonymous and Pseudonymous Literature*, I, 491). The pamphlet was reprinted in 1856 in *A Select Collection of Early English Tracts on Commerce*, published by J. R. MacCulloch.

it in producing goods which could be bought cheap abroad? And by saving labour it would be possible either to create new industries, or to set up within the old a wiser distribution of functions, completed, if necessary, by technical improvements.

'That this thing may not seem a Paradox, the *East-India* Trade may be the cause of doing things with less Labour, and then tho' Wages shou'd not, the price of Manufactures might be abated. If things shall be done with less labour, the price of it must be less tho' the Wages of Men shou'd be as high as ever ... Thus a Ship is navigated with a great number of Hands at very great charge; if by being undermasted and spreading less Canvass the same shou'd be navigated by two-thirds of that number, so as the difference of Speed shall be very inconsiderable, the Ship wou'd be navigated with less charge, tho' the Wages of Sea-men shou'd be as high as ever. In like manner of any *English* Manufacture perform'd by so many Hands, and in so long a time, the price is proportionable, if by the invention of an Engine, or by greater order and regularity of the Work, the same shall be done by two-thirds of that number of Hands, or in two-thirds of that time; the labour will be less, the price of it will be also less, tho' the Wages of Men shou'd be as high as ever.'[1]

How this 'greater order and regularity of the Work' or this 'invention of an Engine' could result from the import of Indian goods, was what seemed extremely obscure to the first readers of this work, so much in advance of its time. So the author hastened to develop and explain his idea: 'The *East-India* Trade is no unlikely way to introduce more Artists, more Order and Regularity into our *English* Manufactures, it must put an end to such of them as are most useless and unprofitable; the People imploy'd in these will betake themselves to others, to others the most plain and easie, or to the single Parts of other Manufactures of most variety; for plain and easie work is soonest learn'd, and Men are more perfect and expeditious in it; And thus the *East-India* Trade may be the cause of applying proper Parts of Works of great variety to single and proper Artists, of not leaving too much to be perform'd by the skill of single Persons; and this is what is meant by introducing greater Order and Regularity into our *English* Manufactures.'[2]

The specialization and division of labour, pushed to the furthest extreme, must end in the employment of artificial means of production: 'Arts, and Mills, and Engines, which save the labour of Hands, are ways of doing things with less labour, and consequently with labour of less price, tho' the Wages of Men imploy'd to do them shou'd not be abated. The *East-India* Trade procures things with less

[1] *Considerations upon the East-India Trade*, pp. 65-6.
[2] Ibid., pp. 67-8.

and cheaper labour than would be necessary to make the like in *England*; it is therefore very likely to be the cause of the invention of Arts, and Mills, and Engines, to save the labour of Hands in other Manufactures. Such things are successively invented to do a great deal of work with little labour of Hands; they are the effects of Necessity and Emulation; every Man must be still inventing himself, or be still advancing to farther perfection upon the invention of other Men; if my Neighbour by doing much with little labour can sell cheap, I must contrive to sell as cheap as he. So that every Art, Trade, or Engine, doing work with labour of fewer Hands, and consequently cheaper, begets in others a kind of Necessity and Emulation, either of using the same Art, Trade, or Engine, or of inventing something like it, that every Man may be upon the square, that no man may be able to under-sell his Neighbour. And thus the *East-India* Trade by procuring things with less, and consequently cheaper labour, is a very likely way of forcing Men upon the invention of Arts and Engines, by which other things may be also done with less and cheaper labour, and therefore may abate the price of Manufactures.'[1] Thus, three-quarters of a century before the event, the anonymous author of a brilliant pamphlet foresaw, as an inevitable result of the extension of trade, the advent of machinery.

The expansion of British trade had very early another and no less important a consequence. It introduced new elements into society, or rather it altered something in the social hierarchy. For a long time there had been rich merchants and powerful financiers, but their wealth and their social position were quite individual. They remained isolated, and did not yet constitute an important and influential class, ranking only below the hereditary aristocracy and almost on an equality with the gentry. We saw the emergence of this class in 1688. 'Trade is so far here from being inconsistent with a gentleman, that, in short, trade in England makes gentlemen: for, after a generation or two, the tradesmen's children, or at least their grandchildren, come to be as good gentlemen, statesmen, Parliament men, Privy Councillors, judges, bishops, and noblemen, as those of the highest birth and most ancient families.'[2] Viscount Barrington was the son of a linen merchant called Shute.[3] Lord Granville, Lord Conway, and even Sir Robert Walpole, did not disdain marriage with the daughters of merchants.[4] During his stay in England Voltaire was struck by the way the old families not only mixed with the trading class but actually took part in their undertakings: 'The younger son of a peer will not look down

[1] *Considerations upon the East-India Trade*, pp. 66-7.
[2] Defoe, *The Complete Tradesman*, p. 74.
[3] Defoe, *Tour*, I, 17.
[4] W. Lecky, *History of England in the Eighteenth Century*, I, 193.

upon business. Lord Townsend, a Cabinet Minister, has a brother who is content with leading a firm in the City. While Lord Orford was governing England, his younger brother kept a warehouse in Aleppo, would never come back, and died there.' Thus they make not only their own fortune but that of their country. 'It is only because the English have taken to trade that London has outgrown Paris both as to its size and the number of its inhabitants, and that England can have two hundred men of war and subsidize allied kings. All this fills the English merchant with justifiable pride, and enables him to compare himself, not unreasonably, to a Roman citizen.'[1]

Whilst the nobility was trying to get rich by trade, the merchant aristocracy was dreaming of that power and ascendancy which, in a country where the land system has long remained so traditional, is only acquired by the ownership of land.[2] Alike in those families who wished to better themselves, and in those who only wanted to keep up their standard, the same object was always kept in view — to found or to increase an estate. In order to bring this about, part of the land had to change hands. Thus, at the same time as an economic revolution, a far-reaching social change was preparing.

---

[1] Voltaire, *Lettres Philosophiques*, Lettre X, 'Sur le Commerce', ed. Moland, XXII, 110-11.

[2] Defoe, travelling in 1724 in Essex, already noted that tendency: 'It is observable that in this part of the country there are several very considerable estates purchased, and now enjoyed by citizens of London, merchants, and tradesmen ... The present increase of wealth in the City of London spreads itself in the country, and plants families and fortunes, which in another age will equal the families of the ancient gentry.'

CHAPTER THREE

THE REDISTRIBUTION OF
THE LAND

THE British reader needs no reminding of the fact that Great Britain is, in western Europe, the classical land of large estates and extensive farms. Whoever travels across the English countryside can recognize certain distinctive aspects of the landscape, familiar from so many descriptions. No motley chequerwork spreads over hills and villages, as in France — a visible sign of small-lot cultivation. Scarcely any ploughed land is to be seen, except in the eastern counties. What could be said of the Roman *latifundium* is still true of the English estate. Far-spreading grazing lands unfold a green mantle, streaked with tall hedges. Farms and dwellings stand wide apart, villages are scarce: the eye may wander sometimes over a broad tract of country without catching sight of a single church tower.

I

Yet up to a comparatively recent date England possessed a considerable class of small landowners and of customary tenants who were almost as strongly attached to the soil as if it had actually belonged to them. They were the *yeomanry*, whose almost total disappearance it became, in the nineteenth century, a kind of ritual to lament. John Stuart Mill wrote with respect of that hard-working, independent peasantry 'who were vaunted as the glory of England while they existed, and have been so much mourned over since they disappeared'.[1] They were, in Macaulay's words, a manly and a true breed. Wordsworth, describing the Lake District, praised its former inhabitants and wrote: 'Till within the last sixty years, towards the head of these dales was found a perfect republic of shepherds and agriculturists, among whom the plough of each man was confined to the maintenance of his own family or to the occasional accommodation of his neighbour. Two or three cows furnished each family with milk and cheese ... Neither high-born nobleman, knight, nor esquire, was here, but many of these humble sons of the hills had a consciousness that the lands which they walked over and tilled had for more than five hundred years been possessed by men of their name and blood.'[2]

[1] John Stuart Mill, *Principles of Political Economy*, I, 300 (1848 edition).
[2] Wordsworth, *A Description of the Scenery of the Lakes in the North of England*, pp. 64-5 (1832 edition).

A yeoman was essentially a freeholder who owned the field on which he lived, and cultivated it himself. But the name also applied to copyholders, whose family had tilled the same bit of land for several generations, and even in certain districts to leaseholders for life.[1] There were great and small yeomen. As a rule, those who deplored the disappearance of the yeomanry were thinking mainly of the latter: they were men whose annual income did not exceed £80 and who compared fairly well with the landowning peasants on the Continent.[2] Above the yeoman stood the squire, beneath him the tenant. The squire, poor though he might be, lived as one of the gentry: he sat as Justice of the Peace, served as an officer in the militia; and if he happened to keep a few hounds he called them a pack.[3] The tenant, rich though he might be, was not master on his land; he could not even forget, as did the copyholder, that the profit out of his work was not for him alone. That which made the yeoman different was his independence. To it he chiefly owed his stalwart character, and the part he played in the ancient days of English history. Out of the yeomanry came, in the Middle Ages, those dreaded archers and pikemen who won the day at Crécy, at Poitiers and at Agincourt. Later, the yeomen became Protestants and Puritans; they were the staunchest supporters of the Reformation and fought in the armies of Fairfax and Cromwell.

Their importance may have somewhat diminished in the course of the seventeenth century.[4] Yet, even after the Revolution of 1688, they still formed a large section of the community.[5] According to the

[1] 'The definite restriction of the word to farmer owners is a comparatively modern usage belonging to the nineteenth century.' Prothero (Baron Ernle), *English Farming, Past and Present*, p. 296 (note). See also Curtler, *The Enclosure and Redistribution of our Land*, p. 71.

[2] *Re* the two classes of yeomen, see H. Levy, 'Der Untergang kleinbäuerlicher Betriebe in England', *Jahrbücher für Nationalökonomie und Statistik*, 1903, pp. 149-50 and 158-9; also W. Hasbach, 'Der Untergang des englischen Bauernstandes in neuer Beleuchtung', *Archiv für Sozialwissenschaft*, XXIV, 6 ff. (1907). Hasbach rightly maintains, on the evidence of Marshall and A. Young, that the word yeomen, at the end of the eighteenth century, applied to rich peasants owning land that yielded incomes of £100 to £600 – quite a distinct class from the small gentry. But H. Levy justly emphasizes the difference between great and small yeomen, which H. L. Gray and A. H. Johnson, in their works based on the Land Tax Assessments, do not sufficiently take into account. See H. L. Gray, 'Yeoman Farming in Oxfordshire from the Sixteenth Century to the Nineteenth', *Quarterly Journal of Economics*, XXIV, pp. 293-326, and A. H. Johnson, *The Disappearance of the Small Landowner*, chap. VII.

[3] Among the many portraits that have been drawn of the English squire, see Macaulay's brilliant sketch, *History of England*, I, 349-55.

[4] Such is the accepted opinion, given by W. Lecky, *History of England in the Eighteenth Century*, I, 7.

[5] A. Eliaschewitsch, *Die Bewegung zugunsten der kleinen landwirtschaftlichen Güter in England*, pp. 7-9, quotes abundant evidence as to the importance in the country of small and middle-sized holdings, at the beginning of the eighteenth century.

approximate statistics published at the time, they numbered no less than one hundred and sixty thousand; together with their families, they amounted to about one-sixth of the total population of the kingdom.[1] Their income varied from £40 to £300; for a large majority of them it hardly exceeded £60 to £80.[2] That was enough to secure to almost all of them a life of comparative ease and comfort. The yeoman did not always draw his income solely from his work on the land: he would often add to that some industrial occupation; his wife and children would card or spin wool.[3] Here was a feature common to him and to the independent small manufacturer who was doomed to disappear almost at the same time. They both belonged to a definite structure of society, which had its foundation in the co-existence and close association between small agricultural production and small industrial production.

When did the final disappearance of the yeomanry take place? The question would involve us in a difficult controversy, in which the last word may not have been spoken yet.[4] In the last years of the eighteenth century we find the yeomanry mentioned by some as an extinct class, who were 'nearly annihilated in the year 1750, and are now but faintly remembered'.[5] This was clearly an exaggeration. If the yeomanry had ceased to exist in 1750, its disappearance must have been sudden indeed. Yet, as early as 1732, the eviction of a great many small landowners was deplored by the author of *An Essay*

[1] Gregory King, 'Natural and Political Observations upon the State of the Nation' (1696), British Museum, Harleian MSS., No. 1898, p. 14; first published by G. Chalmers, *An Estimate of the Comparative Strength of Britain* (1804). See also Charles Davenant, *Essay upon the Probable Methods of Making a People Gainers in the Ballance of Trade* (1697), *Works*, II, 184.

[2] *Report from the Select Committee appointed to Enquire into the Present State of Agriculture* (1833, p. 65).

[3] Wordsworth, op. cit., p. 52; Defoe, *Tour*, I, 37.

[4] See Arnold Toynbee, *Lectures on the Industrial Revolution in England*, first edition, pp. 58-66; H. Rae, 'Why have the Yeomanry perished?' *Contemporary Review*, 1883, II, 548 ff.; H. Levy, 'Der Untergang kleinbäuerlicher Betriebe in England', *Jahrbücher für Nationalökonomie und Statistik*, 1903, pp. 145-67; Id., *Large and Small Holdings*, pp. 30 ff.; W. Hasbach, 'Der Untergang des englischen Bauernstandes in neuer Beleuchtung', *Archiv für Sozialwissenschaft*, XXIV, 11-29, and *History of the English Agricultural Labourer*, pp. 73-6; A. H. Johnson, *The Disappearance of the Small Landowner*, chap. VII. The following should also be consulted: H. L. Gray, 'Yeoman Farming in Oxfordshire from the Sixteenth Century to the Nineteenth', *Quarterly Journal of Economics*, XXIV, and H. C. Taylor, *The Decline of Landowning Farmers in England*, Wisconsin University, 1904.

[5] *A Letter to Sir T. C. Bunbury, Bart., on the Increase of the poor rates and the high price of provisions, by a Suffolk Gentleman* (1795), p. 2. To make sure that his readers will not fail to understand him, the author gives a definition of the yeomanry. In the days of the Revolution 'there existed a race of men in the country, besides the gentlemen and husbandmen, called yeomanry, men who cultivated their own property, consisting chiefly of farms from forty to fourscore pounds a year'.

proving that enclosing Commons and Common Lands is contrary to the Interests. of the Nation; in 1753 Roger North found evidence in the land register that many small properties had been absorbed into larger ones.[1] In 1773 Arbuthnot, although a declared supporter of cultivation on a large scale, lamented the decline of the yeomanry: 'I sincerely regret the loss of that set of men who ... are called yeomen, who really kept up the independence of the nation, and have their lands now in the hands of the monopolizing lords.'[2] As late as 1788, W. L. Marshall mentioned the existence in the valley of Pickering (Yorkshire) of 'about 300 freeholders, principally occupying their small estates, many of which have fallen down by lineal descent from the original purchasers':[3] but to him this appeared as a singular and noteworthy fact. From such contemporary evidence as the foregoing, Karl Marx inferred somewhat hastily that the yeomanry were extinct towards the middle of the eighteenth century;[4] Toynbee, though not going so far, still came to the conclusion that their decline had begun as early as 1770, and was far advanced by the time of the great French wars.

It has been aptly observed that the abundant contemporary literature concerning the changes in the methods of cultivation throws little light on the disappearance of the yeomanry.[5] We have proof of the existence of yeomen towards the end of the eighteenth century, and after 1785 a series of years favourable to agricultural interests made for an increase rather than a fall in the numbers of this class of landowning farmers.[6] But we must insist upon the distinction between the wealthier yeomen, who drew from their farms incomes as high as £400 or even £600, and the small freeholders and

---

[1] *A Discourse of the Poor*, quoted by A. Eliaschewitsch, op. cit., p. 54.

[2] J. Arbuthnot, *An Inquiry into the Connection between the Present Price of Provisions and the Size of Farms*, p. 126.

[3] W. Marshall, *Rural Economy of Yorkshire*, I, 20.

[4] *Das Kapital*, I, 747.

[5] See Prothero (Baron Ernle), *English Farming, Past and Present*, pp. 293-6, quoting the Reports of the Board of Agriculture (1793-1815); W. Hasbach, *The English Agricultural Labourer*, pp. 73-6, and 'Die Untergang des englischen Bauernstandes in neuer Beleuchtung', *Archiv für Sozialwissenschaft*, XXIV, pp. 27-9. As early as 1883 J. Rae maintained that the decline of the yeomanry had not begun in fact until the fall in the prices of agricultural produce which followed on the close of the Napoleonic wars ('Why have the Yeomanry perished?', *Contemporary Review*, 1883, II, 548-53). The same view is taken by H. C. Taylor, *The Decline of Landowning Farmers in England*, Wisconsin University, 1904.

[6] 'During the period 1785 to 1802 there was an increase rather than a decrease of the yeomen proper in all parts of England, except those like Lancashire which were more directly and rapidly affected by the industrial revolution.' (A. H. Johnson, *The Disappearance of the Small Landowner*, p. 144). Cf. H. L. Gray, 'Yeoman Farming in Oxfordshire from the Sixteenth Century to the Nineteenth', *Quarterly Journal of Economics*, XXIV, 306. See W. Marshall, *Rural Economy of Norfolk* (1787), p. 9; H. Holland, *General View of the Agriculture of Cheshire* (1808), p. 79.

copyholders, whose limited incomes left them more exposed to economic changes. To the latter only should be applied the statements made by the authors who, writing at the close of the eighteenth century, show us small properties being absorbed into the neighbouring large estates, or sold to townspeople.[1] These small landowners became either tenants[2] or labourers, while the more enterprising among them went to seek their fortune far from the land that had nourished their race for centuries.

The decline of the yeomanry was not a steady movement; while in some counties they were fast disappearing, they survived in others thanks to the artificial prosperity of English agriculture during the Napoleonic wars.[3] But the crisis that followed on the conclusion of the peace dealt them the final blow; the Parliamentary Report of 1833 on the Condition of Agriculture affords evidence of their becoming extinct throughout the country.[4] For some time yet the Cumberland hills preserved a few remaining yeomen. 'There is a part of England,' John Stuart Mill wrote in 1846, 'unfortunately a very small part, where peasant proprietors are still common: for such are the *Statesmen* of Cumberland and Westmorland, though they pay, I believe generally, if not universally, certain customary dues, which, being fixed, no more affect their character of proprietors than the land tax does. There is but one voice among those acquainted with the country, on the admirable effects of this tenure of land in

---

[1] J. Holt, *A General View of the Agriculture of the County of Lancaster* (1794), p. 12; D. Walker, *A General View of the Agriculture in the County of Hertford* (1795), p. 15; J. Wedge, *A General View of the Agriculture in the County of Warwick* (1794), p. 21; J. Aikin, *A Description of the Country from thirty to forty miles round Manchester* (1795), p. 43; F. M. Eden, *State of the Poor* (1797), II, 30. The fact that part of this information is drawn from Reports of the Board of Agriculture, whose authors were staunch supporters of the new agronomy, removes the imputation of a bias against large scale cultivation.

[2] H. Levy, *Large and Small Holdings*, pp. 30 and 34.

[3] See the Board of Agriculture Surveys, mentioned by Prothero (Baron Ernle), *English Farming, Past and Present*, pp. 293-6, and W. Hasbach, *Der Untergang des englischen Bauernstandes*, pp. 27-9. At the end of the eighteenth century small yeomen were still to be found in Northumberland, Durham, Yorkshire (West Riding), Lincoln, Stafford, Salop, Worcester, Derby, Northampton, Oxford, Nottingham, Cambridge, Essex, Wilts, Cumberland and Westmorland.

[4] *Report from the Select Committee on Agriculture* (1833). Wiltshire: Landowners with incomes from £50 to £300 have disappeared (p. 65). – Yorkshire: All the smaller yeomen disappeared after the war (p. 149). – Cheshire: The yeomen are in a very bad state: their property is nearly gone (p. 272). – Shropshire: All the small farms have been sold (p. 285). – Northumberland and Durham: Many small landowners have become servants and gone into other employment (p. 327). In Hampshire they are burdened with mortgages, ruined, they sell off their land under price (p. 466). In Nottinghamshire not one of them is left (p. 586). Two or three counties were exceptions to the rule, namely: Worcestershire (pp. 84-5), Cumberland (p. 325), Herefordshire (p. 394).

those counties.'[1] But that was merely a survival, noted down with curiosity by the economist − the last vestige of days gone by and soon to be forgotten.[2]

II

If the decline of the yeomanry had not begun before the end of the eighteenth century, it might not unreasonably be looked upon as one of the consequences of the industrial revolution. Did not the decay of the domestic system of industry deprive the rural populations of one of their means of livelihood? Here, no doubt, is one cause, but one that set in at a late stage, and can only have made itself felt at a date when the yeomanry had already lost much ground. For a long time it had been reported that they were becoming smaller in numbers and in importance, when large-scale industry and its consequences began to affect their condition. But the yeomanry did not perish alone. Their fate was but one episode in a great drama, in which all the rural classes of England took a part.

If, taking up the Statutes of the Realm, we survey a period extending over one hundred and twenty years or thereabouts, from the death of William III to the accession of George IV, we shall notice a titleline that recurs ever more frequently in the series of public as well as of private Acts. That titleline reads as follows: 'An Act for dividing, allotting and enclosing the open and common fields, meadows, pastures and common and waste lands, in the parish of ... ': here the name of the parish. The Acts of Parliament opening with that phrase amount to hundreds and thousands.[3] And their number increased year by year as time went on: there were three Acts only in the twelve years of the reign of Queen Anne;[4] from 1714 to 1720, about one every year. During the first half of the century the progress, though gradual, became more marked: thirty-three Acts between 1720 and 1730, thirty-five between 1730 and 1740, thirty-eight between 1740 and 1750. From 1750 to 1760 we find one hundred and fifty-six such Acts; from

[1] John Stuart Mill, *Principles of Political Economy* (1848 edition), I, 300.

[2] Today the yeomanry no longer exist as a class. The Cumberland 'Statesmen' have almost entirely disappeared. Isolated instances of small landowners could still be found in some of the southern counties (Gloucester, Somerset, Devon, Kent) and in the East, where corn is grown (particularly in Lincolnshire). On the last yeomen of Hampshire, cf. Thorold Rogers, *Six Centuries of Work and Wages*, p. 55.

[3] A computation of the actual number was made several times, but incompletely or with little care. Almost all the figures given by Chalmers, *Estimate of the Comparative Strength of Britain*, p. 146, are incorrect. Those given by G. R. Porter, *Progress of the Nation*, p. 148, are correct, but there is nothing earlier than 1760. The statistics in the *Appendix to the Third Report from the Select Committee on Agriculture*, p. 501, afford an excellent means of checking those figures.

[4] The first is 8 Anne, c. 20 (Private Acts), issued in 1709.

1760 to 1770 four hundred and twenty-four; from 1770 to 1780 six hundred and forty-two. Between 1780 and 1790, that is, at the very period when the factory system came into full play, the figure came down to two hundred and eighty-seven. But, between 1790 and 1800, it leapt up to five hundred and six, while between 1800 and 1810 the total reached was much higher still, indeed quite an unprecedented one: during those ten years Parliament passed no fewer than nine hundred and six Acts, with the object of 'dividing, allotting and enclosing'.

The lands that came under the eighteenth century Enclosure Acts extended over considerable areas. If they were not evenly distributed over the whole country it was because, in many regions, there had been no more land to enclose since the end of the previous century. In others, the enclosing had taken place outside the pale of parliamentary procedure by means of private purchases or by bringing farms together on the expiration of leases.[1] The enclosing of the land betokened a transformation so far-reaching that general causes only can account for it.

First of all, a preliminary question should be answered: what were those lands, the dividing up and allotting of which was thus decreed? They were of more than one kind. The Acts applied to them various terms which, albeit different, might easily be mistaken for one another: on the one hand, the words *open fields* and *common fields* are constantly coupled together and appear to be synonymous; on the other those of *common lands*, *common wastes* and *common pastures* are used as an entirely distinct group, never replacing the former, in spite of an obvious kinship with them. Those words belonged to the habitual vocabulary of land legislation, and nothing should be easier than to define their exact meaning.

The author of an *Essay on the Nature and Method of ascertaining the Specific Shares of Proprietors upon the Inclosure of Common Fields* gives the following definition: 'Open or common fields are tracts of land, wherein the property of several owners lies promiscuously dispersed.'[2] The term 'common fields' has the disadvantage of leading to possible

---

[1] G. Slater, *The English Peasantry and the Enclosure of the Common Fields*, p. 73 (map), shows that the regions affected by the Enclosure Acts lay obliquely across Great Britain; the south-east, from the Isle of Wight to Suffolk, the south-west (Devon, Somerset, Cornwall) and the north-west, as well as Wales, did not come under their operation. But at the same time, he explains how enclosures took place without any Act of Parliament (ibid., pp. 152-5 and pp. 187 ff.). – In the south-eastern counties, all the land had been enclosed as early as the seventeenth century. Cf. T. E. Scrutton, *Commons and Common Fields*, p. 114. – Gonner (*Common Land and Inclosure*, p. 123) holds that such was the case also in Northumberland, Durham, Lancaster, Chester, Devon, Cornwall, Salop, Hereford, Somerset and Sussex.

[2] H. Homer, op. cit. (1766), p. 1.

confusion: it calls up an idea of communism. The above definition disposes of that idea altogether: it shows us the *open field* – let us keep to that phrase as less ambiguous – in the hands of several proprietors, each being lawfully entitled to his share; some are freeholders and own the land; others are copyholders, being entitled to occupy it by the possession of a perpetual or very long lease.[1] Their lands are not joined together to form an undivided whole; they are only 'promiscuously dispersed', that is, divided into a large number of lots, all interspersed among one another. Such, in fact, is the most marked characteristic of what is known as the *open field system*.

Let us examine a map showing the distribution of property in an English parish towards the middle of the eighteenth century. One such map has been published – that of the township of Hitchin, Hertfordshire.[2] Its aspect reminds us of a spider's web, showing a divergency and intercrossing of lines that appear to become endlessly complicated. These lines enclose areas which are approximately rectangular in shape, and all but equal to one another in size. If on that map we paint with a distinctive colour the small rectangles representing the different plots that belong to each owner, the result is a strange, broken mosaic made up of straggling fragments. The property of one William Lucas, in 1750, consisted of forty-seven plots, scattered all over the township;[3] and these scattered parts were not even grouped into a more or less definite whole; on the contrary, it would seem that care had been taken to distribute them almost equally over a given area. On the spot, each of the rectangular plots appeared as a long, narrow strip of land, with a thin line of turf between it and the next strip. Its measurements averaged forty rods in length and four rods across – these being the actual dimensions of the English acre. Such strips of land were often divided into two equal parts. Each part was about twenty rods long, and was called a *balk* or *oxgang*;[4] the length showed the direction along which the furrows ran,

---

[1] As to the 'copyhold', see Edward Jenks, *Modern Land Law*, pp. 57 ff.

[2] Cf. F. Seebohm, *The English Village Community*. The map on the frontispiece shows the state of the parish in 1750: that on page 6 bears the date: 1816.

[3] A survival of this mode of parcelling out was very recently shown to exist at Laxton, in the north of Nottinghamshire. (See correspondence published in *The Times*, December 24th and 30th, 1925; January 5th, 7th and 8th, 1926, concerning 'The last Anglo-Saxon Farm'.) The Laxton estate belongs, in fact, to one landowner, Lord Manvers, but is in the hands of about thirty tenants; it is divided into nearly 1,200 plots, which together form one open field, and the system of cultivation is the traditional triennial rotation. – Curtler, *The Enclosure and Redistribution of our Land*, p. 1, mentions a similar instance, at a village called Elmstone Hardwicke (Gloucestershire).

[4] *Oxgang* means literally the space of land ploughed by one ox in one day: it applied to various areas according to districts. – Those words are often found in Acts of Enclosures. – Prothero (Baron Ernle), *English Farming, Past and Present*, pp. 24 ff., gives the different names for those strips of land in different districts.

and at either end a space was left free for the plough to be driven round and back again: this was the *headland*. Interesting evidence of this extraordinary parcelling out can still be found in certain districts. Where the ground was hilly the long narrow plots ran at a right angle to the direction of the slope, to avoid a sliding of the land after each ploughing; they gradually became levelled into narrow terraces that climb the hillsides like steps and that, once formed, have remained there. Such terraces can be seen along the Chiltern Hills and the Sussex Downs as well as in many parts of northern France.[1]

This system of parcelling out the land, strange though it may seem, was nevertheless very prevalent throughout Great Britain, and indeed throughout the greater part of Europe. It was said with truth that 'a traveller met with it from Andalusia to Siberia ... on the Loire and on the plains of Moscow.'[2] In England, prior to the sixteenth century, there were but few exceptions; early in the eighteenth century it still prevailed in most of the counties; in 1794, though it had lost, and was losing, much ground it was still in force in 4,500 parishes, out of a total of 8,500.[3] The wide scope of that system makes the riddle of its origin all the more interesting. An answer to this question has often been sought, but it is not likely that a final solution will ever be forthcoming. The division of the soil into plots, which, if not identical in shape and size, were of one type or pattern, the scattering of properties that left not more than two or three acres together: could all this have been due to mere chance? A suggestion has been advanced that the whole system was the result of a primitive portioning out of the land. The original shares, it is suggested, had been equal, and in order that such equality should be real each man had received as his portion not one lot but a number of different lots, varying in value according to the quality of the soil, situation, aspect and altitude.[4] Certain facts would lead us to believe that periodical redistributions took place, with a view to keeping the shares equal: in the case of some pasture lands, for example, the lots were drawn every year; in others, they were exchanged according to a system of rotation; sometimes, though very

[1] See F. Seebohm, op. cit., pp. 2-6; Ramsay, *The Foundations of England*, I, 159-60; Cunningham and MacArthur, *Outlines of English Industrial History*, p. 170; R. Prothero, *The pioneers and progress of English farming*, p. 5. On sectional property in France under the old régime, see de Foville, *Le Morcellement*, p. 139, 153 and onwards. The existence of terraced fields on the side of hills is naturally a universal fact; it is of interest to us only when the limits of these terraces coincide with those of the old sectional properties.

[2] *General Report on Inclosures* (Board of Agriculture, 1808), p. 25.

[3] In Bedfordshire, 24,000 acres out of 84,000 remained as *open fields*; in Berkshire, the proportion was 220,000 to 438,000; in Cambridgeshire, 132,000 to 147,000. Cf. Prothero (Baron Ernle), op. cit.

[4] This theory is supported by Ramsay, *The Foundations of England*, I, 160.

seldom, the same was the case for plough land.[1] This whole theory, as we know, has been keenly discussed not only in England but also in Germany and in France.[2] Did such a system, enforcing equal possession of the land, ever exist in fact? At what time? When had it arisen? Was its origin Saxon or British, Germanic or Celtic?[3] Had it been at first a village or a tribal institution? These many questions have remained almost unanswerable to this day, and most of them need not even be framed if the primitive community – as is the view of Fustel de Coulanges – belongs merely to romance.

However that may be, any traces of that possible original division still extant in the eighteenth century were being wiped out more and more. Apart from the exceptional cases we have mentioned, the parts making up one property remained always the same. They did not change hands, except as a result of a sale or by inheritance, as is the case with all individual properties. The hazards of sales and successions that now aggregated, now dispersed them, had long since destroyed any real or fictitious equality among the possessors. By the side of a yardland[4] comprising sixty plots, with a total acreage of thirty or forty acres, another would consist solely of a messuage of half an acre, where

---

[1] E. Nasse, *Ueber die mittelalterliche Feldgemeinschaft ... in England*, pp. 9-10. F. Seebohm sees there evidence of two successive systems. Cf. *The English Village Community*, pp. 437-9. As late as the eighteenth century there were still *lot meadows* and *rotation meadows*.

[2] Cf. the controversy between Fustel de Coulanges and Maurer, Glasson and P. Viollet, as to the German *mark*, in *Histoire des Institutions Politiques de l'ancienne France; l'Alleu et le Domaine Rural pendant l'Époque Mérovingienne*, pp. 171, 198. Fustel de Coulanges shows conclusively that there were no village communities in the Merovingian days. As to commons, 'they did not originate in a supposed collective ownership, of which no evidence can be found anywhere; they originated in possession granted to tenants by the actual owner' (ibid., p. 436). Cf. the translation of M. Ashley (*The Origin of Property in Land*, by N. D. Fustel de Coulanges, with an introductory chapter on the English Manor by W. J. Ashley, 1891), Meitzen (*Siedelung und Agrarwesen der Westgermanen und Ostgermanen*, 1895), Maitland (*Domesday Book and Beyond*, 1897) and Kowalevsky (*Œkonomische Entwickelung Europas bis zum Beginn der kapitalistischen Wirtschaftsform*, 1901). More recently still, T. E. Scrutton, inquiring into the origin of the rights of common, came to the conclusion that there never existed any village communities (*Commons and Common Fields*, pp. 1-41). It is, however, to be noted that the *run-rig system*, as practised to this day in the Hebrides, implies a periodical redistribution of the land. (Cf. G. Slater, *The English Peasantry and the Enclosure of the Common Fields*, pp. 166 ff.). The meadow-land was often portioned out in yearly lots, between Candlemas and Midsummer (Baron Ernle, *English Farming, Past and Present*, pp. 25-6). The safest course might be to keep to Maitland's judicious remark (*Domesday Book and Beyond*, p. 340): 'We are among guesses, and little has been as yet proved.'

[3] According to Ramsay (p. 159), the origin of the *open field* was Anglo-Saxon; according to Seebohm (p. 437) it existed prior to the Roman conquest.

[4] The words *yardland* or *virgate* (*virgata terra*) applied to landed property of various sizes according to districts. As to the meaning of *virgate* in the south-eastern counties, see Tait, 'Hides and Virgates at Battle Abbey', *English Historical Review*, 1903, pp. 705 ff.

the dwelling-house stood.[1] Yet something of the early organization remained: the mode of cultivation that had arisen from the open-field system was still almost intact; a transformation of the one would necessarily involve the disappearance of the other.

III

It may now be interesting to compare the English cultivators of our time with those of the open-field days. Today, the Englishman is at home within his hedges, his fields are all of one piece, he does as he pleases with his land. He may, if he chooses, cultivate it or let it lie fallow; he may sow corn or he may sow clover. He may use whatever tools, and decide on whatever process, seem best to him in so far as he can afford them. When ploughing or harvesting he may take his own time, and need have no regard to his neighbour's doings. The husband-man of olden days, on the other hand, was in such close dependence on those around him that he could undertake nothing without their help, or at least their assent. His lands mingled with theirs to such a confusing degree that it required a peasant's life-long habit and unfailing memory to recognize at a glance what belonged to one man and what belonged to another. How could he undertake to cultivate his fifty or sixty acres in his own way, irrespective of what was done in the neighbouring plots? What an amount of time he would waste merely in inspecting his property, if it was at all considerable! Moreover, the situation of each piece of land, shut in as it was amid plots belonging to other men, was the cause of many expensive and burdensome obliga-tions: for instance, no fences could be set up; and, further, it was necessary to have a multitude of paths running from one end of the parish to the other and giving access to the plots, which meant so much arable land wasted. Such a complicated and inconvenient state of things would have led to a hopeless confusion if each owner had insisted on working independently. Hence the excessive parcelling out of land had the paradoxical result that the only possible mode of cultivation was cultivation under common rules.

For that purpose, therefore, all the plots of arable land in each parish were treated as a single estate. They were almost invariably grouped into three *fields*,[2] where crops succeeded one another according

---

[1] A *messuage* is the piece of land lying in the village, on which the house stands. Almost every yardland had its messuage. See the instance quoted by Seebohm, op. cit., p. 26: one yardland at Winslow included a messuage, 68 plots of half an acre, 3 plots of ¼ acre, as well as one acre and 4 half acres of meadow-land. As to the unequal sizes of landed property, cf. ibid., p. 11.

[2] Sometimes two or four. Cf. H. Homer, *Essay on the Nature and Method*, etc., p. 4; *The Advantages and Disadvantages of inclosing waste lands and open fields* (1772), p. 13; Prothero (Baron Ernle), *Pioneers*, p. 5, and *Social England*, V, 103-4. – Instead of three

to an ancient and somewhat clumsy method of rotation. One field
would be sown with wheat or barley, one with oats, peas or beans:
the third would lie fallow. At each new season that portion of the land
that had lain idle for a year was again sown; that which had yielded
one crop was made ready to bring forth a second one, different from
the first; that which had borne two successive harvests was in its turn
allowed to lie fallow. The manuring, ploughing and sowing took place
at dates that had been fixed for the whole parish. For a long time
cultivation in common had been an actual practice, the farmers
agreeing to provide manure, seeds, ploughs, draught-horses or oxen,
according to their means. But that method had been given up gradually since the sixteenth century[1] and had disappeared from most
districts in the eighteenth. If in a few cases it had survived, the individual rights of the owners were nevertheless recognized: the plots
were bounded by narrow bands of untilled land and remained entirely
distinct from one another. When harvest-time came the produce of
each plot belonged indisputably to the lawful owner. It must be said
once more that the open-field system was very far from being communistic.

Between harvest-time and sowing-time, when nothing stood on the
fields but stubble or a few ears that the sickles had spared, or a little
grass growing along the borders, there was no longer any need for the
strict maintenance of individual rights. Then, more than ever, did the
open field put on an appearance of collective property. It became
pasture land, and all the owners, without distinction, sent their pigs,
sheep and geese to graze there. The same was the case with
the meadows, lying generally lower by the water-side, and not looked
upon as part of the open field proper; as soon as haymaking was over
they became common grazing land for the horses, cows and oxen.[2]
Thus, during several months in every year – from the end of July to
Candlemas – the land remained undivided. The lack of any permanent
fences unavoidably caused the yearly recurrence of that state of things.
Now we can realize the full meaning of the words *open fields*; they apply
to unenclosed fields, as opposed to autonomous, enclosed property,

---

[1] See Prothero (Baron Ernle), *English Farming, Past and Present*, p. 25. T. E. Scrutton,
Commons and Common Fields, pp. 115-17. Curtler, *The Enclosure and Redistribution of our
Land*, p. 72, n. 1. For instances of districts where the old custom had been preserved,
see *Journals of the House of Commons*, XXXVIII, 857; LI, 257.
[2] H. Homer, op. cit., p. 7. Those were known as *lammas meadows*. Cf. Cunningham
and MacArthur, *Outlines of English Industrial History*, p. 171.

---

fields, a parish or township might have six, in groups of two: such was the case at
Hitchin. Seebohm, op. cit., pp. 11-12. – H. L. Gray, *English Field Systems*, p. 133,
gives an instance of an eight-course rotation, at Great Tew (Oxfordshire) in the middle
of the eighteenth century.

to which they offered the same contrast as a federation of small states does to a centralized monarchy. And, even as a federal constitution prolongs the existence of small sovereign states, so the open-field system for a long time preserved the existence of small landed properties. Where it had ceased to exist the number of owners was observed to be less, and their lands more extensive.[1] Thus, any cause that tended to maintain or to destroy it affected also the fate of the small landowners, the *yeomen*, whose downfall coincided in fact with the disappearance of the old land system.

IV

There were some lands, in each parish, that remained throughout the year in a state similar to that of the open field during the barren season. They were the *common*, or *waste*, lands. Here we have a case of something more like common ownership, of property that was actually and continually collective property, like the 'biens communaux' which were so often to be found in France in the olden days. To tell the truth, if those lands had no masters it was because they were looked upon as worthless. They lay untilled, as is shown by their name: *wastes*. Moors bristling with brushwood, or gorse, heather and wanton weeds, reed-coated marshes, quaking peat-bogs, woods grown haphazard on sand or rock: the English commons, for the most part, had nothing better to show.[2] In our days many of these long-scorned lands have been broken up and are cultivated with good results. But intensive culture has only recently been put into practice. For centuries men had been content to sow the richer land; and whatever yield it readily gave, they took as an immediate and satisfactory return for their labours.

Although small value was set on the common, and although it had been customary to neglect it and let it lie wild, more than one advantage accrued from it to the peasants. They could drive their beasts there, particularly sheep, since sheep find food even on poor land: this right was known as *common of pasture*, or *right of sheepwalk*. If trees grew on the common the peasants could cut wood and add a few beams to their house, or set up a stile; and that right was known as *common*

---

[1] In Huntingdonshire, at the close of the eighteenth century, the open fields had ceased to exist in some parishes, while in others they had been preserved. In the former case the average income of a farm was £50 to £150; in the latter, £200 to £500. So in Northampton, Oxfordshire, etc. Cf. Marshall, *A Review of the Reports of the Board of Agriculture from the Midland Departments of England* (pp. 334-48).

[2] Sometimes, however, the common included lands of some value – those which, in some villages, were known as the *green common*. Cows grazed there, watched over by a common shepherd. In some cases bulls and stallions were reared, the expense being borne in common. Cf. Seebohm, op. cit., p. 12, and Nasse, op. cit., p. 8.

of estovers.[1] If a pond was included in the common, or a river ran through it, the villagers were entitled to catch fish there: and here was another privilege, known as *common of piscary*. Where there were bogs – and these still covered extensive areas in all the counties of England – they had a right to cut peat for their own use (*common of turbary*).[2] Yet another advantage was that common rights sometimes extended to parts of the parish outside the common land.[3]

Did every inhabitant of the parish enjoy these rights? Was anything in them the legacy of a primitive state of equality? In the first place the common was not, in fact, the land of no master: it belonged legally to the *lord of the manor*, who retained something of his original rights over the whole territory of the parish, and it was sometimes called the *lord's waste*. In fact, the exercise of such rights was in no way exclusive: even as the lord of the manor had, to some extent, made over his rights on the open field to a certain number of freeholders, so he allowed them to share in the enjoyment of the so-called common lands. But it was with the common as with the open field: when once the harvest had been taken in not all the inhabitants were entitled to send their beasts or fowls to feed there, but only those who owned one or more pieces of land in the parish. After carrying out jointly the cultivation of the soil they used it jointly as a common pasture – a natural sequel to the understanding and the daily partnership that bound them together. The common was subject to the same rules: it was common, not to all the villagers but to all the landowners in the village. In spite of appearances it was not free land, the use of which admitted of no restrictions; only in pursuance of certain definite rights, and in proportion with those rights did any man gain admission thereon.

We have now seen that individual rights over the common came under several headings, according to the kind of profits that might be derived from them. They could also be classified according to their origin and to any limitations resulting therefrom. Often they traditionally went with the possession of any land lying within the boundaries of the manor, parish or township (*common appendant*). Such

---

[1] From the medieval French *estovoir, estouvoir* (to be necessary or suitable; or, in a substantive form: what is needed, supplies). That word was used in the old French law with a meaning similar to that of the English phrase: 'Averont tous lor astovoirs en boix batis de Leheicourt.' *Rentes de l'Ecclese de St Hoult* (1258), *Archives de la Meuse*. Quoted by Godefroy, *Dictionnaire de l'ancienne langue française*, III, 634.

[2] Cf. Sir John Sinclair, 'Address to the Members of the Board of Agriculture', *Journals of the House of Commons*, LI, 263 ff. – a very long and exhaustive report, giving a full account of the administration and state of common lands at the time. Cf. also, among the Board of Agriculture publications, the General Report on Enclosures (1808), p. 26; and Edward Jenks, *Modern Land Law*, pp. 160 ff.

[3] 'Common is a profit which a man hath *in the land of another*, as to pasture beasts thereon, to catch fish, to dig turf, to cut wood, or the like.' W. Blackstone, *Commentaries*, II, 32. Cf. W. Hasbach, *History of the English Agricultural Labourer*, pp. 89-90.

was the most frequent case, and that which best illustrates the simili-
tude of the permanent condition of the common to the periodical
condition of the open field. Sometimes these rights were considered to
have originated in a deed of donation from the lord of the manor and
as attaching to the person of the owner rather than to his land (*common
appurtenant*). Sometimes they were personal rights, apart from any
landowning (*common in gross*). Lastly, they might result from an
agreement between the inhabitants of two neighbouring parishes,
whose lands were separated by an ill-defined boundary and subject
to certain joint obligations (*common because of vicinage*).[1] All those provisions made the enjoyment of the common a positive property, and
one that, so far from being shared equally among all the proprietors,
rather served to emphasize their inequality.

A man was seldom entitled to place an unlimited number of cattle,
sheep or pigs on the common. Such was generally the privilege of the
lord of the manor alone, who was nominally the owner of all undivided
lands.[2] As a rule each owner had a right of pasture for a definite
number of animals,[3] that number being in proportion to the extent
of his property: the more plots he occupied on the open field, the
more cattle or sheep he might send on the common.[4] Thus the enjoyment of these lands, called common, not only was not shared by all
the inhabitants but was allotted to each in proportion to what he
already possessed. It meant riches added to previous riches. Nothing,
as we see, could be further removed from an ideal state of equality,
the pattern of which must be sought not in an ill-known or misunderstood past but in speculative theory only.

Although the system of the English commons was little in favour of
equality, yet it conferred on the poorer population some substantial
advantages. Besides those rights that were proportionate to the acreage
or value of landed property there sometimes existed others, the same
for all the inhabitants of the parish. In some districts each family
occupying a house was allowed to graze two or three beasts on the
common: a precious help to poor people whose fortune consisted of
a cow, a few fowls, and a pig that was to be killed when winter set

---

[1] Sir John Sinclair, 'Address to the Members of the Board of Agriculture', *Journals
of the House of Commons*, LI, 263.

[2] See the petition of Lord Talbot, Lord Vernon, Lord Bagehot, etc., relative to the
Needwood Forest commons (Staffordshire), ibid., LVI, 414.

[3] For instance, the property referred to in a bill of inclosure, dated 1783, consisted
of '1,538 acres and 3 roods of field land, 71 acres and 2 roods of meadow-grounds, and
108 horse, 259 cow and 1,681 sheep common' (ibid., XXXIX,110).

[4] Sometimes the number was based on the rent paid by farmers. In Needwood
forest, every £3 worth of farm rent entitled the farmer to graze one head of cattle.
Ibid., LVI, 414; H. Homer, op. cit., p. 2.

in.[1] And, when there was no recognized right, custom did duty for it, being more pliable and often more humane than the law. On ancient sufferance, most of the peasants in England were allowed to benefit by the village common – sometimes in a large measure. There women went to gather dry wood for fuel.[2] There, in some parts of Yorkshire, the poorer weavers spread their pieces of cloth after they had been bleached or dyed.[3] There, again, stood huts, sheds, humble dwellings; these wastes were of such small value that no one would prevent a few people from settling and living there. With no acknowledged right, but acting, so to speak, on an implied permission, they had built cottages from light materials found on the common itself, and such cottages had increased in number as time went on. The cottagers and squatters[4] were fairly numerous, and what they were allowed to take for themselves on those lands which were not their own brought some alleviation to the hard, uncertain plight of those poor field labourers.[5]

Thus a whole class lived, as it were, on the border of property rights. They were not legally entitled to the advantages of the commons; nevertheless, the preservation of the commons was of the greatest moment to them. Just as any alteration of the open-field system must bring about serious changes in the condition of the small land-owners, so any alteration of the common must threaten the very existence of the field labourers. We are now able to realize the full importance of the changes in the land that wrought such perturbation in the structure of rural England during the eighteenth century.

V

The process used to bring about that transformation was *enclosure*. The word is significant. The unenclosed lands of the common and the open field were to become enclosed property; the scattered plots

---

[1] Cf. Sir G. O. Paul, *Observations on the General Enclosure Bill* (1800).

[2] D. Davies reckons that the wood or peat gathered in from the commons did not cost more than one week's work in one year (or 10s.); if the same quantity of fuel had been bought, more than five times the amount would have had to be spent. (*The Case of Labourers in Husbandry* (1795), pp. 15 and 181.)

[3] See the petition against the Enclosure Bill for Armley, near Leeds (1793), *Journals of the House of Commons*, XLVIII, 651.

[4] In most cases the *cottager* had finally become a kind of small landowner or farmer. The *squatter* was a more recent settler, whose position was not so secure. G. Slater (*The English Peasantry and the Enclosure of the Common Fields*, p. 119) has an instance of a parish in Wales (Montgomery) where if any man in one night could erect a hut on the common and light a fire there, so that smoke was seen to come up through the roof at sunrise, that man thereby earned a right of establishment.

[5] Defoe wrote of Surrey, in 1724, that 'abundance of the inhabitants are what we call *cottagers* and live chiefly by the benefit of the large commons and heath-grounds, of which the quantity is so very great'. *Tour*, I, 88.

were to be joined together; the undivided fields portioned out into compact estates that would be entirely independent of one another and surrounded by continuous hedges, the sign and pledge of their autonomy.

Neither the word, nor the fact, was new. The sixteenth-century enclosures, that have been the subject of many learned disquisitions,[1] were part of the great economic development that opened the modern era. The enormous increase in personal estate had reacted upon the condition of real estate. Much land had already changed hands at the time of the Reformation, when the appropriation of Church property took place. Those who benefited by it were the great landowners. Success spurring them on, they sought to complete their fortunes by dividing the commons among themselves. That division was begun all over England, and was achieved, in most cases, by sheer force.[2] From the very beginning of the century complaints were heard on all sides against the enclosures, their unfairness and the sufferings they brought about. Above all, people lamented their habitual consequence — the turning of plough-land into meadow-land. In a large number of parishes corn-growing made way for cattle- or sheep-rearing; many farms and cottages were pulled down or allowed to decay. Bishop Latimer bewailed the fact that 'where have been a great many householders and inhabitants, there is now but a shepherd and his dog'.[3] While Thomas More drew up wondrous schemes for his City of Utopia his eyes rested on a land of rapine and misery, where sheep devoured men.[4]

---

[1] Cf. I. S. Leadam, *The Domesday of Inclosures*, 2 vols. (1897), and 'The Inquisitions of Depopulation in 1517 and the "Domesday of Inclosures",' by Edwin F. Gay, *Transactions of the Royal Historical Society*, New Series, vol. XIV (1900). R. H. Tawney, *The Agrarian Problem in the Sixteenth Century* (1912); Curtler, *The Enclosure and Redistribution of our Land*, pp. 64, 105 ff. E. F. Gay, 'Inclosures in England in the Sixteenth Century', *Quarterly Journal of Economics* (1902-3), pp. 576-97. See also his doctoral thesis in the University of Berlin (*Zur Geschichte der Einhegungen in England*, pp. 7-65).

[2] Karl Marx attempted a summary account of those events in *Das Kapital*, I, 742 ff. For a more exhaustive and more scientific study, see W. J. Ashley, *An Introduction to English Economic History and Theory*, vol. II, chap. IV.

[3] Latimer, *Sermons*.

[4] 'Your sheep that were wont to be so meek and tame, and so small eaters, now, as I hear say, be become so great devourers and so wild, that they eat up and swallow down the very men themselves. They consume, destroy and devour whole fields, houses, and cities. For look in what parts of the realm doth grow the finest, and therefore dearest wool, there noblemen, and gentlemen, yea and certain abbots, holy men God wot, not contenting themselves with the yearly revenues and profits that were wont to grow to their forefathers and predecessors of their lands ... leave no ground for tillage, they enclose all into pastures, they throw down houses, they pluck down towns and leave nothing standing, but only the church to make of it a sheep house ... Therefore that one covetous and insatiable cormorant and very plague of his native country may compass about and enclose many thousand acres of ground together within one pale

It has been shown that complaints as to enclosures had been greatly exaggerated; certain writers have even gone so far as to assert that they had in no way involved the disappearance of corn land. But that argument seems to have been carried too far,[1] and, even though we admit that contemporary grievances were not entirely justified, there remain certain documents which must be taken into account. Those are the laws that were enacted in Parliament as a remedy for an evil, which we can hardly deem to have been imaginary. As early as 1488, in the reign of King Henry VII, an Act ascribed the depopulation of the Isle of Wight to the turning of arable lands to grazing lands and to the engrossing of farms, and set, as a limit to the extent of estates in the Isle, a maximum income of ten marks.[2] It was very soon followed by another, still more far-reaching, the famous *Act against the pulling down of towns*,[3] the preamble of which runs thus: 'The King our sovereign lord … remembereth that among other things great inconveniences daily do increase by desolation, and pulling down, and

---

[1] See, on the subject, the controversy between Gay and Tawney. Gay, on the evidence of the official inquiries of 1517, 1519, 1548, 1566, and 1607, reaches a total figure of 516,000 acres affected by enclosures in the course of the sixteenth century. His conclusion is 'that the specific inclosure movement of the fifteenth and sixteenth centuries, the depopulating inclosure of open-fields with a view to the greater profit of grass-farming, had not by any means the magnitude often ascribed to it; … that, limited in amount, it was also circumscribed in area, being largely confined to the central districts of England, and even here was of a piecemeal character.' *Quarterly Journal of Economics*, p. 596. Such was already Leadam's argument. Tawney shows how difficult it is to give an accurate interpretation of the very incomplete statistics used by Leadam and Gay, and notes that, if they are right, 'it is not easy to explain either the continuous attention which was paid to the question by the government, or the revolts of the peasantry, or the strong views of reasonable and fair-minded men with first-hand knowledge, like John Hales.' (*The Agrarian Problem in the Sixteenth Century*, p. 11.) He concludes definitely that the sufferings denounced by contemporaries were real, and that the movement was an important one, that 'dealt a heavy blow at the traditional organization of agriculture'. A. H. Johnson, *The Disappearance of the Small Landowner*, pp. 44 ff., also raises objections to Gay's method. Baron Ernle (*English Farming, Past and Present*, p. 58) writes that 'it is impossible to doubt the reality of the distress' even though it may have been exaggerated. W. Hasbach (*History of the English Agricultural Labourer*, pp. 33-4) also admits the reality of those evils that were so loudly bewailed in the sixteenth century. It is possible, as mentioned by Curtler (op. cit., p. 109) that the popular discontent was caused not so much by the fact of enclosure as by the increase of meadow land at the expense of plough land: but were not both closely bound together? It should be noted that those changes coincided with an increased cost of living due to a depreciation of the currency.

[2] 4-5 Henry VII, c. 16.

[3] 4-5 Henry VII, c. 19.

---

or hedge, the husbandmen be thrust out of their own, or else either by cunning or fraud or by violent oppression they be put besides it or by wrongs and injuries they be so wearied that they be compelled to sell all.' Thomas More, *Utopia*, Book I, fol. 2 (verso), Louvain, 1516.

wilful waste of houses within this realm, and laying to pasture what customably have been used in tillage, whereby idleness, which is the ground and beginning of all mischief, daily doth increase. For where, in some towns, 200 persons were occupied and lived of their lawful labours, now there are occupied two or three herdsmen, and the residue fall into idleness, so that husbandrie, which is one of the greatest commodities of this realm, is greatly decayed, churches destroyed, the service of God withdrawn, the bodies there buried not prayed for ... the defence of this land against our enemies outward, feebled and impaired.' The law provided that any house to which were appended twenty acres of ploughed land must be kept in a good state of repair and must serve as a dwelling for a peasant family. But neither those provisions, nor the penalties that should have helped to enforce them, seem to have had much effect: for similar laws were passed in 1515, in 1516, in 1533, in 1535, in 1552. Now the repairing of forsaken cottages was prescribed,[1] now the number of sheep to be owned by one man was limited,[2] or a tax was levied on all new pasture lands to the amount of one half the income they brought in.[3] The frequent recurrence of such acts, and the diversity of the remedies they sought to apply for one evil, are the truest sign of their ineffectiveness.[4]

The movement was continued throughout the sixteenth century. Everywhere, the partition of open fields and seizure of common lands brought about an increase of large estates and an extension of pastures. At the same time the holders of moderate-sized and small property were touched by the commercial spirit of the new age, and found it to their advantage to produce wool rather than grow corn. In 1549 there were riots against the enclosures in several counties. Three thousand five hundred rioters were killed, and their leader, Robert

[1] 6 Henry VIII, c. 5 (1514). Any peasant houses that had been pulled down since February 5th, 1514, were to be built up again within one year, and the lands appended thereto must be ploughed again. That Act was made perpetual the following year (7 Henry VIII, c. 17). In 1517 a great inquiry was carried out, the report of which is known as the *Domesday of Inclosures*.

[2] 25 Henry VIII, c. 13 (1533). The maximum number was 2,000. Some landowners, according to the preamble of the Act, owned as many as 24,000 sheep.

[3] 27 Henry VIII, c. 22 (1535) and 5-6 Edward VI, c. 15 (1552).

[4] F. Bacon, *History of King Henry VII, Works* (1878 edition), VI, 94, praises the admirable wisdom of both King and Parliament, who found means whereby to oppose the decay of husbandry. David Hume was the first to question how far those praises were well grounded, showing that the legislation which Bacon admired had been almost entirely without effect. Cf. Curtler, op. cit., p. 92: 'All the Acts were alike evaded, for their administration was in the hands of those most opposed to them ... The Acts were evaded in several ways: that against pulling down houses was nominally obeyed by repairing one room for the shepherd; a single furrow was driven across a field to prove that it was still in tillage, and estates were held in the names of sons and servants.'

Kett, was hanged.[1] Then it was that John Hales wrote: 'Marry, for these inclosures do undoe us all, for they make us paye dearer for our land that we occupie, and causes that we can have no land for our monye to put to tillage: all is taken for pastures, either for shepe or for grazing of cattel. So that I have knowen of late a docen plowes within less compasse than six myles about me laide down in theise VII yeares; and where XL persons had their lyvinges, now one man and his shepherd hath all ... Yes, those shepe is the cause of all theise meschieves, for they have driven husbandrie oute of the countrie, by the which was encreased before all kynde of victuall, and now altogether shepe, shepe.'[2]

The progress of enclosures seems to have slackened down in the second half of the century.[3] But it was never checked, and can be followed throughout the seventeenth century.[4] Along with the operations that were begun in 1626 for draining the fens in the eastern counties, the enclosing of the lands thus recovered was carried out.[5] Elsewhere, the turning of arable land to meadows proceeded for the same reasons as before. In 1622 Lupton wrote: 'Enclosures make fat beasts, and lean poor people.' In 1620 and 1633 the Privy Council ordered inquiries as to enclosures. Large numbers of pamphlets were published on the question, particularly at the time of the Commonwealth:[6] it should be noted that, in answer to complaints similar to those of the sixteenth century, more and more economic arguments were set forth in favour of the enclosures, which some authors declared to be 'not only lawful, but laudable'. In proportion as the notion of agricultural advancement became more definite, and as the desire became keener, among the richer and more enlightened owners, to

---

[1] Curtler, op. cit., pp. 94 ff.

[2] John Hales, *A Discourse of the Commonweal of this Realm of England* (1549), ed. Lamond, pp. 15 and 20. Those words are all the more significant because the author has them spoken by a man who acknowledges the material advantages of enclosures and the profits made by those who turned their tilled land to pastures.

[3] This is one of the clearest results of the statistical tables prepared by Gay.

[4] Cf. Miss Leonard, 'Inclosure of Common Fields in the Seventeenth Century', *Transactions of the Royal Historical Society*, New Series, XIX, 122 ff. Gonner, *Common Land and Inclosure*, pp. 153-86.

[5] T. E. Scrutton, *Commons and Common Fields*, pp. 107 ff. Prothero (Baron Ernle), *English Farming, Past and Present*, pp. 115 ff.

[6] *London and the Country Carbonadoed* (Harleian Miscellanies, IX, 326); J. Bentham, *The Christian Conflict* (1635); Robert Powell, *Depopulation arraigned, convicted and condemned by the Lawes of God and Man* (1636); H. Holland, *Enclosure thrown open* (1650); S. Taylor, *Common Good, or, the Improvement of Commons, Forrests and Chases by Inclosure* (1652); A. Moore, *Bread for the Poor, promised by Enclosures of the Wastes and Common Grounds of England*, 1653; J. Moore, *Crying Sin of England of not caring for the Poor, wherein Inclosure being such as doth unpeople Towns and uncorn Fields is arraigned* (1653); Id., *A Scripture Word against Inclosure* (1656); Pseudomisus, *Considerations concerning Common Fields and Inclosures* (1654); Id., *A Vindication of the Considerations*, etc. (1656).

increase the yield of their land, the old land system became more and more threatened. There lies the whole problem of rural England in the eighteenth century.

VI

Just as some authors have insisted on considering the disappearance of the yeomanry as a consequence of the factory system, so industrial development has been taken by many to be the cause of the reform of agriculture in England. The demands of consumers are said to have given a decisive impulse to agricultural production. The coming into existence of manufacturing centres and the growth of the town population opened up for the producer a new market, with ever-increasing requirements. The days were past when the harvest from one field went no further than the next village or borough. In the crowded cities, round the mines, factories and docks, were working multitudes that turned to the countryside for food. The farms, in their turn, had to become factories where foodstuffs were produced in large quantities, according to improved methods. The progress of agriculture, or its adaptation to the needs of an industrialized society, resulted from an organic necessity, from an indispensable correlation between interdependent functions.[1] At first sight such an explanation is satisfactory, expressing as it does a general truth which could scarcely be questioned and holding true to this day in the case of many facts which we have witnessed in our own time. But does it account truly for the historical origins of the English agricultural movement? In fact, that movement, like the disappearance of the yeomanry, became apparent long before the increase of the population due to the modern factory system. That increase of the population was no sudden development: it was not and could not be simultaneous with the early technical inventions, or, if it did occur then, it must have proceeded from causes entirely unconnected with the factory system. As early as the first half of the eighteenth century, about the time of the first experiments that thirty years later led up to the invention of the spinning machines, English agriculture entered upon a period of change.

It cannot be said that agricultural questions had been entirely neglected in the seventeenth century: the works of Weston and Hartlib at the time of the Commonwealth, of Donaldson after the Revolution, are evidence to the contrary.[2] But there is nothing to show that those

[1] Prothero (Baron Ernle), *Pioneers and Progress of English Farming*, p. 65; Id., *Social England*, V, 106-7; W. Lecky, *History of England in the Eighteenth Century*, VI, 189-90.

[2] Sir Richard Weston was the author of *A Discourse of Husbandry used in Brabant and Flanders* (1652). According to Prothero (Baron Ernle), *English Farming, Past and Present*, pp. 107 ff., Sir Richard Weston was a pioneer, particularly where the rotation of crops,

forerunners of modern agronomy obtained a hearing. In the days when Daniel Defoe wrote his description of England, many provinces were partly lying waste. The west of Surrey was 'not only poor, but even quite sterile, given up to barrenness, horrid and frightful to look on ... Much of it is a sandy desert ... This sand indeed is checked by the heath, or heather, which grows in it ... the common product of barren lands.'[1] In Yorkshire, almost at the gates of Leeds, one entered 'a continued waste of black, ill-looking, desolate moors over which travellers were guided, like race-horses, by posts set up for fear of bogs and holes'.[2] In spite of the draining operations of the previous century, the fens in Cambridgeshire, Huntingdonshire and Lincolnshire still came together, forming one endless swamp. The north of England, above all, remained wild and untilled: from the northern boundary of Derbyshire to that of Northumberland, a line of one hundred and fifty miles as the crow flies could be drawn across uncultivated country.[3]

Where the soil was under cultivation this was often of the most primitive character. The three-year rotation system was practically the only one in use: one year out of three the fields lay bare. Farming implements stood in great need of improvement: in some districts, as is still the case today in the most backward countries, the plough-shares were made of wood, with a mere sheet of metal. Great teams of ten or twelve oxen were still needlessly yoked together for ploughing. Fodder was often lacking and part of the cattle were always killed in the autumn, because there would not have been enough food to keep them through the winter months.[4] The art of cattle-breeding was almost unknown; the domestic breeds were lean and small and differed

[1] Defoe, Tour, I, 84.

[2] Ibid., III, 126.

[3] Prothero (Baron Ernle), Pioneers and Progress of English Farming, p. 56. At the end of the eighteenth century, in spite of some progress, Eden could still write: 'A country disfigured and burthened, as Great Britain everywhere is, with immeasurable heaths, commons and wastes, seems to resemble one of those huge unwieldy cloaks, worn in Italy and Spain: of which a very small part is serviceable to the wearer, whilst the rest is not only useless, but cumbersome and oppressive.' F. M. Eden, State of the Poor, I, xxi.

[4] Ample information as to the manner in which those practices became gradually modified, will be found in Young's Travels. See A Six Weeks Tour through the Southern Counties of England and Wales (1768) and A Six Months Tour through the North of England (1770).

---

based on turnips and clover, was concerned. Samuel Hartlib, a friend of Milton, was protected by Cromwell; he collected a large number of documents bearing on agriculture. He wrote A Design for Plenty by an universal planting of fruit-trees (1652) and The Complete Husbandman (1659). The book called Samuel Hartlib, his Legacy or an Enlargement upon the Discourse on Husbandry (1651) is often ascribed to him; but this, according to W. Cunningham (Growth of English Industry and Commerce, II, 568), is a mistake. Donaldson was the author of Husbandry Anatomized (1697-8).

scarcely from what they might have been in a wild state.[1] Landlords and tenants were equally ignorant and sunken in routine, while mutual suspicion divided them; for the landlord feared that the farmer would exhaust the land by forcing a few richer crops out of his fields during the last years of his tenancy and therefore refused to grant leases for a fixed period, preferring the unstable state of things known as tenure at will. As a result any spirit of enterprise, any undertaking that involved a considerable period for its completion, were out of the question for the farmer, since he lived under the constant threat of instant dismissal and of the loss of a whole year's labours. Thus the effect of backwardness was to make for more backwardness.[2]

In order to reform English agriculture a long series of systematic efforts were necessary. Their starting-point can be traced to the publication of Jethro Tull's book in 1731.[3] The author was not solely a theoretical writer: after studying and comparing the methods used in France, Germany and the Netherlands,[4] he had spent over thirty years on research and practical experiment on his estate, Mount Prosperous, in Berkshire. He was one of the first to conceive the modern idea of intensive culture. He recommended deep hoeing and ploughing, and a system of continuous rotation of crops, thanks to which the land could bear, without exhaustion, a succession of varied harvests, and the wasteful practice of fallows could be suppressed or reduced. He explained the importance of winter food for the cattle and showed to what account could be turned nutritious roots such as turnips and beets. His great originality lay in the fact that he endeavoured to substitute a method grounded on observation and deduction for a changeless tradition. He represented, if not the scientific spirit proper, at least something akin to it — the enlightened empiricism which has often led men to discoveries.

Jethro Tull's theories came at the right moment; the landed nobility, for a whole generation, were going to adopt them and experiment with them on their own estates. Ever since the Revolution the English aristocracy had been possessed with a desire for increased wealth. Their jealousy had been aroused by the rise of the banking and trading middle class. With a strange feeling of mixed pride and avarice they hated the *moneyed men*, and they sought to benefit by their wealth by marrying into their families. At a time when a minister of state boasted that he

[1] Except the breeds of horses, which had always been taken care of, for reasons chiefly military. The rearing of race horses did not begin until the eighteenth century.

[2] The disastrous consequences of tenure at will were seen until a recent date in Ireland, where, as much as absenteeism or even to a greater degree, it set back the development of agriculture.

[3] Jethro Tull, *The New Horse-Houghing Husbandry, or an Essay on the Principles of Tillage and Vegetation*, London, 1731. The date of 1733, given by Prothero (Baron Ernle), *Social England*, V, 107-9, is that of the second edition.

[4] From 1693 to 1699.

had organized the 'jobbing of consciences', they were not backward in taking their share in the plunder of public money. A number of them flung themselves headlong into doubtful undertakings, into notorious swindles, the biggest of which was that of the South Sea Company, and, after reaping large profits, denounced them so as to reap further gains. While the desire to keep up their rank at all costs, in a society where money was becoming more and more the measure of prestige and power, often led those noblemen into dishonourable enterprises, that desire also had the effect of rousing their energy. Instead of looking on all sides for new sources of income, some of them resolved to increase those which they already had at their disposal. Were they not the owners of huge estates, the revenue of which should have been enough to make them powerfully rich? But those estates were ill-managed, ill-cultivated, a prey to slothful, ignorant routine. If the best return was to be obtained from them, methodical exploitation must be undertaken – a great endeavour, demanding much enterprise, attention and perseverance.[1] The court of the Hanoverian dynasty, which was dull and retained much of its German character, did not attract the nobility as the Stuart court of the previous century had done. Moreover, a number of them were looked upon with little favour by royalty because of their Toryism or their alleged loyalty to the cause of the exiled princes. They settled on their estates and devoted themselves to agriculture.

Among those titled farmers, the best known was Lord Townshend. He had been ambassador to the Netherlands, negotiator of the Union between England and Scotland, and, later, of the peace with France, Lord of the Regency at the death of Queen Anne, then Lord Lieutenant of Ireland, twice Secretary of State, and Lord President of the Council; he withdrew from public life in 1730 as a sequel to a famous quarrel with Sir Robert Walpole, and retired to his estate of Rainham in Norfolk.[2] It consisted of vast tracts of wild land, with alternate stretches of sand and bog; the very grass there was thin and scarce.[3] Lord Townshend undertook to cultivate it, taking his inspiration from the methods he had seen practised in the Netherlands. He drained the soil, and improved certain sections by marling and manuring; then he sowed

---

[1] Sombart has clearly shown that one of the characteristics of capitalistic undertaking is the exact computation of ends and means: 'Its symbol is the ledger; the backbone of the system is the debit and credit account.' *Moderne Kapitalismus*, I, 198.

[2] Cf. A. Young, *Annals of Agriculture*, V, 120-1. Young visited the Rainham estate several times (particularly in 1760 and 1786), and described it with admiration as a model to be followed by English landowners and farmers.

[3] It was a province of which King Charles I used to say that it should be divided among all the other counties in England, to make the highroads; it was a fact that, in his time, only clover fields and untilled commons were to be found there: not onetenth of the land was cultivated.' Alexandre and François de La Rochefoucauld-Liancourt, 'Voyage en Suffolk et Norfolk', II, letter dated Sept. 24th, 1784.

crops that succeeded one another in regular rotation, without ever exhausting the land or allowing it to lie fallow. Following the Dutch example he had in view principally cattle and sheep-breeding, for which the neighbourhood of Norwich, the great wool-market, ensured prompt and handsome profits. This object, as much as and even more than Jethro Tull's teaching, determined his partiality for artificial grass land and winter cattle food; at the same time as he improved English agriculture he set it on the road along which, more and more, it was to progress.

At first people laughed at this peer of the realm turned farmer; he was nicknamed Turnip-Townshend. He none the less went on with his work, and in a few years changed a poor, unfruitful district into one of the most thriving in the kingdom. His example was followed by the neighbouring landowners; in thirty years, between 1730 and 1760, the value of land in the county of Norfolk increased tenfold.[1] The Marquess of Rockingham at Wentworth, the Duke of Bedford at Woburn, Lord Egremont at Petworth, Lord Clare in Essex, yet others, like Lord Cathcart and Lord Halifax,[2] played the same part and were in their turn imitated by many. Soon the fashion became universal, and every nobleman boasted that he was personally managing his own estate. All the interest of the preceding generation had been in hunting – their talk, nothing but horses and dogs: the talk of the present one was all manure and drainage, rotation of crops, clover, lucerne grass and field turnips. After the seventeenth-century cavalier, who had fought in the great Civil War, came the gentleman farmer.

Towards 1760 the impulse given by a few noblemen had spread to the whole nation. It was further quickened by the great public works that were then undertaken on all sides – roads being built, canals cut, fens drained.[3] Then a new social class appeared, that of the great farmers, for whom cultivation was an investment and who put into it the same spirit of enterprise and the same close attention as did the tradesman into the management of his business. Coke of Holkham, in 1776, came to live on an estate that was worth about £2,000 a year. When he died it was worth £20,000.[4] He was one of the first to use

[1] Prothero (Baron Ernle), *Pioneers and Progress of English Farming*, pp. 44-7.

[2] See A. Young, *North of England*, pp. 273-305. Id., *Southern Counties*, pp. 62-3; Prothero (Baron Ernle), *Pioneers and Progress of English Farming*, p. 79. Id., *English Farming, Past and Present*, p. 173.

[3] Considerable operations were carried out to that effect in the fens of Cambridgeshire, Bedfordshire, Huntingdonshire and Lincolnshire. Cf. *Statutes at Large*, 30 Geo. II, c. 32, 33, 35; 31 Geo. II, c. 18, 19; 32 Geo. II, c. 13, 32; 2 Geo. III, c. 32; 7 Geo. III, c. 53; 13 Geo. III, c. 45, 46, 49, 60; 14 Geo. III, c. 23; 15 Geo. III, c. 12, 65, 66; 17 Geo. III, c. 65; 19 Geo. III, c. 24, 33, 34, etc.

[4] E. Rigby, *Holkham, its Agriculture*, pp. 21-4. The sons of the duc de La Rochefoucauld-Liancourt visited the estate in 1784 and described it in their 'Voyage en Suffolk', II, letter dated Sept. 24th, 1784.

improved farming implements. He systematically granted long leases, by which alone tenants could feel secure and be encouraged in careful, persevering efforts. He looked upon himself as an educator; he would sometimes call a meeting of the farmers in his neighbourhood, in order to convert them to the new methods. Coke's contemporary, Bakewell, was the pattern for the great modern stock-breeders.[1] He began a systematic improvement of the domestic species, and succeeded, thanks to ingenious crossings. In fact, he initiated the methods of artificial selection, a close study of which was to reveal to Darwin some of the general laws of biology. In 1710 the average weight of oxen sold on Smithfield market was 370 lb., that of calves 50 lb., of sheep 38 lb. In 1795, through the efforts of Bakewell and his followers, the figures had risen respectively to 800 lb., 150 lb., and 80 lb.[2] Certain famous breeds of cattle, such as the Dishley and Durham oxen, date from that period and, better than any document, their build shows what aim the eighteenth-century stock-breeders had in view; the slender bones, short limbs, small head and horns are evidence of the care they took to suppress whatsoever did not conduce to the enormous quantity and superior quality of the flesh. They had realized that the day was near 'when beef would be prized higher than pulling strength, and mutton higher than sheep's wool'.

At the time when the factory system made its appearance modern agriculture was already at work. Only the last supporters of blind tradition remained to be converted. This was the achievement of men such as Arthur Young, whom we see, since 1767, travelling all over England, noting down day after day, mile after mile, what was the state of crops, what improvements were attempted, what good or bad success the efforts of innovators had met with, what was the condition of landlords, farmers and labourers. When, in 1789, he began his famous travels in France, his purpose was only to obtain a series of comparisons between England and the Continent, as a conclusion to the investigation that he had carried out for more than twenty years. An earnest propagandist he has left, besides his travelling notes, a large number of writings:[3] and from 1784 onwards he edited the *Annals of*

---

[1] Léonce de Lavergne, *L'Économie Rurale de l'Angleterre*, pp. 27-9, gives a brief account of the breeding farm at Dishley Grange, from its origin. See A. Young, *On the Husbandry of the three Celebrated Farmers, Bakewell, Arbuthnot and Ducket* (1811).

[2] F. M. Eden, *State of the Poor*, I, 334. Sombart rightly shows the influence of the London market on the transformation of stock-breeding and of agriculture generally (*Moderne Kapitalismus*, II, 155-9).

[3] Here is a list of his principal works (to which should be added the many articles published in the *Annals of Agriculture*, between 1784 and 1809): *Sylvae, or occasional Tracts on Husbandry and rural Economics* (1767); *The Farmer's Letters to the People of England* (1767); *A Six Weeks Tour through the Southern Counties of England* (1768); *Letters concerning the State of the French Nation* (1769); *Essay on the Management of Hogs* (1769); *The*

Agriculture, to which it is said King George III condescended to contribute. With Sir John Sinclair, whose name deserves to be associated with that of Young, he founded in 1793 an important institution, with the aim of encouraging and organizing the advancement of agriculture: this was the *Board of Agriculture*, of which he was for thirty years the enthusiastic secretary, gathering information and ideas from all quarters, and supervising a methodical survey of all the counties in the Kingdom.[1] Although he kept complaining of the tardiness of the most urgent improvements, he was in a position to appreciate the extent of the progress that had been achieved already. The movement of which he had assumed the leadership was no tentative enterprise with an uncertain future: it was powerful already, and was soon to become irresistible. To be convinced of this, it is enough to read a few of the pages describing the state of the French countryside on the eve of the Revolution. It seemed to him to be strangely neglected and wretched, yet it was no worse than his own country had been fifty years earlier.[2]

Arthur Young and his associates witnessed the growth of the factory system; they understood that it was linked with the development of agriculture to which they had devoted themselves. More than once they

[1] From 1794 onward, the Board of Agriculture published a series of reports on the state of agriculture in the different counties. Those reports, numbering about a hundred, are known under their common title of *Agricultural Surveys*. Among the other publications of the Board one at least should be mentioned, the remarkable *General Report on Enclosures* (1808), the editor of which was Sir John Sinclair.

[2] And conversely, England was looked upon as a model by the men who, in the reign of Louis XVI, sought to reform French agriculture. Young men were sent to England to study agronomy.

Expediency of a free Exportation of Corn at this Time (1769); *A Six Months Tour through the North of England*, 4 vols. (1770); *The Farmer's Guide in hiring and stocking Farms* (1770); *Rural Œconomy* (1770); *The Farmer's Tour through the East of England*, 4 vols. (1771); *The Farmer's Calendar* (1771); *Proposals to the Legislature for numbering the People* (1771); *Political Essays concerning the present State of the British Empire* (1772); *Observations on the present State of the waste Lands of Great Britain* (1773); *Political Arithmetic* (vol. I, 1774, vol. II, 1779); *A Tour in Ireland, with general Observations on the present State of that Kingdom*, 2 vols. (1780); *The Question of Wool truly stated* (1788); *Travels in France, Italy and Spain during the years* 1787, 1788 and 1789, 2 vols. (1790-1); *Example of France a Warning to Britain* (1793); *General View of the Agriculture in the County of Suffolk* (1794); id., *in the County of Lincoln* (1799), *Hertfordshire* (1804), *Norfolk*, 2 vols. (1804), *Essex*, 2 vols. (1807), *Oxfordshire* (1809); *The Constitution safe without Reform* (1795); *An Idea of the present State of France* (1795); *National Danger and the Means of Safety* (1797); *An Inquiry into the State of the Public Mind amongst the lower Classes* (1798); *The Question of Scarcity plainly stated* (1800); *Inquiry into the Propriety of applying waste Lands to the better Maintenance and Support of the Poor* (1801); *Essay on Manures* (1804); *On the Advantages which have resulted from the Establishment of the Board of Agriculture* (1809); *On the Husbandry of the three Celebrated Farmers, Bakewell, Arbuthnot and Ducket* (1811); *Inquiry into the progressive Value of Money* (1812); *Inquiry into the Rise of Prices in Europe* (1815).

noted the mutual reactions of those two great simultaneous events.[1] But, though they were inclined to consider the reform of agriculture as a quite recent achievement – even forgetting, sometimes, the efforts of others before them[2] – they would not have made the mistake of representing that reform as a sequel to the industrial movement. It was only towards the end of their lives that they saw, growing out of the very soil, those black and populous cities which, by their rapid progress, were to ruin English agriculture even faster than they had enriched it. Even the improvement in stock-breeding, though obviously stimulated by the demand from manufacturing centres, was due at first to entirely different reasons. The chief cause that had long hindered it, namely, the difficulty of feeding livestock through the winter, had been removed. Less labour is required for the care of cattle and sheep than for the cultivation of most kinds of crops. Here were enough advantages to tempt many farmers, even at a time when meat still sold at a low price,[3] and when its consumption still remained comparatively small. Moreover, had not England from time immemorial been a land of pastures? Her people did but revive, in a more active form, one of her most ancient sources of wealth.

VII

There was one obstacle in the way of the new methods. It was the existence of the open fields. For the greater part those 'unenclosed fields' were very badly cultivated: the arable lands, in spite of fallow years, were exhausted by the monotonous alternation of the same crops – the pastures, left to themselves, were overgrown with heather and gorse. How could it have been otherwise? Each farmer was tied down to the common rules. The system of crop rotation adopted for the whole parish was only suitable for some of the lands, and the other lands suffered thereby.[4] The cattle and sheep fed on weeds, and their pro-

---

[1] In the course of his travels Arthur Young never failed to inquire as to workshops and factories; he noted industrial wages, comparing them with those paid to land labourers; he sought information as to whether the industrial, as compared to the agricultural, population, was increasing or decreasing, etc.

[2] Young wrote in 1770 that more experiments, more inventions and more sense had been made to serve the advancement of agriculture in the past six years than during the previous hundred years. *Rural Œconomy*, p. 315.

[3] Cf. Thorold Rogers, *History of Agriculture and Prices in England*, VI, 284-306 (those tables, which contain statistical documents of great importance, are unfortunately established on the most inconvenient plan). See also the information collected by A. Young, *North of England*, III, 12, 170, 293-313; *East of England*, IV, 311-26. In 1770 the price of beef, according to districts, varied between 2½d. and 3½d. per lb.

[4] 'What system of barbarism can be greater than that of obliging every farmer of the parish, possessing soils perhaps totally different, all to cultivate in the same rotation!' *Board of Agriculture, General Report on Enclosures*, pp. 218-19.

miscuous mixing together was the cause of murrains.[1] As for improvements, any man who attempted them would have ruined himself. He could not drain his fields without the consent and concurrence of his many neighbours. Each plot was contained within fixed limits and was too narrow to admit of cross-harrowing, as recommended by Jethro Tull. Before a farmer could choose his own time for sowing, the custom of allowing the open field to be used as a common grazing ground for several months in every year had first to be abolished.[2] No such thing could be contemplated as growing an unwonted crop, or sowing clover where there had been rye or barley. To all those disadvantages should be added the extraordinary complication of the system, and the endless quarrels and lawsuits that were its inevitable consequence. In the olden days, when farming had been a traditional calling, an accepted inheritance that supported a man year in year out, such a state of things could be put up with. But to the modern farmer, who looks upon agriculture as a business undertaking and reckons up exactly his expense and profits, the compulsory waste on the one hand, and on the other the sheer impossibility of doing anything whatever to increase the produce, are simply intolerable. The open-field system was doomed, therefore, to disappear.[3]

[1] H. Homer, *An Essay on the Nature and Method of ascertaining the Specific Shares of Proprietors.* As to the various disadvantages of the open-field system, see A. H. Johnson, *The Disappearance of the small Landowner,* pp. 96-7.

[2] 'How can a farmer, with all the toils and pains he is capable of, make any considerable improvement in his land, in an open-field state? He can never be paid for his troubles; his expenses, where his land lies intermixed, which is always the case in open fields, are more than his improvements can be, if he had ever so much time or inclination to do it. He is confined to the expensive method of tillage, though the nature of the soil be such as to be turned into good pasture, and capable of becoming of more value to the occupiers at one-tenth part of the expense.' Board of Agriculture, *A View of the State of the Agriculture in the County of Rutland,* pp. 31-2. Cf. *Gentleman's Magazine,* 1732, p. 454; John Sinclair, *An Address to the Members of the Board of Agriculture,* p. 22; *Journals of the House of Commons,* XXV, 511, XXVII, 70, XXXVII, 71, XXXIX, 904, etc.; J. Tuckett, *A History of the past and present State of the labouring Population,* II, 395. All the disadvantages of the open-field system are very aptly outlined by Prothero (Baron Ernle), *English Farming, Past and Present,* pp. 154-6, who analyses the reports of the Board of Agriculture correspondents (ibid., pp. 226-48), with the following conclusion: 'The general impression left by this mass of evidence is that the agricultural defects of the intermixture of land under the open-field system were overwhelming and ineradicable.' See also A. H. Johnson, *The Disappearance of the small Landowner,* pp. 96-7, and Gonner, *Common Land and Inclosure,* pp. 308 ff.

[3] A division of the commons was proposed and supported for the same reasons. See an anonymous pamphlet, published in 1744 under the following title: *A Method humbly proposed to the Consideration of the Honourable the Members of both Houses of Parliament, by an English Woollen Manufacturer:* 'In some parts of this kingdom, there are yet large tracts of uncultivated lands ... which, if inclosed ... would be made, some, good arable, and some, good meadow lands' (p. 5). According to the author, the

Between the sixteenth- and seventeenth-century enclosures and those of the eighteenth century, there was an essential difference. The former had been opposed by the King's administration, the latter on the contrary met with assistance and encouragement from Parliament.[1] Under the Tudors and Stuarts, enclosure was either the result of sheer spoliation or of a mutual agreement between all the landowners of a parish. But the mighty had means at their disposal to suppress any opposition: 'Unwilling commoners are threatened with the risks of long and expensive lawsuits; in other cases they are subject to persecution by the great proprietors who ditch in their own demesne and force them to go a long way round to their own land, or maliciously breed rabbits and keep geese on adjoining ground, to the detriment of their crops.'[2] Once enrolled in Chancery, the agreements could be enforced without any further formality. In the eighteenth century the method was further improved. Whenever it was found impossible to obtain the necessary assent for concluding a *deed of mutual agreement* the legal authorities could step in.[3] All the Acts of Enclosure on the Statute Book, without exception, are evidence of so many cases when the unanimous consent of the landowners could not be secured. But no legal action could be taken unless there was a request for it. Here we shall see on whose initiative and for whose profit the enclosures were made.

The great landowners were the first to undertake a methodical exploitation of their estates according to the precepts of the new agricultural science. They were the men who bore most impatiently the obligations laid on them by the open-field system. And they, in almost every case, initiated the petition to Parliament for a Bill of Enclosure.[4] As a rule they began by holding a conference and choosing an attorney who was to be in charge of the legal side of the proceedings. The next step was to call a general meeting of all the landowners. In that meeting the decision was not reached by a majority of individual votes: the importance of each voter was proportionate to the acreage of his land.

[1] This aspect of eighteenth-century as compared with earlier enclosures was noted by Karl Marx (*Das Kapital*, 3rd edition, I, 749). W. J. Ashley, *An Introduction to English Economic History and Theory*, vol. II, sect. 50, shows that the eviction of customary tenants could be proceeded to without actual violation of any recognized right.

[2] Gonner, *Common Lands and Inclosure*, p. 182. Cf. Prothero (Baron Ernle), *English Farming, Past and Present*, pp. 161-2.

[3] H. Homer, *An Essay on the Nature and Method of Ascertaining the Specific Shares of Proprietors*, p. 42.

[4] A. Young, *North of England*, I, 222.

parcelling out and sale of the commons should bring in at least seven million pounds; to encourage buying he suggested that the purchaser of two lots of land should be made an esquire; of four lots, a knight; of eight lots, a baronet.

For the petition to be considered in order, the number of signatories was of small account: but they must represent four-fifths of the lands to be enclosed.[1] Those who owned the last fifth were often fairly numerous, sometimes they were the majority.[2] Some petitions bore two or three names only, some could be found bearing but a single name. True, they were important, impressive names, accompanied by titles which commended them to the considerate attention of Parliament.[3] If the consent of some small landowner was indispensable, he was asked for it in such a manner that he could scarcely refuse. The local grandees – the lord of the manor, the vicar, the country squires[4] – laid the request before him in tones which, we may surmise, resembled a command rather than an entreaty. If the man resisted he was threatened, and he gave his signature even though he might withdraw it later.[5] But very few occasions arose for taking such action; the villagers scarcely dared show their discontent: what they feared above all things was to 'appear against their superiors'.[6]

Once the petition was duly signed it was brought before Parliament. Then began a series of expensive proceedings of which the wealthier landowners bore the cost.[7] Parliament was all for them: did not their

[1] H. Homer, op. cit., p. 42.

[2] At Quainton (Buckinghamshire) in 1801, there were 34 landowners; 8 petitioned for a Bill of Enclosure, 22 opposed the petition, 4 remained neutral. The amount paid by the eight first together as land tax was £203 5s. 11¾d.; by the 22 opposers, £39 12s. 6¼d.; or an average of £28 8s. 3d. for each man in the first group, and of £1 16s. in the second. *Journals of the House of Commons*, LVI, 544. Cf. ibid., XXIII, 559.

[3] Petition of the Earls of Derby and Aylesford for the enclosing of Meriden (Warwickshire), ibid., XXIX, 904. Petition of the Duke of Marlborough for enclosing Westcote (Buckinghamshire), ibid., XXX, 56.

[4] The signature of the lord of the manor was indispensable. Cf. H. Homer, op. cit., p. 42. Here is the very characteristic beginning of the minutes of the presentation to the House of Commons of one of those petitions: 'A petition from William Sutton and Edmund Bunting, Gentlemen, Lords of the Manor of Faceby in Cleveland, in the county of York; William Deason, clerk, vicar of the parish Church of Faceby aforesaid, and Sir William Foulis, baronet; Edward Wilson, Francis Topham, and Matthew Duane, esquires; John Richatson and David Burton, gentlemen; Margaret Allilee and Mary Allilee, widows, freeholders and landowners within the said manor and township of Faceby, was presented to the House and read.' Ibid., XXV, 511.

[5] Cf. petition of several farmers at Winfrith Newburgh (Dorsetshire): 'Some of the petitioners, by threats and menaces, were prevailed upon to sign the petition for the said bill; but upon recollection, and considering the impending ruin they shall be subject to by the inclosure, beg leave now to have liberty to retract from their seeming acquiescence in the said petition.' Ibid., XXI, 539.

[6] S. Addington, *An Inquiry into the Reasons for and against Inclosing Open-Fields*, pp. 24-5.

[7] Cf. Report on Waste Lands (1800), *Journals of the House of Commons*, LV, 392. The parliamentary fees due for the passing of a Bill of Enclosure amounted to an

own mandatories, their friends and relatives, sit in the House?[1] The heads of the ancient nobility in the House of Lords, as also the many country squires in the House of Commons, were the representatives of the great landed interests. It often happened that the Bill was drafted at once, without any preliminary inquiry.[2] When an inquiry was ordered, its conclusions were almost invariably identical with the desires of the petitioners. Counter-petitions had results in one case only, namely when they, too, originated in the possessing and ruling classes. The claims of the lord of the manor, who would suffer no curtailment of his former rights, those of the vicar, who wanted compensation for his tithes, had every chance of being received favourably.[3] Where a single man owned one-fifth of the acreage to be enclosed his opposition was enough to put an end to the proceedings.[4] Thus, what the great landowners had done could be undone by the great landowners alone.

What happened after the Bill of Enclosure had been passed? Although it was as a rule a lengthy document, burdened with complicated clauses, it did no more than prescribe the general conditions of the operation: on the spot only, and in the presence of the parties concerned, could points of detail be settled. A considerable and most delicate task remained then to be fulfilled. It consisted in actually finding out what was the state of every property, measuring all the plots of land that went to make it up, reckoning the income it brought in, as well as the relative value of the rights of common enjoyed by each owner. It was necessary to consider the whole territory of the parish, the common field together with the open field, to cut it into portions equivalent to the scattered properties for which they were to be substituted; to grant compensation, if the case arose, to direct and supervise the setting up of the fences that were now to divide one man's lands from his neighbours'; to see that undertakings in the common interest

[1] J. L. and L. B. Hammond (*The Village Labourer*, pp. 41-6) mention the case of the Bill of Enclosure for King's Sedgmoor that was of special interest to Lord Bolingbroke, and was referred to a Committee on which sat his brother, Lord St John.

[2] Cf. *Journals of the House of Commons*, XXV, 285, 494; XXX, 56, etc.

[3] Petition from the Duke of Dorset and the Mayor of Stratford-on-Avon against the enclosing of Shottery (Warwickshire), ibid., XXXII, 304. The Bill of Enclosure was withdrawn. For instances of amendments to the Bill adopted at the request of the vicar, see ibid., XXV, 236, and XLIII, 317. Sometimes, on the contrary, the landowners complained that the vicar had been granted too high a compensation; ibid., XLVIII, 217 (Petition of W. Willder against the enclosing of Peopleton, Worcestershire).

[4] A. Young, *North of England*, I, 225.

average of £85 10s. To this should be added the fees due to solicitors and counsels, the expenses involved by the bringing of witnesses before the Parliamentary Committee appointed for inquiring into the case, etc. According to Lecky, *History of the Eighteenth Century*, VI, 199, the total amount varied from £180 to £300.

prescribed by the Act as a complement to the enclosure, such as road-making or mending, drainage, irrigation, were duly carried out.[1] In fact, all this was tantamount to a revolution throughout the parish – the land being, so to speak, seized and dealt out again among the land-owners in an entirely new manner, which, however, was to leave un-touched the former rights of each of them. To ensure that this division should be carried out equitably, that errors and arbitrary measures should be avoided, what minute care, what a fine sense of valuation, and also what impartiality, what detachment from private interest, would have been required!

That very important and delicate task was entrusted to com-missioners, to the number of three, five or seven.[2] As far as the enclosure was concerned, they exercised unrestricted authority. In the words of Arthur Young, 'they are a sort of despotic monarch, into whose hands the property of the parish is invested, to re-cast and re-distribute it at their pleasure'.[3] For a long time there was no appeal from their decisions. It is most interesting, therefore, to know who those com-missioners were, what social class they came from, by whom they were appointed. In theory, they held their authority from Parliament: their names were in the Act of Enclosure.[4] But, since Parliament took no interest in and had no knowledge of the local questions that the com-missioners were to settle, they were in fact nominated by the petitioners: which means that their appointment, even as all the previous proceed-ings, was in the hands of the great landowners. Here once more the same characters played the foremost parts: 'the lord of the soil, the rector and a few of the principal commoners monopolize and distribute the appointments'.[5] They chose men devoted to them, unless they pre-ferred to sit on the Commission themselves.[6] The unlimited authority of the commissioners was no other than their own. It is not very sur-prising that they should have used it to their own advantage.[7]

[1] H. Homer, *An Essay on the Nature and Method*, etc., pp. 60, 99, 102. Sir John Sinclair, 'General Report on the Present State of Waste Lands' (1800), *Journals of the House of Commons*, LV, 384.

[2] H. Homer, op. cit., p. 43. Board of Agriculture, *General Report on Enclosures* (1808), p. 72.

[3] A. Young, *North of England*, I, 226.

[4] At least, such was the practice from 1775 onwards. Cf. *Journals of the House of Commons*, XXXV, 443.

[5] J. Billingsley, *A General View of the Agriculture in the County of Somerset*, p. 42.

[6] *Report respecting the Persons to be appointed Commissioners in Bills of Enclosure*, p. 4 (1801).

[7] Some writers on enclosures have defended the commissioners: 'Taking the conduct of the inclosures and the awards as a whole, there seems to be no ground for alleging a general partiality on behalf of any particular class. The work appears to have been honestly, if not always well, done, and to have been marked by a rough and ready fairness.' Gonner, op. cit., p. 76. 'In spite of some blundering and favouritism,

The abuse was so plain that the most determined supporters of the enclosures, and those least likely to oppose the interests of the great landowners, denounced it emphatically. In 1770 Arthur Young put forward a request that the commissioners be elected in a meeting of all the landowners, and be made responsible to the county magistrates.[1] But his protest did not secure attention, and not till 1801 – when a general Bill was enacted for the purpose of settling once and for all the clauses common to all Acts of Enclosure[2] – were any steps taken to prevent the inflicting of grievous wrongs. It was forbidden to appoint as commissioners the lord of the manor, his stewards, bailiffs or agents either in his service or having left it less than three years before, or 'any proprietor or person immediately interested in such moors, common or waste lands, half-year lands or uninclosed lands, intended to be ... inclosed'.[3] Henceforward, the commissioners were under the obligation of giving a hearing to all complaints and mentioning them in their reports. Any person with a grievance had a right to appeal from the commissioners' decision to the Quarter Sessions.[4] This belated legislation is evidence of spoliations that had been committed and had remained unpunished for a century.

VIII

The small man, whose field was not a capital to him but a bare means of living, could but look on helplessly while those changes took place and his right to his land and the very conditions of his existence were in question. He could not prevent the commissioners reserving the best lands for richer men. He was constrained to accept the lot assigned for him, even though he might not consider it an

[1] A. Young, *North of England*, I, 232.

[2] 41 Geo. III, c. 109.

[3] *Report respecting the Persons to be appointed Commissioners*, p. 4.

[4] Sir John Sinclair, 'Report on the State of Waste Lands', *Journals of the House of Commons*, LV, 382; 'Report from the Committee appointed to amend the standing Orders ... respecting the Bills of Enclosures (1801)', ibid., LVI, 663.

---

there is no reason to think that the commissioners behaved with the gross partiality often attributed to them, and on the whole, they did their work honestly and impartially.' (Curtler, *The Enclosure and Redistribution of our Land*, p. 159). However, Gonner admits that 'there was mismanagement in many cases, and there was much that was arbitrary in the action of some of the commissioners ... ' He adds that 'the allotments were, on the whole, according to legal rights'. But the dismissal, without compensation, of all claims that were not supported by written documents, involved heavy losses for the small farmers: 'Strip the small farms of the benefit of the commons, and they are all on one stroke levelled to the ground.' *Inquiry into the advantages and disadvantages resulting from the Bills of Inclosure* (1780), p. 14.

equivalent of his former property. He lost his rights on the common, which was now to be divided. A portion of that common land was indeed allotted to him; but its size was in proportion to the number of animals he used to graze on the lord's waste. Thus, once more, he that had most received most. Once in possession of his new land the yeoman had to fence it round, and this cost him both labour and money. He had to pay his share of the expenses incurred in carrying out the Act – and those expenses were often very heavy.[1] He could not fail to be left poorer than before, if not actually burdened with debt.[2]

As for the cottager who was traditionally allowed to live on the common,[3] gather his firewood there and perhaps keep a milch-cow, all that he considered as his possession was taken away from him at a blow. Nor had he any right to complain, for after all the common was the property of other men. The possessing classes were unanimous in thinking that 'the argument of robbing the poor was fallacious. *They had no legal title to the common land.*'[4] This was so, no doubt, but they had until then enjoyed the advantages of a *de facto* situation, sanctioned by long tradition. Some writers have maintained that those advantages amounted to very little and that their loss could not seriously injure the cottagers.[5] The law, however, seems to have recognized the grievous

[1] £2,000 was considered an average figure. Cf. *General Report on Enclosures*, pp. 331-4. The repaying of the expense often had to be spread over six or seven years; see A. Young, *A Six Months Tour through the North of England*, I, 230.

[2] S. Addington, *An Inquiry into the Reasons for and against Inclosing Open-Fields*, p. 35. As to the burden laid by the enclosure on the small landowner, see Prothero (Baron Ernle), *English Farming, Past and Present*, p. 251, J. L. and L. B. Hammond, *The Village Labourer*, p. 96, Gonner, *Common Land and Inclosure*, p. 373, Eliaschewitsch, *Die Bewegung zugunsten der kleinen Landwirtschaftlichen Güter in England*, p. 58.

[3] Marx was mistaken when he wrote: 'Sir F. M. Eden, in a cunning defence, described the common as the private property of the great landowners, these having taken the place of the feudal lords: but he disproved his own words when he asked that Parliament should pass a general Bill to approve a division of the commons. Thereby, he not only acknowledged that exceptional legislation would be required to transform them into private property; but he asked Parliament to grant compensation to the evicted poor.' *Das Kapital*, I, 749. (1) The General Act of Enclosures was in no way designed to approve a division of the commons, but to frame general rules for proceeding to that division; (2) compensation granted for the loss of customary possession does not imply the acknowledgment of an actual right. Marx's conception of the status of the English common seems to have been somewhat removed from the real state of things.

[4] Matthew Boulton, a letter to Lord Hawkesbury, April 17th, 1790, quoted by S. Smiles, *Lives of Boulton and Watt*, p. 168. Cf. H. Homer, op. cit., p. 23.

[5] 'The advantages which cottagers and poor people derive from commons and wastes are rather apparent than real; instead of sticking regularly to any such labour as might enable them to purchase good fuel, they waste their time in picking up a few dry sticks ... Their starved pig or two, together with a few wandering goslings ... are dearly paid for, by the care and time and bought food that are necessary to rear them.' F. M. Eden, *State of the Poor*, I, xix. According to Curtler (*The Enclosure*

wrong inflicted on them: an Act of Parliament, passed in 1757, directed the commissioners for enclosures to pay into the hands of the Poor Law authorities certain compensations 'to be applied towards the relief of the poor in the parish or township where ... wastes, woods and pastures had been enclosed'.[1] This implied a recognition of the fact that the dividing up of the common was the cause of hardships. A further step was sometimes taken to alleviate them: a piece of ground was kept undivided for the use of the poorer inhabitants of the parish, the landless cottagers,[2] or else they were awarded small lots whereon to graze their wretched flocks.[3] But such compensation was seldom granted[4] and was in any case illusory: the lots were so very small and inadequate that the cottagers seized the first opportunity to dispose of them and make a little money. Nor had they long to wait.

For, after the enclosure had been made, the shares allotted, the fences set up around each piece of land, all was not yet over. The great landowners had not yet reaped all the profit they expected from the operation. After consolidating their estates they sought to increase them, and when nothing remained to be taken they were prepared to buy. Some wished to add to their ploughed fields or meadows; others wanted to enlarge their parks or their hunting grounds;[5] others yet, in a few cases, would 'buy cottages near their mansions, for no other purpose than to shut them up, and to let them decay, because they did

[1] 31 Geo. II, c. 41.

[2] Cf. the Act of Enclosure for the parish of Walton-upon-Thames and for the manor of Walton Leigh (Surrey), 40 Geo. III, *Local and Personal Public Acts*, c. 86. Any person occupying a cottage with a rent not exceeding £5 was entitled to use the piece of land thus reserved, and to exercise the rights of pasture, woodcutting, etc. In the above case the undivided land covered 260 acres.

[3] The Act of 1801 (41 Geo. III, c. 109) prescribed the distribution of such allotments (art. 13).

[4] 'The poor inhabitants of open-field parishes frequently enjoy the privileges of cutting furze, turves, and the like, on the common land for which they have rarely any compensation made to them upon inclosure. The selfish proprietor insists that they had no right to such privileges, but were only permitted to enjoy them by indulgence or connivance.' H. Homer, op. cit., p. 22 f.

[5] The Earl of Dorchester, after buying up the whole parish of Abbey Milton (Dorsetshire), had the village razed to the ground, and a fish-pond dug out in its place. F. M. Eden, *State of the Poor*, II, 148.

___

and Redistribution of our Land, p. 228) three classes of people 'depended to a considerable extent on their rights of common, the deprivation of which was one of the causes of their great diminution in numbers'. They were (1) labourers cultivating small plots as owners or tenants; (2) small farmers cultivating their holdings with the help of their own families; and (3) the smaller yeomen owning and cultivating farms of less than 100 acres. Cf. A. Eliaschewitsch, *Die Bewegung zugunsten der kleinen Landwirtschaftlichen Güter in England*, p. 46.

not like to have the poor for their neighbours'.[1] And besides those who were already great landowners, others – merchants, bankers, and later, manufacturers – longed to rank with them. The moment was a favourable one. The redistribution of property had caused a wavering among the class that was most closely, most devotedly attached to the soil. The honest, hard-working but shortsighted yeoman, a follower of the beaten track, was bewildered by the changes around him and felt a coming danger in the formidable competition of the great farms run on modern methods. Whether he became discouraged, or chose to seek his fortunes elsewhere, he was tempted by the rich man's offers and sold his land.[2]

Almost everywhere the enclosing of open fields and the division of common land were followed by the sale of a great many properties. The enclosures and the engrossing of farms are two facts which eighteenth-century writers considered as inseparable, whether they wished to speak for or against them. The engrossing of farms was not always a consequence of the enclosure; sometimes, on the contrary, it took place before an enclosure.[3] But whether it was the consequence or the purpose of the operation, we know for certain that the total number of farms had become much smaller in the latter half of the century. One village in Dorsetshire where, in 1780, as many as thirty farms could be found, fifteen years later had the whole of its land divided between two holdings; in one parish in Hertfordshire three landowners had together engrossed no less than twenty-four farms, with acreages averaging between 50 and 150 acres.[4] An admirer of enclosures, little inclined to exaggerate their evil effects, put the number of small farms absorbed into larger ones between 1740 and 1788 at an average of four or five in each parish, which brings the total to forty or fifty thousand for the whole Kingdom.[5] Here was the important fact,

[1] G. F. A. Wendeborn, *A View of England towards the Close of the Eighteenth Century*, II, 287.

[2] 'A steward should not forget to make the best inquiry into the disposition of any of the freeholders within or near any of his Lord's Manors to sell their lands, that he may use his best endeavours to purchase them at as reasonable a price as may be for his Lord's advantage and convenience.' E. Laurence, *The Duty of a Steward to his Lord*, p. 36 (1727). Cf. G. Slater's conclusions in *The English Peasantry and the Enclosure of the Common Fields*, and W. Hasbach, *Die englischen Landarbeiter in den letzten hundert Jahren und die Einhegungen*, pp. 110-11.

[3] According to H. L. Gray, 'Yeoman Farming in Oxfordshire from the Sixteenth Century to the Nineteenth', *Quarterly Journal of Economics*, XXIV, 293, the latter was the more frequent case.

[4] At Durweston, F. M. Eden, *State of the Poor*, II, 148; T. Wright, *A Short Address on the Monopoly of Small Farms*, pp. 3-5.

[5] J. Howlett, *The Insufficiency of the Causes to which the Increase of the Poor and of the Poor Rates have been commonly ascribed*, p. 42. Since 1765 the engrossing of farms was encouraged by the prospect of larger profits, caused by the rise in the price of corn. Cf. H. Levy, *Large and Small Holdings*, p. 10.

undoubtedly more important than the division of the commons, although it disturbed the public opinion of the time much less. It was carried out by means of private deeds, unobtrusively and without any intervention either by Parliament or the local authorities; and it almost escaped notice. But it was the real end towards which efforts of the great landowners were ultimately directed; the enclosures and all their array of legal proceedings were chiefly the means of compelling the farmers to sell their land, or of improving estates that had been enlarged by recent purchases. The figure of forty to fifty thousand farms in less than fifty years, which does not seem exaggerated, shows how far-reaching were the changes wrought in landed property in the course of that half-century.

It is true that the disappearance of a farm did not necessarily mean that of a property. Engrossing often consisted in joining together several small holdings on an estate into one larger farm.[1] But that very change amounted to a revolution, for it involved deep modifications in the method of cultivation and in the use of labour.

During the first two-thirds of the eighteenth century the reduction in the number of small holdings was followed, as in the days of the Tudors, by the extension of pasture land.[2] Arthur Young, in his *Farmer's Letters* (1767) wrote that a farm could make better profits by breeding than by tillage, and cost less labour.[3] A number of counties where cultivation still held its ground, in spite of previous enclosures, now put on a new aspect. Towards the end of the century Leicestershire, that had been famous for its crops, was almost entirely covered with artificial meadows; more than one-half of Derbyshire, three-quarters of Cheshire, three-quarters of Lancashire, had become grazing land.[4] Since 1765 or so the rise in prices stimulated corn-growing, and the movement for transforming tilled land into pastures slackened down.[5]

---

[1] Cf. Hasbach, op. cit., pp. 36-7. A. H. Johnson, after 'a somewhat careful inquiry into the relation of enclosure to consolidation', although he concludes that enclosure was not necessarily followed by an absorption of small holdings, admits that 'during the period up to about 1785, enclosures were often followed by that result' (*The Disappearance of the Small Landowner*, p. 146 f.). According to Laurence, it was the duty of stewards to work for the absorption of small farms into larger ones: 'The steward should endeavour to lay all the small farms, let to poor indigent people, to the great ones ... ' E. Laurence, op. cit., p. 35.

[2] Cf. Prothero (Baron Ernle), *English Farming, Past and Present*, p. 168. A. H. Johnson, *Disappearance of the Small Landowner*, p. 98. W. Hasbach, *Die englischen Landarbeiter*, p. 39.

[3] A. Young, *The Farmer's Letters*, p. 95.

[4] J. Aikin, *A Description of the Country round Manchester*, pp. 18, 44, 69-70; F. M. Eden, *State of the Poor*, II, 531; J. Pilkington, *A View of the present State of Derbyshire*, I, 301.

[5] Cf. H. Levy, *Die Entstehung und Rückgang des landwirtschaftlichen Grossbetriebes*, p. 18 (*Large and Small Holdings*). Prothero (Baron Ernle), *English Farming, Past and*

But even if the cultivation of oats or wheat required more labour than the rearing of sheep, the total number of farm-hands had, in any case, been reduced. Was it not one of the chief aims of the joining together of the plots formerly scattered over the open field, and of the engrossing of farms, to effect such a reduction?[1]

The Bills of Enclosure met with little active opposition; nor is the reason far to seek. Those who had most to complain of dared scarcely lift their voices. If they ventured to put forth a claim or send a petition to Parliament, the only probable result for them was money spent fruitlessly – legal expenses, or the fees of experts, counsels and solicitors. Often they would merely refuse to sign the petition drafted by their neighbours, the great landowners: even then they would at once declare that they did not mean to oppose that petition:[2] an attitude showing that the villager, as the phrase goes, 'knew his betters'. Thus, formal protests were comparatively rare. Yet a few of them have reached us. Sometimes they attacked the very principle of the enclosure, as being 'very injurious to the petitioners, and tending to the ruin of many, especially the poorer';[3] sometimes they denounced its operation as 'partial and unjust ... hurtful to the petitioners in particular and to the community in general'.[4] After 1760 such protests became more frequent and forceful. The suppressed anger of the villagers would break out

[1] Sir John Sinclair acknowledged this: 'In regard to the effect of enclosures on population, it certainly has a tendency to diminish the number of hands employed in agriculture.' Quoted by W. Bowden, *Industrial Society in England towards the end of the Eighteenth Century*, p. 241.

[2] Such facts were very frequent. For instance, cf. *Journals of the House of Commons*, XXX, 607, 608, 613, etc.

[3] Ibid., XXVIII, 1031; XXIX, 563 and 612; XXXI, 539.

[4] Ibid., XXXIII, 459.

Present, p. 168. 'The profits were so great and so immediate to landlord as well as tenant, that every other species of produce was not only diminished, but, as it were, sacrificed, to the design of reaping the superior advantages resulting from the increase of this commodity. For this purpose, the farmer converted every nook and corner of his land into arable, and even the cottager forsook his one little ewe-lamb, and turned his scanty orchard into tillage.' *An Inquiry into the advantages and disadvantages resulting from the Bills of Inclosure* (1780), p. 23. The impression conveyed by this account was much exaggerated, for on comparing the figures in the General Report on Inclosures published by the Board of Agriculture (pp. 229-31 and 232-52) we find, as between the years 1760 and 1800, a slight decrease of the surface under tillage (about 10,000 acres). Eliaschewitsch (op. cit., pp. 23 ff.) shows that, in fact, the rise in prices between 1760 and 1793 was beneficial both to stock-breeding and to culture. With the support of a series of quotations he maintains, against H. Levy, that the eighteenth-century enclosures on the whole resulted in the extension of pasture lands (pp. 34 ff.); and he finds confirmation of his opinion in the following conclusion of the General Report on Inclosures (1808): 'That the fact is so cannot, nor need it be, denied.'

suddenly. In some parishes, the announcement of the enclosure caused riots. Formal notices could not be posted on the church doors, because of the obstruction by riotous mobs who forcibly prevented the sticking up of bills. The constable in charge of those bills was confronted by threatening crowds, armed with cudgels and pitchforks: in a Suffolk village, on three successive Sundays, his notices were torn out of his hands, he was thrown into a ditch and stones were hurled at him.[1]

This passionate opposition, in strong contrast with the villagers' habitual timorousness, may have had no other cause than an instinctive distrust of change. But we find it supported by a full array of documents and facts.[2] According to these the enclosures resulted in the buying up of the land by the wealthier class; they lay at the root of all the evils of the period – the high cost of necessaries, the demoralization of the lower classes and the aggravation of poverty. 'It is no uncommon thing for four or five wealthy graziers to engross a large inclosed lordship, which was before in the hands of twenty or thirty farmers, and as many smaller tenants or proprietors. All these are thereby thrown out of their livings, and many other families, who were chiefly employed and supported by them, such as blacksmiths, carpenters, wheelwrights and other artificers and tradesmen, besides their own labourers and servants.'[3] Not only had the small landowner to give up his land and either to leave the district or fall to the condition of labourer, not only was the cottager evicted from the common,[4] but as the large farms needed comparatively less labour a number of journeymen were left unemployed.[5]

---

[1] *Journals of the House of Commons*, LVI, 333; LVIII, 387. The notices informing all parties concerned that a Bill of Enclosure was to be brought in had to be posted several weeks in advance (cf. ibid., XXXV, 443).

[2] The British Museum Library contains a large collection of pamphlets on enclosures; they are particularly numerous for the period between 1780 and 1790. Here are the titles of a few among the more interesting: *An Inquiry into the advantages and disadvantages resulting from the Bills of Inclosure* (1780); *Observations on a Pamphlet entitled: 'An Inquiry into the Advantages, etc.'* (1781); *A Political Inquiry into the Consequences of enclosing Waste Lands* (1785); *Cursory Remarks upon Enclosures, showing the Pernicious and Destructive Consequences of Enclosing Common Fields* (1786). British Museum, T 1950.

[3] S. Addington, *An Inquiry into the Reasons for and against Inclosing Open-Fields*, p. 38.

[4] How the enclosures affected the different classes interested in the commons is aptly described by W. Hasbach, *History of the English Agricultural Labourer*, p. 107.

[5] The improvement in the methods of cultivation had a similar result: 'Forty years ago, every plough was worked with four horses and two men, or at least a man and a boy, whereas at present, universally over this county, every plough is worked by one man and two horses, without a driver and, according to the best of my observation, the man and the two horses do as much as the two men and the four horses formerly did.' G. Buchan Hepburn, *A General View of the Agriculture in East Lothian* (1794), p. 114.

The result was depopulation, if not everywhere, at least in a number of rural districts. 'Farm houses are pulled down or suffered to drop and perhaps a barn only left in their room. Villages lose their inhabitants ...'[1] An echo of such complaints and accusations rang in Oliver Goldsmith's famous lines:

> Sweet smiling village, loveliest of the lawn,
> Thy sports are fled, and all thy charms withdrawn;
> Amidst thy bowers the tyrant's hand is seen
> And desolation saddens all thy green.
> One only master grasps the whole domain,
> And half a tillage stints thy smiling plain ...
> And trembling, shrinking from the spoiler's hand,
> Far, far away, thy children leave the land ...
> Where then, ah! where shall poverty reside
> To 'scape the pressure of continuous pride?
> If to some common's fenceless limits strayed,
> He drives his flock to pick the scanty blade,
> Those fenceless fields the sons of wealth divide,
> And e'en the bare-worn common is denied ...
> Ye friends to truth, ye statesmen who survey
> The rich man's joys increase, the poor's decay,
> 'Tis yours to judge how wide the limits stand
> Between a splendid and a happy land ...
> Ill fares the land, to hastening ills a prey,
> Where wealth accumulates, and men decay;
> Princes and lords may flourish, or may fade;
> A breath can make them, as a breath has made,
> But a bold peasantry, their country's pride,
> When once destroyed, can never be supplied.[2]

The enclosures also had admirers who dwelt upon their undeniable

---

[1] *An Enquiry into the causes of the present high prices of provisions* (1767), p. 114. See D. Davies, *The Case of Labourers in Husbandry* (1795), pp. 35-6; *Gentleman's Magazine*, LXXI, 809.

[2] Oliver Goldsmith, *The Deserted Village* (1770), lines 35, 64, 265-82 and 303-8. It is difficult to admit that such lines were not suggested by the sight of the enclosures, although this has been contested. F. M. Eden wrote: 'Deserted villages are now only to be found in the pictures of poetry.' *An Estimate of the Number of Inhabitants in Great Britain and Ireland*, p. 49 (1800). 'Dr Goldsmith has been heard to confess that his "Deserted Village" was merely a poetical fiction.' *Gentleman's Magazine*, LXX, 1175. It is quite possible that Goldsmith had not in mind the case of one village in particular. But the terms he used are too definite, and fit in too well with facts known to us from various sources, to make it possible to dismiss the 'Deserted Village' as a pure imagination. If it cannot be quoted as evidence of a fact, it certainly expressed a widespread feeling at the time when it was written.

advantages[1] and strove to prove that most of the evil consequences imputed to them were purely imaginary. The most earnest among them were the writers on husbandry, in whose eyes the distribution of the land had far less importance than its capacity for production. For them the supreme argument was that large holdings offered the best conditions for the practical and theoretical progress of agriculture. Arthur Young compared big farms to big workshops, and, after quoting Adam Smith's famous passage on the manufacture of pins, he added: 'Agriculture will not admit of this, for men cannot be employed their whole lives in sowing, others in ploughing, others in hedging, others in hoeing, and so on, but the nearer we approach to this the better: which can only be on a large farm. In a small one, the same man is shepherd, hogherd, cowherd, ploughman, and sower; he goes about ten different sorts of labour and attention in the same day, and consequently acquires no habitual skill peculiar to himself.'[2] Yeoman farms were ill-cultivated, and 'generally the residence of poverty and misery'.[3] The great landowner had more intelligence and initiative, and above all he could afford to make experiments and undertake more or less expensive improvements. Wherever enclosure had taken place and large farms had been established there had been a rise in rent.[4] This was an unanswerable argument for those students of agriculture who were at the same time economists, and to whom men were of little account[5] when production and profit were at stake.

They could hardly dispute the fact that the consolidation of estates very often resulted in the absorption of small holdings, but they denied that the condition of labourers had become worse in consequence. We

---

[1] See Curtler, *The Enclosure and Redistribution of our Land*, chap. XVI, on the conclusions of the Board of Agriculture Surveys respecting the general results of enclosures: 'Their evidence on two points is overwhelming: they thought the advantages of enclosures incontestable and the disadvantage of commons far outweighed their benefits ... The common was a relic of a primitive agriculture whose chief use was gone ... '

[2] A. Young, 'On the Size of Farms', in *Georgical Essays*, IV, 564-5. *The Farmer's Letters*, p. 56.

[3] A. Young, 'On the Size of Farms', p. 560.

[4] C. Hutsall, *A General View of the Agriculture in the County of Pembroke*, p. 21. A. Young, *Southern Counties*, p. 22: 'About Bishop's Burton is some of the most extraordinary open field I have met with, for it let while open at 18s. and 20s. an acre, and now a bill of enclosure has been passed, it is said to be raised to near 30s. per acre.' Cf. *North of England*, I, 447. A clear distinction should be made between the rise due to enclosures and that which between 1793 and 1815 was connected with the famine prices of agricultural produce.

[5] 'I think population is but a secondary object: the soil ought to be applied to that use in which it will pay most, without any idea of population. A farmer never ought to be tied down to bad husbandry, whatever may become of population. Population which, instead of adding wealth to the State, is a burthen to the State, is a pernicious population.' A. Young, *Political Arithmetic*, I, 122.

know what their opinion was concerning the division of common lands; arguments against it, they thought, were 'grounded upon mistaken principles of humanity'.[1] As for complaints about the reduced demand for agricultural labour and the depopulation of villages, they dismissed them as absurd stories. How could anyone believe that to let part of the land lie fallow and to cultivate the rest as badly as possible was the means of occupying and feeding the greatest possible number of men? 'This appears to my poor understanding a most extraordinary paradox. There is in my neighbourhood a fine heath, consisting of about a thousand acres. In its present uncultivated state, it does not support a single poor family, nor does almost any one receive benefit from it, but some of the farmers around, who occasionally turn a few of their cattle upon it. Whereas, were it enclosed, well cultivated and improved, it would make six or eight good farms, from £70 to £100 a year each. These, besides the farmers and their several households, would require near thirty labourers, who, together with their wives and children, added to the tradesmen and mechanics that would be necessary to supply their respective wants, would raise the population on this single spot, in the course of a very few years, at least two hundred persons.'[2] To make such optimistic calculations more likely, carefully selected figures were brought forward, showing that the ill effects of engrossing were more than compensated by the cultivation of the waste lands.[3] It

[1] *First Report from the Select Committee appointed to take into Consideration the Means of promoting the Cultivation of the Waste Lands* (1795), p. 47.

[2] J. Howlett, *An Examination of Dr Price's Essay on the Population of England and Wales*, pp. 29, 30. This question has been examined and discussed again by some recent writers on enclosures. According to G. Slater (*The English Peasantry and the Enclosure of the Common Fields*, pp. 265-6) the result of enclosure was local depopulation. Professor Gonner, on the contrary, after comparing all the available figures, concludes 'that rural population at the end of the century did not vary with enclosure' (*Common Land and Inclosure*, pp. vi, 411-12 and 448). It should be remembered that there were no statistics of population before 1801, but only estimates.

[3] A. Young, *North of England*, IV. In the pamphlet entitled *The Advantages and Disadvantages of Enclosing the Waste Lands*, p. 42, we find the following figures:

		Quality of the soil		Before the enclosure Wages	Before the enclosure Families	After the enclosure Wages	After the enclosure Families
Open Field	...	...	Good	£400	20	£100	5
„	...	...	Indifferent ...	£400	20	£325	16¼
Common	...	...	Good	£10	½	£100	5
„	...	...	Indifferent ...	£10	½	£325	16¼

Let us examine these figures – although unaccompanied by any mention of date and place, and therefore impossible to verify. They would show a very slight increase in the number of the agricultural population (42¼ families instead of 41) and in the total amount of wages paid (£850 instead of £820). But whatever increase had taken place was due to the enclosure of the common and waste lands; on the contrary the enclosure of the open field resulted in a marked reduction both of population and wages (21¼ families instead of 40 and £425 instead of £800). It remains to be seen what was the general proportion in the country between those two kinds of enclosure. It should be noticed that the families who disappeared from the open

was even maintained that cultivation on a large scale was the system that would give the rural population the best opportunities in respect of both work and wages.[1] At the same time, those who represented the body of opinion hostile to enclosures were committing an error and supplying their adversaries with a ready argument. They believed that all over the Kingdom the population was decreasing, and they represented the alarming fact as a consequence of the enclosures. The party of the agricultural experts had no difficulty in proving that this alleged depopulation of England was a mere fancy, and whenever, on the contrary, they observed an increase in the population of any county they did not fail to ascribe it to the beneficial changes in the distribution of the land.[2] Their triumph was easier still when, as disciples of Adam Smith, they adopted the economic point of view: a system that resulted in the production of the largest quantity of goods at the smallest cost must be the best system for the whole community. If this is not admitted, they said, the Turks rightly object to the introduction of the printing press, which might be prejudicial to the copying profession, 'and all civilized Europe is in error'.[3] Would anyone be so ill-advised as to maintain that the husbandman should lay by the plough and take up the spade to dig the earth, on the plea that this would afford labour for a larger number of men?

Yet they made some significant admissions. In spite of their optimism they bore witness to the wrongs suffered by the poor under their very eyes. A commissioner of enclosures wrote: 'I lament that I have been accessory to injuring two thousand poor people at the rate of twenty families per parish. Numbers, in the practice of feeding on the commons, cannot prove their right; and many, indeed most who have allotments, have not more than an acre, which being insufficient for the man's cow, both cow and land are usually sold to the opulent farmers.'[4] After an impartial inquiry the Board of Agriculture acknowledged that in most cases the poor had been stripped of what little they owned. In some villages they could not even get milk for their children. The available evidence is heartrending in its monotony.[5] The Earl of

---

[1] A. Young, *The Farmer's Letters*, pp. 66-72; J. Howlett, *An Examination of Dr Price's Essay*, p. 20; Sir John Sinclair, 'Address to the Members of the Board of Agriculture', in *Journals of the House of Commons*, LI, 258.

[2] Cf. W. Wales, *An Inquiry into the present state of Population in England and Wales*, pp. 38-41.

[3] F. M. Eden, *State of the Poor*, I, XIV.

[4] *Annals of Agriculture*, XXXVI, 516.

[5] Board of Agriculture, *General Report on Inclosures* (1808), p. 18 – Turvey, Bedfordshire: 'To my knowledge, before the enclosures, the poor inhabitants found no

---

field and those who found work on the divided common could not belong to the same class: the former group certainly included landowners or copyholders, while the latter was formed exclusively of labourers.

Leicester, upon being congratulated on his newly built castle at Holkham, answered with remorseful melancholy: 'It is a sad thing for a man to be alone in the district of his residence: I look around, and can see no other house than mine. I am like the ogre in the tale, and have eaten up all my neighbours.'[1]

Does this mean that those neighbours had disappeared, that they had been wiped out like a nation overrun by barbarous hordes? No, indeed. But a section of the rural population, having been torn away from the land that nourished them, having lost their homes and seen their former ties broken, became unsettled and migratory;[2] the small landowners and farmers on the one hand, the cottagers and journeymen on the other, were ready to leave the countryside if they could make a better, or indeed a plain living elsewhere.

IX

Let us consider these two classes of men in turn. One is none other than the smaller yeomanry, whose decline will now be comprehensible.[3]

[1] Karl Marx, *Das Kapital*, I, 716.

[2] Gonner, while opposing the view that enclosures caused a decrease of the population, admits that their result was 'to change and unsettle a population previously organized on a basis of unyielding custom' (*Common Land and Enclosures*, p. 444).

[3] It should be repeated that on the eve of the nineteenth century the yeomanry was far from having completely disappeared. In the words of E. Halévy (*Histoire du Peuple Anglais au XIXᵉ Siècle*, I, 208), 'the decline of the yeomanry, which had proceeded rapidly in the eighteenth century, seemed to have slackened during the years of agricultural prosperity ending in 1815: after that date it became a headlong fall'.

difficulty in procuring milk for their children; since, it is with the utmost difficulty they can procure any milk at all. Cows lessened from 110 to 40.' – Letcomb, Berkshire: 'The poor seem the greatest sufferers. They can no longer keep a cow, which before many of them did, and they are therefore now maintained by the parish.' – Waddesdon, Buckinghamshire: 'Poverty has very sensibly increased; the husbandmen come to the parish for want of employment; the land is laid to grass.' – Cranage, Cheshire: 'Poor men's cows and sheep have no place, or any being.' – Todenham, Gloucestershire: 'Nothing increased, but the poor: eight farm houses filled with them.' – Norton, Hertfordshire: 'The cottagers have been deprived of their cows, without any compensation.' – Donington, Lincolnshire: 'Cottagers' cows (140) lost by the enclosure.' – Lendham, Norfolk: 'The cottagers have had to sell their cows.' – Passenham, Northampton: 'The cottagers have been deprived of their cows, and are great sufferers by the loss of their hogs.' – Ashford, Staffordshire: 'Much wretchedness.' – Ackworth, Yorkshire: 'The parish belonged to near 100 owners, nearly the whole of whom have come to the parish since the enclosure.' (Pp. 150 ff.) H. Levy, *Large and Small Holdings*, pp. 42-3, observes that Arthur Young, once 'the most zealous advocate of the enclosures', admitted that they had done some harm, regretted the loss of the cottagers' cattle, advocated the revival of allotments, and opposed Malthus's arguments against it. See *Annals of Agriculture*, XXXIV, 251; XXXVI, 515; XLI, 231, etc.

There was no room for them in the system which had been framed by the apostles of the new agriculture and carried out by means of Acts of Enclosure: Arthur Young asked what would be the use to a modern State of having a whole province cultivated by peasant proprietors, as in the early days of Rome, 'except for the mere purpose of breeding men, which of itself is a most useless purpose'.[1] On the large estates, the exploitation of which was methodically conducted by their wealthy owners, a new type of farmer made his appearance who compares with the old-time farmer as the millowner compares with the master manufacturer. He paid a high rent and looked forward to high profits, and the sort of life he was able to lead would have been regarded as extravagant by a country squire of the previous generation.[2] He fed well, and when he had friends to dinner offered them claret or port wine. His daughter was taught to play the harpsichord and dressed 'like the daughter of a duke'.[3] There was now nothing in common between him and the labourer in his employment, and he was very unlike the old yeoman whose place he had taken, although he often sprang from the yeomanry. But, for one small landowner who succeeded in exchanging his former independence for the position of a prosperous tenant, how many were driven either to work as hired labourers or to leave their villages?

The temptation to go in search of work was still greater for unemployed labourers. In many localities the men in need of parochial relief were sent round from one farm to another for employment, part of their wages being paid from the poor rates.[4] They thus formed a somewhat unsettled element, and were ready to go anywhere to find occupation whenever they succeeded in evading the servitude imposed on them by

[1] A. Young, *Political Arithmetic*, I, 47.

[2] 'Squire Charington's father used to sit at the head of the oak table along with his men, say grace to them, and cut up the meat and the pudding. He might take a cup of strong beer to himself when they had none, but that was pretty nearly all the difference in their manner of living.' W. Cobbett, *Rural Rides*, p. 243.

[3] 'Their entertainments are as expensive as they are elegant ... for it is not an uncommon thing for one of these new created farmers to spend £10 or £12 at one entertainment, and, to wash off delicate food, must have the most expensive wines, and those the best of their kind ... As to dress, no one that is not personally acquainted with the opulent farmer's daughter can distinguish her from the daughter of a duke by her dress.' *Cursory Remarks on Inclosures*, p. 21 (1786). See also *Gentleman's Magazine*, LXXI, 588.

[4] 'There seems to be here a great want of employment: most labourers are, as it is termed, "on the rounds", that is, they go to work from one house to another round the parish. In winter, sometimes 40 persons are on the rounds.' – F. M. Eden, *State of the Poor*, II, 29, 30. This was a recent practice: 'An old man of the parish says that, before the enclosure took place, land did not let for 10s. an acre, and that, when he was young, the name of roundsman was unknown in the parish.' Ibid. See on this point W. Hasbach, *History of the Agricultural Labourer*, pp. 188-90, and J. L. and L. B. Hammond, *The Village Labourer*, p. 164.

the Poor Law, which bound the pauper to his parish.[1] This, according
to the supporters of the new system of agriculture, explained the seeming depopulation of the country, which was used as an argument against
enclosures. 'The men were not lost but perhaps, with the ground, better
employed.'[2] If there was less time and labour wasted on the land it was
for the benefit of the towns and of their trades. Before 1760 a movement
of population could already be observed 'from rural parishes to market
towns, and from both of them to the capital city: so that great multitudes of people who were born in rural parishes are continually acquiring settlements in cities or towns, particularly in those towns where
considerable manufactures are carried on'.[3] Industry was in fact the
only refuge for thousands of men who found themselves cut off from
their traditional occupations. The manufactures were to offer them the
living they could no longer earn on the land.

On this movement of rural labour in search of work information is
scanty and unreliable. But whenever such information can be obtained
it reveals the steady movement of land-workers to industrial towns:
'About forty years ago [this was written in 1794] the southern and
eastern parts of this county [Warwick] consisted mostly of open fields,
which are now chiefly inclosed ... Upon all inclosures of open fields the
farms have generally been made much larger. These lands being now
grazed want much fewer hands to manage them than they did of their
former open state: from these causes the hardy yeomanry in country
villages have been driven for employment into Birmingham, Coventry
and other manufacturing towns.'[4] A petition signed by the inhabitants
of a rural parish of Northamptonshire describes the local peasantry as
'driven from necessity and want of employ, in vast crowds, into manufacturing towns, where the very nature of their employment, over the
loom or the forge, may waste their strength, and consequently debilitate
their posterity'.[5]

[1] On the forced settlement of paupers and its abolition in 1795, see Part III,
chap. III.

[2] *An Inquiry into the Connection between the Present Price of Provisions and the Size of
Farms*, pp. 124 and 136; J. Howlett, *An Examination of Dr Price's Essay*, p. 32.

[3] J. Massie, *A Plan for the Establishment of Charity Houses*, p. 99 (1758). S. Addington, after describing the distress prevailing in many districts, adds that sometimes
it could be avoided when work could be found in the neighbourhood owing to some
flourishing industry (*An Inquiry into the Reasons for and against Inclosing Open-Fields*,
p. 38). 'If the land gets into the hands of a few great farmers, the consequence must
be that the little farmers will be converted into a body of men who earn their subsistence by working for others ... There will perhaps be more labour, because there
will be more compulsion to it ... And towns and manufactures will increase, because
more will be driven to them in quest of places and employment.' R. Price, *On Reversionary Payments*, II, 149.

[4] John Wedge, *A General View of the Agriculture in the County of Warwick*, p. 21.

[5] *Journals of the House of Commons*, LII, 661 (1797): 'When did the enclosure take

Thus the enclosures and the engrossing of farms ultimately resulted in placing at the disposal of industry resources in labour and energy which made it possible for the factory system to develop.[1] Industry was becoming, as it were, a new land in the very midst of the country, another America attracting immigrants by the thousand – with this difference: that instead of being a discovery it was a creation, the very existence of that new world being conditioned by the increase of its population. Each newcomer brought with him what he had been able to save before leaving the old country. Those among the yeomen who had suffered least from the redistribution of the land, and had succeeded in getting a fair price for their property, were in possession of a small capital. Having, more or less against their own will, given up their rooted traditions and habits, they were now ready to try their fortune in the new field by launching into ventures which on all sides attracted their enterprise. From their number were to rise many of the first generation of manufacturers who started and led the industrial movement, and were soon to form a class of men rivalling in wealth and influence the great landowners now in possession of their land.[2] But comparatively few, of course, attained that degree of success. Many of the small yeomen and farmers, reduced to the condition of wage-earners, shared the fate of the labourers who came to the towns in search of work. They possessed nothing, and could offer nothing but their labour. These were to form the working population, the anonymous multitude in the factories – the army of the industrial revolution.

The changes in the conditions of rural life had a still more direct influence on the progress of industry. We know that one of the characteristic features of the domestic system of manufacture was the scattering of workshops in the villages, the very basis of that system consisting in a close alliance between cottage industry and the cultivation of small holdings. We have noticed how a weaver would eke out his earnings with the produce of a plot of ground, and how a rural family would in

[1] According to Professor Gonner the cause of the migration to the towns was 'the divorce between agricultural and industrial occupations, and the early growth of factory organization'. *Common Land and Inclosure*, p. 444. This is true of a later period, when the new industries had begun to grow.

[2] See Part III, chap. II. Examples of yeomen becoming manufacturers were particularly frequent in the cotton districts, where the factory system had made more rapid progress than elsewhere: 'The yeomanry, formerly numerous and respectable, have greatly diminished of late, many of them having entered into trade.' J. Aikin, *A Description of the Country from thirty to forty miles round Manchester*, pp. 23 and 48. Compare with J. James, *History of Bradford*, p. 376.

place? – Nine years ago. – Has not the condition of the inhabitants of Harmley greatly improved during these seven years? – I don't know that it has: I know of many who have been obliged to go to a factory to work, who used to work in their own houses.' *Report from the Select Committee appointed to consider the State of the Woollen Manufacture* (1806), p. 22.

the evening spin wool for the merchant manufacturer. The blow dealt to peasant property broke that time-honoured alliance of labour on the land and industrial work. The village artisan, when deprived of his field and of his rights of common, could not continue to work at home. He was forced to give up whatever independence he still seemed to have retained, and had to accept the wages offered to him in the employer's workshop. Thus labour was becoming more and more concentrated, even before the competition of machinery had finally destroyed the old village industries.

There is, therefore, an intimate connection between the movement by which English agriculture was transformed and the rise of the factory system. The connection being of a less simple nature than a mere relation between cause and effect, the two events might at first sight appear to have sprung from entirely different sources, only influencing each other in the course of their respective developments. The disappearance of the yeomanry, for instance, was not caused by the industrial revolution, but the industrial revolution made it more rapid and complete. As for the movement of labour from country to town, it certainly assisted, though it could not have determined, the progress of industry. If one of the two factors had been lacking, would not the other have continued to develop, although most probably its progress would have taken a somewhat different course? Had the bulk of the rural population remained on the land the triumph of the factory system might have come later, but it could not have been indefinitely postponed, as is shown conclusively by what took place in France. Might it not therefore be held that the relation between the transformation of agriculture and that of industry was limited to accidental influences – technical improvements based on entirely different methods accounting in both cases for separate and parallel developments?

But these improvements, independent though their progress may seem to be, were only part of a more general evolution, and their success was largely due to the support they received from each other. The growth of great industrial centres would have been impossible if agricultural production had not been so organized as to provide for the needs of a large industrial population, and agricultural production, on the other hand, could not have developed had not the industrial districts supplied adequate markets with growing numbers of consumers. This was one of the favourite arguments used by the advocates of enclosure: 'By the produce being greater there will be a surplus for manufacturers, and by this means manufactures, one of the mines of this nation, will increase in proportion to the quantity of corn produced.'[1] And, while the two movements were thus connected in their

[1] *An Inquiry into the Connection between the Present Price of Provisions and the Size of Farms*, p. 129.

respective consequences, another and stronger connection was that between their causes. What accounts for the change in rural conditions, for the enclosures, the division of the common lands and the engrossing of farms, is the introduction of a business spirit into the management of agriculture, landowners thereafter considering their land as capital, from which a better income could be drawn by improved methods of exploitation. In agriculture, as in industry, the initiative of the capitalist proved both self-seeking and beneficial to the community,[1] for it did away at the same time with obnoxious routine and with old institutions, to which the working men were still looking for protection. The conditions of all successful business are the reduction of cost and the increase of profit. The enclosures resulted in a reduction of labour and an increase of production. A comparison between their effect and that of the introduction of machinery[2] was well justified, for their ultimate origin was one and the same.

[1] See in the *General Report* of the Board of Agriculture the eulogy of the landowner, liberated at last by the enclosure: 'His talents, his energy, and his capital, are free to be employed for his own benefit,' etc. *General Report*, p. 220.

[2] F. M. Eden, *State of the Poor*, I, XIV.

PART II

Inventions and Factories

CHAPTER ONE

THE BEGINNINGS OF MACHINERY
IN THE TEXTILE INDUSTRY

THE use of machinery, even if not in itself a sufficient definition or explanation of the industrial revolution, remains at any rate the leading fact, in relation to which every other fact in that great historical process must be studied. And this is because every one of them was ultimately swayed by it and had to follow its movement and laws. But we must first be clear as to the meaning of the words we use. If we understand by machinery all artificial means of shortening or facilitating human labour, it would be difficult, if not impossible, to fix an initial date for the facts we mean to study.

I

From time immemorial man has been able to make tools for himself. This is one of the earliest, and perhaps one of the most fundamental characteristics of the human race. But it is very difficult to say where a tool ends and a machine begins. A distaff or a hammer are certainly not machines, whilst a Jacquard loom is undoubtedly something more than a tool. But between these extremes there is room for doubtful cases. How shall we classify a pump or a spinning wheel? Can we define a machine as something which not only helps but does away with and replaces human labour? The answer is that the simplest tool saves a considerable amount of labour. A man with a spade will do as much work as twenty men who only have their nails to scratch the ground with. On the other hand the most perfect automatic machine does not entirely do away with the human element, for it needs a man to look after it.

Yet at this point a distinction becomes evident. The workman in charge of such a machine has to start it, stop it, feed it and keep it in working order. But he has no part in the actual work it does, save to slow it down or to speed it up, or at most to see that it works smoothly without jerks or stoppages. His activity or negligence alter the quantity of work done by the machine rather than the quality. He does not do the work, but is only there to regulate and measure it. On the contrary, a tool is passive in the worker's hands; his muscular strength, his natural or acquired skill or his intelligence determine production down to its smallest details. Can we put this difference into words by saying that the distinctive feature of a machine is its motor power? But supposing it was worked by hand, with a crank, would it no longer be a machine? What would take place in that case is the reduction of the man himself to the part of a mechanical force. The machine, while using the strength of his arms, would render his hands unnecessary. And this it is which constitutes a machine. Instead of being a tool in the workman's hand, it is itself an artificial hand. It differs from a tool not so much by the automatic force which keeps it in motion as by the movements it can perform, the mechanism planned by the engineer's art enabling it to replace the processes, habits and skill of the hand. A spinning wheel is hardly a machine, because even though it spins, the thread has to be drawn out by hand. A pump is a sort of machine, because, in order to make it work, it is only necessary to move the piston backwards and forwards, which can be done by mere brute strength. We can thus define a machine as follows: a mechanism which, worked by any motive power, executes the elaborate movements of a technical operation, which it had previously taken one or several men to do.[1]

This definition easily disposes of many false examples, which would make the first use of machinery appear to go back to the most remote antiquity. We must nevertheless recognize that machinery was used long before modern times. The ancients not only had very complicated and powerful war machinery, but also industrial machinery, as, for instance, the water mill. The characteristic feature of recent economic life is not the occasional use of machines but machine industry. This expression can be used either with reference to a particular industry, or to industry as a whole. Before it became universal, it was only a special, a local phenomenon. Even today, in spite of its immense development, there are still – even in the most highly civilized countries – many exceptions to it. The phrase 'machine industry' could not properly be applied to a branch of trade merely because a machine is used to aid production; it must have become the essential factor in production, the factor which determines the quantity, the quality and the price of the products. From the sixteenth century the iron industry had made use of machinery; forge hammers, worked at first by levers and later by water-wheels;[2] furnace-blowing engines worked by water-wheels or by a gear attached to donkeys or horses.[3] A little later metal lathes, auto-

[1] This definition seems more satisfactory and more complete than that given by Reuleaux: 'A machine is a combination of solid parts, so contrived that by means of it natural forces can be made to cause certain definite motions.' F. Reuleaux, *Theoretische Kinematik*, p. 38.

[2] See the excellent woodcuts in *De Re Metallica*, by Georgius Agricola (Basle, 1546). English translation by H. C. and L. H. Hoover, 1912. A certain number are reproduced in Ludwig Beck, *Die Geschichte des Eisens*, II, 147, 149, 479, 482, 483, 531, etc., together with similar illustrations taken from Vannuccio Biringuccio's *De la Pirotechnia* (Venice, 1558).

[3] See Beck, op. cit., II, 130-42.

matic rolling mills and slitting mills made their appearance.[1] Nevertheless so long as, through lack of fuel, pig iron could only be obtained in
small quantities, and so long as bar iron had to be laboriously hammered, machinery played only a secondary part in influencing the development of industry. Moreover, there are varying degrees of machine
industry. Printing is obviously a machine industry, and was so from
the start, but it has become even more so since rotary presses worked
by steam or electricity have replaced the old-fashioned hand press.
It is becoming even more of a machine industry, as the typesetting
machine gradually relieves the compositor of the material part of his
work.

Apart from printing, which is of interest in connection with the
history of intellectual rather than of economic development, the
textile industries afford the first instance of machine industry, taken in
the most complete sense. The rapid transformation in the cotton
industry, wrought by a succession of technical inventions, made it the
earliest and also the classical example of modern large-scale industry.
This explains why Schulze-Gaevernitz, under the general title of *der
Grossbetrieb*, produced what was simply and solely a monograph on the
cotton industry. Even though its evolution, whose successive stages we
are about to study, was so rapid, yet it did not take place without preparation. A close study will discover continuity of development under
what seems the most startling change. Machine industry, like all other
important facts, had its forerunners, which preceded it and heralded it
from afar.[2]

One of the most interesting, although its consequences were limited,
was the invention in 1598 of the stocking frame by a Cambridge
graduate called William Lee.[3] The stocking frame is undoubtedly one of
those machines[4] which, as they perform a vital operation in an industry,
cannot be introduced without creating in that industry a complete revolution. Can we wonder if the same unhappy destiny befell Lee which
later overtook so many other inventors? His machine was looked upon as
a mischievous contrivance, which threatened to deprive a large number

[1] See the plates in Diderot's *Encyclopédie*, vol. IV, article 'Forges ou Art du Fer'.

[2] We have already referred to the metal industry and have suggested reasons for
putting it in a class apart. We shall come back to it in chap. III of Part II (Iron
and Coal).

[3] For what follows see W. Felkin, *A History of the Machine-wrought Hosiery and Lace
Manufactures*, pp. 23-41, and the article 'Lee (William)' in the *Dictionary of National
Biography*.

[4] 'It is a very ingeniously contrived machine, made of polished iron; it is not
possible to describe its construction here, because of the number and variety of its
component parts, and even a person who sees it will find a real difficulty in understanding how it works.' (*Encyclopédie Méthodique*, 'Manufactures', I, 220). The plates
in Diderot's *Encyclopédie* (vol. II, article 'Métier à faire des bas') give, however, a
fairly clear description of the stocking frame.

of workmen of their livelihood. This objection has been reiterated ever since, and even today it often delays (though it cannot now stop) the progress of industrial technique. Lee, forced to leave England, found refuge in France, where, thanks to the enlightened government of Henri IV, he established himself in Rouen with nine or ten workmen. But after the King's death the inventor, who had become as unpopular in Normandy as in England and was moreover disliked both as a foreigner and a Protestant, was for the second time forced to give up his work. He went to Paris, where he just managed to live, and finally died utterly forgotten. His companions then went back to England and settled in the neighbourhood of Nottingham, where the invention had first been experimented with. There machine knitting, after this period of tribulation, was finally established.

By the following century it had almost entirely displaced hand knitting, and was already a machine industry with most of its usual consequences. It had certainly not resulted in the massing of workers in big workshops. The knitting frame, like the weaving loom, was used at home. But it was too expensive a machine for the workman to own himself. We therefore find that curious system in force, of which the main conditions have been described above.[1] The worker rented his frame, and this 'frame rent' was deducted from his wages. The capitalist, owner alike of raw material and implements, was all-powerful and made his power cruelly felt. Sometimes employers would hire workers without having any work to give them, simply in order to let out some idle knitting frames and secure the frame rent.[2]

This industry revealed a curious mixture of ancient and modern characteristics, some handed down from traditional industries, others the forerunners of impending changes. There was a corporation of stocking-knitters, modelled on the guilds of the Middle Ages. Masters and workmen both belonged to it, affiliation was compulsory and the

[1] See Part I, chap. I, pp. 63 and 80. See *Journals of the House of Commons*, XXXVI, 635, 728, and the preamble to 28 Geo. III, c. 55: 'Whereas the frames for making of framework-knitted pieces, stockings, and other articles and goods in the hosiery or framework-knitted manufactory, are very valuable and expensive machines, and generally the property of the hosier or manufacturer, who lets the same to hire to his workmen or framework-knitters ... '

[2] See *Journals of the House of Commons*, XXXVI, 742, and XXXVII, 370. This abuse was, until recently, a subject of repeated complaints. 'Rent of the machine is exacted by the employer whether the operative is given work or not. Thus, as the framework-knitters allege, when they paid rent for their frames, the employers were tempted to spin out the work over much longer periods than was necessary, doling it out in very small portions in order to keep them paying rent as long as possible. And the Macclesfield silk-weavers complain that they are kept always half-employed, the giver-out of work finding his advantage in getting it done on as many separate looms as possible, from each of which a full weekly rent is derived.' B. and S. Webb, *Industrial Democracy*, I, 316 ff.

number of entries was limited. Masters, journeymen and apprentices were all subject to a complicated system of customs and regulations.[1] But these regulations, based on the industrial legislation of the sixteenth century, became a dead letter as soon as they went against the interests of the employer, who was the owner of all the implements and the dispenser of work. The rules which limited the number of apprentices were constantly violated, for the employer insisted on a plentiful and cheap supply of labour. In this industry we come across the first collective indentures of apprenticeship, by arrangement between manufacturers and parishes. It was a good opportunity for the parish to get rid of its workhouse children and it enabled the manufacturer to obtain free labour, and thus to force down the wages of adult workers.[2] Thus, in spite of the survival of traditional forms, the budding influence of machinery grew stronger, with a tendency to substitute mechanical processes for manual skill and a crowd of labourers for a small number of artisans.

Another instance of the local development of machine industry, with limited results, is supplied by the silk industry. In fact its real beginnings must be looked for outside England, where the silk industry has never been more than partially acclimatized, and the invention which changed it so entirely was an Italian one.

The manufacture of silk materials in the last years of the seventeenth century had undergone rapid development in England. A colony of skilled workmen, driven from France by the repeal of the Edict of Nantes, had just settled in the suburbs of London, and the fame of the Spitalfields silk-weavers was beginning to spread. But English manufacturers had to face serious difficulties. Compelled as they were to buy their raw silk abroad – the British climate putting the cultivation of the mulberry leaf and the rearing of silk worms out of the question – it would have been to their advantage to make their own thrown silk (that is, the silk thread made by twisting together the filaments from the cocoons). But smugglers put such cheap silk thread on the English market that everyone wondered how that thread could have been made.[3] Rumour said that in Italy there were machines for throwing silk. But no one had seen them, or knew how they were made. About 1702 a certain Cotchett of Derby, attempted, without any ideas on the subject, to make one.[4] He failed, and Italian thrown silk continued to be smuggled into the country.

---

[1] On this subject see a fairly complete study in Held's, *Zwei Bücher zur socialen Geschichte Englands*, pp. 484 ff.

[2] Ibid. The Statutes of the Company of Framework Knitters, revised in 1744, are reproduced in the *Journals of the House of Commons*, XXVI, 779-94.

[3] See R. W. Cooke Taylor, *Introduction to a History of the Factory System*, p. 358.

[4] A. Barlow, *History and Principles of Weaving*, p. 30.

These machines did actually exist. No one knows when they were invented. What is certain is that they were described in a treatise on mechanics published in Padua in 1621.[1] But this book, even assuming that it was ever known in England, had apparently been quite forgotten. As for the machines themselves, if we may judge from the mystery which at that time still surrounded the most insignificant manufacturing processes, they must have been jealously guarded. It was a difficult, if not a dangerous venture to go to Italy and discover the precious secret, and it was only natural for the story of such an expedition to be later embellished with romantic details.

The journey was undertaken in 1716 by John Lombe.[2] He went to Leghorn and there succeeded not only in seeing the machines but in making his way into the building where they stood. With the help of an Italian priest he secretly made some drawings and sent them to England hidden in pieces of silk. When his perilous mission was finished he re-embarked and is said to have been nearly caught. A brig was sent after him, but he luckily escaped. Having returned home he died quite young, only a few years later. Rumour said that he had fallen a victim to Italian poison.

In 1717, as soon as he was back, he set up, near Derby, silk-throwing machines built according to the designs he had brought back from Italy.[3] His brother, Thomas Lombe, supplied the necessary capital and in 1718 obtained a patent for fourteen years.[4] Soon after a factory – the first in England – was erected on an island in the Derwent.

The size of the building surprised everyone. Five hundred feet long, five or six storeys high, pierced by four hundred and sixty windows, it resembled a huge barracks. Once inside, astonishment became still greater. The machines were very tall, cylindrical in shape, and rotated on vertical axes. Several rows of bobbins, set on the circumference, received the threads, and by a rapid rotary movement gave them the

[1] Vittorio Zonca, *Nuovo Teatro di Macchine ed Edifici* (Padua, 1621), pp. 68-75 (with plates).

[2] The traditional account is given by William Hutton, *History of Derby*, pp. 161 ff. It has been criticized, particularly by G. Townsend Warner (*Social England*, V, 111-12). According to him the journey was quite unnecessary, since Zonca's description of the machine was available. But it seems rather improbable that John Lombe or any other English trader of that time should have read the *Nuovo Teatro di Macchine*. Warner adds that in 1692 the possibility of introducing throwing mills into England had been discussed. (See *Calendar of Home Office Papers*, 1683-93, p. 293). This shows only that the existence of such machines was known in England, not that their design and working had been disclosed.

[3] With the help of the engineer, George Sorocold. See Defoe, *Tour*, III, 38 (1727 edition), and III, 68 (1742 edition).

[4] *Chronological Index of Patents and Inventions* No. 477. See Wyndham Hulme, 'On the History of Patent Law in the Seventeenth and Eighteenth Centuries', *Law Quarterly Review*, 1902, pp. 280 ff.

necessary twist. At the top the thrown silk was automatically wound on a winder, all ready to be made up into hanks for sale. The vast number of parts which made up the machines, all worked by a single wheel (the motor power for which was provided by the river Derwent), the accuracy and rapidity of the work, and the delicacy of the processes, could not but make a very vivid impression on people who had never seen anything of the kind before. The workman's chief task was to reknot the threads whenever they broke. Each man was in charge of sixty threads.[1] So here we already have a modern factory, with its automatic tools, its continuous and unlimited production, and the narrowly specialized functions of its operatives.

The development of industrial capitalism went hand in hand with that of machine industry. The same facts we have just noted in the stocking-frame industry appear again here, in an even more pronounced and significant manner. The concentration of industry became more clearly defined, the existence of the factory making it concrete and visible. Thomas Lombe's factory employed three hundred workmen. The factories for which this one became the model were often quite as large, if not larger. In 1765, in the course of a parliamentary inquiry on the silk industry, several employers who appeared before the Commission were employing between four and eight hundred persons. A certain John Sherrard declared that he paid wages to as many as fifteen hundred workmen at a time.[2] Some no doubt worked at home, but throwing, at any rate, was done by machines in large workshops. Nathaniel Paterson, of London, had twelve throwing mills all under one roof.[3] The type of the great millowner, as distinct from that of the wealthy merchant with whom up till then he had been still half identified, now stands out clearly. In fifteen years Thomas Lombe made a fortune of £120,000.[4] He became alderman and then sheriff, was

[1] 'Here is a curiosity of a very extraordinary nature, and the only one of the kind in England: I mean those mills on the Derwent, which work the three capital Italian engines for making organzine, or thrown silk, which, before the mills were invented, was purchased by the English merchants with ready money in Italy ... This engine contains 22,586 wheels and 97,746 movements, which work 73,726 yards of silk thread every time the wheel goes round, which is three times in one minute, and 318,504,960 yards in twenty-four hours. The water wheel gives the motion to all the rest of the wheels and movements, of which any one may be stopped separately.' Defoe, *Tour*, III, 67 (1742 edition). A passage from Anderson's *Historical and Chronological Deduction of the Origin of Commerce*, which has been repeatedly quoted, is a mere copy of Defoe's description. See also A. Young, *North of England*, I, 225, William Hutton, *History of Derby*, p. 163, and the drawings in Zonca's book and in the French *Encyclopédie* (Supplement, XI, art. 'Soieries', Plates 8-20). Similar machines were first used in France about the same time as in England, and were known as *Piedmontese mills*.

[2] *Journals of the House of Commons*, XXX, 209-20.

[3] Ibid., XXX, 212-13.

[4] *Gentleman's Magazine*, 1739, p. 4.

knighted, and when in 1732 Parliament at the request of the other manufacturers refused to renew his patent, he was given £14,000 as indemnity and reward.[1] Not only was he a rich and powerful person but he was also regarded as a public benefactor, to whom the country acknowledged itself to be indebted.

It would therefore appear that the journey of John Lombe was the real beginning of the factory system in England. How is it, then, that this important event should have been so neglected, and that the cotton industry should, so to speak, have usurped the place of honour due by rights to the silk industry? Can this be due only to national pride, wanting to give to modern large-scale industry a purely British origin? We must not forget that by the phrase modern factory system we mean a whole economic and social world, considered not as a collection of abstract conditions but as a living reality. We are looking not for its theoretical origin but for its historical beginnings. When we have to define and classify phenomena from the economic or philosophical point of view, it is enough if we only consider their characteristics. But, from the historical point of view, we must also take into consideration what we may call their volume and their weight, their actual effect on surrounding phenomena, everything which determined the material relationship of facts, so different sometimes from the logical chain of principles and consequences.

Even after the introduction of machinery and the birth of great industrial undertakings, the silk industry in England never held any but a secondary position. Several places became centres of production: London, Derby, Stockport near Manchester,[2] Macclesfield, where the manufacture of thrown silk employed, in 1761, nearly two thousand five hundred workmen.[3] But in none of these centres did any industrial change take place comparable to that produced in Lancashire and Derbyshire by the invention of the cotton-spinning machines. The causes which hampered the progress of the English silk industry were the excessively high price of raw silk, especially since the King of Sardinia had forbidden its export, and the discouraging competition of the French and Italian industries whose superiority was partly due to their natural advantages. This led to frequent crises, which were unsuccessfully dealt with by protective measures;[4] to repeated com-

---

[1] 5 Geo. III, c. 8. *Journals of the House of Commons*, XXI, 782-95.

[2] In 1770 there were four factories and a thousand workers in Stockport. *Journals of the House of Commons*, XXXIV, 240.

[3] Ibid., XXX, 215 ff. The ribbon industry of Coventry has its own history.

[4] See 3 Geo. III, c. 21; 5 Geo. III, c. 48. These measures only half satisfied the manufacturers, who several times asked for the complete prohibition of foreign stuffs, together with heavy penalties for smuggling. *Journals of the House of Commons*, XXX, 87, 93, 725.

plaints from the employers, and rioting among the workers;[1] and ultimately to what can be described as the stunting of the industry's growth – a great contrast to the development of the other textile industries.[2]

Technical progress stopped at the same time. The introduction of the silk-throwing machine was the point of departure of no new invention. In the weaving and in the finishing of the material the old processes were maintained, together with the system of small-scale production. The Spitalfields weavers, whose coalitions, strikes and riots we have mentioned before, worked at home. Their employers were merchants and contractors rather than manufacturers, and the reasons for their antagonism were only those which were, slowly and surely, transforming the old industries. John and Thomas Lombe, with their factory on the river Derwent, were precursors rather than initiators. The industrial revolution had been heralded, but had not yet begun.

II

The continuous progress of the cotton industry stands in contrast to this incomplete, or at any rate limited development. From the cotton industry came that decisive impulse which in a few years spread to the whole textile industry, and which is all the more striking as its origins were of a more recent date. For several centuries the word cotton has formed part of the English language. But until the seventeenth century its meaning was different from that which it has nowadays. It was used for certain coarse woollens, made in the north of England.[3] For a long

[1] See Part I, chap. I.

[2] See G. B. Hertz, 'The English Silk Industry in the Eighteenth Century' (*English Historical Review*, 1909, pp. 710-29).

[3] 'As late as 1700 ... cottons were still enumerated among "manufactures of wool"' (11 & 12 Will. III, c. 20). G. W. Daniels, *The Early English Cotton Industry*, p. 7. In an Act of 1552 (5 & 6 Edw. VI, c. 6) which also mentions the 'cottons, rugges and friezes made in Lancashire', the minimum weight of 30 lb. for a piece 22 yards long and ¾ yard broad is clearly meant for woollen fabrics. In 5 Eliz. c. 4 (1563) persons 'inhabiting within the counties of Cumberland, Westmorland, Lancaster and Wales, weaving friezes, cottons, or huswives cloth' are described as woollen cloth weavers. The Lancashire woollen industry had been prosperous since the thirteenth century (*Victoria History of the County of Lancaster*, II, 376). It might seem surprising that the word cotton in England applied to woollens, while in Spain and Italy the words *coton, cotone*, had long been used as they are in our own times. But A. de Candolle observes that a similar confusion lies at the very origin of the word, the Arabic words for cotton (Kutn) and flax (Kattan or Kittan) being practically the same (*Origine des Plantes Cultivées*, p. 325). It should be noticed not only that in Italy and Spain cotton had been spun and woven since the twelfth century, but that in Southern Germany the stuff known as 'barchent', mentioned as early as the fourteenth century, consisted of linen warp and cotton weft. See R. Lévy, *Histoire Économique de l'Industrie Cotonnière en Alsace*, pp. 3, 4, 7, and G. W. Daniels, *The Early*

time the word kept that meaning, and even today it may perhaps still do so in certain districts of Cumberland and Westmorland.[1] We must note that Manchester was one of the best-known districts for the manufacture of cottons.[2] But between the industry mentioned in Camden's *Britannia*[3] and that which in our day has made Manchester's fortune, there is not much in common save the name.

Cotton goods, made in the East, and above all in India, had from time immemorial been imported into the countries on the Mediterranean, whose inhabitants at an early date attempted to imitate them. In northern countries this imitation took place much later. It was only in the fourteenth century that raw cotton, brought by Venetian merchants from the Levant, made its appearance in Flanders. Antwerp was the town where the spinning and weaving of cotton were at first centred. It was an unimportant industry, quite unable to compete in any way with the woollen industry, which then flourished throughout Flanders. In 1585, after the siege and capture of Antwerp by Alexander Farnese, a certain number of workmen emigrated to England. This was, according to Schulze-Gaevernitz, the origin of the English cotton industry.[4]

The first document in which this industry is unequivocally mentioned dates from 1610. It is a petition from a certain Maurice Peeters – a Flemish-sounding name – to the Earl of Salisbury, to denounce daily fraudulent practices 'in the manufacture of bombazine cotton, such as groweth in the land of Persia, being no kind of wool'.[5] Thirty years later

---

[1] See *A Complete History of the Cotton Trade* (1823), p. 40; A. Ure, *The Cotton Manufacture of Great Britain* (1836), I, 30 f. 'A species of coarse cloth, called Kendal cottons.' F. M. Eden, *State of the Poor*, II, 751.

[2] 'The towne at that age (sixteenth century) was of great account for certain woollen clothes there wrought, and in great request, commonly called Manchester cottons.' R. Hollingworth, *Mancuniensis*, p. 64 – a book written in the middle of the seventeenth century, and published by W. Willis in 1839.

[3] 'Hoc circumvicinis oppidis suo ornatu, frequentia, lanificio, foro, templo, collegio a Grislaeis et La Waris, ut ex insignibus deprehendi, constructo longe praecellens. Superiori vero aetate multo praecellentius tum laneorum pannorum honore (quos *Manchester cottons* vocant) tum asyli jure, quod Parliamentaria auctoritas sub Henrico VIII Cestriam transtulit.' William Camden, *Britanniæ Descriptio* (1586), p. 429.

[4] Schulze-Gaevernitz, *La Grande Industrie* (*Der Grossbetrieb, ein wirtschaftlicher und socialer Fortschritt*), p. 27.

[5] *State Papers, Dom.*, LIX, 5. W. H. Price, 'On the Beginning of the Cotton Industry in England', *Quarterly Journal of Economics*, XX, 608-13, quotes a petition of 1620, kept in the London Guildhall Library (*Petitions and Parliamentary Matters*, 1620-1, No. 16), according to which the cotton industry in England dated either from the very beginning of the seventeenth century or the last years of the sixteenth: 'About

---

English Cotton Industry, p. 14. The latter writes: 'It is hard to resist a suspicion that the vegetable fibre, cotton, may have been used in the manufacture of Lancashire cloths … ' Ibid., p. 7.

we find that industry established in Manchester, as is witnessed by Lewes Roberts, 'merchant and captaine of the City of London'. He mentions Manchester's commercial relations with Ireland: 'Neither doth the industry rest here, for they buy Cotten wooll, in *London*, that comes first from *Cyprus*, and *Smyrna*, and at home worke the same, and perfit it into Fustians, Vermilions, Dymities, and other such Stuffes; and then returne it to *London*, where the same is vented and sold, and not seldome sent into forraigne parts, who have meanes at far easier termes, to provide themselves of the said first materials.'[1] It can be therefore said that early in the seventeenth century Lancashire, and Manchester in particular, were in possession of their famous speciality.

During this early period of the cotton industry in England the quality of the product was rather poor, and its quantity insignificant. Almost all the cotton stuffs sold in London and in the chief towns came, more or less directly, from India. Though it is rather difficult to define, there was a very close connection between this old-established import on the one hand and this new-born product on the other. We have seen that the development of the colonial, and especially of the Indian, trade was one of the main characteristics of the great economic movement which took shape towards the end of the seventeenth century. One of the chief products sold to the British public, and for which the demand grew ever greater, was cotton material, flowered fabrics, either painted or printed. Fashion took it up, and soon these stuffs were all the rage: 'We saw our persons of quality dressed in Indian Carpets, which, but a few years before, their chambermaids would have thought too ordinary for them; the chintzes were advanced from lying on their floors to their backs, from the foot cloth to the petticoat, and even the Queen herself[2] at that time was pleased to appear in China and Japan, I mean China silks and calicoes. Nor was this all, but it crept into our houses, our closets and bedchambers; curtains, cushions, chairs, and, at last, beds themselves were nothing but calicoes or Indian stuffs.'[3]

At the same time there arose on all sides a tempest of recriminations and complaints. What was going to become of the staple trade of the Kingdom, the privileged woollen industry, if this foreign competition

[1] Lewes Roberts, *The Treasure of Traffike*, p. 32 (London, 1641).
[2] Queen Mary, wife of William of Orange.
[3] Defoe, *Weekly Review*, January 1708.

---

twenty years past divers people in this kingdom, but chiefly in the county of Lancaster, have found out the trade of making of other fustians, made of a kind of bombast or down, being a fruit of the earth growing upon little shrubs or bushes, brought into this kingdom by the Turkey merchants, from Smyrna, Cyprus, Acra, and Sydon, but commonly called cotton wool ... There is at the least 40 thousand pieces of fustian of this kind yearly made in England ... and thousands of poor people set on working of these fustians.'

was allowed? We know that the woollen industry was not used to submitting patiently to any competition whatsoever. Parliament hastened to its aid. In 1700 an Act was passed forbidding absolutely the import of printed fabrics from India, Persia and China. All goods seized in contravention of this edict were to be confiscated, sold by auction and re-exported.[1]

This drastic step cannot have produced the results expected of it, for very soon complaints were renewed.[2] About 1719 they became very pressing, and again Parliament was besieged with petitions.[3] Many pamphlets were published, in which the manufacturers of woollen goods inveighed against the fashion of printed cottons.[4] And they did not stop at words. Trouble broke out in several places. The weavers, exasperated by continued unemployment, began to attack in the streets people dressed in cotton material, tearing and burning their clothes. Houses were even broken into and sacked.[5] This agitation was only brought to an end after a new Act of prohibition had been passed, even more explicit and far-reaching than the first. 'Whereas it is most evident that the weaving and using of printed, painted, stained and dyed calicoes in apparel, household stuff, furniture and otherwise, does manifestly tend to the great detriment of the woollen and silk manufactures of this Kingdom, and to the excessive increase of the poor, and, if not effectually prevented, may be the utter ruin and destruction of the said manufactures, and of many thousands of Your Majesty's subjects and their families, whose livelihood does entirely depend thereon', all persons resident in England were forbidden to sell or to buy these fabrics, or to wear them or to have them in their possession, under penalty of a £5 fine for private persons and £20 for merchants.[6] Such

---

[1] 11 & 12 Will. III, c. 10. Bales of merchandise for the export trade were temporarily allowed into British ports, but only if they were declared at the customs and put into a bonded warehouse. See Bal Krishna, *Commercial Relations between India and England from* 1601 *to* 1757, pp. 194 ff., and C. J. Hamilton, *Trade Relations between England and India* (1660-1896).

[2] A pamphlet of 1706 deplores 'the wearing of printed or stained callicoes, brought from India'. J. Haynes, *A View of the present State of the Clothing Trade in England*, p. 19.

[3] Very curiously one of these petitions is in opposition to all the others. For it pleads the case for cotton fabrics, in the interest of the cloth trade, showing that a fall in the price of English woollen goods must be followed by an increase in the quantity exported. *Journals of the House of Commons*, XIX, 254.

[4] *The just Complaints of the poor Weaver truly represented* (1719); *A brief State of the Question between printed and painted Callicoes and Silk Manufactures* (1719); *The Weaver's true Case* (1720); *The further Case of the Woollen and Silk Manufacturers* (1720). And for the opposite case: J. Asgill, *Brief Answer to a Brief State of the Question between the Printed and Painted Callicoes and the Woollen and Silk Manufacturers* (1719); *The Weaver's Pretences examined* (1719). We are indebted to Prof. Foxwell for our knowledge of most of these pamphlets.

[5] See *The Weaver's true Case*, p. 40; *The Weaver's Pretences examined*, p. 16.

[6] 7 Geo I, st. I, c. 7.

facts could not help affecting the development of the cotton industry in England. When the import of Indian materials was quite unrestricted, the demand they created already held out the promise of success and fortune to whosoever was capable of imitating them.[1] After the prohibition of 1700 these chances were greatly increased. The public, deprived of a favourite article, or at any rate forced to secure it through unlawful channels, welcomed the still clumsy attempts of English weavers.

Lancashire, where the seeds of this industry had already begun to germinate, offered a most favourable ground for its development. During the preceding century raw cotton had been brought from Smyrna to London, and from London to Manchester. But Liverpool was growing, and received cotton direct from the East and West Indies.[2] For the East no longer had the monopoly of cotton growing. It flourished in the Antilles and in Brazil.[3] Moreover, whilst India and China only exported their surplus crop, practically the whole of the American crop was sent to European ports. In this way a double stream of imports converged on Liverpool – but that would not have been enough to determine the growth of the cotton industry in Lancashire.

[1] Rights of patent were granted in 1691 to one John Barkstead for 'the making of callicoes, muslins and other fine cloathes of the sort out of the cotton wool of the growth and product of their Majesties plantations in the West Indies'. See *Chronological Index of Patents*, No. 276 (Sept. 22nd, 1691).

[2] It was only in the second part of the eighteenth century that Liverpool left London behind as the great cotton market (T. Ellison, *The Cotton Trade of Great Britain*, pp. 170-1). But early in the century much cotton was already imported by Liverpool merchants, and also through the smaller ports of Whitehaven and Lancaster. *Journals of the House of Commons*, XXII, 566-7, quoted by G. W. Daniels, *The Early English Cotton Industry*, pp. 57-8. See also St Dumbell, 'Early Liverpool Cotton Imports and the Organization of the Cotton Market in the Eighteenth Century', *Economic Journal*, XXXIII, 363 ff. By 1752, 106 ships, out of the 220 owned at Liverpool, were engaged in the West Indian and American trade.

[3] The North American colonies only took up cotton growing later on. The cotton imports from Charleston or New York mentioned from time to time after 1747 were probably imports of West Indian cottons in ships which had put in at some North American ports. See T. Ellison, *Cotton Trade of Great Britain*, p. 81, and E. von Halle, 'Baumwollproduktion und Pflanzenwirtschaft in den Nordamerikanischen Südstaaten', *Staats-und socialwissenschaftliche Forschungen*, 15, I, p. 9. This accounts for the surprise shown by the Customs Officers who in 1784 were present at the unloading in Liverpool of eight bales of cotton brought in an American ship, and declared to originate from the United States. They refused to accept this declaration, and seized the bales under the Navigation Act: for cotton from the West Indies, as they believed it to be, was not allowed to be imported under a foreign flag – and this happened a year after the Treaty of Versailles had finally severed the North American colonies from the mother country (J. Bishop, *History of American Manufactures*, I, 354; T. Ellison, op. cit., p. 82). Mention is made of the fact in a contemporary French document ('Considérations sur les Manufactures de Mousseline de Callico dans la Grande Bretagne', Archives des Affaires Étrangères, Angleterre, Mémoires et Documents, LXXIV, fol. 182).

Cotton spinning demands special climatic conditions – a fairly damp atmosphere and no great difference between the maximum and minimum temperatures. These conditions exist in Lancashire. In Bolton the average summer temperature is about 60° Fahrenheit, and the average in winter 40°. The average hygrometric condition is 0.82, that of the wettest month 0.93, and that of the driest month 0.78.[1] The high hills on the east and north of Manchester, towards Ashton and Rochdale, stop the clouds from the sea, their steep slopes receiving most of the rain, which for the whole county reaches an annual average of about 40 inches. It has been observed that factories tend more and more to establish themselves in this wet area, where the constant moisture of the atmosphere makes it possible to spin exceptionally fine counts.[2]

The only things the Lancashire spinners, both male and female, lacked were the supple fingers and the extraordinary skill of the Indian workmen. The counts they spun, with implements as a matter of fact scarcely better than those used in India,[3] were either too coarse or too weak. The custom therefore grew up of making materials of mixed linen and cotton. The linen thread, being stronger, formed the warp, and the cotton the woof.[4] These were the materials which, at the beginning, laid the foundations of Manchester's reputation. Printed by hand with engraved plates, they were able, if not to rival those of India, yet to serve as more or less acceptable substitutes, so that public taste could be satisfied, in spite of prohibitive legislation.

This was exactly what the woollen-cloth merchants had feared. Their campaign of 1715-20 seemed to be directed only against foreign goods, in the name of the British staple industry. As a matter of fact it was really a question of suppressing a competition which was becoming the more dangerous for having been set up in England itself. The selfishness of organized trade interests in our times is probably quite as pitiless as it was then, but it is no longer so artlessly expressed. No one

---

[1] Sir Benjamin Dobson, *Humidity in Cotton Spinning*, pp. 17-22. The plates (pp. 44, 45, 59, 67, 73) show that the cohesion and evenness of the cotton thread varies with the moisture of the atmosphere.

[2] Schulze-Gaevernitz, *La Grande Industrie*, pp. 58 and 108. Mr Chapman seems to undervalue the effect of natural causes when he writes: 'Indeed, the cotton industry itself settled in Lancashire for no particular reason, except perhaps that the woollen industry was already there, that foreigners were kindly received, and that Manchester was not a corporation.' He nevertheless admits that 'as soon as the value of the physical features in certain parts of Lancashire began to be realized, the manufacture in other districts tended to be drawn with increasing force to the main seat of the industry'. S. Chapman, *The Lancashire Cotton Industry*, p. 154.

[3] A few improvements had been adopted from the woollen industry, for example the spinning wheel and metal cards.

[4] See the preamble to 9 Geo. II, c. 4: 'Whereas great quantities of stuffs made of linen yarn and cotton wool have for several years past been manufactured and have been printed and painted within this Kingdom of Great Britain ... '

today would write denouncing as a crime the attempt to establish a new industry in the country: 'As if the Nation was never to want a set of men to undo her, no sooner were the East Indian chintz and printed callicoes prohibited from abroad, but some of Britain's unnatural children set all their arts to work, to evade the law of prohibition, to employ people to mimick the more ingenious Indian, and to legitimate the grievance by making it a manufacture.'[1] When people lamented the fate of those thousands who were going to be deprived of work and bread, some unprejudiced persons could not help remarking that, on the other hand, many were about to obtain work in the new workshops which were being opened.[2] To this it was answered that the number of workmen employed in the cotton industry was very small.[3] But if this industry was so insignificant, how could its competition be represented as a formidable menace to the ancient and powerful woollen trade?

Thus nothing was neglected to kill the cotton industry at its birth. But it survived. The use of painted and printed calico alone was forbidden. The manufacture of the material was uninterrupted. With regard to the printing, we have every reason to believe that it was soon tolerated, for rarely does law triumph over fashion. As early as 1735 manufacturers got Parliament to pass an Act formally exempting from the prohibition of 1721 all stuffs made of mixed linen and cotton, on the ground that it was 'a branch of the ancient fustian manufacture'.[4] Prohibition was maintained against pure cotton fabrics both painted and printed. It only came to an end in 1774,[5] on the request of Richard Arkwright.

This story of the beginnings of the cotton industry is interesting in several ways. It is a clear example of the influence of commercial on industrial development. The new industry was the child of the East Indian trade. Its creation followed the import of a foreign product, and the place and conditions of its establishment were partly determined by the fact that the raw material was imported from abroad. A no less interesting feature is the part played by the ancient textile industry. It was that very industry which, by its blind passion for monopoly, stirred up that competition which it tried to kill a few years later: for it is from the prohibition of 1700 that the success of English-made cotton goods, as a substitute for Indian fabrics, can be said to date. Finally, from that time onwards the contrast between the two industries is very

[1] *The just Complaints of the poor Weaver truly represented*, p. 14.

[2] J. Asgill, *Brief Answer to a Brief State of the Question between the Printed and Painted Callicoes and the Woollen and Silk Manufacturers; The Weaver's Pretences examined; Reasons humbly offered to the House of Commons by the Calico Printers*.

[3] *The just Complaints of the poor Weaver*, p. 25.

[4] 9 Geo. II, c. 4. See short history of the Acts of 1721 and 1735 in G. W. Daniels, *The Early English Cotton Industry*, pp. 20 ff.

[5] 14 Geo. III, c. 72.

clear and enables us to understand the rapid evolution of the one, and
the more difficult and slower development of the other. A new industry
without traditions had, instead of privileges, all the advantages of
freedom. The fact that it was not fettered by tradition and stood outside the regulations which stopped, or at any rate hampered technical
development, made it, so to speak, a field for inventions and for every
kind of initiative. Thus a favourable ground was prepared for the building up of machine industry.

III

In the organization of the work, as well as in its implements, the
cotton industry began by being in every respect like the woollen
industry. It was a cottage industry. The Lancashire weaver worked in
the country, in his own house standing on its own plot of ground.[1] The
women and children carded and span.[2] Nowhere was a close alliance
between agriculture and industry more necessary. The wet and misty
climate and the prevalence of moorlands and marshes forced the
country people to find other means of livelihood besides work on the
land.

Along with the usual features of the domestic system we find here
again traces of that natural evolution which gradually brought in the
capitalist element. Towards 1740 and 1750 a class of men made their
appearance in Lancashire, who in every way resembled the merchant
manufacturers of the south-west; they were called fustian masters.
They bought the raw material, linen thread and raw cotton, and gave
them out to the weavers. The weavers undertook the preparatory
processes of carding, roving and spinning, and they thus became sub-
contractors as well as workmen. Often indeed we find below them a
second class of middlemen, the spinners, who, being paid by the
weavers, had in their turn to pay the carders and rovers.[3] Once woven

[1] Edwin Butterworth, *History of Oldham*, pp. 105-7.

[2] At Mellor in 1770, 'out of fifty or sixty farmers, there were only six or seven
who raised their rents directly from the produce of their farms: all the rest got their
rent partly in some branch of trade, such as spinning and weaving woollens, linen, or
cotton'. As for the cottagers, they were spinners or weavers in winter and worked
in the fields in summer. W. Radcliffe, *Origin of the New System of Manufacture, commonly
called 'Power Loom Weaving'*, pp. 9 and 59-60. 'Farms were mostly cultivated for the production of milk, butter and cheese … And, when that was finished, they busied
themselves in carding, slubbing and spinning wool or cotton, as well as in forming it
into warps for the loom.' S. Bamford, *Dialect of South Lancashire*, pp. iv and v. For a
picturesque description of the domestic system of manufacture in the cotton industry
see L. W. Moffit, *England on the Eve of the Industrial Revolution*, p. 210.

[3] R. Guest, *A compendious history of the cotton-manufacture*, p. 10; Edwin Butterworth, *History of Oldham*, p. 103. Butterworth seems, in some of the facts he quotes,
to have borrowed from Guest.

the material was handed over to the fustian master, who sold it again to the actual merchants.[1] Thus the division of labour was fairly advanced. Moreover, while spinning was still given out in the villages there was a tendency for weaving to concentrate in certain localities, the most important being Manchester.

Thus constituted, the industry made sufficient progress to justify, if not the jealousy and alarm of which it nearly became the victim, at any rate a good opinion of its vitality and its future.[2] Manchester, about the middle of the eighteenth century, is said to have sent cotton goods to Italy, Germany, the North American colonies, to Africa, Asia Minor, and even to China, through Russia.[3] But, according to the Customs Registers,[4] the total value of the cotton goods exported from England did not exceed £46,000; and when, on the occasion of George III's Coronation in 1760, Manchester had a great procession of trades 'with suitable dresses and colours'[5] the cotton spinners and weavers were not represented. The cotton manufacture was still small and weak in comparison with the great woollen industry; but the series of inventions which were to cause its rapid transformation, followed by that of all other textile industries, had already begun.

A mistake we should guard against is the common one of always and everywhere regarding technical inventions as the outcome of scientific discoveries. Of course we do not for a moment deny the decisive influence of science on technical progress.[6] But a closer exami-

---

[1] As in the woollen industry, dyeing and finishing were done at the expense of the merchant. R. Guest, op. cit., p. 11. G. W. Daniels observes that early in the seventeenth century Humphrey Chetham was playing in Manchester the part of master manufacturer (*The Early English Cotton Industry*, pp. 35-6).

[2] See *The late Improvements in Trade, Navigation and Manufactures considered* (1739) in J. Smith, *Memoirs of Wool*, II, 89. See also document of 1751 quoted by Daniels, pp. 25-6, in which it is said of Manchester that 'there is not any town in the nation, excepting our sea ports, that may be compared with it in trade, as appears from the number of packs of goods which go weekly out of the town, which amount by a modest computation to 500'.

[3] W. Radcliffe, *Origin of the New System of Manufacture, commonly called 'Power Loom Weaving'*, pp. 12 and 131-3.

[4] Quoted by E. Baines, *History of the Cotton Manufacture*, p. 215.

[5] *The Manchester Guide* (1804), p. 41.

[6] What follows is by no means in contradiction with the generally accepted idea (so clearly laid down in Sombart's *Moderne Kapitalismus*, II, 60) that the capital economic event of the eighteenth century was the transformation of industrial technique under the influence of science. But that very event had been made possible by an earlier series of inventions of a purely empirical origin. It must be recognized, at the same time, that the interest shown by the enlightened public in the technique of trades (a characteristic feature of the century) helped in finding means to encourage mechanical invention. The foundation of the Society of Arts in England (1754) took place at the same time as the publication of Diderot's monumental descriptions of trades in the French *Encyclopédie*. On the multiplication of such societies and

nation of the subject shows that this progress (prior to the triumph of technique in the nineteenth century) may be divided into two distinct phases. Only in the second of these does science make its appearance. The first is all empiricism and tentative endeavour, and is sufficiently accounted for by economic needs and the spontaneous efforts they call forth. Every technical question is first and foremost a practical question. Before ever it becomes a problem to be solved by men with theoretic knowledge, it forces itself upon the men in the trade as a difficulty to be overcome, or a material advantage to be gained. There is, as it were, an instinctive effort which not only precedes but is a necessary condition to the appearance of conscious effort. 'It is well known,' said Serjeant Adair when pleading for Richard Arkwright in 1785, 'that the most useful discoveries that have been made in every branch of art and manufactures have not been made by speculative philosophers in their closets, but by ingenious mechanics, conversant in the practices in use in their time, and practically acquainted with the subject-matter of their discoveries.'[1]

An idea which flashes suddenly into the mind of a genius, and whose application produces no less suddenly an economic revolution, is what we might describe as the romantic theory of invention.[2] Nowhere do we find evidence of such creations *a nihilo*, bursting forth like miracles, which only the mysterious power of individual inspiration could explain. The history of inventions is not only that of inventors but that of collective experience, which gradually solves the problems set by collective needs.

The first of the inventions by which the textile industries were transformed, and that which must be considered as the origin of all the others, was a simple improvement in the old weaving loom: the invention of the fly shuttle by John Kay, in 1733. Born in 1704, near Bury in Lancashire, John Kay first worked for a Colchester clothier. About 1730 we find him making combs for the looms.[3] He was therefore half weaver and half mechanic, and was accustomed to using the implement which he later on tried to improve. In that same year 1730 he produced his first invention, a new process 'for carding and roving mohair and worsted'.[4] To him also is attributed the introduction of

[1] *R. Arkwright* versus *Peter Nightingale*, pp. 1-2.
[2] J. A. Hobson uses the expression 'heroic theory', *The Evolution of Modern Capitalism*, p. 57. See L. Brentano, *Über die Ursachen der heutigen socialen Not*, p. 30.
[3] Bennet Woodcroft, *Brief Biographies of Inventors*, p. 2.
[4] *Abridgments of Specifications relating to Weaving*, I, 3 (Patent No. 515).

their activities, see W. Bowden, *Industrial Society in England towards the end of the Eighteenth Century*, pp. 10-12, 38 ff. Compare with Henri Sée, 'Les Origines de l'Industrie Capitaliste en France', *Revue historique*, CXLIV (1923), pp. 188 ff.

steel combs, instead of those made of wood or horn, with which the early looms were fitted.[1]

The invention of the fly shuttle was demanded by a practical difficulty which manufacturers daily experienced. It was impossible to obtain material of more than a certain width without employing two or more workmen. The width of the material which a single workman could make by throwing the shuttle from one hand to the other was obviously limited by the length of his arms. Kay arranged for the shuttle to be automatically thrown from one side of the loom to the other.[2] For this purpose he fitted the shuttle with small wheels and set it in a kind of wooden groove, fixed so that it did not interfere with the alternating rise and fall of the warp. On either side, in order to give it a to-and-fro motion, he put two wooden hammers hung on horizontal rods. The two hammers were bound together by two strings attached to a single handle, so that with one hand the shuttle could be driven either way. The arrangement worked in the following manner: with a sharp tap the weaver caused first one and then the other hammer to move on its rod. It hit the shuttle, which slid along its groove. At the end of each rod there was a spring to stop the hammer and replace it in position.[3]

Not only did the fly shuttle enable broader material to be woven, but weaving could also be done much more quickly than formerly. John Kay could not avoid the complaint urged against all inventors, for the Colchester weavers accused him of trying to deprive them of their daily bread. In 1738 he tried his fortune in Leeds. There he met with no less fierce hostility from the manufacturers, who were quite ready to use his shuttle but refused to pay the royalties he claimed. There were endless lawsuits, the manufacturers formed 'the Shuttle Club' to meet the costs, and Kay was ruined by legal expenses.[4] In 1745 he left Leeds and

---

[1] R. W. Cooke Taylor, *Introduction to a History of the Factory System*, p. 405.

[2] The *Dutch loom*, which had been in use for a century, not only was a clumsy contrivance, the shuttle being moved by a system of cog wheels, but could be used only for weaving ribbons.

[3] See the specification attached to the patent and dated May 26th, 1733:

'A new invented shuttle, for the better and more exact weaving of broad cloths, broad bays, sail cloths, or any other broad goods ... which shuttle is much lighter than the former, and by running on four wheels moves over the lower side of the web and spring, on a board about nine feet long put under the same and fastened to the layer; and which new contrived shuttle, by the two wooden tenders, invented for that purpose and hung to the layer, and a small cord commanded by the hand of the weaver, the weaver, sitting in the middle of the loom, with great ease and expedition by a small pull at the cord casts or moves the said new invented shuttle from side to side to pleasure ... ' *Abridgments of Specifications relating to Weaving*, I, No. 542. See the plates in the French *Encyclopédie*, I, vol. III of the supplement, article 'Draperie'.

[4] A. Barlow, *History and Principles of Weaving*, p. 96; Bennet Woodcroft, *Brief Biographies of Inventors*, p. 3; 'Cotton-spinning Machines and their Inventors', *Quarterly Review*, CVII, 49.

returned to Bury, his native place. His opponents' hostility pursued him there, and in 1753 there was even a riot, the mob breaking in and sacking his house. The wretched inventor fled, first to Manchester, which he left, it was said, hidden in a sack of wool,[1] and then to France. In spite of opposition, which still went on for many years, the use of the fly shuttle soon became general, and by 1760 its influence began to be felt in all branches of the textile industry.[2]

This invention had incalculable consequences. The various processes in an industry form one whole, and are comparable to a system of interdependent movements all responding to the same rhythm. The effect of a technical improvement accelerating only one of these operations is to break the common rhythm, upsetting, as it were, the balance of the system. So long as the various operations remain uneven, and do not succeed in regaining their equilibrium, the whole industry remains unstable and subject to oscillations: these slowly become more regular and at length give rise to a fresh rhythm of production.[3] In the textile industry the two chief processes are spinning and weaving. Normally they must work at the same pace. The amount of thread spun in any given time should correspond to the amount of material which can be woven in the same time. The looms must not stand idle for lack of thread, nor the spinning mills run the risk of stoppage because they have spun too quickly.

In the old textile industry the balance was hard to maintain. We know that a single loom provided work for five or six spinning wheels.[4] In spite of imports there was normally an almost constant shortage of thread.[5] As soon as the fly shuttle enabled the weaver to work much faster this shortage became still greater. Not only did the price of thread go up, but it was often impossible to obtain the necessary quantity within a limited time. From this there often resulted delays in the delivery of material, much to the detriment of the manufacturers.[6]

---

[1] Bennet Woodcroft, op. cit., pp. 4-5; *A Complete History of the Cotton Trade*, p. 302.

[2] In London in 1767 there was a violent conflict between the 'narrow weavers' and the 'engine weavers'. See *Annual Register*, 1767, p. 152. In some districts the fly shuttle was only introduced much later. In Wiltshire and Somerset it hardly made its appearance before the nineteenth century. See *Journals of the House of Commons*, LVIII, 885. J. L. and L. B. Hammond (*The Skilled Labourer*, p. 159) mention disturbances caused in Frome as late as 1822 by the introduction of 'spring looms'. The invention in 1760 of the drop box, by Robert Kay (son of John Kay), completed that of the fly shuttle and contributed to its final success.

[3] This process is very well described and analysed in J. A. Hobson's *Evolution of Modern Capitalism*, p. 59.

[4] See Part I, chap. I.

[5] Especially in summer when work in the fields occupied the whole rural population. See the testimony of Henry Hall, President of the Worsted Committee, quoted by J. James, *History of the Worsted Manufacture*, p. 312.

[6] Similar facts took place in Germany for the same reasons and nearly at the

Weavers, who had to pay the spinners, found it hard to make a living. This state of affairs could not last, and a new balance had to be found. Some means had to be devised of spinning yarn quickly enough to keep pace with the weavers. As this necessity became more and more pressing, research became more and more active, until a practical solution was finally discovered.

IV

The cotton industry was specially well adapted as a field for experiments. With regard to the problem of mechanical spinning it afforded especially favourable conditions for inventors. For cotton fibre, being more cohesive and less elastic than wool, is easier to twist and stretch into a continuous thread.

The origin of the spinning machine is still wrapped in some obscurity. Two men, John Wyatt and Lewis Paul, had a hand in it, and it is difficult to determine what part each of them played.[1] Lewis Paul appears as the more important person. He took out in 1738 the original patent, in which Wyatt's name is not even mentioned.[2] He it was whom his contemporaries regarded as the inventor. Nevertheless it is probable that Paul did much less, and Wyatt much more than might be supposed, judging by appearances.

John Wyatt was born in 1700 in a village near Lichfield. He at first became a ship's carpenter.[3] But he was a born inventor, with that special temperament whose manifestations are so closely allied to instinct. He kept inventing all his life, and the variety of his successive schemes was no less astonishing than their number: harpoons shot from a gun, improved weighing machines, machines to mend and level roads.

---

[1] Chas. Wyatt (*On the Origin of Cotton Spinning by Machinery*, Repertory of the Arts, Manufactures and Agriculture, Series II, vol. XXXII, 1818) claims for his father the honour of the invention. R. Cole (*Some Account of Lewis Paul*, published as an appendix to French's *Life and Times of Samuel Crompton*) maintains on the other hand that Lewis Paul was the real inventor. According to E. Baines (*History of the Cotton Manufacture*, pp. 119 ff.) the machine was invented by Wyatt and improved by Lewis Paul. B. P. Dobson is the latest supporter of Lewis Paul's claims (*The Story of the Evolution of the Spinning Machine*, pp. 51-2). But he produces no new evidence disproving that of the manuscripts kept in the Birmingham Central Library (No. 93189), which are quoted below.

[2] *Abridgments of Specifications relating to Weaving*, I, No. 562. Letter from W. James to the bookseller Warren, July 17th, 1740: 'Yesterday we went to see Mr Paul's machine, which gave us all entire satisfaction both in regard to the carding and the spinning.' R. Cole, *Some Account of Lewis Paul*, p. 256.

[3] *John Wyatt, Master Carpenter & Inventor*, pp. 1-4.

---

same time as in England. See J. Kulischer, 'Die Ursachen des Übergangs von der Handarbeit zur maschinellen Betriebsweise um die Wende des 18ten und in der ersten Hälfte des 19ten Jahrhunderts', *Jahrbuch für Gesetzgebung*, XXX, 38-40 (1906).

His notes, which are preserved in the Birmingham Central Library, are full of specifications and drawings.[1] His first invention seems to have been a machine for turning and boring metals, which was purchased by a Birmingham armourer called Richard Heeley.[2] This man got into financial difficulties, and finding himself, apparently, unable to fulfil his engagements he finally made over his rights to a third party. This new owner was Lewis Paul, who thus came into touch with Wyatt. The contract by which these two men bound themselves to exploit the invention abandoned by Heeley is dated September 19th, 1732.[3]

Lewis Paul, the son of a French refugee and the protégé of the Earl of Shaftesbury, was intelligent and pushing; he had the manners of a gentleman, and pretensions somewhat above his station. He was acquainted with some rich or notable persons, as for instance Cave, the editor of the *Gentleman's Magazine*, and Dr Johnson.[4] Wyatt no doubt hoped to make something out of him, and perhaps Paul made him believe he had money.[5] In any case they joined forces, and their association lasted over ten years.

At the time John Wyatt met Lewis Paul he had, if we may believe his son Charles Wyatt, already conceived the idea of a spinning machine. He produced it in the following year (1733): 'In the year 1730, or thereabouts, living then at a village near Litchfield, our respected father first conceived the project and prepared to carry it into effect; and in the year 1733, by a model of about two feet square, in a small building near Sutton Coldfield, without a single witness to the performance, was spun the first thread of cotton ever produced without the intervention of the human fingers,[6] he, the inventor, to use his own words, "*being all the time in a pleasing but trembling suspense*".'[7] Several references in John Wyatt's original papers agree with this account. In

[1] Wyatt MSS., I, 1, 8, 21, and II, 16, 25, 30, 32.

[2] Ibid., I, 4.

[3] 'Articles of agreement indented, had, made, concluded and fully agreed upon the 19th day of September, in the sixth year of the reign of our Sovereign Lord George the Second, by the grace of God, etc., and in the year of our Lord 1732, between Lewis Paul gentleman, of the parish of St Andrews, Holborn, in the county of Middlesex, of the one part, and John Wyatt of the parish of Weeford and county of Stafford, carpenter.' Paul promised Wyatt £500, payable on the production of the invention. Ibid., I, 2.

[4] See the letters published in the *Birmingham Weekly Post*, Nos. of Aug. 22nd, 29th, and Dec. 29th, 1891.

[5] Wyatt did not always have complete faith in him. See letters to his brother of Sept. 25th and Oct. 28th, 1733. Wyatt MSS., I, 8 and 10.

[6] Was it really the first? The catalogue of patents mentions two similar inventions, one made in 1678 by Richard Dereham and Richard Haines (No. 202), the other in 1723 by Thomas Thwaites and Francis Clifton (No. 459). In any case these inventions were followed by no practical consequences.

[7] Chas. Wyatt, op. cit., p. 80.

some of his letters he alludes to a new invention of which he expects great things: 'I think', he wrote to his brother, 'I have a gymcrak of some consequence', and he talks of moving to Birmingham.[1] Then follow two rather puzzling documents dated August 12th and 14th, 1733, laying down the conditions by which Lewis Paul became the sole owner of 'a certain engine, machine or instrument for certain purposes'.[2] This designedly obscure description, together with the importance of the sum promised to Wyatt in exchange for the rights over this mysterious machine,[3] leads us to believe that a secret of great value was involved, although the invention was still incomplete and could give no immediate returns.

Several years went by before it was in a condition to be used practically. The correspondence of the two associates betrays their disappointment. In 1736 their mutual recriminations nearly brought about a rupture. Wyatt complained of the destitution Paul's promises had left him in. He complained of 'being much poorer than a pauper ... It becomes a question to me whether I am not much more to be blamed for an adventurous credulity than for any crime I have been guilty of with respect of you.' Lewis Paul reminded him that he was at his mercy: 'I know your grand secret and can use you as I please.'[4] Moreover, he had no money, and in 1737 he was only just able to help Wyatt, who was starving. He seems to have despaired of carrying through the scheme he had undertaken: 'I suppose you are still entertained with dreams about the bridge to our mutual ruin ... It was a monstrous imprudence in you to hazard all for an undertaking you could in reason have but slight or any hopes of.'[5] In the following year, the machine having no doubt had the necessary improvements made to it, they plucked up courage. The patent was taken out and registered on June 24th, 1738.

This patent is of capital importance in the history of industrial technique. The text is clear enough to give a fairly definite idea of Wyatt's machine, the original models having since disappeared: 'The said machine, engine or invention, will spin wool or cotton into thread, yarn or worsted; which, before it is placed therein, must be first prepared in manner following, to wit, all those sorts of wool or cotton which it is necessary to card, must have each cardful, butt or roll,

---

[1] Wyatt MSS., I, 9. The letter is undated, but it obviously precedes other letters of 1733 where the same word recurs as a familiar term. Later it becomes transformed into a kind of conventional figure: 25 Gymcrak or − 25. Ibid., I, 13.

[2] Ibid., I, 1 and 5.

[3] He was to receive £2,000. If he died within four years his heirs were to receive £450 and his wife a pension of £10. Ibid.

[4] Ibid., I, 23-8 (Letter from Paul to Wyatt undated, p. 24; letters from Wyatt to Paul, April 21st and Sept. 21st, 1736, pp. 25 ff.).

[5] Ibid., II, 69, 71-5 and I, 35-7.

joined together so as to make the mass become a kind of a rope or thread of raw wool ... One end of the mass, rope or thread or sliver is put betwixt a pair of rollers, cylinders, or cones,[1] or some such movements, which, being twined round by their motion, draws in the raw mass of wool or cotton to be spun, in proportion to the velocity given to such rollers, cylinders, or cones; as the prepared mass passes regularly through or betwixt these rollers, cylinders or cones, others, moving proportionally faster than the first, draw the rope, thread or sliver into any degree of fineness which may be required.'[2] This is the essential contrivance which will also be found in the machine said to be Arkwright's. It is easy enough to understand how the thread, passing between rollers which revolved more and more quickly, stretched and became finer and finer. It is harder to understand how it acquired the necessary twist. On this point the text of the patent is rather obscure; there probably lay the weak point of the invention.[3]

Once spun, the thread was wound off on spindles or pins, whose rotation was regulated by that of the fastest turning roller. If required these spindles could be put to another purpose: 'In some cases only the first pair of rollers, cylinders, or cones, are used, and then the bobbin, spole, or quill, upon which the thread, yarn, or worsted is spun, is so contrived as to draw faster than the first rollers, cylinders, or cones give, and in such proportion as the first mass, rope, or sliver, is proposed to be diminished.' In this case the rollers were only used to hold the thread. It was the spindles which, revolving on themselves, stretched and possibly twisted it. This is practically the principle of Hargreaves's jenny. Thus the two capital inventions which thirty years later were to provide the final solution to the problem of mechanical spinning, were both derived from Wyatt's machine.

As for the motor power, this was a question which at first the inventor does not seem to have thought of. But he assumed as a self-evident proposition that the motor power, whatever it was, would be able to work several machines at once. He pictured it to himself as a kind of mill, with wheels turned either by horses, water or wind.[4] Later on it struck him that his invention might be adapted to the needs of small-scale production: 'It may be found useful, where the spinners live remote from the clothiers, or when they have not the conveniency of such mills, to have small moveable ones made to spin the work of a

[1] The surface of one of these cylinders was smooth, the other was 'made very rough, indented, or covered with leather, cloth, shagg, or sometimes with hair or brushes or with points of metal'. Wyatt MSS., I, 45-8. This was what made them adhere together.

[2] *Abridgments of Specifications relating to Weaving*, I, No. 562.

[3] On this subject see the observations of A. Ure, *The Cotton Manufacture of Great Britain*, I, 209.

[4] Wyatt MSS., I, 34.

family or two.'[1] Hargreaves's jenny was later on used in this way, whilst it was Arkwright's machine which gave rise to the big spinning mills.

Wyatt foresaw the factory system and its probable consequences. According to his calculations the use of machinery was to reduce by one-third the labour required, the result being an obvious profit for the manufacturer. But would not this advantage involve a loss for the workers and the public? Wyatt did not think so: 'An additional gain to the clothier's trade naturally excites his industry as well as enables him to extend his trade in proportion to his gain by the machines. By the extension of his trade he will likewise take in some men of the 33 per cent left unemployed ... Then he wants more hands in every other branch of the trade, viz. weavers, shearmen, scourers, combers, etc ... These workmen now having full employ will be able to get more money in their families than they all could before.'[2] The whole nation was to profit by it: 'Every such improvement in trade must certainly be a gain to the country, especially to a country which so much raises its trade as ours ... as a man who can work quicker than his neighbours certainly brings more gain to his family, or if by improvement or by art he can make one of his family gain as much as the whole could before, he certainly gets what the remaining part of his family can get by any other means.'[3]

This invention, which was to enrich England, did not at any rate succeed in enriching its authors. There is no evidence that it was applied before 1740, and meanwhile Lewis Paul had been imprisoned for debt, and the machine seized, together with his furniture.[4] Ultimately, however, a small factory – no doubt provided with capital by Paul's friends – was set up in Birmingham and run by the inventors themselves. The machine was worked by two donkeys, and was tended by ten female workers.[5] It has been asserted that this machine did not work well or produce good thread, which would explain the failure of the undertaking.[6] This does not correspond to evidence given by direct witnesses. Dr James wrote to Warren, the bookseller: 'Yesterday we went to see Mr Paul's machine, which gave us entire satisfaction both in regard to the carding and the spinning ... I am certain that if Paul could begin with £10,000 he must, or at least might, get more money in

[1] Wyatt MSS., I, 34.

[2] Ibid., I, 33 (Oct. 21st, 1736).

[3] Ibid., I, 32.

[4] Letter from Lewis Paul, Jan. 6th, 1739. Letter from Wyatt, April 17th. Ibid., I, 50-7. It was then that Lewis Paul requested the Duke of Bedford to try his machine in the Foundling Hospital.

[5] Ch. Wyatt, op. cit., p. 81, *Local Notes and Queries* (Birmingham Central Library), 1889-93, Nos. 2811, 2815, 2832.

[6] A. Ure, *The Cotton Manufacture of Great Britain*, I, 217.

twenty years than the City of London is worth.'[1] One weak point of the
machine was the frailty of its parts, which caused it to be frequently out
of order, and occasioned expensive repairs.[2]

What is certain is that Paul and Wyatt never got their £10,000, and
the factory, small though it was, had to be closed down. They went
bankrupt in 1742[3] and their invention was sold to Edward Cave, the
editor of the *Gentleman's Magazine*. He tried to run things on a large
scale. He set up a workshop at Northampton containing five machines,
each fitted with fifty spindles. Like the silk-throwing mills in Derby
these machines were worked by water-wheels, driven by water from the
river Nen. Carding was done by cylindrical carding machines, invented
by Lewis Paul.[4] The factory employed fifty workers of both sexes. Half
of them carded the cotton, and the others supervised the machines and
tied the broken threads together.[5] What was lacking this time was not
capital but a no less indispensable factor to the success of an industrial
enterprise, namely good administration, both from the commercial and
the technical point of view. According to Wyatt's calculations the
undertaking should have produced over £1,300 a year profit. But, either
by reason of the deficiency of the machine, or because of the lack of
experience and the carelessness of the managers, it remained an unprofitable business,[6] barely maintaining its existence till 1764.[7] The plant
ultimately was bought up by Richard Arkwright. Although its existence
was always uncertain and attracted little notice, this Northampton
factory was nevertheless the first cotton-spinning mill in England, and
therefore the ancestor of all those factories whose innumerable chimneys
now [1927] surround Manchester and Glasgow, Rouen, Lowell and
Chemnitz, as well as Bombay and Osaka.

In Dyer's poem, which is devoted to a description and a eulogy of the
woollen industry, there is a curious passage referring to Wyatt's invention. The author, while visiting a cloth factory in the Calder Valley, is
shown

> A circular machine, of new design
> In conic shape: it draws and spins a thread
> Without the tedious toil of needless hands.
> A wheel, invisible, beneath the floor,
> To every member of th' harmonious frame

[1] R. Cole, *Some Account of Lewis Paul* (appendix to French's *Life and Times of Samuel Crompton*, p. 256).

[2] See B. P. Dobson, *The Story of the Evolution of the Spinning Machine*, p. 50.

[3] Wyatt MSS., I, 65; II, 82.

[4] Patent No. 636.

[5] Wyatt MSS., I, 76 ff.

[6] *Remarks on Mr Cave's Works at Northampton* (1743), Wyatt MSS., I, 82.

[7] Ch. Wyatt, *On the Origin of Spinning Cotton by Machinery*, p. 81.

> Gives necessary motion. One, intent,
> O'erlooks the work: the carded wool, he says,
> Is smoothly lapp'd around those cylinders,
> Which, gently turning, yield it to yon cirque
> Of upright spindles, which with rapid whirl
> Spin out, in long extent, an even twine.[1]

This is not conclusive evidence that Wyatt's machine was used for spinning wool before 1760. What Dyer probably did was to describe a model factory in which, by a legitimate fiction, he introduced the machine he had seen at work in the Northampton factory, the only one whose existence is an indisputable fact.[2]

What is certain is that Wyatt's invention was not a practical success, and the efforts made to work it were hardly noticed, while weavers went on complaining of the scarcity and high price of thread. In 1761 the Society for the Encouragement of Arts and Manufactures, founded a few years earlier, published a note beginning thus: 'The Society has been informed that our manufacturers of woollen, linen and cotton find it exceedingly difficult, when the spinners are out at harvest work, to procure a sufficient number of hands to keep their weavers employed, and that for want of proper dispatch in this branch of our manufacture the merchants' orders for all sorts of piece goods are often greatly retarded, to the prejudice of the manufacturer, merchant and nation in general ... ': the Society considered that there was every reason for encouraging all research which would put this right, and offered two prizes 'for the best invention of a machine that will spin six threads of wool, flax, cotton, or silk, at one time, and that will require but one person to work it and to attend it'.[3] Thus the problem was still unsolved, while its solution was awaited and demanded with growing impatience. If, twenty years earlier, Wyatt and Paul had met with such an insistent demand, their efforts would no doubt have been rewarded with better results. But they were too early. For an

---

[1] J. Dyer, *The Fleece, a Poem*, Book III, lines 292-302.

[2] See the footnote to line 292: '*A circular machine* — a most curious machine, invented by Mr Paul. It is at present contrived to spin cotton, but it may be made to spin fine carded wool.' This clearly shows that on Dyer's own confession the use of the machine for spinning wool was only a possibility, contrary to what is believed by H. Heaton (*The Yorkshire Woollen and Worsted Industries*, p. 356).

[3] *Transactions of the Society for the Encouragement of Arts and Manufactures*, I, 314-15. 'Robert Dossie, who was well informed concerning the early history of the society, and acquainted with many of its members, tells us that their interest in the problem was aroused by knowledge of the unsuccessful spinning machine patented by Lewis Paul in 1738.' W. Bowden, *Industrial Society in England towards the end of the Eighteenth Century*, pp. 48-9. A man called Harrison in 1764 made a spinning wheel 'whereby a child might spin twice as much as a grown person can do with the common wheel'. A. Warden, *The Linen Trade*, p. 371.

invention will suffer if it appears too long before the moment when the need it is meant to satisfy has reached its climax.

V

This moment had at last arrived. It is a curious thing that the two capital inventions, the success of which revolutionized the textile industry, made their appearance almost simultaneously. Hargreaves's spinning jenny and Arkwright's water frame[1] were produced within a year or two of one another. The invention of the water frame seems to have been made about 1767, and that of the jenny about 1765. Both came into use in 1768, and the patents which, so to speak, notified their official birth were taken out in 1769 and 1770 respectively. They are the double outcome of one current of economic causes.

But though the origins of these two inventions were the same, their consequences were very different. Even though they were in fact simultaneous, yet they represented two successive stages in industrial evolution. Hargreaves's invention was simpler and modified the organization of the work less deeply. It marked the transition between manual work and machine industry, between the domestic system, or small-scale 'manufacture', and the factory system.

We know very little about the life and character of James Hargreaves. Between 1740 and 1760 we find him settled in the neighbourhood of Blackburn in Lancashire, where he combined the trades of weaver and carpenter.[2] It was no doubt in his capacity as carpenter that he came to deal with machinery. At that time, when there were no professional engineers, their place was more or less filled by carpenters, locksmiths, or clockmakers, in fact by anyone who was sufficiently used to working in wood and metal, and who could set up wheelwork or fit parts of machinery together. Among these emergency engineers a special place must be given to the millwrights, whose help was essential to the setting up of the first factories.[3] A millwright knew how to use a turner's, a carpenter's or a blacksmith's tools, he had some knowledge of arithmetic and practical mechanics. He could draw out a plan or calculate the speed and power of a wheel. All difficult cases were

---

[1] Arkwright's claim to the invention was probably unfounded. See chap. II below.

[2] *A Complete History of the Cotton Trade*, p. 77.

[3] 'Their trade was a branch of carpentry (with some assistance from the smith), but rather heavier work, yet very ingenious, to understand and perform which a person ought to have a good turn of mind for mechanics, at least to have some knowledge in arithmetic, in which a lad ought to be instructed before he goes to learn his art: for there is a good deal of variety in mills, as well as in the structure and workmanship of them, some being worked by horses, some by wind, others by water shooting over, and some by its running under and why not in time by fire also, as well as engines?' W. Fairbairn, *Mills and Millwork*, I, V-VI; see Webb MSS., Engineering Trades, I.

submitted to him, be it the mending of a pump, the working of pulleys or the setting up of a water-pipe. He had the reputation of being able to turn his hand to anything, and no one could do without him in any new venture.

Hargreaves had as his next-door neighbour a calico printer, the founder of the great Peel family. In 1762 Hargreaves built a carding machine for him, probably on Lewis Paul's model,[1] and this was the beginning of his career as an engineer and an inventor.

The widening gap between spinning and weaving was producing real uneasiness in the industry. There was much unemployment among weavers, and merchants were always wondering how they could manage to satisfy the ever-growing demand. In Lancashire, where so many were dependent on the textile industry, the question was constantly discussed, and everyone was trying to find an answer.[2] Many attempted the problem which Hargreaves finally solved.[3]

The machine in its original form was very simple, both in its structure and operation. It consisted of a rectangular frame on four legs. At one end was a row of vertical spindles. Across the frame were two parallel wooden rails, lying close together, which were mounted on a sort of carriage and slid backwards and forwards as desired. The cotton, which had been previously carded and roved, passed between the two rails and then was wound on the spindles. With one hand the spinner worked the carriage backwards and forwards, and with the other he turned the handle which worked the spindles. In this way the thread was drawn and twisted at the same time.[4]

Such was the principle of the jenny, the idea of which, according to tradition, Hargreaves had conceived by watching a spinning wheel that had been knocked over lying on its side and still revolving for a few seconds, while the thread, held between two fingers, seemed to go on spinning itself. The jenny had one great advantage over the spinning wheel, from which it was obviously derived,[5] in that a single

---

[1] *A Complete History of the Cotton Trade*, p. 79. Paul's machine was very simple and consisted of a sort of concave trough fitted with metal teeth, and of cylindrical carders worked by a handle.

[2] See the typical conversation between Kay the clockmaker and Richard Arkwright in a public-house at Warrington (*The Trial of a Cause instituted by Richard Pepper Arden Esq. His Majesty's Attorney General by Writ of Scire Facias, to repeal a Patent granted on the Sixteenth of December, 1775, to Mr Richard Arkwright*, p. 63).

[3] Thus Hargreaves could be accused of not being the first or the sole author of his invention. See R. Guest, *The British cotton manufactures*, pp. 176-80.

[4] *Abridgments of Specifications relating to Spinning*, p. 19 (No. 962); *Transactions of the Society for the Encouragement of Arts and Manufactures*, II, 32-5; J. James, *History of the Worsted Manufacture*, pp. 345-6; R. Guest, *A compendious history of the cotton-manufacture*, pp. 13-14; E. Baines, *History of the Cotton Manufacture*, pp. 157 ff.

[5] 'The jenny is merely a many-spindled wheel.' A. Ure, *The Cotton Manufacture of Great Britain*, I, 198.

workman could spin several threads at once. The first models built by Hargreaves had only eight spindles. But this number could be increased without any limit, save that of the motor power. Even during Hargreaves's lifetime jennies with eighty or more spindles were constructed.

Did Hargreaves realize the whole importance of his invention? He at any rate let several years go by before he made it public. At the start he confined himself to trying it in his own house. Only in 1767 did he make a few machines for sale, and at once fell a victim to that unpopularity which inventors in those days seldom escaped. Blackburn workers broke in his door and smashed his machines.[1] He moved to Nottingham. There, as in Lancashire, the textile industry was in the throes of a crisis, due to the insufficiency of the old-fashioned methods of spinning.[2] Then it was that he took out his patent[3] and began to profit by his invention. He sold a large number of jennies, and would have made his fortune had he not, like John Kay, had to contend with the dishonesty of manufacturers. He brought an action against the men who had refused to pay him. The interests involved were already so large that he refused £3,000, which were offered him for his rights in the invention.[4] Unfortunately for him the courts held that the model of his jenny had been used in industry before it was patented, and his rights were therefore declared to have lapsed. Like his predecessors he had, therefore, to endure severe disappointments, but it is quite untrue that he died in want, as Arkwright tried to make out, in order to create sympathy for himself both in Parliament and with the public.[5] On the contrary, we know that Hargreaves, though still poor in 1768, in 1778 left over £4,000 to his heirs.[6] A trifling sum, of course, if compared with the immense amount of wealth produced by the invention of the spinning jenny. Ten years after Hargreaves's death it was reckoned that there were no fewer than twenty thousand of these machines in England, of which the smallest could do the work of six or eight spinners.[7] In Lancashire they spread with astonishing rapidity, and in a few years had completely ousted the spinning wheel.[8] After this the woollen industry, which in

---

[1] Abram, *History of Blackburn*, pp. 205-6.

[2] W. Felkin, *A History of the Machine-wrought Hosiery and Lace Manufactures*, pp. 81-97.

[3] No. 962 (1770).

[4] A. Ure, *The Cotton Manufacture of Great Britain*, I, 197.

[5] 'The Case of Richard Arkwright', in *The Trial of a Cause*, etc., p. 98.

[6] Abram, *History of Blackburn*, p. 209.

[7] *An Important Crisis, in the Callico and Muslin Manufactory in Great Britain, explained*, p. 2 (1788).

[8] J. Kennedy, 'A Brief Memoir of Samuel Crompton', *Memoirs of the Literary and Philosophical Society of Manchester*, Second Series, V, 330; R. Guest, *The British cotton manufactures*, p. 147.

that part of England had never done very well, was almost given up: 'Cotton, cotton, cotton, was become the almost universal material for employment; the hand-wheels ... were all thrown into lumber-rooms, the yarn was all spun on common jennies.'[1] The jenny was a simple machine, and could be built at a slight cost. It took up very little room and so did not involve the setting up of special workshops. It could be worked without any outside motor power, and its use did not interfere much with the worker's habits. Outwardly, at any rate, it did not cause any great alteration in the organization of the industry. This was certainly one of the reasons why it was so quickly successful. Far from destroying the cottage industry, it seemed at first to revive it. It was found in the workshops managed by small employers who worked with their own hands, and in farms where the spinning wheel had for generations added its earnings to those of the plough. But the rapid increase of the output, and the importance of mechanical equipment, as compared with labour, already heralded the coming of the factory system. And, while in cottages Hargreaves's jenny was taking the place of the old-time spinning wheel, in Nottingham, Cromford, Derby, Belper, Chorley and Manchester, Richard Arkwright's spinning mills were being built.

[1] W. Radcliffe, *Origin of the New System of Manufacture, commonly called 'Power Loom Weaving'*, p. 61 (describing the conditions in the village of Mellor).

CHAPTER TWO

THE FACTORIES

Arkwright's name is one of the few which from the beginning shone like stars in the twilight which has long surrounded so many of the events and personalities of economic history. In him tradition sees not only the prototype of the great manufacturer, made rich by his own toil and his own inventions, but the true founder of the modern factory system.[1] About 1830 he became the hero of political economy,[2] and even literature did not despise him. Carlyle has sketched a vivid picture of this 'plain, almost gross, bag-cheeked, pot-bellied Lancashire man, with an air of painful reflection, yet also of copious free digestion ... O reader, what a historical phenomenon is that bag-cheeked, pot-bellied, much enduring, much inventing barber! French Revolutions were a-brewing: to resist the same in any measure imperial Kaisers were impotent without the cotton and cloth of England; and it was this man that had to give England the power of cotton.'[3] But these lines refer only to the immediate consequences of the transformation of industry which, according to Carlyle, were due to Arkwright's genius. We should have to turn to another of Carlyle's books[4] to find a vivid description of the new world, born of the industrial revolution, that new world which he compared so bitterly with his idealized picture of the past. Our task here is to define exactly the part which Arkwright actually did play. If we can determine the place he really deserves to occupy, we shall help to solve a more important problem. For in order to appreciate correctly the share of individual action in the genesis of social changes we should first separate the facts from legends which have grown up round them, and which often lay too much stress upon the individual factor, as compared with more general causes.

I

Richard Arkwright was born at Preston on December 23rd, 1732, the youngest of a large and poor family.[5] While still quite young he was

[1] See for instance the story of his career in *A Complete History of the Cotton Trade*, pp. 92 ff.

[2] See A. Ure, *Philosophy of Manufactures*, pp. 15 ff.

[3] T. Carlyle, *Chartism*, chap. VIII (New Eras). *Miscellaneous Essays*, Chapman & Hall edition, p. 166.   [4] *Past and Present*.

[5] R. Guest, *A compendious history of the cotton-manufacture*, p. 21; Whittle, *History of Preston*, II, 213; Hardwick, *History of the Borough of Preston*, pp. 361 ff.; E. Baines, *History of the Cotton Manufacture*, p. 148.

apprenticed to a barber and wig-maker, and just found time in which to learn to read and write. At fifty, he was taking lessons in grammar and spelling. In 1750 he set up at Bolton, a few miles from his small native town, where for a long time he plied his trade of barber, first of all in a basement and then in a very humble shop. He was married twice. His second wife came from Leigh, between Warrington and Bolton[1] – a detail of some interest. She brought him some money, which enabled him to leave his shop and to go in for a more paying occupation, that of a dealer in hair. He attended markets, and visited farms in order to buy the hair of country girls. He then treated it with a dye of his own making and resold it to the wig-makers who, in that century of wigs, were ready buyers.[2]

This story of Arkwright's early life is not only interesting in itself but gives us an insight into his character and thus helps us to judge of the part he actually played. We must first note that there was nothing about him which suggested an inventor's career. He had no technical experience, for he was not a weaver like John Kay and Hargreaves, or a carpenter and mechanic like Wyatt. He must have learnt everything he knew of the textile industry, of its needs and of the crisis it was undergoing, through conversations in his barber's shop or during his rounds in Lancashire villages. On the other hand he displayed very early those qualities which explain his success. He was anxious to better himself, he had fertile brains for devising means of rising in the world, and he knew how to drive a good bargain, the sort of diplomacy in which he had been trained being akin to that of the pedlar or the horse-dealer.

The origins of his main invention are wrapped in a curious obscurity. Not that it is difficult to understand how he came to be interested in the problem of mechanical spinning, for everyone in Lancashire knew that there was a fortune to be made out of it. But though he was several times asked to prove his claim as an inventor, he was never able to give any but vague and embarrassed explanations, and this for very good reasons.[3] No end of ridiculous and conflicting stories, which he was careful never to deny, were circulated during his lifetime by his admirers. According to some people the principle of the spinning machine had been suggested to him by a cylindrical wire-drawing machine, which drew out a bar of red-hot iron.[4] According to others

---

[1] R. Guest, *The British cotton manufactures*, p. 14.

[2] Id., *A compendious history of the cotton-manufacture*, p. 21.

[3] See p. 227 below, the history of the case which ended in the cancelling of his patent. In the course of the proceedings evidence was given that his chief invention had been borrowed, to used a polite word, from a certain Thomas Highs of the village of Leigh in Lancashire.

[4] *Beauties of England and Wales*, III, 518 (information given by the son of Jedediah Strutt, one of Arkwright's partners). It is hardly necessary to point out that no serious comparison can be made between the drawing out by compression of a

he had studied at Derby the working of the silk-throwing machines,[1] or, in his barber's shop, he had overheard a sailor describe a machine used by the Chinese,[2] or he had learnt a precious secret from a certain Brown, a cabinet-maker, who had himself discovered it no one knew how, and who, for equally mysterious reasons, was unable to make use of it.[3] An equally improbable story shows us Arkwright seized, about 1768, by a sudden and unexpected passion for mechanics, and put on the track of his invention by researches into the problem of perpetual motion.[4]

While the history of the invention is so obscure, the story of Arkwright's ventures is clear and easy to follow. The machine was made, in 1768, in a room adjoining the Free Grammar School at Preston.[5] Arkwright had enlisted the help of a Warrington clockmaker, a namesake of Kay the inventor of the fly shuttle. As we shall see, this collaboration accounts for many things. Apparently Arkwright had had great difficulty in raising the necessary funds. He first turned to a scientific instrument-maker, who refused to take him seriously,[6] and then to one of his friends, a publican called John Smalley.[7] The next year he took out his patent of invention, valid for fourteen years.[8]

We can not only read the text of this patent but also see the original model of the machine itself, preserved at the Science Museum, South Kensington.[9] It is made entirely of wood, and is about thirty-two inches high. As far as we can judge it is very like the machine invented in 1733 by John Wyatt, and improved by Lewis Paul. A wheel sets in motion four pairs of rollers of increasing rapidity of rotation. The top cylinder

---

[1] *Gentleman's Magazine*, LXII, 863. This analogy again is quite superficial. The throwing process only strengthens a thread already made by the silk worm, who in this case plays the part of spinner.

[2] *Wool encouraged without Exportation, or practical Observations on Wool and the Woollen Manufacture* (1791), p. 50.

[3] *Mechanics' Magazine*, VIII, 199.

[4] R. Guest, *A compendious history of the cotton-manufacture*, p. 21; A. Ure, *The Cotton Manufacture of Great Britain*, p. 225. The story is quoted, probably from R. Guest, in an article on 'Cotton-spinning Machines and their Inventors', *Quarterly Review*, CVII, 59.

[5] 'The Case of Richard Arkwright', in *The Trial of a Cause*, etc., p. 98. The date has never been questioned, and Arkwright, to whose interest it would have been to have had it put a year or two earlier, never did so.

[6] E. Baines, *History of the Cotton Manufacture*, p. 150.

[7] Publican and house painter. See Guest, *Compendious history*, p. 22; Whittle, *History of Preston*, II, 216.

[8] No. 931 (July 3rd, 1769).

[9] Science Museum, South Kensington, gallery 24.

---

solid mass of metal and that of making thread out of the fibres of cotton or the staples of wool.

of each pair is covered with leather, whilst the lower one is ribbed or grooved lengthwise. After it has gone through the rollers, whose progressive acceleration stretches it more and more, the thread is twisted and wound on vertical spindles. Generally speaking, this machine differs from that of Wyatt only in its details. These trifling differences cannot explain Arkwright's triumphal success in a line where more ingenious men than he had been hopeless failures. His success was due to his business capacity, of which he gave proof almost at once.

It was, above all, necessary to raise capital. Smalley was not rich enough, and Arkwright already dreamed of big business. For this reason, following the example of Hargreaves whose misadventures he was familiar with, he migrated to Nottingham.[1] We know that this town was the centre of the stocking frame industry, in which a capitalistic organization had followed the development of mechanical equipment. Arkwright succeeded in interesting in his schemes the local bank of Wright Brothers. There were still very few of these provincial banks, and they were therefore all the more important in the districts they catered for. But profits no doubt did not follow rapidly, or the success of the venture was not so great as the dazzling promises of the inventor had pictured it, for at the end of a year the Wrights withdrew their support.[2] Arkwright knew how to extricate himself from his difficulties. In 1771 he entered into a contract with two rich hosiers, Need of Nottingham and Strutt of Derby.[3] Need and Strutt belonged to the class of merchant manufacturers. They employed a large number of workers in their own homes, and also had workshops where stockings were knitted on frames. Thus it was on a system of production akin to 'manufacture', if not on 'manufacture' itself, that the factory system was grafted.

II

The first workshop set up by Arkwright at Nottingham was hardly larger than the one Wyatt and Paul had established in Birmingham thirty years before. It had but a few machines, which were worked by horses.[4] It was in 1771, the year he joined forces with Need and Strutt, that Arkwright settled at Cromford, near Derby. Cromford lies on the Derwent, at a point where the river runs swift and powerful through a narrow gorge quite close to the picturesque hills of its origin. A little

[1] 'The Case of Richard Arkwright', in *The Trial of a Cause*, etc., p. 98.

[2] F. Espinasse, *Lancashire Worthies*, I, 387; J. Tuckett, *A History of the past and present State of the labouring Population*, I, 212.

[3] On Jedediah Strutt, see W. Felkin, *A History of the Machine-wrought Hosiery and Lace Manufactures*, pp. 89-97.

[4] Espinasse, *Lancashire Worthies*, I, 390.

way above, the hot waters of Matlock flow into it and prevent it from ever freezing in winter. It was therefore a suitable place for building a mill. The word *mill* continued to mean a factory long after steam had almost everywhere taken the place of water power. The brothers Lombe's factory, a few miles away, was the model taken for the building and the workshops.[1] In a few years the Cromford spinning mill had grown up, and by 1779 it contained several thousand spindles and employed three hundred workmen.[2]

That which made the success of the undertaking quite certain was not only the rapidity but the quality of the production. The new machine (the water frame[3] as it was called, to distinguish it from the jenny, which was worked by hand) produced a much stronger thread than the most skilled spinner could have made with a spinning wheel. Instead, therefore, of weaving materials which were partly linen and only partly cotton, it became possible to weave pure cotton goods, which were as perfect in every respect as their Indian models. At first the Cromford factory was only an appendage to those of Need and Strutt. All the thread it spun was used solely for making stockings. But in 1773 Arkwright and his partners set up weaving workshops in Derby, where, for the first time, pure cotton calicoes were made.[4]

At this point an obstacle arose. The small manufacturers, who had viewed this dangerous competition with great dislike, thought that at last they had found a way of putting a stop to it. The Act of 1735, which allowed the manufacture of mixed materials, had confirmed the prohibition of printed cotton goods; the possibility of a similar industry being established in England had not been foreseen. It was possible, therefore, to maintain that the Act applied to the case of Arkwright and his partners, and their cotton goods, already subject to a heavy excise duty,[5] ran the risk if they were made into the then fashionable prints of being seized as prohibited goods.

Arkwright defended his industry before Parliament. Should a law which was intended merely to prevent foreign goods from coming into the kingdom be enforced against goods made in England by English workmen? Properly licensed, and subject to moderate taxation, this new industry could not fail to become a source of wealth for the whole country: 'The said manufacture, if not crushed by so heavy a

[1] R. Guest, *A compendious history of the cotton-manufacture*, p. 22.

[2] R. March, *A Treatise on Silk, Wool, Worsted, Cotton and Thread* (1779), Foxwell Library; Edwin Butterworth, *History of Oldham*, p. 118.

[3] A model of a water frame with eight spindles is exhibited at the Science Museum, South Kensington, gallery 24.

[4] 'The Case of Richard Arkwright', in *The Trial of a Cause*, etc., p. 99; *A Second Letter to the Inhabitants of Manchester on the Exportation of Cotton Twist*, p. 9; *A Complete History of the Cotton Trade*, p. 101.

[5] 6d. a yard. See *Journals of the House of Commons*, XXXIV, 496-7.

duty, will rapidly increase and find new and effectual employment for many thousand British poor, and increase the revenue of this Kingdom. ... Cotton goods so made wholly of cotton will be greatly superior in quality to the present species of cotton goods, made with linen yarn warps, and will bleach, print, wash and wear better.' Arkwright therefore requested that 'leave might be given to bring in a Bill for ascertaining the rate of duty on the said white cotton stuffs, wholly made of cotton wool, and manufactured within the Kingdom of Great Britain, when printed, painted, stained, or dyed, at 3d. per yard only, and for the free vending, wearing and using by all persons, in apparel, household stuff, furniture, or otherwise, any sort of the said cotton stuffs ... '[1] Parliament, after a short inquiry,[2] agreed to these very justifiable requests.[3] From that time onwards the cotton industry, and with it machine industry, was able to develop without impediment.

The following year (1775), Arkwright took out his second patent,[4] the very long and obscure text of which was to give rise to endless difficulties. It described several distinct inventions of varying importance, and of which some seemed only to have been included (as was afterwards pointed out) in order to puzzle and put off too inquisitive readers.[5] The most important were the carding machine, the crank and comb, the roving frame and the feeder. The carding machine consisted of three cylinders of different diameters, covered with bent metal teeth. The first, with teeth bent in the direction of its revolution, caught up the cotton fibres. The second, revolving in the same direction but much faster, carded the fibres by contact with the third, whose teeth and motion were in the opposite direction.[6] The crank and comb completed the carding machine, by detaching the carded cotton in such a way that it came off as a continuous sheet. As its name indicates it was a kind of comb fitted to an elbow-shaped joint, which, at regular intervals, came in contact with the teeth of the third cylinder and thus disengaged the cotton without tearing it.[7] The roving frame was a machine which turned the ribbon of carded cotton into a cylindrical strand slightly twisted on itself, and ready for conversion

---

[1] *Journals of the House of Commons*, XXXIV, 497 (1774).

[2] Ibid., 709.

[3] 14 Geo. III, c. 72. The text of this Act reproduces almost word for word the terms of Arkwright's petition save with regard to export bounties which he asked for but did not obtain.

[4] No. 1111 (Dec. 16th, 1775). See *Abridgments of Specifications relating to Spinning*, p. 19. The writ of the case of 1785 gives the full text of the patent. See *The Trial of a Cause*, etc., pp. 4-10.

[5] For instance, that which appears as the heading to the specification: 'A hammer for beating flax.'

[6] Science Museum, South Kensington, gallery 24.

[7] Ibid.

into thread. Its structure resembled the spinning machine, but it was simpler, and the acceleration between one pair of cylinders and the other was much less. Instead of winding itself off on spindles the cotton went into a revolving cone, which gave it the necessary twist.[1] Finally, the feeder was nothing but a band of material in perpetual revolution, which carried the raw cotton to the carding machine as it was fed to it by a sloping hose. We venture to go into all these details, at the risk of incurring the criticism of experts, in order to show what part machinery already played in the cotton industry. We see that as early as 1775 textile machinery had developed into a system, the interdependent parts of which were able to perform all the successive operations of the industry, save the last and most difficult, that of weaving.

In the specification attached to his new patent, Arkwright had been careful to insert several articles relating to real or pretended improvements of the spinning machine. In this way he hoped to extend for a few years the validity of his first patent, which would expire in 1783. Confident of the future, he went on and multiplied his ventures. In 1776 he set up a third spinning mill at Belper, between Cromford and Derby.[2] At that time, therefore, his various factories were concentrated in a small area, along the Derwent and the Trent, and all outside Lancashire. Yet it was in Lancashire that the English cotton industry had first developed, and that its growth still found the most favourable conditions. Arkwright, who was poor and unknown when a few years before he had left his native county, went back already rich and famous. He founded several factories there. One at Birkacre near Chorley[3] was supposed to be the largest factory yet built in England.[4] It was sacked and burnt down in 1779 during the anti-machine riots, to which we shall have to return later. The loss was estimated at £4,400.[5] Another spinning mill, set up in 1780 in Manchester, was equally, if not more, important: the buildings alone, which could hold six hundred workmen, cost over £4,000.[6] Arkwright's partnership with Need and Strutt, the stocking manufacturers, could not supply him with the necessary capital for all his new undertakings. He was able to find other partners as he needed them, and very skilfully limited their rights. He alone was present

[1] Science Museum, South Kensington, gallery 24.

[2] F. Espinasse, *Lancashire Worthies*, I, 420; A. Ure, *The Cotton Manufacture of Great Britain*, I, 256 f., 273. The Milford spinning mill, which belonged to Jedediah Strutt, was built about the same time.

[3] Between Preston and Wigan.

[4] It could hold 500 workmen. Edwin Butterworth, *History of Oldham*, p. 118.

[5] See *Manchester Mercury* of Oct. 12th and 16th, 1779, and Arkwright's petition to the House of Commons, *Journals of the House of Commons*, XXXVII, 926.

[6] F. Espinasse, *Lancashire Worthies*, I, 421.

everywhere, took part in every concern, and in fact managed them all.[1]

His two patents of 1769 and 1775 gave him the exclusive owner-ship of the water frame and the accessory inventions. But he could authorize their use by other persons, who had to pay a stipulated royalty.[2] In this way, between 1775 and 1780 a certain number of new undertakings were started, which were more or less subsidiary to his. Amongst others, we may mention those of Altham, of Burton and of Bury, which belonged to the two Robert Peels, the grandfather and father of the statesman.[3] But jealousy, as well as the desire for money, led spinners to dishonest practices. They racked their brains to construct machines which differed, even though only in detail, from those of Arkwright.[4] In 1781 he adopted the course of bringing an action for infringement of patent against nine of them.[5] They defended them-selves by pointing to the suspicious obscurity of the patent. How could they know what belonged to the inventor, when he himself either would not or could not define it clearly? Arkwright lost his case, and his patent rights were in consequence suspended before reaching the date of their normal expiration.

He would not be beaten. On February 6th, 1782, he addressed a petition to Parliament, asking not only for a confirmation but for an extension of his rights.[6] At the same time he brought out a memoran-dum[7] in which he pointed out the importance of his inventions, re-called the sacrifices he had made for them, referred again to the fraudulent manœuvres of his competitors, and exalted his own merit. He allowed that the patent of 1775 was not perfectly clear, but said he had drawn it up in this way because of his patriotic scruples, and in order to prevent foreigners from profiting by such an inexhaustible

[1] Edwin Butterworth, op. cit., p. 118, mentions the firm of Arkwright, Simpson & Whittenbury of Manchester. In Scotland, Arkwright was at one time the partner of David Dale, Owen's father-in-law (R. Dale Owen, *Threading My Way*, p. 7). His association with Need and Strutt only lasted till 1781: see W. Felkin, *A History of the Machine-wrought Hosiery and Lace Manufactures*, p. 96.

[2] *The Trial of a Cause*, etc., p. 99.

[3] Sir Lawrence Peel, *A Sketch of the Life and Character of Sir Robert Peel*, p. 20; Wheeler, *Manchester*, pp. 519-20.

[4] *The Trial of a Cause*, etc., p. 101.

[5] There were nine distinct summonses. But only one case was heard, that of Arkwright v. Mordaunt. See Baines, *History of the County Palatine and Duchy of Lancaster*, II, 447.

[6] *Journals of the House of Commons*, XXXVIII, 687.

[7] This memorandum was probably drafted by one of his lawyers. It appears in extenso in *The Trial of a Cause*, etc., pp. 97 ff., 'The case of Messrs Richard Arkwright & Co. in relation to Mr Arkwright's invention of an engine for spinning cotton, etc., into yarn, stating his reasons for applying to Parliament for an Act to secure his right in such invention, or for such other relief as to the Legislature shall seem meet.'

source of wealth. Surely he who would rather lay himself open to unjust suspicion than compromise the fortunes of his country, deserved to receive help against his enemies. But Parliament turned a deaf ear to his entreaties.

Arkwright then applied again to the courts. He began a fresh action against one of his competitors, Peter Nightingale. In February 1785, the case was heard in the Court of Common Pleas. The arguments centred entirely on the obscurity of the specification attached to the second patent. Arkwright again boasted of his patriotism, referred to the French (this took place just after the American war) who would have been only too glad to possess themselves of an industry which till then had been purely British. Several important witnesses gave evidence in his favour. James Watt, the inventor of the steam engine, declared that after having read the document under dispute it seemed to him to be sufficiently clear, and that, if necessary, he would undertake the construction of the various machines mentioned in the patent without further explanations.[1] This time Arkwright won his case. The Court confirmed the validity of his rights and granted the shilling damages he had asked for.

But this judgment interfered with so many vested interests[2] that it was bound to be contested. The Lancashire and Derbyshire spinners[3] combined to fight out the cause they had first won and then lost, for there was an obvious contradiction between the judgments of 1781 and 1785. They had the case brought before the Court of King's Bench by a writ of *scire facias*. There they not only attacked the terms of the patent, but they tried to prove that its obscurity, intentional or otherwise, concealed a fraud.

III

The incident on which the whole case hinged, and which decided the issue, was the appearance in court of Thomas Highs.[4] This man declared on oath that as early as 1767 he had, in his own village of Leigh, built a spinning machine which was identical with the one of

---

[1] *Richard Arkwright* versus *Peter Nightingale* (Court of Common Pleas, Feb. 17th, 1785), pp. 3*-7*. See also evidence of Wilkinson, pp. 2*-3*; John Stead, p. 9*; Erasmus Darwin, p. 15*; Th. Wood, p. 19*.

[2] E. Baines, *History of the Cotton Manufacture*, p. 184. The undertakings started by Arkwright's competitors represented then a capital of about £300,000.

[3] The list of names will be found in Wheeler, *Manchester*, pp. 521 ff. Robert Peel is there, and also Peter Drinkwater, who was one of the first spinners to make use of the steam engine.

[4] In the report (*The Trial of a Cause*, etc., pp. 57 ff.) his name is spelt Hayes, but R. Guest spells it Highs, as written in the parish register of the village of Leigh (*The British cotton manufactures*, p. 18).

which Arkwright pretended to have been the inventor. He had been helped in the adjustment of the various parts by a clockmaker, who turned out to be that very John Kay of Warrington who had been employed by Arkwright a year later.[1] This statement was confirmed by that of Kay himself. He related how in 1768 he had made the acquaintance of Arkwright, who was then a barber and hair-dealer. Arkwright had called on him, had given him some trifling job, and had then taken him off to a public-house. There the conversation had turned on the question with which the whole neighbourhood was humming, that of spinning by rollers: 'He said: That will never be brought to bear; several gentlemen have almost broke themselves by it. I said: I think that I could bring that to bear. That was all that passed that night.' Early the next morning Arkwright came to him again, asking whether he could build a model of a spinning machine. 'I went and bought a few articles, and made a small wooden model, and he took it with him to Manchester.'[2]

The reader will remember that Arkwright had married a woman from Leigh. He had known Highs for several years,[3] and had no doubt heard of his invention. Moreover, it was not by chance that he called on Kay at Warrington. It was only a little while after this interview that he suddenly, and without any preparation, appeared as an inventor. Moreover, his relations with Kay in the following years were somewhat unaccountable. He began by taking him into his service. Then they suddenly fell out. Arkwright accused Kay of theft and embezzlement, and the latter fled.[4] This would naturally have roused some suspicion of Kay's evidence, and Adair, Arkwright's counsel, did not miss the opportunity. Could anyone hesitate between the word of a well-known and respected man and that of a workman dismissed for dishonesty, who was trying to avenge himself?[5] But it must be noted that the charge against Kay had remained indefinite, and had never led to any prosecution or inquiry. His flight is quite sufficiently explained by threats, whether justified or not, which had been levelled at him, for 'there is not a more miserable or dangerous situation for a poor man than to be in possession of a secret of which a powerful and rich man dreads the discovery'.[6]

But if Highs was really the author of the machine attributed to Ark-

---

[1] *The Trial of a Cause*, etc., pp. 57-8.
[2] Ibid., pp. 62-3.
[3] Ibid., p. 59.
[4] Ibid., pp. 65-6.
[5] Ibid., p. 109.
[6] Bearcroft, counsel for the Crown in *The Trial of a Cause*, etc., pp. 166-7. It is not unlikely, as supposed by Guest (*The British cotton manufactures*, p. 43), that Kay had made himself inconvenient, perhaps by demanding a partnership in Arkwright's business.

wright, why did he wait twenty years before asserting his rights?[1] It is certainly very surprising, but it becomes less so when we know the life and character of the man. He belonged to that class of born inventors whose type we are familiar with. He was a simple uneducated mechanic, working by instinct, at home only in his workshop, and knowing nothing of business. He several times tried to set up a spinning mill on his own account, but he always came to grief for lack of capital and business ability.[2] Above all, he lacked the strenuous will to make a fortune which gave Arkwright his resolution and his power. He was content to rise from the rank of a workman comb-maker[3] to that of an engineer in the employ of millowners. He several times gave proof of his inventive talent. In 1772, on the Manchester Exchange, he exhibited a double jenny with fifty-six spindles, for which he won a two-hundred-guinea prize.[4] According to witnesses, whose belated and somewhat questionable evidence was collected after his death by his biographer and apologist Richard Guest, he was not only the inventor of the water frame, but, before Hargreaves, of the jenny, and the name of this machine, which has never been explained, was that of one of his daughters.[5]

---

[1] This is the most serious argument used by G. W. Daniels (*The Early English Cotton Industry*, p. 110) to disprove the evidence given in Court by John Kay and by Thomas Highs himself: 'The great difficulty is to explain why [Highs's] claim was allowed to lie so long in abeyance, seeing that he was not without friends in Manchester, men moreover who, it may be assumed, would not have been slow to attack Arkwright's patent, had the slightest opportunity been offered.' There can be no doubt about the feelings and desires of Arkwright's competitors. But how is it that Arkwright, or his counsel, made no use of this argument; but simply declared that Kay and Highs were false witnesses? G. W. Daniels thinks that Arkwright may have known something of Lewis Paul's (or Wyatt's) machine: but is it not again surprising that Arkwright should never have said a word about it, when it might have saved both his patent and reputation, and that he never gave any clear and satisfactory account of the origin of his invention? G. W. Daniels writes that the evidence put forward by Guest (in 1823) on behalf of Highs rests mainly on statements made by old men sixty years after the event (op. cit., p. 96): we shall simply observe that all the evidence quoted here is taken from the report of the case published the same year (1785), the value of its corroboration by Guest's witnesses remaining an open question.

[2] R. Guest, op. cit., pp. 203-5.

[3] He made combs for the weaving looms.

[4] R. Guest, op. cit., p. 203.

[5] R. Guest, op. cit., pp. 176-80 (being the evidence given by T. Leather and T. Wilkinson before the parish clerk of Leigh on Aug. 29th, 1823, and Nov. 1st, 1827). What prevents us from unreservedly believing the evidence of these two witnesses is that when the events in question had taken place, half a century before, they were only twelve and fourteen years old respectively. A. Held (*Zwei Bücher zur socialen Geschichte Englands*, p. 591) believed he could conclude that the jenny was invented by Highs and improved by Hargreaves. In this case I am inclined to share G. W. Daniels's scepticism.

Even if this were an established fact it would not follow that Hargreaves should be regarded as a mere pirate. He may have rediscovered something which someone else had invented before him, and of which he was unaware. The case of Arkwright is quite different. The fact that he previously had no knowledge either of spinning or mechanics, and his suspicious dealings with Kay, make it fairly clear how he may have come into possession of another man's invention. Moreover, he seems to have tried to ward off suspicion: when he took out his first patent he described himself falsely as a clockmaker, probably in order to suggest that he had some knowledge of mechanics.[1] An even more interesting document is the account by Highs of an interview between him and Arkwright which took place at Manchester in 1772: 'We fell into conversation and I began to tell him he had got my invention. I told him I had shown the model of it to Mr John Kay, the method I intended to use the rollers, because John Kay's wife had told me that before, how it happened, and Mr Arkwright and them could never deny it ... He said very little about it: when I told him, he never would have had the rollers but through me, he put his hand down in this way, and never said a word ... Also he told me, when I told him it was my invention: Suppose it was, he says, if it was, he says, if any man has found out a thing, and begun a thing, and does not go forward, he lays it aside, and another man has a right in so many weeks or months (I forget now) to take it up, and get a patent for it.'[2] What can be thought of Arkwright's silence in court, when faced with such definite accusations? His counsel, in his name, said that both Highs and Kay were false witnesses, but Arkwright never produced any satisfactory explanation of the origin of his invention.

For lack of any proof to the contrary[3] we must therefore admit that Arkwright's chief invention, to which he owed most of his wealth and fame, was not really his. As to the minor inventions, enumerated in the patent of 1775, if we are to believe the evidence of the many witnesses against him at the trial of 1785, he could not claim these either.

[1] 'Richard Arkwright of Nottingham in the County of Nottingham, clockmaker.' See *Calendar of Home Office Papers*, 1766-9, p. 425. Ure, who has heaped most exaggerated praise on Arkwright, tries to justify him. 'As Mr Arkwright had thus [by making Kay's acquaintance] evidently directed his attention to clock-making, *and naturally enough supposed himself the author of some improvements in that art* [italics ours] he chose to designate himself clock-maker in the drawing-roller patent of 1769 — a very pardonable assumption.' A. Ure, *The Cotton Manufacture of Great Britain*, I, 231. A very artless explanation.

[2] *The Trial of a Cause*, etc., p. 59.

[3] The only fact of importance produced in Arkwright's favour was this: Highs acknowledged (*Trial*, p. 58) that he did not give his cylinders their final form (one half grooved and the other covered with leather) till 1769, one year after the construction of Arkwright's model. But there was nothing new about this arrangement, as John Wyatt had used it in 1738. See Wyatt MSS., I, 45.

According to them the feeder had been invented in 1772 by the Quaker John Lees of Manchester,[1] the crank and comb was Hargreaves's,[2] and the carding machine was almost identical with the one for which Daniel Bourne had taken out a patent in 1748.[3] As for the roving frame, its cylinders were borrowed from Highs's machine, and its conical box revolving on a vertical axis had been used by Benjamin Butler since 1759.[4] We can understand now why the 1775 specification had been drawn up in such vague terms, that it required the genius of a Watt to guess its meaning. Arkwright had only tried, as well as he could, to conceal his thefts. But the proceedings in June 1785 made them manifest. After the brilliant pleading of Adair for Arkwright, and of Bearcroft for the Crown, the jury did not hesitate to condemn Arkwright, and to declare his patent to have lapsed and the action of his competitors to be right and proper.[5]

This trial, together with the judgment, would have utterly crushed any other man than Richard Arkwright. But he was not so easily daunted. Deprived of his patent, he was still the richest cotton-spinner in England, and his factories were the most numerous, the most important and the best run. He went on developing his undertakings. In 1784, with David Dale,[6] he founded the New Lanark spinning mills, which derived their power from the falls of the Clyde. He set up others at Wirksworth and Bakewell near Cromford, and he did not neglect the old ones, whose buildings he enlarged and whose plant he renewed. It was in Nottingham, which had witnessed the beginnings of his industrial career, that he first made use of the steam engine. Honours too became his portion. In 1786 Margaret Nicholson's outrage provided the occasion for Arkwright, at the head of a deputation of notables, to present the King with a congratulatory address, and he was knighted shortly after. The following year Sir Richard Arkwright was called on to fill the high office of Sheriff of the County of Derby.[7] He died in 1792, leaving a capital of half a million. One of his

---

[1] Evidence of Lees, T. Hale and H. Marsland, *Trial*, pp. 38-40.

[2] Evidence of Elizabeth and George Hargreaves, *Trial*, pp. 41-5. Evidence of Whittaker, pp. 45-8, contested by the author of the article on Hargreaves, in the *Dictionary of National Biography*. 'We know now that Arkwright was, as he claimed, the author of these improvements, about which Hargreaves was informed by one of Arkwright's workmen' (E. Lipson, *History of the Woollen and Worsted Industries*, p. 151).

[3] Patent No. 628 (Jan. 20th, 1748).

[4] Bennet Woodcroft, *Brief Biographies of Inventors*, p. 11.

[5] *Trial*, pp. 107-87.

[6] Robert Dale Owen, *Threading my Way*, pp. 7 and 13: David Bremner, *The Industries of Scotland*, p. 280. David Dale, Robert Owen's father-in-law, is best known as a philanthropist. See Part III, chap. IV.

[7] R. Guest, *A compendious history of the cotton-manufacture*, p. 28.

factories, that at Bakewell, brought his heirs in £20,000 a year.[1] These were big figures, in days when great millionaire manufacturers had not yet been heard of. Such a fortune, built up in so few years, such unprecedented success in a man risen from nothing, were enough to justify Arkwright in the eyes of his generation.[2]

His success, in fact, best illustrates what he really achieved, and what his place in economic history should be. He was no inventor. At the most he arranged, combined and used the inventions of others, which he never scrupled to appropriate for his own ends. The praise once lavished on him by rash admirers, today seems slightly misplaced. It was plainly absurd to compare him either to Newton or to Napoleon,[3] and rather unfortunate to quote him in order to prove that capitalism is founded entirely on personal merit and on laborious honesty. Arkwright's real claim to fame lies in the fact that he was successful. He was the first who knew how to make something out of other men's inventions, and who built them up into an industrial system. In order to raise the necessary capital for his undertakings, in order to form and dissolve those partnerships which he used successively as instruments with which to make his fortune,[4] he must have displayed remarkable business ability, together with a curious mixture of cleverness, perseverance and daring. In order to set up large factories, to engage labour, to train it to a new kind of work and to enforce strict discipline in the workshops, he needed an energy and an activity not often met with. These were qualities which most inventors never had, and without which their inventions could not have resulted in the building up of a new industrial system. It was Arkwright who, after the inconclusive or unsuccessful attempts of the brothers Lombe, of Wyatt and of Lewis Paul, really created the modern factory. He personified the new type of the great manufacturer, neither an engineer nor a merchant, but adding to the main characteristics of both, qualifications peculiar to himself: those of a founder of great concerns, an organizer of production and a leader of men. Arkwright's career heralded a new social class and a new economic era.

[1] *Gentleman's Magazine*, LXII, 771 (August, 1792); F. Espinasse, *Lancashire Worthies*, I, 463.
[2] See the evidence of Sir Robert Peel before the Commission of Enquiry of 1816: 'A man who has done more honour to the country than any man I know ... I mean Sir Richard Arkwright.' *Report of the Minutes of Evidence taken before the Select Committee on the State of the Children employed in the Manufactories of the United Kingdom* (1816), p. 134. Peel had been one of Arkwright's opponents in 1785.
[3] A. Ure, *Philosophy of Manufactures*, pp. 16 and 252.
[4] 'Arkwright succeeded very unaccountably in finding fresh partnerships, though former ones were dissolved in consequence of their not answering, and he always came richer from the misfortune, like Anteus, who in his falls gained strength from his mother earth.' R. Guest, *A compendious history of the cotton-manufacture*, p. 20.

His name will always be associated with the beginnings of the modern factory system. At the end of the eighteenth century all the factories in Lancashire and Derbyshire were built in imitation of his establishments. 'We all looked up to him', said Sir Robert Peel.[1] He knew it, and seemed deliberately to try and lead the way in hard work and limitless ambition. He worked ceaselessly all day and often part of the night.[2] He had to travel constantly in order to supervise his many factories, and worked on the road in his post-chaise, drawn by four horses, which were always driven at top speed.[3] His plans for the future were boundless. He once said that if he had the privilege of living long enough his capital could one day repay the whole national debt.[4]

IV

With Arkwright machine industry ceased to belong solely to the realms of technical history and became an economic fact, in the widest sense of the word. Yet, even in the cotton industry, it was still far from having reached complete development. The main feature of the period we are describing was the very extensive use of the jenny,[5] which did not make any great difference either to the organization of labour or to the life of the working people. On the other hand no new improvements had been made in the loom since the invention of the fly shuttle, and it was therefore now the weaver who lagged behind the spinner. The two inventions which finally transformed the textile industry were those of Samuel Crompton and Edmund Cartwright.

Crompton's 'mule',[6] as its name suggests, was a compound machine; that is to say, it combined two principles, that of the jenny and that of the water frame. From the water frame it borrowed the rollers between which the thread was drawn, and from the jenny the moving carriage which slid backwards and forwards. The spindles were fixed to it and were thus given an alternating motion, first moving away, so as to stretch the thread after it had passed between the rollers, then moving back whilst they rotated rapidly on their own

---

[1] *Report of the Minutes of Evidence ... on the State of the Children employed in the Manufactories of the United Kingdom*, p. 134.

[2] When he was over fifty he found two hours every day to improve his spelling and his grammar.

[3] F. Espinasse, *Lancashire Worthies*, I, 467.

[4] Ibid.

[5] 'The yarn or twist for warps was spun from cotton in the water-frame factories, whilst the weft was spun by the families of the weavers on the jenny.' R. Guest, *A compendious history of the cotton-manufacture*, p. 17.

[6] Or mule-jenny.

axis, and thus at the same time both twisting and winding the thread. The thread which the water frame produced was strong but rather coarse. The thread produced by the jenny was fine, but was too weak and broke too easily. The mule gave both strength and extreme fineness.[1]

In many respects it was a final invention, for, in spite of modifications due to the various needs of the different textile industries, and to the development of engineering knowledge, its main characteristics are still to be found in the delicate and complicated machinery of the most up-to-date type.

The inventor of the mule, Samuel Crompton, belonged to a Lancashire family of small landowners.[2] The old house near Bolton, where he was brought up and where he worked at his invention between 1774 and 1779, can still be seen, and has now been transformed into a museum. It is a fine building with gables, high chimneys and mullioned windows, which reminds the visitor of the prosperous days of an extinct class.[3] In Crompton's time the smaller yeomanry was becoming more and more divorced from the land. His father was still a farmer as well as a spinner and a weaver, but Crompton himself never did any agricultural work. Had he an opportunity of seeing and studying the water frame, or did he reinvent it as Highs did with Wyatt's invention?[4] In any case he knew Arkwright personally, for he had met him when Arkwright was still a barber at Bolton.[5] As for the jenny, he had often used it, and it was in order to improve it that he began his researches.[6]

Unlike Arkwright, he had not worked out in advance the profit his

[1] In 1792 John Pollard of Manchester was able, with the aid of the mule, to turn a pound of raw cotton into 278 hanks of yarn with a total length of about 212,000 yards. *Edinburgh Review*, XLVI, 18.

[2] 'His father held a farm of small extent, and, as was customary in those days, employed a portion of his time in weaving, carding and spinning.' 'Brief Memoir of Samuel Crompton', in *Memoirs of the Literary and Philosophical Society of Manchester*, Second Series, V, p. 319.

[3] G. French, *Life and Times of Samuel Crompton*, pp. 27, 43, 48, 51; Bennet Woodcroft, *Brief Biographies of Inventors*, p. 13. The popular name of Crompton's house was 'Hall i' th' Wood' (Drawing in G. W. Daniels, *The Early English Cotton Industry*, p. 115).

[4] This is asserted by Kennedy, 'Brief Memoir of Samuel Crompton', pp. 325-6. But the terms of the petition of Mar. 5th, 1812 (*Journals of the House of Commons*, LXVII, 175) do not tally with this hypothesis. Crompton was evidently acquainted with the water frame, since he said he had invented the mule to remedy the defects of that machine, which was 'utterly incapable of spinning weft of any kind, or of producing twist of very fine texture'.

[5] French, *Life and Times of Samuel Crompton*, p. 46.

[6] He was born in 1753. In 1779, the date of the invention, he was therefore 26 years old.

invention would bring him. For some time he only used the machine himself, in the little workshop where he was at once engineer, workman and employer. But the extreme fineness of his thread attracted the attention of the neighbouring manufacturers. He at once became the object of much curiosity, mingled with a great deal of jealousy and covetousness. Ladders were used to peep in at his windows and holes were bored in his walls.[1] He realized that he would not be able to keep his secret very much longer. He had no patent and perhaps would have found it difficult to take one out, as part of his invention was simply an adaptation of the water frame, and Arkwright was still in possession of his patent rights: 'I was under the necessity of making it public or destroying it, as it was not in my power to keep it and work it, and to destroy it was too painful a task, having been four and a half years, at least, wherein every moment of time and power of mind, as well as expense, which my other employment would permit, were devoted to this one end, the having good yarn to weave: so that destroy it I could not.'[2] He preferred to make a present of it to the public. The manufacturers had promised him a voluntary subscription as compensation, and the subscription was actually made, its total amount being £67 6s. 6d.[3] But some of the subscribers, once they had got hold of the model, did not feel bound to keep their word.

After this experience of the generosity and good faith of his neighbours, it is hardly surprising that Crompton should have become discouraged and misanthropic. A few years later he invented a carding machine, but it was hardly finished before he smashed it to pieces, exclaiming, 'They shall not have this too.'[4] Being a poor man, with very little talent for business, he was doomed to disappointment. He succeeded in setting up a little spinning mill, first at Oldham near Bolton, and then, in 1791, in Bolton itself. But the manufacturers, fearing his competition, enticed away his best workmen;[5] one of them, Robert Peel, once offered to take him into partnership but was refused.[6] In 1802 a new subscription list was opened for him and produced about £500.[7] Finally, in 1812, his friends persuaded him to apply to Parliament for a grant, such as had often been awarded to less

[1] Bennet Woodcroft, *Brief Biographies of Inventors*, p. 15; French, *Life and Times of Samuel Crompton*, p. 77.

[2] Letter from Crompton, quoted by E. Baines, *History of the County Palatine and Duchy of Lancaster*, II, 453.

[3] This is the figure given by French, p. 85, and by the *Dictionary of National Biography*, XIII, 149. Woodcroft, op. cit., p. 15, and Kennedy, op. cit., p. 320, give £106 and £50 respectively.

[4] French, op. cit., p. 106.

[5] Bennet Woodcroft, op. cit., p. 16.

[6] 'Cotton-spinning Machines and their Inventors', *Quarterly Review*, CVII, 70-1.

[7] Kennedy, op. cit., p. 321, and *Journals of the House of Commons*, LXVII, 838.

deserving persons. The support of the Prince Regent had been solicited and Parliament granted Crompton £5,000,[1] most of which he spent in paying his debts, for he died poor.

Crompton was a man of remarkable intelligence and some culture,[2] probably much above most of those who profited by his invention. But he was unable to reap any benefit from it. His very independent character, combined with a modesty which almost amounted to shyness, were not qualities which made for success: and he lacked some other qualities, such as the gift of organization and of leadership. The contrast between his life and that of Arkwright shows the difference there is between original research and discovery, and their clever adaptation to practical ends. In the South Kensington Museum the portraits of the two men hang side by side. Arkwright, with his fat vulgar face, his goggling heavy-lidded eyes, whose expressionless placidity is belied by the vigorous line of the brow and the slight smile on the sensual and cunning lips, is the matter-of-fact business man who knows how to grasp and master a situation without too many qualms of conscience. Crompton, with his refined and emaciated profile, his fine forehead from which his brown hair is tossed back, the austere line of his mouth and his large eyes, both enthusiastic and sad, combines the features of Bonaparte in his younger days with the expression of a Methodist preacher. Together they represent invention and industry, the genius which creates revolutions and the power which possesses itself of their results.

Like the jenny, the mule was at first made of wood, and its small size made it suitable for use in cottages. About 1783 larger ones were made, with metal rollers and wheels.[3] In 1790 a Scotch manufacturer called William Kelly made automatic mules, set in motion by a water-wheel like Arkwright's machine, and fitted with as many as three or four hundred spindles.[4] From that time forward the mule became the spinning machine *par excellence*, and took the place, in current use, of Hargreaves's jenny. In 1812, before presenting his petition to Parliament, Crompton, in order to collect information on the success of his invention and the importance of the interests it had created, visited the chief centres of the textile industry and noted that the mule was used in

[1] The petition was brought in on March 5th, 1812, and the Bill passed on March 25th. *Journals of the House of Commons*, LXVII, 175 and 476. See G. W. Daniels, *The Early English Cotton Industry*, pp. 155-8.

[2] Mr Daniels, after studying Crompton's original correspondence, has been led to the same appreciation: 'Crompton can only be regarded as a working man, but that he had fully utilized his limited opportunities of education, his letters and other attainments show.' *Early English Cotton Industry*, p. 149.

[3] Kennedy, op. cit., pp. 329-30.

[4] Ibid., pp. 337 ff.; E. Baines, *History of the Cotton Manufacture*, p. 205, mentions as one of the authors of this improvement William Strutt, son of Jedediah Strutt.

many hundreds of factories, with a total of four or five million spindles.[1] The jenny, which twenty years before had been so popular, now only played a comparatively unimportant part in the industry as a whole. And with the jenny the last remains of the old cottage system finally disappeared from the cotton-spinning industry, which had become the most flourishing industry in England.

Not only was spinning transformed by Crompton's invention but its consequences were felt in weaving as well. The water frame had made it possible to weave calicoes in England, while previously they had to be imported from India. The mule, thanks to the extreme fineness of the thread it produced, enabled British manufacturers to outdo the renowned skill of the Indian workers and to manufacture muslins of incomparable delicacy.[2] This was a new industry, whose centres were Bolton in Lancashire, and Glasgow and Paisley in Scotland.[3] By 1783 it occupied over a thousand looms in Glasgow alone,[4] and in 1785 the output of muslins in Great Britain was estimated to be about fifty thousand pieces.[5] As was observed by the author of a contemporary pamphlet, the muslin industry 'is of the greatest importance from a national point of view, because the whole process consists of labour alone, in many instances performed by women and children, and the value of the raw material applied to this article is generally increased from 1,000 to 5,000 per cent'.[6]

V

Meanwhile the unequal speed of industrial processes, which had once already set in motion technical progress, was again making itself manifest. While spinning was now done by machinery, weaving was still done by hand. About 1760 weavers found it difficult to get enough thread to keep themselves in constant employment. Thirty years later the opposite was the case: there was a scarcity of weavers and their wages rose rapidly. Those who wove fancy muslins at Bolton were paid in 1792 as much as 3s. or 3s. 6d. a yard, while the weavers of cotton

[1] Kennedy, op. cit., p. 322; Bennet Woodcroft, *Brief Biographies of Inventors*, p. 17.

[2] Crompton in his petition of 1812 points out this advantage, due to the use of his mule. See *Journals of the House of Commons*, LXVII, 175.

[3] D. Macpherson, *Annals of Commerce*, IV, 80; *A Complete History of the Cotton Trade*, p. 102; J. Aikin, *A Description of the Country from thirty to forty miles round Manchester*, p. 166; R. Guest, *A compendious history of the cotton-manufacture*, p. 31.

[4] Among the Glasgow muslin manufacturers, a certain number were merchants or shipowners, who had gone into industry during the war with America. See La Rochefoucauld-Liancourt, 'Voyage aux Montagnes', vol. II, letter dated May 8th, 1786.

[5] A. Anderson, *An Historical and Chronological Deduction of the Origin of Commerce*, IV, 655.

[6] *An Important Crisis, in the Callico and Muslin Manufactory in Great Britain, explained*, p. 9.

velveteen earned 35s. a week.[1] So they gave themselves great airs, and could be seen parading about the streets, swinging their canes and with £5 notes ostentatiously stuck in their hatbands. They dressed like the middle class and would not admit workmen of other trades to the public houses they patronized.[2] It is true that their prosperity was short lived. In 1793 the general industrial crisis in England caused a drop in wages.[3] But this only changed the aspect of the problem. The disproportion between the output of spun yarn and of material became so great that spinners were forced to export.[4] This exportation gave rise to some alarm, as many people feared that a weaving industry, supplied by English cotton thread, might be set up in neighbouring countries, particularly in France. A vigorous campaign was conducted against the export of cotton thread, and there was even some talk of prohibiting it altogether, for the same reason as the export of wool.[5]

Just as in the period before the spinning machines were invented, great discomfort was experienced in the whole textile industry. It became worse as the disproportion between the two branches of the industry increased, and reached its height in 1800. By then the remedy had already been known for several years, but its effect was not felt as yet, nor was it seriously applied until the need for the invention had reached its highest point. In this way the interplay of economic needs and technical inventions produced a succession of oscillations within the industry, each one of which marked a step forward.

[1] *Fifth Report from the Select Committee on Artizans and Machinery*, p. 392 (1824); *Minutes of the Evidence taken before the Select Committee appointed to report upon the Condition of the Hand Loom Weavers*, p. 389 (1835).

[2] Place MSS. (British Museum, Add. MSS. 27828), p. 199.

[3] Price of weaving muslins at Bolton per yard:

1792	...	...	...	3s. 0d.	1797	...	...	...	1s. 6d.
1793	...	...	...	2s. 0d.	1798	...	...	...	1s. 3d.
1794	...	...	...	1s. 9d.	1799	...	...	...	1s. 2d.

This drop was mostly due to the rapid increase in the number of weavers attracted by the high wages. *Fifth Report from the Select Committee on Artizans and Machinery*, p. 392.

[4] 'The demand for cotton cloth was equal, during this period, to take off the whole produce of the spindle, if weavers could have been found to weave it into cloth; but, this being impossible, the spinners began to export the surplus to the manufacturers abroad.' *Report on Dr Cartwright's Petition* (1808), p. 7. This exportation made it possible to keep down the wages of weavers at home, in spite of a great demand for labour. About 1800, 'there was not a village within thirty miles of Manchester, on the Cheshire and Derbyshire side, in which some of us were not putting out cotton warps, and taking in goods, employing all the weavers of woollen and linen goods who were declining those fabrics as the cotton trade increased; in short, we employed every person in cotton weaving who could be induced to learn the trade.' W. Radcliffe, *Origin of the New System of Manufacture, commonly called 'Power Loom Weaving'*, p. 12.

[5] W. Radcliffe, op. cit., pp. 78-84, 163-72, etc. Radcliffe was one of the leaders of this movement in Lancashire. On the discussions on this subject in the Manchester Chamber of Commerce, see E. Helm, *Chapters in the History of the Manchester Chamber of Commerce*, pp. 17 ff.

Power loom weaving was a problem which had already tempted many investigators. The difficulty seemed great, but not insuperable. The motions of the two frames on which the warp was stretched, and the shuttle which passed between them to form the woof, were fairly simple problems. In England and Germany, as early as the seventeenth century, a power loom was used for the weaving of ribbons.[1] A crank drove the shuttle backwards and forwards, while a system of counterweights stretched and tightened the threads.[2] But the process was slow and complicated, and even if steps had not been taken in various countries at the request of the weavers to prohibit its use,[3] the 'Dutch loom', as it was called,[4] would never have revolutionized the textile industry.

The same can be said of the loom made in 1678 by de Gennes, a Frenchman, in which two horizontal shafts passed the shuttle from one to the other side of the loom.[5] As for the one made by Vaucanson (the model of which is at the Conservatoire des Arts et Métiers in Paris), its main interest[6] lies in the fact that, half a century after it was invented, it served as a starting point for Jacquart's researches.

None of these inventions was of any practical value.[7] If in France or England power loom weaving shops had existed, they must have disappeared almost at once, for it is very difficult to find any traces of them.[8] At any rate it is fairly certain that Edmund Cartwright, the inventor of the power loom, knew nothing of them. The youngest son of a Nottingham gentleman, and early destined for the Church, he had done brilliantly at Oxford, and in 1764 had been made a fellow of Magdalen.[9] For a long time he thought of nothing but literature. He

---

[1] The invention has been attributed to one Anton Muller, who lived at Danzig at the end of the sixteenth century. See Beckmann, *Beyträge zur Geschichte der Erfindungen*, II, 527.

[2] See the description of the ribbon-weaving loom in the *Encyclopédie Méthodique*, 'Manufactures', II, ccii ff., and in its *Recueil de Planches*, VI, 72 ff. Also in A. Barlow, *History and Principles of Weaving*, pp. 217-27 (with plates).

[3] In Germany there had been regular riots against this machine. See Karl Marx, *Das Kapital*, I, 438.

[4] It was also called swivel loom.

[5] See *Journal des Savants*, year 1678, No. XXVII; *Philosophical Transactions of the Royal Society*, XII, 1001 ff., and *Abridgments of Specifications relating to Weaving*, Intro., p. xxxv.

[6] It is not even mentioned in the article on silk in the *Encyclopédie Méthodique*.

[7] John Kay, the inventor of the fly shuttle, took out a patent for a weaving machine in 1745, but it does not appear that his efforts in this direction had any material consequence. F. Espinasse, *Lancashire Worthies*, I, 310-18.

[8] R. Guest, *A compendious history of the cotton-manufacture*, p. 44, mentions the establishment created by Garside at Manchester in 1765. The failure of that undertaking was due to the fact that the use of defective machines resulted in an increase rather than in a reduction of expenses. See J. James, *History of the Worsted Manufacture*, p. 351.

[9] *Memoir of Edmund Cartwright*, pp. 7-12. His family had lived in Nottinghamshire for

even produced, in Pope's style, some verse whose chilly elegance was not entirely devoid of distinction.[1] When he left Oxford for a country living,[2] being an intelligent and active man, he took a keen interest in the condition of the rural population amongst whom he lived. He studied medicine and agriculture, and instructed his parishioners in the newest remedies for fever and the latest methods of cultivation.[3] In this way he first showed that enterprising spirit which was to transform a classical scholar lost in a country vicarage into an inventor and a manufacturer.

In the course of a chance conversation, whilst on a holiday at Matlock, Cartwright's attention was directed to the cotton industry, and the crisis with which it was threatened. He relates how he 'fell in company with some gentlemen of Manchester, when the conversation turned on Arkwright's spinning machinery. One of the company observed that as soon as Arkwright's patent expired, so many mills would be erected, and so much cotton spun, that hands never could be found to weave it. To this observation I replied, that Arkwright must set his wits to work and invent a weaving mill. This brought on a conversation on the subject, in which the Manchester gentlemen unanimously agreed, that the thing was impracticable.'[4] Cartwright disagreed, and undertook to prove his case.

His first efforts were very clumsy. He knew nothing of mechanics and had never even seen a weaver at work. Nevertheless, with the help of a carpenter and a blacksmith he succeeded in fitting up a loom which worked somehow: 'The warp was placed perpendicularly, the reed fell with a force of at least half a hundredweight, and the springs which threw the shuttle were strong enough to have thrown a Congreve rocket. In short, it required the strength of two powerful men to

---

[1] *Constantia* (1768), *Almine and Elvira* (1775), *The Prince of Peace, with other Poems* (1779), *Sonnets to Eminent Men* (1783). 'Mr Cartwright was once Professor of Poetry at Oxford, and really was a good poet himself. But it seems he has left the barren mountain of Parnassus and the fountain of Helicon for other mountains and other vales and streams in Yorkshire, and he has left them to work in the wild, large and open field of mechanics.' Letter from S. Salte (a cotton-goods merchant in London) to S. Oldknow, Nov. 5th, 1787, G. Unwin, *Samuel Oldknow and the Arkwrights*, p. 99.

[2] First at Brampton in Derbyshire, and then at Goadby Marwood in Leicestershire.

[3] *Memoir of Edmund Cartwright*, p. 18; J. Burnley, *Wool and Woolcombing*, p. 110; Bennet Woodcroft, *Brief Biographies of Inventors*, p. 21.

[4] *Encyclopædia Britannica*, first edition, article 'Cotton' (reproduced in the eleventh edition, VI, 500). See W. Radcliffe, *Origin of the New System of Manufacture commonly called 'Power Loom Weaving'*, pp. 52 ff.

---

three hundred years. Of his three brothers, two served with distinction in the army and the third was a member of Parliament, where he became famous for his advanced opinions. E. Halévy considers him to be the founder of English radicalism (*La Formation du Radicalisme Philosophique*, I, 223-4).

work the machine at a slow rate, and only for a short time.'[1] This was the invention which Cartwright patented in 1785.[2] He at once realized how much was still needed to render it really useful. By successive improvements he produced a machine which was easily worked, stopped automatically every time a thread broke, and could be used, with a few modifications, to weave any kind of material.[3] What remained to be done was to bring it into general use in the industry, which seemed to be waiting and crying out for it, and Cartwright had no doubt but that he would be immediately successful.

Then his troubles began. He had money[4] and wanted to work his invention himself. So in 1787 he set up a small factory at Doncaster. There were twenty looms, eight for weaving calicoes, ten for muslins, one for cotton checks and one for coarse linen.[5] As in the early spinning mills the motor power was at first supplied by animals, but in 1789 Cartwright introduced a steam engine from Birmingham. Unfortunately, though well equipped, the factory was badly run, for Cartwright had not, and never acquired, a business capacity.[6] It was the same melancholy story, true of most inventors, told over again. In 1791 he thought he had found the road to fortune, for he came to an agreement with some Manchester spinners, the brothers Grimshaw. They were to set up a big factory which was to contain no fewer than four hundred looms, worked by steam. Large buildings were put up for the purpose.[7] But the first machine had hardly been fitted when the weavers' violent hostility broke loose. The owners received threatening letters,[8] and a month later the whole place was burnt to the ground. Not only did Cartwright lose all profits from his contract with the brothers Grimshaw, but after that no one was found bold enough to be willing to renew the experiment.[9]

[1] *Encyclopædia Britannica*, loc. cit.; *Memoir of Edmund Cartwright*, pp. 63-4.

[2] *Abridgments of Specifications relating to Weaving*, No. 1470, April 4th, 1785.

[3] Patents No. 1565 (Oct. 30th, 1786), No. 1616 (Aug. 1st, 1787), No. 1676 (Nov. 12th, 1788).

[4] 'A very ample fortune.' Petition of Edmund Cartwright, clerk, D.D., Feb. 24th, 1809. *Journals of the House of Commons*, LXIV, 97.

[5] *Memoir of Edmund Cartwright*, p. 77; J. Burnley, *Wool and Woolcombing*, p. 112.

[6] He also suffered from his lack of an early training in practical mechanics: 'Cartwright's loom proved of little service, and was of value principally as a starting point for other inventors ... It was not until the machine had been taken in hand by actual mechanics and weavers that any satisfactory progress was made.' 'Cotton-spinning Machines and their Inventors', *Quarterly Review*, CVII, 78.

[7] These buildings were known as Knott Mills. See A. Barlow, *History and Principles of Weaving*, pp. 40 and 236; Wheeler, *Manchester*, p. 166.

[8] Here is the text of one of these letters, dated March 1792: 'We have sworn together to destroy your factory, if we die for it, and to have your lives for ruining our trade, and if you go on, you know the certainty.' *Report on Dr Cartwright's Petition* (1808), p. 4.

[9] See petition of Feb. 24th, 1809, *Journals of the House of Commons*, LXIV, 97.

Between 1792 and 1800 the power loom was both necessary and un-popular. It could not force itself into general use, because it was as much opposed as it was wanted and because the fall in wages had made the demand for mechanical weaving less urgent. Cartwright, com-pletely ruined and forced to hand his patents over to trustees, was struggling with merciless creditors and dishonest debtors.[1] He brought a series of actions against those who were trying to deprive him of the profits of his second invention, a machine for combing wool. But the force of necessity was at work, bringing final success. It first began in Scotland, where in 1793 James Lewis Robertson set up in Glasgow two power looms, the power being supplied by a Newfoundland dog;[2] a year later a workshop fitted with forty power looms was opened at Dumbarton; and in 1800 John Monteith, renewing the efforts of the Grimshaw brothers, set up in one factory two hundred looms worked by steam.[3] The campaign against the export of spun yarn hastened this tardy development. In 1803 Horrocks of Stockport produced some power looms made entirely of metal, which shortly after were in use in several Lancashire towns.[4] For Cartwright it was 'an agreeable surprise' to see the resurrection, if not the final triumph, of his invention. When in 1809, three years before Crompton, he petitioned Parliament for a grant, he was able in support of his request to point out that his machines 'were now in such use in the county of Lancaster alone as to be considered of great national importance'.[5]

A full study of the consequences of Cartwright's invention would take us far beyond the limits of the present book. It would include the history of power loom weaving as far as 1839, the date of the famous report of the Royal Commission on the condition of hand loom weavers.[6] This report, together with the evidence given before the Commission, illustrates both the growth of machine industry in this branch of the

[1] Inquiry into the Petition of Mar. 18th, 1801, *Journals of the House of Commons*, LVI, 271-2 (John Cartwright's evidence).

[2] We must also mention the efforts of Robert Miller and of Andrew Kinloch (1793). Webb MSS., Textiles, V, 1.

[3] R. Guest, *A compendious history of the cotton-manufacture*, p. 46; E. Baines, *History of the Cotton Manufacture*, p. 231.

[4] Hardwick, *History of the Borough of Preston*, pp. 374 ff. On the improvements intro-duced by Peter Marsland and Miller of Glasgow, see Wheeler, *Manchester*, p. 167, and 'Cotton-spinning Machines and their Inventors', *Quarterly Review*, CVII, 78.

[5] *Journals of the House of Commons*, LXIV, 97. On June 7th the petition was referred to the Supplies Committee (ibid., p. 391) which on June 8th granted Cartwright £10,000 (ibid., p. 393). Cartwright's misadventures had not made him a man-hater like Crompton. With his £10,000 grant he bought a farm in Kent, and occupied the last years of his life with experiments in agriculture, chemistry and mechanics. See E. Lipson, *History of the Woollen and Worsted Industries*, p. 168.

[6] *Minutes and Reports from H.M.'s Commissioners and Assistant Commissioners on the Condition of the Hand Loom Weavers* (1839-41).

textile trade and the causes owing to which its final triumph was delayed. The appalling misery of the weavers who, in 1839, still used hand looms, had become worse and worse as the grinding competition of machinery increased. But the worse it became the more it delayed the universal use of the new equipment, for wages sunk so low that it paid better to use men than machines. More recently a repetition of the same phenomena has been witnessed in certain industries which have not been completely transformed by the industrial revolution. There lies the explanation of the survival of a belated technique in small domestic workshops, the last home of the sweating system. But the obstacles which machinery raised against its own progress could never be anything more than temporary.

At the beginning of the nineteenth century the development of power loom weaving had hardly begun. Against the several million spindles already at work in the spinning mills there were in all England no more than a few hundred power looms.[1] But the results were plainly visible. Two steam looms, looked after by a fifteen-year-old boy, could weave three and a half pieces of material, while in the same time a skilled weaver, using the fly shuttle, wove only one.[2] Even though the textile industry had not yet found that organic balance, which successive inventions had for sixty years sought to restore, the problem was now solved. We have seen how the equipment of the spinning mills gradually grew up, like the interdependent organs of a living body. Before Cartwright's invention the system was still incomplete. Now all the essentials were there, and in that particular branch of production the triumph of machine industry was an accomplished fact.

Machinery now not only seized on and changed the fundamental processes of industry but made its way into all details and special operations. Up till that time materials had been printed by means of plates engraved in relief, which were stamped by hand on linen or calico, as many times over as was necessary[3] – a slow and expensive process. Materials printed in the roughest way and showing the simplest patterns in crude colours (a geometrical design, a leaf or an arabesque) were sold in 1780 at 3s. or 3s. 6d. a yard.[4] But in 1783 Thomas Bell, a Scotsman, replaced the plates, so laboriously applied

[1] R. W. Cooke Taylor, *The Modern Factory System*, p. 95, gives the following figures: in 1813, 100 steam looms; in 1820, 14,000; in 1829, 60,000; in 1833, over 100,000. According to S. Chapman, *The Lancashire Cotton Industry*, p. 28, the number of power looms in the country in 1813 amounted to 2,400, part of them being probably worked by water power.

[2] See R. Guest, *A compendious history of the cotton-manufacture*, pp. 47-8.

[3] In order to print 28 yards of linen, the plate, which was 10 inches long by 5 inches broad, had to be applied nearly 450 times. G. Townsend Warner, in *Social England*, V, 471-2.

[4] See *The Callico Printers' Assistant* (1790).

by hand, by copper cylinders, and one revolving press could do the work of a hundred workmen.[1] In Lancashire large calico-printing works were erected. Meanwhile the bleaching and dyeing industries were reaping the benefits of scientific progress. Berthollet's discovery of the bleaching properties of chlorine dates from 1785,[2] and was almost immediately taken up by James Watt, who made it known in England.[3] Its use in industry was realized some years later by Tennant of Glasgow,[4] and in a few years the process was universally adopted: the sight of pieces of stuff spread out in the open air for months together, and if looked at from a distance glittering in the sun like ponds, round all weaving villages, now vanished for ever. About the same time Taylor of Manchester rediscovered the secret of Oriental dyes, and produced 'Turkey reds', which soon became as popular as Indian prints.[5] Velveteen made its appearance, owing to John Wilson of Ainsworth.[6] A complete description of all these secondary improvements would cover many pages.[7]

But far from bringing the evolution to an end they only extended its scope. The effect of each fresh invention was to tighten the bond between all the various technical processes, and the more dependent they became on one another the more did any improvement in one have an immediate and profound effect on all the others. Thus their common development, that contagious and incessant progress which more than any static quality marks the factory system, was determined and quickened.

---

[1] There had been others before Bell, as early as 1764 or 1765. See *Gentleman's Magazine*, XXXV, 439 (1765). In 1785 his machine was introduced into Lancashire; Wheeler, *Manchester*, p. 169.

[2] 'Description du blanchiment des toiles par l'acide muriatique oxygéné', *Annales de Chimie*, II, 151; VI, 204 ff. 'Action de l'acide muriatique oxygéné sur les matières colorantes', ibid., VI, 210.

[3] On the relations of James Watt with French and English chemists, Berthollet, Black, Priestley, etc., see S. Smiles, *Lives of Boulton and Watt*, pp. 141-2. The same year (1786) the Literary and Philosophical Society of Manchester in its *Memoirs* (III, 343 ff.) published T. Henry's essay on 'The Theory of Dyes'. The Soho MSS. contain a letter from Watt to Berthollet (Feb. 25th, 1787) of which the beginning is in French: 'Monsieur – L'accumulation des affaires, suite nécessaire de notre longue absence de chez nous, m'a empêché jusqu'à présent de me prêter à votre affaire de blanchiment, mais je n'ai pas oublié cette importante affaire, ni non plus nos promesses de vous aider tant qu'il nous serait possible.'

[4] E. Baines, *History of the Cotton Manufacture*, p. 249.

[5] Note on Charles Taylor in the papers of the Owen Collection, LXXX, 74, Manchester Central Library.

[6] *A Complete History of the Cotton Trade*, pp. 71-3.

[7] Special mention should be made of an American invention, *the cotton gin* (1793), the use of which speeded up considerably the preparation of the raw material for industrial treatment. On the cotton gin and its inventor, Eli Whitney, see M. B. Hammond, *The Cotton Industry, an essay in American economic history*, I, 25-31.

VI

Even though the cotton industry developed so quickly we can distinguish several different stages. The first is the period immediately following on Hargreaves's invention. Between 1775 and 1785 a fever of production seized on certain districts. While thousands of jennies were at work in the cottages, the number of weavers and looms increased enormously, without being able to cope with the work. 'The old loom-shops being insufficient, every lumber-room, even old barns, cart-houses and outbuildings of any description, were repaired, windows broke through the old blank walls, and all fitted up for loom-shops. This source of making room being at length exhausted, new weavers' cottages with loom-shops rose up in every direction; all immediately filled ... '[1] There were still very few factories, for capitalistic organization had not yet taken on the shape which was soon to make it conspicuous. At least in appearance, that was the golden age of domestic industry.

The second period began with that memorable trial which ended in the cancelling of Arkwright's patent.[2] From that moment factories became general throughout the textile industry. The use of highly complicated and delicate machinery, which took up a great deal of room and was very expensive, was incompatible with cottage industry. But until then, in spite of its obvious advantages from the point of view of organization and supervision, the bringing together of many workmen in large workshops had never been in general use. In short, the system of 'manufacture', if by that term we mean a system of production which really prevailed at any given time, never existed in England at all. The factory system, on the other hand, was the necessary outcome of the use of machinery. Plant which consisted of many interdependent parts, and which was worked from one central power station, could only be set up in one main building, where it could be supervised by a disciplined staff. This building was the factory, which admits of no other definition.[3]

---

[1] W. Radcliffe, *Origin of the New System of Manufacture, commonly called 'Power Loom Weaving'*, p. 65.

[2] On the impression in Lancashire made by the decree, see *Manchester Mercury* of June 28th, 1785: 'The country is liberated from the dreadful effects of a monopoly in spinning', etc. G. Unwin observes that the cancelling of Arkwright's patent was shortly followed by the publication of Crompton's invention, both together giving 'an immense stimulus to the manufacture of the finer cotton fabrics' (*Samuel Oldknow and the Arkwrights*, p. 2).

[3] See *An Important Crisis, in the Callico and Muslin Manufactory in Great Britain, explained*, p. 4. According to this pamphlet (which, like many of the economic pamphlets of the eighteenth century, cannot be unreservedly relied upon) there were in 1788 in Great Britain, 143 spinning mills fitted with automatic equipment, 550 mules of 90 spindles, and 20,070 jennies of from 8 to 80 spindles.

The first spinning mills, compared with the great textile factories of the present day, would seem small indeed. Yet the labour they employed was fairly numerous: between a hundred and fifty and six hundred hands.[1] Apart from their gradual extension, the four- or five-storeyed brick buildings hardly changed at all during the following half-century.[2] The main characteristic of that time was the use of water for motor power. Arkwright's machine, being worked by water, was usually described as 'the water frame'. We have mentioned above the typical site of the Cromford spinning mill, which possessed all the essential conditions of which a manufacturer had to make sure. This had an important consequence, for it meant that no factory could be established far from a stream powerful and swift enough to set the machines in motion. For this reason it was not in towns that the mill-owners at first established their factories, but near the hills, in narrow valleys where by using dams it was easy to create an artificial waterfall. The beginnings of the modern factory system are to be found in small hamlets, far removed from those great industrial centres round which the mass of the working population has since gathered. These small places were scattered along the foot of the Pennine range, on all three sides of it; on the west towards Manchester and the Irish Sea, on the south towards the Trent valley, and on the east towards the Yorkshire plain and the North Sea.

But this dispersion was only comparative. The cotton industry, which differed in this respect from the old woollen industry, tended to establish itself almost exclusively in two or three districts: in southern Lancashire, in the north of Derbyshire and in the Clyde valley between Lanark and Paisley. The first of these districts was by far the most important, for in 1788 it contained more than forty spinning mills.[3] This was due to the abundant water power, for the high hills on the south-east run very steeply down to the low and marshy country which stretches right across to the coast. From time immemorial the Lancashire rivers have turned many wheels: at the beginning of the eighteenth century there were sixty mills established on the Mersey below Manchester within a distance of three miles.[4] Even though we can say that the geographical position and the climate, as well as the prosperity of the port of Liverpool, favoured the growth of the cotton industry in Lancashire, yet it is the existence of streams providing the necessary power which explains why the earliest factories

[1] A spinning mill employing 600 workmen was opened at Manchester in 1780. See Edwin Butterworth, *History of Oldham*, p. 118.

[2] W. Fairbairn, *Mills and Millwork*, II, 113.

[3] *An Important Crisis, in the Callico and Muslin Manufactory of Great Britain, explained*, p. 4.

[4] See W. Stukeley, *Itinerarium Curiosum*, p. 58.

grew up round Blackburn, Bury, Bolton, Oldham and Manchester.[1] The same observation applies to the Derbyshire and Glasgow districts. It is, of course, true that this essential condition was found in many other districts as well. And, indeed, between 1785 and 1800 factories were set up in a large number of counties. But these experiments, which were actuated by the success and the rapidly acquired fortunes of the northern manufacturers, were not followed by extensive consequences.[2] Far from resulting in the spread of the cotton industry over the whole country they only threw into relief its localization, which, as time went on, became ever more pronounced.

While its geographical concentration was only one of the external features of the new industrial system, an even more fundamental concentration was taking place within: the concentration of undertakings bound together by their common need for raw materials and markets, and that of capital, the importance of which grew with that of mechanical equipment. Each factory represented a capital of several thousand pounds,[3] and it was not uncommon for one man to own several. For instance, we know that Arkwright ran eight or ten at a time.[4] The second Peel employed almost the whole population of Bury in his spinning, dyeing and printing works, while the weaving was carried on by the cottagers in the neighbouring villages.[5] He also owned other

---

[1] There were spinning mills at Bury from 1774, at Chorley from 1776, at Preston from 1777, at Oldham from 1778. See Edwin Butterworth, *History of Oldham*, pp. 117-18; Id., *History of Ashton-under-Lyne*, pp. 142-3.

[2] The author of *An Important Crisis* gives the following table (1788):

England	Spinning Mills	Scotland	Spinning Mills
Lancashire	41	Lanark	4
Derbyshire	22	Renfrew	4
Nottinghamshire	17	Perthshire	3
Yorkshire	11	Midlothian	2
Cheshire	8	Ayrshire	1
Staffordshire	7	Galloway	1
Westmorland	5	Annandale	1
Flintshire	3	Bute	1
Berkshire	2	Aberdeenshire	1
Surrey	1	Fife	1
Hertfordshire	1		
Leicestershire	1		
Worcestershire	1		
Pembroke	1		
Gloucestershire	1		
Cumberland	1		

The spinning mills of Cheshire, Flintshire and Westmorland can be regarded as part of the Lancashire group, while those of Staffordshire formed part of the Derbyshire group. *An Important Crisis, in the Callico and Muslin Manufactory in Great Britain, explained*, p. 5.

[3] On that point G. Unwin warns us against contemporary exaggerations (*Samuel Oldknow and the Arkwrights*, p. 115).

[4] Those at Nottingham, Cromford, Belper, Bakewell, Wirksworth, Derby, Chorley, Manchester and Lanark.

[5] 'Some of these are confined to the carding, slubbing, and spinning of cotton; others to washing the cottons with water wheels which go round with great velocity

factories in over twelve different places.[1] In 1802 he employed more than fifteen thousand persons, and he paid into the Treasury £40,000 in excise duties.[2] At Stockport, Samuel Oldknow, a muslin manufacturer, was towards the end of the century popularly reputed to be earning £17,000 a year.[3] Between 1792 and 1797 the Horrocks set up three factories in Preston alone.[4]

The large amount of capital which was needed for such undertakings did not in each case belong to one individual. Joint capitalist enterprises increased, especially in the earlier period, before great individual fortunes had been made in industry. The reader no doubt remembers the numerous contracts which Arkwright so cleverly turned to good account in order to bring his various schemes to a successful conclusion. Peel, too, had several partners,[5] and his firm was commonly referred to as 'the Company of which that very respectable gentleman, Robert Peel, Esq., member of parliament for Tamworth, is the head'.[6] It is important to note that in this case the word 'company' was not used in its usual sense of a joint-stock company. This form of organization had so far only been used in, and was only deemed suitable for, a few important banking, insurance or public works undertakings.[7] Adam Smith considered this as an unquestionable principle.[8] When in 1779

[1] At Bolton, Warrington, Manchester, Blackburn, Burnley, Walton, Stockport, Churchbank and Ramsbottom in Lancashire; at Bradford in Yorkshire; at Tamworth and Lichfield in Staffordshire, etc.

[2] R. W. Cooke Taylor, *Life and Times of Sir Robert Peel*, I, 16.

[3] On Samuel Oldknow see Robert Owen, *The Life of Robert Owen, written by Himself*, p. 40; J. Kennedy, 'Brief Memoir of Samuel Crompton', *Memoirs of the Literary and Philosophical Society of Manchester*, Second Series, V, 339, and the interesting book on *Samuel Oldknow and the Arkwrights*, written from original records, by G. Unwin with the assistance of A. Hulme and G. Taylor.

[4] Hardwick, *History of the Borough of Preston*, p. 366.

[5] See Wheeler, *Manchester*, pp. 528 ff.

[6] J. Aikin, loc. cit.

[7] See G. Schmoller, 'Die geschichtliche Entwickelung der Unternehmung', *Jahrbuch für Gesetzgebung, Verwaltung und Volkswirtschaft*, 1893.

[8] 'The only trades which it seems possible for a joint-stock company to carry on successfully, without an exclusive privilege, are those in which all the operations are capable of being reduced to what is called a routine, or to such a uniformity of method as admits of little or no variation. Of this kind is, first, the banking trade; secondly, the trade of insurance from fire and from sea risks, and capture in time of war; thirdly, the trade of making and maintaining a navigable cut or canal; and,

... Boiling and bleaching the goods are performed at other works. In short, the extensiveness of the whole concern is such as to find constant employ for most of the inhabitants of Bury and its neighbourhood, of both sexes and all ages, and notwithstanding their great number, they have never wanted work in the most unfavourable times.' J. Aikin, *A Description of the Country from thirty to forty miles round Manchester*, p. 268; Wheeler, *Manchester*, p. 521; F. Espinasse, *Lancashire Worthies*, II, 90-103.

the question of starting a company for the manufacture of linens and printed calicoes was discussed,[1] the scheme was promptly allowed to drop. As in other industries, joint-stock enterprise only came into being at a much later period. Capitalism in its early days retained an essentially individual character. The employer was both the owner and the director of an industrial undertaking, and in his own person combined the powers and the prerogatives which in a joint-stock company would be divided between the shareholders on the one hand and the directors on the other.

In this way, through the introduction of machinery and the consequent concentration of the means of production, the hold of commercial capital was riveted on industry, and the manufacturer in the modern sense of the word took the place of the merchant-manufacturer. Between the two extremities of this rapid evolution there lay a whole series of intermediate stages. Sometimes the fustian master would merely gather together in one workshop a certain number of hand machines: this was the 'spinning room', which belongs more to the stage of 'manufacture' than to that of the modern factory.[2] Sometimes the raw material and the plant were owned by different people. Small spinning mills received the raw cotton from the merchants and returned it to them in the shape of yarn,[3] and thus the two successive systems of production formed a temporary alliance, the factory merely carrying out the tasks formerly entrusted to home workers. So long as hand and power loom weaving existed side by side part of the industry was bound to remain subject to those conditions which had in the beginning ruled the whole industry; but great weaving establishments, which often belonged to owners of spinning mills, competed in many places with the cottage industry.[4] And lastly, it must not be forgotten that from 1780 onwards the mule, which replaced the jenny and was, like it, adapted

---

[1] Petition to the House of Commons, *Journals of the House of Commons*, XXXVII, 108. We must also note the scheme described in a pamphlet of 1798, 'The Outlines of a Plan for establishing a United Company of British Manufacturers'. The plan was an extremely ambitious, not to say a chimerical one: the author conceived a great federation of all industries, partaking of the joint-stock company and of the *News from Nowhere* community, with the workers housed and paid in subsistence tickets and a share of social capital, a scientific office for the organization of production, etc.

[2] See Edwin Butterworth, *History of Ashton-under-Lyne*, p. 82. This type of work was very common before 1785.

[3] Schulze-Gaevernitz, *La Grande Industrie*, pp. 53 ff., compares this system with the one which existed for so long and which still exists today [1927] in the Saxon Oberland.

[4] Like that set up at Derby by Arkwright, Need and Strutt in 1773. See p. 224.

---

fourthly, the similar trade of bringing water for the supply of a great city.' Adam Smith, *Wealth of Nations*, Book V, chap. I. On the failure of several industrial companies founded in the eighteenth century see W. Cunningham, *Growth of English Industry and Commerce* (third edition), II, 519.

for use in the cottages, spread throughout the country, and thus for some time still kept the domestic system of production alive. In the cotton materials which were produced about that time the warp, spun on a water frame, was usually made in a factory, whilst the woof was spun on a mule in a cottage.[1] In this way we see how the old and the new methods of industry crossed and intercrossed, so closely were they bound up with one another.

It was during this decisive period that the main lines of the factory system were laid down. By the time when, in the following period, steam came into general use the factory system was fully grown, and it was altered by this new invention very much less than we might be led to suppose. Now that after long neglect man is again turning to account natural forces, now that factories are once more built by running water in lonely valleys, the difference in appearance, which formerly was so marked, begins to fade away and enables us to see the identity of the underlying principle. There was more difference between a spinning mill and a domestic workshop as they existed side by side between 1780 and 1800, than between a factory of that date and a modern one.

VII

It was difficult then to realize the whole importance of this change, the social results of which could not yet be foreseen. What struck people chiefly was the immediate material result: the birth of great undertakings, the unlimited growth of production, all that unprecedented development, which they could not but contrast with the stagnation of the traditional industries.[2] In 1795 John Aikin thus began his *Description of the Country from thirty to forty miles round Manchester*: 'The centre we have chosen is that of the *cotton manufacture*; a branch of commerce, the rapid and prodigious increase of which is, perhaps, absolutely unparalleled in the annals of trading nations.'[3] Someone else compared this sudden progress to the bursting forth of a hidden force.[4] Others refused to see anything more in it than an extraordinary,

---

[1] J. Kennedy, 'Rise and Progress of the Cotton Trade', *Memoirs of the Literary and Philosophical Society of Manchester*, Second Series, III, 126.

[2] 'The whole nation has observed it with wonder.' *Thoughts on the Use of Machines in the Cotton Manufacture* (1780), p. 12.

[3] J. Aikin, *A Description of the Country from thirty to forty miles round Manchester*, p. 3.

[4] 'The cotton manufacture, although generally believed to be very extensive, yet the magnitude of this trade, and the national advantages derived from such a combination of human labour with ingenious machinery, can scarce be supposed to have made an impression equal to the importance of the object, because the progress has been rapid beyond example. It has burst forth, as it were, upon the country in a moment.' *An Important Crisis, in the Callico and Muslin Manufactory in Great Britain, explained* (1788), p. 1.

and perhaps a disastrous, accident. For England did not herself produce cotton, and must therefore buy it, and according to the theory of the balance of trade, all imports which were not compensated for by an equal or greater quantity of exports were a loss to the country. For this reason it seemed impossible that the cotton industry should ever become a permanent asset to the wealth of the nation.[1]

But in order to form an idea of the progress that had been made already, we need not confine ourselves to such more or less arbitrary impressions and arguments. No statistics of production are available, but the consumption of raw material is shown by the figures of imports recorded in the Custom House Registers. In 1701 the weight of raw cotton imported into Great Britain did not exceed a million pounds. Fifty years later it was scarcely three million. In 1771 it reached 4,760,000 lb. and in 1781, 5,300,000. In the six following years the figures went up so quickly that we cannot wonder at the astonishment then felt by the public. By 1784 the 1781 figure was doubled (11,482,000 lb.), and by 1789 it was six times as great (32,576,000 lb.). A slackening followed on this rapid growth, which was resumed, however, after 1798. The import of cotton rose from 32 million lb. to 43 million in 1799, to 56 million in 1800, and in 1802 to 60,500,000 lb.: over thirty times what it was in the preceding century, when the competition between the cotton and the woollen trades was denounced as a national peril.[2] The export of manufactured goods developed on parallel lines. In 1780 it was still insignificant, and its total value did not reach £360,000. By 1785 it exceeded one million sterling; by 1792, two million; in 1800, five and a half million; in 1802, £7,800,000,[3] more than twenty times the value of British cotton goods exported twenty-two years before.

Let us look more closely at the curve of the movement. Its general upward direction is by no means uniform. Between 1780 and 1800 it shows, at almost regular intervals, depressions which correspond with as many industrial crises. Two, at any rate, of these crises were serious. In 1788-9 most of the new factories had to dismiss part of their hands, and some even had to close down. Distress prevailed in Lancashire and Cheshire villages, where the jenny had become the inhabitants' chief source of income.[4] In 1793 the situation was

---

[1] 'Cotton can be no staple.' See *The Contrast, or a Comparison between our Woollen, Silk and Cotton Manufactures* (1782).

[2] See *Journals of the House of Commons*, LVIII, 889, 892, 894; MacCulloch, *Dictionary of Commerce*, article 'Cotton'; E. Baines, *History of the Cotton Manufacture*, pp. 215-16.

[3] E. Baines, op. cit., pp. 349-50.

[4] 'The utmost distress prevails among the cotton spinners in many of the populous towns in Lancashire and Cheshire, who spin upon the jennies.' *An Important Crisis, in the Callico and Muslin Manufactory in Great Britain, explained*, p. 23. 'In the course of the last twelve months, the petitioners have been compelled to discharge a great number

even more serious: about a dozen cotton spinners went bankrupt,[1] and the import of raw material fell suddenly from 35 to 19 million lb. It is true that each one of these crises was followed by renewed activity, as was stated by a manufacturer who had been through the whole period of the formation of the British cotton industry: 'I have seen a great many overthrows in the cotton manufacture. In 1788 I thought it was never to recover. In 1793 it got another blow, and in 1803 again, and in 1810, but every time that it received a blow, the rebound was quite wonderful.'[2]

The curious recurrence of these crises, coupled with the vigorous growth both before and after each one of them, at once suggests a simple explanation. Are these not the earliest instances of over-production due to machine industry? And have we not thus at its very birth hit on one of the most characteristic features of the modern factory system? We know already that more yarn was spun than could be woven in the country, and the fall in prices, due to the new methods of manufacture, was thereby greatly increased. No. 100 cotton yarn, which in 1786 was still worth 38s. a pound, by 1788 was only worth 35s., by 1793 only 15s., by 1800 only 9s. 5d., and by 1804 only 7s. 10d.[3] No doubt this fall did increase the consumption both in England and on the Continent. But the supply increased more rapidly than the demand. Machinery was gaining ground, and new undertakings were springing up everywhere. As prices fell, cotton spinners, in order to maintain their profits, had to produce ever larger quantities of yarn, which only added to the congestion of the market. In the circumstances periodical collapse was inevitable. And when the ruin of a number of firms, the forced slowing down of machinery and unemployment of part of the population, had brought production down to its normal level, then a fresh period of prosperity would set in, to be followed after a few years by another catastrophe, the same causes bringing about the same consequences.

Such is the explanation which would be given of these recurring crises, if we allowed ourselves to indulge in hasty generalizing. The next step would be to look for an economic law accounting for this periodic recurrence. But anyone who realizes the great complexity of the facts, even in this early stage when they had not attained their full develop-

[1] Wheeler, *Manchester*, p. 244.

[2] A. Ure, *Philosophy of Manufactures*, p. 441.

[3] E. Baines, *History of the Cotton Manufacture*, p. 357.

of the men, women and children which they employed at that business, the mills in general have been reduced to half work: some have been totally abandoned in consequence of the stagnation of trade.' *Journals of the House of Commons*, XLIV, 544-5. See Patrick Colquhoun, *An Account of Facts relating to the Rise and Progress of the Cotton Manufacture in Great Britain* (1789), pp. 3 ff.

ment, will not be satisfied with so simple and abstract an explanation. For a more careful study of each of these crises shows that over-production does not sufficiently account for their appearance. That of 1788 is, in fact, the only one of which this explanation can be given, for it occurred very soon after the great expansion of the industry which took place as soon as Arkwright's patent was cancelled, after that period of feverish activity and unbounded speculation, when hundreds of undertakings both great and small had been set up all over the country, and when the humblest manufacturer had entertained hopes of success and wealth. That the cause of the crisis was clear to the cotton spinners is sufficiently shown by their attacks against the importation of Indian goods:[1] the English market was becoming too small: 'there was', as they rather naively expressed it, 'a want of consumption'.[2] This was only another way of saying that too much was being offered for sale, that there was, in fact, over-production. In 1793 the case was quite different. To begin with, the crisis was not confined to the cotton industry, nor even to those industries whose system of production had recently undergone great changes. It was a general crisis. The total number of bankruptcies in the United Kingdom, whose annual average between 1780 and 1792 was not more than 530, rose in 1793 to over 1,300.[3] It would be impossible to attribute this general disaster to the still very limited influence of machine industry and large-scale production. It began, as a matter of fact (and this explains its universal character) by a financial crisis. In February 1793 several important banks stopped payment. This caused great nervousness, and a few weeks later brought about the failure of about a hundred provincial banks.[4] A general panic broke out. No more credit was given, and people hid their money at the bottom of their chests, 'terror created distrust, distrust impeded circulation'.[5] Transactions were reduced to a bare minimum. Goods were left in the shops, not because

---

[1] An Important Crisis, in the Callico and Muslin Manufactory in Great Britain, explained, pp. 12-13. The unpublished memorandum preserved at the French Foreign Office under the title of 'Considérations sur les manufactures de mousseline de callico dans la Grande Bretagne' (Mémoires et documents, Angleterre, LXXIV, fol. 182-92) describes those complaints and admits their being founded. The author seems to have been inspired by the pamphlet we have just referred to.

[2] Patrick Colquhoun, An Account of Facts relating to the Rise and Progress of the Cotton Manufacture in Great Britain, p. 4. On the crisis of 1788, see Unwin, Samuel Oldknow and the Arkwrights, pp. 85-102 (original letters exchanged between S. Oldknow, S. Salte, Richard Arkwright Jun., etc.).

[3] G. Chalmers, Estimate of the Comparative Strength of Britain, p. 291. See J. H. Francis, History of the Bank of England, pp. 213-15, and D. Macpherson, Annals of Commerce, IV, 266. Of those 1,300 bankruptcies very few affected the cotton trade (thirteen according to Wheeler, Manchester, p. 244).

[4] D. Macpherson, Annals of Commerce, IV, 266 ff.; Chalmers, op. cit., p. 297.

[5] Chalmers, op. cit., p. 295.

there were too many for the usual consumption but only because no one would buy. The remedy, too, was a financial one. After having talked the matter over with the chief London bankers, Pitt decided to issue Treasury bonds up to five million sterling.[1] This step, which threw non-depreciated securities into the market, helped to re-establish confidence and to restore credit. From that moment matters slowly readjusted themselves and gradually reverted to their normal state.

What was the cause of this financial crisis? Was it the war with France, which broke out at the beginning of February? War certainly made matters worse; but it did not create the trouble, since its first symptoms had been discernible a year before.[2] The most alarming of these was the depreciation of the notes issued for an excessive amount by the county banks. How was it that these banks, so few of which existed forty years before, had increased far beyond the real needs of the country? In order to find the reason we must turn to that great economic movement in which all England was taking part, and in which not only industry but agriculture and trade, both at home and abroad, were equally involved.[3] Side by side with the opening of new factories estates were changing hands, and fresh lines of communication were opened from one end of the kingdom to the other. The reader will remember the 'canal fever' which raged after 1792, the multifarious schemes and hastily established undertakings to which speculation lent artificial and ephemeral vitality. In short, the 1793 crisis seems to us to have been the outcome of a combination of many interconnected facts, and the extent of its effects can be easily explained by the complexity of its causes. In the language of modern business the 'crash' succeeded the 'boom', a sudden depression was caused by an abnormal expansion of trade. Over-production was only one manifestation of this expansion, in the same way as machinery was only one of the factors in the industrial revolution. The early history of the cotton manufacture should not be separated from that of the more general development in which it was included, and its various stages interest us in so far as they announce or accompany those of a greater and more general growth. But they do not account for that

[1] See 'Report from the Select Committee on the State of Commercial Credit', *Parliamentary History*, XXX, 740-66; *Journals of the House of Commons*, XLVIII, 702-7.

[2] W. Ederson, in his *Letter to the Spinners and Manufacturers of Cotton Wool upon the present Situation of the Market* (1792), complains of the state of the market, of the fluctuations of prices, due, according to him, to speculation.

[3] The above considerations do not substantially differ from the conclusion arrived at by Dr Bouniatian, although he does not confine the use of the word over-production to purely industrial phenomena, but extends it to any excessive expansion of trade (M. Bouniatian, *Geschichte der Handelskrisen in England*, chap. V, pp. 151-72). The same book should be consulted on the crises of 1783 (pp. 144-50), 1797 and 1799 (pp. 173-99).

growth as a whole. Moreover, as is the case with any fact taken separately, they were surrounded by many circumstances, which should be eliminated before the underlying law can be discovered.

VIII

If this law does not stand out clearly it is because too many adventitious elements combine to alter and complicate it. By these we do not only mean accidental happenings, such as good or bad harvests, the peace of 1783 or the war of 1793, but also the many forms of official intervention – regulations, fixation of prices, tariffs and prohibitions, which, more tightly than today, held fast the whole economic life of the country as in a fine-meshed net. Even the cotton industry, whatever may have been said to the contrary, did not escape the bonds of official protection and constraint. To a certain extent it benefited by the one, while it had often to contend with the other. As soon as the doctrine of *laissez-faire* had established itself, it became the fashion to say that this industry, which had in so few years become the most flourishing in the country, owed everything to liberty.[1] This statement cannot be unreservedly accepted. We must above all draw a distinction between tariffs, which were based upon the theory of mercantilism, and regulations originating in medieval tradition.

Nothing is less accurate than to say that the English cotton manufacture grew up without any artificial defence in the face of foreign competition. For the very prohibitions which had nearly stopped the early growth of that industry were later used for its protection. The import of printed cottons from whatever source remained forbidden.[2] No protection could be more complete, for it gave the manufacturers a real monopoly of the home market. The prohibition did not extend to yarns or undyed materials, and the East India Company continued to import certain foreign materials into England, such as muslins from Dacca, famous for their fineness. But the English manufacturers very soon began to raise protests against this, for they meant to be protected. They repeatedly sent in petitions to ask that a duty should be levied on all materials of foreign origin, and in the end they had their way.[3] And not only was the home market reserved for them, but steps

---

[1] See E. Baines, *History of the Cotton Manufacture*, pp. 321 ff.; Schulze-Gaevernitz, *La Grande Industrie*, p. 40; Leone Levi, *History of British Commerce*, p. 24.

[2] 'As the law now stands, no printed cotton, other than the manufacture of Britain, can be worn in this Kingdom. The wear of all others is forbidden by positive statute. The cotton therefore enjoys a monopoly over the whole island; the law admits no rival to it.' *Parliamentary History*, XVII, 1155.

[3] The details of the various tariffs is given by Baines, *History of the Cotton Manufacture*, pp. 322-31. Between 1787 and 1813 the duties were raised from 16.5 per cent to 85 per cent *ad valorem* for calicoes, and from 18 per cent to 44 per cent for muslins.

were taken to help them to gain markets abroad. A bounty was given on every exported roll of calico or muslin,[1] a privilege that might have been considered unnecessary, seeing that from the technical point of view England had a twenty-five or thirty years' start over all continental countries.

So great was the superiority of English production that neighbouring countries could hardly have kept out English goods save by a policy of strict prohibition, which, as a matter of fact, they never adopted. Before the great wars of the French Revolution and of the Empire disturbed the whole economic life of Europe, opinion tended if not to free trade, as it was understood by the Cobdens and Brights of the following century, at any rate to commercial treaties, and to international agreements founded on mutual concessions. The Anglo-French treaty of 1786 is the most interesting example of this policy. One of its results was to throw open the French market to Manchester and Paisley goods. It is true that in return cotton materials manufactured in France were, for the first time, admitted into England.[2] But this system of reciprocity could not fail to benefit chiefly the country which, thanks to its technical progress, could produce a greater quantity of goods at a lower price.

This, it will be said, was the result of free competition. But English manufacturers had not yet learnt to substitute this new formula for the old protectionist tradition. They were still suspicious of free trade, even when it was to their advantage. This attitude is illustrated by the campaign waged against the export of yarns. Some spinners, like William Radcliffe, actually refused to sell to foreign buyers.[3] At several meetings held at Manchester in 1800 and 1801 they vehemently denounced 'that baneful practice, which threatened the English cotton manufacture with complete ruin'. The Board of Trade was approached with a view to obtaining complete prohibition, or at any rate severe restric-

---

[1] 21 Geo. III, c. 40 and 23 Geo. III, c. 21. This bounty varied from ½d. to 1½d. a yard, according to the quality of the material. See *Journals of the House of Commons*, XXXVIII, 465, and XXXIX, 294, 387.

[2] See de Clercq, *Recueil des Traités de la France*, I, 146-65, and *Parliamentary History*, XXVI, 233-54, Art. VI, para. 7: 'All sorts of cotton manufactured in the dominions of the two Sovereigns in Europe, and also woollens, whether knot or woven, including hosiery, shall pay, in both countries, an import duty of twelve per cent *ad valorem*.' For the Parliamentary debates on the ratification of the treaty, see ibid., pp. 381-514 (House of Commons) and 534-96 (House of Lords). A special study of the treaty has been made by F. Dumas (*Étude sur le traité de commerce de 1786 entre la France et l'Angleterre*), (1904).

[3] W. Radcliffe, *Origin of the New System of Manufacture, commonly called 'Power Loom Weaving'*, pp. 10-11.

On the frequent appeals of the cotton manufacturers for protection, see E. Helm, *Chapters in the History of the Manchester Chamber of Commerce*, pp. 17, 22, etc.

tions of the export of yarns.[1] Only the vigorous opposition of several influential manufacturers, including Sir Robert Peel, prevented these measures being actually put into force.[2] So the export of yarns was still permitted, though other protective measures were either introduced or maintained. For many years a law against the employment of English workmen abroad had been in force.[3] Its regulations were specially renewed for the benefit of the cotton industry, and very strictly enforced.[4] As for the new machinery, stern measures were enacted to prevent its exportation to foreign countries. An Act passed as early as 1774 made it an offence to export 'tools or utensils used in manufacturing cotton or cotton and linen mixed'.[5] Another Act, in 1781, extended the same prohibition to sketches, models or specifications.[6]

Such a state of things was indeed very different from freedom of trade as defined later by the liberal school of political economy – that is, complete mobility of goods and labour spontaneously moving to wherever the highest wages or profits are to be found. If it be true that the history of the cotton industry can provide arguments for the doctrine of *laissez-faire*, these will certainly not be found during this early period, in which we see nothing but a struggle between contradictory and half-conscious tendencies. But this very contradiction shows that fresh wants were growing up and were beginning to be felt. They grew up all the quicker because they had not to break down too many habits and traditions.

The fact is, that with regard to this new industry the government had no definite policy at all. It did not at first think of it as anything but

[1] Many pamphlets were published dealing with this subject. See *A Letter to the Inhabitants of Manchester on the Exportation of Cotton Twist* (Manchester, 1800); *A Second Letter to the Inhabitants of Manchester on the Exportation of Cotton Twist*, by Mercator; *Observations founded upon Facts on the Propriety or Impropriety of exporting Cotton Twist, for the Purpose of being manufactured into Cloth by Foreigners* (London, 1803); *A View of the Cotton Manufactories in France* (Manchester, 1803).

[2] W. Radcliffe, op. cit., pp. 163 ff.

[3] 5 Geo. I, c. 27. For a first offence the hirer was given 3 months' imprisonment and £100 fine; for further offences 12 months' imprisonment and such fine as the Court would think fit to impose. If a workman settled abroad he was warned by the Embassy and had to go home within six months. If he did not do so he ceased to be a British subject and all his property in England was confiscated.

[4] 22 Geo. III, c. 60 (1782). The penalties were as much as £500 fine and one year of imprisonment and for further offences £1,000 and 5 years. The export of tools or machinery was punished by a fine of £500. On sentences given against German subjects in 1785 and 1786 see Wheeler, *Manchester*, p. 171.

[5] 14 Geo. III, c. 71.

[6] 21 Geo. III, c. 37. Similar legislation was enacted for the metal trades in 1785 and 1786 (25 Geo. III, c. 67, and 26 Geo. III, c. 89) and a General Act was passed in 1795 (35 Geo. III, c. 38). See W. Bowden, *Industrial Society in England towards the end of the Eighteenth Century*, pp. 130-1.

a new source of wealth, which could supply revenue to the State. When, in 1784, Pitt wanted to find some more money to balance his budget, he bethought himself of increasing the excise duty on cotton materials. For when he considered the flourishing state of the cotton industry, its eighty thousand workers and the many fortunes made by millowners, he felt that it could easily bear more taxation.[1] The new tax was therefore decided on.[2] The extent and power of the interests which had grown up with the industry were shown by what followed. A chorus of lamentations arose. Lancashire manufacturers of calicoes and fustians, Glasgow and Paisley manufacturers of muslins, weavers, printers and dyers all sent petitions to Parliament.[3] A Committee to get the new taxes repealed was set up in Manchester.[4] This Committee organized an agitation in the affected districts and sent delegates to London to approach both the Government and the opposition. There was a debate in the House of Commons, when Fox and Sheridan spoke in defence of the manufacturers, and Pitt, after some resistance, gave way and did as he was asked.[5] The delegates had a triumphal return to Manchester. A procession of two thousand people turned out to meet them, in which every branch of the cotton industry was represented, carrying banners with topical mottoes: 'Let Commerce flourish for ever! Freedom restored! May Industry never be cramped!'[6]

But was liberty the real object of that movement? To justify their protest against the imposition of a burdensome tax the cotton manufacturers needed no other principle than that of self-interest, as it has been understood in all ages and under all systems of government.[7] The intervention of the Whig party was the only thing which might have created some illusions in the matter. For the first time it came out as

---

[1] Speech of April 20th, 1785, *Parliamentary History*, XXV, 481. See the report of the Committee of Ways and Means in 1784, *Journals of the House of Commons*, XL, 410.

[2] 24 Geo. III, c. 40. Each roll of calico, muslin, etc., had to pay when bleached, dyed or printed, a tax of 1d. a yard if its value was less than 2s. a yard, and of 2d. if its value was over 2s. This tax was in addition to the previous excise duty of 3d. per yard.

[3] 'If these laws are allowed to continue, they will go far in extirpating these branches, particularly the British muslins, and the cotton machinery ... The hazards and inconveniences attending the introduction of a new branch of trade are manifestly obvious, and the necessary and unavoidable struggle to bring the same to perfection point out, in strong colours, the cruelty of disturbing infant manufactures in their progress to maturity.' *Journals of the House of Commons*, XL, 484 and 748. See also 749, 760, 768, 780, 835.

[4] See *A Report of the Receipts and Disbursements of the Committee of the Fustian Trade*, Manchester, 1786.

[5] *Parliamentary History*, XXXV, 478-91.

[6] Owen MSS., LXXX, 7; Wheeler, *Manchester*, p. 170.

[7] We must refer, however, to a pamphlet of 1785, *Manufactures improper Subjects of Taxation*, in which the argument for the cotton industry assumes the appearance of a general theory.

the defender, or rather as the ally, of large-scale industry. But this alliance, which later was to throw such a weight into the political scales, had not yet become permanent. The Tory Government had still many partisans among the northern manufacturers. Sir Robert Peel was both an admirer and a personal friend of William Pitt.

From the very beginning there was, however, one sphere in which the history of the factory system and of free trade were one, namely the sphere of production. Manufacturing regulations, gild statutes, and even Acts of Parliament, such as the Statute of Artificers of 1563,[1] had always been measures with special and limited applications; they only applied to one or more specified trades. By the very fact of its novelty any recently created industry was beyond their hold, and unless it became in its turn the subject of special regulations it could grow up in complete freedom. This was the case in the cotton manufacture. We have seen the difficulties in spite of which it found a footing in England, where it was at first treated as a foreign industry. By the time that its existence had become recognized and authorized, the old industrial legislation, if not quite discredited, had at any rate become much weaker. In the woollen industry it had great difficulty in coping with smuggling, and it was in vain that penalties were increased and that a system of mutual spying was set up among manufacturers.[2] It was useless to make the meshes of the net finer, for it was impossible to arrest the stream which continued to pour through it. Adam Smith, who on so many points was far in advance of his time, on this subject merely gave expression to a growing feeling.[3] It was hard enough to maintain

[1] 5 Eliz., c. 4. Article XXV mentions land labourers; Article XXVII, haberdashers, drapers, goldsmiths, embroiderers, ironmongers; Article XXIX, blacksmiths, wheelwrights, ploughwrights, millwrights, carpenters, masons, plasterers, sawyers, lime burners, brick makers, brick layers, tile-makers, linen-weavers, turners, cowpers, millers, potters, weavers 'weaving huswives or house-hold cloth only and none other cloth', fullers, distillers and thatchers. We follow the order, or rather the disorder, of the original text.

[2] 17 Geo. III, c. 12 (1777) set up general assemblies of manufacturers, who themselves selected committees, working under the Justices of the Peace. This institution which was first set up in Lancashire, Yorkshire and Cheshire, was in 1784 extended to Suffolk (24 Geo. III, c. 3), in 1785 to Huntingdon, Bedford, Northampton, Leicester, Rutland and Lincoln (25 Geo. III, c. 40), and in 1790 to Norfolk (30 Geo. III, c. 56).

[3] He was not alone in this respect. See James Anderson (*Observations of the Means of Exciting a Spirit of National Industry*), (1777), p. 427: 'If it be difficult for gentlemen of ordinary station to acquire a perfect knowledge of the detail of mechanical arts, it is surely more difficult still for Ministers of State and others in the highest departments of civil affairs, to attain a perfect knowledge of these *minutiæ*; so that when they assume to themselves a sort of dictatorial power, and prescribe positive rules for regulating the practice of individuals, they descend from their own sphere and enter upon another, in which it is impossible they can have a sufficient degree of knowledge to be certain that they are acting with propriety, so that they frequently do hurt to the particular art they mean to encourage.'

the old regulations, and it was becoming quite impossible to set up new ones. Thus, from its birth, the cotton industry was free of the heavy yoke which weighed on the older industries. No regulations prescribed the length, the breadth or the quality of its materials, or imposed or forbade methods of manufacture. There was no control save that of individual interest and of competition. Because of this, machinery quickly came into general use, bold ventures were made and many kinds of goods were manufactured. There was the same freedom with regard to labour. Neither the trade gild, with its time-honoured traditions, nor the system of apprenticeship with its strict rules, ever existed in the cotton industry. This condition of things made it easier to recruit labour for the factories, but it also accounts for certain grievances which we shall have to record.[1]

This internal freedom is the one thing modern industry cannot do without. As soon as that is taken away industry ceases to move, and movement is its basic law: continual change, irresistibly carried forward by technical progress, and continual expansion, which shows itself in the increase of production and the extension of markets. This change and this expansion, though bound up with one another, are two quite separate phenomena, and, though either can start the other, yet logically the second follows from the first. In the same way economic freedom takes two different shapes, freedom of production and freedom of exchange. Without freedom of production large-scale industry was impossible, and the justifiable restrictions which have been imposed on it have never questioned that fundamental necessity. Freedom of exchange developed later and in a more halting way. If it is a feature of the new world created by the industrial revolution, it certainly was not among the early factors which went to its formation.

IX

From the cotton manufacture the use of machinery spread in a very short while to all the other textile industries. We shall confine ourselves to describing shortly the principal stages of its development in one of these, the most important as well as the most ancient and the most traditional of all. The slow evolution which in the woollen industry was imperceptibly developing capitalistic organization, received a sudden impulse against which the combined forces of interest and tradition were to prove powerless.

One of the main causes which held back the progress of this industry was the fact that it was so scattered. Every little technical improvement, before it reached the small country workshops, took years to spread from town to town and from village to village. The fly shuttle

[1] See Part III, chap. IV.

did not reach the country districts of Wiltshire and Somerset till seventy years after the date of its invention.[1] Until the end of the eighteenth century, the history of the woollen industry remained essentially provincial and local. Even the industrial revolution assumed in that industry the aspect of a local event, for it took place almost wholly in one district, exclusively to its advantage, and enabled it to remain the chief centre of the English woollen industry to this day. There, in that small area, stand the cities of Leeds, Bradford, Huddersfield and Halifax, whose fame has long since consigned to oblivion the towns of the east and south-west, Norwich and Colchester, Frome and Tiverton.

Two different and opposite explanations have been given of these contrasting fortunes. According to M. Laurent Dechesne, the woollen industry developed in Yorkshire because wages were lower than in the southern counties.[2] According to Dr Cunningham it was the rise of wages in Yorkshire which forced the manufacturers to use machinery, while in the south the comparative cheapness of labour made them careless of technical improvements.[3] This contradiction is only an apparent one, for the two statements, in fact, relate to two distinct and successive stages. Manufacturers who had been first drawn to Yorkshire by the cheapness of labour had to raise wages as the prosperity of their industry increased, chiefly because of the competition in the labour market of the cotton industry in the neighbouring counties of Derbyshire and Lancashire.[4] They thereupon tried to increase their profits by making use of the machinery to which the competing industry owed its then unrivalled progress.

Above all, the prosperity of the West Riding must be attributed to

---

[1] *Report from the Committee to whom the Petition of several Persons concerned in the Woollen Trade of Somerset, Wilts and Gloucester was referred* (1803), *Journals of the House of Commons*, LVIII, 884-5: T. Joyce, a weaver at Freshford (Somerset), declares 'that he does not use the spring shuttle, but it was introduced about two years ago by a person who had been in the North of England to work'. The fly shuttle made its appearance at Stroud in 1795, to the great alarm of the weavers. Webb MSS., Textiles, V, 1.

[2] Laurent Dechesne, *L'évolution économique et sociale de l'industrie de la laine en Angleterre*, pp. 108-11. He quotes the following figures: A weaver's wages in 1771: at Norwich 7s., at Leeds 6s. 3d.; in 1790: Norwich 11s., Bradford 10s. These figures are somewhat higher than those given by A. Young, *Southern Counties*, p. 65, and *North of England*, I, 137.

[3] W. Cunningham, *Growth of English Industry and Commerce*, II, 462 (second edition: not repeated in the following editions). What cannot be disputed is that the industrial importance of the West Riding had begun before machinery was introduced into the woollen manufacture. The growing prosperity of its towns between 1770 and 1780 is witnessed by the erection of Cloth Halls (Bradford Piece Hall, 1773; Colne Piece Hall, 1775; Tanney Hall, Wakefield, 1776; Manufacturers' Hall, Halifax, 1779). *Victoria History of the County of York*, II, 417-19.

[4] In Halifax, female spinners who in 1770 were paid at the rate of 5d. or 6d. a day, received in 1791 1s. 3d. to 1s. 4d. Ibid. (third edition), II, 657.

its position and its contact with the new centres of industrial life. Once it was established, new advantages made themselves felt and made the future of the industry secure. The upper reaches of the Yorkshire rivers have as much water and power as those on the other side of the watershed. Their pure water, which had been used for many years in fulling and finishing cloth, turned the wheels of the first spinning mills.[1] Later on, when the steam engine replaced hydraulic power, Yorkshire found fresh wealth in its rich coal deposits, which in some places lay at an inconsiderable depth. Thus every phase in industrial progress brought fresh prosperity to this favoured spot, whilst on the other hand it made more and more inevitable the decay of other districts, with less running water and no coal. Whilst water was still the driving power of machinery those districts could continue to hold their own, but the use of steam finally ruined them. About 1785 the Norwich woollen manufacture was still prosperous. Business had improved after the bad crisis caused by the American war, and there seemed every indication of a future which would be worthy of the city's past record.[2] But only a few years later Eden observed various symptoms of decay. Manufacturers were dissatisfied, and wages were very low.[3] That industry has now entirely disappeared, and Norwich, once so well known for her fine worsted goods, has no more spinning or weaving mills. Their place has been taken by the manufacture of foodstuffs, while the worsted industry has migrated to the north, particularly to Bradford, whose population in one century increased from 13,000 to 200,000.

The jenny, the simplest of all spinning machines, was used in Yorkshire about 1773,[4] a few years only after its invention, but its use does not seem to have been very general before 1785, that is before the time when in the cotton industry it was already being supplanted by the mule and the water frame.[5] As in Lancashire, and

---

[1] Another advantage was 'the possession of a population which could not produce by tillage of the bleak slopes all that was necessary for sustenance, and which, by the inherited skill of generations, was especially suited for industrial work'. H. Heaton, *The Yorkshire Woollen and Worsted Industries*, p. 281.

[2] 'The manufacture in the last two centuries has been constantly increasing in importance, but at no time has it been so thriving as it is now: *callimancoes* go to Germany, Poland and Spain; *camlets* to Flanders, Spain, the West Indies and South America.' A. and F. de la Rochefoucauld-Liancourt, 'Voyage en Suffolk et Norfolk', II, letter dated Sept. 24th, 1784. We must not trust quite unreservedly to the admiring descriptions of young travellers: according to J. James, *History of the Worsted Manufacture*, p. 270, the decline of Norwich had begun about 1760.

[3] F. M. Eden, *State of the Poor*, II, 477.

[4] *Report from the Committee on the State of the Woollen Manufacture* (1806), p. 113.

[5] Ibid., p. 73. Technical reasons probably account for the delay: 'It arose partly from the weakness of the material, which broke more readily than cotton when subjected to any strain.' J. L. and L. B. Hammond, *The Skilled Labourer*, p. 145.

for similar reasons, it was for some time unpopular. Riots against machinery broke out in 1780 in Leeds, only a few months after Arkwright's factory at Chorley was burnt down.[1] But this hostility was serious and lasting only with the workmen, who feared a fall in wages. On the contrary the jenny was welcomed by the master-spinners, of whom there were so many in the West Riding, for it enabled them to increase the output of their workshops without making any alterations in their traditional organization. Far from favouring the progress of capitalism, the jenny seemed to have provided the small master with a new weapon with which to safeguard his independence. This was the secret of its success in a country which was, above all others, the home of small-scale industry.

In the south-west the merchant manufacturers, having little technical knowledge, did not realize how much their interests hinged on a rapid change of equipment, and how much they were to lose by having put it off until it was too late. So long as the operatives carried out their prescribed duties for a fixed wage they felt sure of their profits, the implements and the methods of manufacture being left for the men to choose according to their preferences or their habits. A few isolated attempts were made at Tiverton, at Shepton Mallet and at Leicester,[2] but they met, as we should expect, with the usual hostility from the workers. It was only after 1790, when the competition of the northern towns became alarming, that the people of Devonshire and Wiltshire, of Somerset and Gloucester,[3] finally made up their minds to the use of the jenny. But it was too late. In Yorkshire spinning mills with automatic equipment had already made their appearance, and these very soon made impossible the position of the manual worker, who was bound to the antiquated methods of cottage industry.

The first of the great Yorkshire spinners was Benjamin Gott, of Leeds.[4] He began his career when Arkwright was ending his. He did not meet with the same difficulties, and found it unnecessary to pass himself off as an inventor. He had only to be an intelligent capitalist, guided by the light of a neighbouring industry. His business seems to have rapidly become very important: he had a good supply of capital and was therefore able to set up two large factories in the suburbs of Leeds. He carried out there all sorts of experiments, which it would have been too difficult or too expensive for smaller men to undertake: for instance, he tried the most recent methods of chemical dyeing.

---

[1] The Skilled Labourer, p. 81.

[2] Harding, History of Tiverton, I, 198; The humble Petition of the poor Spinners in the Town and County of Leicester (1787); Webb MSS., Textiles, V, 1.

[3] Between 1790 and 1794 at Frome, Shepton and Taunton. Before 1791 at Barnstaple, Annals of Agriculture, XV, 494, and G. Billingsley, A General View of the Agriculture in the County of Somerset, pp. 90 and 167.

[4] J. Bischoff, A Comprehensive History of the Woollen and Worsted Manufactures, I, 315.

His success was immediate and decisive. In order to meet the demand, which grew even more quickly than the supply, Gott soon found himself like the Lancashire manufacturers compelled to resort to night work, and the machines, several of which were worked by steam, often worked for four days on end.[1] Very few years elapsed before Gott found himself with many rivals. Among those who in the last years of the eighteenth century founded the most active and prosperous businesses, we must mention Fisher, Holbeck, Brook of Pudsey, and William Hirst of Leeds, who boasted that he had been the first man to use the mule in spinning wool.[2]

Most of these men were cloth merchants who had become manufacturers. The very position of their factories suggests it. Leeds, round which they were gathered, had never until then been looked upon as an important manufacturing centre, but rather as a commercial one, a market to which all the weavers from the surrounding villages came to sell their cloth. Now they were to come to Leeds as workers in a master's workshop. While in the south-western counties the encroachments of capital on the producer's independence had been slow and gradual, in Yorkshire they were felt all at once and in an unmistakable manner. The small manufacturers saw the danger. A petition which, as early as 1794, they presented to the House of Commons, put their case with remarkable foresight. After pointing out the advantages of the system of cottage industry as it had existed till then in the West Riding, they went on to say: 'This system, which so fortunately for the trade in general, the individuals concerned in it, and' the public at large, has so happily long prevailed in Yorkshire, is now in danger of being broken in upon, and destroyed, by the introduction of the modes which have prevailed in other parts of the Kingdom, where the inconveniences and mischiefs resulting from it have been frequently and most severely felt; which modes are founded on monopoly erected and supported by great capitalists, and set on foot by that description of persons concerned in the woollen trade in Yorkshire, called cloth merchants, becoming cloth makers; and of late several such merchants in and near the towns of Leeds and Halifax, in the said Riding, have commenced clothiers, or cloth makers, and others have manifested a disposition to follow their

---

[1] *Report on the Woollen Manufacture* (1806), pp. 43, 72, 76, 118, 445; *Abridgments of Specifications relating to the Steam Engine*, I, 106.

[2] Ibid., pp. 45, 71; W. Hirst, *History of the Woollen Trade for the last Sixty Years*, p. 39. The first worsted mill in Yorkshire was established at Addingham near Skipton in 1787, motive power being supplied by the river Wharfe. There was no spinning mill in Bradford before 1794. *Victoria History of the County of York*, II, 421. Marshall's great linen factory, which in 1806 employed nearly 1,100 workmen, was founded about the same time. On the introduction of machinery into the linen industry, see A. Warden, *The Linen Trade*, pp. 690-3.

example, by establishing large factories for making woollen cloth. And the consequence of this procedure must, as the petitioners believe, be highly prejudicial to them, who, with a very trifling capital, aided by the unremitting labour of themselves, their wives, and children, united under one roof, decently and independently have maintained themselves and families ... And from this comfortable and independent situation, should such innovation prevail, the petitioners must separate from their families, and be reduced to a state of servitude, to gain bread for themselves, and their dearest relatives.'[1]

They did not confine themselves to vain complaints, but implored Parliament to defend them from the competition of the great manufacturers. Accustomed as they were to the legal protection which at all times had been so generously extended to the woollen trade, such a request seemed to them quite natural. They succeeded in getting a Bill introduced which forbade cloth merchants to open workshops.[2] This Bill was an anachronism, for the type of legislation to which it belonged was becoming obsolete and was very soon to lose what little strength it had left. The Bill was thrown out, like the Bill which sought to enforce the old apprenticeship regulations, like those against the use of machinery, which the workers were always clamouring for, and like all those others by which it was attempted to revive an almost forsaken policy.[3] But the small Yorkshire manufacturers persisted in their resistance. One of them, Robert Cookson, advocated in 1804 the passing of an Act similar to that of 1557, which limited the number of looms to be owned by any one employer.[4] It was only after repeated rebuffs that they finally gave up the attempt to persuade the public authorities to intervene in favour of domestic industry and against the factory system.

The dangers which they anticipated did not, as a matter of fact, seem very imminent. In 1806 the Parliamentary Commission in charge of a general inquiry into the condition of the woollen industry found that the number of manufacturers had not diminished. Eighteen hundred still had their places reserved in one or other of the cloth

---

[1] *Journals of the House of Commons*, XLIX, 275-6.

[2] Ibid., 432. It was to be supplemented by local regulations laid down by the cloth halls in each town. Aikin refers to this effort and adds: 'It is evident that merchants concentrating in themselves the whole process of a manufactory, from the raw wool to the finished piece, have an advantage over those who permit the article to pass through a variety of hands, each of which takes a profit. This some persons in the vicinity of Leeds now see, and are adopting the same plan ... Numbers of the small manufacturers, who made perhaps a piece in a week, find it more advantageous to work at these factories, where their ingenuity is well rewarded.' J. Aikin, *A Description of the Country from thirty to forty miles round Manchester*, p. 565.

[3] See Part III, chap. IV.

[4] *Journals of the House of Commons*, LIX, 226.

halls at Leeds.[1] Moreover, in spite of the competition of the factories, the bulk of the trade was still in their hands. In 1803 only one-sixteenth of all the pieces of cloth woven in the West Riding was produced by large factories, controlled by capitalists. All the rest, about 430,000 pieces, came from the workshops of master weavers.[2]

These figures are most significant, for they show the fight which this old industry put up against the same change which had taken place so easily and so completely in the cotton manufacture. There was still much vitality in thousands of small independent businesses, and it took a long time before they were finally absorbed or suppressed. Indeed, many of them survived until the middle of the nineteenth century.[3] But this was only possible when they adapted themselves, as far as they could, to the new conditions of production. Machine industry gradually permeated, before it finally destroyed them. About 1800 the Yorkshire manufacturers were almost all using the jenny or the mule for spinning and the fly shuttle for weaving. Carding, too, was done by machinery, but in special workshops to which the master workman, who did not own the necessary implements himself, sent his raw wool in the same way as from time immemorial he had sent his cloth to the fulling mills.[4] In this way a fusion, or rather a temporary compromise, was come to between manual work and machinery, between small- and large-scale industry.

In the worsted industry, capitalist organization had not waited for the introduction of machinery. But there the manufacturers had to take the wool-combers into account, as their technical skill and their strong organization enabled them to be exacting in their demands. Their clubs, which had branches all over England, helped them when they had to move about, or in case of unemployment.[5] Their

---

[1] *Report from the Committee on the State of the Woollen Manufacture in England* (1806), p. 8. But many of them only earned a bare subsistence wage and often got into debt. Ibid., p. 75.

[2] Ibid., p. 11. J. Bischoff, *A Comprehensive History of the Woollen and Worsted Manufactures*, II, table 4.

[3] In 1851 the Huddersfield Cloth Hall was still patronized by 287 small manufacturers. Laurent Dechesne, *L'évolution économique et sociale de l'industrie de la laine en Angleterre*, pp. 65 and 71.

[4] *Report on the State of the Woollen Manufacture* (1806), p. 446: 'I believe the number of mills, which I would call domestic mills, manufacturers' mills, in the district I am acquainted with, have been increased more than three times, perhaps more than four times; those which I speak of are the mills to which the domestic clothiers resort ... Whenever I go into the country I find a new mill, or a small steam engine erected wherever there is any water; on the smallest brook they erect a wheel to carry two or three engines; they have erected machines up to a thirty horse engine, principally for scribbling and carding.'

[5] See William Toplis's petition to the House of Commons (1794), *Journals of the House of Commons*, XLIX, 395.

frequent strikes were often successful, for it was difficult if not impossible to do without them, and they made their employers feel it. At certain times a mere threat to stop work was enough to force concessions from the employer which he would never have granted of his own accord, so that the wool-combers had succeeded in gaining for themselves a higher rate of pay than any other class of workers in the woollen trade, up to 28s. a week.[1] The invention of the combing machine completely altered this condition of things.

This invention was Cartwright's achievement.[2] It was brought out five years after the power loom, and the needs it was intended to meet were no less urgent; but, like the earlier invention, it was not immediately made use of. It did not, in fact, come into general use until much later, between 1825 and 1840,[3] but its existence was enough to set a limit to the extortions of the wool-combers. Their apprehension of its subsequent effect is shown by the desperate efforts they made to secure its prohibition.[4] Manufacturers, having now such an infallible weapon at their disposal, appear to have thought that they could hold it in reserve and spare themselves the expense of setting up an elaborate plant worked by water-wheels or by steam engines. Yet Cartwright had set forth the advantages of his invention in the most convincing language: 'A set of machinery consisting of three machines will require the attendance of an overlooker and ten children, and will comb a pack, or 240 lbs., in twelve hours. As neither fire nor oil is necessary for machine-combing, the saving of those articles, even the fire alone, will in general pay the wages of the overlooker and children, so that the actual saving to the manufacturer is the *whole* of what the combing costs by the old imperfect mode of hand-combing.'[5]

The first factory to use the combing machine was the one which was managed by the inventor himself at Doncaster, not far from Sheffield. The machine was nicknamed 'Big Ben' after a popular prize-fighter, because its jerky motion reminded people of a boxer's action.[6] It was still imperfect, and could not deal equally well with various qualities of wool. The disappointment felt by the manufacturers who used it before

---

[1] *Journals of the House of Commons*, XLIX, 395.

[2] See *Memoir of Edmund Cartwright*, pp. 99 ff.; J. Bischoff, *A Comprehensive History of the Woollen and Worsted Manufactures*, I, 316 ff.; J. James, *History of the Worsted Manufacture*, pp. 555-6; and J. Burnley, *Wool and Woolcombing*, pp. 113 ff.

[3] See W. Cunningham, *Growth of English Industry and Commerce*, II, 761.

[4] See Part III, chap. III. Over forty petitions were sent by the workmen to Parliament. The employers retaliated with counter petitions drawn up by a Committee formed for the purpose, the 'Worsted Committee'.

[5] J. Burnley, *Wool and Woolcombing*, p. 115.

[6] *Memoir of Edmund Cartwright*, p. 106. The word is found in the song which was made up by a workman on the day the machine was first used, and which is quoted by Burnley, op. cit., p. 126.

it had been improved is perhaps a sufficient explanation of the delay in its final success.[1] It was, nevertheless, in use in a good many factories by the beginning of the nineteenth century, especially around Nottingham and Bradford.[2] For this change, like all the earlier ones, was to benefit chiefly the towns of the midlands and the north. When in 1794 Garnett introduced the mule and Ramsbotham the combing machine[3] into Bradford, it was still a sleepy little town with grass growing in the streets.[4] Ten years later it already had several large factories[5] and was becoming a dangerous rival to the ancient industry of Norwich.

By then the superiority of the northern industrial centres was so firmly established that they were held up as examples to the rest of England: 'If the experiment of twenty years already in the use of spinning by water at Manchester has produced such general employment and activity there, as that hardly any person can be found in want of employ; and if in Yorkshire, by dint of such machines and engines, they not only use all their wool, but send down into the West Country and buy it up out of the very mouths of the wool dealers and clothiers; then it must necessarily follow that the general introduction and use of them in the Western Counties, and every other part of the Kingdom also, must be advantageous to the poor, and likewise eventually to the community at large.'[6] What Yorkshire was to the backward districts of Devonshire and Norfolk, Lancashire was to Yorkshire. For the cotton industry continued to lead the way for all the other textile industries. 'In my humble opinion', a manufacturer wrote in 1804, 'the woollen cannot too closely follow the steps of the cotton trade: that nation which brings forth its goods the best and the cheapest will always have a preference, and it is only by means of the adoption of every possible improvement that pre-eminence can be secured.'[7]

But in order to do this the first step was to change the whole spirit which still ruled this time-honoured industry. The tradition of extreme protection which bound it to routine had to be destroyed and it became necessary to do away with the antiquated legislation still in force, with the old system of apprenticeship strictly regulating the recruiting of labour, as well as with the trade regulations, which made it difficult to introduce new equipment and to abandon obsolete methods of

[1] Ibid., p. 127.

[2] *Report on the Woolcombers' Petitions* (1794), pp. 5 ff., and *Journals of the House of Commons*, LVI, 272.

[3] J. James, *Continuation to the History of Bradford*, p. 222. Garnett was the founder of one of the great manufacturing families of the district. Id., *History of the Worsted Manufacture*, pp. 328-9.

[4] *Continuation to the History of Bradford*, p. 91.

[5] Ibid., p. 366, and *History of Bradford*, p. 283.

[6] *Wool Encouraged without Exportation* (1791), pp. 69-70.

[7] *Observations on the Cotton Weavers' Act* (1804), p. 20.

production: 'In the beginning of the nineteenth century it would be a gratifying circumstance to have old prejudices removed, and to see a committee of the House of Commons occupied in clearing the Statute Book of all the Acts concerning that important manufacture ... Thus it would be at once freed from the fetters which have so long bound it, and henceforward its operations would go on as unconstrained as those of another trade, which has risen to at least an equal magnitude, without being scarcely noticed on the Journals of either House of Parliament.' The fulfilment of this wish was soon to remove the last obstacle in the path of the industrial revolution.

CHAPTER THREE

COAL AND IRON

THE country and the period that witnessed the extraordinary growth of the cotton manufacture, the birth of machine industry and the organization of the factory system, witnessed also a parallel development in the iron industry. This simultaneous progress is a most interesting fact, for the two industries concerned are totally different. They have nothing in common either in their material or their essential processes; and their technical advancement had therefore to proceed by quite different methods. Only deep-lying causes could make them participate in one general evolution. Moreover, the changes in the textile and the metal-working industries are connected by something more than a merely simultaneous development, which we might be tempted to consider as a pure coincidence, for they are mutually complementary, like the different parts of an organized body. The beginnings of machine industry belong to the history of the textile trades, but its final triumph throughout the world was made possible only by the development of the metal industries.

These undoubtedly hold a quite special position in the modern factory system, the key position as it were, for they produce most of the equipment required by other industries and are the indispensable allies of every branch of applied mechanics. Hence every improvement in the metal industries has a reaction on the whole of industrial production. By metal industries we mean above all the iron and steel industries. Their early importance has been, and is still, growing with the manifold uses of iron and steel. To the iron and steel industries are due some of the striking material features of our present civilization, as shaped by the industrial revolution. They provide the framework of our most gigantic buildings, they span the broadest rivers with metal bridges, and launch ships like floating cities, while railway lines form a network over the whole earth. The history of iron and steel is not that of a single industry, but can from a certain point of view be identified with that of the factory system itself.

I

When that great series of changes first began in England the country was not, as she afterwards became and for many years remained, the chief metal-working country in the world. She could not in this respect compare with either Sweden or Germany. The wealth of English iron-ore deposits does not seem to have been realized, and many remained unworked. Far from being able to export, as nowadays, great quantities of pig and bar iron, England had to import them, mainly from the Baltic countries but also in a small degree from Spain and the American colonies.[1]

The iron industry falls naturally into two main divisions. The first includes mining and smelting operations, and the second, the working of the metal in its endless variety. The first, which is much the more important, as otherwise metal has to be imported in a semi-manufactured state, was at the beginning of the eighteenth century in such a bad state that people despaired of ever seeing it revive. There were in England about 1720 only some sixty blast furnaces, which produced annually 17,000 tons of pig iron.[2] This small output, vastly below that of a single one of our big blast furnaces,[3] was, moreover, spread over many districts. Here, again, we notice that dispersion of industry which was such a characteristic feature of the old textile trades. The chief ironworks were distributed over eighteen or twenty different counties.[4] Some, like Yorkshire, Warwickshire and Glamorganshire, are today among the main metal-working centres of the country. Others, on the contrary, have long ago lost what little industrial value they then still possessed.

[1] H. Scrivenor, *History of the Iron Trade*, pp. 325-7: between 1710 and 1720 the import of iron ore varied from 15,000 to 22,000 tons, while the export was scarcely more than 4,000 tons. Import grew steadily till 1765 (57,000 tons) and then became stationary, Swedish iron of superior quality alone accounting for nearly three-quarters of the total figure. See A. Anderson, *An Historical and Chronological Deduction of the Origin of Commerce*, III, 217.

[2] D. Mushet, *Papers on Iron and Steel*, p. 42. About 18,000 tons in 1737, according to a Parliamentary inquiry (see *Journals of the House of Commons*, XXIII, 109 ff.). We should like to be able to compare these figures with those of preceding periods: but for the seventeenth century we have only estimates like those of S. Sturtevant (*The Treatise of Metallica*, pp. 3-4, 1612) and of Dud Dudley (*Metallum Martis*, Preface). The country's output before the Great War was about 10,000,000 tons (10,425,000 tons in 1913).

[3] In 1921 the United States had 331 blast furnaces with a daily capacity of 126,115 tons (*Statesman's Year Book*, 1925, p. 471). In 1925 the American production of pig iron was 37,288,000 tons.

[4] Here is a list of these counties, classified by districts: (1) South-east: 15 blast furnaces (Kent, 4; Sussex, 10; Hampshire, 1); (2) Forest of Dean and district: 11 furnaces (Gloucestershire, 6; Herefordshire, 3; Monmouthshire, 2); (3) South Wales: 5 furnaces (Breconshire, 2; Glamorganshire, 2; Carmarthenshire, 1); (4) Midlands: 12 furnaces (Shropshire, 6; Worcestershire, 2; Warwickshire, 2; Staffordshire, 2); (5) Sheffield District: 11 furnaces (Yorkshire, 6; Derbyshire, 4; Nottinghamshire, 1); (6) North-west: 5 furnaces (Cheshire, 3; Denbighshire, 2). D. Mushet, *Papers on Iron and Steel*, p. 42. To this list we ought to add Cumberland with one or two blast furnaces: see Swedenborg, 'Regnum Subterraneum, sive Minerale: de Ferro' (*Collected Works*, III, 160).

Among these latter we must mention Sussex. Formerly covered with forests which provided its ironworks with fuel, it was, in the sixteenth and seventeenth centuries, extremely prosperous: 'Sussex', Camden wrote in 1607, 'is full of mines everywhere, for the casting of which there are furnaces up and down the country, and abundance of wood is yearly spent. Many streams of water are drawn into one channel, and a great deal of meadow ground is turned into pools for the driving of mills ... which, beating with hammers upon the iron, fill the neighbourhood day and night with their noise.'[1] Noble families, like the Howards, the Nevilles, the Percys and the Ashburnhams, owned ironworks in Sussex. Others made a fortune out of it and rose to social rank through industrial success; for instance, the Fuller family, whose coat of arms showed a pair of tongs with the motto: 'Carbone et forcipibus'.[2]

By the beginning of the eighteenth century this industry was already on the decline. In 1724 Defoe still admired 'the many large ironworks' of eastern Sussex, in the wooded parts of the Weald.[3] There they still made kettles, fire-backs and also artillery.[4] On the other hand we know that at that time the number of blast furnaces in Sussex had been reduced to ten, each of which produced an annual average output of 140 tons of pig iron.[5] Two of them were hardly enough to smelt the railings round St Paul's Cathedral.[6] Slowly they went out, one after the other, and only a few place names, between the villages of Hawkhurst and Lamberhurst, still remind us of this extinct industry.[7] Another iron-working district, the Forest of Dean, between the upper Wye and the mouth of the Severn, after having been completely given up has more recently come to life again. It once contained fairly rich deposits, which were known of and worked by the Romans,[8] and which are not quite exhausted. If we can believe Andrew Yarranton, the Forest of Dean under the Restoration still supported a numerous population of miners and blacksmiths.[9] But is this evidence anything more than an echo of

[1] W. Camden, Britanniæ Descriptio, II, 105 (1607 edition).

[2] S. Smiles, Industrial Biography, pp. 35-7. A blacksmith, Leonard Gale, born in 1620, was able to make his son a lord of the manor and a Member of Parliament. Interesting information on the old Sussex iron industry can be found in a book by M. A. Lower, Contributions to Literature, Historical, Antiquarian and Metrical, pp. 132 ff.

[3] See R. Budgen's map of Sussex (Actual Survey of the County of Sussex, 1724) in which the sites of the chief ironworks are indicated.

[4] Defoe, Tour, I, 106.

[5] W. Fairbairn, Iron: its history, properties and processes of manufacture, p. 283.

[6] M. Lower, op. cit., pp. 132 and 136. These railings weighed about 200 tons.

[7] Forge Wood, Furnace Wood.

[8] These were situated near Bath (Aquæ Sulis) where the Emperor Hadrian had established a 'fabrica', that is an armourer's shop for the use of the British legions. See H. Scrivenor, History of the Iron Trade, p. 29.

[9] Andrew Yarranton, England's Improvement by Sea and Land, Part I, p. 57.

ancient fame? The fact is that between 1720 and 1730 this district, like Sussex, did not contain more than about ten blast furnaces, which often, instead of smelting ore from the mines, made use of the slag from the Roman foundries.[1] And we may look in vain in all England for a more important centre. In the districts producing small iron ware, round Birmingham and Sheffield, there were a few blast furnaces, but not enough to provide the existing workshops with raw material. Everywhere else, in South Wales, in the Severn Valley, in Cheshire and Cumberland, there were only a few scattered works leading a precarious existence and hardly able to meet purely local needs.

Let us pass from the main industry to the secondary ones. These were much more prosperous and also more definitely localized. The two cities of Birmingham and Sheffield owed to those minor trades their ancient fame. From the Middle Ages Sheffield had been in possession of her world-famous speciality, for Chaucer's often-quoted lines from the 'Canterbury Tales' already mention the Sheffield cutlery.[2] The whole of the surrounding district, known as Hallamshire, took part in this manufacture. There was plenty of mill-stone grit, and the small rapidly flowing streams from the high and rocky Peak were used both to temper the steel and to turn the mill wheels.[3] The vicinity of the port of Hull enabled the cutlers to import, at comparatively small expense, Swedish iron, which was the easiest to make into steel by the processes then in use. Hallamshire produced not only knives and scissors, but axes, hammers, files and tools of various description. Birmingham, too, worked in steel. In the seventeenth century the Birmingham sword cutlers had supplied Cromwell's armies with thousands of pikes and swords.[4] But Birmingham's real speciality was ironmongery, including every kind of article, some of daily use and others which varied with the fashion. They ranged from nails and locksmiths' necessities to metal buttons, shoe buckles,[5] and included the whole Birmingham toy industry, which was so popular in England and

---

[1] H. G. Nicholls, *Iron Making in the Olden Times*, pp. 48-54.

[2] A ioly popper baar he in his pouche
Ther was no man for peril dorst him touche.
A Sheffield thwytel baar he in his hose.
Round was his face and camuse was his nose.

Chaucer, 'Canterbury Tales' ('The Reeve's Tale', lines 13 ff.), *Complete Works of Geoffrey Chaucer* (Skeat edition), IV, 114.

[3] Defoe, *Tour*, III, 81, points out that this use of water power was comparatively recent.

[4] S. Timmins, *The Resources, Products and Industrial History of Birmingham and the Midland Hardware District*, p. 210; S. Gardiner, *History of the Great Civil War*, I, 107.

[5] Counterfeit coin was also manufactured there. See the trial of false coiners in the *Birmingham Gazette* of Nov. 15th and Dec. 16th, 1742. The industries of Birmingham at the end of the eighteenth century are enumerated by L. W. Clarke, 'History of Birmingham', III, 30 and 160.

later on throughout Europe. The inhabitants were reputed to be as industrious as they were clever, and it was said that the sound of hammering was to be heard at three o'clock in the morning.[1] Birmingham, like Sheffield, was the chief centre of an industrial district. In what is now the Black Country, disfigured by mines and blast furnaces, workshops were already multiplying round a few places like Dudley, Wednesbury and Wolverhampton,[2] villages which have since grown into as many towns.

But those two favoured centres of production, although comparatively important, certainly did not hold in their industry a much higher place than a town like Norwich or a district like the West Riding did in the woollen industry. For there were other centres, which we may divide into two classes. Those in the first class had specialized industries and supplied an extensive market, as, for instance, the manufacture of pins at Bristol and Gloucester, and of knives 'after the manner of Sheffield'[3] at Newcastle. The others, on the contrary, supplied the general needs of local markets. They produced, as best they could, everything which it did not pay to bring from a distance, at a time when the transport of heavy goods was both difficult and expensive. There were many of these small centres of production, which, being scattered over the country, were too unimportant for precise information to be available about them; but a description of the iron industry in the first half of the eighteenth century would be very inadequate if the part played in scores of market towns and villages by the tinker and the farrier was left out. In Scotland almost the whole metal industry was still in their hands.[4]

The geographical concentration of the industry, in short, and its specialization in different branches, varied according to districts and to the nature of the technical processes. In the same way its internal organization was the heterogeneous product of most varied economic conditions. Simple though its methods were, mining could not be undertaken without comparatively large capital. For this reason mining companies[5] were founded at an early date. Their organization re-

[1] 'I was much surprised at the place, but more at the people. They were a species I had never seen ... I had been among dreamers, but now I saw men awake: their very step along the streets showed alacrity ... I was each morning by three o'clock saluted with a circle of hammers.' William Hutton, *History of Birmingham*, pp. 90-1.

[2] Already most of the typical Birmingham industries were represented in or round Wolverhampton. See *Journals of the House of Commons*, XXIII, 15, and XLVI, 202.

[3] Defoe, *Tour*, III, 194. Important ironworks were established there in the course of the century: see A. Young, *North of England*, III, 10-15.

[4] W. Ivison MacAdam, *Notes on the Ancient Iron Industry of Scotland*, p. 89. In 1760 the output of pig iron in Scotland was valued at 1,500 tons (David Bremner, *The Industries of Scotland*, p. 33).

[5] The first was founded in 1561 in Northumberland. W. Cunningham, *Growth of English Industry and Commerce*, II, 59.

sembled that of trading companies, and they enjoyed the same sort of constitution and privileges. These undertakings, directed by 'governors' or 'captains' and distributing annual dividends among their shareholders, were fairly numerous but of varying importance. Some of them, like the Company of Mine Adventurers of England and the Royal Mines Company, had interests in different parts of the country and formed ambitious schemes, though with only partial success.[1] Others, like the Cornish ones, were small associations with slender resources, most of them being incapable of working more than one or two shafts at a time.[2] It is obvious that this system was far from having reached its full development, especially as it did not apply to the whole of the mining industry. Companies worked the copper mines, which, as they were often very deep, demanded considerable capital outlay both in the initial cost and the upkeep.[3] On the contrary, coal mines were nearly always worked by private persons. These were sometimes the owners themselves, many of whom belonged – and still belong [1927] – to the great landed nobility. The Duke of Bridgewater, who built the Worsley canal to ship the coal from his mines to Manchester, was a typical example. They were more often let to contractors in exchange for a royalty based on the amount of coal extracted.[4] In Yorkshire, persons known as 'banksmen' sometimes played the part of agent or foreman in the employ of the owner, and sometimes in the guise of tenant managed the work as they chose.[5] There seems to have been little difference in that respect between the coal mines and the iron mines, but the latter were so closely bound up with the working of ironworks and foundries that it is impossible to study them apart.

[1] At the beginning of the eighteenth century the Company of Mine Adventurers was much in debt and would have gone to pieces if it had not been reorganized and given new powers by an Act of Parliament (9 Anne, c. 24).

[2] On the small companies of 'adventurers' in Cornwall, see S. Smiles, *Lives of Boulton and Watt*, pp. 230 and 349-50.

[3] One of these mines at Ecton Hill (Staffordshire) is described in the *Annual Register* for 1769. The deepest gallery was about 400 yards beneath the top of the hill. It was reached by very badly kept ladders. This was a copper mine: in the iron-ore mines the shafts were often not more than 15 to 18 yards deep. See Aikin, *A Description of the Country from thirty to forty miles round Manchester*, p. 81.

[4] When it was a question of entailed property Parliament had to intervene in order to confirm the lease. Example: 'An Act for confirming a Lease of Mines between Charles, Duke of Queensberry and Dover, and Patrick Crawford, and for enabling the said Duke and his Heirs of entail to grant Leases in Terms of the said Contract.' 7 Geo. III, c. 44 (private Act).

[5] See G. Lister, 'Coal Mining in Halifax' (*Old Yorkshire*, series II, pp. 274 ff.). The material for this curious monograph has been drawn from family archives. The organization of the mining industry in the seventeenth century has been dealt with by H. Levy (*Monopoly and Competition*, pp. 10 ff.), but in a sketchy way, so that a complete monography of the subject has still to be undertaken. On the Cornish copper mines see the same book, pp. 146 ff.

Mine and blast furnace were as a rule parts of the same undertaking. The ore was smelted on the spot, and the amount extracted was limited by the demand of the ironworks in the immediate neighbourhood. If we may be allowed the expression, the ironmaster was likewise the mine master. And conversely, the owner of an iron-ore deposit could only develop it by becoming an ironmaster. This explains the part which was taken in industry by noble families in the south of England. For them it was a means of improving their estates. Lord Ashburnham's seat still lies near the place where his ancestors made ordnance for the royal army two or three hundred years ago.[1] But a mine, one or two blast furnaces and often an ironworks in the same hands, necessarily amounted to a capitalist undertaking. And this was emphasized by the nature of the equipment. For as early as the fifteenth century the wind-swept open charcoal fires at the crossing of valleys or on the tops of hills, had been superseded by blast furnaces with bellows worked by water-wheels.[2] The sentence from Camden's *Description of Britain*, which has been quoted above, shows that at the end of the sixteenth century hydraulic hammers were used in Sussex ironworks.[3] We have already mentioned machines for rolling and cutting iron, an equipment which foreshadowed that of the factory system. But we should not forget that there was little life in the British iron industry and that its progress had practically stopped, the average output of a blast furnace not exceeding five or six tons a week. In spite of appearances these capitalist undertakings remained small-scale businesses.

In the subsidiary metal-working industries the conditions were quite different. They were full of life and activity, and the division of labour was far advanced. But we must be quite clear as to what is meant here by division of labour. For the phrase is used with two different if not opposite meanings. Sometimes it applies to the distribution of special tasks for the achievement of one piece of work, and sometimes it only means the creation of special trades, each of which may be regarded as complete in itself. In the first case, division of labour tends

---

[1] Ashburnham Place is in east Sussex, about 10 miles from Hastings. Compare some great Midland families, like the Dudleys. At the age of 20, Dud Dudley was sent by his father to take charge of a forge at Pensnet Chace in Worcestershire. Dud Dudley, *Metallum Martis*, p. 5.

[2] See Ludwig Beck, *Die Geschichte des Eisens*, II, 186. On the methods of the metal industry before the sixteenth century, see T. Lapsley, 'An Account Roll of a Fifteenth-century Iron Master', *English Historical Review*, XIV, 509-29 (1899). In the eighteenth century wooden bellows were used, made of two pieces fitted one into the other. See Beckmann, *Beyträge zur Geschichte der Erfindungen* (Leipzig, 1780-1805), I, 319-30.

[3] They were usually shaped like ordinary hammers, and moved round horizontal pivots. But already tilt hammers falling perpendicularly were being made and used. See Ludwig Beck, *Die Geschichte des Eisens*, II, 479, 482-3, 531 (with plates).

to industrial concentration and unity, whilst in the second it tends to economic dispersion. It was the latter which prevailed in the early period of the metal trades. The varied articles of ironmongery and English cutlery were produced in a great number of small specialized workshops. Very little or no capital, very simple technical equipment with the necessary complement of great manual skill, these were the usual conditions of production. In Sheffield the number of wage-earners hardly exceeded that of employers, the latter working at home, with their own hands, and with the help of their children and apprentices.[1] The domestic system of manufacture was thus kept up in Sheffield as well as among the woollen weavers in the neighbouring valley of Halifax, but with even more medieval features, being associated as it still was with a very strict corporate organization. The Company of Cutlers of Hallamshire, whose regulations had been in 1624 confirmed by Act of Parliament,[2] was modelled on the local gilds of the Middle Ages, and included all the master cutlers of the district, no one being allowed to settle there if he had not been formally admitted to membership. Each workshop received a trade mark from the Company. It was forbidden to employ other than local labour, and every man had to serve a seven years' term of apprenticeship. It was forbidden to sell knife blades without handles to a stranger, to lend him a grindstone or any tool whatsoever. These regulations, together with many others concerning the processes of manufacture and the quality of the goods, remained in force till the end of the eighteenth century.[3] The Company of Cutlers of Hallamshire was one of the last trade organizations to preserve its effective authority.[4] This was due to the existence of domestic industry, which it no doubt helped to keep alive, by keeping it stationary in the traditional setting in which it had originally developed.

The transition from a natural division of work among independent workshops to the organized division of labour in manufacture, took

[1] J. Hunter, *Hallamshire: the History and Topography of the Parish of Sheffield*, p. 173: 'Within the recollection of an aged inhabitant most of the cutlers' houses were small abodes with a shop and forge in the yard behind. You entered the low doorway by a step downwards, and the small written orders from the chapman who came round ... were stuck in the leaden casements of the windows and formed a subject for comment by the passers-by. Very few of the manufacturers ventured to leave the town in search of custom.'

[2] 21 James I, c. 31. The Company's official title was 'The Holy Fellowship and Company of Cutlers and Makers of Knives within the Lordship of Hallamshire in the county of York'. It included actual cutlers only (see petition of the edge-tool makers and saw makers against a Bill which brought them under its jurisdiction, *Journals of the House of Commons*, XLV, 274).

[3] See *Journals of the House of Commons*, XLIV, 223, and XLVI, 12.

[4] In order to understand how discredited most of them were, see W. Cunningham, *Growth of English Industry and Commerce*, II, 322.

place gradually. As in the textile industry it was commerce and commercial capital which brought about the change. At Sheffield and at Birmingham the merchant who at stated intervals visited the small manufacturers was an indispensable figure.[1] Production was regulated by his orders,[2] and things went on just as though the master artisan had only been a foreman in his employ. Sometimes this dependence was carried a step further, the merchant providing the raw material. In that case the producer, although still nominally independent, was in fact no more than a piece-work operative who still used his own tools.[3] Only those manufacturers who were richer or more enterprising than the others were able, thanks to the improvement in transport, to enter into direct communication with London, or even with continental markets.[4] But as soon as they became traders, in order to satisfy their customers they were forced to bring together branches of the industry which had previously been kept separate. In 1765 Joseph Hancock owned six workshops in Sheffield, in which all the chief industries of the town were represented, including the new industry of gold and silver plating.[5] One more step towards capitalist concentration and we reach the stage of 'manufacture'. Long before his partnership with James Watt, Matthew Boulton was the head of an important establishment which, apart from its plant, had already much in common with a modern factory. Iron, copper, silver and tortoiseshell were worked there and a great variety of articles were produced, such as ornamental bronzes, metal buttons, snuff-boxes and watchchains.[6] Thus one establishment, in the hands of one man, offered as it were a picture of the whole Birmingham industry.[7]

This grouping together of different and previously separate branches of work was only one of the results of that tendency towards concentration which manifested itself in all industries at the same time. Another,

[1] J. Hunter, op. cit., p. 168.

[2] Manufacturers were always afraid of producing on too large a scale. 'Their trade was inconsiderable, confined, and precarious. None presumed to extend their traffic beyond the bounds of this island ... ' J. Aikin, *A Description of the Country from thirty to forty miles round Manchester*, p. 547.

[3] In a great number of workshops Sheffield workmen until recently owned their tools, and paid a kind of rent for the use of the benches and motor power. (Information supplied in 1902 by Mr R. Holmshaw, Secretary of the Scissor Grinders' Union.)

[4] Aikin, op. cit., p. 548.

[5] See Hunter, op. cit., pp. 156, 169.

[6] On Matthew Boulton, see chap. IV, below.

[7] A similar, and equally important undertaking was that of John Taylor, a remarkable man whom W. Hutton in a transport of admiration calls 'the Shakespeare or the Newton of his times'. The main merit of this Shakespeare or Newton was to excel in the manufacture of shoe-buckles and lacquered snuff-boxes. He left a fortune of £200,000. See William Hutton, *History of Birmingham*, p. 103, and the *Local Notes and Queries* in the Birmingham Central Library (1885-8, No. 1906).

and probably a more important result (certainly a more far-reaching one) was the subdivision of technical processes within each branch into an ever-increasing number of fragmentary operations, each of which was entrusted to a special workman or group of workmen. This classical form of the division of labour showed itself nowhere earlier or more clearly than in the secondary metal-working industries. It was from one of them that Adam Smith took the well-known example which is described in the first page of his *Essay on the Nature and Causes of the Wealth of Nations*.

But this development towards 'manufacture', as is shown by most of the facts quoted above, only became marked towards the middle of the eighteenth century. Before that period the chief characteristic of the iron industry was, on the contrary, its conservative tendency. So long as production remained inconsiderable and was rather decreasing than increasing, no change in the old system was likely to take place. The British metal trade was in a poor state, and, if some of the secondary industries still had comparative vitality, this was maintained only by the import of Swedish and Russian ores. As she could not be self-sufficient, England thought that she could at least obtain all her raw or semi-manufactured material from her dependencies, whilst maintaining against them a strict monopoly in manufactured products. To encourage the production of pig or bar iron in those dependencies, whilst on the other hand forbidding all competition with the industries of Sheffield and Birmingham, was the policy adopted from 1696 by the home government. It was applied successively to Ireland[1] and the American colonies.[2] But Irish resources soon came to an end and, as we know, the Americans did not submit meekly to the measures it was attempted to enforce against them. The only real remedy for the languishing condition of the English iron trade was the introduction of modern technique.

II

Why was there such a scarcity of iron in a country containing such plentiful deposits of iron ore? Why were rich iron-working districts,

[1] The duties on bar iron from Ireland were abolished by two Acts of 1696 and 1697 (7 and 8 Will. III, c. 10, and 8 and 9 Will. III, c. 20). On the development of the iron industry in Ireland at the end of the eighteenth century, see William Petty's *Political Anatomy of Ireland* (1691). Sir William Petty owned ironworks in Co. Kerry.

[2] See Paul Busching, *Die Entwickelung der handelspolitischen Beziehungen zwischen England und seinen Kolonien bis zum Jahre* 1860, pp. 34-7. The Act of 1750 (23 Geo. II, c. 29) allowed the free import of American iron to the port of London. In 1757 (30 Geo. II, c. 16) this permission was extended to all English ports. At the same time the colonies were forbidden to work iron or to make it into steel. All workshops opened in defiance of this law, and all machines for hammering or drawing metal, were declared to be 'common nuisances' and had to be destroyed within thirty days.

which previously had been prosperous, slowly declining? The reason is not far to seek: it was the lack of fuel.

The only kind of fuel which at that time it was possible to use in smelting ore was charcoal. This accounts for blast furnaces being situated in the wooded parts of southern England, and also for the complete abandonment of certain deposits which happened to lie too far from any forests. A great deal of wood was needed for an ironworks, and round each of them a perfect massacre of trees had taken place. Thus the development of the iron industry seemed to have as its inevitable result the cutting down and the final destruction of woods and forests. This, at any rate, was the reason given for their gradual decrease, which was as a matter of fact chiefly due to the clearing for cultivation and to the extension of pasture. It had been for many years a matter of great public anxiety, as it was feared that there would soon not be enough timber for naval construction.[1] As early as 1548 a commission had been appointed to inquire into the destruction of wood and timber by the Sussex ironworks, and had reported that the shortage of wood was so great that the Channel ports were threatened with a complete lack of fuel, 'and that the fishermen would not be able to dry their clothes or warm their bodies when they came in from the sea.'[2] In the reign of Elizabeth several Acts were passed to protect the forests by limiting the number of ironworks allowed to be set up in certain counties and by forbidding any to be established within a radius of twenty-two miles round London.[3] But these Acts conflicted with a need which could not be suppressed, and, on the other hand, did nothing to mitigate the real and active causes of deforestation. The work of destruction went on faster than ever: 'He that hath known the welds[4] of Sussex, Surrey and Kent, the grand nursery especially of oak and beech, shall find such an alteration in less than thirty years as may well strike a fear lest few years more, as pestilent as the former, will leave few good trees standing in those welds.'[5] The work of destruction which appears to have begun in the southern counties

---

[1] Dud Dudley was much concerned with this danger. 'Now if wood and timber should decay still and fail, the greatest strength of Great Britain, her ships, mariners, merchants, fishings, and His Majesty's navies and men of war for our defence and offence would fail us, which before and since '88 made his Sacred Majesty's predecessors to make laws for the preservation of wood and timber ... so greatly consumed by ironworks.' *Metallum Martis*, p. 2.

[2] T. S. Ashton, *Iron and Steel in the Industrial Revolution*, p. 9 (quoting *Sussex Arch. Coll.*, XV, 21, and *Hist. MSS. Comm., Hatfield House*, XIII, 19-24).

[3] 1 Eliz., c. 15 (1558), 23 Eliz., c. 5 (1581), 27 Eliz., c. 19 (1585), 28 Eliz., c. 3 (1588). The Act of 1581 forced some of the Sussex ironmasters to move: several went to Wales. See S. Smiles, *Industrial Biography*, pp. 41-2.

[4] The name of the Weald of Sussex still preserves the memory of a formerly wooded country, where at present only hedges and parks survive.

[5] John Norden, *The Surveyor's Dialogue*, p. 214 (1607).

soon extended to the west and the midlands: 'The waste and destruction of the woods in the counties of Warwick, Stafford, Hereford, Worcester, Monmouth, Gloucester and Salop, by their ironworks, is not to be imagined.'[1] Similar complaints were heard concerning Ireland: 'Within these sixty years, Ireland was better stocked with oak timber than we now are; but the ironworks since set up there have, in a few years, swept away the woods to that degree, that they have not small stuff enough to produce bark for their tanning, nor timber for common uses, insomuch that at present they are forced to have bark from England, and building timber from Norway, and to suffer their large hides to be exported untanned ... '[2]

The point had been reached when people seriously began to wonder whether iron deposits could be reckoned as part of England's wealth at all. Andrew Yarranton wrote: 'I am sure I shall draw a whole swarm of wasps about my ears, for, say some (and many, too, who think themselves very wise), it were well if there were no ironworks in England, and it was better when no iron was made in England, and the ironworks destroy all the woods.'[3] He fought hard against this view, and tried to show that the iron industry could not be held responsible for the conversion of forests into fields and pastures.[4] Whether or not this deforestation was due to the iron industry, it was followed by disastrous consequences to the industry itself, for the blast furnaces disappeared with the woods. Scarcity of fuel sent up the cost of production of the metal. All protection against foreign competition was entirely useless, as the amount produced at home was far less than the national consumption. The English iron trade had to find a solution to this problem, or die.

The solution seemed obvious. Was there not coal to take the place of charcoal? Coal had been known and used in England for centuries. In

[1] Text quoted from an unknown source by H. Scrivenor, *History of the Iron Trade*, p. 69 (written between 1720 and 1730, as shown by the import figures).

[2] Ibid. A rather different opinion was expressed in 1749 by the Sheffield tanners who petitioned against the Bill allowing the import of American iron: 'If the Bill should pass the English iron would be undersold; consequently a great number of furnaces and forges would be discontinued; in that case the woods used for fuel would stand uncut, and the tanners be deprived of oak bark sufficient for the continuation of their occupation.' *Journals of the House of Commons*, XXV, 1019. See similar petitions from the Gloucester and Southwark tanners, ibid., pp. 1048 and 1051.

[3] Andrew Yarranton, *England's Improvement by Sea and Land*, I, 56.

[4] Ibid., II, 163-4. The same question existed in France until a much more recent date. See Bonnard, 'Mémoire sur les procédés employés en Angleterre pour le traitement du fer par le moyen de la houille', *Journal des Mines*, XVII, 245 (An XIII): 'The many ironworks now in existence in every part of France, while hardly sufficient for the growing needs of our agriculture, manufactures and arsenals, consume each year a staggering quantity of wood. It cannot unfortunately be doubted that this consumption of wood exceeds the proportion in which it should be allowed to continue, considering the present decay of most of our forests.'

a charter of 852, quoted in the *Anglo-Saxon Chronicle*, a certain Wulfred agreed to provide the monks of the Abbey of Medhamstead with, among other annual tributes, 'sixty loads of wood, twelve loads of coal (grœfa) and six loads of peat' (sixtiga fothra wuda, and twœlf fothur grœfan, and sex fothur gearda).[1] During all the Middle Ages coal was largely used in English towns.[2] It was brought from the deposits on or near the coast, and this accounts for the rather odd expression 'sea coal', which was used in texts previous to the eighteenth century.[3] Coal used in London mostly came from Newcastle and was the basis of a very important trade, which made Newcastle a great port and one of the main centres for recruiting for the Royal Navy. The trade even included foreign countries and was so profitable that in this respect it was compared to colonial ventures. The Northumberland mines[4] were already 'the Black Indies'.[5]

The importance of Newcastle and its trade could not be explained if coal had only been used to warm houses and for other domestic purposes. It was, as a matter of fact, used in a great number of industries. A petition of 1738, requesting Parliament to take steps to prevent the excessive rise in the price of coal, was signed by the 'glass makers, brewers, distillers, sugar bakers, soap boilers, smiths, dyers, brick makers, lime burners, founders and calico printers'.[6] It will be

---

[1] *Anglo-Saxon Chronicle*, ann. DCCCLII. The word *grœfa, grœfan* is derived from the teutonic root *grab* (German, *grab*, mod. Engl. *grave*). See the word *Grœfa* in Bosworth's *Dictionary of the Anglo-Saxon Language*.

[2] People complained very much of its smell and smoke. Edward I wanted to prohibit its use in London. See W. Cunningham, *Growth of English Industry and Commerce*, I, 173. On its use in the Bishopric of Liège, in the twelfth and thirteenth centuries, see Ludwig Beck, *Die Geschichte des Eisens*, II, 101.

[3] See for instance the well-known passage in the *Merry Wives of Windsor*, Act I, Sc. IV: 'Go, and we'll have a posset for it soon at night, in faith, at the latter end of a seacoal fire.'

[4] The Welsh mines were also worked at an early date. Defoe mentions the town of Swansea, which sent great quantities of coal to Somerset, Devon, Cornwall and Ireland. *Tour*, III, 82.

[5] According to Brand, *History of Newcastle upon Tyne*, II, 273, in 1705 this trade employed 1,277 ships of all tonnage: 'The coal mines must be reckoned among the chief causes of the progress of shipping in England, for that branch of trade alone occupies more than 1,500 ships from 100 to 200 tons, and is looked upon as the nursery of the English navy. This is why those mines are called "The Black Indies".' Dudley already had described Great Britain, with its wealth of ores and deposits, as 'our Northern Indies'.

[6] *Journals of the House of Commons*, XXIII, 263. In some of these industries coal only seems to have been introduced at the end of the sixteenth or the beginning of the seventeenth century: 'Brickmaking, brewing, dyeing, casting of brassworks, etc., were, not many years since, done altogether with the fuel of wood and charcoal, instead whereof seacoal is now used as effectually and to as good use and purpose.' S. Sturtevant, *The Treatise of Metallica*, Preface, p. 8. Coal had from an earlier date been in use in forges: 'The blacksmith long ago forged all his iron with charcoals (and

noted that the smiths and smelters appear on this list. Is this not a sufficient proof that the metal trade did at that period usually make use of coal? There is no doubt that it did, but only for some of its processes. In forging or working metals coal had more or less the same qualities as charcoal, but this was not the case in smelting ores, and specially iron ore. Iron ore, when in contact with the sulphur compounds which coal contains in a variable quantity and which are set free by combustion, deteriorates, yielding only impure and brittle pig iron, which it is quite impossible to hammer. No one knew how to get over this difficulty, and so the very industry in which coal should have been of the greatest assistance was unable to make use of it. Ironworks went on consuming charcoal which was becoming ever scarcer and dearer, while immense reserves of coal lay untouched at their very door.

How could good workable iron be obtained by using coal instead of charcoal? This was the problem the solution of which was actively sought for by several generations of investigators. The story of their efforts is an extremely interesting one, though it is rather difficult to appreciate exactly how far each of them attained practical results. In 1612 a certain Simon Sturtevant, of German origin, obtained by letters patent the exclusive right of smelting iron ore with coal.[1] He left behind him a curious book which, in a somewhat scholastic fashion although not without clever hints and suggestions, deals with inventions in general and with his own in particular.[2] Any new technical process,

---

[1] Ludwig Beck, *Die Geschichte des Eisens*, II, 1247, quotes similar privileges awarded in 1589 to Thomas Proctor and William Peterson, and in 1607 to Robert Chantrell. But did they use 'stone coal, sea coal, pit coal and peat coal' to smelt the ore or only to forge the metal? The text of Sturtevant's patent is reproduced *in extenso* in *The Treatise of Metallica*, pp. 5 ff.

[2] In what he called heuretics (from the Greek εὑρίσκω) he distinguished two factors, the scientific and the mechanic: 'The scientific is that part of Heuretica which prescribeth precepts general to all liberal arts, the end of which arts is chiefly science or knowledge, and not any real visible work or sensible thing ... The mechanic part is this part of Heuretica which prescribeth precepts general to all illiberal arts, the

---

in some places where they are cheap they continue this course still); but these many years small seacoal hath and does serve the turn as well and sufficiently.' Ibid. See the passage in which Agricola in 1546 enumerates the various uses of coal: 'Etenim fabri aerarii et ferrarii carbonum, quod eis multo diutius duret, vice ipso utuntur. Sed quia sua pinguitudine inficit ferrum et fragile facit, qui subtilia opera efficiunt hoc non utuntur, nisi eorum qui ex ligno fiunt magna fuerit penuria. Eodem bitumine hi, quos ligna deficiunt, cibos coquunt, caldaria, in quibus hieme degunt vitam, calefaciunt, calcem urunt, vitium vero foetoris plerumque sale, in ignem injecto, corrigunt. Agricolae eodem vites oblinunt, quod vermes illarum oculos rodentes interficiat. Eodem, decoris gratia, quidam tingunt palpebras et capillos. In medicinae vero uso exsiccat et digerit. Atque ex duro polito figurantur effigies hominum, globuli quibus numerantur preces, gemmae annulis inferendae, aut funda claudendae.' Georgius Agricola, *De Natura Fossilium*, Book IV, p. 237 (1546 edition).

he said, must fulfil at least three conditions with reference to the process it replaces, for it must guarantee a production at least equivalent in respect of quantity, quality and price.[1] Its real usefulness only begins, and its success is only probable, when this minimum has been passed and when production is made greater, better or cheaper. The invention which Sturtevant claimed to have made had, according to him, two of these advantages. It made it possible to effect a considerable economy in manufacture. The use of coal in a blast furnace costing £500 a year in charcoal would reduce this expense to one-tenth.[2] Thereafter nothing would interfere with the rapid and unlimited development of the metal-working industries. At the same time the forests would be saved, which, far from being only a matter of minor importance, was the fact which probably came home to people at that time more than any other.[3]

Sturtevant had therefore understood, and had very definitely pointed out, the immense advantages which the iron industry would derive from the use of coal. But did he go further? Was he really an inventor or only a projector? We have a good deal of information as to what he thought, but very little as to what he did. He had probably given up the idea of using raw coal, for he refers to a preparation, 'the object of which was to remove from it whatever could spoil or corrupt the metal'.[4] Whether he did really succeed in making coke is very doubtful: what is certain is that he did not manage to make anything out of this first invention, for, at the end of less than a year, his patent was declared to have lapsed on the ground that he had failed to use it.[5] His rights were then transferred to a protégé of the Prince of Wales[6] called John Rovenzon, who in his turn made all sorts of fine promises and was no more successful than his predecessor in fulfilling them.

[1] Sturtevant, p. 82: 'Equi-sufficiency, equi-excellency, equi-cheapness.'

[2] Ibid., p. 2.

[3] Sturtevant mentions it several times with marked insistence in his treatise, pp. 2, 8, 105.

[4] Ibid., p. 106. See Percy, *Iron and Steel*, p. 882.

[5] John Rovenzon, *A Treatise of Metallica, but not that which was published by Mr Simon Sturtevant upon his Patent*, p. A. Ludwig Beck, *Die Geschichte des Eisens*, II, 1253-4, takes sides against Sturtevant, calling him a humbug and a swindler.

[6] Henry Stuart, the eldest son of James I, who died in 1613.

end of which is a real visible work or sensible thing. And an invention of this kind is called an invention mechanic.' *The Treatise of Metallica*, pp. 50-1. According to Sturtevant, inventions could be divided into 'mixed' and 'pure'. The first were new applications of a principle already known (for instance, windmills, invented after water-mills), the second, on the other hand, were based on a new principle (for instance, printing). Ibid., p. 56.

This repeated failure was of ill omen. But the difficulties it bore witness to did not stop research, which was stimulated by practical necessity, from going on. The man who seems to have got nearest to the final solution was Dud Dudley, a most extraordinary character, the value of whose work has been admitted by some technical writers and questioned by others.[1] He has left us the story of his own life.[2] The natural son of Edward, Earl of Dudley, he was, fresh from Oxford, put at the head of his father's ironworks in the forest of Pensnet in Worcestershire. There in 1619 he began his first experiments: 'Wood and charcoal growing then scant, and pit coals in great quantities abounding near the furnace, did induce me to alter my furnace, and to attempt, by my new invention, the making of iron with pit coal ... I found such success at first trial [as] animated me ... After I had made a second blast and trial, the feasibility of making iron with pit coal and sea coal, I found by my new invention the quality to be good and profitable, but the quantity did not exceed above three tons per week: ... [though I] doubted not in the future to have advanced my invention to make quantity also.'[3] He sent samples to King James, which were recognized as 'good merchantable iron', and, as Sturtevant's and Rovenzon's patent had lapsed, he was able to take out a new patent at once in the name of his father Lord Dudley.[4]

We will not follow him through all the vicissitudes of his chequered career. He endured the usual disappointments of inventors. The blast furnaces he set up near Stourbridge in the Birmingham district were swept away by floods.[5] Later, having settled at Sedgeley in Staffordshire, he became the object of the jealousy of the ironmasters, who excited their workmen against him, and his works were broken into and sacked.[6] In the midst of all his troubles Charles I showed some interest in his endeavours, and in 1638 even agreed to the renewal of his patent.[7] But civil war broke out almost immediately, and Dudley, a passionate Royalist, left his ironworks for Prince Rupert's cavalry. There he distinguished himself by his bravery and became a colonel.

[1] D. Mushet, *Papers on Iron and Steel*, pp. 43 and 400-3, and Percy, *Iron and Steel*, pp. 884-5, take Dudley very seriously. T. S. Ashton, *Iron and Steel in the Industrial Revolution*, pp. 11-12, is very sceptical.

[2] In the book called *Metallum Martis, or Iron made with Pitcoal, Seacoal, etc., and with the same Fuel to melt and fine imperfect Metals, and refine perfect Metals* (1665).

[3] Ibid., pp. 5 ff.

[4] In 1621 this patent was renewed for a period of fourteen years. See *Abridgments of Specifications relating to the Manufacture of Iron and Steel*, p. 1 (Patent No. 18).

[5] *Metallum Martis*, p. 13.

[6] Ibid., p. 16.

[7] 'My dear master, our sacred martyr Charles the First of ever blessed memory, did animate the author by granting him a patent Anno 14 of his reign, for the making of iron, and melting, smelting, extracting, refining and reducing all mines and metals with pit coal, sea coal, peat and turf. Ibid., pp. vii and 17-18.

But as the war was ended by the King's defeat and death, Dudley found himself alone, ruined and under suspicion.[1] There could be no question of defending his patent rights, and he even agreed to help other persons who were working at the same problem. The first was one Captain Buck, who in partnership with Edward Dagney, 'an ingenious glazier', had settled in the Forest of Dean. Their method was to keep the ore apart from the coal by putting it into earthenware crucibles. But the crucibles exploded and the experiments, in which Cromwell had taken an interest, were given up.[2] Copley, who in 1656 made similar experiments near Bristol, met with no more success. For him Dudley had made big forge bellows, 'that one man may blow with pleasure the space of an hour or two'.[3] The whole matter was still in the same state when the Restoration renewed Dudley's hopes of recovering his rights and of being able to start his works again.

His applications were coldly received, and he then wrote and dedicated to 'His Majesty's Right Honourable Council' his book entitled *Metallum Martis*, which was both an autobiography and a vindication of his work. He recalled the anxiety felt for so many years at the destruction of forests, and the laws which had been vainly passed to prevent it. The remedy he offered, far from injuring the metal industry, was such as to promote its growth. He laid stress on the existence of many important coal deposits, often situated in the immediate neighbourhood of the iron mines, and he instanced the country in which he had lived and worked from his youth up. Near Dudley Castle he had found strata of coal and veins of ore overlying each other, the ore almost on the surface, and the other hardly ten yards deep, while in the same district the ironworks were at a standstill for lack of wood.[4] The encouragement and help he asked for, after all his sacrifices, would benefit the public more than himself: he entreated his readers to believe that he was prompted by no 'private or politic design', but by 'mere zeal, becoming an honest man, *patriæ, parentibus et amicis*'.[5] Whatever the merit of his case, Dudley's tried devotion to

---

[1] *Metallum Martis*, pp. 17-20. His ironworks had been destroyed again, this time by the republican army.

[2] Ibid., pp. 21-5. Captain Buck's patent is dated March 1st, 1651. A series of earlier patents, some of which infringed on the first one given to Dudley, bear witness to the repeated efforts made in the same direction. See *Abridgments of Specifications relating to the Manufacture of Iron and Steel*, pp. 2-3. The same experiments were being made in France about the same time. See *Le Parallèle des Bois et Forests avec les Terres à brusler, Verbal de l'Invention du vray Charbon de Terre par toute la France* (Anonymous, Paris, 1627), and C. Lamberville, *Œconomie ou Mesnage des Terres inutiles propres à brusler et faire Charbons de Forge* (Paris, 1631).

[3] *Metallum Martis*, p. 26.

[4] Ibid., pp. xv, 2, 9, 38-9.

[5] Ibid., pp. 1-11.

the Royalist cause should have helped him to win Charles II's favour. But Restorations are proverbially ungrateful to some of their early supporters, and Dudley was one of these. His offer met with a polite refusal, and, broken by this last disappointment, he gave up all attempts to make use of his invention. He died unnoticed in 1684, and his secret, if he had one, died with him.

His evidence on his own achievements, although unsupported by contemporary records, was in the nineteenth century accepted by men with technical knowledge.[1] He claimed that he had actually produced pig iron of a good quality at a cost price of £4 per ton, the usual cost being between £6 and £7.[2] This would have been enough to bring about a revolution in the iron trade. It is surprising that with such an advantage over all competitors he should not have succeeded in the end. Moreover, as has been observed by the most recent historian of the industrial revolution in the iron trade, 'if he was a high-minded patriot actuated only by a desire to save the timber vital to England's security, it is strange that he allowed his knowledge to die with him ... No mention is made in his treatise of any attempt to coke the coal, and, with the blowing apparatus of the seventeenth century, it would appear to have been impossible to produce sound iron with raw fuel.'[3] We shall probably never know whether Dudley partly anticipated the invention that was to revolutionize the industry in the following century, or was a mere adventurer and dreamer who knew how to give an interesting and romantic account of himself.

After Dudley the series of abortive experiments began all over again. In 1677 a German called Blauenstein set up a blast furnace near Wednesbury, 'so ingeniously contrived, that many were of opinion he would succeed in it'.[4] It was a reverberatory furnace, in which the flames only licked the ore. But being laden with sulphurous vapours they deteriorated the iron almost as much as actual contact with coal in combustion.[5] Blauenstein used coal without treating it in any way,

---

[1] See D. Mushet, *Papers on Iron and Steel*, p. 43; Percy, *Iron and Steel*, p. 885; Ludwig Beck, *Die Geschichte des Eisens*, II, 965.

[2] *Metallum Martis*, pp. 14 and 15. He sold it for as much as £12 a ton.

[3] T. S. Ashton, *Iron and Steel in the Industrial Revolution*, p. 11.

[4] R. Plot, *Natural History of Staffordshire* (1686), p. 128. The patent granted to Blauenstein (under the anglicized name of Blewstone) is dated Oct. 25th, 1677. *Abridgments of Specifications relating to Iron and Steel*, p. 3.

[5] R. Plot, loc. cit. J. Becher, *Närrische Weisheit und Weise Narrheit*, p. 34, maintains that Blauenstein overcame this difficulty: 'I have lately at Prince Rupert's seen the proof. It is an instrument which, made of metal smelted according to this method, presents all the characteristics of malleable cast iron.' But firstly Plot's testimony is later than Becher's (1686 instead of 1683), and in the interval it had become possible to estimate the real value of the invention; and secondly, Plot, living in England and taking as his subject the history of the country where the experiments were made, was probably able to obtain more direct and complete information;

though the use of coke was spreading more and more, and had already become quite habitual in some industries: brewers, for instance, preferred it to charcoal.[1] It was with coke that between 1726 and 1730 William Wood made his unlucky experiments. He was a well-known character in his time: it was against him that Swift in 'The Drapier's Letters' displayed a wit as brilliant as it was unjust. The coining of copper halfpence for Ireland, which brought down on his head this storm of abuse from the formidable satirist, was only one of his many ventures. He owned ironworks and hardware manufactures, and had leased all the mines throughout the crown lands.[2] Used to ambitious schemes, he dreamed, by improving the technique of the iron industry, of building up a huge monopoly for his own advantage.

In 1726 he set up ironworks at Whitehaven in Cumberland, and tried to produce pig iron by mixing ore and powdered coke in a reverberatory furnace.[3] If we may trust the opinion of a competent judge, Swedenborg, who before he founded a religion was an Inspector of Mines and wrote books on the chemistry of metals,[4] the results were far from satisfactory. Wood, nevertheless, maintained that he would very soon be able to produce excellent malleable iron in unlimited quantities. He talked of borrowing a million sterling and of erecting a hundred blast furnaces.[5] In 1728 he contracted with the Royal Company of Mines to deliver them 30,000 tons of bar iron at £11 to £12 a ton.[6] He would never have made such a contract had he not believed himself to be on the verge of success. But it was rash of him to discount the future in this way, for when in 1729 he applied for an exclusive privilege, which would perhaps have enabled him to save himself by buying up the existing blast furnaces, he was at once challenged to produce proof of his discovery. Raillery and abuse were

[1] 'They have a way of charring coal in all particulars the same as they do with wood ... The coal thus prepared they call coake, which conserves as strong a heat almost as charcoal itself, and is as fit for most other uses, but for melting and refining of iron.' R. Plot, loc. cit.

[2] *The present State of Mr Wood's Mine Partnership* (1720); A. Anderson, *An Historical and Chronological Deduction of the Origin of Commerce*, III, 124.

[3] Patent dated Sept. 18th, 1728 (No. 502). *Abridgments of Specifications relating to Iron and Steel*, pp. 5-6.

[4] 'Tentamen novum Angliae venam ferri fundendi in caminis reverberii per carbones lapideos sive fossiles.' *Regnum Subterraneum: de Ferro*, Swedenborg's Works, III, 160-1.

[5] *To all Lovers of Art and Ingenuity*, p. 2; *A Letter from a Merchant at Whitehaven to his Friend in London*, p. 3.

[6] *A Letter from a Merchant*, p. 2. The price of Bilbao iron in the London market was as much as 15s. 6d., that of Swedish iron 16s. 6d. Thorold Rogers, *History of Agriculture and Prices in England*, VII, 387.

thirdly, Becher, a compatriot of Blauenstein (he is careful to mention that the latter was a German, 'ein Teutscher'), may have been partial to him.

showered on him, he was accused of theft, it was said that the iron he showed the experts was made with charcoal and that the pig iron produced by his wonderful invention was black, coarse and brittle. All the ironmasters who had tried it vowed they would not use it, even as a gift. Sham prospectuses were issued which, on the strength of these wonderful results, invited the public to subscribe fantastic sums: 'Even Mr Wood's Irish pennies will be accepted.'[1] A test before witnesses which he was forced to make put him to complete confusion.[2] Even this, however, did not prevent one William Fallowfield from making, the same year, a great stir over a similar invention, so urgent was it to find the solution of a problem which involved the very existence of the English iron trade.[3]

A family, or rather a dynasty of ironmasters, the Darbys of Coalbrookdale, finally discovered what had been vainly sought after for a century. The invention has now been proved to have been made by the first Abraham Darby, who died in 1717. He was a Quaker, the son of a farmer, who had begun life as a millwright and then undertaken to make cast-iron pots. During a journey in 1704 he noted the methods of Dutch smelters, and in 1707, with another Quaker called John Thomas, he took out a patent 'for casting iron bellied pots and other iron bellied wares in sand only without loam or clay'.[4] In 1709 he settled at Coalbrookdale, not far from Wolverhampton, on the edge of the Midlands, which may be said to have been the home of metal inventions, as that of textile inventions was Lancashire. The valley of the Coldbrook, a small tributary of the Severn, had been an iron-working centre, but the old works by the beginning of the eighteenth century were almost abandoned, although wood was still plentiful in the neighbouring district. There were close at hand considerable and easily worked coal deposits. Whether Darby did or did not fully realize all the advantages of the site before he settled there, it is a fact that he lost no time in turning them to account.

The date of the invention cannot be exactly determined. In a letter written many years after the event and only recently brought to light, Abiah Darby, wife of the second Abraham Darby, gives the following account of her father-in-law's achievement: 'About the year 1709 he came into Shropshire to Coalbrookdale and with other partners took a lease of the works, which only consisted of an old blast furnace

[1] *A Letter from a Merchant in Whitehaven to an Iron Master in the South of England; An Account of Mr Wood's Iron made with Pulverized Ore and Pit Coal; Beware of Bubbles* (British Museum, 816 m. 13).

[2] *Gentleman's Magazine*, 1731, pp. 187 and 219.

[3] *Mr William Fallowfield's Proposal for making Iron with Peat at Ten Pounds a Ton, in Pursuance of a Patent granted to him by His late Majesty* (1731).

[4] S. Smiles, *Industrial Biography*, p. 81; T. S. Ashton, *Iron and Steel in the Industrial Revolution*, p. 27.

and some forges. He here cast iron goods in sand out of the blast furnace that blowed with wood charcoal; for it was not yet thought of to blow with pit coal. Sometime after he suggested the thought, that it might be practable [*sic*] to smelt the iron from the ore in the blast furnace with pit coal: upon this he first tried with raw coal as it came out of the mines, but it did not answer. He, not discouraged, had the coal coked into cinder as is done for drying malt, and it then succeeded to his satisfaction.'[1]

This account would tally with the mention made in Darby's *Memorandum Book* of the use he made in 1713 of a mixture of coke, peat and coal dust.[2] But from records kept at the works it appears that as early as 1709 coal was regularly purchased, while very few entries are found relating to the purchase of charcoal: in the same year sums were paid 'for charking coals', which means that coke was then made and used at Coalbrookdale. It seems likely, however, that it took some time to overcome the difficulties which had so long proved insuperable.

The problem was not a simple one,[3] and much probably remained to be done after Abraham Darby's untimely death. His son, who took over the management of Coalbrookdale only in 1730, improved the methods of coking, strengthened the bellows, which were worked by water-wheels, and in order to prevent any deterioration of the metal during the process of smelting, conceived the idea of adding to the ore limestone and other reagents. While his father had always remained a cast-iron manufacturer, he successfully undertook to make bar iron 'from pit coal pigs'.[4] But many years were to elapse before a discovery, which had been so much clamoured for, was to become really popular.[5]

[1] T. S. Ashton, op. cit., p. 250. The first edition of the present book followed Dr Percy's version, based upon a family tradition, according to which the invention had been made by the second Abraham Darby about 1735 (see Percy, *Iron and Steel*, p. 888). Mrs Darby's evidence disposes of that story, of which clearly she had never heard.

[2] H. Scrivenor, *History of the Iron Trade*, p. 56, and Ludwig Beck, *Die Geschichte des Eisens*, III, 160-1. Both authors give 1713 as the date of the invention.

[3] 'To produce a satisfactory metal with mineral fuel it was therefore necessary, first, to contrive methods of removing some of the impurities by coking; second, to construct a furnace of such a size that the ironstone could remain in contact with the fuel for a longer period than was the practice in charcoal smelting; and third, to increase the temperature by means of a more powerful blowing apparatus.' T. S. Ashton, op. cit., p. 31.

[4] Percy, op. cit., p. 888, and T. S. Ashton, op. cit., p. 251.

[5] Ibid. No public mention of the invention appears to have been made previous to Professor Mason's communication to the Royal Society in 1747: 'Several attempts have been made to run iron ore with pit coal; I think it has not succeeded anywhere … but Mr Ford, of Coalbrookdale in Shropshire, from iron ore and coal, both got in the same dale, makes iron brittle or tough as he pleases, there being cannon thus cast so soft as to bear turning like wrought iron.' *Philosophical Transactions of the Royal Society*, XLIV, 305. Ford was Abraham Darby's son-in-law and partner.

The story of this vital invention has more than one feature in common with the textile inventions. In both cases the change in technique was made necessary by an economic crisis, and this crisis was brought about by the upsetting of the balance between the different branches of the industry. The activity of the small workshops around Sheffield and Birmingham, which needed raw material, and the arrest in the growth of, or rather the decline in, the mining and blast-furnace industry, which could no longer provide it, these were the causes of the movement in which Abraham Darby's invention marked the critical stage. As to the results, they could even then be foreseen, at any rate as far as England was concerned. 'Nature has given us immense plenty both of iron ore and pit coal ... British pit coal will come almost as cheap near our collieries as charcoal does in Sweden or Russia.'[1] The partnership thus contracted between coal and iron opened the most brilliant prospects to the English metal industry.

III

Once the spinning jenny had been invented, hand looms could no longer keep up with the work. In the same way, as soon as coal enabled pig iron to be produced in large quantities, a new problem arose. How was this pig iron to be converted into malleable iron? The process of open hearth refining[2] only enabled small quantities to be dealt with at a time. Moreover, and there lay the chief difficulty, only charcoal could be used. Thus, while the production of pig iron increased rapidly that of bar iron was limited. This resulted in a kind of periodical congestion in production, which caused the ironmasters great anxiety.[3] The only way of putting an end to it was to complete the work of Abraham Darby and find a way of using coal in the refining of pig iron as well as in the treatment of the ore.

[1] Postlethwayt, *Considerations on the making of Bar Iron with pitt or sea coal fire* (1747), p. 5.

[2] Open hearth refining was used directly on rich ores, and was carried out by melting the iron in a crucible, placed on the ground, under a continuous blast. See Ludwig Beck, *Die Geschichte des Eisens*, III, 113-31, and A. Ledebur, *Manuel de la Métallurgie du Fer* (French trans.), II, 335 ff.

[3] Some people tried to find a solution abroad, particularly in Sweden. On Samuel Garbett's journey in 1763, see the documents quoted in the *Calendar of Home Office Papers*, 1760-5. No. 1359.

According to MacCulloch, *Literature of Political Economy*, p. 238, the process was not in general use before 1780. Complaints as to the lack of fuel went on long after the invention had made them unjustified. See *The State of the Trade and Manufactory of Iron in Great Britain considered* (1750). Mr Ashton notes that the use of coke pig iron in Worcestershire did not begin until about 1750, and explains that 'the iron-smelter who wished to sell his product to forgemasters had no incentive to advertise the fact that it had been made with mineral fuel'. Op. cit., p. 36.

The period of research and trial was comparatively short. In 1762 John Roebuck, the founder of the Carron Iron Works, obtained encouraging results. He was an intelligent and cultivated man who had studied chemistry as well as medicine at Edinburgh and Leyden.[1] As far as we can make out, he nearly anticipated the invention of puddling.[2] We do not know in what particular respect he failed, but it would seem that the metal he obtained was not pure enough to compete with Russian and Swedish iron. In 1766 a similar process was discovered by two Coalbrookdale workmen, Thomas and George Cranage, with the help of their employer Richard Reynolds, the second Darby's son-in-law. They built a reverberatory furnace, similar to that which had been erected by Blauenstein in the same district about a century before.[3] Their experiments, like Roebuck's, were only partially successful. Did they clearly understand what had to be done? This is very unlikely, for the presence of carbon in pig iron and the process of decarbonization in order to isolate the pure metal are quite modern notions, and it is a well-known fact that chemistry hardly existed before Priestley and Lavoisier.

But once more, under the pressure of economic necessity, practice outstripped theory. The high price of the bar iron imported from Sweden and Russia,[4] which was indispensable so long as England did not produce enough, was one of the facts which caused researches to be undertaken simultaneously in different parts of the country.[5] Puddling was invented within a period of only a few months both in South Wales and at Fontley, near Portsmouth. The two inventors did not know one another and their ways lay far apart. Peter Onions[6] was a foreman in an iron mill at Merthyr Tydvil and remained unknown.

[1] On Roebuck, see *Dictionary of National Biography*, and Jardine, 'Account of John Roebuck', *Transactions of the Royal Society of Edinburgh*, IV, 65 ff.

[2] Patent of Oct. 25th, 1762 (No. 780): Pig or other cast iron was melted 'in a hearth heated with pit coal by the blast of bellows' and the metal was worked 'until reduced to nature'. Then it was taken out of the fire and broken into pieces. The metal was then 'exposed to the action of a hollow pit coal fire' under a strong blast, 'until it was reduced to a loop' which could be hammered into bar iron. *Abridgments of Specifications relating to the Manufacture of Iron and Steel*, p. 9.

[3] Patent of June, 1766 (No. 851). In Sweden there were many reverberatory furnaces, which were chiefly used to heat bar iron before forging it for the second or third time. See Josiah Wedgwood's papers in the British Museum, Additional MSS., 28311, p. 9.

[4] A great rise had taken place since 1770 (see G. Townsend Warner in *Social England*, V, 465). The latest reliable figures collected by Thorold Rogers are dated 1763 (Stockholm £17 to £22 and Gothenburg £17 a ton). *History of Agriculture and Prices in England*, VII, 389). In 1791, according to H. Scrivenor, *History of the Iron Trade*, p. 93, Oregrund iron was worth £24.

[5] We can quote those of John Cockshutt (1771). See *Abridgments of Specifications relating to the Manufacture of Iron and Steel*, p. 13.

[6] Patent of May 7th, 1783 (No. 1398), *Abridgments*, p. 19.

Henry Cort, contractor to the Admiralty and in touch with important persons, was able to make his process known at once and to undertake its commercial development.[1] Even if he was not the only man to deserve credit for the invention, he was chiefly responsible for the important changes in the iron industry which that invention was to cause.

It may be convenient here to give a short description of puddling.[2] Pig iron, in its impure state, is first broken up and refined over a coke fire, which causes it to lose some of its carbon. It is then put into a reverberatory furnace together with clinkers rich in oxides of iron. As soon as it melts, the carbon it still contains unites with the oxygen. In order to stimulate this process the molten metal is stirred with a hook called a clinker bar. After some time the metal seems to boil, and this is accompanied by the emission of a bluish flame, due to the combustion of the oxide of carbon. The incandescent mass is still stirred while the heat of the fire is made to vary from time to time. Gradually the pure metal collects into a spongy 'loop'. This 'loop' is gathered up, hammered to expel the slag and finally rolled between cylinders. The use of the rolling mill was perhaps the most original part of Cort's invention. It greatly shortened the laborious process of hammering, and both speeded up production and enabled large quantities to be produced.[3] Such is the process, arrived at by quite empirical methods, by which since 1784 immense quantities of iron have been obtained. The chemical discoveries of the following century supplied a scientific explanation of the process, without causing it to be substantially modified.[4]

Its practical success was immediate. The first samples of puddled iron, when submitted to the naval experts, were declared, 'to be equal or superior in quality to the best Oregrund iron'.[5] James Watt, who in 1782 had invited Cort to Soho,[6] at once realized the importance of his inven-

[1] Patent of Feb. 13th, 1784 (No. 1420), *Abridgments*, p. 21. An excellent account of Henry Cort's career and inventions is found in T. S. Ashton's book, chap. IV.

[2] This description is taken from Bonnard, 'Mémoire sur les procédés employés en Angleterre pour le traitement du fer par le moyen de la houille', *Journal des Mines*, XVII, 270 ff. (An XIII). We have of course not taken into account the recent improvements mentioned in technical treatises like Ledebur's.

[3] See T. Webster, 'The Case of Henry Cort', *Mechanics' Magazine*, New Series, II, 53, and petition of Cort's sons to the House of Commons in 1812. *Journals of the House of Commons*, LXVII, 77. It took twelve hours to hammer a ton of iron; whilst during the same time fifteen tons could be put through the rolling mill. Scrivenor, *History of the Iron Trade*, p. 122.

[4] An almost immediate improvement consisted in putting sliding iron 'soles' at the bottom of the puddling furnaces, so that the metal could be taken out at will. Robert Gardner's patent, No. 1642.

[5] Trials were made at Portsmouth, Plymouth, Woolwich and Sheerness. See T. Webster, op. cit., p. 85.

[6] Letter from Watt to Boulton, Dec. 14th, 1782: 'We have had a visit today from a Mr Cort of Gosport, who says he has a forge there and has found out some grand

tion and wrote about it to his countryman Joseph Black, the chemist.[1] The great ironmasters lately established in the Midlands and in Wales were at first incredulous. Watt wrote: 'Cort is treated shamefully by the business people, who are ignorant asses, one and all.' But very soon they asked the inventor to come to some arrangement with them with regard to his patent. The results were even better than had been anticipated: at Richard Crawshay's works at Cyfarthfa the production of bar iron rose from ten to two hundred tons a week.[2] Cort had arranged to be paid a royalty of 10s. a ton,[3] and, if the contracts entered into between 1786 and 1789 had been faithfully carried out, his total gains during the legal duration of his patent would have amounted to £250,000.[4]

But just at the moment when the future of his undertaking seemed most promising, Cort was struck down by sudden misfortune. In order to enlarge his Fontley ironworks he had borrowed capital from an Admiralty official, one Adam Jellicoe, Deputy Paymaster of seamen's wages,[5] whose son had been Cort's partner since 1775. In August 1789, Jellicoe suddenly died, and it was said that he had committed suicide to escape prosecution as he had embezzled public money for which he was responsible. The government took possession of whatever property he had left, including sums due from third parties, and Cort, being called upon to redeem his debt at short notice, lost everything. His very patent was either sold or confiscated, and the ironmasters who were in his debt took the opportunity of not paying the royalties due to him.[6] It was the end of his industrial career: a ruined man, he obtained, thanks to Pitt's protection, a small pension on which he lived till 1800.[7] But the fate of his invention was not bound up with his personal fortunes. On the contrary, the premature lapse of Cort's patent rights helped it to spread rapidly, as happened with the water frame after the case which resulted in the cancellation of Arkwright's patent. Puddling very soon became the usual process throughout Great

---

[1] Letter of June 6th, 1784, quoted by Webster, p. 52.

[2] T. Webster, op. cit., p. 118.

[3] Say 2½ to 3 per cent of the trade price, which was about £18 a ton. D. Mushet, *Papers on Iron and Steel*, p. 39.　　　　[4] T. Webster op. cit., p. 387.

[5] On this episode see T. Webster, pp. 387 ff., and F. Espinasse, *Lancashire Worthies*, II, 234-6.

[6] Among others the Crawshays of Cyfarthfa saved £10,000 in this way. Percy, *Iron and Steel*, p. 639.

[7] In 1811 a subscription for his widow brought in £871 10s.

---

secret in the making of iron, by which he can make double the quantity at the same expense and in the same time as usual. He says he wants some kind of engine, but could not tell what; wants some of us to call on him and said he had some correspondence with you on the subject. He seems a simple goodnatured man, but not very knowing.' S. Smiles, *Lives of Boulton and Watt*, p. 327.

Britain: the production of bar iron[1] could thus keep pace with that of pig iron, whilst both, reacting on one another, entered on that era of gigantic development the end of which is not yet in sight.[2]

It was much later, about the middle of the nineteenth century, that steel began to occupy its commanding position in the world of industry. We should, however, mention with those inventions the history of which we have just outlined that of cast steel made by Benjamin Huntsman. As early as 1722 Réaumur had managed to make steel by mixing malleable iron and pig iron in a crucible, but his experiments led to no practical consequences.[3] Huntsman was a clockmaker at Doncaster in Yorkshire, who dabbled in mechanics and surgery. The story goes that he was struck by the difficulty of obtaining finely tempered steel for watch springs,[4] and that he tried to remedy the deficiency. He had, no doubt, already begun his researches when in 1740 he left Doncaster to settle near Sheffield. They proved very laborious, and were only completed about 1750.[5] In order to obtain homogeneous and flawless metal Huntsman smelted it at a very high temperature in sealed fireclay crucibles, together with small quantities of charcoal and ground glass which acted as reagents.[6] Even today this process is in use in a few metal-working factories where crucible steel is still produced.

Huntsman hoped to sell his steel to the Sheffield manufacturers. But they were suspicious of novelties and refused to buy it. He found a readier welcome in France, but the Hallamshire cutlers, fearing foreign competition, at once went in a body to Sir George Savile, one of the local members in the House of Commons, and urged him to induce the Government to forbid the export of cast steel.[7] Thus they hoped to limit the results of the unwelcome invention, which threatened their

[1] In 1812 the weight of puddled iron produced in English and Scotch ironworks amounted to 250,000 tons. See the petition from Cort's sons, *Journals of the House of Commons*, LXVII, 77.

[2] In 1784 Sir John Dalrymple wrote: 'The advantages of the above discoveries ... give the command of the iron trade of the world to Britain, and take it for ever, or, at least, as long as the industry and liberty of Britain remain, from the Northern Kingdoms and America; because Britain is the only country hitherto known in which seams of coal, iron stone or iron ore and lime stone (the three component parts or raw materials from which iron is made) are frequently found in the same field and in the near neighbourhood of the sea, or of short water carriage to the sea.' *Address and Proposals from Sir John Dalrymple, Bart., on the Subject of the Coal, Tar, and Iron Branches of the Trade*, p. 8.

[3] See his *Traité sur l'art de convertir le fer en acier et d'adoucir le fer fondu*, Paris, 1722.

[4] S. Smiles, *Industrial Biography*, p. 103.

[5] B. Huntsman, *Historique de l'Invention de l'Acier fondu en* 1750 (published in French in 1888).

[6] Ibid. See Ludwig Beck, *Die Geschichte des Eisens*, III, 272; F. le Play, *Annales des Mines*, 4th Series, III, 636; *Victoria History of the County of York*, II, 396.

[7] S. Smiles, *Industrial Biography*, p. 108.

interests after having come near to interfering with their methods. But Sir George Savile refused his support, and at the same time some Birmingham manufacturers having heard of Huntsman's work asked him to come and settle near them.[1] This would undoubtedly have been a most serious blow to Sheffield's prosperity, but the cutlers finally realized the danger and submitted to the dreaded novelty which was to make their fortunes as well as that of their city. Their hostility gave place to a self-interested curiosity, and Huntsman, who had no patent, had to take endless precautions against spying. He worked at night and employed only men on whom he could rely. Even thus he could not keep his secret for long,[2] though the excellence of his manufacture was never equalled and his trade-mark soon became famous and was much sought after throughout Europe. His factory at Attercliffe,[3] which does not seem to have been very large, was the first that could be described by the modern name of steelworks. Its prosperity began about 1770, at the time when thirty or forty miles away the first spinning mills were being started.[4]

We must again stop to compare those two great industries, the development of which took place almost at the same time. The history of technical progress brings out their differences rather than their likenesses. The evolution of the textile industry is due to mechanical inventions, that of the metal-working industry to chemical inventions. In the one case machinery replaced manual work, whilst in the other processes were introduced which increased the quantity or improved the quality of the output without appreciably diminishing the part played by labour. The two series of facts are, from some points of view, so different that it is really difficult to draw a parallel between them. How can Abraham Darby's invention be compared with that of Wyatt or of Hargreaves? Yet their consequences were, if not identical, at any rate very similar. The industrial revolution cannot be summed up in one simple formula: whether we look at it from the technical or the economic point of view it comprises factors and circumstances too different for any such simplification to be possible. Even the use of machinery, which we are sometimes tempted to consider as the alpha and omega of

[1] B. Huntsman, *Historique de l'Invention de l'Acier fondu en* 1750, p. 12.

[2] Samuel Walker, an ironmaster, succeeded in making his way into Huntsman's workshop in a beggar's clothes. The whole story was misunderstood by the Swedish traveller Proling (referred to by Beck, *Die Geschichte des Eisens*, III, 277 ff.): he believed that Walker (whom he called Walter) was the inventor, and that Huntsman had only followed him.

[3] Today Attercliffe is a suburb of Sheffield.

[4] In 1774 two other Sheffield firms used Huntsman's process. See *Victoria History of the County of York*, II, 397. Huntsman died in 1776. He was a Quaker like the Darbys, and, scorning all dignities, he even refused to become a member of the Royal Society. The activity and enterprise of dissenters have often been noted.

the whole modern factory system, does not sufficiently account for its beginnings. How could such an explanation be made to cover the vital fact of the use of coal in the smelting and working of iron?

Later on the influence of machinery did indeed pervade the metal-working industry as it pervaded all other industries, and did so perhaps to an even greater extent. But at this most decisive stage of its development machines were only an element of secondary importance. Moreover, their use in the metal industry was not so novel as in other trades. Equipment already in use adapted itself to the new conditions of production, rather than determined what they were to be. Some of the improvements which thus completed more important inventions are worth mentioning. First of all, efforts were made to increase the power of the forge bellows so as to build larger blast furnaces and thus to take full advantage of the use of coal. It was in 1761, at the Carron ironworks, that air cylinders were first used. They consisted of four air pumps twenty-one feet long and four and a half feet in diameter, whose pistons were worked by a water-wheel. They were built by Smeaton, one of the first professional engineers to place his knowledge at the disposal of that industry.[1] Thanks to the powerful and continuous blast of air which these bellows provided, a furnace which had previously produced ten to twelve tons of pig iron a week was now able to produce over forty.[2] We have mentioned above the rolling mills used by Cort instead of hydraulic hammers to work the iron after it had been puddled.[3] Almost at the same time Watt built a small steam hammer for John Wilkinson's ironworks. It weighed a hundred and twenty pounds and could strike a hundred and fifty blows a minute.[4]

[1] See Jardine, 'Account of John Roebuck', *Transactions of the Royal Society of Edinburgh*, IV, 73. On Smeaton, see S. Smiles, *Lives of the Engineers*, II, 61. Faujas de Saint-Fond thus describes the working of the Carron bellows: 'Four blast furnaces, forty-five feet high, devour day and night immense quantities of coal and ore. We can therefore realize the amount of air needed to keep alive these fiery furnaces which, every six hours, pour forth streams of liquid iron. Each furnace is kept going by four air-pumps of the largest size, in which the air, compressed in iron cylinders, and driven on to the flame through a single tube, produces such a piercing whistle and such a violent disturbance, that anyone who did not know what was coming would certainly feel terrified. These wind machines, a kind of huge bellows, are set in motion by the action of water. A considerable volume of air is indispensable in order to keep a column of coal and ore forty-five feet high in the most intense state of incandescence. The current of air is so rapid and strong that it produces a live and bright flame ten feet above the top of the furnace.' Faujas de Saint-Fond, *Voyage en Angleterre, en Ecosse et aux Iles Hébrides*, I, 212 ff.

[2] H. Scrivenor, *History of the Iron Trade*, p. 85.

[3] He had them patented in 1783 (Patent No. 1398, see *Abridgments of Specifications relating to the Manufacture of Iron and Steel*, p. 19).

[4] Letters from Watt to Boulton, May 3rd, Nov. 26th and 28th, 1782, Soho MSS. According to R. Thurston, *A History of the Growth of the Steam-Engine*, p. 111, Watt probably offered to make a steam hammer for Wilkinson as early as 1777.

New machines were added to those already in use for drawing, cutting and working the metal: drills for boring cannon,[1] and metal-turning lathes, in which the main improvement was in 1797 the carriage invented by Henry Maudslay.[2] To these should be added more complicated and specialized machines, such as a machine for forging nails and another for turning screws.[3]

These inventions not only resulted in a speeding up of the work and a saving in labour, but they ensured that perfect precision of execution, that absolute uniformity of shape which previously it had been possible to do without but which now became indispensable. These machines helped in the making of other machines, and so, by developing its own equipment, the metal industry assisted in the improvement of all other industries. But all this development, with its incalculable consequences, was made possible by inventions which owed nothing to machinery, such as the use of coal in blast furnaces, puddling and Huntsman's process for making steel. From these must be dated the era of large-scale metal production.

IV

Large-scale production and large undertakings — these are almost synonymous expressions. During the sixteenth and seventeenth centuries, what prevented founders from extending their control over the whole iron trade was the limitation imposed on production by the shortage of fuel. The concentration in one place of several blast furnaces meant the systematic cutting down of an extensive wooded area. As soon as this difficulty was removed nothing more stood in the way of the founding of great ironworks. On the contrary, everything seemed to point to that direction. It was not only possible but essential to produce large quantities, and the men who were first in the field gained such an advantage that their wealth increased very rapidly.

The first example of this is that of the Darby family. In 1750 the ironworks at Coalbrookdale were the only ones to use coal.[4] They were already so important that the little river along which they stood was no longer strong enough to work their forge-bellows. A Newcomen engine[5]

---

[1] Previously cannons were cast hollow, only the touch hole being drilled with the help of a kind of wimble, or of an auger worked by a drill-bow. See plates in Diderot's *Encyclopédie*, vol. IV, article 'Fonte des canons'.

[2] On Henry Maudslay, see S. Smiles, *Industrial Biography*, pp. 198-235.

[3] Nail-making machines were invented by Thomas Clifford in 1790 and S. Guppy in 1796. See Ludwig Beck, *Die Geschichte des Eisens*, III, 447-8. The first screw-making machine was Maudslay's. See S. Smiles, op. cit., p. 226.

[4] The author of the 1750 pamphlet entitled *The State of the Trade and Manufactory of Iron in Great Britain considered* complains of the scarcity and dearness of wood, and does not mention the use of coal.

[5] See chap. IV below.

had to be used to create an artificial waterfall, which worked a driving wheel twenty-four feet in diameter.[1] New blast furnaces were put up, one after another, in neighbouring localities.[2] As early as 1754 the Horsehay furnace produced twenty to twenty-two tons of pig iron a week.[3] Richard Reynolds, who took over the management in 1763, was a great manufacturer in every sense of the word.[4] He first directed the Coalbrookdale concern during the minority of the second Darby's sons, and remained their partner for many years after, though he conducted at the same time establishments of his own. The firm had shops in London, Liverpool, Bristol and at Truro in Cornwall.[5] In 1784 they owned, around Coalbrookdale, eight blast furnaces and nine ironworks, and received coal and iron ore from mines leased and worked by themselves. To enable their heavy trucks of coal and ore to move over this extensive area they had made and laid rails of pig iron of a total length of twenty miles.[6] The output, which at the death of the first Abraham Darby was hardly more than five or six hundred tons a year, rose at the end of the century to thirteen or fourteen thousand tons,[7] nearly three-quarters of the whole English output before coal had taken the place of charcoal.

The fortune of the Darby dynasty was the work of three generations, and its history during eighty years sums up that of the whole English metal-working industry. The first steps were made easier for those who, coming later, profited by the impulse which they had given and by

[1] Ludwig Beck, *Die Geschichte des Eisens*, III, 363.

[2] At Horsehay, Ketley, Madeley Wood, Donnington Wood.

[3] J. Phillips, *General History of Inland Navigation*, pp. 126-7.

[4] Rathbone's *Memoir of Reynolds*, frequently quoted by T. S. Ashton, contains many extracts from Richard Reynolds's correspondence.

[5] At Truro he chiefly sold Newcomen pumps to pump water out of the mines. See S. Smiles, op. cit., p. 86.

[6] Ibid., p. 93. Before pig-iron rails, wooden ones had been used, notably round the Newcastle mines. See A. Young, *North of England*, III, 9: 'The coal waggon roads from the pits to the water are great works, carried over all sorts of inequalities of ground, so far as the distance of nine or ten miles. The track of the wheels is marked with pieces of timber let into the road, for the wheels of the waggons to run on, by which means one horse is enabled to draw, and that with ease, fifty or sixty bushels of coal.' In the Parliamentary papers relating to the making of canals, 'railways' or 'railroads' constructed at the same time as the canals and meant to connect them up, are often mentioned. See *Journals of the House of Commons*, XXXIV, 604 (connection between the Middleton mines and the River Aire), XL, 240 (between Bilston and Birmingham), LVII, 182 (between the mines of the Forest of Dean and the Severn).

[7] This figure is the result of a comparison between the 'table of blast furnaces burning coke in May, 1790' given by H. Scrivenor, *History of the Iron Trade*, p. 359, and the statistics of the production of iron in 1796, ibid., pp. 95-6. As early as 1776 'the turnover of each of the furnaces at Coalbrookdale, Madeley Wood, Lightmoor, Horsehay and Ketley was said to exceed £80,000 a year'. T. S. Ashton, op. cit., p. 43, quoting Whitworth, *The Advantages of Inland Navigation*, p. 37.

the results already achieved. John Wilkinson was a typical example of the men of this second period, who were not inventors but men quick to note new inventions, to realize their practical value and to use them for their own profit. His father, Isaac Wilkinson, seems to have been one of the first to set up a coke furnace similar to those at Coalbrookdale.[1] In 1775 John Wilkinson was the first to order a steam engine from Boulton and Watt's for purposes other than pumping.[2] By 1770 he and his brother William were in possession of three important ironworks – at Broseley, Bersham and Bradley. He gradually extended the Broseley works, and connected them with the Birmingham canal.[3] There he built one after another five or six blast furnaces,[4] and obtained coal from deposits which he owned and worked himself. He had interests in foundries in South Wales and was a shareholder in Cornish tin mines. He owned a big warehouse in London with five or six landing stages on the Thames.[5] His activities were extended to France, where in 1777 he set up ironworks at Indret, near Nantes, and where in 1778 he built furnaces for the Creusot foundry.[6] The whole made up a kind of kingdom, an industrial State, which Wilkinson governed with a strong and autocratic hand.[7] This State, more important and much richer than many Italian or German principalities, enjoyed a credit which they might well envy and, like them, coined its own money. Between 1787 and 1808 copper and silver tokens, stamped with the effigy of John Wilkinson, were in use in several midland and western counties. They show a profile of the great ironmaster. His rather heavy homely face might remind us of Arkwright's vulgarity were it not for the haughty eyebrows and the scornful mouth. And round it run the simple words: WILKINSON, IRON MASTER.[8]

[1] A. N. Palmer, *John Wilkinson and the old Bersham Iron Works*, p. 8. F. Nicholson, 'Notes on the Wilkinsons, Ironmasters', *Memoirs of the Literary and Philosophical Society of Manchester*, 1905, No. 15.

[2] See chap. IV (Steam). He took out patents in his own name for the manufacture of lead pipes (1790, No. 1735), for a rolling mill, a steam lathe (1792, No. 1857), and for certain improvements in smelting processes (1794, No. 1993).

[3] Palmer, op. cit., p. 16. Ashton, pp. 44-5.

[4] See H. Scrivenor, *History of the Iron Trade*, p. 359.

[5] Palmer, p. 18.

[6] G. Bourgin, 'Deux documents sur Indret', *Bulletin d'Histoire économique de la Révolution française*, 1917-19, pp. 467 ff. T. S. Ashton, op. cit., p. 54.

[7] His despotic temper was the cause of his quarrels with his brother William, who left him in 1776-7, and settled at Nantes. The Soho MSS. give some information as to the difficulties between the two brothers (Correspondence between J. Watt and J. Wilkinson, Nov., 1795). See T. S. Ashton, op. cit., chap. III (Watt, Boulton and the Wilkinsons), and H. W. Dickinson, *John Wilkinson, Ironmaster*.

[8] See the photographic reproductions of these tokens in Palmer's *John Wilkinson and the old Bersham Iron Works*, pp. 24 ff. Various types were issued in 1787, 1788, 1790, 1791, 1792 and 1793. The 1787 token has on the reverse side a workman putting a piece of iron under an automatic hammer; that of 1788 has a ship; that of 1790 a

New metal-working centres were being formed wherever three essential conditions were found: the presence of iron, the presence of coal and the vicinity of streams for supplying power. South Wales combined these three qualities, but for a long time its possibilities were almost unknown, while communication with the rest of the kingdom was difficult for lack of good roads. In 1765 an iron merchant called Anthony Bacon obtained from Lord Talbot a concession of all mines within an area of forty miles round Merthyr Tydvil for an annual rent of £100.[1] During the American War of Independence, Bacon made a fortune thanks to orders for artillery given by the British Government. In 1782, when he retired, he owned four prosperous works, at Dowlais, Cyfarthfa, Plymouth and Pen-y-Darran. The two most important became the property of Samuel Homfray and of Richard Crawshay, who were the first ironmasters to use the puddling process, and they grew rich while Cort was ruined. Crawshay founded a dynasty of iron-masters,[2] and enjoyed the same kind of fame as some great industrialists of our times. When he drove in his four-in-hand from London to Cyfarthfa, all the countryside hastened to see 'the Iron King' pass.[3]

Another district of which the metal-working industry took possession about the same time was the Lowlands of Scotland, a country rich in ores with an intelligent and hardworking population. The first and the most famous of the great Scotch ironworks was the Carron works founded in 1760 by John Roebuck.[4] The site was happily chosen, where the central plain of Scotland meets the hills and quite near the Firth of Forth.[5] There was coal on the spot in great quantities and costing only the labour of digging it out. When Roebuck settled there he was no novice as regards inventions and undertakings. At Birmingham,

[1] J. Lloyd, *Early History of the Old South Wales Iron Works* (1760-1840), p. 48.

[2] The Cyfarthfa ironworks belonged successively to Richard Crawshay, to his son William Crawshay, to his grandson also called William, and to his great-grandson Robert Thompson Crawshay, who died in 1879, leaving the business to his son. See J. Lloyd, op. cit., pp. 63 ff.

[3] S. Smiles, *Industrial Biography*, p. 132. See T. S. Ashton, op. cit., pp. 94 ff. In 1803 the Cyfarthfa works alone employed 2,000 men.

[4] The few blast furnaces built between 1730 and 1760 (at Bunawe, Goatfield, Abernathy, etc.), burnt charcoal. See W. Ivison MacAdam, *Notes on the Ancient Iron Industry of Scotland*, p. 89.

[5] Power was provided by a small left-hand tributary of the Forth, the Carron Water (David Bremner, *The Industries of Scotland*, p. 42).

woman leaning on a cog wheel and holding an auger; that of 1791 a naked man, seated, raising a hammer over the anvil; that of 1792 a harp with the inscription, NORTH WALES; that of 1793 a woman holding a pair of scales with the motto MEA PECUNIA. Wilkinson also issued guinea notes. It will be remembered that during the same period 'monnaies de confiance' were issued in France by traders or manufacturers, amongst others those of the brothers Monneron, which were coined in Boulton's works at Soho.

where he had first practised as a doctor, he had joined Samuel Garbett in 1747 to work at what would now be called industrial chemistry. In 1749 he had set up at Prestonpans, near Edinburgh, a sulphuric acid factory.[1] He wanted to make the Carron works into a model establishment, and he enlisted for that purpose the help of the best engineers of the time. He employed Smeaton to set up hydraulic bellows. Later on James Watt, who was still unknown, joined him, and Roebuck provided him with the means to carry on his investigations and to take out his first patent.[2] Roebuck's mistake was to try too many experiments at once. The working of the coal mines and salt pans he had rented on the Duke of Hamilton's estate proved disastrous. He sunk a great deal of money in them and finally went bankrupt in 1773.[3] But the prosperity of the Carron works, in the hands of a company of English and Scotch capitalists, 'the Carron Company', continued uninterrupted.[4] The amount subscribed at the beginning by Roebuck's partners was limited to £12,000. This soon rose to £130,000 and then to £150,000,[5] whilst the name of Carron became a household word throughout Europe with the fame of the 'carronades'.[6]

In Yorkshire, around Sheffield, and in Northumberland, around Newcastle, great enterprises were also growing up. We can read the notebook of Samuel Walker of Rotherham, in which he recorded the chief events in his industrial career.[7] In 1741 he had set up 'in an old nail-shop' a small forge, which he and his brother worked together. They found partners who brought in a little money and in 1746 they were able to build their first blast furnace. In 1748, having by underhand means discovered Huntsman's secret, Samuel Walker began to make cast steel. This was the beginning of his fortune. The value of his

[1] There it was that leaden receivers were first used for the condensation of sulphurous gas. See Jardine, 'Account of John Roebuck', *Transactions of the Royal Society of Edinburgh*, IV, 69. The price of sulphuric acid fell to 25 per cent of its former value.

[2] See chap. IV below.

[3] Jardine, op. cit., p. 75; S. Smiles, *Lives of Boulton and Watt*, pp. 150-8.

[4] In 1788 the output was 4,000 tons, in 1796, 5,620. See H. Scrivenor, *History of the Iron Trade*, pp. 87 and 96.

[5] Ludwig Beck, *Die Geschichte des Eisens*, III, 364.

[6] 'It is the largest iron foundry in Europe.' Faujas de Saint-Fond, *Voyage en Angleterre, en Ecosse et aux Iles Hébrides*, I, 209. Faujas de Saint-Fond describes the carronades as 'huge guns, short and broad in the breech'. Ibid., p. 210. The works had been described before by another French expert, G. Jars, in his *Voyages Métallurgiques*. Amongst other metal-working establishments founded in Scotland between 1770 and 1800, we must mention the Devon Ironworks, the Clyde Ironworks and John Wilson's factory at Wilsontown. See St John Vincent Day, *The Iron and Steel Industries of Scotland*, p. 34, and E. Svedenstjerna, *Reise durch einen Theil von England und Schottland in den Jahren* 1802 *und* 1803, pp. 155 ff.

[7] 'A Sketch of the Proceedings of the Foundry &c which was in an Old Nailer Smithy, at Grennowside, about Nov., 1741', by Saml. and Aaron Walker. Published by J. Hunter, *Hallamshire*, pp. 211-12.

annual output, which in 1747 he estimated at £900, had risen by 1750 to £2,400; by 1755 to £6,200; by 1760 to £11,000. He had workshops not only at Rotherham but in all the neighbouring villages, at Holmes, Conisborough, and Masborough where he built himself a princely residence. He died in 1782 and was succeeded by his sons. By 1796 the Rotherham foundries represented a capital of over £200,000.[1]

A question at once arises with reference to the organization and ownership of these great concerns: how far were they individual and how far collective undertakings? The company which after Roebuck's failure bought up the Carron works was no exception. Companies similar to those which had long existed for working mines set up, or undertook the management of, ironworks in various parts of the kingdom. Let us examine the composition of one of them. The Low Moor Company which in 1788 purchased the Low Moor Mines not far from Leeds, and in the following year set up the Bowling Foundries, consisted originally of three partners.[2] Later, their number for a short time rose to six. About 1800 there were again only three men to share the risks and profits of the business: John Lofthouse, a Liverpool merchant, John Hardy, a Bradford solicitor, and Joseph Dawson, a Protestant clergyman.[3] Thus this 'Company' was nothing but a mere trade association of the oldest and most traditional kind. The only thing it had in common with a modern joint-stock company was the fact that it was not described (as it might well have been) by the names of the partners. On the other hand, businesses known by the name of their founder or the man who actually managed them did not always belong to him alone. Considerable capital was needed to set up or to develop great ironworks. In order to obtain that capital the ironmasters took in sleeping partners, whose good or bad fortunes often decided the fate of the firms they were interested in. The reader will not have forgotten the story of Henry Cort, dragged down in the fraudulent bankruptcy of his creditor Jellicoe. Such sleeping partners, being frequently manufacturers themselves, as often as not became active partners and took part in the management of the business. Roebuck and Walker had several partners, Wilkinson worked for a long time with his brother William, Richard Reynolds with his brother-in-law, the third Abraham Darby. But none of these facts carry us beyond the realm of individual enterprise. A few men, working either individually or

[1] J. Hunter, *Hallamshire*, p. 212.

[2] Richard Hird, John Preston and John Garratt, *Fortunes made in Business*, pp. 91-2. Compare with the description of several 'Companies' of the same kind in T. S. Ashton's book (the Darbys and Reynolds, the Wilkinsons, Roebuck's Carron Company, etc.).

[3] This Dawson was a curious character. He was interested in the physical sciences and had relations with Priestley. More taken up with business than religion, he used to pay his workmen on Sunday mornings. Ibid., p. 94.

in small groups, were responsible for the creation of the great establishments in the metal-working industry, just as in the textile trades.

V

Thus, as regards the iron industry, England's inferior position had in a short period been changed into an ascendancy which was promptly recognized throughout Europe. Several of the foreigners who, at the end of the eighteenth and beginning of the nineteenth century, came to Great Britain to study the new processes of the metal industry, wrote notes of their travels. In these notes they described, with an admiration justified by the novelty of the sight, the activity of the places they had visited and their general appearance, as well as the details of their technical organization. Apart from size, the description given by these observers does not essentially differ from what a traveller might write today [1927] after visiting an important metal-working district.

In 1802-3 Erik Svedenstjerna visited the foundries of Wales, the Midlands and the Scotch Lowlands. He was an intelligent man who knew how to observe and to collect information. He saw a great deal, learned even more and went home full of admiration: 'Round Swansea such a number of copper works, coal mines, water tanks, canals, aqueducts and railroads can be seen crowded together, that a new visitor will hardly know to what object he should first give his attention.'[1] He went to Merthyr Tydvil: 'Some twenty years ago it was but an insignificant village, but the works, now established there have in a few years made it one of the most interesting places of the whole kingdom.' There, on a length of half a Swedish mile in the narrow Taff Valley, he counted thirteen blast furnaces, each producing an average of forty tons of pig iron a week.[2] In the Pen-y-Darran works alone he was shown three blast furnaces, three refining furnaces and twenty-five puddling furnaces. The mechanical equipment was most impressive. At Cyfarthfa, the water-wheel which worked the forge bellows was fifty-two feet in diameter. There were steam engines everywhere — seventy, eighty horse-power engines.[3] The factories seemed towns filled with hurrying people — one, with its dependent mines, employing nine hundred workmen. The owner, Samuel Homfray, was said to employ in his various works about four thousand men.[4]

It is interesting to compare Svedenstjerna's accounts, written with

[1] Erik Svedenstjerna, *Reise durch einen Theil von England und Schottland in den Jahren 1802 und 1803*, p. 40.

[2] Ibid., pp. 49 ff.

[3] Ibid., p. 57.

[4] Ibid., p. 56. On the Severn group (Coalbrookdale, etc.), see pp. 68-80; on Newcastle, pp. 115-17.

all the accuracy of a technical man, with the probably less exact but very graphic and often picturesque descriptions from less expert observers. The French mineralogist, Faujas de Saint-Fond, was in 1784 permitted to visit the Carron works. He saw the workshops where the famous carronades were made: 'Amongst these warlike machines, these terrible death-dealing instruments, huge cranes, every kind of windlass, lever and tackle for moving heavy loads, were fixed in suitable places. Their creaking, the piercing noise of the pulleys, the continuous sound of hammering, the ceaseless energy of the men keeping all this machinery in motion, presented a sight as interesting as it was new.'[1] 'There is such a succession of these workshops that the outer air is quite hot; the night is so filled with fire and light that when from a distance we see, here a glowing mass of coal, there darting flames leaping from the blast furnaces, when we hear the heavy hammers striking the echoing anvils and the shrill whistling of the air pumps, we do not know whether we are looking at a volcano in eruption or have been miraculously transported to Vulcan's cave, where he and his cyclops are manufacturing lightning.'[2] The sight of these great factories revealed, in the most concrete and striking manner, the revolution which had just taken place in the English metal-working industry.[3]

The many new uses to which iron could be put made people even then foresee the consequences of this change. Since the output of iron and steel was no longer restricted within narrow limits, these metals, because of their unique qualities of cohesion and strength and their capacity for taking any shape and keeping it for a practically indefinite time, were becoming the best raw material for many industries. We have seen how Richard Reynolds, as early as 1767, replaced the wooden rails connecting together the Coalbrookdale blast furnaces and mines by iron ones. But the man who is really entitled to the name of pioneer, who first had a presentiment of the unbounded future of the metal industries and proclaimed it to his astonished contemporaries with enthusiasm, was John Wilkinson, 'the father of the iron trade'. Before him Isaac Wilkinson had used at Bersham bellows the sides of which were made of iron.[4] Following his father's example John

---

[1] Faujas de Saint-Fond, *Voyage en Angleterre, en Ecosse et aux Iles Hébrides*, I, 210-11.

[2] Ibid., pp. 216-17.

[3] In 1788 the output of pig iron in Great Britain was 68,000 tons; in 1796 it was 126,000 tons, in 1804, 250,000 tons, while the number of blast furnaces increased from 85 to 121 and 221. *Parliamentary Debates*, VII, 81 and 88.

[4] 'I grew tired of my leathern bellows and determined to make iron ones. Everybody laughed at me. I did it, and applied the steam engine to blow them, and they all cried: Who could have thought it?' S. Smiles, *Lives of Boulton and Watt*, p. 213. The steam engine mentioned here must have been a Newcomen pump, which was used for bringing water to the wheel. In 1757 Isaac Wilkinson had taken out a patent

Wilkinson first made iron chairs, vats for breweries and distilleries, and iron pipes of all sizes. In 1776 the question of building a bridge across the Severn, between Broseley and Madeley, was discussed. Wilkinson, as one of the local captains of industry, was directly concerned. It was he who, together with Darby of Coalbrookdale, undertook the execution of the plan.[1] He suggested that instead of building a stone or a brick bridge they should, at any rate for part of the work,[2] make use of iron, which was the staple product of the district and which, by the very increase of trade it had brought about, had made new lines of communication necessary. This was not an entirely new idea, for it had already been put forward several times and in various countries by scientists and engineers.[3] But it had never been put into practice. Wilkinson and Darby boldly upheld its practicability and decided to put it at once to the test. The plans were drawn up with the help of Pritchard, a Shrewsbury architect.[4] The various parts of the framework were cast under Darby's supervision, his factory being close by. The bridge was opened to the public in 1779. It was made entirely of cast iron, consisted of one arch with a hundred-foot span, had a height of forty-five feet[5] and became the object of universal curiosity.[6] The second metal bridge was built at Sunderland in 1796,

[1] Their names appear in the authorizing Act of Parliament (16 Geo. III, c. 17). In 1777 they appear again on an altered list, together with that of Francis Homfray, brother of the Homfray of Pen-y-Darran.

[2] On this matter no immediate decision was come to. The Act of 1776 says that the bridge may be made 'of cast iron, stone, brick, or timber'.

[3] At the beginning of the seventeenth century the Venetian engineer, Faustus Verantius (Veranzo), had made designs for a suspension bridge with metal chains and for a bridge made of bronze. See Ludwig Beck, *Die Geschichte des Eisens*, III, 758-9. In 1779 one Calippe submitted to the Consulate of the city of Lyons plans for a metal bridge, at which, he said, he had been working since 1755 with the help of a Lyons botanist called Goiffon. The text of the proposal entitled 'Plans for a single span bridge, a noble and simple metal structure of a new design, arranged to span a great river without endangering the safety of navigating vessels', together with the correspondence between the Lyons Consulate and the inventor, are preserved in the Lyons Municipal Archives (Series D). The model of the bridge Calippe wished to build was exhibited at the Académie des Sciences in 1779.

[4] S. Smiles, *Lives of the Engineers*, II, 356.

[5] 'We crossed the river by an iron bridge, with a single arch of a hundred-foot span and of a height of forty-five feet above the level of the water. It is eight yards wide and a hundred yards long, and consists of iron parts, each of which has been cast separately, their total weight amounting to fifty tons.' *Tournée faite en 1788 dans la Grande Bretagne par un Français parlant la langue anglaise*, p. 100.

[6] Rozier, *Observations sur la Physique, l'Histoire Naturelle et les Arts*, XXXV, 16-19 (1789). (Account given by M. Prévost-Dacier, of Geneva.)

for a system by which 'a furnace, forge, or any other works may be blowed from any waterfall ... to several miles distant ... by means of a pipe'. (T. S. Ashton, op. cit. p. 22.)

over the river Wear. It was much longer than the first and was high enough to allow sea-going ships with all their rigging to pass under it.[1] The third, over the Severn a little above Broseley, dates from 1797.[2] The advantages of this method of construction were so obvious that the most ambitious schemes were already being built upon it. In 1801, when the question arose of building another bridge for London in order to relieve the traffic on the old one, which had for many years been inadequate to the needs of the city, the Parliamentary Commission set up to go into the matter heard the evidence of the great ironmasters of the time. They not only offered to build an iron bridge but to build it with only one arch, with a span of about seven hundred feet.[3]

The idea of building an iron bridge had nothing in it to upset accepted opinion, but the idea of floating iron ships seemed a challenge to common sense. When Wilkinson first mentioned it, people shrugged their shoulders and said he was smitten with a new kind of insanity: iron madness. Trusting in Archimedes he followed up his scheme, and in July 1787 launched on the Severn a boat made of plates of iron bolted together. He wrote to a friend: 'It answers all my expectations, and has convinced the unbelievers, who were nine hundred and ninety-nine in a thousand. It will be only a nine days' wonder, and afterwards a Columbus' egg.'[4] The first boats built in this way were small twenty-ton lighters for inland navigation.[5] A less surprising novelty, but one which deserves to be mentioned, was the use of cast iron in making water pipes. In 1788 Wilkinson carried out an order, the size of which to the previous generation would have appeared fantastic: he had forty miles of cast-iron pipes made for the water supply of the city of Paris.[6] We can understand that such results filled him with ever-growing passion for his industry and unlimited faith in its future. Towards the end of his life he liked to repeat that iron was destined to take the place of most of the materials then in use, and that the day would come

[1] It had a span of 236 feet, a height above the water of 108 feet. See *Annales des Arts et Manufactures*, II, 166-73.

[2] See S. Smiles, *Lives of the Engineers*, II, 360. Svedenstjerna mentions an iron bridge built in 1796 at Laasan in Silesia, op. cit., p. 73.

[3] See *Report on the Improvements of the Port of London* (1801), which contains evidence given by Rennie, Watt, Reynolds, Wilkinson, etc.

[4] Letter to Stockdale, July 14th, 1787, in S. Smiles, *Lives of Boulton and Watt*, p. 213.

[5] Svedenstjerna in 1802 saw some on the canals round Birmingham, *Reise durch einen Theil von England und Schottland in den Jahren* 1802 *und* 1803, p. 87.

[6] D. Macpherson, *Annals of Commerce*, IV, 176. These were the articles mentioned in *L'examen et débat des comptes tant de l'ancienne que de la nouvelle administration des eaux de Paris, à partir de l'origine de cette entreprise jusqu'au* 10 *Août*, 1793 (*vieux style*), *par le citoyen G. D. David, liquidateur, ci-devant homme de loi*, pp. 27 and 92 (Archives Nationales, O¹ 1596).

when everywhere would be seen iron houses, iron roads, and iron ships. When he died in 1805 he was buried, in accordance with his wishes, in an iron coffin.[1]

With the reign of iron and steel came also that of machinery, one being the indispensable condition of the other. Watt would never have been able to build the steam engine which in 1775 Wilkinson ordered for his Bradley ironworks, had not Wilkinson provided him with metal cylinders of perfectly accurate shape which could not have been made by old-fashioned methods[2] — a most significant occurrence which illustrates the essential interdependence of these two simultaneous facts, the development of the iron industry and that of machinery. This was certainly the most important of the many new uses to which iron was put. In early machines, for instance those shown on the fine plates of Agricola's *De Re Metallica*, every single part, except for a few springs, was made of wood.[3] The result was irregular motion and rapid wear. As might have been expected, it was in the ironworks and iron foundries that metal equipment was first used. Such machines as rolling mills, metal lathes and hydraulic hammers could only be made of iron, and by preference of very hard iron.[4] Later on cast-iron fly-wheels made their appearance, the great weight and geometrical shape of which had the double advantage of great power together with uniform and regular motion. The steam mills known as Albion Mills, which were built between 1785 and 1788 by John Rennie on plans drawn up by Watt, were supposed to have been the first important establishment in which every piece of the plant and equipment, axles, wheels, pinions and shafts, were made of metal.[5] But the evidence given by French travellers who came to England just at that time shows that this was not exceptional, for all over the country wooden machines were being replaced by iron ones. In the spinning mills this change by that time was almost completed.[6] Thus these complex phenomena, which

---

[1] *Dictionary of National Biography*, article 'Wilkinson (John)'.

[2] Wilkinson had the year before patented a new method of boring cannon, by which he could obtain a bore of unequalled accuracy (Patent No. 1063, 1774). On the co-operation of John Wilkinson with Boulton and Watt, see T. S. Ashton, op. cit., pp. 63-8.

[3] Arkwright's machine, the model of which may be seen at the Science Museum, South Kensington, was also all made of wood.

[4] See J. Paine's patent (No. 505): 'The bars, being heated in a long hot arch or cavern are to pass between two large metal rollers, which have proper notches or furrows on their surface' (1728).

[5] See note by James Watt in Robison, *Steam and Steam Engines*, p. 137.

[6] 'I here admired [in a Paisley cotton mill], as in all the large factories I have had the chance of seeing in England, their skill in working iron and the great advantage it gives them as regards the motion, lastingness and accuracy of machinery. All driving wheels, and in fact almost all things, are made of cast iron, of such a fine and hard quality that when rubbed it polishes up just like steel ... There is no doubt

together went to make up the modern factory system, seemed all to be spontaneously advancing in the same direction. A new factor of incalculable power, steam, was now to bind their movements together and to quicken their common progress.

---

but that the working of iron is one of the most essential of trades and the one in which we are the most deficient. It is the only way by which we can manufacture on a large scale and qualify ourselves to compete on equal terms with the English. For it is impossible for, say, our spinning mills, to attempt to compete with those machines, and for our wooden machinery to try to rival that made of iron.' A. and F. de La Rochefoucauld-Liancourt, 'Voyage aux Montagnes' (letter dated May 9th, 1786).

CHAPTER FOUR

THE STEAM ENGINE

IN the metal as in the textile industry, most of the inventions on which modern technique is based were the result not of abstract speculation but of practical necessity and professional experience. With the steam engine science first made its appearance, and the empirical period of the industrial revolution was followed by the scientific one. This is one of the facts which account for the capital importance of this invention, as it forms a part of the history of science as well as of technology. But it is no part of our plan to study it from this double point of view, for which the knowledge both of the physicist and of the engineer would be needed. We must limit ourselves to drawing on the recognized authorities for the elementary data needed to understand the facts which belong to our own field of study. For the purposes of the present book the discovery of steam-power is an economic phenomenon. What need called forth the discovery, and how did it materialize? When was the steam engine introduced into various industries, giving rise at the same time to a wholly new industry? These are the questions to which an answer can and must be found. Documents of first-rate importance are available: those from Boulton and Watt's works in Soho,[1] the greater part of which have been fortunately preserved owing to the enlightened interest of a great industrial firm.[2] They enable us to reconstruct the industrial and commercial history of the steam engine at its first critical stages.

I

The use of motive power other than the muscular strength of men or of animals is one of the essential features of the modern factory system. Without it, though there might have been machines, yet there could have been no machine industry; and production could only have developed within comparatively narrow limits. The gap between 'manufacture' and the factory could in fact never have been bridged. The very existence of the great industrial establishments, whose beginnings are described in the foregoing chapters, was in fact dependent on a motive power, that of water. The reader will remember the significant name of 'water frame' given to Arkwright's machine.

[1] Now at the Central Library, Birmingham.
[2] Messrs Tangye, of Birmingham.

The old water-wheel, which for many centuries had worked flour mills, and since the end of the Middle Ages had been used to work the mallets of fulling mills, the bellows and hammers of ironworks or pumps for supplying and draining water, in the eighteenth century took on a character of universal utility.[1] It was found wherever a branch of industry was being either created or transformed. It made it possible to work, in one building, numerous and powerful machines. It enabled work to be organized in large workshops, where the men were brought under that strict discipline which was the necessary and immediate outcome of machine industry.

This period of industrial history, which we may call that of water power as distinct from that of steam power, was of some duration. The fact that in England it came to an end before the opening of the nineteenth century must be attributed to several distinct causes, whose combined action explains the immediate success of Watt's invention. The use of water power limited industries to certain localities, as a water mill could not be built except near a plentiful stream of swiftly running water. This condition was fulfilled at the foot of the Pennine range where the earliest spinning mills were set up, and in Scotland and Wales[2] where, as has been shown before, the metal industry knew how to make use of natural advantages. But the rest of England consists of flat country, alternating with gently sloping hills and valleys, through which slow rivers flow. This was one difficulty, and the other was that even in those places where water power did exist it was often insufficient. The clumsy systems of wheels and troughs which were used to collect and transmit it wasted a good deal, and the modern resource of obtaining additional energy from a distance by means of electricity was, of course, not available. The only practicable method which then existed of increasing the supply of power on the spot, was to create artificial waterfalls. But then the water had to be raised to the level of a reservoir by means of a pump, and this is how the steam engine first came to be used.

The fact is that originally the steam engine, or fire engine as it was called for many years, was nothing more than a pump. We need only mention the first researches into the expansion of steam by Salomon de Caus, by the Marquis of Worcester and by Denys Papin.[3] Practical

---

[1] We must note some efforts which were made in imitation of the Dutch to try and use wind power. A mechanical saw mill worked by a wind-mill was built at Limehouse, east of London, in 1766. But it was destroyed in 1768 by a riotous mob. See *Journals of the House of Commons*, XXXII, 160 and 194.

[2] The Severn ironworks may be considered as forming part of the Welsh district to which Wrekin Hill, north of Coalbrookdale, belongs geologically.

[3] Salomon de Caus, in his *Raisons des forces mouvantes* (Frankfurt, 1615), p. 4, was the first person to point out the possible practical use which could be made of the properties of steam. He made a machine which was reminiscent of the *aeolipylos*

applications of the principle, apart from unsuccessful experiments, only began with Savery's invention. Thomas Savery, an officer in the British Army, came from Cornwall.[1] He was familiar with the ever-growing difficulties of working copper mines, where, after a certain depth had been reached, it became almost impossible to get rid of the water which flooded the galleries; the pumps which had to be used one above the other were expensive to set up and did not answer very well.[2] It was in order to replace them that Savery invented his engine, the model of which was presented to William III at Hampton Court during the summer of 1698.[3]

This machine, although very simple, made use of two different forces: atmospheric pressure to raise the water and the expansion of steam to lower it again. Its main parts consisted of a boiler (B), connected with a tank (T). At its lower end the tank was fitted with two pipes, a downward one (P) and an upward one (P[1]), both closed by valves. The steam issuing from the boiler filled the tank, the tap

[1] R. Thurston, *A History of the growth of the Steam-Engine*, pp. 31 ff.; C. Matschoss, *Die Entwicklung der Dampfmaschine* (second edition), I, 292-3.

[2] As Torricelli discovered as early as 1640, the height of a column of water which can be raised by a suction pump is limited by the intensity of the pressure of the atmosphere. It cannot be raised more than about 33 feet 11 inches under an atmospheric pressure corresponding to 30.4 inches of mercury. In order to raise it 180 feet, at least six pumps had to be used, each one pumping its water into a tank from which the water was drawn up by the pump immediately above. This method of pumping water up had been known empirically, and used in mines, long before Torricelli's discovery. See the diagrams in Agricola's *De Re Metallica*.

[3] Communication to the Royal Society (June 14th, 1699); see *Transactions of the Royal Society*, XXI, 228 (with plates). The patent is dated July 23rd, 1698 (No. 356): 'A new invention for raising of water and occasioning motion to all sorts of mill work by the impellent force of fire, which will be of great use and advantage for draining mines, serving towns with water, and for the working of all sorts of mills where they have not the benefit of water nor constant winds.' Savery left a pamphlet called *The Miner's Friend, or, an Engine to raise Water by Fire described, and the Manner of fixing it in Mines, with an Account of the several Uses it is applicable unto, and an Answer to the Objections against it* (1707). Finally we must note the contemporary descriptions given by Harris, *Lexicon Technicum* (article 'Engine'), by Desaguliers, *Experimental Philosophy*, II, 465, and by J. Leupold, *Theatrum Machinarum Hydraulicarum*, III, 302-4.

invented by Hero of Alexandria. About 1660 the Marquis of Worcester made use of steam pressure to raise water into tanks in order to work fountains. A fountain worked by steam and invented by him was built at Whitehall, and in 1669 was visited by the Grand-Duke of Tuscany. See Henry Dircks, *The Life, Times and Scientific Labours of the Second Marquis of Worcester*, pp. 264 ff. The account given by the Marquis himself in his famous *Century of Inventions*, Nos. 68 and 100, is very vague. Papin's 'digesteur' dates from 1680, and his first works on steam as motive power from 1690 ('Nova Methodus ad Vires motrices validissimas levi Pretio comparandas', published in the *Acta Eruditorum* of June, 1690).

between the two was then closed and cold water was poured on the sides of the tank. This condensed the steam, leaving a partial vacuum in the tank. As a result the atmospheric pressure raised the water in the downward pipe (P). This was the first part of the proceeding. When the tank was nearly full of water, steam was again admitted, which in its turn exercised pressure on the water and drove it up the upward pipe (P¹). We need hardly say that this description is very much simplified, as is our diagram, details being purposely omitted. We must, however, mention the arrangement which gave Savery's pump its characteristic shape. Instead of having only one tank it had two of equal capacity, which filled and emptied alternately.

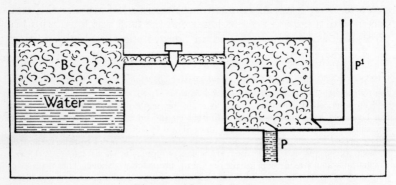

Diagram of Savery's Engine

In Savery's mind his engine was to serve many purposes; it was to drain marshes, to pump water out of mines, to supply water to towns and houses, to put out fires and to turn the wheels of mills.[1] It was indeed used in mines, first in Cornwall in the copper mines of Huel Vor, then in 1706 in Staffordshire, in the Broadwater collieries near Wednesbury.[2] But it occasioned some disappointment to those who first used it, for it only pumped the water up about a hundred feet at most, and if greater pressure was used the boiler burst. Savery was more successful with less powerful engines, in private houses or in gardens. About 1712 several were set up in London and the suburbs. We must mention the one at Sion house, bought by Lord Chandos, and the one at Camden House which pumped up fifty-two gallons a minute to a height of fifty-eight feet.[3] Another was used by the Company which supplied a part of London with water from the

[1] See the patent and *The Miner's Friend*, pp. 22 ff.
[2] S. Smiles, *Lives of Boulton and Watt*, pp. 55 and 56.
[3] *Abridgments of Specifications relating to the Steam Engine*, I, 32-3.

River Thames: but it did not apparently come up to expectation.[1] Savery's pump was indeed far from perfect. It worked slowly and its power was limited. Moreover, its use was not without danger, as no one knew how to prevent explosions in the absence of any pressure gauge, or regulator to lessen the pressure. As soon as Newcomen's engine became known the earlier one was at once abandoned.

The essential difference between the two inventions (and from the point of view of theory the difference is all in Savery's favour) was that Newcomen did not make use of the expansion of steam. In fact, he only made use of steam to create through condensation a vacuum in the tank. The most appropriate name for his engine would be an atmospheric engine. The principle was as follows: The boiler (B) communicated with a cylinder (C) in which worked a piston (P). The piston rod was attached to one of the ends of a beam (D) oscillating in a vertical plane. The other end was connected with a second piston rod (R) working a suction and force pump. While at rest a counter-weight (N) kept the beam in a slanting position. In order to put it in motion the cylinder (C) was cooled by cold water being poured on it. The steam condensed, the atmospheric pressure lowered the piston (P) and, by the action of the beam, raised the piston rod (R). The opposite effect was produced as soon as the steam was admitted into the cylinder (C). The atmospheric pressure no longer came into play, and the piston (P) was raised by the counter-weight. Thus a regular to-and-fro motion was set going and worked the pump.[2]

The invention was a few years later than Savery's.[3] Its author, Newcomen, was a blacksmith and locksmith at Dartmouth in Devonshire. He had no doubt heard of Savery, whose experiments had taken

[1] It replaced a water-wheel under London Bridge. See *Journals of the House of Commons*, XXIX, 883, and *Abridgments*, I, 34. From the seventeenth century London's water supply was in the hands of privileged companies. They had done a great deal to justify their monopoly: in 1724 Defoe praised 'the great convenience of water being everywhere laid in the streets in large timber pipes ... There are two great engines for the raising of the Thames water, one at the bridge, and the other near Broken Wharf. They raise so great a quantity of water, that, as they tell us, they are able to supply the whole city in its utmost extent, and to supply every house also, with a running pipe of water up to the uppermost story. However, the New River, which is brought by an aqueduct or artificial stream from Ware, continues to supply the greater part of the city with water, only with this addition by the way, that they have been obliged to dig a new head or basin at Islington on a higher ground than that which the natural stream of the river supplies, and this higher basin they fill from the lower, by a great engine worked formerly with six sails, now with many horses constantly working.' Defoe, *Tour*, II, 150.

[2] See *Abridgments of Specifications relating to the Steam Engine*, I, 35. A model of Newcomen's engine, made in 1740 by Desaguliers, is preserved in the museum of King's College, London. Another may be seen in the Science Museum, Kensington.

[3] It dates from 1705 or 1706. See S. Smiles, *Lives of Boulton and Watt*, p. 63; Ludwig Beck, *Die Geschichte des Eisens*, III, 91, and C. Matschoss, op. cit., I, 304 ff.

place not far off.[1] It has been supposed that he knew of Papin's work, and he was said to have corresponded on the subject with Robert Hooke, one of the most learned men of his time and country, then permanent secretary of the Royal Society.[2] It is more likely that the invention had a far less scientific origin. Newcomen's partner when the engine was first built, a glazier named John Calley, belonged as did

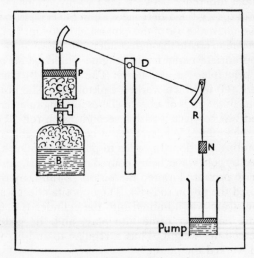

Diagram of Newcomen's engine

Newcomen himself to the class of skilled workmen or small manu-facturers.[3] The engine as first produced was very clumsy. The piston did not fit exactly into the cylinder; condensation, which was obtained by watering the outside of the cylinder with cold water, was very incomplete; while the tap had to be opened and closed by hand seven or eight times a minute. Successive improvements partly remedied these defects. Condensation was accelerated and made more perfect by the introduction of a siphon, by which cold water was sprayed into the cylinder and came into contact with the steam. The speed of the machine was increased by a system of strings and bars

[1] At Modbury, near Plymouth.

[2] In his article on the steam engine in the *Encyclopædia Britannica* (fourth edition, 1810) Robison upholds this story, which is quite unsupported by any written document. In any case there was nothing of the scientist about Newcomen. According to Desaguliers, both Newcomen and his partner Calley were so ignorant of mathematics and of the principles of physics (which Desaguliers calls 'philosophy') that much in their success must be due to mere chance. *Experimental Philosophy*, II, 532.

[3] Or Cawley. See *Abridgments*, loc. cit. According to the *Dictionary of National Biography*, article 'Newcomen', he was a landowner and a *grazier*, not a *glazier*.

which, by connecting up the taps with the beam, made their alternating motion quite automatic. Later on it was said that this improvement was due to the laziness of a young workman called Humphrey Potter, who while in charge of a Newcomen engine invented this method of lessening his labours. Finally, the danger of explosion was done away with by fitting the engine with a safety valve, which was added in 1717 by Henry Beighton of Newcastle.[1] By about 1720 the engine had been sufficiently improved to give satisfaction, and it remained practically unaltered for over half a century.[2]

As early as 1711 a company had been formed to build and sell Newcomen's engines,[3] and their use spread very quickly, on the Continent as well as in England.[4] One, working at Griff near Coventry, developed power equivalent to that of fifty horses at one sixth of the cost.[5] The engine at the York Buildings, bought in 1720 by the Thames Water Supply Company to replace Savery's machine, was fairly powerful, the capacity of the boiler was 450 cubic feet, the cylinder was $2\frac{1}{2}$ feet in diameter and 9 feet high, while the cost of the coal consumed annually amounted to £1,000.[6] Contemporary wonder cannot have lasted long, for very soon there were 'fire engines' everywhere, not only in the mines, where they very soon became indispensable,[7] but beside canals, where they were used to feed reservoirs and locks,[8] and in towns, which they supplied with drinking water. In 1767 there were nearly seventy such engines in and around Newcastle.[9]

Newcomen's engine could without great alterations have been

[1] See Desaguliers, op. cit., II, 481, 533. The story of the boy Potter is open to doubt. Perhaps it only comes from a kind of pun on the words 'buoy' and 'boy'. See *Dictionary of National Biography*, article 'Newcomen'.

[2] See the plates in the French *Encyclopédie*, vol. IV, article 'Hydraulique', and in C. Matschoss, op. cit., I, 47, 308, 309, 310.

[3] It was described as 'A Company of the proprietors of the invention for raising water by fire'. *Abridgments*, I, 36.

[4] As early as 1722 a Newcomen engine was set up at Cassel, in the landgraviate of Hesse, and another at Königsberg in Hungary. Ludwig Beck, *Die Geschichte des Eisens*, III, 166.

[5] Desaguliers, op. cit., II, 470 ff. (detailed description with plates). An engraving of 1712, representing a steam engine set up near Dudley, was in the latter part of the nineteenth century in the private collection of Mr Samuel Timmins at Birmingham.

[6] See the description (with plates) given by Johann Weidler, in his *Tractatus de Machinis hydraulicis toto Terrarum Orbe maximis Marlyensi et Londiniensi*, Wittenberg, 1728.

[7] See *A Treatise upon Coal Mines* (1769), pp. 100 ff.

[8] Sometimes one pump performed the double duty of pumping the water from a mine and of filling a canal. See *Journals of the House of Commons*, XXXV, 210. In the Acts giving permission to make canals there was sometimes a clause insisting that mine owners with mines on the course of the canal should pump the water from their mines into it. See 16 Geo. III, c. 28.

[9] R. Thurston, *A History of the Growth of the Steam-Engine*, p. 71.

made into a driving engine, as all that was needed was to connect the beam to some transmitting apparatus. In 1758 a certain Fitzgerald did write to the Royal Society on this very subject.[1] But though the idea was easy to apply it was not turned to any practical use, as it was found simpler to pump up water into a reservoir and then to use it to turn a wheel. About the middle of the eighteenth century this combined use of the fire engine and the water-wheel was found everywhere. To the loss of power which resulted from this mongrel contrivance was added the loss of heat due to the continual cooling of the condensing cylinder, the consequence being a consumption of fuel quite out of proportion to the results. Many efforts were made to remedy this defect, to which Brindley and Smeaton, two of the best engineers of the day, devoted some attention.[2] But the problem could be solved only by Watt's scientific genius.

II

From the glory surrounding the name of James Watt, from the place he occupies among great men not only in his native land but in the whole civilized world, and above all from the development and lasting consequences of his work, it is plain that he did not belong to the common race of inventors and pursued other ends. His scientific curiosity awoke early. On the walls of the house where he was born,[3] at Greenock in Scotland, he could as a boy see portraits of Isaac Newton and of Napier, who invented logarithms. These had belonged to his grandfather Thomas Watt, a teacher of mathematics.[4] His father was an architect and a shipbuilder, an intelligent and educated man, for a long time Treasurer of the Borough of Greenock and a town magistrate.[5]

In spite of his delicate health, and of the continual and intolerable headaches which racked him all his life, James Watt very early showed not merely a marked inclination but a positive passion for study. His mechanical bent soon developed, for at the age of thirteen he was making models of machines in his father's workshop.[6] When he had to choose a trade he elected to become a maker of scientific instruments, and he settled in Glasgow. He had some difficulties with the local

---

[1] *Philosophical Transactions of the Royal Society*, L, 370 (1758).

[2] S. Smiles, *Lives of the Engineers*, I, 330-3, and II, 73. On the improvements of Newcomen's engine, see C. Matschoss, *Die Entwicklung der Dampfmaschine*, I, 313, 334 (with plates).

[3] Jan. 19th, 1736.

[4] S. Smiles, *Lives of Boulton and Watt*, p. 81.

[5] Williamson, *Memorials of Watt*, p. 91. He was also a maker of nautical instruments, telescopes, compasses, sextants, etc. S. Timmins, *James Watt*, p. 4.

[6] Williamson, op. cit., pp. 152 ff.

authorities because he was not a native of the city. But the University, needing his services, extended its protection to him and gave him, within its own ground, a workshop where he could work in peace.[1] There he became acquainted with several distinguished scientists, among whom was Black the chemist, whose lectures he attended at the time when he was developing his theory of latent heat.[2] Robison, who met him for the first time in 1758 (he was then twenty-two), was struck by his extensive knowledge and by his intellectual grasp: 'I saw a workman and expected no more: I found a philosopher.'[3] In order to be able to read foreign scientific books Watt thoroughly mastered French, Italian and German.[4] From then onwards, and throughout his life, he kept up with all scientific developments and took part in important discoveries. First with Black, and afterwards with Roebuck, he investigated the composition of salt and of hydro-fluoric acid and sought to improve the barometer and the hygrometer. Later on, at the same time as Cavendish and Priestley, he worked at the analysis of water.[5] Nor was his culture, any more than his intelligence, that of a narrow specialist. In his middle age persons who met him were struck by his knowledge of ancient history, law and the fine arts. He read German metaphysics, was interested in poetry and passionately fond of music.[6] His speculative genius drew nourishment from all the science and all the thought of his time.

He has himself explained the origin of his invention.[7] There is no question here of any precocious or sudden inspiration, such as legends so easily attribute to great men. It was not by chance, as he watched a kettle boil, that Watt discovered the power of steam. Conversations with his friend Robison directed his attention to a problem which had been known to exist for a long time, and in 1761 or 1762 he began a series of systematic experiments on the pressure of steam, using Papin's 'digesteur'. During the winter of 1763-4 he had to mend a small

[1] S. Timmins, op. cit., p. 5.

[2] A. Ure, *The Cotton Manufacture of Great Britain*, I, 175. Ure had it from Watt himself.

[3] Robison, *Steam and Steam Engines*, p. 108.

[4] S. Smiles, op. cit., pp. 145-6.

[5] Discussions over this point are well summed up in the article 'Watt' in the *Dictionary of National Biography*. The documents by which Watt's claim is made good were published by J. Muirhead, *Correspondence of the late James Watt on the Discovery of the Composition of Water*.

[6] See Notice on Watt in the Timmins MSS. (Birmingham Central Library). The Soho MSS. contain many letters in French written by Watt. Svedenstjerna, who visited him in 1802, saw a fine collection of mineralogical specimens, which he had formed and classified, 'though putting forward no claim to the name of minera-logist'. Svedenstjerna, *Reise durch einen Theil von England und Schottland in den Jahren 1802 und 1803*, p. 89.

[7] Watt's note included in Robison's *Steam and Steam Engines*, pp. 118-20.

model of Newcomen's engine belonging to the University of Glasgow that was used in the practical physics course. This led him to a critical study of its mechanism. The loss of energy, which was its obvious defect, seemed to him to proceed from two main causes. On the one hand, after each stroke of the piston a quantity of fuel had to be consumed to raise the temperature again within the cylinder. On the other hand, condensation was incomplete owing to insufficient cooling. How could these two defects be remedied? Watt's invention was the answer to this question, worked out in a laboratory by scientific methods.

Here is that answer in the inventor's own words: 'To avoid useless condensation, the vessel in which the steam acted upon the piston ought always to be as hot as the steam itself ... To obtain a proper degree of exhaustion, the steam must be condensed in a separate vessel, which might be cooled to as low a degree as was necessary without affecting the cylinder.'[1] There we have the whole principle of the condenser, thereafter distinct and separate from the cylinder, while in Newcomen's engine they were one and the same. This first improvement led to an even more important one: 'In order to prevent the necessity of using water to keep the piston air-tight, and also to prevent the air from cooling the cylinder during the descent of the piston, it was necessary to employ steam to act upon the piston in place of the atmosphere.'[2] Thus, as a conclusion completes a process of sound logical reasoning, so the capital transformation took place by which the 'atmospheric engine' became a steam engine.

From that moment the main lines of the invention were fixed. As Watt had sketched them out in 1764, so do we find them in the specifications attached to his first patent of 1769.[3] The modest title he gave

[1] Watt in Robison's *Steam and Steam Engines*, p. ix.
[2] Ibid.
[3] No. 913. The patent is dated Jan. 5th and the specification April 29th. The text is quoted in full in the Act of 1775 (15 Geo. III, c. 61), which extended its period of validity. The specification begins as follows: 'My method of lessening the consumption of steam, and consequently fuel, in fire engines, consists of the following principles: (1) That vessel, in which the powers of steam are to be employed to work the engine, which is called the *cylinder* in common fire engines, and which I call the *steam vessel*, must, during the whole time the engine is at work, be kept as hot as the steam that enters it; first by enclosing it in a case of wood, or any other material that transmits heat slowly; secondly, by surrounding it with steam, or other heated bodies, and thirdly by suffering neither water, or any other substance colder than the steam, to enter or touch it during that time; (2) In engines that are to be worked wholly or partially by the condensation of steam, the steam is to be condensed in vessels distinct from the steam vessels or cylinders, although occasionally communicating with them: these vessels I call condensers, and, whilst the engines are working, these condensers ought to be kept as cold at least as the air in the neighbourhood of the engines.'

his invention very exactly indicated its original purpose, which had been merely to 'lessen the consumption of steam, and consequently fuel, in fire engines'. Watt, who was by nature diffident of his own abilities, only mentioned quite casually and as a minor hypothesis the really new and fruitful result of his researches, which was the use of steam, not as an auxiliary power to create a vacuum in the barrel of a pump but as an active motive power.[1] It was only thirteen years later, after a prolonged series of experiments, that the expansion of steam was brought to the foreground and the use of atmospheric pressure finally abandoned.

We need not go into all the minor inventions by which Watt completed his masterpiece. Some, like 'Watt's governor', or the slide valve in the double action engine, were intended to ensure a maximum of power with a minimum of irregularity.[2] The purpose of other devices was to make use of this power, and to turn it to various practical uses. To these more particularly we must direct our attention, for on them, at a certain moment, the industrial future of the steam engine depended. Had it merely remained what it was in the beginning and what the machines were from which it developed, that is to say an automatic pump, then its influence on the progress of industry would have been a very limited one. At the most it would have been an accessory to the water mill, used simply to pump up the water that worked the wheels. To make it able to work directly all kinds of machinery and to perform the most varied technical operations, a series of problems had to be solved, of which this was the first: how could the oscillation of the beam be converted into rotary motion? Watt, resuming Fitzgerald's researches, found not only one but several solutions.[3] The best was adapted from one of the oldest and simplest machines in existence, the knife grinder's treadle wheel.[4] A more complicated one, which for commercial reasons Watt had to adopt, is fairly well described by the expressive phrase 'sun and planet motion'.[5] One more invention must be mentioned, of which

[1] 'I intend in many cases to employ the expansive force of steam to press on the pistons, or whatever may be used instead of them, in the same manner as the pressure of the atmosphere is now employed in common fire engines; in cases when cold water cannot be had in plenty, the engines may be wrought by this force of steam only.'

[2] Patent of March 12th, 1782, No. 1321. See C. Matschoss, op. cit., I, 359-66.

[3] Five were put forward in the patent of Oct. 25th, 1781, No. 1306.

[4] There was the same arrangement in the treadle spinning wheel, known as the saxon wheel. To apply it to the steam engine, as Watt put it in his usual colloquial way, 'was like taking a knife to cut cheese which had been made to cut bread'. S. Smiles, *Boulton and Watt*, p. 287.

[5] A shaft, attached to the beam, had a small cogwheel at the end. This small wheel set in motion a second much larger wheel by coming into gear round its axis. This invention was due to William Murdock, who was foreman in the Soho factory. Papers and designs relating to this invention are to be found in the Soho MSS.,

Watt was very proud. This was known as 'Watt's parallelogram', and became a starting point for many ingenious improvements. For Watt had one of those rare minds which can master the details as well as the whole, and which are never satisfied with the mere enunciation of a principle but follow it out into all its applications: for which, in a word, science is at once the end and the means.

III

It is one thing to make an invention, but as we have already seen it is quite another to turn it into an industrial and commercial success. Special difficulties were connected with the steam engine, as practically a new industry had to be created, together with its personnel and equipment. A body of highly specialized workmen, fit for difficult work which demanded muscular strength, intelligence and great steadiness of hand, were needed to replace the occasional engineers of former times – locksmiths, tinsmiths and millwrights. Cylinders of geometrical accuracy, properly fitted pistons, gears as accurate as those of a watch, had to take the place of the rough and often ill-assembled parts which made up the earlier machines and which were often the cause of their failure. This necessary change was made possible by the progress of the industry. But it could be effected only with the help of men bold enough to risk their capital in a new and uncertain venture, and endowed with the commercial gift which makes for practical success. An invaluable invention such as the steam engine was bound to succeed. No one today could conceive of its being ignored. But, like so many other inventions, it might have succeeded only after the death of the inventor. Watt was lucky enough to meet with two remarkable men able to understand and to help him, and who deserve to share with him, if not in the glory of the actual discovery, at any rate the honour of having brought it from the realm of theory into that of practical use. These two men were John Roebuck of Carron and Matthew Boulton of Soho.

Watt was introduced to Roebuck in 1765 or 1766 by a mutual friend, Professor Black of Glasgow University.[1] At that time he had almost entirely given up his research work, which he could no longer afford to pursue. Penniless and loaded with debt he had been obliged,

[1] S. Smiles, op. cit., p. 139.

---

commercial correspondence, years 1780-2. Watt gave up any idea of using the simple eccentric, because Matthew Washborough, one of his competitors, had patented it in 1779. On the accusation of piracy brought against Washborough by Watt, see J. Muirhead, *Mechanical Inventions of James Watt*, II, 128. Several of Watt's machines built between 1782 and 1800 at Soho, and fitted with sun and planet wheels, are shown at the Science Museum, Kensington. A small model can be actually worked.

in order to make a living, to become a surveyor and engineer, and he was then engaged in drawing up the plans for the Caledonian Canal.[1] It was as an engineer that he first had dealings with Roebuck, as the latter needed pumps for coal mines, the concession of which he had just obtained at Borrowstounness on the right bank of the Forth.[2] The reader is already acquainted with his intelligence and his enterprise. Hearing of Watt's work he at once realized its importance and offered to help him to carry it on. Watt accepted, and an agreement was signed by which Roebuck undertook to pay the debts of his new partner up to £1,000, and to provide sufficient capital for completing the experiments and for turning them to practical account. In exchange he was to receive two-thirds of the profits.[3]

The contract marked a stage in the history of steam. From that day on, through Roebuck's initiative and boldness, it left the laboratory for the world of industry which it was to revolutionize. Watt was constantly doubtful and displeased with himself, and always needed someone by his side to encourage him and urge him on. Roebuck played this part with indefatigable zeal. Towards the end of his life Watt was wont gratefully to acknowledge his debt to him: 'To his friendly encouragement, to his partiality for scientific improvements and to his ready application of them to the processes of art, to his intimate knowledge of business and manufactures, and to his extended views and liberal spirit of enterprise, must in a great measure be ascribed whatever success may have attended my exertions.'[4]

The first steam engine was set up at Kinneil House,[5] near Edinburgh, in 1769. Its construction had been difficult. The Carron ironworks, in spite of their improved equipment, had not been able to carry out correctly all that Watt asked of them; and this engine, the imperfect embodiment of an idea which was not yet fully developed, was known as Beelzebub. With its one cylinder and its beam oscillating in a vertical plane it very much resembled a Newcomen pump, and was used for the same purpose.[6] Its working was so defective that it very soon had to be given up. Roebuck's financial difficulties

[1] See summary of his report in the *Journals of the House of Commons*, LVIII, 1007. He was also given the task of sounding the Clyde and he worked at improving the port of Glasgow. Williamson, *Memorials of Watt*, pp. 172-7.

[2] S. Jardine, 'Account of John Roebuck', *Transactions of the Royal Society of Edinburgh*, IV, 75 (1787).

[3] *Abridgments of Specifications relating to the Steam Engine*, I, 56; J. Lord, *Capital and Steam-Power*, p. 80.

[4] Note by Watt quoted by Robison, *Steam and Steam Engines*, p. 144.

[5] This house, which belonged to Roebuck, was later inhabited by Dugald Stewart the philosopher. S. Smiles, *Industrial Biography*, p. 134.

[6] This machine was destroyed in a fire in 1777.

began about the same time. The mines of which he had so rashly undertaken the working kept being flooded in spite of all pumps, both of the old and of the newer type: they had already cost him and his friends large sums of money. All the ventures he was engaged in at the time felt the effects of this disaster. For some time he struggled against the ruin with which he was threatened; Watt went back to his surveying: his invention, still incomplete and with its faults shown up by actual experience, remained at a standstill. In 1773 Roebuck's bankruptcy put an end to this melancholy state of affairs, and was the origin of the partnership between Watt and Boulton.

Boulton had known Watt for some years. Being a friend of Roebuck he was informed by him of Watt's experiments, in which he took a special interest. He hoped they might result in solving a question with which he was much concerned. His Soho workshops lacked motive power, and he had been thinking of creating it artificially, either with the aid of a Newcomen engine or in some other way. In 1766 he had asked for the advice of two men whose opinion in scientific matters carried weight, Benjamin Franklin and Dr Erasmus Darwin.[1] In 1767 Watt, on his way to Birmingham, visited the Soho workshops and admired the accurate work, the need of which he felt so keenly.[2] The following year Boulton asked Watt to come and see him, and after a long conversation offered to become his partner. Roebuck, when consulted, was in favour of accepting the offer, but on condition that the scope of the agreement should be limited and that Boulton should only be allowed the use of the patent rights in Warwickshire, Staffordshire and Derbyshire. This suggestion shows how far Roebuck was from realizing the full extent of the Soho manufacturer's views and the hopes he based on this new invention: 'The plan proposed to me' – Boulton answered – 'is so different from that which I had conceived that I cannot think it a proper one for me to meddle with ... My idea was to settle a manufactory near to my own, by the side of our canal, where I would erect all the conveniences necessary for the completion of engines, and from which we would serve the world with engines of any size ... It would not be worth my while to make for three counties only, but I find it well worth my while to make for all the world.'[3] Roebuck's failure gave Boulton

---

[1] On this correspondence see S. Smiles, *Boulton and Watt*, pp. 182-5. Erasmus Darwin, physician, naturalist and poet, was the grandfather of Charles Darwin. A letter from Boulton to Franklin, dated Feb. 22nd, 1766, is quoted in Lord's *Capital and Steam-Power*, p. 96.

[2] S. Timmins, *James Watt*, p. 9; S. Smiles, op. cit., p. 187; Lord, op. cit., p. 93.

[3] February 1769. Quoted by S. Timmins, *James Watt*, pp. 11-13. The same letter gives interesting sidelights on Boulton's collaboration with Watt: 'I presumed that your engine would require money, very accurate workmanship, and extensive correspondence, to make it turn out to the best advantage, and that the

the opportunity of reopening the subject. Roebuck owed him £1,200: he offered to forgo that debt in exchange for his debtor's partnership with Watt. It may be said that this was a cheap way of acquiring incalculably valuable rights. But we must remember that their value was still doubtful and that the results of the enterprise, however sanguine Boulton might be about them, were thought to be still remote. 'The thing is now a shadow, it is merely ideal, and it will cost money to realize it.'[1] The arrangement was easily made, the Kinneil engine was taken down and sent to Soho, and Watt himself came and settled there as soon as he had completed his survey for the plans of the Caledonian Canal in May 1774.[2]

IV

The Soho factory, situated north of Birmingham on a height now covered with factories, and black with coal and smoke, had been founded in 1759.[3] At that time Matthew Boulton was already a rich and important man. His father, a Birmingham toymaker,[4] had put him into business early, but not before he had received a fairly good education which he completed for himself later on. The workshops of Boulton & Son manufactured metal buttons, watch-chains and shoe-buckles of engraved steel. These last were the object of a curious form of trade, due to the prevailing fashion: they were sent to France, to be reimported as French articles.[5] Boulton had married an heiress, the daughter of an 'esquire',[6] and after his marriage he could easily have

[1] Letter from Boulton to Watt, March 29th, 1773. S. Smiles, *Boulton and Watt*, p. 197. It must also be remembered that among Roebuck's other creditors 'none value the engine at a farthing' (Letter from Watt to Small, July 25th, 1773, quoted by J. Lord, *Capital and Steam-Power*, p. 86).

[2] Ibid.

[3] When Boulton leased it, it was 'a barren heath, ȯn the bleak summit of which stood a naked hut, the habitation of a warrener'. *Memoir of Matthew Boulton, Esq., late of Soho*, p. 5.

[4] Ibid., Clarke MSS. (Birmingham Central Library), V, 65.

[5] Ibid.

[6] S. Smiles, op. cit., p. 166. The word 'esquire' in the middle of the eighteenth century still had some significance. It was only given to men who were members of the lesser gentry or who came of well-established middle-class families.

best means of doing the invention justice would be to keep the executive part out of the hands of the multitude of empirical engineers, who, from ignorance, want of experience, and want of necessary convenience, would be very liable to produce bad and inaccurate workmanship ... We could engage and instruct some excellent workmen who (with more excellent tools than would be worth any man's while to procure for a single engine) could execute the invention 20 per cent cheaper than elsewhere, and with as great a difference in accuracy as there is between the blacksmith and the mathematical instrument maker.'

settled down as a country gentleman. But he loved industry, to which he had been brought up, and he devoted his fortune to creating model works. The building of his great factory which, though begun in 1759 was not finished till 1765, cost him £9,000.[1] It comprised five buildings and could hold six hundred workmen, while a reservoir on the top of the hill provided the water for working a large wheel which 'communicated motion to an immense number of different tools'.[2] We know that mechanical equipment was already much advanced in the metal trades, although its importance was not so vital as it became later. Boulton was determined to have the most up-to-date machines and he took pains to adapt them to the special needs of his industry.[3] As early as 1763 the figures of his sales reached £30,000 in one year.[4]

The products of the Soho manufacture were of many kinds. To the usual articles of the Birmingham toy trade Boulton added others, such as ornamental bronzes, vases, chandeliers, tripods, silver and plated wares, and imitation gold and tortoiseshell work.[5] About 1768 he even thought of making china, and Wedgwood, the great Staffordshire potter, prepared to compete with the man he called 'the first manufacturer in England'.[6] Boulton deserved this title as much for the quality of his goods as for the size of his business. He had set himself the task of wiping out Birmingham's bad reputation, and he spared no efforts in its accomplishment. He would only use the best materials and the most skilled workmen, and he personally supervised the work in the shops with utmost care.

On the commercial side he was seconded by Fothergill, who had been his partner since 1762. Fothergill was in touch with foreign markets, knew the tastes of clients in various countries, and when necessary travelled about in search of new patterns and fresh orders.[7] Thanks to his activity their markets grew steadily wider and the firm acquired a

---

[1] *Memoir of Matthew Boulton, Esq., late of Soho*, p. 6; J. A. Langford, *A Century of Birmingham Life*, II, 147.

[2] Erasmus Darwin, *The Botanic Garden* (1768), p. 287.

[3] Ibid., 'The mechanical inventions for this purpose are superior in multitude, variety and simplicity to those of any manufactory in the whole world.'

[4] *Memoir of Matthew Boulton*, p. 5.

[5] Invoices preserved at the Birmingham Central Library (Timmins MSS.); *Journals of the House of Commons*, XXXIV, 191-3.

[6] Letter from J. Wedgwood to R. Bentley, Nov. 27th, 1768: 'If Etruria cannot stand its ground, but must give way to Soho, and fall before her, let us not sell the victory too cheap, but maintain our ground like men, and endeavour, even in defeat, to share the laurels with our conqueror. It doubles my courage to have the first manufacturer in England to encounter with. The match likes me well. I like the man, I like his spirit.' Correspondence, Wedgwood Museum, Stoke-on-Trent. As a matter of fact, Boulton did not follow up his idea and contented himself with making gilt bronze decorations for Wedgwood's vases.

[7] S. Smiles, *Boulton and Watt*, p. 172.

European reputation. In 1765 Boulton received tempting offers to move to Sweden.[1] But he had no wish to leave England. He already held an important position in the country, while the artistic element, which was then as important a feature of his production as the scientific element was to be later, won for him valuable sympathies. He was patronized by the aristocracy. Horace Walpole, Lord Shelburne, Lord Dartmouth and the Duke of Northumberland lent him antique bronzes to copy, while Lord Cathcart recommended him to the Empress of Russia.[2] Encouraged as he was by well-deserved success, we can understand that with his bold enterprising nature he should have conceived ambitious schemes: 'I am fond' — he wrote — 'of all those things that have a tendency to improve my knowledge in mechanical arts, in which my manufactory will every year become more and more general, and therefore wish to know the tastes, the fashions ... that prevail in all the different parts of Europe, as I should be glad to work for all Europe in all things that they may have occasion for: gold, silver, copper, plated, gilt, pinchbeck, steel, platina, tortoise-shell, or anything else that may become an article of general demand.'[3] Thus the reader can realize what the Soho business was like when, after Roebuck's bankruptcy, Watt came into it. Never had the two systems of 'manufacture' and factory so nearly approximated, and never had the transition from the one to the other been more imperceptible and the distinction between the two (which remains sound enough when only a general classification is required) harder to make without becoming involved in subtleties and arbitrary distinctions. Boulton was able to provide Watt with the resources, and very nearly with the power of the modern factory system.

Watt at once set to work. By November 1774 the engine from Kinneil House, overhauled and put right by the skilled workers trained by Boulton, was at last able to work tolerably well. Watt wrote about it to his father: 'The business I am here about has turned out rather successful, that is to say, the fire engine I have invented is now going and answers much better than any other that has yet been made, and I expect that the invention will be very beneficial to me.'[4] But before final success could be achieved he and his partner had to be prepared for prolonged efforts and considerable expenses. It was five years since Watt had taken out his patent, which was to expire in 1783, and meanwhile he had to fear the competition of similar inventions, or of more or less dissembling imitations. He decided to apply to Parliament for an extension of his patent rights, and on February

[1] *Calendar of Home Office Papers*, 1760-5, Nos. 1818, 1821, 1919.
[2] S. Smiles, op. cit., pp. 172-4.
[3] Letter to Wendler, ibid.
[4] J. Muirhead, *Mechanical Inventions of James Watt*, II, 79.

23rd, 1775, he sent to the House of Commons a petition[1] which, thanks to his scientific friends and also thanks, no doubt, to Boulton's aristocratic connections, was most carefully considered. The Committee in charge of the bill heard the evidence of Roebuck, who did full justice to the invention, the practical value of which he had been the first to recognize: 'It will at least do double the work of a common fire engine at the same expense … and it may be applied with advantage wherever any kind of mechanical power is wanted.'[2] At the same time he bore witness to the sacrifices which it had already called for and would still demand before any profit could be made out of it. First he and then Boulton had already spent in experiments, constructions and trials over £3,000, whilst the total expense in view amounted to at least another £10,000. But what was such a sum when set against the profits to be derived from the invention by England and the whole world? The patent was extended for a period of twenty-five years;[3] though not without some opposition, for, just as the vote was about to be taken, Burke rose and protested in the name of liberty against the institution of this new monopoly.[4]

But for several years more this monopoly was far from being profit-

---

[1] *Journals of the House of Commons*, XXXV, 142.

[2] Ibid., 168. Boulton gave evidence more or less on the same lines: 'It is not only the cheapest mechanical power yet invented except wind and water mills, but it may be applied to an infinite number of purposes to which the common fire engine is not at all applicable.'

[3] 15 Geo. III, c. 61. The preamble runs as follows: 'Whereas his Most Excellent Majesty King George III, by his letters patent under the great seal of Great Britain, bearing date the 5th of January, in the ninth year of his reign, did give and grant unto James Watt, of the City of Glasgow, merchant, his executors, administrators, and assigns, the sole benefit and advantage of making and vending certain engines by him invented, for lessening the consumption of steam and fuel in the fire engines … Whereas the said James Watt has employed many years, and a considerable part of his fortune, in making experiments upon steam, and steam engines, commonly called fire engines, with a view to improve those very useful machines, by which several very considerable advantages over the common steam engines are acquired; but upon account of the many difficulties which always arise in the execution of such large and complex machines, and of the long time requisite to make the necessary trials, he could not complete his invention before the end of the year 1774 … And whereas, in order to manufacture these engines with the necessary accuracy, and so that they may be sold at moderate prices, a considerable sum of money must be previously expended in erecting mills and other apparatus; and as several years and repeated proofs will be required before any considerable part of the public can be fully convinced of the utility of the invention and of their interest to adopt the same, the whole term granted by the said letters patent may probably elapse before the said James Watt can receive an advantage adequate to his labour and invention … '

[4] It was only after the renewal of Watt's patent rights had been granted that his association with Boulton took its final shape. See the terms of their agreement, signed for twenty-five years from June 1st, 1775, in Muirhead's *Mechanical Inventions of James Watt*, II, 98.

able. The expenses very much exceeded Roebuck's estimate.[1] It was the other industries, which Boulton never gave up when he went into partnership with Watt, which enabled the expensive manufacture of steam engines to go on, while some little help was derived from a time-saving invention of Watt's, that of the copying press.[2] The firm went through difficult, and even critical times. In 1778 and 1780 Boulton had to bring in some sleeping partners, after having sold some of the property that had come to him from his father and his wife. At the end of the financial year 1781 Boulton and Watt had not enough to pay their Christmas balances nor their workmen's wages, but received money from Boulton and Fothergill for those purposes.[3] In 1782 Watt was so worried by the ever-increasing weight of debt contracted with the bankers Lowe, Vere and Williams that he wrote to his partner: 'I am almost moved, if they will free me from any demands on my future industry, to give up my present property altogether and trust to Providence for my support. I cannot live as I am with any degree of comfort.'[4] It was not before 1786 or 1787 that the firm, having paid off their debt, could at last begin to reap the profits of their costly venture.

Yet orders were not too slow in coming in. In 1775 a pumping engine from the Soho works was set up at the Bloomfield collieries near Birmingham, which pumped out the water three times as fast as a Newcomen engine and at the same cost.[5] Shortly after, Wilkinson ordered an engine to blow his blast furnaces at Broseley: this was the first application of Watt's invention to purposes other than pumping.[6] Another early order came from the New River Company.[7] In 1777 Watt went to Cornwall where, in spite of some hesitation on the part of the mine owners and some disappointments due to the difficulty of setting up the engine on the spot, he did succeed in erecting a number of large steam pumps. The engine supplied to the Chacewater mines in 1778, owing to its power and easy working, did much towards overcoming local prejudice.[8] The same year the Soho factory was visited

[1] According to a note in the Timmins MSS. the construction, equipment, etc., cost about £47,000. We have not been able to check the accuracy of this figure by the Soho MSS. as these latter do not begin before 1780 as regards correspondence, and 1795 as regards books.

[2] Soho MSS., Commercial Correspondence, 1780-5; J. Lord, *Capital and Steam-Power*, p. 132.

[3] M. Boulton to G. Matthews, June 19th, 1782, quoted by J. Lord, op. cit., p. 130, from the Tew MSS.

[4] S. Smiles, *Boulton and Watt*, pp. 262-3, 314; J. Lord, op. cit., p. 114.

[5] *Birmingham Gazette*, March 11th, 1776.

[6] Ludwig Beck, *Die Geschichte des Eisens*, III, 1079, and T. S. Ashton, *Iron and Steel in the Industrial Revolution*, p. 70.

[7] C. Matschoss, *Die Entwicklung der Dampfmaschine*, I, 126-7.

[8] S. Smiles, op. cit., pp. 242-8. See the description of another machine set up at Gwenham near Truro. 'The fire engine which works the pump is extremely large and

by the brothers Périer, who asked Watt to provide them with an engine for the Paris water supply. In 1779 it was set up on the bank of the Seine at the end of the Cours-la-Reine, and was known for many years as 'the Chaillot fire-pump'. In the following century that engine was replaced by more modern machinery, which went on working on the same spot until quite recently.[1] Some German engineers sent by Frederick the Great also came to see the Soho works, although steam engines were only introduced into Germany a few years later, in 1785.[2]

Boulton and Watt's terms were very reasonable. They asked the purchasers to pay only the cost of building and setting up each engine, together with a third of the economy in fuel obtained by its use, in comparison with the consumption of coal made by a Newcomen engine of the same power.[3] Thus they relied for their profit on the tried superiority of the steam engine and the advantages derived from its use. But after the dislike of using the new engine had been overcome a no less marked dislike to pay for its advantages immediately became apparent. The owners of the Cornish mines were particularly notorious for their recalcitrance and their bad faith when it came to paying the stipulated royalty. For years there was perpetual conflict between

[1] The drawings of the engines for the Périer brothers are preserved in the Soho MSS. The agreement between them and Boulton and Watt is dated Feb. 12th, 1779. The engine was to pump 57,000 hogsheads of water in 24 hours. Between 1779 and 1793 the inventor's royalties amounted to £48,000. *Examen et débat des comptes tant de l'ancienne que de la nouvelle administration des eaux de Paris, à partir de l'origine de cette entreprise, en 1778, jusqu'au 10 Août 1793, par le citoyen G. D. David, liquidateur, ci-devant homme de loi*, p. 22, Arch. Nat. O^{1}1596^2. The Périers claimed that they had set up their engines themselves: 'Messrs Périer have never claimed the invention, but the execution is another matter. No Englishman ever had a hand in the setting up of the Chaillot machines, they are the sole work of Messrs Périer ... Moreover Messrs Périer are the men who have built every engine of that kind in France.' *Second plaidoyer des sieurs Périer frères contre les administrateurs des eaux*, p. 8, Arch. Nat., A.A. 11. It is possible that Watt did only provide the drawings. But the Périers admit that they began by having the larger metal parts sent from English foundries, 'the only ones of their kind in Europe'. Ibid., p. 8. The relations between Boulton and Watt and the Périers are described by Lord, op. cit., pp. 210 ff.

[2] Ludwig Beck, *Die Geschichte des Eisens*, III, 541.

[3] Boulton and Watt, *Proposals to the Adventurers*, p. 1 (Prospectus dated 1800, Birmingham Central Library, No. 69,672.)

indescribably powerful. The main pipe is 65 inches in circumference. It is a double action pump, and usually gives eight strokes a minute and can give twelve, although the water is 120 fathoms deep, that is 720 feet. Each stroke sucks up 100 gallons of water, or 400 pints, of which part goes into the big tank which supplies the steam, and the rest becomes a stream which disappears at the foot of the hills.' *Tournée faite en 1788 dans la Grande Bretagne par un Français parlant la langue anglaise*, p. 53. By 1783 Watt's engine had replaced Newcomen's in practically all the Cornish mines. See Matschoss, op. cit., I, 126, and *Victoria History of the County of Cornwall*, p. 550. The list of the engines used in Cornwall in 1782 is given by Lord, op. cit., pp. 155 ff.

them and the Soho manufacturers.[1] In 1780 a movement was started in the county to petition Parliament to cancel the patent. Watt complained bitterly about it: 'They charge us with establishing a monopoly, but if a monopoly, it is one by means of which their mines are made more productive than ever they were before ... They say it is inconvenient for the mining interest to be burdened with the payment of engine dues, just as it is inconvenient for the person who wishes to get at my purse that I should keep my breeches-pocket buttoned ... We have no power to compel anybody to erect our engines. What, then, will Parliament say to any man who comes there to complain of a grievance he can avoid?'[2] The step was never taken but interminable lawsuits began, and in 1799 Boulton and Watt, having at last won their case, received a lump sum of over £30,000 in unpaid dues.[3]

On the other hand they had to protect themselves against competitors of varying degrees of scrupulousness. The most formidable was Jonathan Hornblower, who was by no means a mere counterfeiter. He was ahead of Watt in his study and use of high pressure. His engine, more complicated than Watt's, had two cylinders which filled with steam alternately.[4] He was successful enough to give Boulton and Watt a good deal of anxiety. They decided to sue Hornblower, who lost his case and was ruined.[5]

Other difficulties, and not the least, were those of organization. They were overcome chiefly owing to Boulton's gift of leadership. Much diplomacy was also needed, for Boulton and Watt's methods implied close co-operation with other firms. No steam engine was sold ready-made from their works. They acted chiefly 'as designers and erectors of engines, and as consultants to the firms making use of their invention. The individual business which required an engine was usually free to make its own arrangements with founders and smiths for the supply of materials, and the Soho firm provided the skilled labour as well as those parts of the mechanism which required special

---

[1] The various incidents of those litigations may be followed in the voluminous correspondence of Boulton and Watt with their Cornish agents Murdock, and later Wilson (Soho MSS.). Watt himself spent some time in Cornwall in order to look after the interests of the firm.

[2] Letter of Watt to Boulton, Oct. 31st, 1780. S. Smiles, op. cit., pp. 279 ff.

[3] Ibid., p. 420.

[4] Patent dated July 13th, 1781, No. 1298. According to Hornblower himself, the invention dated from 1776. See his petition to the House of Commons, *Journals of the House of Commons*, XLVII, 417 and 478. A good description of this machine can be found in R. Thurston, *A History of the Growth of the Steam-Engine*, pp. 135 ff.

[5] Wrongly, according to the engineer J. Bramah, who wrote in Hornblower's defence, *A Letter to the Right Hon. Sir James Eyre, Lord Chief Justice of the Common Pleas, on the subject of the cause Boulton & Watt v. Hornblower & Maberly* (1797).

care in manufacture.'[1] Most of the cylinders were supplied by Wilkinson, whose accuracy in boring was unequalled and who for that reason was always strongly recommended by Boulton and Watt.[2]

They were admirably seconded by the foremen they had trained. At least one of these men, William Murdock, had greater capacity than his position warranted. The son of a Scotch millwright, he had asked as a favour to be allowed to become a workman in the Soho works.[3] Being intelligent, industrious and inventive he was soon noticed by his employers, who sent him to supervise the setting up of their engines, particularly in Cornwall. He displayed incredible energy and worked day and night at setting up, inspecting and repairing the engines, while he watched over the interests of his employers with tireless vigilance and guarded them against the coalition of hostile interests.[4] In his spare time he looked for and discovered technical improvements: it was he who suggested to Watt the idea of 'sun and planet' motion. He was almost the first man in Europe, and certainly the first in England, to use steam as a means of traction, and in 1784 he built a little model locomotive that did eight miles an hour.[5] He also shared with the Frenchman Lebon the honour of discovering and using coal gas. The Soho factory was lighted by gas as early as 1798. Murdock, who might have made a fortune by his inventions, preferred to spend his whole life with Boulton and Watt who trusted him completely and to whom he was entirely devoted.[6] His help was most valuable in those difficult times when the future of the steam engine, which was to justify the most sanguine hopes, was as yet but dimly perceptible.

V

Boulton had never had any doubts as to the success of the undertaking, and in this respect he was very different from Watt, who was

[1] T. S. Ashton, *Iron and Steel in the Industrial Revolution*, p. 64.

[2] In a letter to a customer dated July 27th, 1795, the younger Watt wrote about Wilkinson: 'In the course of twenty years we have not erected more than three or four engines the cylinders of which were not of his manufacture.' Ibid.

[3] S. Timmins, *William Murdock*, p. 2. He entered the Soho works in 1774, about the same time as Watt himself.

[4] Soho MSS., Commercial Correspondence, years 1780 ff.

[5] S. Timmins, *William Murdock*, pp. 7 ff. R. Thurston, *A History of the Growth of the Steam-Engine*, p. 153. This invention is mentioned in one of Watt's patents (No. 1432, April 18th, 1784). Cugnot's steam carriage, preserved at the Conservatoire des Arts et Métiers in Paris, was built as early as 1769.

[6] His wages were more those of a foreman than of an engineer. Until 1780 he only earned 20s. a week. In 1793 he was sent to set up an engine at Cadix under the following conditions: his travelling expenses were paid, he was to receive a fee of £50 and a wage of a guinea a week. Agreement signed April 20th, 1793, Timmins MSS.

always despondent and pessimistic.[1] In 1781 he at last perceived the first signs of the development he had expected for ten years: Watt's invention was attracting attention and arousing general curiosity. 'The people in London, Manchester and Birmingham are steam-mill mad.'[2]

The same year Watt took out his second patent, that for the rotary motion. Until then the steam engine had been no more than an improved 'fire engine', and it was in that capacity that it had been used in mines and for the supply of water. The invention of the rotary motion converted it into a source of motive power, the uses of which could be indefinitely varied. From that moment the whole field of industry was thrown open to it. It was first used in its new capacity at Soho, where bellows, rolling mills and hammers were all worked by steam. Almost at once Wilkinson ordered similar engines for his Bradley works, and so did Reynolds and the Coalbrookdale Company. Their example was followed by all the great ironmasters in England and Scotland.[3] Then did the metal works, already equipped with all kinds of machines, take on their characteristic aspect, and the irresistible alliance of steam and iron was finally sealed.

The steam engine was early used in flour mills, in malt mills for breweries,[4] in flint mills for the earthenware and china industry,[5] and in mills for crushing sugar-cane for the West Indian refineries.[6] Among many instances we should mention the Albion flour mills. These mills were built in London in 1786 and their equipment was arranged by Watt himself with the help of John Rennie, who later was to design Waterloo Bridge. It consisted of fifty pairs of millstones set in motion by two engines.[7] The output was expected to reach sixteen thousand bushels of flour a week. The opening of this mill created a great sensation in London and it became the fashion to go and see it, which

[1] 'Through the whole of this business Mr Boulton's active and sanguine disposition served to counterbalance the despondency and diffidence which were natural to me.' Watt's notes on Boulton, in S. Smiles, *Boulton and Watt*, p. 485.

[2] Boulton to Watt, June 21st, 1781. Ibid., p. 293.

[3] Ibid., pp. 301 and 317. The Soho MSS. contain many letters between Boulton and Watt and the ironmasters Wilkinson, Reynolds, Walker, Homfray, etc. On the first uses of the steam engine in the iron industry, see T. S. Ashton, op. cit., pp. 72 ff.

[4] The engine sold to Whitbread & Co. (1785) went on working till 1887. Timmins MSS.

[5] An engine was sold to Wedgwood as early as 1782. See J. Lord, *Capital and Steam-Power*, p. 179, n. 1.

[6] Letter from James Watt to Fermin de Tastet, Sept. 3rd, 1794, Timmins MSS.

[7] Note by J. Watt, in Robison's *Steam and Steam Engines*, p. 137. According to Robison, each engine was of 50 h.p. But this is not confirmed by the figures collected by J. Lord, according to which the total power of the six engines supplied to corn mills between 1785 and 1795 amounted only to 68 h.p. Lord, *Capital and Steam-Power*, p. 175.

annoyed Watt very much.[1] The millers were much alarmed by this unexpected competition, but in 1791 a fire broke out which perhaps was not a mere accident, and the whole place was burnt to the ground together with all it contained. The losses were valued at £10,000.[2]

In the textile industry the steam engine was at first only an accessory to the hydraulic machine. About 1780 Richard Arkwright used a Newcomen pump in his Manchester factory.[3] In 1782 a spinning firm established at Burton-on-Trent asked Watt to provide them with an engine. He received their order with marked coldness: 'From their letter and the man they have sent here' — he wrote to Boulton — 'I have no great opinion of their abilities ... If you come home by way of Manchester,[4] please not to seek for orders for cotton-mill engines, because I hear that there are so many mills erecting on powerful streams in the North of England, that the trade must soon be overdone, and consequently our labour may be lost.'[5] He had no idea that the industrial expansion he was witnessing could develop beyond a certain limit, which he thought had almost been reached, and he did not realize that he had done more than anyone else to remove any such limitations. In any case he very soon changed his mind. By 1784 he agreed that the rotative engines 'are certainly very applicable to the driving of cotton mills, in every case where the conveniency of placing the mill in a town, or ready-built manufactory, will compensate for the expense of coals and of our premium'.[6] Experience was not long in confirming the opinion so tentatively expressed.

The first steam spinning mill was set up for Robinson at Papplewick in 1785.[7] Then the Warrington and Nottingham manufacturers ordered machinery from Soho. Their example was followed in 1787 by Robert Peel, in 1789 by Peter Drinkwater of Manchester, in 1790 by Richard

[1] 'What have Dukes, Lords, and Ladies to do with masquerading in a flour-mill?' Letter to Boulton, April 17th, 1786, S. Smiles, op. cit., p. 357.

[2] Ibid., pp. 358-9.

[3] E. Baines, *History of the Cotton Manufacture*, p. 226. For some time Watt's machine was used in the same way. See the evidence of a French traveller in 1784: 'In most of these mills, the water is pumped up by fire pumps improved by Mr Woite [*sic*], which consume 2/3 less coal than the others.' Marquis de Biencourt, 'Mémoire sur ... l'Angleterre', Affaires Etrangères, Mémoires et Documents, LXXIV, fol. 28.

[4] Boulton was then in Ireland.

[5] Letter from Watt to Boulton, December 1782. S. Smiles, op. cit., pp. 326-7.

[6] Letter from Watt to MacGregor of Glasgow, Oct. 30th, 1784. Williamson, *Memorials of Watt*, p. 181. Eight to ten horse-power were needed for every thousand spindles.

[7] In Nottinghamshire, A. Ure, *The Cotton Manufacture of Great Britain*, I, 274. The *Victoria History of the County of Lancaster* (II, 386) mentions the existence of a cotton mill worked by steam as early as 1777, but the fact would be very surprising, as Watt's patent for the rotative engine was taken out only in 1781.

Arkwright and by Samuel Oldknow.[1] In Yorkshire, and generally in those districts where the woollen industry predominated, development was slower and met with much more opposition. Not only the workmen but many of the employers openly showed their hostility. John Buckley of Bradford, who in 1793 wanted to introduce a steam engine into his spinning mill, met with a kind of ultimatum from his neighbours, threatening if he carried out his intentions to sue him for damages in respect of the noise and smoke caused by the engine.[2] Nevertheless, from 1794 onwards the steam engine gradually won its way into the woollen spinning mills, closely following on the adoption of machinery.

Thus by the end of the eighteenth century Watt's steam engine was everywhere beginning to supersede hydraulic power. In 1802 Svedenstjerna expressed his surprise at meeting so many of these engines during his journey through the industrial districts of England: 'It is no exaggeration to say that this sort of engine is as commonly used, or more, than water-mills and wind-mills in our country.'[3] Several were frequently built close together in a small area, and used for the most diverse purposes. For instance, at Swansea 'some are used for pumping water out of the mines, others for hauling up the coal, and others still for moving, grinding and rolling mills'. In 1800 there were eleven steam engines[4] in Birmingham, twenty in Leeds and thirty-two in Manchester.[5]

It should be remembered that in this great technical revolution Watt and Boulton did not work alone. Murdock, their faithful helper; Hornblower, their unsuccessful competitor; John Wilkinson, who was the first to realize and to obtain the accuracy needed in the making of modern machinery; Cartwright, who, after inventing the weaving and the combing machines, had turned his ingenious mind to other prob-

---

[1] E. Baines, loc. cit. Arkwright had corresponded with Boulton and Watt since 1785 (Letter from Arkwright to Watt, Jan. 30th, 1785, Soho MSS., Commercial Correspondence). The engine supplied to Samuel Oldknow was for his spinning mill at Stockport. See Unwin, *Samuel Oldknow and the Arkwrights*, p. 123.

[2] J. James, *History of Bradford*, p. 282: 'Take notice that if either you or any person in connexion with you shall presume to erect and build any steam engine for the manufacture of cotton or wool in a certain field in Horton near Bradford, called or known by the name of the Brick Kiln Field, we whose names are hereunto subscribed shall, if the same be found a nuisance, seek such redress as the law will give.' (Jan. 23rd, 1793.)

[3] Erik Svedenstjerna, *Reise durch einen Theil von England und Schottland in den Jahren 1802 und 1803*, p. 44. According to J. Lord (op. cit., p. 176) the total number of engines constructed by Boulton and Watt for England, Scotland, Wales and Ireland between 1775 and 1800 amounted to 321.

[4] Clarke MSS., III, 150.

[5] P. Gaskell, *Artisans and Machinery*, p. 35. E. Baines's *History of the Cotton Manufacture*, pp. 226 ff.

lems;[1] Adam Heslop, who tried to improve and to revive the atmospheric engine;[2] all these, together with a host of others many of whom were quite unknown, either assisted or rivalled them. But the Soho firm, protected by the Act of 1775, remained the sole centre from which steam engines were ordered for the whole country. In its workshops, containing over a thousand workmen,[3] the new industry grew up in the midst of Birmingham's traditional trades, which after assisting it were in their turn transformed by its powerful influence: 'Every branch of the metallic trade' — a visitor wrote — 'is carried on there ... Almost every part of the work is performed by the assistance of machinery. Those operations where force is required, such as the rolling out of plates by means of cylinders, the cleansing and polishing of the metal, etc., are effected by the help of large wheels, which are kept in motion by a steam engine.'[4]

Among some of the most interesting uses of steam in the Soho works we must mention the automatic coining of money. This idea was Boulton's, and was one of which he was especially proud. His hatred of the forgers who had injured Birmingham's good name had filled him with the desire to produce a perfect currency, proof against the counterfeiting which the old-fashioned methods made so easy. He built a steam coining press in which the coins, held in place by a steel clamp, were stamped with absolute accuracy. Each press, tended by one man, could stamp from fifty to a hundred and twenty coins a minute.[5] This invention met with great success. Boulton received orders from the East India Company; from France, during the first years of the Revolution;[6] from Russia, where in 1799 he was allowed to set up a Mint;[7] and finally from the British Government whom in ten years, between 1797 and 1806, he supplied with over four thousand tons of copper coin.[8] The advantages were not only rapid output and the almost complete absence of manual labour, but also

[1] Patents dated Nov. 11th, 1797 (No. 2202), and Feb. 5th, 1801 (No. 2471).

[2] Patent dated July 7th, 1790 (No. 1760). A Heslop machine was at work at Whitehaven until 1878. It is now in the Science Museum, Kensington.

[3] J. G. A. Forster, *Voyage philosophique et pittoresque en Angleterre et en France*, p. 88. Faujas de Saint-Fond, *Voyage en Angleterre, en Ecosse et aux Iles Hébrides*, II, 387.

[4] Duke of Rutland, *Journals of a Tour to the Northern Parts of Great Britain*, quoted in the *Local Notes and Queries*, in the Birmingham Central Library, years 1889-93, No. 2438.

[5] Patent dated July 8th, 1790 (No. 1757). Announcement of the 'coining mill' in the *Moniteur Universel*, Supplement to the No. of Jan. 27th, 1791.

[6] It was at the Soho workshops that the so-called 'Monnerons' coins were made. They were issued by the Monnerons, the Paris bankers, by permission of the French Government. See E. Dewamin, *Cent ans de Numismatique Française*, Plates 7, 10 and 11.

[7] 39 Geo. III, c. 96.

[8] S. Smiles, *Boulton and Watt*, pp. 398-9. Machines supplied by Boulton were working at the London Mint until 1882. *Dictionary of National Biography*, article 'Boulton'.

accuracy and regularity in finish. This was an instance of what could be done in all industries by the use of machinery, now set in motion by a powerful and obedient force, which man could produce, increase, move about and regulate at will.

VI

With this great new event, the invention of the steam engine, the final and most decisive stage of the industrial revolution opened. By liberating it from its last shackles, steam enabled the immense and rapid development of large-scale industry to take place. For the use of steam was not, like that of water, dependent on geographical position and local resources. Wherever coal could be bought at a reasonable price a steam engine could be erected. England had plenty of coal, and by the end of the eighteenth century it was already applied to many different uses, while a network of waterways, made on purpose, enabled it to be carried everywhere very cheaply: the whole country became a privileged land suitable above all others for the growth of industry. Factories were now no longer bound to the valleys, where they had grown up in solitude by the side of rapid-flowing streams. It became possible to bring them nearer the markets where their raw materials were bought and their finished products sold, and nearer the centres of population where their labour was recruited. They sprang up near one another, and thus huddled together gave rise to those huge black industrial cities which the steam engine surrounded with a perpetual cloud of smoke.

As a matter of fact this concentration was merely the development of a movement which had already begun. It did not alter the geographical distribution of industries, which had been determined between 1760 and 1790 by machine industry in its first stage of development, that of water-power: a most remarkable fact, that throws light on the origins of large-scale industry in England. The movement of the chief centres of economic activity towards the northern counties and the formation of the new textile and metal-working districts both took place before steam was first used in industry. The appearance of the steam engine did no more than hasten this development by strengthening the influences which had caused it. It might be objected that this continuity was only accidental, that it merely happened that coal was found to be plentiful in those districts where for quite other reasons the new industries had been established, and those industries were therefore able to stay there even after the proximity of mines had become of greater value than that of running water. But was that a pure coincidence? Even before Watt's invention, coal had played a sufficiently important part in industrial life for manufacturers to prefer building their factories where there was plenty of cheap coal. To believe that coal, like a hidden treasure, was suddenly discovered precisely in the districts where factories had just been erected would be entirely to disregard its comparatively long history previous to that period.

Steam did not create the modern factory system, but it lent that system its power and gave it a force of expansion as irresistible as itself. Above all, it gave it unity. Up till that time the various industries were much less interdependent than they are now. From the technical point of view they had little in common, and they developed separately along their own lines. The use of a common motive power, and especially of an artificial one, thenceforward imposed general laws upon the development of all industries. The successive improvements in the steam engine reacted equally on the working of mines and of metals, on weaving and on transport. The industrial world came to resemble one huge factory, in which the acceleration, the slowing down and the stoppage of the main engine determines the activities of the workers and regulates the rates of production.

James Watt's contemporaries did not live to see all the consequences of the great event which they had witnessed. But they could already have a glimpse of them. They felt that they were on the threshold of a new era, full of possibilities, which could be measured by no comparisons with past developments. Eden wrote in 1797: 'With regard to mechanical knowledge, it is probable that we are still in our infancy, and when it is considered that, fifty years ago, many inventions for abridging the operations of industry, which are now in common use, were utterly unknown, it is not absurd to conjecture that, fifty years hence, some new contrivance may be thought of in comparison with which the steam engine and spinning jennies, however wonderful they appear to us at present, will be considered as slight and insignificant discoveries.'[1]

[1] F. M. Eden, *State of the Poor*, I, 44.

PART III

The Immediate Consequences

CHAPTER ONE

THE FACTORY SYSTEM AND POPULATION

Iᶠ the industrial revolution had meant no more than a series of technical improvements, and if its consequences had not gone beyond changes in machinery and production, it would only have been an event of secondary importance and would not occupy much space in general history. But through the medium of material things, which are the visible expression of the needs, designs and activities of men, it reacted on man himself. It set its stamp, first in England and then in all civilized countries, on the whole of modern society. To admit this is not necessarily to accept without reserve the materialistic interpretation of history. Whether we look at society from the outside and as a whole, as composed of a population whose growth and distribution follow definite laws, or whether we study its internal structure, with the formation, functions and relationships of its various classes, on all sides we find traces of this great movement which in changing the system of production changed at the same time all the conditions of life for the whole of society.

I

The rapid and continuous growth of population is not a phenomenon peculiar to our industrial civilization. It can and does occur in quite other surroundings, as for instance in China, where the system of small holdings and intensive agriculture supports the densest population in the world. We may add that the extraordinary increase of population in Western countries which has taken place in the last hundred years cannot be attributed to one cause alone. It is encouraged by everything which tends to add to general prosperity and individual security. But what must be pointed out is that no such increase was noticeable before the era of the modern factory system. Nowadays a stationary or slowly increasing population causes surprise and anxiety. A hundred and fifty or two hundred years ago the opposite fact would have caused astonishment. In his *Observations on the State of England*, written in 1696, Gregory King thus predicted how the population of England would increase during the coming centuries: 'In all probability the next doubling of the people in England will be in about six hundred years to come, or by the year of our Lord 2300, at which time it will have eleven millions of people ... The next doubling after that will not be, in all probability, in less than twelve or thirteen hundred years, or by the year of our Lord 3500 or 3600. At which time the Kingdom will have 22 millions of souls … in case the world should last so long.'[1]

Gregory King was an optimist. During the whole of the eighteenth century the accepted theory was that the population of England was decreasing,[2] and people talked as though it was a fact which had actually been proved, while statesmen like Lord Shelburne and Lord Chatham publicly expressed the fears they felt on this score.[3] This supposed evil was ascribed to most various causes: to the excessive increase of armed forces, to the wars, to emigration, to over-taxation, to the rising price of foodstuffs, to the engrossing of farms.[4] But as the increasing wealth of the country became more apparent an opposite theory was put forward, which argued, *a priori*, that an increase of population must go hand in hand with economic progress. Some curious discussions took place on the subject between 1770 and 1780, at the very time when the new factory system was beginning to display its wonderful creative activity.[5]

These discussions were only possible because of the lack of any reliable statistics. The first official census of population in England was taken in 1801.[6] Before then people had to rest content with more or less plausible estimates. These were based either on taxation returns, which contained the enumeration of hearths or houses, or on parish

[1] Gregory King, *Natural and Political Observations and Conclusions upon the State and Condition of England*, p. 41. In 1921 the population of England and Wales was 32,526,075 souls.

[2] 'It has of late years been a common idea that the population of England is declining very fast, and that this declension has been so considerable as to lessen our numbers above a million and a half since the Revolution … an opinion not only found in political pamphlets, but which often occurs in Parliament.' *Observations on the present State of the Waste Lands* (1773), p. 5.

[3] See their speeches on the losses during the American war, *Parliamentary History*, XIX, 599, and XXI, 1036.

[4] R. Price, *Essay on the Population of England*, pp. 27 ff.; *La Richesse de l'Angleterre*, pp. 9, 84. See also *Considerations on the Trade and Finances of the United Kingdom* (third edition, 1769).

[5] On those discussions and on the methods of estimation used on both sides, consult E. C. K. Gonner's interesting paper, 'The Population of England in the Eighteenth Century', in the *Journal of the Royal Statistical Society*, LXXVI, pp. 261-303 (1912-13). That paper contains an extensive bibliography of the question.

[6] The bill for a census of the population, introduced in 1753, met with violent and unreasonable opposition: 'I did not believe that there had been any set of men, or, indeed any individual of the human species as presumptuous and abandoned as to make the proposal we have just heard.' It was said that a census would reveal the weakness of England to her enemies, that it concealed tyrannical schemes for compulsory military service, and was 'totally subversive of the last remnants of English liberty'. *Parliamentary History*, XIV, 1318-22.

registers, in which a record of christenings, marriages and burials was kept. From these data calculations were made of the average number of inhabitants per house or of the birth and death rates, and these figures became the basis for multiplication sums. This was Gregory King's method. Under the date of March 25th, 1690, he had found in the hearth tax returns the figure of 1,319,115 houses. That total number could, he thought, be divided into several categories. There were the houses in London, those in the suburbs of London, those in other towns in England and Wales, and finally those in the villages and hamlets. He assumed that a house in each category contained a certain number of inhabitants, which varied between four and five and a half. By this figure he multiplied the number of houses in the corresponding area. Adding the results together, he arrived at a total of 5,318,000 souls. By throwing in the strength of the land and sea forces, and an additional number to make up for probable omissions in the registers, he reached the figure of 5,500,000 inhabitants.[1]

It is obvious that arbitrary assumptions played a considerable part in such computations. Moreover, the figures themselves, although taken from authentic documents, were far from reliable. Even the best kept parish register could only supply incomplete returns, for there was no compulsory registration of births, marriages and deaths. It was still mainly a religious matter, the Church in each parish registering the christenings, the marriages and the burials of its members. But the Church took no account of nonconformists, who in some districts were very numerous, sometimes even more numerous than members of the Church of England.[2] The figures, too, which were taken from taxation registers, are open to doubt. The Treasury officials who were responsible for the making of these registers regarded them from a purely practical point of view. For them, houses which paid neither hearth nor window tax did not exist, and as a rule they did not even trouble to count them. Such documents, taken just as they stood and read without criticism, were bound to lead those who utilized them to the most unfounded conclusions.

These were the documents used to prove that the population of England was decreasing. The main argument, which was developed at great length by Richard Price in his *Essay on the Population of England*

---

[1] G. Chalmers, *Estimate of the Comparative Strength of Britain*, p. 56, thinks this too low a figure. But it more or less tallies with those given by more recent hypotheses, based on the study of the data of population and on the actual results of several successive censuses. See J. Rickman, *Abstract of the Answers and Returns to the Population Act*, 11 *Geo. IV*, Preface, xlv; G. R. Porter, *Progress of the Nation*, pp. 13 and 26, and R. Price Williams, 'On the Increase of Population in England and Wales', *Journal of the Statistical Society*, XLIII, 462 (1880).

[2] *Abstract of the Answers and Returns to the Population Act*, 11 *Geo. IV*, I, xxxii.

(1780),[1] was as follows: In the reign of William III there were in the kingdom, exclusive of Scotland and Ireland, about thirteen hundred thousand houses. By 1759 this figure had fallen to 986,482, by 1767 to 980,692, and by 1777 to 952,734.[2] How was it possible to avoid the conclusion that the population of England was decreasing? It must have fallen twenty-five per cent in less than a century. Price overlooked only one detail. The figures on which he based his comparisons were taken from different sources. The earliest figure was taken from the hearth tax registers. But in 1696 the hearth tax had been abolished and its place taken by a tax on house property, which was based on the number of windows. This new tax had resulted in the creation of a new set of statistics, the figures of which did not agree with the data of an earlier period.[3] Hence a sudden and apparently inexplicable drop. According to the hearth tax register in 1690 London had a total of 111,215 houses. According to the window tax registers in 1708 it had only 47,031.[4] Must we therefore assume that about the beginning of the eighteenth century some sudden disaster, unobserved by contemporaries and unknown to history, had destroyed half London? This *reductio ad absurdum* is enough to show the ridiculous fallacy of this method of making estimates, a method finally condemned by Arthur Young in his *Political Arithmetic*.[5]

It is, nevertheless, unlikely that the depopulation theory would have been attacked merely on the ground of statistical method had not visible signs of general prosperity suggested a presumption in favour of the opposite theory. How was it possible to believe that a country was growing weaker and losing its people, when its activity and its resources grew greater every day? Arthur Young wrote: 'View the navigation, the roads, the harbours, and all other public works. Take notice of the spirit with which manufactures are carried on ... Move your eye on which side you will, you behold nothing but great riches and yet greater resources ... I have proved the nation to be in

[1] Already outlined in 1772, in his *Observations on Reversionary Payments*, II, 280 ff. He found additional proofs in the decrease of excise revenue, the complaints about rural depopulation, etc.

[2] R. Price, *Essay on the Population of England and Wales*, pp. 14-18.

[3] The number of 'hearths' was in fact different from the number of houses. See Gonner, op. cit., p. 269.

[4] See the table setting out the two lists of figures for all the counties in Chalmers, *Estimate of the Comparative Strength of Britain*, p. 216.

[5] 'Upon the whole, we may determine that the facts upon which the arguments for our depopulation are founded are absolutely false, that the conjectures annexed to them are wild and uncertain, and that the conclusions which are drawn from the whole can abound in nothing but errors and mistakes.' A. Young, *Political Arithmetic*, I, 90. See the critical observations made by W. Eden, *Letters to the Earl of Carlisle* (1780), pp. 21-9, and J. Howlett, *An Examination of Dr Price's Essay on the Population of England and Wales*, pp. 43-62.

possession of a vast income, highly sufficient for all demands, to possess a vigorous agriculture, flourishing manufactures, and an extended commerce; in a word, to be a great industrious country. Now, I conceive that it is impossible to prove such points without proportionally proving the Kingdom to be a populous one. It is in vain to talk of tables of births, and lists of houses and windows, as proofs of our loss of people: the flourishing state of our agriculture, our manufactures, and commerce, with our general wealth, prove the contrary.'[1]

This was, of course, only an impression. In order to turn it into a proven fact, sources of information were needed which, in those days, were not available. People like William Eden, Howlett and Wales[2] made the mistake of adopting the methods they had themselves so justly criticized, and their conclusions were no more convincing than those of their opponents.[3] Others for want of facts to prove their case relied on abstract reasoning, like the economists whose disciples they were, and, from what had at first only been an opinion, they ultimately evolved a theory.

That theory is implied in the lines we have just quoted from Arthur Young, and is explained and developed in other passages of the same book. According to him the increase of wealth and the growth of population are interdependent facts. Wherever men can make a living they increase and multiply: 'It is employment that creates population. There is not an instance in the whole globe of an idle people being numerous in proportion to their territory, but, on the contrary, all industrious countries are populous, and proportionably to the degree of their industry. When employment is plentiful and time of value, families are not burdens, marriages are early and numerous ... It is an absolute impossibility that, in such circumstances, the people should not increase[4] ... The increase of employment will be found to raise men like mushrooms.'[5] The fear that undertakings might grow too quickly and that there would be a shortage of labour was purely imaginary: 'No industrious nation need ever fear a want of hands for executing any of the most extensive plans of public or private improvement. It would be false to assert that such plans could anywhere be executed at a given expense, or at a certain rate of wages,

---

[1] A. Young, *North of England*, IV, 404-6, 416.

[2] The author of *An Inquiry into the present state of Population in England and Wales* (1781).

[3] See the most sensible remarks made in a pamphlet called *Uncertainty of the Present Population of this Kingdom* (1781), p. 4. The author observed that it was impossible to decide with any degree of certainty whether the population of England had increased or diminished in the preceding hundred years, and whether that population, when he wrote, was between eight and nine millions or only between four and five.

[4] A. Young, *North of England*, IV, 411.

[5] Ibid., I, 173.

but wherever employment exists, that is, money to be expended, workmen can never be wanting ... Let but the requisite money be found, men can never be wanting.'[1]

Moreover, economic progress would be impossible were it not accompanied by, at any rate, an equivalent increase in population. For if agriculture or industry could only count on the minimum amount of labour required to supply their immediate demands, it is probable that a shortage would soon be felt: 'The increase of population must be out of proportion to the increase of employment, or some of the demands would be unsupplied. For instance, five hundred hands are employed by husbandry; public works are set on foot, which would take three hundred, upon the average of work done by labourers among the farmers; but as the increase of wages occasions a new species of idleness, the works would be at a stand if only three hundred more were drawn forth, so that three hundred and fifty or four hundred must possibly be created by the rise of wages to do the work of three hundred.'[2] When Young asserted that the population must increase more rapidly than the amount of work to be done, was this merely the outcome of logical reasoning, or was it a kind of foreboding of a state of things as yet hardly apparent but discernible already by the far-sighted? This excess of population, regarded as both the result and the necessary condition of economic development, was to supply what Marx a century later called 'the reserve army of the factory system'.

The arguments over the population of England were still going on when in 1798 Malthus's famous book was published.[3] It did not deal with England only. The law governing the growth of population, which Malthus set out to prove, was supposed to be a general law for all ages and all countries.[4] It should be noted that among the facts on which Malthus built his theory, very few were taken from England. He surveyed every nation and every degree of civilization, in order to show that his theory was (or seemed to be) confirmed in the most dissimilar cases. We cannot forget, however, that this book was written in England in the last years of the eighteenth century. Ideas are not born of ideas alone, and Malthus's thought was moulded quite as much by environment and circumstances as by his study of Adam Smith, Condorcet or Godwin. By 1798 the factory system had already come into being. Industrial centres were developing and the class of

[1] A. Young, *North of England*, I, 178.

[2] Ibid., I, 177.

[3] *Essay on the Principle of Population as it affects the future Improvement of Society*, London, 1798.

[4] On the abstract origins of the Malthusian theory see E. Halévy, *L'Évolution de la doctrine utilitaire de 1789 à 1815*, pp. 136-56.

factory workers was making its appearance. The country was at the same time going through a most serious crisis. In 1795 and 1796 a succession of bad harvests, the consequences of which were made worse by the war at sea, sent up the price of foodstuffs to famine level.[1] The increase of destitution can be estimated by the growth of the poor rate. In eight years it rose from two and a half million pounds to nearly four million. The reform of the poor law, which had begun in 1782,[2] was again taken up. Malthus wrote his book during this period of rapid growth and acute distress, and attempted to prove that the former was the cause of the latter. Thus the fear of depopulation was followed by the fear of seeing England over-populated and doomed to pauperism, not so much because wealth was badly distributed as because the people were too many.

The problem which Malthus thought he had solved has remained unsolved to this day. The true law of population (if it be admitted that one law can account for such complex phenomena) is still unknown, and can be discovered only by patient inductive work conducted on strictly scientific lines. As to the actual historical question regarding the growth of the population of England in the eighteenth century, that question was answered by the 1801 census. At that date the population of England and Wales was found to be 8,873,000 and that of the United Kingdom 14,681,000.[3] If we compare these figures with Gregory King's fairly reasonable estimate for the end of the seventeenth century,[4] we must conclude that in a hundred years the population had grown by 60 per cent in England, while that of the whole kingdom had been nearly doubled. The country was, nevertheless,

			£	s.	d.
[1] Price of a quarter of corn in	1791	2	15	6
,,	,,	1792	2	19	7
,,	,,	1793	3	2	8
,,	,,	1794	3	0	9
,,	,,	1795	4	11	8
,,	,,	1796	4	10	4
,,	,,	1797	3	9	9
,,	,,	1798	3	9	9
,,	,,	1799	4	5	1
,,	,,	1800	7	2	10

Abstract of the Answers and Returns to the Population Act, 11 *Geo. IV*, I, 211. The figures in the Eton records, published by T. Tooke, *History of Prices*, II, 389, are about 10 per cent lower than these.

[2] Under the law known as 'Gilbert's Act'. W. Cunningham observes that while at the time of the Restoration the parish had been given means of defence against the pauper's claims, it was provided with ample means of assistance on the eve of the industrial revolution. *Growth of English Industry and Commerce*, II, 578.

[3] *Abstract of the Answers and Returns to the Population Act*, 41 *Geo. III*, I, 3 ('Observations on the Results').

[4] Professor Gonner, on the basis of the hearth tax registers, arrives at the approximate total of 5,860,000 inhabitants (see article quoted above, pp. 282-3), while a critical study of Rickman's estimate, based on the parochial registers of baptisms and burials, leads to the figure of 5,740,000, instead of 5,500,000 as conjectured by Gregory King.

far from being over-populated: it only contained between one-third and one-fourth of its present population, the average number of inhabitants to the square mile being under 120. The census returns only confirmed the impression created by Malthus's theory. There was no longer any talk about the depopulation of the country, which many people had believed without any definite reason. From that moment a steady increase in population was regarded as normal, and its slackening or its cessation as an unhealthy condition. Nowadays this idea has become a dogma which has nowhere found more adherents than in England. Upon it are based the most ambitious hopes of British expansion: according to a creed which has found its apostles and its fanatics,[1] the wealth and power of the Empire will indefinitely increase with its population, so that one day Canada, Australia and South Africa will contain hundreds of millions of people, a whole new race, speaking the English language and still forming one great Commonwealth under the Union Jack. As a matter of fact it is quite possible that this growth in the population, which began in the eighteenth century, may go on for a long time yet. But we must not forget that it is quite a modern development, bound up with historical conditions which have not always existed and which in the future may very well alter or even disappear.

As for the past, it is impossible to be very definite on this point, since we have to deal more with conjectures than with facts. It would appear that until 1750 the population of England increased but slowly. We will quote, with all reserve, the figures put forward by Rickman in his preface to the census tables of 1831.[2] According to him, England and Wales in 1600 had five million inhabitants, about 1650 five and a half million, in 1700 six million, and in 1750 six and a half million. Therefore in a hundred and fifty years the population had only increased by less than fifteen hundred thousand inhabitants. But during the following half-century, from 1750 to 1801, it increased by two and a half million. Thus the rate of increase was four times as great as in the preceding period.[3]

---

[1] Written in 1927.

[2] *Abstract of the Answers and Returns to the Population Act*, 11 *Geo. IV*, Preface, I, xlv.

[3] On the progress of medicine since 1750, and its consequences, see Talbot Griffeth, *Population Problems in the Age of Malthus*, and M. Dorothy George, 'Some Causes of the Increase of Population in the Eighteenth Century', *Economic Journal*, XXXII, 325 ff. Owing to the improvement of agriculture it became possible to eat butcher's meat in winter, and, in spite of the many deaths caused by smallpox and typhoid fever, there was a marked decline in the effect of epidemics. Cf. L. C. A. Knowles, *Industrial and Commercial Revolutions in Great Britain during the Nineteenth Century* (third edition), p. 67.

II

As the population grew its centre of gravity moved, and the direction of this movement is a sufficient indication of its cause. If, on the map of England proper, a line is drawn from the mouth of the Humber to that of the Severn, following approximately the Jurassic hills north and west of the London geological basin, that line will divide two regions of more or less equal size.[1] The one on the north-west includes today almost all the great centres of English industry: the Midlands, Yorkshire, Lancashire, the Northumbrian and Durham coal deposits, and the manufacturing centres round Manchester, Liverpool, Leeds, Sheffield and Newcastle. The south-eastern part has a less concentrated and less active economic existence. Few large cities are to be found there apart from London, whose gigantic growth corresponds to that of a world-wide Empire. But on the other hand that part of England is full of ancient towns, proud of their colleges, their castles and cathedrals, but stunted and sleepy, as though wrapped in themselves within their old walls. The contrast, which it is enough to mention, is most clearly marked by statistics. In 1901, just a hundred years after the first census, the seventeen north-western counties had a population of 16,718,000 inhabitants. The twenty-four south-eastern counties had only 14,254,000, of which nearly a third (exactly 4,536,000) were in the County of London.[2] The first group contained twenty-one towns with a minimum population of a hundred thousand, of which three had a population of over 500,000 and twelve of over 200,000.[3] The second group contained only eight, including London and two of its suburbs, West Ham and Croydon.[4] The average density of population in the north-west was 720 inhabitants to the square mile, while in the south-east it was 530, or if we exclude the County of London, only 360.

It was quite otherwise in the eighteenth century. On the following maps we have tried to indicate the distribution of population in 1700, 1750 and 1801. The documents attached to the 1801 census have enabled us to make this attempt, which is not open to the same

[1] 26,827 square miles (south-eastern counties) as against 23,194 square miles (north-western counties).

[2] The County of London was established in 1888.

[3] Birkenhead, 110,926 inhabitants; Birmingham, 522,182; Blackburn, 127,527; Bolton, 168,205; Bradford, 279,809; Bristol, 328,842; Derby, 105,785; Gateshead, 109,887; Halifax, 104,993; Hull, 240,618; Leeds, 428,933; Leicester, 211,574; Liverpool, 684,947; Manchester, 543,969; Newcastle, 214,803; Nottingham, 239,753; Oldham, 137,238; Preston, 112,982; Salford, 220,956; Sheffield, 380,717; Sunderland, 145,565.

[4] Brighton, 123,478 inhabitants; Croydon, 133,855; Norwich, 111,728; Plymouth, 107,509; Portsmouth, 189,160; Southampton, 104,911; West Ham, 267,308; London, 4,536,036.

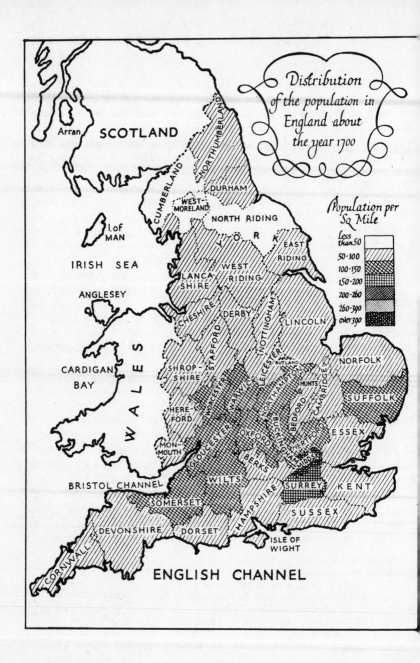

Distribution of the population in England about the year 1700

Population per Sq Mile

Less than 50
50-100
100-150
150-200
200-260
260-390
over 390

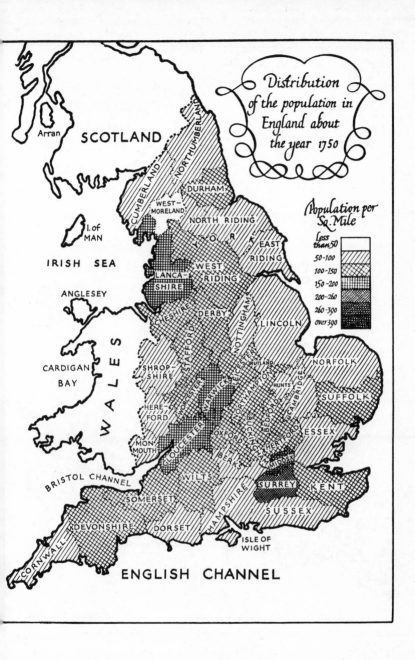

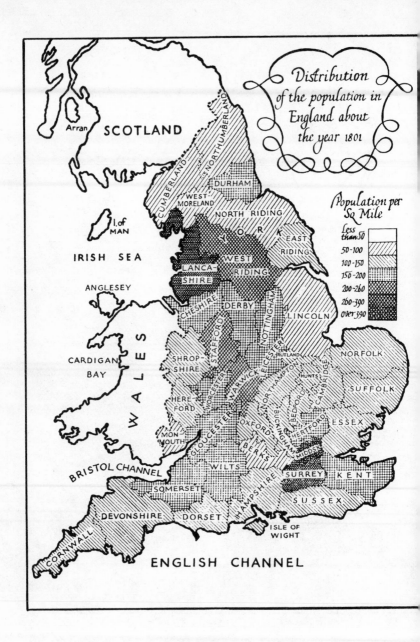

Distribution of the population in England about the year 1801

Population per Sq Mile
Less than 50
50-100
100-150
150-200
200-260
260-390
Over 390

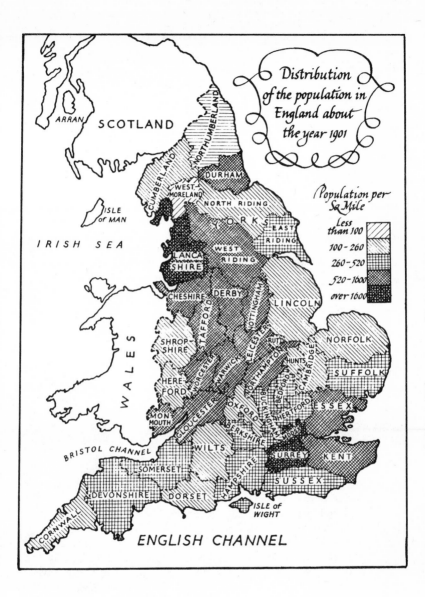

Distribution of the population in England about the year 1901

Population per Sq. Mile

Less than 100
100 – 260
260 – 520
520 – 1600
over 1600

SCOTLAND

ARRAN

ISLE of MAN

IRISH SEA

WALES

CUMBERLAND

NORTHUMBERLAND

DURHAM

WEST-MORELAND

NORTH RIDING

YORKS

EAST RIDING

WEST RIDING

LANCASHIRE

CHESHIRE

DERBY

STAFFORD

NOTTINGHAM

LINCOLN

SHROPSHIRE

WORCESTER

WARWICK

LEICESTER

RUTLAND

NORTHAMPTON

HUNTS

NORFOLK

SUFFOLK

CAMBRIDGE

HEREFORD

BEDFORD

MONMOUTH

GLOUCESTER

OXFORD

BUCKINGHAM

HERTFORD

ESSEX

BERKSHIRE

WILTS

HAMPSHIRE

SURREY

KENT

BRISTOL CHANNEL

SOMERSET

SUSSEX

DEVONSHIRE

DORSET

ISLE of WIGHT

CORNWALL

ENGLISH CHANNEL

objections as the estimates of the seventeenth and eighteenth centuries: this kind of construction seems to us reasonably justified when undisputable and complete data supplied by an official census are available for purposes of comparison.[1] The point which at once arrests attention on looking at the first of these maps is the low average density of the population as compared with today. Apart from London and its immediate neighbourhood, not a single county had 160 inhabitants to the square mile. The distribution of population is clearly marked. The most densely populated counties formed a continuous zone, running from the Bristol Channel to the Suffolk coast. That narrow strip of country contained over three-fifths of the whole population of England. The northern counties were sparsely populated, Lancashire and the West Riding of Yorkshire having only 80 to 110 inhabitants to the square mile.

In 1750 the trend of population towards the north and west had begun to show itself. It seemed to be moving towards the Atlantic, drawn thither by the development of the maritime trade and the growing wealth of Liverpool and Bristol. The most densely peopled district formed a triangle with its broad base in the West, and stretching northwards to the county of Durham. By 1801 the whole face of the map had changed. London, with its suburbs, forms on that map an isolated patch in the angle facing the Continent, while a dark band, widening out towards the north, stretches over the midland and western counties to the foot of the mountains in Cumberland and Wales. Had it not been for London, with her 900,000 inhabitants, the north-western group would even at that date have rivalled that of the south-east, for it had a population of 3,895,000 as against 4,711,000. Let us now turn to the map showing the distribution of the population of England in 1901. Here we find the same characteristics, more marked but quite recognizable. From 1801 to 1901 the trend is continuous and the direction always the same. In 1700 it had not yet begun.

What is the meaning of this migration towards the north and west? To understand it a more detailed study becomes necessary. Look for instance at Wiltshire, which was typical of the ancient order of things, with cottage industries scattered throughout the country and little towns where employers and merchants lived. In 1700 Wiltshire, with 130 persons to the square mile, was the third most densely populated county after Middlesex and Surrey. Its population hardly varied during the eighteenth century: in 1750 it had fallen to 127, and in 1801 had risen again to 133 to the square

---

[1] See *Abstract of the Answers and Returns to the Population Act*, 41 *Geo. III*, I, 11 ff. ('Observations on the Results'). Little difference will be found between our maps and those drawn up by Professor Gonner (*Journal of the Royal Statistical Society*, LXXVI, 289-91).

mile. In some purely agricultural counties, as in Rutland or Lincoln-shire, the final result was about the same, after more marked fluctua-tions: in a hundred years their populations only rose from 104 to 109 and from 65 to 75 inhabitants to the square mile. Let us now turn our attention to those districts where the new industries were de-veloping and where machine industry and large-scale undertakings were making their appearance. Warwickshire and Staffordshire, both contiguous to the mining and metal-working Birmingham district, had a population of 224,000 in 1700, of 285,000 in 1750, and of 447,000 in 1801. Thus the population had nearly doubled: but in Lancashire it had become almost three times as great, for from 240,000 in-habitants the figure had risen to 672,000. It is a significant fact that three-quarters of this considerable increase took place in the second half of the century.

Then it was indeed that, wherever it could develop under favour-able conditions, the factory system brought about the rise of these mighty centres of population, whose monstrous growth is still going on under our own eyes. At first they were rather less concentrated, as were the industries round which they were growing up: it was the steam engine which finally fixed and consolidated them. The early factories, with machinery worked by water-wheels, were usually out-side the towns. Yet they had to be near a town, as serious difficulties of communication and transport made it essential for them to be close to a market, both for buying and selling purposes. Labour was needed, not only for the actual work in the factory but also for the subsidiary domestic industries without which work in the factory could not be carried on. For there was a period before the invention and the general use of the power loom when cotton and wool, which were machine spun, had to be hand woven, and the country weavers were too scattered to meet the requirements of the industry. Thus, even before the time of the steam engine, it became possible for the centres of the factory system to find their geographical position and to develop with a rapidity which foreshadowed their future greatness.

III

Among the towns mentioned on almost every page of this book, and to which the factory system owes as much as they owe to the factory system, the cotton towns showed the earliest and the most remarkable development. And by far the most important and famous of them all, which remains today the classical type of an industrial town, is Manchester.

It does not follow that Manchester is a creation of modern times. On the contrary it is a very ancient city, the Mancunium of the

Roman period.[1] It commanded the line of communication between the Pennine range and the impassable bogs which stretched down to the sea.[2] Its position on the banks of the Irwell, not far from the river's junction with the Mersey and in the centre of the crescent of hills round south Lancashire, marked it out as a centre for local trade. One of the main causes of its industrial success was the rapid flow of the streams which run down from all sides into the natural depression where the city lies. Towards the end of the Middle Ages the weaving of cloth and of coarse woollen goods known as 'cottons', which for many years remained a speciality of the district, brought great prosperity to Manchester. Two buildings, still in existence in the modern city, bear witness to this fact.[3] Its reputation during the epoch of the great cloth merchants of the Renaissance was far above its actual importance.[4] For Manchester was always spoken of as though it were a considerable town, while as a matter of fact it was then not much more than a wealthy village.[5]

In the seventeenth century the cotton industry made its appearance. Then it was that Manchester really became a town, though for a long time it was not officially recognized as such. It had no municipal corporation, and sent no representative to the House of Commons.[6] For this reason, in 1727 Defoe still referred to it as 'one of the greatest, if not the greatest mere village in England'.[7] Far from desiring in this way to belittle the town, he put his estimate of its population at the absurdly high figure of 50,000 inhabitants. At the outside the correct figure was actually no more than nine or ten thousand.[8] The

---

[1] See the *Itinerarium Antonini Augusti* (Iter Britannicum), *Monumenta Historica Britannica*, I, xxii. John Whitaker's comments (*History of Manchester*, I, 3 ff.) do not supply a very helpful elucidation of the text.

[2] Even at the end of the eighteenth century, those bogs were still very extensive. See Aikin's description of them: 'In dry weather the upper crust of turf will bear the foot, but for a large space round the ground shakes with the tread, and horses or cattle cannot venture upon it. In wet seasons the mosses are impassable.' J. Aikin, *Description of the Country from thirty to forty miles round Manchester*, p. 16.

[3] Namely the Chetham Hospital building, which contains a fine fifteenth-century library, and a church, lately erected into a cathedral, dating from the early fourteenth century.

[4] Manchester 'hath for a long time been a town well inhabited ... well set to work in making of cloths, as well of linen as of woollen, whereby the inhabitants of the said town have gotten and come into riches and wealthy livings, and by reason of great occupying, good order, strict and true dealing of the inhabitants of the said town, many strangers, as well of Ireland, have resorted thither.' 33 Henry VIII, c. 15 (preamble).

[5] This is the phrase used by Sir William Ashley.

[6] Manchester was first represented in Parliament after the Reform Act of 1832.

[7] Defoe, *Tour*, II, 69, and III, 209-11.

[8] T. Percival, *Observations on the State of Population in Manchester and Salford*, p. 1, for the year 1717, puts the figure at 8,000. Practically the same result is reached if

impression of numbers was probably given by the activity of the surrounding district. For Manchester was the market for an industrial area extending to ten or fifteen miles round the little town. Woollens, coarse linens and felt hats were still made there, but above all cotton goods of every kind and quality: calicoes, fustians and brightly coloured piece goods, which Liverpool merchants exported to Africa and to the American colonies.[1] After the first critical period, during which the laws of prohibition were passed, the cotton industry developed steadily and without setbacks, while the growth of the population followed a parallel curve. By 1753 the two churches in Manchester were no longer large enough, and the inhabitants petitioned for authorization to build a new one.[2] In 1757 another petition showed the new requirements of the growing population: they asked to be relieved of the obligation to have their grain ground at the School Mill, which since the Middle Ages had served as a common mill and for many years had been inadequate for the local needs. In order to supply facts in support of this request a town census was taken, and the population of Manchester and Salford was found to be about 20,000 inhabitants.[3] When compared with the huge tract of country now covered by these twin cities, the area actually built over at that time seems absurdly small: a few dark and narrow lanes clustered round Cannon Street where the chief merchants had their shops, and round Deansgate, which followed the old Chester road, both leading to the one bridge over the Irwell. Across the bridge and in the curve of the river lay Salford, then hardly covering more ground than the big Exchange Station does today. The Royal Infirmary, founded in 1752, stood outside the town. Open country lay all around, and trout was still caught in its streams, the Irk and the Medlock, which today are as polluted and black as the Bièvre in Paris.[4]

Two of the events which contributed most to the growth of the city were the cutting of the Worsley Canal, which enabled the inhabitants

[1] J. Aikin, *Description of the Country from thirty to forty miles round Manchester*, pp. 158-61.

[2] Petition from the Warden and the Fellows of the Collegiate Church. *Journals of the House of Commons*, XXVI, 556.

[3] J. Aikin, op. cit., p. 156; T. Henry, 'Observations on the bills of mortality for the Towns of Manchester and Salford', *Memoirs of the Literary and Philosophical Society of Manchester*, III, 159; T. Percival, *Observations on the State of Population in Manchester and Salford*, p. 1.

[4] See the series of historical maps of Manchester in the Map Section of the British Museum.

we base our calculations on the Parish Registers (*Summaries and Abstracts of Answers and Returns to the Population Act*, 41 *Geo. III*, II, 149) and compare them with the figures of the local census of 1773 (three manuscript volumes in Chetham's Library).

to buy cheap coal, and of the Mersey Canal, which made trade with Liverpool easier and more regular. During the following years steps were taken to improve the roads, to light the streets and to provide against fire.[1] This was evidence of the development that was taking place, even though as yet it was only beginning. In 1773 a group of private persons, led by John Whitaker who wrote the first *History of Manchester*, organized a new census, the results of which make it possible to realize how much the town had progressed. Manchester had then 3,402 houses and 22,481 inhabitants, and Salford had 866 houses and 4,765 inhabitants, giving a total of a little over 27,000 persons.[2] These statistics are of special interest because they were taken just at the time when the technique of the textile industry was beginning to change. The use of the jenny was becoming general throughout Lancashire and the neighbouring counties, but the factory at Cromford had hardly been running two years, while Manchester had as yet no single spinning mill. It will be argued from these facts that it was not machine industry which had caused the population to increase threefold in fifty years. This is true, but machine industry and the increase of population were results of the same forces that were shaping the new economic evolution and giving the first impetus, which was to determine both the direction and speed of its movement. And when machine industry did finally come into being, this increase of population, which had begun shortly before, showed a significant acceleration. In 1790 Manchester had 50,000 inhabitants. In 1801 it had 95,000.[3]

The whole appearance of the city was also changed. More and more large factories were built, especially after the steam engine had replaced water power. In 1786, according to a contemporary writer, only one chimney, that of Arkwright's spinning mill, was seen to rise above the town.[4] Fifteen years later Manchester had about fifty spinning mills, most of them worked by steam.[5] Near them, like a belt round the old town, rows of working-class dwellings had been hastily built, where space was already lacking for the crowded population. Fevers were endemic in the dark, damp streets.[6] On the other

[1] See *Journals of the House of Commons*, XXX, 159.

[2] Census of Manchester and Salford (1773), Chetham's Library. It will be seen that each house on an average had six or seven inhabitants.

[3] This includes the suburban population. See Wheeler, *Manchester*, p. 250. The official figure was 84,020. *Abstract of the Answers and Returns to the Population Act*, 41 *Geo. III*, 173.

[4] *Report of the Minutes of the Evidence taken before the Select Committee on the State of the Children employed in the Manufactories of the United Kingdom* (1816), p. 317.

[5] Erik Svedenstjerna, *Reise durch einen Theil von England und Schottland in den Jahren* 1802 *und* 1803, p. 188.

[6] T. Henry, op. cit., pp. 161-2, and Aikin, op. cit., p. 192. See chap. III, 'The

hand the centre of the town, where the shops were, had been greatly improved by wide streets with high brick houses.[1] Outside and south-east of the city, fine villas standing in their own gardens had made their appearance; there resided the new aristocracy, the upstart and wealthy 'cotton lords'.[2] For many years Manchester retained these characteristics which during the nineteenth century were re-produced in every large industrial town in England, and which recent improvements in transport facilities have only made more con-spicuous. It is difficult to make out, at any rate during the period we are speaking of, whence the increase in the population of Man-chester came. Many men, attracted by the comparatively high wages of the cotton industry, came in from the neighbouring counties.[3] This influence was also felt at a distance, for the Irish element began to make its appearance not only in Manchester but throughout the whole of Lancashire.[4]

Due allowance being made for differences in size and importance, the history of Manchester is typical of what took place in most of the towns around it. About 1760, Oldham was a village of 300 or 400 inhabitants.[5] The people were weavers of wool and cotton and used the recently introduced fly shuttle. The earliest factories were built between 1776 and 1778.[6] By 1788 there were twenty-five within the parish boundaries, and the village had grown into a town with a thickly populated countryside all round.[7] In 1801 the township contained 12,000 inhabitants and the parish 20,000. In 1753, when Samuel Crompton was born, Bolton consisted of a single rough and ill-paved street, with thatched cottages standing in their own gardens down each side. The country weaver brought in his stuffs for sale in 'wallets balanced over one shoulder, while on the other arm there was often a basket full of fresh butter'.[8] By 1773 the population figure was already

[1] J. Aikin, op. cit., pp. 182, 192, 373. Until 1760 or 1770 almost all the houses in the town were built of wood or clay.

[2] Ibid., p. 203.

[3] The average agricultural wage between 1789 and 1803 was 10s. a week. Thorold Rogers, *Six Centuries of Work and Wages*, p. 510. The average industrial wage in Man-chester was 16s. a week. F. M. Eden, *State of the Poor*, II, 367.

[4] *A Second Letter to the Inhabitants of Manchester on the Exportation of Cotton Twist* (1800), p. 11.

[5] Edwin Butterworth, *History of Oldham*, pp. 110-11.

[6] Ibid., p. 117. Of the first six, three had water-wheels and the others used horses to work their machinery.

[7] Ibid., pp. 132, 148.

[8] French, *Life and Times of Samuel Crompton*, p. 9. In 1727 Defoe only mentioned Bolton as a place from which a title of nobility was taken. *Tour*, III, 217.

Industrial Revolution and Labour'. In 1790 it was decided to build a new work-house (*Journals of the House of Commons*, XLV, 194, 544).

over 5,000: by 1789 it had reached 12,000,[1] and by 1801, 17,000. The same is true of Rochdale, Bury, Blackburn, Preston, Wigan, Stockport, Ashton, Stalybridge. Everywhere on this poor soil the same fruitful seeds gave a harvest of cities.[2]

We must also remember that, far from being confined to the towns alone, industry spread all round them, the population often increasing more quickly in the industrial suburbs than in the towns themselves. In 1780 the hamlet of Tyldsley, south of Bolton, consisted of two farms with eight or nine cottages. In 1795 it had no fewer than 162 houses, a church and 976 inhabitants, of whom 325 were weavers. All this was due to the enterprise of one Mr Johnson, who some time before had put up there a six-storeyed factory, including a spinning mill and dye works fitted with the most up-to-date machinery.[3] Men who witnessed such developments felt that industry, to use Arthur Young's telling phrase, was 'raising men like mushrooms'.

In those districts where the woollen industry was predominant the industrial revolution, with its accompanying characteristics of an increasing population and growing cities, came later and more gradually. At the beginning of the eighteenth century Leeds was somewhat larger than Manchester.[4] But in 1775 it had only 17,000 inhabitants,[5] while Manchester had 30,000 at least. Its growth only began about 1780, when the jenny was first introduced into Yorkshire, and did not accelerate until the opening of the first factories in 1793 and 1794. Then it was that Leeds ceased to be merely the centre of an extensive manufacturing district with a scattered cottage industry, a market

---

[1] J. Aikin, op. cit., p. 260.

[2] See Edwin Butterworth, *History of Ashton-under-Lyne*, pp. 81 ff.; J. Aikin, *Description of the Country from thirty to forty miles round Manchester*, pp. 260 ff.; F. M. Eden, *State of the Poor*, II, 298. On the industrial revolution in Stockport, see Unwin, *Samuel Oldknow and the Arkwrights*, chap. II, pp. 21-41. The census of 1801 gave the following figures:

	Town	Parish
Ashton	5,000	15,000
Rochdale	7,000	29,000
Bury	5,500	22,300
Blackburn	10,000	14,300
Preston	11,000	33,000

[3] J. Aikin, op. cit., p. 299. Aikin congratulates the manufacturer on his choice of a site 'having great plenty of coal, fine water, being in the centre of some thousand weavers, and only distant four miles from the Duke of Bridgewater's canal at Worsley'. This shows very clearly what were then the essential conditions demanded by those who built factories.

[4]	MANCHESTER		LEEDS	
	Christenings	Burials	Christenings	Burials
1700	259	195	290	274
1710	212	260	284	253
1720	298	298	305	186
1730	351	574	569	519
1740	402	622	573	582
1750	653	818	770	548

Abstract of the Answers and Returns to the Population Act, 41 *Geo. III*, II, 149 and 371.

[5] F. M. Eden, *State of the Poor*, II, 847.

where every week several thousand weavers came to sell the pieces of stuff they had woven themselves, and became the home of a centralized industry. But this centralization was far from being complete, for side by side with the factories, still few in number, a great many domestic workshops remained in existence. In 1801, of the 53,000 inhabitants of the parish more than 20,000 lived in cottages outside the town proper.

If from Leeds, where the influence of machine industry was already perceptible, we turn to the neighbouring parish of Halifax, a striking contrast can be immediately observed. No important changes had taken place there, and small-scale production, small holdings and cottage industry still survived and were carried on practically without any alteration.[1] Thus throughout the whole of this extensive parish the population, already fairly numerous, increased but slowly. From 50,000 inhabitants in 1760,[2] the figure in 1801 scarcely reached 63,000. The town itself developed still more slowly. Its old stone houses, clustered round the Gothic church, were still standing, and the town continued to be what it had been for so many centuries, the meeting-place for all the weavers of the district who still gathered in the great Cloth Hall built in 1779.[3]

In the industrial centres of the east and south-west growth did not merely slow down, it actually stopped altogether. Norwich, once the third largest town in the Kingdom after London and Bristol, was in 1801 only the tenth.[4] But at any rate it was still, and still remains, an important town. In the south-western counties the collapse was complete and irretrievable.[5] Their day was over: they could not resist the competition of the northern districts. It was useless for the manufacturers of Tiverton, Frome and Exeter to fight against the tide by introducing machinery into their work-shops, or even by trying to run the cotton and woollen industries side by side.[6] Their towns, which until the very eve of the industrial revolution had ranked among the wealthiest in the country, were now doomed to decay. The population of Tiverton fell from 9,000 to 7,000.[7] Frome, as described in 1795 by Eden, cut a very poor figure

[1] See *Report from the Select Committee on the Woollen Manufacture* (1806), p. 9.

[2] *Journals of the House of Commons*, XXVIII, 133.

[3] J. James, *History of the Worsted Manufacture*, p. 616. The neighbouring town of Bradford, nowadays so much more important than Halifax, remained insignificant until the end of the eighteenth century. See J. James, *History of Bradford*, pp. 185 ff., and *Continuation to the History of Bradford*, pp. 189 ff.

[4] *Abstract of the Answers and Returns to the Population Act*, 11 *Geo. IV*, Preface, p. xxiii.

[5] Written in 1927.

[6] Harding, *History of Tiverton*, I, 191. In 1793 a cotton-spinning mill was set up at Tiverton, but the owner did very badly and had to give it up. See J. Billingsley, *A General View of the Agriculture in the County of Somerset*, pp. 90 and 167.

[7] F. M. Eden, *State of the Poor*, II, 142. Even today there are hardly 10,000 inhabitants in Tiverton.

compared with the great northern cities: no new buildings, and old, winding, dirty, unpaved streets with grass growing in them.[1] Very soon modern life passed these towns by altogether, and left them to silence and sad decay, and the memories of a life which had gone from them for ever.

IV

The iron towns grew up more slowly than the cotton, and faster than the wool towns. Unlike the former they did not benefit by the creation and growth of a wholly new industry, but their old industries were transformed rapidly and without much difficulty. It is true that the essential changes took place outside the towns and far from them. Most of the large ironworks, such as Darby's at Coalbrookdale, Roebuck's at Carron, Wilkinson's at Bersham and Bradley, Homfray's and Crawshay's in Wales, were established at a distance from the old centres of the iron trade. It was in towns like Birmingham and Sheffield, with their innumerable small specialities, that the old methods of production still lingered.[2] Even so they soon felt the influence of the great ironworks, which by providing the small workshops with the raw material they so much needed changed the scale, if not the system, of production. The use of coke in blast furnaces, puddling and Huntsman's steel-making process, may not have immediately affected the technical traditions of Birmingham hardware manufacturers and Sheffield cutlers, but they greatly contributed to the success of their undertakings and to the growth of their towns.

During the first half of the eighteenth century it seems that Birmingham had a larger population than Manchester. In 1740 it probably had 25,000 inhabitants, and in 1760 about 30,000.[3] But during the period between 1760 and 1800, when the population of Manchester increased fourfold, that of Birmingham scarcely doubled. At the census of 1801 it had a population of 73,000 inhabitants. The town, built without any regard to plan (and it was to remain so until the important improvements undertaken in the latter part of the nineteenth century) was fairly extensive already. It covered an area of about

[1] *State of the Poor*, II, 644.

[2] In 1780, Birmingham had 6 awl makers, 104 button makers, 23 copper founders, 26 buckle makers, 8 cutlers, 9 scale makers, 12 candlestick makers, 29 die sinkers, 15 file manufacturers, 21 armourers, 9 hinge makers, 8 iron founders, 14 wholesale locksmiths, 46 platers, 9 ring makers, 12 saw and edge-tool makers, 24 blacksmiths, 40 toymakers, 26 jewellers, 17 chainmakers. S. Timmins, *Dr Priestley in Birmingham*, p. 3.

[3] See William Hutton, *History of Birmingham*, pp. 57-9 (somewhat exaggerated figures); Clarke MSS., III, 46; *Abstract of the Answers and Returns to the Population Act*, 41 *Geo. III*, II, 319 (figures taken from the parish registers).

one square mile, bounded by the Wolverhampton, Worcester and Warwick Canals.[1] Alongside these canals, which supplied Birmingham with coal and iron ore, new quarters had grown up, and it was near a fourth canal leading to Tamworth and the Grand Trunk that the great Soho factory stood. Even at that date, and in spite of its unattractive appearance and the ugliness of its small brick houses built haphazard on uneven ground, Birmingham was one of the richest towns in the kingdom, as was witnessed by its two theatres and its library built by public subscription.[2] But this wealth was very unequally distributed, for of the eight thousand houses recorded in 1780 by the Poor Law officials only two thousand eight hundred were taxed.[3]

In the surrounding districts the distribution of population was already showing its present-day characteristics. In the southern corner of Staffordshire and north-west of the city lay a densely populated district, rich in coal, where all day the anvils rang and where at night the sky was lit up by the glow of furnaces. This was the Black Country, lying between Dudley and Wolverhampton, and already worthy of its name. There, within a limited area, Svedenstjerna in 1802 counted about forty blast furnaces.[4] In every other direction there was no transition between a densely populated industrial district and meadowland dotted with one or two villages, while in the distance could be seen the slender spires of Coventry and the battlemented walls of Warwick Castle reflected in the peaceful waters of the Avon.

Sheffield developed more slowly than Birmingham. Was this because industry, besides being as in Birmingham split up among small specialized workshops, was bound to its antiquated traditions by the regulations which the Hallamshire cutlers defended so jealously? More probably it was a result of its geographical position, which was less convenient because it was a less central one. Whatever the reason, Sheffield was soon outstripped by the rival town. In 1760 its population was only about 20,000, and in 1801, 45,000.[5] But how many towns of 45,000 inhabitants had there been in England a hundred years before?

[1] Map of Birmingham in 1795 in W. Hutton's *History of Birmingham*, p. 80. Map by Sheriff (1805); compare with the map drawn up by Bradford in 1750. (British Museum, Maps Nos. 72,830 and 72,835.)

[2] W. Hutton, op. cit., pp. 165 and 196-200. On the building of new churches, see *Journals of the House of Commons*, XXXIII, 494, and LVIII, 365.

[3] *Journals of the House of Commons*, XXXVII, 576.

[4] E. Svedenstjerna, *Reise durch einen Theil von England und Schottland in den Jahren 1802 und 1803*, p. 83. Many nail and hardware making workshops were still scattered about the villages. See W. Pitt, *A General View of the Agriculture in the County of Stafford*, pp. 160 ff. (1794).

[5] Eden's speculative figures (*State of the Poor*, II, 869) are too low when compared to the reliable statistics of 1801. See *Journals of the House of Commons*, XXVIII, 497.

To make such a comparison it is not even necessary to go back a whole century. Before 1750 any locality with more than 5,000 inhabitants was called a large town. Defoe, describing Devonshire, wrote that it was 'full of great towns'.[1] The fact was that the bulk of the population lived in villages and market towns containing less than three hundred hearths. And among these 'great towns' of a hundred and fifty or two hundred years ago, how many have lived up to their expectations? On the other hand, those towns whose development dates only from the industrial revolution have never ceased to grow. Their fate was bound up with that of the factory system, which irrevocably determined not only their position but their actual structure and aspect. By the end of the eighteenth century they looked very much as they did a hundred years later, black and ugly, wrapped in smoke, their ill-built suburbs like shapeless tentacles reaching out on all sides, but also full of life, wealthy and getting wealthier every day. They had connections in every part of Europe, where they poured out the ever-growing surplus of their production. In these new cities a kind of life grew up which the England of former days had never known. There within two generations sprang up new men, new classes and almost a new nation: first, the great obscure mass of factory workers, filling the industrial ant-hill with their disciplined activity; above this class, and turning to its own profit the whole mechanism of the factory system, the manufacturing aristocracy, the powerful class of capitalists, the founders and owners of the factories. After noting the changes in population which the industrial revolution produced we must now describe the various social classes to which it gave rise, classes whose needs, growth and conflicts fill the annals of recent history.

[1] Defoe, *Tour*, I, 81. See Part I, chap. I.

CHAPTER TWO

INDUSTRIAL CAPITALISM

To seek for the origins of capitalism in the industrial revolution would involve a singular misunderstanding of history. The more closely those origins are studied the further do they recede, and they are probably quite as old as trade and currency or the distinction between rich and poor. What is characteristic of the factory system is the use of capital in the production of goods, the creation of capital by means of industrial production, and the existence of a class of capitalists whose interests are identified with those of industrial development.

I

Hitherto, capital had been the product either of mere thrift or of the exploitation of land, or of a direct or indirect exchange of goods. It was based either on land, or on finance, or on trade. If we inquire who owned these various forms of capital before the end of the eighteenth century, we are brought face to face with three different types of men. First there were the owners of landed property, laymen or ecclesiastics. This was a numerous class of men, with more influence in the country than any other, and its economic power, strengthened by ancient privileges, was still very great. Then came the small group of dealers in money, changers, bankers and brokers. Their wealth and activity, and their connection with the government to whom they lent money, had already given them a considerable status in the country. The part they played, though still a highly specialized one and confined to a limited field, was losing more and more that character of something occasional and exceptional which it had possessed in the days of the great bankers of Augsburg and Florence. Finally there was the merchant class who in their undertakings at home or abroad, whether individual or collective, often handled and accumulated considerable amounts of capital. In the commercial towns the richest often formed an aristocracy of its kind. In an earlier chapter we have shown how they gradually acquired the control of industry. But once they had thus established their supremacy over production they still remained merchants, less concerned with manufacture than with buying and selling again. Landowners, bankers and merchants: apart from a few exceptions, every example of capitalism previous to the industrial revolution can be classified under one or other of these three heads.

We must admit that there were exceptions. They all belong to that early form of large-scale production which, after Marx, we have called 'manufacture'. The great cloth merchants of the sixteenth century,[1] or the Sussex ironmasters,[2] were something more than traders and entrepreneurs. They owned both plant and industrial buildings, they organized and supervised the work themselves, and enforced a uniform discipline on their numerous workpeople: in short they organized production. But these cases were exceptions, which have been observed and noted just because they were exceptions. It is an undisputable fact that before the era of the factory system a few men from time to time played the part of manufacturers, but they never formed a manufacturing class. There was not even a word for such a thing in the English language. The word 'manufacturer' was used indiscriminately to mean either workman or master, and more usually meant the former.[3] About 1720 an 'eminent manufacturer' of Manchester would go down to his workshop at six o'clock in the morning, breakfast with his apprentices on oatmeal porridge and then set to work with them.[4] Having gone into business without capital he earned his living from day to day, and if after years of hard work he managed to save a little money he put it by and made no change in his daily habits.[5] He rarely left his workshop or his shop and only drank wine once a year at Christmas time. His favourite pastime was to go of an evening, in company with others like himself, to an alehouse where the custom was to spend fourpence on ale and a halfpenny on tobacco.[6]

[1] See Introduction.　　　　[2] See Part II, chap. III (Coal and Iron).
[3] Arnold Toynbee, *Lectures on the Industrial Revolution in England*, p. 53: 'The manufacturer was literally the man who worked with his own hands in his own cottage.' See id., *Industry and Democracy*, p. 183.
[4] *A Complete History of the Cotton Trade*, p. 170; J. Wheeler, *Manchester, its Political, Social and Commercial History*, p. 149.
[5] J. Aikin, *Description of the Country round Manchester*, p. 181: 'The trade in Manchester may be divided into four periods. The first is that, when the manufacturer worked hard merely for a livelihood, without having accumulated any capital. The second is that, when they had begun to acquire little fortunes but worked as hard and lived in as plain a manner as before, increasing their fortunes as well by economy as by moderate gains. The third is that, when luxury began to appear, and trade was pushed by sending out riders for orders in every market town in the kingdom. The fourth is the period in which expense and luxury had made a great progress, and was supported by a trade extended by means of riders and factors through every part of Europe.' It should be noticed that these various periods are distinguished here from one another by advances not in industrial technique, but in home and foreign trade. Aikin's manufacturers were, above all, traders.
[6] Ibid., p. 190. At the end of the century a great manufacturer kept a valet, owned both a town and a country residence, and patronized Bath or Brighton. See W. Lecky, *History of England in the Eighteenth Century*, VI, 185.

In Yorkshire, where industry was very scattered, there was practically no distinction between master and man.[1] The thousands of small manufacturers who lived around Leeds, Bradford and Halifax had the master's independence and the workman's way of living. Many of them owned some land and worked on it, and therefore belonged to the farming class, much as the town manufacturer belonged to the trading class. Thus the various social classes, whose interests the industrial revolution was about to separate and oppose, were still intermingled and hardly distinguishable.

By the end of the century this separation had taken place, but not completely, any more than the small workshops were swept away all at once by the great factories. There was already a large number of important industrial establishments, mines, foundries, spinning and weaving mills, every one of which, with its costly equipment, its hundreds of working men and women, needed a large capital. Between the man who owned and used this capital and the wage-earner whose labour he bought for a low wage, between the man who directed the whole undertaking and his humble helper kept to one narrow groove, the gulf was becoming almost impassable. The manufacturer now was so high above his workmen that he found himself on the same level as those other capitalists, the banker and the merchant. He needed them both, one to give him credit and the other customers, while in return he provided the one with investments and the other with goods. But he never merged his own individuality in theirs. He had his own special work, which was to organize industrial production, and his own special interests, to the aid of which he very soon learnt to turn political power. With the factory system a new class, a new social type came into being.

II

What did this class consist of? It was certainly made up of very different elements. Like a newly discovered gold mine the factory system attracted men from all over the country. Such was the case in Lancashire during the years which followed the invention of the spinning jenny. These were years of feverish activity and of limitless ambition. Industry, developing with what in those days seemed incredible rapidity, appeared to progress in a series of bounds: a period of prosperity, during which undertakings were founded and developed and fortunes made in a few years, was followed by disaster. Progress was held up for a moment, but then it again went forward more eagerly than ever. During the seasons of prosperity, one of which set in after Arkwright's patent was cancelled in 1785, who would not

[1] See Part I, chap. I.

have tried his luck? Every man who owned some capital, however small, shopkeepers, carriers, innkeepers, all became cotton-spinners.[1] A few were successful and made a fortune, but many failed and either went back to their old trades or else joined the growing throng of factory workers.

Most of these extemporized manufacturers knew very little of the industry of which they expected so much. In 1803, during an inquiry into the state of the cotton industry, the following question was asked: 'Are manufacturers in general sufficiently acquainted with the process of weaving, to be able to determine a dispute which arises on the badness of the material?' This was the answer: 'No, they are not capable of deciding those disputes that relate to bad materials: the reason of it is, that the master was never acquainted with the art of weaving. He just puts in a man who understands the trade, invests his capital, and when he gets the price of the market, he goes forward.'[2] The manufacturer who thus regarded the part he had to play was almost identical with a merchant entrepreneur. His work was mainly that of a trader, and the essential condition of success for him was to have a good business head, a quality which has nothing to do with technical knowledge.

Here is another significant point. One might expect to find, in this first generation of great manufacturers, the men who by their inventions had started the industrial revolution. But nothing of the sort happened. Arkwright's name immediately suggests itself, but we know that his real achievements were not those of an inventor. Neither Hargreaves, nor Crompton, nor even Cartwright in spite of his repeated efforts,[3] was able to found a great industrial concern. The Darbys are an instance of a family-of manufacturers whose fortunes were built up on a great invention. But it is perhaps the only one in the whole period, and against it we must set the tardy and partial success of Huntsman, and the failure of Cort. It is true that James Watt directed the Soho factory and was both a scientific genius and one of the foremost manufacturers in England. But in that respect he certainly owed much to his partner Matthew Boulton. This seems to point to the conclusion that the improvement in the means of production brought about by inventors mainly profited business men, and that the

[1] See Edwin Butterworth, *History of Oldham*, p. 178. Examples: Arkwright the barber, Yates the innkeeper, partner of the second Peel. See W. Cooke Taylor, *Life and Times of Sir Robert Peel*, I, 6.

[2] *Minutes of the Evidence taken before the Committee to whom the several Petitions presented to the House in this Session, relating to the Act of the 39th and 40th year of His present Majesty for settling Disputes between Masters and Workmen engaged in the Cotton Manufacture, were referred* (1803), p. 26.

[3] On Cartwright's undertakings, see *Memoir of Edmund Cartwright*, pp. 115, 119, 133, etc.

nineteenth-century industrialists were simply the successors of the merchant manufacturers of the eighteenth. No conclusion would be more plausible, for the merchant manufacturers by possessing themselves of the raw material and of part of the equipment, and by gradually forcing the small independent producer into the position of a mere wage-earner, had already advanced half-way towards the factory system. The theory thus expounded is very tempting because it seems to leave nothing unexplained;[1] but it would be unwise to accept it unreservedly.

In the woollen industry, the districts where the supremacy of commercial capital was most clearly marked were those in the east and the south-west, in Norfolk, Devonshire, Wiltshire and Somerset. It would therefore seem natural, according to the above theory, that the first wool-spinning mills and weaving sheds should have been put up in those counties, and that development in the north where production was still distributed among many small men, should have been slower. But just the contrary actually took place, and it was in Yorkshire, side by side with a still vigorous cottage industry, that the factory system first made its appearance. Apart from the general causes which forced the industrial centres to shift from the south towards the north of England we must also reckon with the difficulties involved in changing from one economic system to another, even when the latter appears to be the natural outcome of the former. Between their logical relationship and the actual change from one to the other, there is room for every kind of resistance which self-interest and prejudice can suggest. The merchant manufacturers, accustomed as they were to the methods their fathers had used before them, found it hard to change. The outlay in equipment and building demanded by a factory frightened them.[2] Why should they incur such heavy charges when they could, or thought they could, earn just as much with less expense and fewer risks? The distance between them and the captains of industry was not great, but they never thought it worth their while to cover it. They soon had to bear the consequences of their timidity.

It was therefore not exclusively from these men that the class of manufacturers was recruited, even though the distance between them was so small. Especially in districts such as Lancashire and Yorkshire, where there was no transition between domestic industry and the factory system, we must look elsewhere for the origins of that class.

[1] On this question see Held's very judicious remarks, *Zwei Bücher zur socialen Geschichte Englands*, p. 566: 'Every commercial capitalist, whether he understands the technical side of his business or not, is always a trader. It is trade which decides what commodities shall be produced, where they shall be produced and how they shall be produced.'

[2] See *Report from the Select Committee on the State of the Woollen Manufacture* (1806), p. 11.

The best way to arrive at a complete solution of this problem would be to set out one by one the genealogies of all the manufacturers of this period. This can be done at any rate in a few cases, and one fact of general significance at once emerges. Many of them, particularly in the cotton industry, were of country stock and came of that semi-agricultural, semi-industrial class which up to that time had formed a large part, perhaps more than one-half, of the population of England. And, if we go further back still, we often arrive at the peasant stock, at the old race of yeomen, now hidden though not extinct.

The Peel family is a striking instance. The father of the Prime Minister, Sir Robert Peel, was a cotton-spinner and manufacturer of printed calicoes at Bury in Lancashire. He died in 1830 and left a substantial fortune made entirely in the cotton industry.[1] The grandfather, born in 1723,[2] was a manufacturer, one of Arkwright's first imitators and competitors.[3] Before he became a spinner he used to sell woollen stuffs and hand-printed cottons, which he had begun by manufacturing himself in his own house.[4] At the same time he farmed land which had been in his family's possession since the fifteenth century, for the Peels had been for many generations peasant proprietors, of that comfortable yeoman class which was 'too high for the office of constable, too low for that of sheriff'.[5] From farmers they became both farmers and weavers, and were gradually drawn into industry. It was only in 1750 that the first Robert Peel finally left the country for the town.

The Peel family were particularly befriended by fortune, for their wealth and social rank grew steadily, and they never experienced any of those ordeals which befell many yeomen families when divorced from their native soil and from the life they had lived for centuries. For many people the industrial revolution presented itself as an opportunity for advancement after a difficult period. William Radcliffe, born in 1761 in the village of Mellor, came of a family of landed proprietors who had once been among the wealthiest in the parish. Their downfall began with the civil wars of 1642-9, and was completed

---

[1] His personal estate came to £1,400,000, on which more duties were paid than in any previous case. See *Gentleman's Magazine*, 1830, I, 557-8. On the life of the first Sir Robert Peel, see W. Cooke Taylor, *Life and Times of Sir Robert Peel*, I, 6 ff.; Sir Lawrence Peel, *A Sketch of the Life and Character of Sir Robert Peel*, p. 33; F. Espinasse, *Lancashire Worthies*, II, 84-7.

[2] Espinasse, op. cit., II, 52. Thus he was Arkwright's contemporary, born in 1732, a few years after him.

[3] His first spinning mills were at Altham and then in 1779 at Burton-on-Trent. J. Wheeler, *Manchester*, p. 519. Sir Lawrence Peel, op. cit., p. 20.

[4] One of these was a pattern of parsley, which earned him the nickname of 'Parsley Peel'. Espinasse, op. cit., II, 67.

[5] Sir Lawrence Peel, op. cit., p. 6.

by the Enclosure Acts and the ensuing growth of large estates.[1] The Radcliffes took to weaving as a means of earning their living. While still quite a child William learned carding and spinning in the family workshop, where his father and brothers were weaving. As soon as his legs were long enough he was set down to a loom.[2] He has left a description of his first start in modern industry: 'Availing myself of the improvements that came out while I was in my teens, by the time I was married (at the age of 24, in 1785), with my little savings, and a practical knowledge of every process from the cotton-bag to the piece of cloth, such as carding by hand or by the engine, spinning by the hand-wheel or jenny, winding, warping, sizing, looming the web, and weaving either by hand or fly-shuttle, I was ready to commence business for myself; and by the year 1789 I was well established, and employed many hands both in spinning and weaving, as a master manufacturer.'[3] By 1801 he was giving work to over a thousand weavers.[4]

If further instances are wanted we shall quote that of Joshua Fielden, who in 1780 was still living as a peasant in his native village of Todmorden.[5] He owned and farmed the family holding, but the best part of his income came from the two or three looms set up in his house. He sold the cloth himself from time to time in the Halifax market. Meanwhile, the development of the cotton industry began to make a stir in the district. Fielden bought some jennies and set up work in three small cottages, where his nine children made up the whole of the labour supply. By the end of the century this embryo spinning mill had turned into a five-storey factory.[6] Jedediah Strutt, one of Arkwright's first partners, was the son of a small landed proprietor and was a farmer until he set up at Derby as a stocking manufacturer.[7] As a child, David Dale used to look after the cattle at Stewarton in Ayrshire.[8] Isaac Dobson, who founded one of the great cotton-spinning firms of Lanca-

---

[1] W. Radcliffe, *Origin of the New System of Manufacture, commonly called 'Power Loom Weaving'*, p. 9.

[2] Ibid., and Bennet Woodcroft, *Brief Biographies of Inventors*, p. 32.

[3] W. Radcliffe, op. cit., p. 10: 'After the practical experience of a few years, any young man who was industrious and careful might then from his earnings as a weaver lay by sufficient to set him up as a manufacturer, and, though but few of the great body of weavers had the courage to embark in the attempt, I was one of those few.'

[4] Ibid., p. 16.

[5] Between Rochdale and Halifax. *Fortunes made in Business*, I, 414-18.

[6] John Fielden, one of his sons, was a member of Parliament. He was one of the leaders in the campaign for factory legislation, and the author of a book with the significant title of *The Curse of the Factory System* (1836).

[7] W. Felkin, *A History of the Machine-wrought Hosiery and Lace Manufactures*, p. 89.

[8] R. Dale Owen, *Threading My Way*, p. 2. Dale seems to have belonged rather to cottager than to yeoman stock.

shire, was the youngest child of an old yeoman family, established in Westmorland since the fourteenth century.[1]

Among the successful ironmasters many came from small local workshops: 'Aaron Walker was a nailer; William Hawks of Newcastle and John Parker of Staffordshire began their industrial life as blacksmiths; Peter Stubs, the founder of the well-known firm at Rotherham, was originally a filemaker and innkeeper at Warrington; Spencer, who held Barnby Furnace in Yorkshire, began as a maker of hay-rakes; and George Newton of Thorncliffe was a maker of spades and shovels ... To steel-making came Benjamin Huntsman from the manufacture of clocks ... Samuel Garbett began life as a brass worker; Roebuck's father was a manufacturer of small wares in Sheffield ... Reynolds was the son of an iron merchant of Bristol ... '[2] But a further inquiry into the origins of their families would more than once bring us back to the country and the peasant class. John Wilkinson's father, Isaac Wilkinson, was a Lake District farmer who became the foreman of a neighbouring ironworks at 12s. a week.[3] Richard Crawshay, later known as the Iron King, came of farming stock. Their farms at Normanton near Leeds probably did not yield enough to feed all the children, for young Richard was very early packed off as an apprentice to a London hardware manufacturer.[4] Henry Darby, the father of the first Abraham, was a locksmith, but about 1670 John Darby, the ancestor of the Coalbrookdale dynasty, was a farmer in a Worcestershire village.[5] The Boulton family came from the essentially agricultural county of Northampton. Impoverishment obliged them to move to Lichfield and then to Birmingham, where they went into industry.[6]

In the industrial districts the yeomanry had no need to move. Its transformation took place on the spot. Until the middle of the eighteenth century Oldham was surrounded by farms which the freeholders occupied and worked. Fifty years later the same families were at the head of the town's chief manufactures. The Lees, Broadbents, Hiltons, Taylors, who had become spinners, and the Boultons and Joneses, who were working the coal mines, were all yeomen or the sons of yeomen.[7] Here we see actually at work a process which in many cases can only be guessed at.

[1] B. P. Dobson, *The Story of the Evolution of the Spinning Machine*, p. 88.

[2] T. S. Ashton, *Iron and Steel in the Industrial Revolution*, p. 210.

[3] A. N. Palmer, *John Wilkinson and the Old Bersham Iron Works*, p. 7. Cf. J. Lord, *Capital and Steam-Power*, p. 26.

[4] S. Smiles, *Industrial Biography*, p. 130. J. Lloyd, *Early History of the Old South Wales Iron Works*, pp. 63 ff.

[5] Percy, *Iron and Steel*, p. 887.

[6] *Dictionary of National Biography*, article 'Boulton'.

[7] Edwin Butterworth, *History of Oldham*, pp. 33, 40, 42, 47, 53, 57, 61, 125, 130.

We have shown above how the redistribution of the land, the dividing up of common land and the engrossing of farms, had altered the condition of the country people. We have tried to explain the decline of the yeoman class, and we are now beginning to realize what became of them. They provided building materials, so to speak, for the construction of a new class. For when the traditional alliance between small holdings and home industry, on which their very existence was based, broke down, they instinctively turned to the side which seemed to offer the best opportunities. The industrial revolution opened up a new career for unemployed energy, and the most enterprising or the luckiest yeomen entered it in a spirit of adventure and conquest.

As soon as their fortunes were made they hastened to become landowners again. They bought land from the gentry who had previously looked down on them, and old historic homes became their country seats. Or else they would build near them lordly residences, monuments to their new wealth and their ancient pride.[1]

III

Such a transformation cannot be effected without difficulties. It comes about through a stern process of weeding out, which only allows the fittest to survive. To succeed, these village agriculturists, blacksmiths, weavers and barbers who made up the first generation of great English manufacturers, must have possessed in a high degree certain qualities fitting them for their new task, and these qualities, which they had in common, gave them a certain mutual likeness. Their distinguishing feature was not inventiveness but a gift for turning other people's inventions to practical results. They were not all, like Arkwright, lucky or audacious enough to take complete possession of them and to secure a monopoly protected by patent rights. But following the dictates of self-interest they worked untiringly to reduce the inventor's legitimate rights to nothing. This conduct, questionable though human enough, is abundantly illustrated by the behaviour of

[1] Robert Peel in 1797 bought Drayton Manor (F. Espinasse, *Lancashire Worthies*, II, 95). Arkwright and his sons made their home in Willersley Castle: 'Smedley Hall was once the seat and property of the last of the family of Cheethams of Cheetham. It is now owned by James Hilton esq ... Ordsall Hall was once owned by a family of Ratcliff. This moated mansion is now occupied by Mr Richard Alsop ... Ancoats Hall, a very ancient building in wood and plaster, but in some parts rebuilt with brick and stone, is now occupied by William Rawlinson esq., an eminent merchant in Manchester.' J. Aikin, *Description of the Country round Manchester*, pp. 207, 208, 211.

The same is true of the Wedgwoods, farmers and potters at the same time. See Eliza Meteyard, *Josiah Wedgwood*, I, 180-5.

the spinners to Hargreaves and Crompton,[1] of the ironmasters to Henry Cort,[2] and by the innumerable lawsuits Boulton and Watt had to bring against those who used their engines.[3] We must, however, not exaggerate the incompetence of these manufacturers in technical matters, since it was by no means general. Even though they were not the originators of any important invention, yet several of them introduced improvements of great practical value. Strutt invented a special device in the knitting-frame for making ribbed stockings.[4] John Wilson of Ainsworth introduced several new processes for dyeing and finishing cotton goods.[5] William Radcliffe, with the help of Thomas Johnson, one of his workmen, invented the dressing machine.[6] Arkwright himself could claim to have skilfully combined other people's inventions and to have obtained practical results where they had failed.

The manufacturer's distinctive quality was that of an organizer. He had first to raise the necessary capital, for men who had no need to borrow money, like Matthew Boulton or Roebuck, the sons of already wealthy manufacturers, were quite exceptional. But investors were not easy to find, especially at first, while machinery and factories were still looked upon unfavourably as novelties with no certain future. Arkwright knew extremely well how to bring off these difficult negotiations: the reader will remember the successive partnerships on which he rose to fortune. Moreover, he did really give something in return for the money lent to him, namely his patents, the value of which soon became unquestionable. But those men who had neither patents nor capital were in a much worse position. They had to begin in a very small way, with no capital but their own savings. Radcliffe thus began, in 1785, with the money that he had saved out of his weaver's wages;[7] Kennedy, previously apprenticed to a Manchester cotton-spinner, in 1791 started a workshop where, having only two men to help him, he worked with his own hands.[8] In the textile industry these very modest beginnings were not at all uncommon. For they were made easy by the simplicity of the equipment then required. It cost little to set up, in any house, a few mules or jennies worked by hand. The more elaborate machines, the water frames or power looms, came later, as soon as profits had made it possible. And with those machines came water power or steam, the use of the heavy and high-power plant of the factory proper. Thus within a short period a single

---

[1] See Part II, chap. I, and chap. II.

[2] Ibid., chap. III.

[3] Ibid., chap. IV.

[4] W. Felkin, op. cit., pp. 91-3.

[5] See *A Complete History of the Cotton Trade*, pp. 71-3.

[6] W. Radcliffe, op. cit., pp. 20-3.

[7] Ibid., p. 10.

[8] S. Smiles, *Industrial Biography*, p. 321.

undertaking would pass through every stage from domestic industry to 'manufacture', and from 'manufacture' to the factory system. After the first few years some of the men who had been trained as managers in the early cotton mills began to rise to the position of manufacturers, with the advantage of practical experience.[1]

Once the problems of capital and plant had been solved, that of labour arose. How was it to be recruited and governed? Men used to working at home were generally not inclined to go to the factory. In the early days factory labour consisted of the most ill-assorted elements: country people driven from their villages by the growth of large estates, disbanded soldiers, paupers, the scum of every class and of every occupation.[2] All these unskilled men, unused to collective work, had to be taught, trained, and above all disciplined by the manufacturer. He had so to speak to turn them into a human machine, as regular in its working, as accurate in its movements, and as exactly combined for a single purpose as the mechanism of wood and metal to which they became accessory. Hard-and-fast rules replaced the freedom of the small workshops. Work started, meals were eaten and work stopped at fixed hours, notified by the ringing of a bell.[3] Within the factory each had his allotted place and his strictly defined and invariable duty. Everyone had to work steadily and without stopping, under the vigilant eye of a foreman who secured obedience by means of fines or dismissals, and sometimes by more brutal forms of coercion.[4] This discipline was not altogether a new thing. It had been enforced for many years in a few workshops where extreme division of labour had for its counterpart a strong central management.[5] Now the introduction of machinery

---

[1] G. Taylor's 'Handloom Weavers at Stockport' in G. Unwin, *Samuel Oldknow and the Arkwrights*, p. 51. See the striking account by Robert Owen of his work as manager in Drinkwater's cotton mill (*The Life of Robert Owen, written by Himself*, p. 39).

[2] Schulze-Gaevernitz, *La Grande Industrie*, p. 67. In the calico-printing factories 'herds of Lancashire boors' were engaged for very low wages, *The Callico Printers' Assistant* (1790), Q. 4.

[3] In Manchester, the bells of the spinning mills began to ring at half-past four in the morning. *Minutes of the Evidence taken before the Select Committee on the State of the Children employed in the Manufactories of the United Kingdom* (1816), pp. 127-8. The Wedgwood factory was the first important establishment in Staffordshire to use a bell to notify the starting and closing times. It was known in the neighbourhood as 'The Bell Works'. S. Smiles, *Josiah Wedgwood*, p. 44; Eliza Meteyard, *Josiah Wedgwood*, I, 330; Ll. Jewitt, *The Wedgwoods*, I, 132.

[4] See Part III, chap. IV.

[5] In the Royal Manufactories of France. See Germain Martin, *La Grande Industrie en France sous le règne de Louis XIV*, p. 14 (Manufacture of cloth at Villenouvette in Languedoc). Thus at Abbeville under Van Robais, who employed 600 workmen: 'All the employed are governed with great decorum and regularity. They all come to work and leave it at the beat of a drum. If a workman gets fuddled or commits any offence, he is suspended his work by the foreman of the branch to which he belongs,

made the enforcement of strict discipline an absolute necessity. The great manufacturers of the eighteenth century did not initiate the system, but they organized it with remarkable intelligence and energy. Here again Arkwright is our outstanding example.[1] His most original achievement was the discipline he established in his mills. He made his presence felt everywhere, watching his men and obtaining from them the steadiest and most careful work. Although rough in his behaviour and speech, and pitiless to those whom he considered inefficient or careless, yet he did not make the mistake of overworking his employees. The working day in his factories did not exceed twelve hours,[2] at a time when the average in factories set up after his was fourteen hours or more.[3]

The management of a factory means government, and the manufacturer is in every sense of the word a captain of industry. In the Soho factory, Boulton's workmen were trained to such regularity that any break in the usual steady noise of wheels and hammers was said to be enough to warn him of a stoppage or an accident.[4] Boswell, who came to see him in 1776, was much impressed by his power. As he vividly expressed it, he saw him as 'an Iron Captain in the midst of his troops'. Wedgwood the potter, when he tried to enforce a strictly regulated division of labour in his workshops, had to fight not only the ill-will but the open hostility of his workpeople. He succeeded, however, in breaking down all opposition.[5] The high quality of his wares, which made his trade-mark famous throughout the world, was only achieved by his tireless energy together with his constant supervision of every detail. He stumped about everywhere on his wooden leg, breaking with his own hand any pot which showed the least flaw, and chalking on the careless workman's bench: 'This won't do for Josiah Wedgwood.'[6]

Lastly, the producer was brought face to face with a problem which the small manufacturer had hardly needed to consider at all: the

---

[1] This is one of the main reasons for the excessive praise which was lavished on him by the individualistic school of the following generation. 'To devise and administer a successful code of factory discipline, suited to the necessities of factory diligence, was the Herculean enterprise, the noble achievement of Arkwright.' A. Ure, *Philosophy of Manufactures*, p. 15.

[2] *Minutes of Evidence ... on the State of the Children employed in the Manufactories*, etc. (1816). Evidence of A. Buchanan, p. 8.

[3] Ibid., pp. 96-8.

[4] S. Smiles, *Boulton and Watt*, p. 482.

[5] Eliza Meteyard, *Josiah Wedgwood*, I, 260.

[6] S. Smiles, *Josiah Wedgwood*, p. 145.

---

every branch being under the conduct of a distinct foreman, who disciplines the workmen so as to make them excel in every branch of the whole.' *An Essay on Trade and Commerce*, p. 131 (1770).

problem of markets. The large-scale manufacturer could not, as his predecessor had done, take his goods for sale to the nearest town. The local demand was much too small, and even that of the entire home market was scarcely sufficient to absorb the ever-growing supply. If he was not a born trader he had to become one, and learn how to extend his connections over the whole country and beyond. We have been able to look through the correspondence of a great industrial firm of the eighteenth century: the Soho establishment. It reveals a commercial activity in many ways comparable to that of a first-class modern firm. Boulton and Watt had business dealings with every manufacturer of their day. Steam engines were supplied to the mine-owners in Cornwall, to the ironmasters of Wales, to the cotton-spinners of Manchester, Derby and Glasgow, and to the potters of Staffordshire. The firm took many orders from France, from Belgium and Holland, Germany, Spain and Russia. It is true that a time came when they had very little to do in order to attract custom. Buyers came of themselves, and accepted their terms without haggling. But at the start matters were very different. The reader will remember their struggles in Cornwall and the help they received from their faithful and indefatigable agent William Murdock.[1] Boulton, and even Watt himself, though his natural pessimism made him a timorous business man, were often obliged not only to negotiate an agreement but to supervise its execution personally.[2] The form of the agreements, which made their profit dependent on the amount of fuel and money the buyer saved by the use of their engine, was very cleverly thought out. Thus their success was due not only to a technical invention but to a commercial system as well.

Thus the manufacturer, being at the same time a capitalist, a works manager and a merchant, set a new pattern of the complete business man. Often enough he was nothing else. Robert Owen, who knew the 'cotton lords', as he called them, better than anyone, had no great opinion of their intelligence outside their particular sphere of activity: 'The manufacturers were generally plodding men of business, with little knowledge and limited ideas, except in their own immediate circle of occupation.'[3] There were, however, a few who besides their practical knowledge and activity had other and higher qualities. In the midst of this aristocracy of wealth, these formed an intellectual élite. Whether we look upon them as original and exceptional people, or as outstanding representatives of their class, they deserve more detailed study.

[1] See Part II, chap. IV.
[2] Watt spent several years in Cornwall. Boulton often visited the industrial districts. Hence the correspondence between the two partners.
[3] Robert Owen, *The Life of Robert Owen, written by Himself*, pp. 31 and 37.

IV

The most interesting among them were those whose professional activity brought them into contact with the scientific or artistic life of their times. Technical problems, which owed their origin to purely practical needs, became linked towards the end of the century to scientific research and speculation. On the other hand, some of the products of industry, pottery for instance, are not only useful things. They have, or at any rate can have, an artistic value as well. A few manufacturers realized this, and their conception of their own occupations was thereby widened and changed. For them industry ceased to be only the means of acquiring wealth and power. When they tried to improve their equipment or their methods of production, it was not only to gain a victory over their less conscientious or less careful competitors. It was also because technical progress, bound up as it was with the development of science and art, seemed to them a desirable end in itself. Such purposes, higher than those of the mass of their rivals, did much to ennoble their lives and characters.

Matthew Boulton was one of them. Even before he became James Watt's not unworthy partner he had given proof of those rare qualities which account for his success. When, about 1765, he undertook the manufacture of ornamental bronzes, he had before him the masterpieces of French decorative art. He determined to equal them, even if it meant forcing the approval of a public used to less refined work.[1] In order to succeed he left no stone unturned. He had copies of some of the finest antique work sent to him from Italy, and visited the private collections of his aristocratic patrons.[2] He made it a point of honour to sell nothing which had not been approved by the most fastidious connoisseurs, and the reader will remember that at one time Wedgwood feared his competition. Twenty-five years later he lavished the same meticulous care on the coining of money by the process he had invented. On that occasion James Watt wrote: 'Had Mr Boulton done nothing more in the world than he has accomplished in improving the coinage, his name would deserve to be immortalized; and if it be considered that this was done in the midst of various other important avocations, and at enormous expense, for which at the time he could have had no certainty of an adequate return, we shall be at a loss whether most to

---

[1] In connection with two of his clocks which had not found a buyer in London, he wrote to his wife: 'I have brought back my two fine clocks, which I will send to a market where common sense is not out of fashion. If I had made the clocks play jigs upon bells, and a dancing bear keeping time, or if I had made a horse-race upon their faces, I believe they would have had better bidders. I shall therefore bring them back to Soho, and some time this summer will send them to the Empress of Russia, who, I believe, would be glad of them.' S. Smiles, *Boulton and Watt*, p. 174.

[2] See Part II, chap. IV.

admire his ingenuity, his perseverance, or his munificence. He has conducted the whole more like a sovereign than a private manufacturer, and the love of fame has always been to him a greater stimulus than the love of gain.'[1]

Boulton was a cultured man, and some of the most distinguished men of the day were his friends: Dr Darwin, who was at the same time a physician, a botanist and a poet; the astronomer William Herschel, Priestley, whose advanced views on religion and government he shared, and Sir Joseph Banks, President of the Royal Society. Others were less famous, for instance Small the chemist, the printer Baskerville, and the Queen's learned librarian de Luc.[2] Boulton liked to invite them to meet in the house he had built for himself close to the Soho factory, 'the inn of friendship on Handsworth Heath', as he used to call it in his private letters. After a time these meetings became periodical, taking place every month at the full moon, so as to make the walk there and back through country lanes easier. For this reason they jokingly called themselves the Lunar Society.[3] Wedgwood sometimes came from Burslem or Etruria.[4] Watt was, of course, one of the most constant members during the years he spent in Birmingham. Each meeting had its agenda, and scientific questions were the most frequent topics. Boulton showed himself quite capable of taking part in the discussion with his guests. His factory was one huge laboratory of applied mechanics, in which he worked as Watt's disciple and emulator. The coining machine was made from his designs. He was the first person to think of tubular boilers,[5] long before they were actually designed and made by the French inventor Marc Séguin. He was deeply interested in the development of chemistry, and made a great number of original experiments.[6] He also dipped into political economy and was made a member of the Society of Economists at St Petersburg.[7] Such studies, far from drawing him away from his industrial work, only fitted him to do it better.

His private correspondence reveals the breadth of his outlook as well as the uprightness of his character. His favourite maxim was Poor Richard's optimistic motto, 'Honesty is the best policy.' With reference to an agreement to be concluded with some of the firm's customers he wrote to his partner James Watt: 'You must not be too

[1] Watt, 'Memoir of Matthew Boulton', in S. Smiles, op. cit., p. 399.

[2] S. Smiles, op. cit., p. 201; S. Timmins, *Matthew Boulton*, p. 4.

[3] S. Smiles, op. cit., pp. 369-75.

[4] Eliza Meteyard, *Josiah Wedgwood*, II, 558. The distance was too great (about 40 miles) for him to be able to attend regularly.

[5] S. Timmins, *Matthew Boulton*, p. 10.

[6] 'Chemistry has for some time been my hobby horse.' Letter to James Watt, July 3rd, 1781, S. Smiles, op. cit., p. 373.

[7] He was also a member of the Royal Societies of London and Edinburgh.

rigid in fixing the dates of payment. A hard bargain is a bad bargain.'
'Patience and candour should mark all our actions, as well as firmness
in being just to ourselves and others.'[1] He completed his children's
liberal education by advice founded on lofty moral principles:
'Remember I do not wish you to be polite at the expense of honour,
truth, sincerity, and honesty, for these are the props of a manly
character, and without them politeness is mean and deceitful. Therefore be always tenacious of your honour. Be honest, just and benevolent,
even when it appears difficult to be so. I say, cherish those principles,
and guard them as sacred treasures.'[2] And he taught them not by
advice only, but by the example of his own life.

He was the implacable foe of all those industrial frauds of which the
Birmingham manufacturers were only too fond. The fight that he put
up against the false coiners is well known: 'I will do anything short of
being common informer against particular persons, to stop the mal-
practices of the Birmingham coiners.'[3] In 1795, at a meeting of manufacturers he spoke against the adulteration of goods: 'I will not
expatiate upon the impolicy, the dishonour and the immorality of the
act itself, nor upon the inevitable consequences that must ensue,
such as ruin to the trade, and disgrace to the name of Birmingham
... Let it be remembered that honesty is the best policy, and that fair
dealing must in the end prove most advantageous both to the town and
to individuals.'[4]

He was personally most scrupulous in these matters. He never used
reprisals against people who tried to entice his men away,[5] and however
keen the competition he never cut his prices below a certain level, for
that would have meant lowering the quality of his goods and thus
destroying the confidence of his customers.[6] Thus he actually put in
practice utilitarian principles before they were formulated by Jeremy
Bentham.

He was famous for his generosity. When Priestley became the victim
of riots occasioned in Birmingham by hatred of the French Revolution,
Boulton, though himself suspected of holding advanced opinions,
headed a subscription list for Priestley, so that he could live and go
on with his work.[7] When the Birmingham dispensary was started in
1792 he became treasurer, saying: 'If the funds of the institution are

[1] Letters to Watt, quoted in S. Smiles, *Boulton and Watt*, p. 271.
[2] Ibid., pp. 340-1 (letter to his eldest son, written from Cornwall).
[3] Ibid., p. 178.
[4] *Birmingham Gazette*, Dec. 28th, 1795.
[5] Letter to J. Taylor, Jan. 23rd, 1769, S. Smiles, op. cit., p. 178.
[6] Ibid., pp. 374-5.
[7] One of the chief subscribers was John Wilkinson, who sent £500. A. N. Palmer,
John Wilkinson and the Old Bersham Iron Works, p. 33. On this subject see S. Timmins's
pamphlet, *Dr Priestley in Birmingham*.

not sufficient for its support, I will make up the deficiency.'[1] As regards his workpeople his attitude was that of an emotional reader of Richardson and Rousseau, rather than of a disciple of those economists in whose eyes labour was only a commodity. A benevolent autocrat, he was loved by his workpeople for his frank and simple ways and for his fair dealing. He kept them with him for many years, and the son often succeeded the father in his employment.[2] As he knew them all personally he took an interest in them. He started a sick club, each man subscribing from a halfpenny to fourpence a week, according to his wage.[3]

Such benevolence and philanthropy were not incompatible with pride. Boulton's attitude was that of a great lord to his retainers. When his eldest son came of age festivities took place at Soho. From early morning the bells were ringing in Handsworth and Birmingham. At one o'clock all the factory hands, headed by music and divided into groups according to their trades, marched by in procession. In the evening 700 of them sat down to a banquet and drank the health of their present and future masters.[4] Thus a wealthy squire in his ancestral seat, surrounded by his tenants, would celebrate the coming of age of his heir. Boulton was well qualified to play the part, for his presence suggested dignity and magnificence, on account of which as much as for his generosity he was sometimes called 'princely' Boulton.[5] A tall man with a prepossessing countenance and eyes lit up by intelligence and kindliness, he had the rare gift of attracting people as well as impressing them.[6] This captain of industry had the qualities of a leader of men. To the material power of capital he added something which always and everywhere makes an aristocrat: he had prestige.

Boulton, the friend of art and science, was above all a manufacturer. But in Wedgwood we have an artist, and, some would main-

---

[1] J. A. Langford, *A Century of Birmingham Life*, II, 143.

[2] They were generally engaged for four or five years on a renewable contract. For instance, a man called Gavin MacMurdo, who entered Boulton and Watt's service in 1793, had his contract renewed in 1796, 1799 and 1810.

[3] Apprentices earning 2s. 6d. a week paid ½d., those who earned 5s. paid 1d., and so on up to those who earned 20s. a week and over, who paid 4d. See *Local Notes and Queries* (Birmingham Central Library), 1885-8, No. 1917, and S. Smiles, op. cit., p. 482.

[4] *Birmingham Gazette*, Aug. 15th, 1791.

[5] Eliza Meteyard, *Josiah Wedgwood*, II, 99-100.

[6] Portrait of Boulton by Sir W. Beechy, R.A., in the front page of S. Smiles's *Boulton and Watt*. There are several other portraits in the Timmins collection in the Birmingham Library. He had a high and rather sloping forehead, curly powdered hair, prominent, clear and expressive eyes, a somewhat protruding nose, a firm mouth with clearly marked corners, broad full cheeks and a fat chin resting on an ample frill.

tain, a great one.[1] True, the delicate masterpieces which bear his name are not the work of one man. The figures on them were designed and executed by a whole body of painters, sculptors and decorators who worked for him and under his orders.[2] But even those pieces which he did not touch himself bore the stamp of his personality. For he had decided on their shape, colour and decoration, and had given them a style of their own in keeping with the classical taste of his day. The very material of which they were made was his creation: earthenware with bright, unfading glaze, or with dull black or red surfaces, biscuit wares of pale green, blue or purple, upon which white designs stood out like cameos. The beauty of that material would alone be enough to justify Wedgwood's claim to artistic fame.[3]

Wedgwood was a self-educated man. Apprenticed to his elder brother Thomas at the age of nine,[4] he used the leisure provided by illness to educate himself.[5] At thirty he had read many books, and kept himself informed of the latest productions. He was one of the first English readers of Rousseau's *Émile*,[6] and it was through books that he learnt to know the arts of Greece and Rome. Caylus's *Collection of Egyptian, Etruscan, Greek, Roman and Gallic Antiquities*, which came to his

[1] Novalis compared his work to that of Goethe: 'Goethe's poetry is a quite practical one. He is in his books like the English artist in his pottery, simple, neat, convenient and lasting. He did for German literature what Wedgwood did for English art.' Quoted by W. E. Gladstone, *Wedgwood, An Address delivered at Burslem, Staffordshire,* Oct. 26th, 1863, p. 5.

[2] John Bacon, John Voyez, Coward, Stothard, Hackwood, Stringer, Burdett, Mrs Wilcox, etc. See Eliza Meteyard, *J. Wedgwood*, I, 493; II, 65, 84, 89, 91, 170, 233, and K. E. Farrer's edition of the *Correspondence of Josiah Wedgwood*. Flaxman was also one of Wedgwood's collaborators. Ibid., II, 321.

[3] Here is a list of the chief kinds of material used in Etruria in 1776: (1) 'Queen's pottery', cream colour with glazed surface; (2) 'Terra cotta', dull red colour like some Japanese pottery; (3) 'Basalt', black like some vases found in Etruria; (4) 'Jasper', a background of various colours, azure, pale blue, green or mauve, ornamented with white medallions, garlands, etc. – this was Wedgwood's most original idea, and the one which has been most admired and imitated; (5) 'Bamboo', brown with fluted surfaces; (6) 'Biscuit', white, of a hard texture. The chief collection of Wedgwood's works is at the Wedgwood Museum, Stoke-on-Trent.

[4] On the death of his father, a Burslem potter. S. Smiles, *Josiah Wedgwood*, p. 24; Eliza Meteyard, op. cit., I, 219-22. According to Ll. Jewitt, *The Wedgwoods*, p. 89, he only started work at eleven. In any case his early education was very limited: in fact 'scarcely any person in Burslem learned more than mere reading and writing'. Shaw, *History of the Staffordshire Potteries*, p. 180. Cf. Frances Julia Wedgwood, *Personal Life of Josiah Wedgwood* (1915).

[5] In 1742 he had smallpox, and after that had constant trouble with one leg, which was finally amputated in 1768.

[6] Letter to his partner Bentley, dated Oct. 26th, 1762: 'If you have seen Rousseau's *Émile*, I should be glad to know your thoughts of that piece, and now it is translated, I should be glad by your recommendation to purchase it.' Wedgwood Museum, Stoke-on-Trent.

notice in 1767,[1] first gave him the idea of making those copies which after some time led to his most original creations. His new factory, built in 1769 a little way out of Burslem, he called Etruria, and all the pieces made on the opening day were engraved with the motto 'Artes Etruriæ renascuntur'.[2] He corresponded with many literary men and archæologists, particularly with Sir William Hamilton, the English Ambassador at Naples, whose collections were then famous.[3] Wedgwood's letter to him dealing with the arrival in London of the Barberini vase, now in the Gallery of Gems in the British Museum, shows a high degree of culture and a finely tempered critical sense.[4]

His study of the art of antiquity was closely bound up with his industrial activities, and the same was true of his chemical investigations which he carried very far. Starting from results obtained in his own furnaces, from combinations which resulted in the evolution of new clays and which determined or modified their colours, he was gradually drawn into the investigation of more general questions. His whole soul was in it: 'The fox hunter does not enjoy more pleasure from the chase than I do from the prosecution of my experiments.'[5] His work on the measurement of high temperatures and his invention of the pyrometer are his chief claims to scientific reputation.[6] He was made a member of the Royal Society at the same time as Priestley, whom he had known for many years, and whose genius he had been one of the first to discover.[7]

---

[1] Eliza Meteyard, op. cit., I, 480. About the same time he also saw the collection of plates published by Sir William Hamilton.

[2] These pots, several of which may be seen in the above-mentioned collections, are also engraved with the following inscription: 'June XIII, MDCCLXIX, one of the first day's productions at Etruria in Staffordshire by Wedgwood and Bentley.'

[3] On June 8th, 1773, Sir William Hamilton wrote to Wedgwood that he was sending him drawings of the finest vases in the collection of the Grand Duke of Tuscany; a month after (July 6th, 1773) he sent him a long letter on the study of Greek and Etruscan models. Wedgwood Museum, Stoke-on-Trent.

[4] Letter to Sir William Hamilton, Jan. 24th, 1786. The Barberini vase is today better known as the Portland vase. Wedgwood made some very fine copies of it in jasper ware. (The original is made of opaque glass.)

[5] S. Smiles, Josiah Wedgwood, p. 90.

[6] Communications to the Royal Society: 'The Pyrometer or Heat-measuring Instrument', Philosophical Transactions, LXXII, 305 (1782); 'Attempt to Compare and Combine with the Pyrometer the common Mercurial Thermometer', ibid., LXXIV, 358 (1784); supplementary observations on the same subject, ibid., LXXVI, 390 (1786). Wedgwood's papers show that he had been occupied with many other researches. On his Commonplace Book and his Memorandum Book, see S. Smiles, op. cit., pp. 181-2. The British Museum (Add. MSS. 28309 to 28318) contains nine manuscript volumes of extracts from the proceedings of the Royal Academy of Science at Upsala, made by him or for him.

[7] Letter from Wedgwood to Bentley on electrotyping, Oct. 9th, 1776, Wedgwood Museum, Stoke-on-Trent.

He was very open-minded, and showed great independence both in thought and language. Like Boulton and Wilkinson he held democratic views. The American war filled him with violent indignation against the Government: 'Somebody should be made to say distinctly what has been the object of the present most wicked and preposterous war with our brethren and best friends ... I am glad that America is free, and rejoice most sincerely that it is so, and the pleasing idea of a refuge being provided for those who choose rather to flee from, than to submit to, the iron hand of tyranny, has raised much hilarity in my mind.'[1] The French Revolution won his sympathy from the first. 'Politicians here say that we shall have no cause to rejoice of this Revolution; for if the French become a free people like ourselves, they will immediately apply themselves to the extension of manufactures and soon become more formidable rivals to us than it was possible for them to do under a despotic government. For my own part I should be glad to see so near neighbours partake of the same blessing with ourselves, and indeed should rejoice to see English liberty and security spread over the face of the earth, without being over-anxious about the effects they might have upon our manufactures or commerce, for I should be very loth to believe that an event so happy for mankind in general could be so injurious to us in particular.'[2] Like his partner Thomas Bentley,[3] he took an active part in the anti-slavery campaign. He was an early member of the Society for the Abolition of Slavery and made the Society's seal, the design of which became its regular emblem.[4]

Philanthropy was fashionable, but for many manufacturers it ended on the threshold of the factory. Their sympathy with the negroes in the colonies, which indeed cost them very little, entirely exhausted their fount of human kindness: but imputations of this kind could not be made against Wedgwood. Although he was sometimes at strife with his men[5]

---

[1] Letter to Bentley, March 3rd, 1778, Wedgwood Museum, Stoke-on-Trent.

[2] Letter to Eden, July 5th, 1789. This sets forth the principle that the real interests of nations are fundamentally identical, which lies at the basis of the whole of Adam Smith's political economy and of Bentham's utilitarian philosophy. It is a well-known fact that English radicalism has developed out of utilitarianism. See E. Halévy, *La Jeunesse de Bentham*, pp. 159-60.

[3] On Thomas Bentley, see Eliza Meteyard, *Josiah Wedgwood*, I, 469-73; II, 15-16 and 415-16; Ll. Jewitt, *The Wedgwoods*, pp. 195 ff. Bentley was a very intelligent man. For many years a contributor to the *Monthly Review*, and the founder of the Warrington Academy, his chief concern was the commercial side of the business. It was he who managed the shop in Greek Street, London.

[4] The seal represented a chained negro in a supplicating attitude, with the device 'Am I not a man and a brother?'

[5] For instance in 1772, when, after a period of over-production, he tried to reduce hours and wages. Letter from Wedgwood to Bentley, Sept. 8th, 1772, Wedgwood Museum, Stoke-on-Trent.

he always behaved towards them as an enlightened and liberal-minded man. Like Boulton at Soho he set up a sick club at Etruria. He also opened a library there and contributed largely to the cost of establishing schools in the district.[1] He never forgot that he too had worked with his hands, and that when he came of age his whole capital had consisted of twenty pounds left him by his father, the Burslem master potter.[2]

In the care he lavished on the manufacture of his pottery he showed the scrupulousness of the artist combined with the judgment of the business man. With even more reason he preached the same gospel as Boulton: 'Though an ordinary piece of goods for common use is always dearer than the best of the kind, yet an ordinary and tasteless piece of ornament is not only dear at any price, but absolutely useless and ridiculous.'[3] Far from fearing competition he welcomed it, if he felt it would help art or the public: 'So far from being afraid of other people getting our patterns, we should glory in it, throw out all the hints we can, and if possible have all the artists in Europe working after our models. This would be noble, and would suit both our dispositions and sentiments much better than all the narrow mercenary selfish trammels.'[4] He steadfastly refused to take out any patent, except on one occasion when he thought he had rediscovered the secret of encaustic painting, which had been lost since ancient times.[5]

This disinterestedness, which his consciousness of superiority over most of his competitors made an easy matter for him, did not prevent him from doing good business. He did not make only expensive museum pieces but manufactured goods for the everyday market, which sold in large quantities. He provided all Europe with table china: 'In travelling from Paris to St Petersburg, from Amsterdam to the farthest point of Sweden, from Dunkirk to the southern extremity of France, one is served at every inn from English earthenware. The same fine article adorns the tables of Spain, Portugal, and Italy; it provides the cargoes of ships to the East Indies, the West Indies, and the American continent.'[6] As early as 1763 the Burslem workshops exported over

[1] See Shaw, *History of the Staffordshire Potteries*, pp. 193-4.

[2] Ll. Jewitt, *The Wedgwoods*, pp. 90-1 (Testament of Thomas Wedgwood, June 26th, 1739). Josiah Wedgwood, at his death, left large landed property and about £240,000 in personal estate. Ibid., pp. 413-20.

[3] 1774 *Catalogue*, at the end.

[4] Letter from Wedgwood to Bentley, Sept. 27th, 1769. He did not, however, like people trying to spy out his methods of production. See letter to Nicholson, Oct. 25th, 1785, on foreign spies.

[5] 'A patent for the purpose of ornamenting earthen and porcelain ware with a peculiar species of encaustic painting of various colours, in imitation of the ancient Etruscan and Roman earthenware' (No. 939).

[6] Faujas de Saint-Fond, *Voyage en Angleterre, en Ecosse et aux Iles Hébrides*, I, 112.

550,000 articles.[1] Even while planning his best artistic creations Wedgwood was thinking of industrial processes which should open new and boundless markets to his industry: 'I have a fine letter to answer by this post from my good old friend Paul Elers esq., who has cut out a trifling job for me, which, when I engage in, will lift me as far above intaglios, cameos and such trifling trinkets as certain steam engines have lifted a good friend of ours above his watch-chain and sleeve-button business ... The business is not less than making earthen water pipes, for London first and then for all the world.'[2] Shortly after he started the manufacture of earthenware drains and water pipes,[3] which developed on such an immense scale that it became later one of the great industries of the country.

The prosperity of the district known today as 'the Potteries' dates from the days of Wedgwood's inventions and undertakings. When he was born there in 1730 the country was poor and backward. A clay soil discouraged agriculture and scarcely fed a thinly scattered population. The roads were few, and so bad that goods had to be carried on men's shoulders. There were no towns, only a few villages of thatched cottages. There were some fifty potters at Burslem and seven at Hanley, while Stoke consisted of less than ten houses.[4] Nevertheless, the local industry had improved a little since the middle of the seventeenth century. Salt glaze, introduced about 1690 by German potters, the brothers Elers,[5] and the combination of calcined silicate with plastic clay used for the first time by Astbury[6] about 1720, had opened the way for improvements. Side by side with the heavy coarse stoneware and clumsy earthenware decorated with trivial designs,[7] more delicate if not more artistic products were making their appearance, such as white porcelains and imitation marble, agate and tortoiseshell, which were used for the lids of snuff-boxes and the handles of knives. But the

[1] Letter from Josiah Wedgwood to John Wedgwood, Feb. 19th, 1765. 'The bulk of our production goes to foreign markets ... The principal of these markets are the continent and islands of North America.' Letter to Sir W. Meredith, March 2nd, 1765, John Rylands Library, Manchester.

[2] Wedgwood to Bentley, Oct. 20th, 1779, John Rylands Library, Manchester.

[3] See Arthur Young's letter of Nov. 6th, 1786, in connection with drain pipes supplied by Wedgwood. John Rylands Library, Manchester.

[4] Shaw, *History of the Staffordshire Potteries*, pp. 4 ff.; J. Ward, *The Borough of Stoke-upon-Trent*, p. 42; Eliza Meteyard, op. cit., I, 106. Until 1750 Burslem had only five shops. In 1740 the post was an old woman who came every Sunday from Newcastle-under-Lyme.

[5] On the Elers, see Ll. Jewitt, *The Ceramic Art of Great Britain*, I, 100 ff. The collections referred to above contain good specimens of their red pottery, which is not unlike some of the Japanese.

[6] See the traditional story of this invention in A. Anderson's *An Historical and Chronological Deduction of the Origin of Commerce*, IV, 698-9.

[7] As for instance the sample in the Bateman collection reproduced in Eliza Meteyard, op. cit., I, 117.

organization of the industry was still very primitive, for it was a domestic industry pure and simple. The largest workshops only employed about half a dozen men.[1] One man shaped the pots, another made the handles and put them on, whilst the others did the decoration, the glazing and the firing. But they were none of them specialists, for a good workman had to know everything and to be able to turn his hand to anything. The Staffordshire potters were poor and ignorant. Their habits were brutal and they delighted in cock-fights and bull-fights. When John Wesley preached to them for the first time they pelted him with mud.[2]

In a very few years, thanks to the growth of the industry of which Wedgwood was the principal creator, to improvements in the roads and to the building of the Mersey-Trent Canal, the whole face of the country was altered. Large towns had grown up round the factories built by Wedgwood and his rivals,[3] and had gradually spread until they became 'one large scattered town'.[4] The fame of the Staffordshire potteries, due entirely to Wedgwood, had resulted in a great addition to the wealth and well-being of the district. The great potter, speaking to a new generation of inhabitants, could justly say: 'I would request you to ask your parents for a description of the country we inhabit when they first knew it; and they will tell you that the inhabitants bore all the marks of poverty to a much greater degree than they do now. Their houses were miserable huts, the lands poorly cultivated and yielded little of value for the food of man or beast, and these disadvantages, with roads almost impassable, might be said to have cut off our part of the country from the rest of the world, besides rendering it not very comfortable to ourselves. Compare this picture, which I know to be a true one, with the present state of the same country, the workmen earning near double their former wages, their houses mostly new and comfortable, and the lands, roads, and every other circumstance bearing evident marks of the most pleasing and rapid improvements ... Industry has been the parent of this happy change.'[5] Without speaking of himself Wedgwood was glorifying his

[1] J. Ward, *The Borough of Stoke-upon-Trent*, p. 46; Shaw, op. cit., p. 166; S. Smiles, *Josiah Wedgwood*, p. 173. Wedgwood's grandfather employed six workmen, whom he paid at the rate of 4 to 6 shillings a week.

[2] John Wesley, *Journal*, II, 500. (Everyman's Library.)

[3] Among others, Spode of Stoke-on-Trent, who according to Aikin was the first man to use the steam engine to crush the silica used in English pottery. J. Aikin, *Description of the Country round Manchester*, p. 522.

[4] 'The manufacture has still continued to increase and has spread over a district in the North part of Staffordshire of about nine miles in extent, the whole of which is now so covered with manufactories and dwelling houses, that it has the appearance of one large scattering town.' D. Macpherson, *Annals of Commerce*, III, 383 (1805).

[5] Josiah Wedgwood, *An Address to the Young Inhabitants of the Pottery*, pp. 21-2. This pamphlet was written in 1783, in the hope of stopping the agitation caused

own work, and he was indeed justified in being as proud of it as he could be of his artistic triumphs.

Men like this, whose practical ability works in harmony with the highest intellectual and moral qualities, and whose productive ability has not self-interest for its sole object, do honour to the class to which they belong. But we should not form an opinion on the first generation of modern manufacturers from such exceptional examples. Indeed, most of the great manufacturers of the day were not like them in their finer qualities. They deserved admiration for their initiative and activity, their power of organization and their gift of leadership. But their one aim was money, men and things alike being only tools for the attainment of this single object. The following chapter gives illuminating details as to how their workpeople were often treated. The consciousness of power made them tyrannical, hard, sometimes cruel: their passions and greed were those of upstarts. They had the reputation of being heavy drinkers and of having little regard for the honour of their female employees.[1] They were proud of their newly acquired wealth and lived in great style, with footmen, carriages and gorgeous town and country houses.[2] But their generosity was not proportionate to the luxury in which they lived. At the beginning of the nineteenth century £2,500 were collected in Manchester for the foundation of Sunday schools. The total sum contributed by the chief cotton-spinners of the district, who employed about 23,000 people, was £90.[3] Their whole energies were given up to money-making, and while they certainly displayed the ambition, the daring and the tireless energy of the conqueror they also resembled him by their egotism.

V

In spite of its recent origin, of the dissimilar elements which had gone to its making and of the unequal moral value of its members, the manufacturing class soon became conscious of its own existence. Such class-consciousness, which is based on common interest, can make its appearance only where it is able to find expression. In this respect

---

[1] *Report on the State of the Children*, etc. (1816), pp. 104 ff.

[2] See, for instance, Robert Blincoe's account of one of his employers, Ellice Needham: 'He is said to have arisen from an abject state of poverty ... Of his primeval state it was his weakness to be ashamed. By the profusion of his table and the splendor and frequency of his entertainments, he seemed to wish to cover and conceal his mean descent. His house, lawns, equipage, and style of living completely eclipsed the neighbouring gentry.' J. Brown, 'Memoir of Robert Blincoe', in *The Lion*, I, 181.

[3] *Report on the State of the Children employed in the Manufactories* (1816), p. 337.

---

by the high price of corn. Riots actually took place, and had to be suppressed by the use of force. See *Derby Mercury*, March 20th, 1783.

conditions in England were more favourable than in any other country. The freedom of the political system, and above all the traditional habit of petitioning, gave ample scope for advancing collective demands. For many years it had been customary for Englishmen to unite according to their needs or their opinions, to present complaints or suggestions to Parliament. In the records of the two Houses of Parliament some trace can be found of every conceivable temporary or permanent alliance, of every association which economical, political or religious interests could suggest to a community. Thus it was natural and in conformity with innumerable precedents that the leading manufacturers should unite together for certain practical ends.

They were keen critics of William Pitt's fiscal policy. Shortly after his accession to power he had announced his intention of creating fresh taxes in order to improve the country's financial position, which had suffered seriously through the American war. Among other proposals a tax was to be levied on raw materials, particularly on iron, copper and coal.[1] The mining and metal working industries were in a ferment. Without actually forming an association they agreed to act together, to approach the Minister and to lay their objections before him. Reynolds of Coalbrookdale drew up a memorandum, in which he pointed out the growth of the iron-smelting industry since coal had been used: did the Government want to run the risk of impeding or of stopping this development?[2] Boulton formulated his opinion in terms which Adam Smith might have made his own: 'Let taxes be laid upon luxuries, upon vices, and if you like upon property; tax riches when got, and the expenditure of them, but not the means of getting them. Of all things, don't cut open the hen that lays the golden eggs.'[3]

Pitt granted him an audience and appears to have listened to him. But, although an adept of the new political economy, he regarded the new taxes as a necessary expedient for balancing his budget. The move-

[1] At the same time as on cotton fabrics: see Part II, chap. II.

[2] 'The advancement of the iron trade within these few years has been prodigious. It was thought, and justly, that the making of pig iron with pit coal was a great acquisition to the country by saving the wood and supplying a material to manufactures, the production of which, by the consumption of all the wood the country produced, was formerly unequal to the demand, and the nail trade, perhaps the most considerable of any one article of manufactured iron, would have been lost to this country had it not been found practicable to make nails of iron made with pit coal. We have now another process to attempt, and that is to make bar iron with pit coal; and it is for that purpose we have made, or rather are making, alterations at Donnington Wood, Ketley, and elsewhere, which we expect to complete in the present year, but not at a less expense than £20,000, which will be lost to us, and gained by nobody, if this tax is laid upon our coals.' S. Smiles, *Industrial Biography*, p. 93.

[3] Letter from M. Boulton to J. Wilson, Dec. 16th, 1784. S. Smiles, *Lives of Boulton and Watt*, pp. 342-3.

ment of the cotton interest against the so-called fustian tax, which has been mentioned in a preceding chapter, succeeded only after months of strenuous effort in which every branch of the cotton trade took part.[1] The coal tax, however, disappeared before the fustian tax, which was still an object of controversy when further trouble arose on account of the Irish treaty.

The commercial treaty of 1785 between Great Britain and Ireland was based on the principle of reciprocity, one of its effects being to equalize import duties on manufactured goods.[2] The treaty was favourably received in Ireland. But in England it met with violent protests. Every industry was involved,[3] and very soon the general opposition crystallized into a definite organization. Wedgwood took the lead. He went to Boulton in Birmingham and urged him to set up 'a committee of delegates from all the manufacturing places in England and Scotland to meet and sit in London all the time the Irish commercial affairs are pending'.[4] The idea gained ground rapidly, and most of the great manufacturers joined the movement. The 'General Chamber of Manufacturers' (such was the committee's title) met in the spring of 1785 with Wedgwood as chairman. It immediately attacked the treaty, which had not yet been finally approved by Parliament. It distributed broadcast over the country circulars and pamphlets, one of which was written by James Watt.[5] Its representatives appeared before the Privy Council and before the Parliamentary Committee in charge of the Irish resolutions. Wedgwood was heard by both these bodies and also had private conversations with the heads of the Government and of the Opposition. He conferred with Pitt and the Duke of Portland, with Fox and Sheridan.[6] Finally, after a series of amendments which had considerably modified the original text, the Anglo-Irish treaty was given up.[7]

---

[1] On that movement see W. Bowden, *Industrial Society in England towards the end of the Eighteenth Century*, pp. 172-3. Three hundred and fifty subscriptions were received in a short time. The dyers and bleachers threatened to stop work till relief was granted.

[2] The question was raised in England by the King's Speech of Jan. 20th, 1785. *Journals of the House of Commons*, XL, 453.

[3] According to W. Bowden (ibid., pp. 175 ff.), that opposition was not unjustified, particularly on the part of the new industries, the interests of which had been overlooked by Pitt or his advisers.

[4] Josiah Wedgwood to Matthew Boulton, Feb. 21st, 1785. See Eliza Meteyard, *Josiah Wedgwood*, II, 540.

[5] *An Answer to the Treasury Paper on the Iron Trade of England and Ireland*, 1785.

[6] Correspondence, March-April 1785, Wedgwood Museum, Stoke-on-Trent.

[7] *Parliamentary History*, XXV, 311-75, 409-14, 575-778, 820-85, 934-82. The third reading of the Bill was adjourned sine die after the King's Speech of Jan. 24th, 1786, which announced the failure of the Irish negotiations. Ibid., p. 985. See the many petitions in connection with this matter in vol. XL of the *Journals of the House*

On this issue the General Chamber of Manufacturers stood for an alliance of interests, rather than for a general opinion. Fundamentally the manufacturers were far from being in complete agreement. Some were afraid that Ireland would emerge from the economic slavery to which English jealousy had condemned her for so many centuries,[1] while others were anxious to see the barriers between the two countries completely broken down. The traditional policy of extreme protection still had its adherents, especially among men in the older industries who had become accustomed to receiving privileges and thought they could not do without them. But the leaders of the new industries were beginning to realize that their main interests lay in obtaining cheap raw materials and free markets for the sale of their goods. This difference of opinion was noticeable when in 1786 the commercial treaty with France was concluded. The Chamber of Manufacturers was divided. Wedgwood supported the Government,[2] and was followed by the Birmingham metal-workers and the Manchester and Derbyshire spinners.[3] It would be an anachronism to use the term 'free trade' with reference to this period, but the aspiration towards unlimited commercial expansion was already being felt wherever machine industry and large-scale production had made their appearance, and thus every

[1] The cotton manufacturers, who were at the same time fighting for the abolition of the fustian tax, turned to account anti-Irish prejudice. See W. Bowden, op. cit., p. 176, who gives a well-studied account of the formation and action of the Chamber of Manufacturers. See also T. S. Ashton, *Iron and Steel in the Industrial Revolution*, pp. 170 ff. (showing the difference of opinion between ironmasters on the subject of the French treaty and on the treaty generally), F. Dumas, *Étude sur le traité de commerce de 1786 entre la France et l'Angleterre* (Toulouse, 1904), and J. H. Rose, 'The Franco-British Commercial Treaty of 1786', *Engl. Hist. Review*, XXIII, 709 ff. (1908).

[2] He had an allegorical bas-relief made by Flaxman to commemorate the event. It is worth noting that throughout the lengthy debates in both Houses on this subject not a word was said about the recent changes in industry. *Parliamentary History*, XXVI, 381-514 and 534-96.

[3] Watt wrote to him: 'I am very sorry to see by the public papers that there are two opinions in the Chamber of Manufacturers about the treaty with France. As your opinions on the subject seem to coincide with my own, I thought it might be some small support to you to inform you of it and also to assure you that Mr Boulton, Mr Garbett and I believe all the town of Birmingham are of the same sentiment. At least I was present some time ago at a public meeting with about 100 of the principal inhabitants, merchants and manufacturers, where success to the treaty and a perpetual peace with France were drunk and followed by three unanimous cheers.' Letter from J. Watt to Wedgwood, Feb. 26th, 1787, Soho MSS.

of Commons. The Chamber of Manufacturers' action at the time of the Irish resolutions served as an example: in 1794 the Commercial Society of Manchester, which had been recently established, conveyed to the Government observations on the commercial treaty which it was proposed to conclude with Spain. See E. Helm, *Chapters in the History of the Manchester Chamber of Commerce*, p. 17.

measure which made expansion easier was bound to win the support of the more enlightened manufacturers.[1] A foreign market was their first need, and if foreign Governments demanded reciprocity, then these industries trusted to their better technique to protect them against competition. Thus the tendency was revealed which was soon to set the manufacturers, hostile to the old protectionist system, in opposition to the landowners, whose interests were involved in maintaining it. The approval with which the leaders of the new industries greeted the treaty of 1786 foreshadowed the support which fifty years later their successors extended to the teachings of the Manchester School.[2]

The official attitude towards the organized manufacturers showed a rapid change. In 1785, representatives of the cotton trade who came to complain of the fustian tax were received in government offices 'with a humiliating condescension'. But less than two years later Pitt, although he contemptuously referred to the Chamber of Manufacturers as a body absurdly attempting to take from Parliament 'the trouble of legislation', admitted that the manufacturers' representations, in matters affecting their interests, 'must indeed carry the most powerful weight'. And when he prepared his treaty with France he was careful to take their advice and to conform to their views.[3]

If the manufacturers did not always agree as to the commercial policy which was most beneficial to general trade interests, they could be relied upon to agree whenever their class interests were concerned. To their employees they already presented a firm and united front. For instance, in 1782 a committee of cotton manufacturers demanded, and induced Parliament to pass, drastic legislation against workers who when on strike broke up looms or destroyed goods.[4] Like the acts of violence which it aimed at suppressing this law was simply a class weapon. In 1799 Bolton weavers complained that some of them could no longer find work in the district, as their names were entered in

[1] See the petition from the cotton spinners and weavers in 1788-9, the date of the over-production crisis: 'From the great reduction of the price, and the improved quality of the goods, it is only necessary to open a fair and unfettered transit of the British-made calicoes and muslins into foreign countries, in order to obtain such an increase of consumption as would completely renovate the trade.' *Journals of the House of Commons*, XLIV, 544.

[2] In his *Address to the Young Inhabitants of the Pottery*, p. 10, Wedgwood declared himself to be in favour of the free import of grain.

[3] W. Bowden, op. cit., pp. 172, 187, 207.

[4] Circular of the Committee of Manufacturers, Dec. 10th, 1782, Owen MSS. (Manchester Central Library), LXXX, 3. List of the members of the Committee in 1782, ibid., p. 4. The law is the Act of 1782 (22 Geo. III, c. 40), by which wilful damage to property committed by workmen was included among capital crimes 'without benefit of clergy'.

the employers' 'black book'.[1] This black book was the outcome of a special agreement to which about sixty firms were parties. According to the manufacturers its object was to stop the theft of raw material, an offence often complained of in the domestic system of industry.[2] We may note that this typical instance of a union of employers took place at the same date as the passing of the law which, at the instance of the employers, forbade any combination among workmen under penalty of fine or imprisonment.[3]

But it was over the old laws which regulated employment, and above all over the apprenticeship laws, that the opposition between the manufacturers and workmen was most clearly marked. Deprived as they were of the right of combination by which they could have pressed their claims themselves, the men had hoped that these laws, which had almost fallen into disuse, could be revived and used by them as a protection against economic oppression. But immediately and throughout the kingdom the employers asked for their repeal, and obtained prompt satisfaction. The reader will find below an account of this struggle, the outcome of which, being in favour of the employers' policy, meant the triumph in Great Britain of the system of *laissez-faire*.

The interests of manufacturers were naturally opposed to regulation of any kind, whether of persons or things, of technical processes or of labour conditions. They were determined to be the sole masters of production, unfettered by any limitation or control. In this their partisan view coincided with the ideas of their generation. At the time of the industrial revolution the doctrine of *laissez-faire* was just leaving the realm of theory for that of practical application. It was no economist, but a statesman, William Pitt himself, who in 1796 said from the Treasury Bench: 'Look to the instances when interference has shackled industry, and when the best intentions have often produced the most pernicious effects ... Trade, industry and barter

---

[1] 'Enquiry into the Condition of the Cotton Weavers (1800)', *Journals of the House of Commons*, LV, 492; 'Report from the Committee to whom the Petitions of Masters and Journeymen Weavers were referred (1800)', ibid., p. 15.

[2] Several laws were passed to put a stop to this kind of 'embezzlement', for instance 13 Geo. II, c. 8 (1740), and 22 Geo. II, c. 27 (1759). The latter contained the following penalties: for a first offence a public whipping and fourteen days imprisonment; for further offences, imprisonment for two or three months. Receivers of the stolen goods ran the risk of a whipping and of fines varying from £20 to £40. Another Act of the same kind was passed in 1777, with special reference to the worsted industry (17 Geo. III, c. 11), and the master manufacturers in Yorkshire formed the so-called Worsted Committee to see that the provisions of that Act were enforced against offenders. H. Heaton (*The Yorkshire Woollen and Worsted Industries*, p. 435) justly observes that the whole legislation against 'frauds and embezzlements' was linked up with the domestic system of industry.

[3] See chap. IV below.

will always find their own level, and be impeded by regulations which violate their natural operation and derange their proper effect.'[1] This was the very language spoken by the manufacturing class when, in the following century, power and government fell into their hands.

VI

As the factory system developed, this class, a child of yesterday but rich, industrious and ambitious, gradually became more and more essential to the economic life of the country. But what was their recognized position in society, in that English society which even today still retains, almost untouched, its ancient order of precedence with the feelings or prejudices it involves? Did these newcomers who, not only by their wealth but by their power and the number of persons under their control, more and more equalled the landed aristocracy, realize their actual position in a world transformed by the industrial revolution? From certain facts it would seem that this class of upstarts was of little account, faced as it was by contempt from above and by snobbery from below. A list of English worthies of the eighteenth century which was drawn up in 1805, does not mention a single inventor or manufacturer.[2] About the same time Wedgwood's son and heir, when Sheriff of Dorsetshire, had to endure the scarcely concealed contempt of the local gentry; for after all he was only a potter.[3] Many of them were Nonconformists, a fact which created a further barrier between them and the upper classes of society.[4] But foreigners, coming from countries where large-scale manufacture had not yet been introduced and who were therefore in a better position to appreciate its essential features, were struck by the important position which some at any rate of the chief manufacturers already held in the country. After visiting a calico-printing works[5] a Frenchman wrote: 'With us a man rich enough to set up and run a factory like this would not care to remain in a position which he would deem unworthy of his wealth. He would at once want to become a "Conseiller au Parlement", or a "Maître des

---

[1] Speech in the House of Commons, Feb. 12th, 1796. *The Speeches of the Right Honourable William Pitt* (1816 edition), II, 368.

[2] *Gentleman's Magazine*, LXXIII, 161-70.

[3] Eliza Meteyard, *A Group of Englishmen*, p. 187. Compare with what Bowden writes about the 'disdainful attitude' of the gentry towards the new industrial aristocracy. *Industrial Society in England towards the end of the Eighteenth Century*, pp. 154 ff.

[4] This applies particularly to the ironmasters. T. S. Ashton calls attention to the Biblical christian names of many of them: Abraham Darby, Benjamin Huntsman (both of them Quakers), Isaac Hawkins, Shadrach Fox, Samuel, Aaron and Jonathan Walker, Sampson and Nehemiah Lloyd, David Mushet, Jeremiah Homfray, etc. *Iron and Steel in the Industrial Revolution*, p. 212.

[5] That belonging to Sterling, at Cordale near Dumbarton in Scotland.

Requêtes".[1] And he would be right, for it is natural to desire the dignity conferred by position, seeing that none is ever obtained by personal merit. In this country Mr Boulton of Birmingham, Mr Wedgwood of Etruria, Mr Sterling of Cordale and other manufacturers of their standing, command such credit and respect that in the eyes of everyone they are on a level with the greatest in the land.'[2]

This influence rested mainly on local power. We will not stress the time-worn comparison between manufacturers and feudal lords, but they had this much in common, that certain localities, certain districts did belong to them. This was not only true of the factories which they ruled but of the village or town into which they breathed life and prosperity, and of the county which came to depend on their industry; while the whole population more and more regarded them as its natural leaders. After the great landowners, to whom their titles gave an added ascendancy, the men who really counted were the spinners of Lancashire and Derbyshire, the ironmasters of Birmingham, of the Severn and of South Wales, and the potters of Staffordshire. Whenever a question arose of carrying out some important scheme of public utility by which the whole district would benefit, they were the men with the greatest interests at stake and ready to take the lead. Thus, following the Duke of Bridgewater's example, they played a prominent part in the creation of a network of canals throughout England. On the committees which drew up the plans, obtained the necessary permits from public authorities and organized the whole enterprise, manufacturers sat side by side with the leading men of the local aristocracy.[3] Both classes had many and devoted adherents, who never thought to reproach them for working primarily for themselves.

But outside his own district, where he displayed his activity and where the measure of his importance was determined by the benefits

---

[1] Judicial titles in use before the French Revolution.

[2] *Tournée faite dans la Grande Bretagne en 1788 par un Français parlant la langue anglaise*, p. 158.

[3] Lord Stamford, Lord Grey, Lord Gower and the Duke of Bridgewater were on the Committee of the Grand Trunk Canal, together with Wedgwood, Garbett, Bentley, Boulton, etc. See E. Meteyard, *Life of Josiah Wedgwood*, I, 410; S. Smiles, *Lives of the Engineers*, I, 433, and *Lives of Boulton and Watt*, p. 179. Wedgwood describes his visit to the Duke of Bridgewater in 1766 as follows. 'I have been waiting upon His Grace the Duke of Bridgewater with plans respecting inland navigation. Mr Sparrow went along with me. We were most graciously received, we spent about eight hours in His Grace's company, and had all the assurances of his concurrence of our designs that we could wish. His Grace gave me an order for the completest set of table service of cream colour that I could make. He showed us a Roman urn, 1,500 years old at least, made of red china, which has been found by his workmen in Castle Field near Manchester. After His Grace had dismissed us, we had the honour and pleasure of sailing on his gondola some nine miles along his canal ... ' Letter to John Wedgwood, July 6th, 1766, Wedgwood Museum, Stoke-on-Trent.

which he was felt to have conferred, the manufacturer did not meet with the same consideration, but was judged on his personal merits. Nevertheless, it was a sign of the times that a great lord should treat a plain manufacturer, even though he was a remarkable man, otherwise than as a tradesman. It is true that from the beginning of the eighteenth century the 'philosophers', both in France and England, had outdone one another in trying to restore the prestige of arts and crafts and even of manual labour.[1] The regard shown to the founders of the factory system was perhaps more due to this fashion than to a true appreciation of their real place in modern society.

As an artist, or at any rate as a producer of luxuries sought after by amateurs, Wedgwood stands apart from other manufacturers. In patronizing him the gentry and nobility merely followed the tradition of all aristocracies. But they went beyond patronage, for in the relations of the Gowers, the Cathcarts and the Talbots with him there was a touch of friendly courtesy.[2] Boulton, although he was even more a manufacturer than an artist, was received several times by George III and Queen Charlotte, and each time they conversed with him for a long time and were lavish in their compliments and congratulations.[3] When Catherine II came to England in 1776 she condescended to accept the hospitality of the Soho manufacturer for a few days.[4] Later on he was invited in the most flattering way to visit Paris with his partner.[5] He went at the expense of the French Government and

[1] In England as in France it was the fashion for young men from the best families to learn a trade. Lord Chatham used to say that Lord Stanhope, his son-in-law, could earn his living as a blacksmith or a millwright. S. Smiles, *Lives of the Engineers*, I, 142.

[2] When he had his leg amputated, in May 1768, Sir William Meredith, Sir George Saville, Lord Bessborough, Lord Cathcart, the Duke of Bedford and the Duke of Marlborough sent every day to his London house for news of him. Eliza Meteyard, *Josiah Wedgwood*, II, 42.

[3] 'Never was man so much complimented as I have been ... The Queen showed me her last child, which is a beauty ... The Queen, I think, is much improved in her person, and she now speaks English like an English lady. She draws very finely, is a great musician, and works with her needle better than Mrs Betty. However, without joke, she is extremely sensible, very affable, and a great patroness of English manufactures. Of this she gave me a particular instance, for, after the King and she had talked to me for nearly three hours, they withdrew, and then the Queen sent for me into her boudoir, showed me her chimney-piece, and asked me how many vases it would take to furnish it.' Boulton to his wife, quoted by S. Smiles, *Boulton and Watt*, pp. 174-5.

[4] Ibid., p. 216.

[5] The letter from the French Embassy in London ran as follows: 'Gentlemen, I have the honour, by order of my Court, to inform you that if your business should permit of your visiting Paris, His Majesty would provide for the expenses of your journey, and that you would further receive, on behalf of the Government, all the welcome which you could desire, and which persons of your distinction and reputation are entitled to expect. It gives me, gentlemen, all the greater pleasure to discharge this order from my Court, that it affords me the special privilege of renewing

was received with attentions reserved only for distinguished visitors.[1]

This favoured treatment of a few outstanding men cast a reflected glory on the class to which they belonged and, so to speak, confirmed the actual position which the power of capital gave to the manufacturers. But this was not enough for them. Their interests, as well as their pride, urged them to higher ambitions, and they already coveted political influence. The life of the first Sir Robert Peel enables us to study this double conquest of wealth and power.[2]

He began very modestly in 1772 as partner with his uncle Haworth, a calico-printer at Bury. On the look-out for every new fashion and displaying incredible activity,[3] he made his fortune in a few years. By 1780 he was employing, either in his workshops or in their homes, almost the whole population of Bury. In 1788 he built a factory on the land which he had just bought at Tamworth in Staffordshire, and it was for that district that he became Member of Parliament. A great admirer of William Pitt, whom he regarded as above all an enlightened protector of industry, 'the true source of national greatness',[4] he supported him with passion during the worst times of the war against France. In 1797, when at the height of the financial crisis Pitt called on private individuals to help to eke out the resources of the State, Peel sent him £10,000. He, moreover, at his own expense fitted out eight companies of volunteers (the Bury Loyal Volunteers) and was put at their head with the rank of lieutenant-colonel. He was rewarded with a baronetcy, and took for his motto 'Industria'.[5]

[1] 'When I look back on the state of intoxication in which we were kept at Paris by the very flattering civilities and attentions and unmerited praises we received, and the good wine we drank, I am afraid we were guilty of many rudenesses and incivilities.' Watt's letter to the Abbé de Calonne, Feb. 17th, 1787, Soho MSS.

[2] See W. Cooke Taylor, *Life and Times of Sir Robert Peel*, I, 6 ff.; Sir Lawrence Peel, *A Sketch of the Life and Character of Sir Robert Peel*, pp. 33-42; F. Espinasse, *Lancashire Worthies*, II, 82-125; J. Wheeler, *Manchester*, pp. 520 ff.

[3] 'He was a man of untiring energy. For many a day his life was one of hard incessant labour. He would rise at night from his bed, when there was a likelihood of bad weather, to visit the bleaching grounds, and one night in each week he used to sit up all night, attended by his pattern drawer, to receive any new patterns which the London coach, arrived at midnight, might bring down.' Sir Lawrence Peel, op. cit., p. 34.

[4] See his speech of May 7th, 1802, in the House of Commons, *Parliamentary Register*, New Series, XVIII, 248-9: 'I have the honour to be a member of the commercial world, and have had occasion to transact with the late Chancellor of the Exchequer business of great importance and difficulty. From personal knowledge, I am therefore enabled to state that no minister ever understood so well the commercial interest of the country. He knew that the true sources of its greatness lay in its productive industry, and he therefore encouraged that industry.'

[5] Arkwright had been only knighted and his title, therefore, died with him.

my assurance of all the feelings of consideration and devotion with which I have the honour to be, etc.' See letter from Watt to Boulton, Oct. 3rd, 1786, Soho MSS.

He did not take much part in the proceedings of the House of Commons, save on one memorable occasion when, in 1802, he introduced and carried the bill dealing with apprenticeship in the spinning mills, which was the beginning of all factory legislation. He had little time for politics, as all his energies were devoted to building up the fortunes of his family on a solid foundation. All his ambition in the political field was on behalf of his son. While the second Robert Peel was still a child his father had dedicated him to the service of his country.[1] As soon as the young man was through the University he found him a rotten borough in Ireland. Soon after, he had him appointed to an under-secretaryship in the Spencer-Percival government. He was able to follow the successive stages of that great career. In 1812 his son became Secretary for Ireland, in 1820 Secretary of State for Home Affairs, in 1828 leader of the House of Commons. He had hoped before he died to have seen him Prime Minister,[2] but this was the only one of his dreams which he did not live to see.

In one generation a family of manufacturers had attained the foremost rank in the country. But it took longer for the manufacturing class as such to gain political power. The Peels, new men though they were, were quick to join the party of tradition. They were proud to belong to the party of the old aristocracy and of social conservatism, which had been strengthened by its great and ultimately victorious struggle with the French Revolution.[3] Their Toryism, which ultimately became so broad as almost to become Liberalism, began by being strict and exclusive. They did not wish the door by which they had entered to be left too widely open for their successors. The great opponent of the Reform Bill of 1832, that Magna Charta of the English middle class, which in the realm of politics crowned the industrial revolution, was Sir Robert Peel, the Bury manufacturer's son.

---

[1] 'Every Sunday after church, he would set the child on a table and make him repeat the sermon he had just heard. He thought he could not begin too soon in giving him that difficult practice of memory and of speech, which helps so much in the formation of great orators.' F. Guizot, *Sir Robert Peel*, p. 7.

[2] He died in 1830 and his son became Prime Minister for the first time in 1834.

[3] Sir Robert Peel had at first approved of the Revolution. He became afraid of it when its period of armed propaganda began.

CHAPTER THREE

THE INDUSTRIAL REVOLUTION
AND LABOUR

IT now remains for us to show what the first effects of the industrial revolution were on the conditions of labour and on the life of the working class. To do this it is not enough to contrast the picture of industrial aristocracy with that of 'factory proletariat'. For our attention should not be concentrated exclusively on the factory and factory hands. The great body of manual workers, although for a long time they remained outside the new system of industry, were nevertheless almost immediately affected by its all-pervading influence.

I

At first that influence was an object of fear. The reader will remember what mistrust and anger was roused in the working class by the first appearance of machine industry. The struggle against machinery, and generally against all the technical improvements, is the best known incident of this whole phase of history. Further, it is not peculiar to any one period or country. We need hardly remind the reader of the often quoted episodes of the destruction of Papin's steamboat by the Fulda boatmen, or of Jacquart's loom broken to pieces by the Lyons silk workers. Even today, in spite of new habits brought about by a long succession of inventions and improvements, changes in industrial equipment frequently meet with resistance from the men, and who can wonder at it?[1] Their attitude has often been condemned in the name of progress and of rational political economy, and been called ignorant and uncivilized. Yet nothing could be more natural. The workman's sole capital being his labour and his technical skill, anything that depreciates their value deprives him of part of his only property. The whole advantage of machinery, and its actual *raison d'être*, is the saving in labour which it makes possible.

---

[1] The opponents of the English trade unions used until quite recently to accuse them of making improvements in technical processes almost impossible – an accusation which in our opinion exaggerates the facts. See 'The Crisis in British Industry', articles which appeared in *The Times* of Nov. 21st, 1901, and Jan. 16th, 1902. On the real tactics of trade unions, see Sidney and Beatrice Webb, *Industrial Democracy*, Part II, chap. VIII (New Processes and Machinery), and Paul Mantoux and Maurice Alfassa, *La Crise du Trade-Unionisme* (1902), pp. 127, 134, 142, 150, 163.

But the workman may justifiably regard this saving as made at his expense. The orthodox answer to this popular objection is that by lowering prices machinery increases consumption; that the increase in demand hastens industrial development, and that ultimately labour, far from being eliminated, plays an ever larger part in more numerous and larger workshops. But it was impossible for the workmen when first brought into contact with machinery to appreciate this reasoning, which long experience has vindicated. The one thing which struck them was that they would have to fight an overwhelming competition, that many of them would lose their employment and that, in any case, their wages would fall. And if, instead of looking at the immediate results of the introduction of machinery, we look at what these have brought forth after more than a century, these fears do not always appear as unfounded as might have been thought. If the men by their violent opposition stood in the way of progress, and opposed the public inter-est without benefiting themselves in any way, can we attribute it only to their stupidity and brutality? Is it not rather due to the imperfection of a social system in which an increase in production may be followed, if only for a short time, by an increase in the misery of the producers, and where inventions destined to lighten human labour make it harder for the workers to live?

The men had not yet discovered the real cause of their troubles. They only knew one thing, and that was that machinery threatened their livelihood. They therefore reasoned that machinery must be destroyed. We need not refer again to the unpopularity of inventors and to the way in which they were persecuted. Indeed some of them were not far from sharing the opinions, or, if the reader prefers, the prejudices of the men. Ten years before Hargreaves, Lawrence Earnshaw invented a cotton-spinning machine, but destroyed it as soon as it was made, saying that he did not desire to take the bread out of the mouths of the poor.[1] But this altruism, besides being mistaken, was rare if not unique. Excesses committed against inventors did more harm to them than to their ideas. Machinery satisfied real and pressing economic needs. Moreover, to those who had the necessary capital, it offered an incomparable opportunity for making handsome profits or even a fortune. After having in vain attacked the inventors the men were confronted by the manufacturers, whose interest lay in the maintenance and extension of machinery. Their instinctive reaction was again the same: it was to fight the factories and break up the machinery.

Long before machinery made its appearance it had been a common thing in disorderly strikes for tools to be destroyed. But when the

[1] S. Smiles, *Lives of the Engineers*, I, 390. See a similar story about T. Benford of Kettering, *Gentleman's Magazine*, LXI, 587 (1791).

stocking knitters revolted against their employers and broke their knitting frames, it was not done to stop the frames being used. They bore no malice against the frames but against the owners, and they only broke them up as being the property of greedy employers who were levying the cruel frame rent on them. Moreover, the men (and this shows clearly which were their real intentions) destroyed tools and products with equal impartiality. Weavers were very often punished for having torn or burnt woven stuffs, either in the workshops where they were employed or in the houses of others into which they had broken.[1] But the riots against machinery, which began in the second half of the eighteenth century, had a quite different meaning.

The first Act specially passed to put them down is dated 1769. A mechanical saw mill in Limehouse, built on the same plan as the Dutch ones, had shortly before been stormed and destroyed by the mob.[2] It was while this incident, which took place at the very gates of London, was still fresh in the people's minds that the Act was passed. Just about the same time the workmen at Blackburn were breaking up James Hargreaves's jennies and forcing him to fly to Nottingham. The wilful destruction of any building containing machinery, either by a single person or by an 'illegal and seditious' mob, was made a felony, the penalty being the same as for arson, which meant death.[3]

This drastic law did not, however, prevent the recurrence of riots, which became more frequent and more serious as the use of machinery spread. In Lancashire, where machinery had developed most quickly, these disturbances in 1779 became really alarming.[4] Wedgwood, who was in the district when the riots broke out, wrote in one of his letters an account of them which has the value of evidence given by an eye-witness: 'In our way to this place (Bolton), a little on this side Chowbent, we met several hundred people in the road. I believe there might be about five hundred; and upon inquiring of one of them the occasion of their being together in so great a number, he told me they had been destroying some engines, and meant to serve them all so through the country. Accordingly they have advice here today that they must expect a visit tomorrow, the workmen in the neighbour-

---

[1] In this last case the penalty under the Acts 12 Geo. I, c. 33, and 22 Geo. II, c. 37, was death.

[2] See C. Dingley's petition and the report of the Committee of Inquiry, *Journals of the House of Commons*, XXXII, 160, 194, 388.

[3] 9 Geo. III, c. 29.

[4] One of the incidental consequences of the American War was to cause a crisis in the cotton industry, because exports to Spain and her colonies were stopped, and the Mediterranean was closed to British ships, while trade with Africa and the West Indies was very much reduced. This condition of things caused unemployment, which the introduction of machinery threatened to make worse. See G. W. Daniels, *The Early English Cotton Industry*, p. 89.

hood having mustered up a considerable number of arms, and are casting bullets and providing ammunition today for the assault tomorrow morning. Sir Richard Clayton[1] brought this account here today, and, I believe, is in the town now, advising with the inhabitants upon the best means for their safety, and I believe they have concluded to send immediately to Liverpool for part of the troops quartered there.'[2]

Wedgwood had met on the road only the vanguard of the rioting workmen. 'On the same day in the afternoon a capital engine or mill in the manner of Arcrites [sic] and in which he is a partner, near Chorley, was attacked, but from its peculiar position, they could approach to it by one passage only, and this circumstance enabled the owner, with the assistance of a few neighbours, to repulse the enemy and preserve the mill for that time. Two of the mob were shot dead upon the spot, one drowned and several wounded. Accordingly they spent all Sunday and Monday morning in collecting firearms and ammunition and melting their pewter dishes into bullets. They were now joined by the Duke of Bridgewater's colliers and others, to the number, we were told, of eight thousand, and marched by beat of drum and with colours flying to the mill where they had met with a repulse on Saturday. They found Sir Richard Clayton guarding the place with fifty armed invalids, but this handful were by no means a match for enraged thousands, so they contented themselves (the invalids) with looking on, while the mob completely destroyed a set of mills valued at £10,000.[3] This was Monday's employment. On Tuesday morning we heard their drums at about two miles' distance from Bolton, a little before we left the place, and their professed design was to take Bolton, Manchester and Stockport on their way to Cromford, and to destroy all the engines not only in these places, but throughout all England.'[4] Arkwright had already made preparations for the defence of Cromford.[5] Similar disturbances took place at the same time in various localities; Peel's cotton-printing factory at Altham was

[1] One of the County magistrates.

[2] Letter to Thomas Bentley, Oct. 3rd, 1779, Wedgwood Museum, Stoke-on-Trent. Quoted by Eliza Meteyard, A Group of Englishmen, pp. 13 ff.

[3] See the petition addressed to Parliament by R. Arkwright, Journals of the House of Commons, XXXVII, 926. The damages are there assessed, not at £10,000 but at £4,400 only.

[4] Letter to T. Bentley, Oct. 9th, 1779, Wedgwood Museum, Stoke-on-Trent.

[5] 'All the gentlemen in this neighbourhood being determined to support Mr Arkwright in the defence of his works, which have been of such utility to this country, fifteen hundred stand of small arms are already collected from Derby and the neighbouring towns, and a battery of cannon raised of nine and twelve pounders, with great plenty of powder and grape shot ... Five or six thousand men, miners, etc., can at any time be assembled in less than an hour.' Letter published in the Manchester Mercury of Oct. 12th, 1779.

taken by storm, the engines were smashed and thrown into the river.[1]

Prompt and stern repression followed. The troops sent from Liverpool dispersed the rioters without difficulty. Some were caught, tried by the Grand Jury and sentenced to the gallows.[2] But most of them escaped punishment. Public opinion was disposed to be indulgent, if not sympathetic. The middle class, either because they disliked new departures or because they were afraid of the reduction of wages being followed by a corresponding increase of the poor rate,[3] showed almost as much hostility to the machines as did the working men themselves. As in Mellor Church the vicar was referring to the recent disturbances, and inveighing against them for the spiritual benefit of the congregation, an old yeoman rose to his feet and said to the unwelcome preacher that he would do better to keep to his text rather than meddle with such worldly affairs.[4] On the other hand, the Justices of the Peace in the quarterly sessions held at Preston passed a resolution which went right against the popular prejudice: 'Resolved that the sole cause of great riots was the new machines employed in the cotton manufacture; that the country notwithstanding has greatly benefited by their erection; that destroying them in this country would only be the means of transferring them to another country, and that, if a total stop were put by the legislature to their erection in Britain, it would only tend to their establishment in foreign countries, to the detriment of the trade of Britain.'[5]

As a matter of fact the 1779 riots were followed by attempts to secure by legal methods the prohibition of spinning machinery. There were precedents for this. In 1552 an Act had been passed forbidding the use of the gig mill,[6] while in 1623 a royal proclamation had forbidden the use of a needle-making machine.[7] These steps, in keeping with the spirit of early industrial legislation, were taken not so much to protect the worker as to maintain the high quality of the finished article, which, it was considered, might be endangered by any change in the traditional methods of manufacture. In the petition which the cotton spinners placed before the House of Commons in 1780 they made use of this obsolete argument,[8] but without producing much impression. There

---

[1] *A Complete History of the Cotton Trade*, pp. 80-1.

[2] *Manchester Mercury*, Oct. 26th, 1779.

[3] J. Kennedy, 'On the Rise and Progress of the Cotton Manufacture', *Memoirs of the Literary and Philosophical Society of Manchester*, Second Series, III, 121.

[4] W. Radcliffe, *Origin of the New System of Manufacture, commonly called 'Power Loom Weaving'*, p. 55 note.

[5] Webb MSS. (Textiles, I, 277). The resolution was taken on Nov. 11th, 1779.

[6] 5 and 6 Edw. VI, c. 22.

[7] See W. Cunningham, *Growth of English Industry and Commerce*, II, 295.

[8] 'The work executed by the patent machines is so very inferior to that performed by manual labour, that the quality and credit of our manufacture ... are greatly

was more justification for their complaints about unemployment and the fall in wages.[1] But these could be explained by the general depression due to the American war.[2] The Committee appointed to consider the petition reported against it, and in doing so used the same arguments as the Lancashire magistrates.[3]

At the same time a pamphlet was published in Manchester, written by one of the magistrates, Dorning Rasbotham, who signed himself 'A Friend of the Poor'.[4] In this leaflet he tried to explain to the men the actual nature of their troubles. He represented them as being by their very nature of a transitory character: 'All improvements in trade by machines do at first produce some difficulties to some particular persons ... About ten years ago, when the spinning jennies came up, old persons, children and those who could not easily learn to use their own machines did suffer for a while ... ' Was not the first effect of the printing press to deprive many copyists of their occupation? 'What mean those riots and tumults which we saw a few months ago? What mean the petitions to Parliament to suppress or tax the machines? We might just as well ask to have our hands lopped off or our throats cut.'[5]

The rapid growth of the cotton industry, and the corresponding increase in the number of people employed, helped to spread these new ideas. In this industry the men's hostility to machinery very soon made way for a quite opposite sentiment.[6] In the woollen industry it lasted longer, as the change was made with greater difficulty. As in Lancashire, violent outbreaks occurred more than once in the West Riding and in the south-west. In 1796 certain Yorkshire spinning

---

[1] In 1764 a woman spinner earned ten to fifteen pence a day; in 1780, three to five pence. During the same period, men's wages fell from seventeen to ten pence a day. See *Journals of the House of Commons*, XXXVII, 926.

[2] In 1774 the figure for foreign trade (exports and imports) was over 33,000,000. In 1779 it had fallen to 25,000,000. A. Anderson, *An Historical and Chronological Deduction of the Origin of Commerce*, IV, 694.

[3] *Journals of the House of Commons*, XXXVII, 926.

[4] *Thoughts on the Use of Machines in the Cotton Manufacture, addressed to the Working People in that Manufacture and to the Poor in general, by a Friend of the Poor*, Manchester, 1780. On D. Rasbotham's authorship, see W. Radcliffe, op. cit., p. 55.

[5] *Thoughts on the Use of Machines*, pp. 9, 11, 20.

[6] Wendeborn in 1791 thought the population in the cotton districts had become so accustomed to the use of machines that 'perhaps riots would ensue if an attempt were made to prohibit them'. G. F. A. Wendeborn, *A View of England towards the Close of the Eighteenth Century*, II, 235.

---

depreciated thereby and in danger to be lost.' *Journals of the House of Commons*, XXXVII, 804-5. See the cloth-workers' petition against the gig mill, ibid., XLI, 599.

mills had to be garrisoned. The use of the gig mill in 1802 gave rise to serious disturbances in Wilts and Somerset.[1] These outbreaks, always followed by stern repression, became very frequent during the critical years of the struggle against Napoleon, and especially after the proclamation of the continental blockade. The description in the famous pages of *Shirley* of an attack on a spinning mill has kept alive the memory of those troublous times.[2] But during the war period, in which so many different forces reacted upon one another, the facts become so complex that a special and elaborate study would be necessary to interpret them correctly. The Luddite riots, for instance, which in 1811 and 1812 spread terror throughout the industrial Midlands and seriously alarmed Lord Liverpool's government, were not directed against machinery. While the shearers in the north of England were destroying the machines, which they declared were lowering their wages, the Midland stocking knitters[3] when they broke up their frames were simply resorting to their customary weapon against their employers.[4] As a matter of fact they were all of them suffering chiefly from the abnormal situation caused by the continuation of the war with France, from the obstacles to the expansion of British trade offered by the continental blockade, the rigorous application of which began in 1810, from the dearth caused by the difficulties of supply and from the continuous rise in the price of foodstuffs. But these local disturbances,

[1] *Report from the Committee on the State of the Woollen Manufacture in England* (1806), pp. 3 ff. Laurent Dechesne, *L'évolution économique et sociale de l'industrie de la laine en Angleterre*, p. 144.

[2] Currer Bell (Charlotte Brontë), *Shirley*, I, chaps. 2 and 8, and II, chap. 2. See L. Cazamian, *Le Roman Social en Angleterre*, pp. 419 ff.

[3] It was to these especially that the name Ludd was given. The word was said to be derived from the surname of a certain Ned Ludlam, but King Ludd himself was a myth (see R. W. Cooke Taylor, *The Modern Factory System*, p. 158, and J. L. and L. B. Hammond, *The Skilled Labourer*, pp. 259-60, 292, 310). It would seem that more than one person was nicknamed King Ludd. See the short and excellent account of the movement given by E. Halévy, *Histoire du Peuple Anglais au XIXᵉ Siècle*, I, 313-15.

[4] W. Cunningham, *Growth of English Industry and Commerce*, I, 663, shows the difference between the riots in the woollen district of Yorkshire and the Luddite riots of 1811: while in the first instance the mob attacked exclusively the factories where machinery was used, the Luddite movement was directed against manufacturers whom their rapidly acquired wealth or their harsh treatment of their men had made unpopular. J. L. and L. B. Hammond, after a careful study of the Luddite movement, arrive at the same conclusion: 'It has often been assumed that the Nottingham Luddites were venting their anger against new and improved machinery, whereas, in truth, there was no new machinery in use, although, amongst other grievances, there was a new and, as it seemed to the men, an illegitimate adaptation of an old machine.' J. L. and L. B. Hammond, *The Skilled Labourer*, p. 257. See *Report from the Committee of Secrecy on the Disturbances in the Northern Counties* (1812) and *Annual Register*, 1812 (Chronicle), pp. 39, 51, 114.

which threatened at one time to unite into an industrial *Jacquerie*, do not belong solely to the history of the factory system.[1]

While fresh riots against machinery were breaking out, petitions, the futility of which the workers in the cotton industry had already discovered, were being laid before Parliament. In 1794 the wool-combers petitioned against the use of Cartwright's combing machine. Their request, which was cleverly presented, met at first with a fairly favourable reception. But then the employers put forward the irresistible argument that the industry needed machinery and that the interests of the industry were the interests of the whole country, and thus once again they carried the day.[2] A few months later, at the time of the

---

[1] Byron mistook the Luddite riots for a revolutionary movement and wrote for the Midland insurgents his fierce 'Song for the Luddites'.

> As the Liberty lads over the sea
> Bought their freedom, and cheaply, with blood
> So we, boys, we
> Will die fighting, or live free,
> And down with all kings but King Ludd.
>
> When the web that we weave is complete,
> And the shuttle exchanged for the sword,
> We will fling the winding sheet
> O'er the despot at our feet,
> And dye it deep in the gore he has poured.
>
> Though black as his heart its hue,
> Since his veins are corrupted to mud,
> Yet this is the dew
> Which the tree shall renew
> Of liberty, planted by Ludd!

'Miscellaneous Poems', *Works*, Chandos Classics edition, p. 667.

[2] Both sides of the arguments are shown very clearly in the petitions presented at the same time by the men and by their employers. The wool-combers wrote: 'The petitioners have hitherto been considered as useful members of the community, who, by their industry and manual labour, have provided for themselves with as little assistance from parochial bounty as any class of manufacturers of their numbers within these Kingdoms; but they beg leave to state to the House that by the invention and practice of a new machine for combing of wool, which diminishes labour to an alarming degree, the petitioners entertain serious and just fears that themselves and families will speedily become a useless and heavy burthen to the State. It appears to the petitioners that one machine only, with the assistance of one person and four or five children, will perform as much labour as thirty men in the customary manual manner. The reasons adduced in support of machines employed in other manufactures, such as the cotton, silk, linen, etc., will not apply to the woollen, for almost any quantity of the raw materials can be procured to supply the manufactures of the former, which, by enlarging their trade, still retain an equal or greater number of persons in employ, whereas but a specific quantity can be obtained of the latter, scarcely sufficient to employ the manufacturers engaged in that branch in the manner hitherto practised. And in consequence of the introduction of the said machine the great body of woollen manufacturers will almost immediately be deprived of their business and employ, the whole trade will be engrossed by a few powerful and wealthy

Wiltshire outbreak, Parliament was flooded with petitions against mechanical shearing, and especially against the use of the gig mill. Was this the same machine the use of which had been forbidden in 1552? Probably the name was the only likeness between the two.[1] But that

[1] The early gig mill performed an operation, which consisted in picking over the cloth in order to do away with the knots in the weft. The gig mill mentioned in petitions about or after 1802 was used for raising a nap on the cloth. See *Journals of the House of Commons*, LXVIII, 885. On the protest against the use of the gig mill in

adventurers, and after short competition the surplus profit arising from the annihilation of manual labour will be transferred into the pockets of the foreign consumers. The machines of which the petitioners complain are rapidly multiplying throughout the Kingdom, the pernicious effects of which have already been sensibly felt by the petitioners, numbers of whom thereby are in want of occupation and food; and it is with the most heartfelt sorrow and anguish the petitioners anticipate that fast approaching period of consummate wretchedness and poverty, when fifty thousand of the petitioners, together with their distressed families, by a lucrative monopoly of the means of earning their bread, will be inevitably compelled to seek relief from their several parishes.'

The most significant passages of the employers' petition read as follows: 'It appears to be the general right of the subject, which the wisdom of the legislature has for ages admitted, that he be at liberty to exercise his art and profession in that way which appears to be the most conducive to his interest, nor offends against the law or the right of others; that of his interest he is himself in all instances the fittest judge, and that from this unfettered and well directed pursuit of individual interest has arisen, and ever will arise, the greatest aggregate of national benefit. Under the protection of the law, vesting in some of the petitioners and others the right of certain patents, the public has become possessed of a very valuable improvement in the combing of wool by machinery ... Great benefit has already resulted from that improved method of combing, but in no proportion to what is expected to result, whereby a great saving in the production of yarn will be obtained ... On a moderate estimation the price of combing of the lower wools is reduced by this improvement from 2½d. or 3d. to 1d. per lb., and, when the finer wools shall be subjected to the same operation, the reduction of price will most probably be from 6d. or more to 1d. or 1½d. per lb. ... If the petitioners should be compelled to abandon the combing of wool by machinery, they will severally be subjected to the ruinous obligation of producing their yarns at an expense of from £1,500 to £2,000 per annum more than the production of the same yarn will cost by machinery. If in the progress of time the machine combing, being unrestricted by law, should supersede the use of hand combing, the saving to the national produce would, on a moderate calculation, greatly exceed £1,000,000 per annum; and, if the machine combing be suppressed, the national manufactures must in consequence be charged with this additional load ... The good policy of the law in leaving manufactures to their natural course was strikingly evinced in the business of cotton, in the spinning of which the application of machinery threatened to deprive of their maintenance a much more considerable body of artizans, while in the progress the artizans found employment and the cotton manufactures of the Kingdom were carried to a height both of excellence and extent, and the national wealth was multiplied, beyond all example. The woollen manufactures may, in all probability, from the same causes, reach the same height of prosperity and excellence, if unchecked by prohibition laws.' *Journals of the House of Commons*, XLIX, 545-6. Many similar petitions were presented to the House. See ibid., 104, 135, 152, 158, 201, 249, 280, 307, 322, 331, 395-6, etc.

did not prevent the men from insisting on the revival of this obsolete law.[1] Beaten once, they tried again when the great Parliamentary Inquiry on the woollen industry was set up, whose proceedings were published together with the famous report of 1806. But their demands were adversely reported on by the Commission: 'It has been given in evidence before your Committee, and even acknowledged by some of the petitioners themselves, that alarms, similar in nature to those which are now conceived of the gig mill and shearing frame, attended the first introduction of several of the machines which are now generally used with acknowledged advantage in different processes, formerly performed by hand, of the woollen manufacture. Hitherto these alarms have after a time subsided, and the use of the machines has been gradually established, without, as it appears, impairing the comforts or lessening the numbers of the workmen.'[2]

But this optimistic view hardly took into consideration the sufferings of the men who had been thrown out of work by machinery, for hardship was none the less for being only temporary. But the resistance which the workers sought to offer to the progress of machinery could not supply a remedy to their troubles. Whether this resistance was instinctive or considered, peaceful or violent, it obviously had no chance of success, as the whole trend of events was against it. The only result it sometimes achieved was to force the manufacturers to pay attention to the men made desperate by unemployment, and to find work for them in order to prevent a recurrence of disturbances which might threaten their own property and even their lives.[3]

II

Intermixed with the men's grievances against machinery was their hatred of the factory. The feeling of repulsion which it aroused is

[1] At Leeds, Huddersfield and Halifax, committees to organize petitions were set up. Other trades sent them money, among others the coalminers, the brickmakers and the shoemakers. See *Report from the Committee on the Woollen Clothiers' Petition* (1803), and *Report on the State of the Woollen Manufacture in England* (1806), pp. 241, 355. The manufacturers' views are expressed in a pamphlet by J. Anstie, *Observations on the Importance and Necessity of introducing improved machinery into the woollen manufactory* (1803).

[2] *Report on the State of the Woollen Manufacture in England* (1806), p. 58.

[3] See the resolutions passed by a meeting of manufacturers held at Bath on Aug. 16th, 1802. After having decided to defend their machinery against any kind of opposition, they promised to find decently paid work for all their men who might be thrown out of work through the introduction of machinery. See *Report from the Committee on the Woollen Clothiers' Petitions* (1803), p. 12.

Yorkshire and the south-western counties between 1802 and 1806, see J. L. and L. B. Hammond, *The Skilled Labourer*, pp. 171 ff.; E. Lipson, *History of the Woollen and Worsted Industries*, pp. 188-90.

easily understood, as to a man used to working at home or in a small workshop, factory discipline was intolerable. Even though at home he had to work long hours to make up for the lowness of his wage, yet he could begin and stop at will,[1] and without regular hours. He could divide up the work as he chose, come and go, rest for a moment, and even if he chose be idle for days together.[2] Even if he worked in the master-manufacturer's house, his freedom though less complete was still fairly great.[3] He did not feel that there was an impassable gulf between himself and his employer, and their relations still retained something of a personal character. He was not bound by hard and fast regulations, as relentless and as devoid of sympathy as the machinery itself. He saw little difference between going to a factory and entering a barracks or a prison. This is why the first generation of manufacturers often found real difficulty in obtaining labour.[4] They would have found it still more difficult had there not been a floating population available, which the changes in rural conditions were driving from agriculture into industry and from the country to the towns. Other workers were attracted from the poorer parts of the Kingdom, from the bogs of Ireland and from the mountains of Scotland or Wales.[5] Thus the origin of factory labour is to be found partly in a

[1] 'A tender man, when he had his work at home, would do it at his leisure. There you must come at the time: the bell rings at half-past five, and then again at six.' *Report on the State of the Woollen Manufacture* (1806), p. 111.

[2] He did so, in fact, as soon as he had earned a little money. All witnesses, whether for or against the men, are agreed about this. See Part I, chap. I. Between 1790 and 1800 the spinners who worked at home with the jenny or the mule 'frequently spent two or three days in the week in idleness and drinking, while the children they employed were often waiting on them at the public-houses, till they were disposed to go to their work; and when they did go they continued it sometimes almost night and day'. *Second Report from the Central Board of H.M.'s Commissioners ... on the Employment of Children in Factories* (1833), p. 36.

[3] It should be noticed, however, that since 1777 a series of Acts and regulations against embezzlement had created a system of supervision which tended deeply to alter the character of the domestic system in a number of trades. See Unwin, *Samuel Oldknow and the Arkwrights*, p. 35.

[4] David Dale, when he set up in New Lanark in 1784, could not get workmen from among the neighbouring population. Robert Owen, *The Life of Robert Owen, written by Himself*, p. 58.

[5] 'You have been a witness of growth of the operative class in these parts; you have seen it grow from nothing into a great body in the space of a few years. How was it recruited? Of what was it composed? What were the spinners taken from? – A good many from the agricultural parts; a many from Wales; a many from Ireland and from Scotland. People left other occupations and came to spinning for the sake of the high wages. I recollect shoemakers leaving their employ and learning to spin. I recollect tailors, I recollect colliers, but a great many more husbandmen left their employ to learn to spin ... ' Evidence given by an inhabitant of Bolton before the Factory Commission of 1834 (*Supplementary Report*, I, 169). See W. Bowden, *Industrial Society in England towards the end of the Eighteenth Century*, p. 97.

class of men forcibly uprooted from their employment, and partly among populations to whom industry offered better opportunities than did their former employment.

In the textile trades the manufacturers found another way out of the difficulty, by resorting largely to woman and child labour.[1] Spinning was quickly learned and needed little strength, while for certain processes the small size of the children and their delicacy of touch made them the best aids to the machines.[2] They were preferred, too, for other and more conclusive reasons. Their weakness made them docile, and they were more easily reduced to a state of passive obedience than grown men. They were also very cheap. Sometimes they were given a trifling wage which varied between a third and a sixth of an adult wage;[3] and sometimes their only payment was food and lodging. Lastly they were bound to the factory by indentures of apprenticeship for at least seven years, and usually until they were twenty-one. It was obviously to the spinners' interest to employ as many as possible and thus to reduce the number of workmen. The first Lancashire factories were full of children. Sir Robert Peel had over a thousand in his workshops at once.[4]

The majority of these wretched children were paupers, supplied (one might almost say sold) by the parishes where they belonged. Especially during the first period of machine industry, when factories were built outside and often far from the towns, manufacturers would have found it impossible to recruit the labour they needed from the immediate neighbourhood. And the parishes on their side were only too anxious to get rid of their paupers.[5] Regular bargains, beneficial

---

[1] On the question of the employment of children in factories, see *Minutes of Evidence taken before the Select Committee on the State of the Children employed in the Manufactories of the United Kingdom* (1816); *Report from the Select Committee on the Bill to regulate the Labour of Children in Mills and Factories* (1832); John Fielden, *The Curse of the Factory System* (1836); O. Weyer, *Die englische Fabrikinspektion* (1888); R. W. Cooke Taylor, *The Factory System and the Factory Acts* (1894); B. L. Hutchins and A. Harrison, *History of Factory Legislation* (1903) and J. L. and L. B. Hammond, *The Town Labourer*, chaps. VIII and IX (1917).

[2] For instance 'the piecers', whose duty it was to join the broken threads, were always children.

[3] In a calico-printing factory in 1803, an adult earned 25s. a week and an apprentice 3s. 6d. to 7s. *Minutes of the Evidence taken before the Select Committee to whom the Petition of the Journeymen Calico Printers was referred* (1804), p. 17.

[4] See Sir Robert Peel's evidence before the 1816 Committee, *Report from the Select Committee on the State of the Children employed in the Manufactories*, p. 132.

[5] The custom was no new one, as the parishes had always tried to find places for their pauper children, not so much in the interest of the children as to keep down their own expenses. An Act of 1697 (8 and 9 Will. III, c. 30) obliged employers, chosen by the Justices of the Peace, to take such children as apprentices, under penalty of a £10 fine. See inquiry of 1767, *Journals of the House of Commons*, XXXI, 248. According to Miss O. J. Dunlop, the hiring of parish apprentices was a current

to both parties if not to the children, who were dealt with as mere merchandise,[1] were entered into between the spinners on the one hand and the Poor Law authorities on the other.[2] Lots of fifty, eighty or a hundred children were supplied and sent like cattle to the factory, where they remained imprisoned for many years. Certain parishes drove even better bargains and stipulated that the buyer should take idiots in the proportion of one to every twenty children sent.[3] At the beginning these 'parish apprentices' were the only children employed in the factories. The workmen, very justifiably, refused to send their own.[4] But unfortunately this resistance did not last long, as they were soon driven by want to a step which at first had so much horrified them.

The only extenuating circumstance in the painful events which we have now to recount as shortly as we can, was that forced child labour was no new evil. In the domestic system of manufacture children were exploited as a matter of course. Among the Birmingham ironmongers apprenticeship began at seven years of age.[5] Among the weavers of the north and the south-west children worked at five or even four years old, as soon in fact as they were considered capable of attention and obedience.[6] Far from regarding this with indignation, men at that time thought it an admirable system. Yarranton recommended the establishment of 'industrial schools' such as he had seen in Germany. There, two hundred little girls under a matron's rod sat spinning without a moment's relaxation and in complete silence, and were beaten if they did not spin quickly or well enough: 'In these parts I speak of, a

---

[1] A form of obtaining their consent was gone through, but the reader may imagine how much it was worth and to what frauds it gave rise: 'It was gravely stated to them ... that they were all, when they arrived at the cotton mill, to be transformed into ladies and gentlemen; that they would be fed on roast beef and plum pudding, be allowed to ride their masters' horses, and have silver watches, and plenty of cash in their pockets. Nor was it the nurses, or other inferior persons of the workhouse, with whom this vile deception originated, but with the parish officers themselves.' J. Brown, 'Memoir of Robert Blincoe', in *The Lion*, I, 125.

[2] A typical example is Samuel Oldknow's bargain with the parish of Clerkenwell for a supply of seventy children (1796). Some of the children's parents hearing of the destination had 'come crying to beg [to] have their children out again rather than part with them so far off'. Unwin, *Samuel Oldknow and the Arkwrights*, p. 71.

[3] 1816 *Report*, p. 39.

[4] Ibid., p. 8. See Alfred, *History of the Factory Movement*, I, 16. 'When the first factories were erected, it was soon discovered that there was in the minds of the parents a strong repugnance to the employment thus provided for their children ... For a long time it was by the working people themselves considered to be disgraceful to any father to allow his child to enter the factory.'

[5] *Journals of the House of Commons*, XXVIII, 496.

[6] Defoe, *Tour*, II, 20; III, 101.

---

practice at the time of Henry VII (*English Apprenticeship and Child Labour*, pp. 248 ff.). See also W. Hasbach, *History of the English Agricultural Labourer*, p. 83, and Hutchins and Harrison, *History of Factory Legislation*, pp. 3-6.

man that has most children lives best; whereas here he that has most is poorest. There the children enrich the father, but here beggar him.'[1] When Defoe visited Halifax he was lost in admiration at the sight of four-year-old children earning their living like grown-up people.[2] William Pitt's statement on child labour, which Michelet with his usual exaggeration of sentiment and language quoted against him as though it were a crime, was only a commonplace reference to an accepted opinion.[3]

It might be said that in the earlier forms of industry the child was at any rate an apprentice in the true sense, for he learned a trade instead of merely being a part of the plant, as he was in the factory. But real apprenticeship could only begin when the child was old enough to benefit by it, and therefore for several years the child could only be a workman's drudge, paid either nothing or next to nothing. It might also be said that the conditions under which the child lived were less unfavourable to its physical development; but with regard to hygiene we know only too well the condition of the domestic workshop. Was it kindly treated and not overworked? Under the sting of necessity parents were often the most exacting, if not the harshest of taskmasters.[4]

---

[1] Andrew Yarranton, *England's Improvement by Sea and Land*, I, 45-7.

[2] 'Hardly anything above four years old but its hands are sufficient to itself.' Defoe, *Tour*, III, 101.

[3] See Michelet, *Le Peuple*, pp. 90-1: 'When at the time of the great struggle between England and France the English manufacturers warned Pitt that owing to the high wages they had to pay their workmen, they were unable to pay their national taxes, Pitt returned a terrible answer: "Take the children." That saying weighs like a curse upon England.' As a matter of fact, those words were never spoken. On the only occasion when Pitt mentioned that question in public he spoke as follows: 'Experience has already shown how much can be done by the industry of children, and the advantages of employing them in such branches of manufactures as they are capable to execute. The extension of schools of industry was also an object of material importance. If anyone would take the trouble to compute the amount of all the earnings of the children who are already educated in this manner, he would be surprised when he came to consider the weight which their support by their own labour took off the country, and the addition which by the fruits of their labour, and the habits to which they were formed, they made to its internal opulence.' William Pitt, *Speeches*, II, 371 (discussion on Whitbread's Minimum Wage Bill, Feb. 12th, 1796). About the same time 'a benevolent Anglican clergyman having an exceptional interest in the welfare of the laboring classes [the Rev. David Davies] recommended the general adoption of the rule applied in Rutland in 1785, "that no persons be allowed any relief ... on account of any child above six years of age who shall not be able to knit, nor on account of any child above nine years of age who shall not be able to spin either linen or woollen." ' W. Bowden, *Industrial Society towards the end of the Eighteenth Century*, p. 276.

[4] W. Cooke Taylor, *Notes of the Manufacturing District of Lancashire*, p. 141. According to an old man who had begun work about 1770 'the creatures were set to work as soon as they could crawl, and their parents were the hardest of taskmasters'. Another

But, even with these reservations, we must acknowledge that the fate of these parish apprentices in the early spinning mills was particularly miserable. Completely at the mercy of their employers, kept in isolated buildings, far from anyone who might take pity on their sufferings, they endured a cruel servitude. Their working day was limited only by their complete exhaustion, and lasted fourteen, sixteen and even eighteen hours.[1] The foreman, whose wages were dependent on the amount of work done in each workshop,[2] did not permit them to relax their efforts for a minute. In most factories forty minutes were allowed for the chief or the only meal of the day, and of these about twenty were taken up in cleaning the machines.[3] In some factories work went on ceaselessly day and night, so that the machines might never stop. In such cases the children were divided up into shifts, and 'the beds never got cold'.[4] Accidents were very common, especially towards the end of the overlong day, when the exhausted children almost fell asleep at their work. The tale never ended of fingers cut off and limbs crushed in the wheels.

[1] 1816 *Report*, pp. 89, 146, 252. In Manchester the average working day was fourteen hours (twenty-two instances given, pp. 96 and 97). David Dale, who was a philanthropist, made his apprentices work thirteen hours a day. Ibid., p. 27, and *The Life of Robert Owen, written by Himself*, p. 116.

[2] John Fielden, *The Curse of the Factory System*, p. 10.

[3] *Report of* 1816, p. 97; J. Brown, 'Memoir of Robert Blincoe', in *The Lion*, I, 183. See J. L. and L. B. Hammond's admirable study of the question in *The Town Labourer*, chap. VIII.

[4] 1816 *Report*, p. 115. We have been unable to obtain accurate information as to the system in use in the English spinning mills at the end of the eighteenth century. Probably, to judge by the length of the working day, shifts relieved one another in thirds, each working for sixteen hours and resting for eight hours. In a few spinning mills the apprentices only worked twelve hours, as, for instance, in the Paisley mills, which were visited in 1786 by the son of the duc de la Rochefoucauld-Liancourt: 'They work twelve hours straight off, without the necessary intervals for food and rest. When they have finished they are immediately relieved by others, so that work only ceases on Sunday ... I inquired whether this work did not have ill effects on their health, but I was assured that this was not so.' La Rochefoucauld-Liancourt, 'Voyage aux Montagnes', II (Letter of May 9th, 1786). Samuel Oldknow made his apprentices work from 6 a.m. to 7 p.m. But he 'was generally recognized as an exceptionally humane employer', fed the children fairly well and made them take exercise in the meadows near the factory. See Unwin, *Samuel Oldknow and the Arkwrights*, pp. 173-4. In 1784 the Manchester magistrates (showing an exceptional sense of responsibility) decided not to apprentice children to any mill where they had to work more than ten hours a day. Hutchins and Harrison, *History of Factory Legislation*, p. 9.

witness said that 'he would not accept an offer to live his whole life again, if it were to be accompanied by the condition of passing through the same servitude and misery which he had endured in his infancy'. It should be recognized that the old system of apprenticeship entailed all sorts of legal and moral obligations of which the manufacturers, in the first period of the factory system, felt entirely free; but that system had been gradually relaxing long before the industrial revolution began.

Discipline was savage, if the word discipline can be applied to such indescribable brutality, and sometimes such refined cruelty as was exercised at will on defenceless creatures. The well-known catalogue of the sufferings of the factory apprentice, Robert Blincoe, makes one sick with horror.[1] At Lowdham (near Nottingham), whither he was sent in 1799 with a batch of about eighty other boys and girls, they were only whipped. It is true that the whip was in use from morning till night, not only as a punishment for the slightest fault but also to stimulate industry and to keep them awake when they were dropping with weariness.[2] But at the factory at Litton matters were very different. There the employer, one Ellice Needham, hit the children with his fists and with a riding whip, he kicked them, and one of his little attentions was to pinch their ears until his nails met through the flesh.[3] The foremen were even worse and one of them, Robert Woodward, used to devise the most ingenious tortures. It was he who was responsible for such inventions as hanging Blincoe up by his wrists over a machine at work so that he was obliged to keep his knees bent up, making him work almost naked in winter with heavy weights on his shoulders, and filing down his teeth. The wretched child had been so knocked about that his scalp was one sore all over. By way of curing him his hair was torn out by means of a cap of pitch.[4] If the victims of these horrors tried to escape their feet were put in irons. Many tried to commit suicide, and one girl, who took advantage of a moment when the supervision relaxed and threw herself into the river, thus regained her freedom: she was sent away, as her employer was 'afraid the example might be contagious'.[5]

Of course, not all factories witnessed such scenes, but they were less rare than their incredible horror would lead one to suppose[6] and were repeated until a system of strict control was set up.[7] Even if they had

[1] Robert Blincoe was discovered in 1822 by J. Brown, who was engaged in making an inquiry into the moral and social effects of the factory system throughout the industrial centres. The account of his wretched childhood was published in 1828 in *The Lion*, a radical periodical, run by R. Carlile, and in 1832 in *The Poor Man's Advocate*. Blincoe's was certainly an extreme case, and Carlile was a violent partisan.

[2] *The Lion*, I, 125.   [3] Ibid., I, 191-2.
[4] Ibid., I, 189-90.   [5] Ibid., I, 219.

[6] William Hutton has left an account of his sufferings in the factory started by the Lombe brothers at Derby: 'To this curious, but wretched place, I was bound apprentice for seven years, which I always considered the most unhappy of my life ... Low as the engines were, I was too short to reach them. To remedy this defect, a pair of high pattens were fabricated and lashed to my feet, which I dragged after me till time lengthened my stature. The confinement and the labour were no burden, but the severity was intolerable, the marks of which I yet carry and shall carry to the grave.' William Hutton, *History of Derby*, p. 160.

[7] Justices of the Peace had the power of cancelling indentures for bad treatment of apprentices. 32 Geo. III, c. 5 (1792), lays an obligation on the employer, in such a case, to leave the apprentice the clothes he had been given and to pay his family

not been ill-treated, excessive labour, lack of sleep and the nature of the work forced on children during the critical period of their growth, would have been quite enough to ruin their health and deform their bodies. The food, too, was often bad and insufficient. They had black bread, oatmeal porridge and rancid bacon.[1] At Litton Mill the apprentices used to struggle with the pigs fattening in the yard in order to get some of the food in their troughs.[2] The factories were usually unhealthy, as their builders cared as little for health as they did for beauty. The ceilings were low in order to economize as much space as possible, the windows were narrow and almost always closed.[3] In the cotton mills fluff filled the air and gave rise to serious lung diseases.[4] In flax-spinning mills, where wet spinning was usual, the air was saturated with moisture and the workers' clothes were dripping wet.[5] Overcrowding in unventilated rooms, where the atmosphere was further vitiated by candle smoke at night, favoured the spreading of a contagious disorder resembling prison fever. The first cases of this 'factory fever' broke out near Manchester in 1784.[6] It very soon spread to nearly all the industrial districts and there were many deaths. Lastly, the promiscuity of both workshops and dormitories gave scope for immorality,[7] and this was unfortunately encouraged by the

[1] *The Lion*, I, 149, 184; Statement of a Clergyman, in Alfred, op. cit., I, 25. Oldknow gave his apprentices wheaten bread and milk porridge, meat almost every day and fruit from his orchard. Unwin, op. cit., pp. 173-4.

[2] Ibid., I, 214-15. In 1801, an action brought against the owner of a silk-spinning mill at Watford (Hertfordshire) revealed the fact that he was literally letting his apprentices die of starvation. He committed suicide in order to escape criminal proceedings. *Gentleman's Magazine*, LXXI, 1157.

[3] *A Short Essay written for the Service of Proprietors of Cotton Mills and the Persons employed therein* (1784), p. 9; Sir Benjamin Dobson, *Humidity in Cotton Spinning*, p. 8.

[4] *A Short Essay written for the Service of Proprietors of Cotton Mills and the Persons employed therein* (1784), p. 9; Gaskell, *Manufacturing Population of England*, p. 260.

[5] *First Report from the Central Board of H.M.'s Commissioners on the Employment of Children in Factories* (1833), p. 328.

[6] 'There has been a contagious disorder in a cotton mill in the neighbourhood of Manchester, which has destroyed many persons. It was a malignant fever: it ran through whole families, equally affecting people of all ages, but most fatal to the men.' *A Short Essay written for the Service of Proprietors of Cotton Mills and Persons employed therein*, pp. 4-5. Blincoe saw forty out of a hundred and sixty apprentices sick at the same time. The mortality was so great that 'Mr Needham felt it advisable to divide the burials' between different cemeteries. *The Lion*, I, 183.

[7] This question has been gone into at great length by P. Gaskell, *Manufacturing Population of England*, pp. 64 ff. See 1816 *Report*, p. 104.

or his parish an indemnity, which might be as much as £10. An Act passed the following year (33 Geo. III, c. 55) lays a further penalty on the guilty employer in the shape of a fine at the discretion of the judge. But such Acts were hardly ever enforced. See *The Lion*, I, 225. The 1832 inquiry reveals the continuation of the trouble they were supposed to cure. See Alfred, *History of the Factory Movement*, I, 279, 284-6, 305, etc.

bad behaviour of some of the employers and foremen, who took advantage of it to satisfy their low instincts.[1] Thus to a puritan conscience the factory, with its mixture of depravity and suffering, of barbarity and vice, offered a perfect picture of hell.[2]

Among those who lived through the cruel period of apprenticeship, many bore its brand for life in the shape of crooked backs, and limbs deformed by rickets or mutilated by accidents with machinery. With 'flaccid features, a stunted growth, very often tumid bellies',[3] they were already marked down as the victims of all the infections to which, during their later life, they were but too frequently exposed. Their moral and intellectual condition was no better. They left the factory ignorant and corrupt. During their miserable period of servitude not only did they receive no teaching of any kind, but in spite of the formal clauses of their indenture of apprenticeship they did not even acquire enough technical knowledge to enable them to earn their living. They had learned nothing beyond the mechanical routine to which they had been bound during so many long hard years,[4] and they were thus condemned to remain mere slaves tied to the factory as of old the serf to the soil.

It must not be assumed that the status of all workers under the factory system was like that of the apprentices in the spinning mills. But, even though adults were not treated with quite the same revolting cruelty, their life in the factory was hard enough. They, too, suffered from too many working hours, from overcrowded and unhealthy workshops, and from tyrannical foremen and overseers. With them the despotic employer, instead of physical violence, resorted to fraud; one of the most frequent abuses of which the workmen had to complain was that, in order to lengthen the working day of which every minute meant money to the employer, they were literally robbed of their rest hours. During the dinner hour the speed of the factory clock appeared miraculously to accelerate, so that work was resumed five or ten

---

[1] 'The shamelessness and grossness in constant practice in some cotton mills exceed that of the lowest prostitutes ... The masters have cognizance of it, but it would be unsafe to inquire into the practice of it ... It is known to all who are conversant with cotton mills that managers, overseers, and others in command have in a vast many instances been its chief promoters.' F. Place, Additional MSS. (British Museum), 27827, p. 192.

[2] In 1789 one Lancashire spinning mill was known as 'Hell's Gate'. 'It can only be considered as so much pure unmixed evil, moral, medical, religious, and political. In great manufactories, human corruption accumulated in large masses seems to undergo a kind of fermentation which sublimes it to a degree of malignity not to be exceeded out of hell.' *Gentleman's Magazine*, LXXII, 57 (1802).

[3] P. Gaskell, *The Manufacturing Population of England*, p. 195. See evidence before the 1832 Commission.

[4] *The Lion*, I, 181-2.

minutes before the hour had actually struck.[1] Sometimes the means used to the same end were even simpler and less hypocritical: the meal times and closing times were at the discretion of the employer, and the workers were forbidden to carry watches.[2]

Here we come to the real cause of the evils attributed to machine industry, namely the absolute and uncontrolled power of the capitalist. In this, the heroic age of great undertakings, it was acknowledged, admitted and even proclaimed with brutal candour. It was the employer's own business, he did as he chose and did not consider that any other justification of his conduct was necessary. He owed his employees wages, and once those were paid the men had no further claim on him: put shortly, this was the attitude of the employer as to his rights and his duties. A cotton spinner, on being asked whether he did anything to help sick apprentices, answered: 'When we engage a child, it is with the approbation of the parents, and it is an engagement to give a certain quantity of money for a certain quantity of labour. If the labour is not performed, the child is supported by the parents. – Then there is no security afforded to the child, that in sickness the master will support it? – It is an act of bounty in the master.' Pure bounty, indeed, on which it was wiser not to count. The same man, when questioned as to why he had decided to stop his machinery at night, explained that he did it in order to allow water to accumulate in a tank, as the stream of the neighbouring river was insufficient: 'Then if the stream had been more ample, you would have continued your night work? – As long as the trade had been sufficiently lucrative. – Then there is nothing now to restrain you from working day and night, but want of water or want of trade? – I know of no law to restrain me for so doing: I never heard of any.'[3] This was unanswerable, so long as the law remained unchanged.

[1] 'I have heard it said that the minute hand used to tumble when it got to the top at dinner time: it very seldom tumbled at any other time. I have seen it drop myself, happen five minutes, so that when it was really twelve o'clock it would drop to five minutes after twelve. This was in the dinner hour. I can't tell what it was for: we always considered among ourselves it was to shorten our meal times. We had got wind of it, and one day a dozen of us looked at a window just at the time, and it was so.' *First Report from the Central Board of H.M.'s Commissioners ... on the Employment of Children in Factories* (1833), p. 9.

[2] 'I worked at Mr Braid's mill ... There we worked as long as we could see in summer time, and I could not say at what hour it was that we stopped. There was nobody but the master and the master's son who had a watch, and we did not know the time. There was one man who had a watch, I believe it was a friend who gave it him. It was taken from him and given into the master's custody because he had told the men the time of the day ... ' Alfred, *History of the Factory Movement*, I, 283.

[3] *Report of* 1816, p. 115 (evidence of William Sidgwick). The Act of 1802 (42 Geo. III, c. 73) had forbidden night work for apprentices. But the manufacturers got round it by engaging young workmen without indentures of apprenticeship. Ibid., p. 137.

III

In 1797 a disciple of Adam Smith thus described the position of the manual worker: 'The man who has only the unsubstantial property of labour to offer in exchange for the real visible produce of landed property, and whose daily wants require daily exertion, must, it may be said, from the very nature of his situation, be almost entirely at the mercy of his employer.'[1] So it was even before the industrial revolution began. We have seen how the weavers of the south-west, the London tailors and the Nottingham stocking-knitters were entirely in the power of the manufacturers, who doled out the work which they did at home. In the same way day labourers were in the hands both of the farmers and the landlords, on whom they were dependent both as workmen living on a daily wage and as cottagers settled on the land of an owner by his indulgence. The opposition of capital to labour is many centuries older than the industrial revolution. But it had never before been so clearly marked. On the one hand the manufacturer, the owner of the factories and machinery, was infinitely more powerful than the former types of employer had ever been before. He owned capital, which increased rapidly by the accumulated value of labour, and he owned mechanical equipment, which was like an army of slaves under his command, and against which it would have been both futile and disastrous to fight. On the other hand the worker, faced by this overwhelming power, knew himself to be weaker than ever. Even if formerly it had usually been impossible for him to bargain about his wage, yet there had at any rate been an appearance of a contract, individually, if not freely, discussed between his master and himself. Under the factory system the individual contract was only the means by which a man finally signed away his personal freedom and became a unit lost in a crowd, or, if the reader prefers, a soldier enrolled in a regiment and having *nolens volens*, to accept the conditions common to all.

What were these conditions, and how far did they differ from those offered to workmen before the factory system came into being or outside the factories? How did they react on wages in the small-scale industry, which still gave work to a large number of people? These are most important questions, and it would be desirable to answer them accurately and completely. Unfortunately the statistics, not only

---

[1] F. M. Eden, *State of the Poor*, I, 476. The idea that the worker's condition was the result of a sort of economic fatality, was, from then onwards, referred to as though it were scientifically proved: 'It is not probable that the arguments of philanthropists ever will have much weight in persuading the great mass of employers to increase the wages of the employees, for it is by imperious circumstances alone, which neither master nor workman can control, that the demands of the one and the concessions of the other are regulated.' Ibid., p. 494.

for the period we are describing but for all periods previous to the great inquiries and regular censuses of the nineteenth century, are so incomplete as to render their use both difficult and deceptive. The last volume of Thorold Rogers's *History of Prices*,[1] which is open to more than one criticism,[2] contains no reference to industrial wages.[3] We can rely on the accuracy of certain data, as for instance the figures actually noted on the spot by reliable observers, such as Arthur Young and the Board of Agriculture's correspondents; or the figures collected by Eden between 1790 and 1797 for his monumental work on the state of the poor;[4] or those scattered in great numbers throughout Parliamentary documents; and lastly, on those found in the account books of old industrial firms which by some miracle have escaped the usual fate of useless papers, and which in the last few years have been explored more and more.[5] But this is not enough, for as soon as one tries to classify them huge gaps appear, leaving whole districts and periods in the shadow. Conclusions based on such incomplete statistics cannot be accepted without reservation: we know very well how widely wages and prices vary in different districts,[6] and the most authentic figures become very misleading as soon as we try to calculate averages

[1] Thorold Rogers, *A History of Agriculture and Prices in England* (1259-1793). Volume VII (1703-93), in two parts, published after the author's death through the care of Mr Arthur G. L. Rogers, 1902.

[2] Some of these criticisms, in a concise form, will be found in our communication to the Société d'Histoire Moderne. See *Bulletin de la Société d'Histoire Moderne* (First Series), pp. 98-9.

[3] Beyond agricultural wages, the tables of the cost of labour (pp. 493-528) only give us the wages in the building trade. Tables drawn up with the aid of Young's *Journeys* are entirely devoted to agricultural wages. It is true that Thorold Rogers's book is entitled *A History of Agriculture and Prices*, but it might, at any rate, contain industrial wages as well as the daily prices of shares in the East India Company. (See pp. 803-83.)

[4] On his sources, see *State of the Poor*, Preface, pp. i-iv.

[5] Invaluable research work has been done in that direction by G. Unwin and his collaborators, who brought to light the records of the Oldknow firm; by T. S. Ashton, who studied the Soho, Coalbrookdale, Huntsman, Horsehay and Thorncliffe manuscripts; by J. L. and L. B. Hammond, who extracted so much valuable information from the Home Office papers; and by J. Lord, who had access to the Tew Park documents, containing part of the correspondence between Boulton and Watt. A comprehensive study of the history of industrial wages in the first decades of the factory system, based on such documents and on town records, remains to be undertaken.

[6] A. Young had thought he could draw up a general table of agricultural wages, showing that wages decreased according to the distance of the district from London. *North of England*, IV, 293-6. But Bowley's tables (*Wages in the United Kingdom*, Appendix) show that there were several high-wage centres, for instance in the East (*Norfolk and Suffolk*) and in the Midlands (*Warwick, Leicester, Nottingham*). The extreme figures were:

In 1770	9s. (Surrey and Nottingham)	and 6s. (York)
In 1793	10s. (Surrey)	and 7s. (Cumberland)
In 1795	11s. (Kent)	and 7s. (Cornwall)

and to deduce general statistics from them. We have to be content with this rough approximation, but without deceiving ourselves as to its real worth and without forgetting that its truth is never more than partial and local.

The fact that no complete statistics are available adds to the difficulty of interpreting those at our disposal, a difficulty which, even if they were more abundant and more reliable, would still be very great. If we want to discover not the nominal wage, i.e. the money paid for a certain time or for a certain piece of work, but the actual wage, together with its purchasing power, we are tackling a difficult and complicated problem the solution of which can only be obtained by comparing a number of different data. We ought first to know a man's total wage for a month, a season or a year, and how far it was reduced by either voluntary or compulsory unemployment. For a man may be well paid and yet earn very little, if he does not work every day. Then we should know whether he had any other source of income, as was the case with village workers, who when comparatively well off cultivated their plots of land or grazed their cows on the common, and who when very poor received help from the parish. We should also want to know what each member of the family contributed to the annual family budget. Then, even assuming that we have been able to solve that part of the problem, a no less difficult problem remains to be solved, for we should want to find out how this income was actually spent. And it would not be enough to know what were the price of foodstuffs and the rents. For unless we knew what kinds of food were actually consumed, and the relative quantities of each which the needs and habits of the consumers demanded,[1] such a list of prices would not be of much use. In order, therefore, to be able to draw any conclusions we should need to have at our disposal a great collection of facts which nearly always are missing, except for our own times. We are really able only to grasp some rough relationships between the phenomena. For instance we can find out the difference between nominal wages in several trades, their variations over a given period of time, and whether the variations in price of any given foodstuff follow their curve or not. It sometimes happens that these variations are so clearly marked that one can draw a definite conclusion from them, as when, for instance, there was a considerable rise in prices without a rise in wages, or vice versa. But usually the interpretation is difficult, and, however much one tries

[1] W. Cunningham points out that, during the Middle Ages, day labourers could get certain daily necessities (as, for instance, firewood) for nothing, which nowadays they would have to buy, and they had no knowledge of certain commodities such as tea and tobacco which have now become almost indispensable to the English working class. See *Growth of English Industry and Commerce*, II, 937-42. We must also reckon with the ever-growing importance of meat and of the money spent on alcoholic drinks.

to avoid such a fault, more or less arbitrary. It would, indeed, be impossible without the help of descriptive documents, which though perhaps less precise often bring us nearer reality than incomplete statistics.

Let us try to disentangle the main facts. One of the most striking, before as well as after the introduction of the factory system, is that the wages of industry were higher than those of agriculture.[1] A day labourer in 1770 earned 5s. to 6s. a week in winter and 7s. to 9s. in summer. In harvest time he earned as much as 12s.,[2] but that was only for a very short time and only in certain localities. At the same period a Manchester cotton weaver was earning from 7s. to 10s. a week,[3] a Leeds cloth weaver about 8s.,[4] and a Braintree drugget weaver 9s.,[5] while a Witney blanket weaver or a Wilton carpet maker received 11s. or more.[6] Wool-combers, thanks to their small numbers, to their technical skill, and also no doubt to their early organization, held a special position among textile workers and easily earned 13s. a week: this wage was about the same all over the country, as their habits were nomadic and they travelled from town to town in search of work and always supported one another.[7] Furnace keepers at Horsehay earned about 12s. a week, Rotherham blacksmiths 13s., Sheffield cutlers, 13s. 6d.,[8] Newcastle miners 15s.,[9] Staffordshire potters from 8s. to 12s., according to the nature of their work.[10] Among the worst paid were the frame knitters, who were badly exploited by the employers. In 1778 those in Leicestershire, with a fifteen-hour day, only earned 5s. 6d. a week. In Nottingham they complained that when all their workshop expenses had been deducted from their piece wage they hardly had 4s. 6d. left after a whole week's work.[11] But even in this

---

[1] This circumstance undoubtedly helped in the recruiting of labour for the factories. See W. Bowden, *Industrial Society in England towards the end of the Eighteenth Century*, pp. 253 ff.

[2] As, for instance, all round London and in the eastern counties, the cereal country. A. Young, *Southern Counties*, p. 62, and *North of England*, I, 171; III, 345. Wages in cash were slightly decreased when the day labourer received, according to custom, a measure of small beer. For farm hands it was halved, as they received board and lodging.

[3] A. Young, *North of England*, III, 190.

[4] Ibid., I, 137.

[5] Id., *Southern Counties*, p. 65.

[6] Ibid., p. 270.

[7] Ibid.; T. S. Ashton, *Iron and Steel in the Industrial Revolution*, p. 190.

[8] A. Young, *North of England*, I, 115 and 123.

[9] Ibid., IV, 322, and Brand, *History of Newcastle upon Tyne*, II, 681.

[10] A. Young, *North of England*, III, 255; and Ll. Jewitt, *The Ceramic Art of Great Britain*, II, 167-8.

[11] In one week they made twelve pairs of drawers, at an average wage of 7d. per pair (7s. a week). But from this 7s. deducted 9d. for frame rent, 3d. for workshop rent, 4d. for needles, 2d. for the assistant who got the work ready, 5d. for firing and

extreme case, made worse by a temporary crisis,[1] the nominal wage was scarcely lower than the normal wage of most agricultural labourers during two-thirds of the year.

By the end of the century the difference was not only maintained, but had perceptibly increased. During those twenty-five or thirty years which witnessed such changes in the economic and social order, agricultural labourers' wages rose a good deal. The average rates had become 7s. to 8s. in winter and 8s. to 10s. in summer.[2] But industrial wages had increased still more rapidly. In 1795, in spite of many days of unemployment, the workmen in the cotton spinning mills in Manchester, Bolton, Bury and Carlisle were earning an average weekly wage of 16s.,[3] while specialists, like printers of Indian muslins, earned as much as 25s. a week.[4] Metalworkers in Birmingham, Wolverhampton and Sheffield earned from 15s. to 20s.: this was the wage which Boulton and Watt paid their men.[5] These high wages were due to the flourishing condition of the textile and metal industries, and

[1] The following year the average wage rose from 4s. 6d. to 6s. or 7s. *Journals of the House of Commons*, XXXVII, 371-2.

[2] F. M. Eden, *State of the Poor*, II, 11, 17, 24, 45, 136, 275, 280, 379, 395, 424, 589, 712. Eden's figures refer to 1795 and 1796. For the preceding years, see the *Agricultural Surveys of the Board of Agriculture* published in 1794.

[3] Eden, *State of the Poor*, II, 60, 294, 360: 'They rarely work on Mondays, and many of them keep holiday two or three days in the week. It must, however, be confessed that at present constant and regular employment cannot be procured by all who are inclined to work.' Ibid., II, 357.

[4] *Minutes of the Evidence taken before the Committee to whom the Petition of several Journeymen Calico-Printers ... was referred* (1804), p. 17. Radcliffe describes them as 'well clad, the men with each a watch in his pocket, and the women dressed to their own fancy' and having at home 'a clock in elegant mahogany or fancy case, handsome tea services in Staffordshire ware, with silver or plated sugar-tongs and spoons'. W. Radcliffe, *Origin of the New System of Manufacture, commonly called 'Power Loom Weaving'*, p. 67.

[5] Eden, op. cit., II, 655, 739, 873. Boulton and Watt men were all engaged by written contracts for a period of four or five years. Many of these contracts have been preserved among the Soho MSS. Wages were generally increased over the whole period on a previously arranged scale. Joseph Hughes, blacksmith and fitter, engaged on July 27th, 1795, was to earn 16s. a week for the first year, 17s. for the second and so on up to 20s. In 1800 he renewed his contract for a four-year period on the understanding that he should be paid a fixed wage amounting to 21s. a week. In the contracts signed between 1780 and 1790 the wages, perceptibly lower, varied between 11s. and 15s. The same kind of document is also to be found among the Wedgwood MSS. in Stoke-on-Trent. A very interesting synopsis of documents concerning wages at Mellor in 1792 and 1793 is given by Unwin, *Samuel Oldknow and the Arkwrights*, pp. 167-9.

---

light during work hours, and 7d. for the sewing; so that expenses amounted to about 2s. 6d. Petition from the Stocking Frame Knitters, *Journals of the House of Commons*, XXXVI, 740.

to the rapid development which had followed on the change in equipment and technical processes. It is easy to understand how strong an
attraction they exercised on country folk, at a time when so many other
causes were working together to take them away from the land.

From the above figures it must not be assumed that the introduction of the factory system caused a general rise in wages. We
shall soon realize that this rise was more apparent than real, and that
in most industries it was followed by a fall which was particularly
disastrous owing to the great influx of labour during the good years. It
was in this way that the sad tribulations of the English weavers began.
Just after the invention of spinning machines the weavers were in a
very strong position, as in the whole of England there were not enough
shuttles to weave all the thread spun by the jennies and water frames.[1]
But this did not last long. The year 1792 was the high-water mark of
their short-lived prosperity. Then the calico and fustian weavers were
earning 15s. to 20s. a week and the velvet and fine-muslin weavers 25s.
to 30s.[2] But in the following year their wages were immediately affected
by the crisis in the cotton industry. In order to limit the rapid spread
of unemployment the Bolton manufacturers fixed among themselves
a maximum quantity of work for each home worker, corresponding
to a wage of 10s. a week.[3] From then onwards the fall was rapid.
In 1792 a weaver was paid £4 for weaving a piece of velvet. In 1794
he was only paid £2 15s., in 1796 £2, and in 1800 £1 16s., while at
the same time the piece grew longer, for instead of forty it was now
fifty yards long. Thus a good workman, working 14 hours a day, was
hardly able to earn 5s. or 6s. between one Sunday and the next.[4]

Why did this fall take place? The crisis of 1793 was obviously only
an incidental factor. At that date and in that branch of industry
there can have been no question of the competition of machinery: the
use of the power loom was still so rare that when the men laid their
grievances before Parliament they did not once mention it. The sole
cause of the fall in wages was the overcrowding of the labour market.
At first there were too few weavers, but then their numbers increased
out of all proportion. And among the new-comers were many country
labourers, used to low wages and quite ready to submit without

---

[1] Between 1780 and 1790 the price of a loom increased threefold. See *Journals of the House of Commons*, LVIII, 884-5.

[2] *Report upon the Petitions of Masters and Journeymen Weavers* (1800), pp. 11-13. *Journals of the House of Commons*, LV, 487 and 493 (evidence of James Holcroft, a Bolton weaver, and of Daniel Hurst, an Oldham weaver).

[3] *Report from the Committee ... on the Petitions of several Cotton Manufacturers and Journeymen Cotton Weavers* (1808), p. 21.

[4] *Journals of the House of Commons*, loc. cit. *To the Nobility, Gentry and People of Great Britain* (weavers' pamphlet), Place MSS., British Museum, Additional MSS., 27828, p. 199.

complaint to the conditions dictated by the manufacturers.[1] Drawn into the industry during the period of high wages, they intensified competition and therefore accelerated the fall in wages, which was very soon increased again by the introduction of machinery.

In the woollen industry, where development always lagged behind that of the cotton industry, the same causes brought about the same results, though at a slower pace. There was no rise in wages comparable to that which occurred during the expansion of the cotton industry, save in a few districts where it only happened for quite local reasons. While in 1796, in Leeds, the weekly wage of a weaver was as much as 18s.[2] and in some parts of Wiltshire a guinea,[3] everywhere else it was hardly more than 11s. or 12s.[4] The fall, even during the Napoleonic wars, was also less. But a fact which does not appear from statistics is that unemployment (for many years a recurrent evil in places like Norwich which had ceased to develop industrially, and where life was dying down) was now becoming general. The best workers were still able to make a living, as they benefited by piecework, but it was at the expense of a number of less able men who could no longer find employment. This was of course to the advantage of the employers. According to one of the witnesses before the Select Committee in 1806, 'the opulent clothiers [in Yorkshire] have made it a rule to have one third man more than they could employ, and then we have had to stand still part of our time'.[5] Thus as early as the first years of the nineteenth century the weavers' complaints began. Their discontent was already manifesting itself by underground agitation and frequent appeals to public authorities.[6] But they were still far from having reached the wretched state of destitution that made them, thirty years later, the typical instance of the old-world artisan crushed by the industrial revolution.

At the time, however, machinery only affected the weavers indirectly, but others were directly hit. Among them were the woolcombers, who had for so long held a proud and privileged position

[1] This is well brought out in P. Gaskell's *Artisans and Machinery*, p. 34. Hence the grave situation which after 1815 resulted from the end of the state of war, causing a new afflux of labour. Cf. S. Chapman, *The Lancashire Cotton Industry*, p. 46.

[2] F. M. Eden, *State of the Poor*, II, 847.

[3] At Chippenham and Bradford-on-Avon. *Report from the Committee on the State of the Woollen Manufacture in England* (1806), p. 483; Eden, op. cit., I, 782.

[4] Eden, II, 753 (Kendal 8s. to 12s.), 810 (Bradford 7s. to 11s.), 820 (Halifax 7s. to 11s.).

[5] *Report on the Woollen Manufacture* (1806), p. 111.

[6] In eight years four inquiries were set up as a result of their petitions. That of 1800 resulted in the setting up of a system of arbitration between employers and employees. That of 1802 dealt with the use of the gig mill in the south-western districts, that of 1806 dealt with the state of the woollen industry, and that of 1808 with the idea of a minimum wage.

among textile workers.[1] Cartwright's invention broke their pride by lowering the value of their recognized technical skill. Their wages, which previously had been 50 to 60 per cent higher than those of weavers, fell to about the same level.[2] In fact the combing engine was not in general use until much later.[3] But the mere threat to introduce it was a weapon in the employer's hands, enabling him to silence demands and crush resistance. The cloth shearers, another set of skilled workers, were similarly affected by the invention of the shearing machine. Their anxiety and anger when they found themselves threatened with reduction to the rank of labourers, mere tenders and slaves of machinery, was shown by the part they played in the riots of 1811-12.

As usual the lowest wages were earned by the women and children, and this was why the factories employed them in preference to men. The parish children seldom received a money wage. It was enough if they were housed and fed, and we know how that was done in many cases. The apprentices who did not live in the factory had to be paid. As 'doffers' and 'piecers'[4] in the spinning mills they received, according to their age, from one to four shillings a week.[5] The women, spinning with either a jenny or a mule, earned hardly more, their maximum wage being about five shillings a week.[6] However low these wages seem to us, there is no doubt that they were at least as good as those paid in the preceding period.[7] The work of women and children had never been in such demand before, and it was just this, the employment of cheap and inferior labour, which becoming more and more general constituted a real danger to the adult workers. That danger was first created but later lessened by machinery which as it developed became more difficult to tend, so that the system of filling the mills with parish apprentices had to be given up. It was the period of

[1] They insisted on being called 'gentlemen wool combers' and at the ale house they would not drink with the other men. S. and B. Webb, *History of Trade Unionism*, pp. 44 ff.

[2] 13s. a week in 1770. A. Young, *Southern Counties*, p. 270. 9s. to 10s. in 1795. Eden, *State of the Poor*, II, 385, 810, 820.

[3] After the great strike in 1825. See S. and B. Webb, *History of Trade Unionism*, p. 100.

[4] The 'doffer' looks after the carding machine and collects the cotton as it comes out. The 'piecer' joins up the broken threads during the spinning.

[5] Wirksworth spinning mill near Derby, 1797. F. M. Eden, *State of the Poor*, II, 130.

[6] The women wool spinners at Kendal earned 4s.; at Leicester, from 2s. to 4s.; at Newark (Nottinghamshire), from 1s. 6d. to 5s.; near Northampton, 3s. 1d. Ibid., pp. 385, 563, 753, and J. Donaldson, *General View of the Agriculture in the County of Northampton* (1794), p. 12.

[7] The women spinners round Manchester in 1770 earned 2s. to 5s. a week. A. Young, *North of England*, III, 192.

transition which here, as in all periods of far-reaching changes, caused the greatest difficulties and sufferings to individuals. This transitional period lasted for years, years full of misery though marked also by economic progress, and in spite of the benefits which it undoubtedly brought, it justly earned the instinctive curse of the common people.

IV

Its evils were made worse by England's other difficulties between 1793 and 1815. The nominal rise of wages, which has been noticed in most industries, bore no proportion to the rise of prices due to the war. A large proportion of foodstuffs was already being imported, especially cereals, the imports of which had greatly increased since 1770.[1] The slightest disturbance of the ordinary course of maritime trade now threatened the people of England with starvation. The first two-thirds of the eighteenth century had been a period of comparative prosperity and cheap living.[2] It was then that 'comfort', a new word and a new thing, made its first appearance not only in the middle class but in the working class, with leather shoes and white bread. The years 1765 to 1775 mark a halt in the progress of general prosperity. After a series of bad harvests the country rang with complaints of the high price of food.[3] During the summer of 1773 the price of wheat, which since 1710 had hardly ever been higher than 45s. a quarter, and on several occasions had fallen below 25s., rose to 66s. in the London market.[4] Disturbances took place in many districts, the crowd breaking into and looting corn mills, shops and markets.[5] Prices fell after a time, but never

[1] See Part I, chap. III. This import varied greatly from year to year according as to whether the harvest had been good or bad. In 1781 it rose as high as 160,000 quarters, in 1785 it was only 94,000 quarters, in 1790 it was 216,000 and in 1793, 480,000. *General Report on Enclosures*, p. 355.

[2] See Thorold Rogers, *Six Centuries of Work and Wages*, pp. 484 ff. The extreme figures for the cost of wheat during that period, in the records of Eton College, are 53s. 4d. in 1757 and 22s. 1d. in 1744.

[3] Eton Records, published by T. Tooke, *History of Prices*, II, 387-9. F. M. Eden, *State of the Poor*, III, 75-8, and *Abstract of the Answers and Returns to the Population Act*, 11 *Geo. IV*, I, lii, give somewhat different figures. Compare with Thorold Rogers's tables in *History of Agriculture and Prices in England*, VII, 4-229.

[4] See the many petitions in the *Journals of the House of Commons*, XXX. Among the pamphlets dealing with this subject we may quote: *An Inquiry into the Causes of the High Price of Provisions*, 1767, and *An Inquiry into the Connection between the Present Price of Provisions and the Size of Farms*, by a Farmer (J. Arbuthnot), 1773. See A. Young, *Political Arithmetic*, I, 42.

[5] At Bath and Malmesbury the rioters seized sacks of grain and sold them at 5s. a bushel; at Oxford, flour taken from the mills was distributed on the high road; at Leicester, they tried to force the prison doors; near Kidderminster there was a skirmish and eight men were killed. *Annual Register*, 1766 (p. 140). Similar disturbances took place in Birmingham: for a few hours the mob gained possession of the city and

again to the level of the earlier period. A poor harvest was enough to cause local scarcity, as was seen in 1783, and it was after a riot of this kind which broke out in Staffordshire[1] that Wedgwood wrote his 'Address to the Young Inhabitants of the Pottery'. Thus the position of the working class was already very precarious when in 1793 the war with France broke out.

During the first two years the war had no appreciable effect on the price of foodstuffs. Wheat, which in 1792 cost 47s. a quarter, rose in 1793 only to 50s. and in 1794 to 54s. But in 1795 and 1796 bad harvests caused an unprecedented rise. The average price rose to over 80s. In August 1795 it reached 108s.[2] This perilous crisis was followed by a period of quiet. Exceptionally good harvests, even more than the steps taken to encourage the import of grain,[3] brought a return of plenty. In 1797 wheat stood at 62s. a quarter and in 1798 at 54s. At one moment it even fell below 50s. But after the hard winter of 1798-9 the price rose again more than ever. In 1799 it went up to 75s. 8d., in 1800 to 127s. and in 1801 to 128s. 6d.[4] This was literally a famine price: the quartern loaf cost 1s. 10d., 5½d. a pound. Parliament, flooded with endless petitions, held one inquiry after another[5] and the Govern‧ment looked anxiously for some remedy. To save grain, all distilleries and starch factories were closed.[6] Individuals were requested to reduce their consumption of bread to a minimum, and it was proposed to

---

[1] Boatloads of flour and cheese were held up on the Grand Trunk Canal. A company of Welsh Fusiliers, sent to re-establish order, met with resistance and fired. It resulted in several convictions, one of them a death sentence. *Derby Mercury*, March 20th, 1783. Neither Thorold Rogers (VII, 183) nor the Eton Records enable us to say that there was a general rise in 1783. For the winter of 1782 Thorold Rogers quotes prices of 53s. to 58s.: but in Aug. 1782, we already find a price of 57s. and in May 1781, 55s. 6d. (pp. 176 and 179).

[2] T. Tooke, *History of Prices*, II, 182. Natural and artificial causes are here so entangled that it is difficult to analyse their separate effects. The most reasonable supposition is to attribute the variation in prices from one year to another to seasonal differences, and their general rise to the scarcity of imports during the war.

[3] In 1796 bounties were given on imports to the amount of £573,418 4s. 9d. *Report from the Select Committee appointed to consider the most effectual Means of facilitating the Enclosure and Improvement of the Waste, Uninclosed and Unproductive Lands* (1800), p. 224.

[4] Tooke, op. cit., I, 188, and II, 387 ff.

[5] The Committee on the High Price of Provisions presented six reports in 1800 and seven in 1801, which deserve to be studied. See also the debates in the House of Commons (Nov. 12th and 26th, 1800) and in the House of Lords (Nov. 14th and Dec. 15th, 1800), *Parliamentary History*, XXXV, 786-832 and 837-54.

[6] 41 Geo. III, c. 3.

---

fixed a maximum price for all foodstuffs. L. W. Clarke, 'History of Birmingham', III, 60-1.

encourage the planting of potatoes by a special bounty.[1] The Act of
1801, making the necessary procedure for enclosure cheaper and more
expeditious, was passed with the same end in view. It was hoped that
an improvement in agriculture would prevent a recurrence of famine.
But there was only one thing which could really prevent it and that was
the conclusion of peace, for which the whole nation cried aloud. As soon
as the preliminaries, the news of which was received with enthusiasm,
had been signed in London, the price of wheat fell to 72s. and then to
66s.[2] But this improvement was as short lived as the peace itself. And
it was, moreover, only comparative. Prices which in 1802 seemed
moderate and were thankfully received were the prices which, thirty
years before, had caused riots in many districts.

The prices not only of cereals but of all vital foodstuffs had risen
to such an extent that it was almost impossible for the poor man to live.
Between 1770 and 1775 meat cost 3d. to 4d. a pound, cheese 3½d., beer
8d. a gallon, potatoes 1s. 1d. to 1s. 4d. a bushel.[3] Between 1795 and
1800 meat cost, in different districts, 5d., 6d. or 8d., cheese 7d. or 8d.,
a gallon of beer 10d. or 1s., while potatoes were 2s. or 3s. a bushel.
And this was only at the beginning of the lean years, when corn was not
yet more than 80s. a quarter.[4] But, in our opinion, it would be rash to
attempt to draw a general price curve on the basis of such approximate
figures, as it could only be done at the expense of scientific honesty;
and *a fortiori* an attempt to make any mathematical comparison

[1] This bounty was to have been distributed among the cottagers by the Justices
of the Peace. *Reports from the Committee appointed to consider the present High Price of
Provisions*, p. 132.

[2] *Gentleman's Magazine*, vols. LXXI and LXXII, 1801-2 (monthly tables of
prices in the London market).

[3] See A. Young, *Southern Counties*, pp. 48, 62, 65, 152, 154, 157, 171, 187, 193,
253; *East of England*, IV, 311-26; *North of England*, I, 171, 313; II, 225; III, 12, 25,
134, 255, 278, 349; IV, 275 ff. Compare with Thorold Rogers's figures, VII, 291
and 557-8.

[4] F. M. Eden, *State of the Poor*, II, 11, 17, 24, 29, 74, 130, 275, 357, 379, 385, 565,
753, 782, 810, 812, etc.; Thorold Rogers, VII, 351 and 591. If we compare extremes
the difference is even more clearly marked. Here is a list of Nottingham food prices
in 1742 and 1796-1806, taken from documents consulted by S. and B. Webb:

	1742	1796-1806
4 lb. loaf of bread	3d.	1s. 2d.
1 lb. cheese	2d.	8d.
1 lb. butter	3½d.	1s. 3d.
1 lb. salt	1d.	4½d.
1 lb. beef	3d.	9d.
1 lb. mutton	1½d.	7d.
1 lb. veal	1½d.	8d.
1 lb. pork	2d.	8d.
1 lb. bacon	3½d.	1s. 0d.
1 fat goose	1s. 2d.	5s. 6d.
2 ducks	1s. 2d.	5s. 6d.
2 chickens	8d.	4s. 6d.
1 lb. soap	3½d.	10d.
1 lb. candles	4d.	10d.
1 bushel barley	1s. 0d.	4s. 4d.
1 bushel oats	8d.	3s. 1½d.
1 bushel malt	1s. 6d.	8s. 6d.

between the movements of prices and wages could only result in mystification. In order to realize the condition of the English workman at the end of the eighteenth century we must turn to the descriptive evidence of eye-witnesses.

When Arthur Young was in France, on the eve of the Revolution, he found that the condition of his own people compared favourably with the misery and sufferings of the French. Every page of his book is full of his proud consciousness of the enviable superiority of England over France and all continental countries. There was undoubtedly a considerable difference, although it should not be exaggerated. In England the labourer was better housed and dressed, and he fasted less often than in France. But his life was far from being luxurious. In the south he often had only bread and cheese to eat from one year's end to the other. In the north he also had barley or oatmeal porridge with skimmed milk.[1] Although potatoes had been cultivated in England much earlier than in France,[2] yet the place they occupied in the national diet still varied considerably in the different parts of the country.[3] On the other hand, the consumption of tea had increased surprisingly during the eighteenth century,[4] tea having become the ordinary drink of those for whom beer was too expensive. Rather than go without it, the poorest drank it without sugar. Meat was very seldom eaten.[5] When in 1795 the Hampshire magistrates wished that agricultural labourers could have meat at least three times a week, they were expressing an ideal which seemed to be far ahead of the times.[6]

[1] F. M. Eden, *State of the Poor*, I, 496, and II, 812; *Annals of Agriculture*, VII, 50.

[2] In Lancashire towards 1770 it is already so important that 'the husbandman often depends more upon a good crop of potatoes than of wheat or any other grain'. W. Enfield, *History of Liverpool*, p. 5. Thorold Rogers quotes potato prices in 1734, *History of Agriculture and Prices*, VII, 555.

[3] See family budgets of 1795-6 given by Eden, II, 767, 770, and III, cccxxxix ff. In four families of Bedfordshire agricultural labourers the amount spent on potatoes varied from 3d. to 1s. 3d. a week.

[4] In the budget of a Kendal weaver in 1795, the expenditure on tea and sugar was twice that on beer and almost half that on bread and flour. Ibid., II, 767. The use of tea sometimes replaced that of milk, which had become too expensive. (D. Davies, *The Case of Labourers in Husbandry*, p. 37.) In such cases it did not denote an improvement in the condition of the consumers.

[5] 'The food of poor people: bread and cheese and milk or water. Some small beer. Meat never, except on Sundays.' *Annals of Agriculture*, VII, 50 (Breconshire, Wales, 1787).

[6] 'Animal food and beer are necessary parts of the proper subsistence of labourers, to enable them to do justice in their work to themselves, their employers and the community. The labourer should have meat once a day, or, at least, three times a week. To the want of sufficient subsistence or animal food and malt liquor are to be attributed several pernicious habits, particularly the use of spirits.' Ibid., XXV, 365 ff.

In that respect the town worker was rather better off, as meat for him was no longer a luxury,[1] and he would have been able to buy meat even more frequently if he had reduced his consumption of beer and gin. But it should be borne in mind that alcoholism, which had been the curse of the country for many years, was the result as well as the cause of misery. 'Straw houses', where anyone could get drunk for a few pence, and where the innkeeper provided fresh straw for nothing, for the benefit of customers who were unable to walk home,[2] can hardly be considered as a sign of working-class prosperity. Drunkenness in famine years did not decrease in anything like the same proportion as public distress increased. The men went on drinking gin whilst they had no food for their children save bread and mouldy potatoes.[3]

The industrial revolution was not the cause of these sufferings, which the industrial England of 1800 felt far less than the rural France of 1789. In so far as the use of machinery resulted in a reduction of labour it did, no doubt, make matters worse. But a more immediate and more baneful consequence of the industrial revolution was the creation of a distressing housing problem. The rapid growth of large industrial centres immediately gave rise to overcrowding in its worst form. Working-class districts with dismal narrow streets and tumbledown houses, too small for the pale and emaciated population which thronged them, already existed in Manchester before 1800. Many people lived in cellars, without light or air. A medical report written in 1793 states that 'In some parts of the town the cellars are so damp that they are unfit for habitation ... I have known many laborious families who, after a short stay in damp cellars, were lost to the community ... The poor mostly suffer from the insufficiency of the windows in cellars. Fever is the usual effect, and I have known very often cases of consumption

---

[1] Eden, op. cit., II, 60 (Carlisle cotton operatives), 753 (Kendal wool weavers), 873 (Sheffield ironworkers).

[2] Place MSS., British Museum, Additional MSS., 27825, p. 186. The first attempts to cope with this evil were made in 1736. That was the date of the famous pamphlet, *Distilled Liquor the Bane of the Nation*. As the result of a petition from the Middlesex Justices of the Peace, Parliament intervened. A very high excise duty was put on spirits and the sellers had to buy a licence. The sale of gin was even forbidden for a little while, but this was very difficult to enforce, and gave rise to disturbances in London and other cities.

[3] See T. Carter, *Memoirs of a Working Man*, p. 43: 'My father's wages were but ten shillings and sixpence per week, and my mother's little school brought from two to three shillings more. With very little besides this scanty income, they had to provide for the wants of themselves and four children, while bread was sold at the enormous price of 1s. 10d. for the quartern loaf. We were consequently forced to put up with very insufficient food ... Potatoes also were excessively dear, and moreover were of bad quality through the wetness of the preceding summer [1799]. A quarter of a peck of these, which cost 4d., with a little melted suet poured over them, and a very small allowance of bread, constituted the dinner of the family.'

which can be traced to such causes.' Conditions were still worse in low-class lodging houses, where new-comers took beds by the night. 'The horror of these houses cannot easily be described: a lodger fresh from the country often lies down on a bed filled with infection by its last tenant, or from which the corpse of a victim to fever has only been removed a few hours before.'[1] The picture which fifty years later was laid before a frightened public by philanthropists and reformers was even worse.[2] The evil grew in extent, if not in gravity, with the growth of industrial towns, while its nature and causes remained the same.

Yet, badly housed and fed as he was, the working man did not succeed in reducing his expenses to meet the rise in prices and was usually unable to make both ends meet. The budget of a working-class family with children almost always showed a deficit during a crisis,[3] and in order to meet the deficit they had to rely on public assistance. This is why no study of the working class in England would be complete without some reference to the Poor Law and the workhouse.

V

The Poor Law, one of the most original branches of English legislation,[4] dates from the time of Elizabeth.[5] Like the earlier measures, which it only followed and completed, its original object seems to have

---

[1] Paper addressed by Dr Ferriar to the Committee for the regulation of the police in Manchester (1790). (Quoted from Aikin, *A Description of the Country from thirty to forty miles round Manchester*, p. 193.) Dr Ferriar, a Manchester physician, did pioneer work in the study of health conditions in the industrial district where he practised his profession. See W. Bowden, *Industrial Society in England towards the end of the Eighteenth Century*, pp. 265-6, and Dr Ferriar's *Medical Histories and Reflections*, 3 vols., London, 1792.

[2] J. P. Kay, *The Moral and Physical Condition of the Working Classes* (1832); P. Gaskell, *The Manufacturing Population of England, its Moral, Social and Physical Conditions* (1833); *Artisans and Machinery* (1836, a new edition of the previous book); A. E. Buret, *De la Misère des Classes laborieuses en France et en Angleterre* (1840); W. Cooke Taylor, *Notes of the Manufacturing Districts of Lancashire* (1842); F. Engels, *Die Lage der arbeitenden Klasse in England* (1845).

[3] F. M. Eden, *State of the Poor*, II, 767-70, and III, cccxxxix.

[4] W. J. Ashley (*An Introduction to English Economic History and Theory*, II) shows that the English Poor Law, although original, was not unique. Similar institutions have existed in the Netherlands, in France and in Germany. But from the end of the seventeenth century they developed on different lines.

[5] It was not drawn up all at once. The 1536 Act (27 Henry VIII, c. 25) made it an obligation for the parishes to help the destitute. The 1572 Act (14 Eliz., c. 5) levied a poor rate and empowered the Justices of the Peace to appoint 'overseers' whose duty it was to organize the parish relief. The 1576 and 1597 Acts (18 Eliz. c. 3, and 39 Eliz. c. 3) made reformatories general. They had at first only existed in London. The 1601 Act (43 Eliz., c. 2), which collected and completed earlier stipulations, is the 'Poor Law' which, in spite of many successive alterations, has actually survived until our own time. See G. Nicholls, *History of the English Poor Law*, I, 160 ff., and E. M. Leonard, *The early History of English Poor Relief*, pp. 36 ff.

been the suppression of beggary and vagrancy, as much at least as the relief of distress. It was prompted both by Christian charity and by strong social prejudice. The idea that charity was a pious act and atoned for sins caused a great deal of money to be given and spent quite indiscriminately, but did not prevent those who received charity from being looked upon with fear and suspicion. Thus rigour and weakness alternated in the enforcement of the law, though as a rule it was rigour that prevailed. The object was to suppress the dangerous class of professional beggars which, about the middle of the sixteenth century, was growing to alarming proportions.[1] Every person receiving parish relief, unless a hopeless cripple, was made to work, and this provision was supported by stern penalties. The first offence was punished by a whipping or by sentence to the reformatory. Further offences were treated by the lash or by branding with red-hot iron.[2] Later on, the workhouse in which the paupers were confined came to be much more like a prison than a refuge. The fear it inspired was relied on to frighten away all who had not reached the last stage of destitution.

One of the reasons why this charitable institution became so inhumanly severe was because it was organized on a strictly local basis. Each parish only reckoned on having to support its own poor and not new-comers, who were looked on as intruders. There is little doubt but that some parishes did try to rid themselves of their obligations at the expense of richer or less miserly ones.[3] To remedy this the 'Act of Settlement' was passed in 1662.[4] Anyone leaving his residence could be officially sent back to the parish where he was legally 'settled'. His removal was ordered by two Justices of the Peace at the request of the overseer of the poor rate. And for this measure to be taken it was not necessary for the person concerned to be in need of immediate relief and a burden to the parish. It was enough that this should be considered as a likely occurrence.[5]

[1] On vagrants and sturdy beggars during the sixteenth century, see Ashley, op. cit., II, pp. 386-95.

[2] This was the first penalty for vagrancy (14 Eliz., c. 5). For the third offence the penalty was hanging.

[3] See F. M. Eden, State of the Poor, I, 144.

[4] 14 Chas. II, c. 12: The preamble runs thus: 'By reason of some defect in the laws poor people are not restrained from going from one parish to another, and therefore do endeavour to settle themselves in those parishes where there is the best stock, the largest commons or wastes to build cottages, and the most woods for them to burn and destroy, and when they have consumed it, then to another parish, and at last become rogues and vagabonds, to the great discouragement of parishes to provide stocks where it is liable to be devoured by strangers.'

[5] Thorold Rogers compares the condition of labourers under the Act of Settlement to serfdom, and explains how the great landowners took advantage of it to secure cheap labour from the parishes adjoining their estates: 'The law of settlement not only fixed the tenant to the soil, but enabled the opulent landowner to rob his neighbour and to prematurely wear out the labourer's health and strength. All this,

Thus the law safeguarded the interests of the parishes. But at what a cost! The whole working class found itself deprived of one of its most valuable rights: the right to move about freely. If a labourer left his village because he could find no work and went to another village, he ran the risk of being turned out as 'likely to become chargeable'.[1] He was thus deprived of his sole chance of earning his living, and lest it might become necessary to give him assistance he was condemned to hopeless destitution, with no other means of livelihood but public or private charity. The law was, of course, not always enforced, but it often was, and in some cases with incredible brutality: 'Coming up to town last Sunday I met with an instance shocking to humanity: a miserable object in the agonies of death crammed into a cart to be removed lest the parish should be at the expense of its funeral. Other instances every day met with are the removals of women with child and in labour, to the danger of both their lives, lest the child should be born in the parish.'[2]

This passionate protest was made in a speech delivered in 1773. Almost at the same time Adam Smith was violently attacking a system which from his point of view was the height of absurdity.[3] But twenty

[1] As a proof of where he was legally 'settled', a man had to produce a certificate signed by the churchwarden and the overseers of his parish, and countersigned by two Justices of the Peace. He was then allowed to settle in his new home, the parish authorities keeping the right to turn him out of the parish if he became 'actually chargeable' (8 & 9 Will. III, c. 30). There was such a desire on the part of ratepayers to prevent any increase of the poor tax that in many districts the farmers hired labourers for fifty-one weeks only, so as to make it impossible for them to become 'settled' in the locality of their employment by a full year's residence. See J. L. and L. B. Hammond, *The Village Labourer*, pp. 112 ff. 'It was claimed that the industrial parishes in need of labor were allowing laborers to come, but were refusing settlement, and, whenever they seemed likely to become dependent upon the rates, were sending them back to the parishes whence they came.' W. Bowden, *Industrial Society towards the end of the Eighteenth Century*, p. 258. W. Hasbach (*History of the English Agricultural Labourer*, pp. 172-3) observes that removals were not a daily occurrence, and quotes figures from Eden's *State of the Poor* (I, 181 and 296), according to which there were in a year only two removals from Ashford (2,000 inhabitants), three from Kendal (8,000 inhabitants), and twenty from Sheffield (35,000 inhabitants). But the explanation may be that many paupers were prevented from leaving their parish.

[2] *Parliamentary History*, XVII, 844 (Speech by Sir William Meredith). The same matter was debated in 1775. Ibid., XVIII, 541-6.

[3] Adam Smith, *Wealth of Nations*, Book I, chap. X. Arthur Young described that system as 'the most false, mischievous, and pernicious system that ever barbarism devised'. *Political Arithmetic*, I, 93.

---

too, was done when the patriots and placemen chattered about liberty and arbitrary administration, and fine ladies and gentlemen talked about the rights of man and Rousseau and the French Revolution, and Burke and Sheridan were denouncing the despotism of Hastings. Why at his own door Burke might have daily seen serfs who had less liberty than those Rohillas, whose wrongs he described so dramatically.' Thorold Rogers, *Six Centuries of Work and Wages*, p. 434.

years went by before that system disappeared. What destroyed it was the irresistible pressure of the new conditions brought about by the industrial revolution. For large-scale production on modern lines a free circulation of labour was absolutely necessary. The new industries had been able to develop only because the law of settlement had been constantly broken, and because the trend of the population towards the towns was so great and so universal that individual measures were unable to stop it. But as the factory system grew it became more and more impatient of the fetters which hampered its development, and thus a change which had not been conceded through humanitarian considerations was ultimately agreed to through utilitarian ones, founded on the doctrine of *laissez-faire.* 'The law of settlement,' William Pitt said in the House of Commons, 'prevents the workman from going to that market where he could dispose of his industry to the greatest advantage, and the capitalist from employing a person who is qualified to procure him the best returns for his advances.'[1] The Act of 1795 took away from the parish authorities their power of preventive expulsion. Only persons without means of subsistence and actually on the rates could be sent back to the parish of their origin, and time had to be allowed before the removal if they were sick or crippled.[2] Thus the trammels to industry were abolished, together with the intolerable oppression of the working population. In so far as man (a less inert factor than capital and commodities) obeyed the economic laws of supply and demand, the mobility of labour was now complete.

Another reform, which took place just about the same time, had less happy results though dictated by the best motives, viz. the distribution of money allowances to supplement low wages. As a matter of fact this was no new practice, though for a long time the law had set its face against it — so much so that, under an Act of Parliament passed in 1723, local authorities had to build workhouses, and to refuse relief to anyone who was not willing to work there.[3] Nevertheless, and in spite of the law, the parishes in certain cases had gone on giving out-relief. By doing so they avoided the necessity of entirely supporting families

---

[1] William Pitt, *Speeches,* II, 369 (Feb. 12th, 1796).

[2] 35 Geo. III, c. 101: 'Whereas many industrious poor persons, chargeable to the parish, township, or place where they live, merely from want of work there, would in any other place where sufficient employment is to be had maintain themselves and families without being burthensome to any parish, township or place, and such poor persons are for the most compelled to live in their own parishes, townships, or places, and are not permitted to inhabit elsewhere, under pretence that they are likely to become chargeable to the parish, township or place, into which they go for the purpose of getting employment, although the labour of such poor persons might, in many instances, be very beneficial to such parish, township, or place ... '

[3] 9 Geo. I, c. 7.

who though not completely destitute yet had not enough to live on. But to many people this seemed merely conniving at, and pandering to, laziness and disorder.[1] In the second half of the eighteenth century the poor were treated with much less severity, and this was due to that wave of sentimentalism which so deeply affected the European mind. People ceased to regard destitution as the mere consequence of improvidence and vice, and were moved by the thought of so much undeserved suffering.[2] This new spirit was embodied in an Act of 1782, known as Gilbert's Act,[3] which improved poor-law administration and introduced less narrow and more humane regulations. The parishes were empowered to give out-relief to able-bodied persons, the workhouses being reserved for children, old people and cripples. Parish officers were to find work for them in the farms and if the wages were inadequate, to supplement them from the poor rate.[4] Thus the community appeared not only to recognize the right to work but also the right to live.[5]

These regulations were not put into force at once throughout the country. In fact, Gilbert's Act was based on the principle of local option, every parish being free either to apply the new system or to abide by

[1] 'It is the opinion of this Committee, that the present method of giving money out of the parochial rates to persons capable of labour, in order to prevent such persons claiming an entire subsistence for themselves and their families from the parishes, is contrary to the spirit and intention of the laws for the relief of the poor, is a dangerous power in the hands of parochial officers, a misapplication of public money, and a great encouragement to idleness and intemperance.' *Report from the Committee on amendments to the Poor Law, Journals of the House of Commons*, XXVIII, 599 (1759).

[2] In 1753 Fielding wrote these famous lines: 'The sufferings of the poor are less known than their misdeeds, and therefore we are less apt to pity them. They starve and freeze and rot among themselves, but they beg and steal and rob among their betters.' See his two pamphlets: *An Enquiry into the Causes of the late Increase of Robbers* (1751) and *A Proposal for making an Effectual Provision for the Poor* (1753). A few years later J. Massie wrote: 'Many people are reduced to that pitiable way of life by want of employment, sickness or some other accident: and the reluctance or ill success with which such unfortunate people do practise begging is frequently manifested by a poor and emaciated man or woman being found drowned or starved to death; so that though choice, idleness, or drunkenness may be reasons why a number of people are beggars, yet this drowning and perishing for want are sad proofs that the general cause is necessity.'

[3] 22 Geo. III, c. 83. It was due to the initiative of T. Gilbert, a member of the House of Commons. His main object was to group the parishes into Unions for the collection and spending of the poor rate. These Unions (which could sue and be sued) were managed by guardians and visitors appointed by the Justices of the Peace. Parishes were forbidden to contract with private persons for the distribution of poor relief except under strict supervision. G. Nicholls, *History of the English Poor Law*, II, 83-8.

[4] This was the origin of the *roundsmen*, who have been mentioned above (Part I, chap. III).

[5] See E. Halévy, *L'Evolution de la doctrine utilitaire de* 1789 à 1815, p. 98.

the earlier regulations. Circumstances completed what had been thus begun, for famine at the end of the century produced a terrible increase of pauperism. What was to be done to mitigate these evils and these dangers? This was the problem before the Berkshire magistrates who in May 1795 gathered at the Pelican Tavern in the village of Speen-hamland.[1] In the south-west the general distress caused by the rise in the cost of living had been aggravated by a crisis in the woollen industry, which at the time was thought to be only temporary, but was, in fact, the beginning of an irretrievable decay, finally to deprive the country people of one of their traditional resources. Disturbances had already broken out in market places. Shops and warehouses here and there had been plundered by the mob.[2] The magistrates, assembled to consider the situation and to devise a remedy,[3] gave it as their opinion that 'the present state of the poor required further assistance than had generally been given them'. Such assistance, in order to be equitable, was to vary with the cost of living. A scale was drawn up which made the minimum cost of living dependent on the price of corn:

'When the gallon loaf of seconds flour, weighing 8 lb. 11 oz., shall cost 1s., then every poor and industrious man shall have for his own support 3s. weekly, either procured by his own or his family's labour, or an allowance from the poor rates, and for the support of his wife and every other of his family, 1s. 6d. When the gallon loaf shall cost 1s. 6d., then every poor and industrious man shall have 4s. weekly for his own support, and 1s. 10d. for the support of every other of his family; and so in proportion as the price of bread rises or falls, that is to say, 3d. for the man and 1d. to every other of his family on every 1d. which the loaf rises above 1s.'[4]

This was the famous decision known as the Speenhamland Law. It was, as a matter of fact, observed as a regular law, at first in the county concerned and later throughout the whole kingdom.[5]

The men who drew up the Speenhamland Law only meant it as a

[1] Near Newbury in Berkshire.

[2] J. L. and L. B. Hammond call these disturbances 'the revolt of the housewives'. *The Village Labourer*, p. 121.

[3] Their meeting was held in consequence of a resolution taken at the General Quarter Sessions of Berkshire in the preceding month. Ibid., pp. 161-2.

[4] *Reading Mercury* of May 11th, 1795. The complete table is given in Eden's *State of the Poor*, I, 577. Similar tables, with slightly different figures, were drawn up in other counties.

[5] As early as October 1795 Arthur Young wrote in a circular letter to the correspondents of the Board of Agriculture: 'It having been recommended by various quarter sessions that the price of labour should be regulated by that of bread corn, have the goodness to state what you conceive to be the advantages or disadvantages of such a system.' *Annals of Agriculture*, XXV, 345.

temporary expedient. They were probably actuated chiefly by the fear of a popular rising, the French Revolution having given the gentry much to think about. In any case, the principle was a very bold one. The Berkshire magistrates affirmed that every man has the right to a minimum of subsistence, and that if he can earn only part of it then society owes him the difference.[1] This principle, implied in the Act of 1782, was here formally expressed. Almost at once it received legal confirmation, for the 1723 Act was repealed and out-relief was authorized in all parishes.[2] This reform of poor relief was to have very noticeable, if not very satisfactory, effects on the condition of the working class.

Its popularity is not to be wondered at. The crisis through which England was passing had wiped out all distinctions between the poor and the destitute. Not only among country people, who were feeling the enclosures and the decline of small rural industries, but also among workshop and factory hands distress was great and applications for relief numerous. This can be seen by the increase in the poor rate. In 1785 it was £2,000,000, in 1801 £4,000,000, and in 1812 6½ millions.[3] In many cases people came to rely on out-relief as a usual and necessary help, when formerly they would have tried to earn their own living. Arthur Young wrote: 'There was formerly found an unconquerable aversion to depend on the parish, inasmuch that many would struggle through life with large families, never applying for relief. That spirit is annihilated.'[4] Such was the first deplorable result of a seemingly generous policy. Too many English working men became paupers and felt the degrading influence of charity: 'It becomes a struggle between the pauper and the parish, the one to do as little and to receive as much as possible, and the other to pay by no rule but the summons and order of the Justice. The evils resulting are beyond all calculation, for the motives to industry and frugality are cut up by the roots, when every poor man knows that, if he does not feed himself, the parish must do it for him, and that he has not the most distant hopes of ever attaining independency, let him be as industrious and frugal as he may be.'[5] Thus relief given to destitution was becoming a premium on improvidence and laziness.[6] There is no doubt that in

[1] In practice out-relief simply replaced the wages formerly earned in domestic industry.

[2] 36 Geo. III, c. 23. At one time Pitt thought of getting Parliament to pass the Speenhamland Law. On his Bill of 1797 and Bentham's criticism of it, see E. Halévy, op. cit., pp. 101 and 152.

[3] F. M. Eden, *State of the Poor*, I, 363-72; G. Nicholls, *History of the English Poor Law*, II, 133.

[4] *Annals of Agriculture*, XXXVI, 504.

[5] Ibid.

[6] It also sometimes happened that the poor rate, being distributed without discrimination, went to swell the savings of some hardworking and wily workman:

spite of, or perhaps because of the fundamental fallacy of the system, its immediate object was attained, for the alleviation of the workers' distress removed all danger of serious disturbances. Thus the country remained comparatively quiet during the critical years of the Napoleonic wars, while the new Poor Law removed some of the obstacles which stood in the way of the great economic change, which was steadily progressing regardless of revolutions and European wars. In some districts the opposition to machinery was almost suppressed by parish relief, which partly made up for the loss of earnings previously derived from cottage industry and had the advantage of entailing no effort. Some country women were known to break their spinning wheels with their own hands.[1]

As a matter of fact the system worked largely at the expense of the very persons whom it was supposed to help. When the owning classes complained of the poor rate becoming heavier and heavier they overlooked the fact that it really amounted to an insurance against revolution, while the working class, when they accepted the scanty allowance doled out to them, did not realize that it was partly obtained by a reduction of their own legitimate earnings. For the inevitable result of 'allowances' was to keep wages down to the lowest rate, and even to force them below the limit corresponding to the irreducible needs of the wage-earner.[2] The farmer or the manufacturer relied on the parish to make up the difference between the sum he paid the men and the sum on which the men could live. For why should they incur an expense which could so easily be foisted on to the body of ratepayers? On the other hand, those in receipt of parish relief were willing to work for a lower wage, and thus made competition quite impossible to those who

---

[1] *Annals of Agriculture*, XXV, 635.

[2] A complete list of charges against the system will be found in the *Report from ... His Majesty's Commissioners appointed to inquire into the Administration and practical Operation of the Poor Laws* (1834). See W. Hasbach, *History of the English Agricultural Labourer*, pp. 183-4, whose conclusion is that the operation of Gilbert's Act and of the Speenhamland Law was 'a veritable curse to the labourer'.

'In my native village in Hampshire I well remember two instances of agricultural labourers who raised themselves through the machinery of the allowance system to the rank and fortune of small yeomen ... They had their allowances, lived on their fixed wages with the profit of their bye labour, one being pig killer to the village, and therefore always busy from Michaelmas to Lady Day at a shilling a pig, and the offal, on which his family subsisted, with the produce of their small plot for half the year. In the end the allowance, saved scrupulously, and, I presume, made a profound secret, was invested in land by each. The one bought forty acres of poor soil, on which he got an independent and comfortable living, the other some twenty, on which he did still better, for the land was some of the best in the village.' Thorold Rogers, *Six Centuries of Work and Wages*, pp. 502-3.

received no parish help.[1] The paradoxical result arrived at was that the so-called 'poor rate' meant an economy for the employers, and a loss for the industrious workman who expected nothing from public charity. Thus the pitiless interplay of interests had turned a charitable law into a bond of iron.

Its worst effects were felt by the rural population,[2] for it completed the evolution which had begun in consequence of the enclosures and of the engrossing of farms. Destitution and idleness broke the last links that bound the countryman to the land, and drove him, demoralized and indifferent to the total loss of his independence, to the labour market in the cities. The industrial population was apparently less affected by the endemic plague of pauperism, as it was partly protected by the progress of industry and a comparatively high rate of wages. But there was always the risk of unemployment, which involved parish relief with its worst consequences. Thus the influence of that system pervaded the whole working class, and everywhere had the same results, creating more distress than it alleviated, enslaving and humiliating a considerable part of the nation. This was the price paid for the peace of mind of the ruling classes during a grave crisis, and for England's triumphs abroad — the victories of Nelson and Wellington. And poor-law money, extorted partly from the public and partly from the poor themselves, was one of the foundations upon which the great fortunes of industrial capitalism were erected.

[1] The authors of the 1834 report found that manufactures where normal wages were paid proved unable to compete with establishments which employed assisted paupers, so that 'a manufacturer in Macclesfield could be ruined in consequence of the defective administration of the Poor Laws in Essex'. *Report from ... His Majesty's Commissioners appointed to inquire into the Administration and Practical Operation of the Poor Laws*, p. 43.

[2] Most of the facts quoted in the report of 1834 relate to rural parishes.

CHAPTER FOUR

INTERVENTION AND
LAISSEZ-FAIRE

THE Poor Law, the working of which has just been described, was a remedy often worse than the disease itself. Even had it been better conceived or better administered it could never have been more than a palliative. For the industrial revolution created a problem which even the most ingenious devices of charity could never solve. How was it possible to improve the condition of the working multitude, who had so small a share in the wealth created by their labours? For the artisan, who after having served a master hoped to become a master himself, this question did not arise. But for the workman, a mere tool in a huge undertaking which he had not one in a thousand chances of ever managing himself,[1] this was, on the contrary, the essential question. His future and that of his family, the only future to which he could ever look forward, was involved. So far his claims had no revolutionary character.[2] He did not question the established order of things, and the thought of obtaining a freer and better life by a complete overthrow of the social structure had never occurred to him. What he asked for was a higher wage (and in most cases indeed he merely resisted a reduction); some security against unemployment due to the introduction of machinery or an excessive number of apprentices; and milder or less arbitrary discipline in the workshop. In all these things his interests were in direct opposition to those of his employer, which were to reduce wages to a minimum, to lower the cost of production by the use of mechanical equipment and cheap labour, and to maintain his uncontrolled authority in and about the

---

[1] This was the point made in 1804 by the Committee who reported on the calico printers' petition against the Combination Law: 'The legislature could never mean to injure the man whose only desire is to derive a subsistence from his labour, and that indeed is all a journeyman calico printer can look to, for from the particular nature of his trade, differing much from others, he cannot, from the capital required, ever calculate upon becoming a master.' *Report on the Petition presented by the Journeymen Calico-Printers* (1804), p. 7.

[2] Schulze-Gaevernitz, *La Grande Industrie*, p. 42, writes on the contrary that 'there was in England in the first decades of the nineteenth century a labour party with socialistic and revolutionary tendencies, far stronger and more dangerous than any similar movement seen later on the Continent'. It seems difficult to justify such an opinion. Riots which broke out here and there, the most serious of which were the Luddites', were never actuated by consciously revolutionary ideas. And as for communistic doctrines worked out by individual theorists like Thomas Spence, they do not appear to have had the least influence on popular opinion.

factory. Class contest was the inevitable result of this opposition. The workers had already begun to organize, and very soon their organization became strong enough to alarm the government, and to induce it to take exceptional measures against their activities.

I

In a previous chapter we have shown the difference between the temporary combinations, formed under special circumstances to remedy special grievances and breaking up as soon as the case was either won or lost, and permanent combinations, ready to protect the interests of their members on every occasion that might arise.[1] The former, like the spontaneous revolts which gave them birth, and with which as a rule they came to an end, belong to no particular period or economic system. The latter, on the other hand, have a clearly defined origin: they made their appearance at the moment when the producer was divorced from the means of production.[2] They represent the lasting opposition of capital and labour, which had been previously so closely intertwined as to be sometimes hardly distinguishable. The earliest combinations appeared some fifty years before the beginning of the modern industrial system, being connected with that gradual development of capitalistic organization which immediately preceded the era of machinery and factories. But it was the factory system which gave the movement its magnitude and its direction. It formed the workers into a class bound together by common grievances. It showed them that they must combine and help one another, since the only weapon of the wage-earners against the power of capital lay in the strength of numbers.

The first workers' associations were formed between 1700 and 1780 in the woollen industry: they were those of the combers, the weavers and the stocking-frame knitters.[3] The cotton industry soon followed suit. In 1787, when the Glasgow muslin manufacturers tried to take advantage of the surplus of labour to cut down piece rates, they were met by organized resistance. The men combined and refused to work for less than a certain minimum rate. Employers who refused to pay that mini-

---

[1] See Part I, chap. I.

[2] See S. and B. Webb, *History of Trade Unionism*, pp. 25 ff.

[3] Mention should also be made of the organization of the small-ware weavers, who, as early as 1753, formed a union divided into 'shops', each one of which sent a delegate to a central executive committee. A pamphlet, preserved in the Manchester Central Library, contains the rules of this Society: *The Worsted Small-Ware Weavers' Apology, Together with all their Articles which either concern their Society or Trade; to which is added a Farewell Discourse made by their first Chairman, all faithfully collected together* (Manchester, 1756). The author used the pseudonym of Timothy Shuttle.

mum were boycotted. The struggle ended in rioting and street shooting, but the way in which the opposition was organized and sustained seems to show that the men had behind them an organization strong enough to control and discipline its members.[1] In 1792 a similar dispute between the Bolton and Bury manufacturers and the cotton weavers ended in a real collective agreement. The employers bound themselves not to change the 'counts' of yarn used for various classes of goods without raising wages in proportion to the fineness of the material. The men in return agreed to give up the 1½d. in every shilling which they had been receiving to defray the cost of accessory requisites, hitherto supplied by them. This agreement was observed by both parties for six years, 'until manufacturers began to multiply, and every new hand found out some new invention to reduce the price of weaving'.[2]

These organizations, at first quite local, rapidly spread and joined up with one another. In 1799 a Society of Cotton Weavers exerted its influence throughout Lancashire and, perhaps, even beyond. Its main object was to lay the men's complaints before the public authorities. Far from concealing the existence of their society they boldly appealed to public opinion. Thanks to William Radcliffe[3] we can read the text of a manifesto issued by their general committee, sitting at Bolton on May 23rd, 1799. It began by setting forth the policy which the society proposed to follow: 'The present existing laws that should protect weavers &c. from imposition being trampled under foot for want of a union amongst them, they have come to a determination to support each other in their just and legal rights, and to apply to the legislature of the country for such further regulations as it may in its wisdom deem fit to make, when the real state of the cotton manufactory shall have been laid before it.' This preamble was followed by protests against the fears and suspicions to which the very notion of a great workers' union gave rise: 'Ye who are our enemies … are you afraid that we should approach Government and there tell the truth, that ye use the mean artifice of stigmatizing us with the name of Jacobins, that ye raise your rumours of plots, riots, etc? We disdain your calumny and look upon you with that contempt you merit[4] …

---

[1] David Bremner, *The Industries of Scotland*, p. 283.

[2] *Report from the Select Committee on the Handloom Weavers' Petitions* (1835), p. 448.

[3] *Origin of the New System of Manufacture, commonly called 'Power Loom Weaving'*, pp. 73-6.

[4] We should also note that they had been accused of being unpatriotic and of having a secret understanding with foreign revolutionaries. 'How unjustly do those calumniate us who assert that our meetings are calculated to sacrifice the independence of our country. It is the reverse, for should the clarion ever sound "To arms! England is in danger!" we know what is our duty and what is our interest, and not only ours, but the duty and interest of every individual.' Ibid.

Rioting, or any illegal behaviour we detest, and are firmly attached to our King and country, and to promote their prosperity shall ever be the object most dear to our hearts ... Is there anything to fear by us meeting together? We shall neither interfere with Church nor State, but strictly confine ourselves to a private grievance, which we wish to lay before Government, and it will remain to be determined by it whether or not our case merits redress.'

With the weavers' grievances we are already familiar. They complained not only of the fall in the rates of wages but of the growing demands of the manufacturers, who had already several times increased the length of the piece.[1] While the society's main object was to lay the case for the men before Parliament, yet it was at the same time trying to find some way of coming to an understanding with the employers: 'If the manufacturers would think proper to condescend so far as to call a meeting, the committee of the association will send a deputation to wait upon them ... The weavers do not consider themselves in opposition with the masters: on the contrary, they entertain the same sentiment that certain prejudicial practices prevail that incommode the regular progress of the trade.'[2] Thanks to this conciliatory tone, and to its declared policy of submitting to the decision of Parliament, the Cotton Weavers' Society was enabled to survive when workmen's unions were forbidden by an Act which came into force within a year of the Society's foundation.

The example set by the men in the south-west had for a long time little influence in one of the most important woollen districts, the West Riding of Yorkshire. But gradually as the industry changed (and the change originated in Yorkshire) small groups were formed, consisting not only of workmen but also of small manufacturers, who were frightened by the development of machinery.[3] Such was 'the Community' or 'Institution' of the wool workers which, founded in 1796,[4] soon spread throughout the north of England. One witness before

---

[1] 'We will suppose a man to be married in the year 1792. He at that period received 22 shillings for 44 yards of cloth. We will follow him year after year, his family increasing, together with the price of every necessary of life, whilst his wages for labour decrease. Let us look at him in the year 1799, and we shall perhaps find him surrounded with five or six small children, and lo! instead of forty-four yards they have increased the length to sixty and give him only eleven shillings for it; and (to make it worse) he must work it with finer weft. No wonder that poor rates increase.' W. Radcliffe, *Origin of the New System of Manufacture*, p. 76. This last argument was meant for the ratepayers and especially for the landlords.

[2] This referred mainly to the export of yarn, which was opposed by many manufacturers. William Radcliffe was one of the leaders in the campaign, and that is why he quoted this weavers' manifesto, as he considered them as his allies.

[3] A. Held, *Zwei Bücher zur socialen Geschichte Englands*, p. 441; S. and B. Webb, *History of Trade Unionism*, pp. 36 and 67.

[4] It was not completely organized before 1803. See Held, op. cit., p. 442.

the Commission of Inquiry of 1806 said: 'I believe there was not two in Halifax or its neighbourhood that were not in it.'[1] The necessary funds for the expenses entailed in bringing a case before Parliament, in calling witnesses and in paying lawyers, were raised by regular subscriptions. The Institution possessed also less expensive and more drastic weapons. It was powerful enough to insist on the men leaving the shops it boy-cotted,[2] and those who refused to do so, or members who left the association, incurred brutal punishment. They were called 'snakes',[3] and were threatened, attacked and even sometimes besieged in their houses. The manufacturers lived in constant dread of this secret organization, of which it was rumoured that it fomented riots against machinery and sent advice to fire-insurance companies not to insure the factories.[4]

The first unions among the ironworkers were formed about the same time. The Sheffield industry, whose great variety gives it even today a peculiarly scattered character, had for many years been divided up among hundreds of independent workshops, all under the time-honoured control of the Company of Hallamshire Cutlers. But towards the end of the century the old regulations which had pro-tected the small men were relaxed and finally disappeared altogether,[5] thus giving capitalist enterprise a free field. The men immediately combined to resist the demands of their new masters. In 1787 the cutlers boycotted a certain Watkinson because he tried to force them to deliver thirteen knives a dozen.[6] In 1790 the manufacturers accused the knife grinders of forming unlawful associations for the purpose of raising the price of labour.[7] As a result five of them were prosecuted and con-victed of 'conspiracy', a crime recognized by criminal law long before special measures against workmen's combinations were ever contem-plated.

Similar events took place in widely differing industries and districts. In 1795 the Kent papermakers were highly organized. They had a

[1] *Report and Minutes of Evidence from the Committee on the State of the Woollen Manu-facture in England* (1806), pp. 231 and 353.

[2] Ibid., p. 181.

[3] Ibid. This name was later replaced by that of 'blackleg'.

[4] Ibid., p. 36.

[5] Particularly those which limited the number of apprentices in each workshop.

[6] J. Hunter, *Hallamshire*, p. 220. The affair roused popular feeling in Sheffield. A violent song against the unpopular manufacturer was sung by working men:

> Then may the odd knife his great carcase dissect,
> Lay open his vitals for men to inspect
> A heart full as black as the infernal gulf
> In that greedy, bloodsucking, bonescraping wolf.

[7] *Sheffield Iris*, Aug. 7th and Sept. 9th, 1790. See S. and B. Webb, *History of Trade Unionism*, p. 39.

strike fund which had several times enabled them successfully to fight the employers.[1] They used to refuse to work with men outside their union, and would leave the workshop in a body if the others were not dismissed.[2] The millwrights adopted the same tactics and were even more successful, as they were trained men who had served a long apprenticeship to a skilled trade and could not be replaced at will. Even the agricultural labourers, though without any definite organization, held meetings asking Parliament to regulate their wages. The agenda of one of these meetings, which was held in a village church in Norfolk, included a proposition to organize for common action all the labourers of the county, and those of other counties were invited to follow their example.[3]

The agitation, which then seemed to spread gradually throughout the whole working class, could not fail to make the government uneasy. Not only were the manufacturer's interests endangered but, in the circumstances, this unrest seemed to be a serious political and social danger. At a time when the fear of a revolution, such as was taking place in France, haunted so many heads and disturbed the minds of ministers, every popular association, whatever its professed aims might be, naturally became an object of suspicion. The same spirit which had led to the concession of out-relief as a means to prevent disturbances, now introduced the Act of 1799 against combinations.[4] As a matter of fact this Act did no more than renew and complete a whole series of previous provisions. To say nothing of early enactments, dealing with the 'conspiracies' of merchants and artisans, the penal clauses of which could be, and actually were on several occasions, used

---

[1] There were strikes in Dover in 1789, 1794 and 1795. See the petition from the paper manufacturers, *Journals of the House of Commons*, LI, 589.

[2] Ibid., p. 595 (Inquiry into the Manufacturers' Petition).

[3] *Annals of Agriculture*, XXV, 504. The resolutions may be summarized as follows (Nov. 5th, 1795):

'(1) The labourer should be properly paid, and the current practice of selling to him flour below the market price is both a degrading and deceptive mode of relief; (2) the wages should be proportioned to the price of bread [a table is given]; (3) a petition asking Parliament to regulate wages according to that principle shall be prepared forthwith and all labourers in the county invited to support it; (4) each person approving the movement shall pay 1 shilling to cover expenses; (5) as soon as the Secretary of the Committee is informed of the opinion of a majority of the labourers in the county, he shall call a general meeting; (6) in that meeting two or three parishes may send one representative, who shall receive 2s. 6d. per day for his time and as much for his expenses; (7) Adam Moore, the secretary of the present meeting, shall publish the present resolutions with the signatures in one London and one Norwich newspaper.' Such an organization, formed with the sole object of appealing to public authority, should not be mistaken for a trade union.

[4] Almost at the same time an Act was passed against 'debating societies'. 39 Geo. III, c. 79.

against the men's combinations,[1] there was a number of recent and no less severe Acts aimed directly at these combinations: 'Indeed ... Parliament was from the beginning of the eighteenth century perpetually enacting statutes forbidding combinations in particular trades.'[2] Among others we may quote those which specially affected the tailors (1720),[3] the weavers and wool-combers (1725),[4] the hatters (1777),[5] the papermakers (1796).[6] That which distinguished them both in principle and in extent from the Act of 1799, was that almost without exception they followed directly on official labour regulations, which they merely supplemented. S. and B. Webb have made this point very clear: 'It was assumed to be the business of Parliament and the Law Courts to regulate the conditions of labour, and combinations could, no more than individuals, be permitted to interfere in disputes for which a legal remedy was provided.' Thus by uniting in order to defeat labour regulations fixed by law, or at any rate in conformity with the law, the men were committing an act of rebellion. In 1799 the state of things was quite different. Intervention was becoming more and more discredited, and *laissez-faire* was already the guiding principle in most industries. The authority of the trade guilds hardly existed any longer, and the State refused to interfere. The idea that a contract should be simply the outcome of an agreement between the two interested parties was not far from being accepted and propounded as a dogma. To forbid the men to combine, at the very time when any hope of legal protection was withdrawn, was to place them at the mercy of the employers.

The Act was prepared and passed with a rapidity denoting the anxiety of its authors. On April 5th, 1799, a petition had been received from the master millwrights, asking for protection against the 'dangerous combination' that had for some time existed among their men. The rules of the House were waived to allow that petition to be read at once 'in consideration of the particular circumstances'. When the committee to whom the petition had been referred submitted their report,

---

[1] We have already referred to the decision of the Lancashire Justices of the Peace in 1725. It was based on an Act of 1549 (2 & 3 Edw. VI, c. 15) entitled *Bill of Conspiracies of Victuallers and Craftsmen*, and was meant to stop the artificial raising of prices of goods. S. and B. Webb quote the much more recent case of the cotton spinners who, in 1818, were sentenced to two years' imprisonment under a law enacted in 1305. *History of Trade Unionism*, p. 67.

[2] Ibid., p. 68. According to Whitbread there were in 1800 forty such Acts on the Statute Book.

[3] 7 Geo. I, st. I, c. 13. See F. W. Galton, *Select Documents illustrating the History of Trade Unionism* (I. *The Tailoring Trade*), p. 16.

[4] 12 Geo. I, c. 34.

[5] 17 Geo. III, c. 55.

[6] 36 Geo. III, c. 111.

Wilberforce, who always combined philanthropy with most unrelenting social conservatism, suggested the enacting of a General Combination Law. That suggestion was promptly acted upon by William Pitt, who on June 17th, 1799, brought in the Workmen's Combination Bill, in order 'to provide a remedy to an evil of considerable magnitude'. The first reading took place the following day: 'By July 1 the Bill had passed all stages in the House of Commons, and twenty-four days after its introduction in the House of Commons it had received the Royal Assent.'[1]

One voice was heard against it in the House, that of Benjamin Hobhouse, who contrasted the condition it was proposed to make for the working men with the unrestricted freedom of employers' combinations. He protested against the provision which made the offenders liable to summary conviction by a Justice of the Peace: but his amendment, providing for the presence on the Bench of at least two magistrates, was rejected without a division.[2] A petition against the Bill was sent to the Lords by the London calico-printers.[3] Lord Holland rose to support it, and attacked with great force legislative provisions which he considered 'unjust in their principle, and mischievous in their tendency ... It was always the tendency of the master to impute a conspiracy to his workmen who fairly endeavoured to raise their wages ... Circumstances might arise that might render an increase of the workmen's wages necessary on principles of justice and humanity, but if such a Bill as this should be suffered to pass, no fair attempt could ever be made on the part of the journeymen to get their wages increased without subjecting them to the pains and penalties of this Act.' It was dangerous to give exclusive jurisdiction to local magistrates, who might be influenced by personal interest: 'He would put the case of a magistrate in a manufacturing town, who was a master of workmen, and had a neighbour who was also a master manufacturer and a Justice of the Peace: see how these two could play into each other's hands. One might be the witness for the other, and thus they might commit to prison or hard labour such of their workmen as did not think proper to accede to the terms they might offer them.' The right of appeal to Quarter Sessions was purely nominal, as the appellant was to give bail for £20 and pay costs if his appeal was rejected: 'Could poor workmen ever appeal under these circumstances?' Nobody took the trouble of answering Lord Holland's objections, and the Act was finally passed without any amendment.[4]

[1] See J. L. and L. B. Hammond, *The Town Labourer*, p. 123.

[2] June 26th, 1799, *Parliamentary Register*, LXXI, 65-6.

[3] *A full and accurate Report of the Proceedings of the Petitioners against the Combination Laws, by one of the Petitioners*, London, 1800.

[4] 39 Geo. III, c. 81. The preamble reads as follows: 'Whereas great numbers

Workers in every trade were forbidden to combine for the purpose of obtaining higher wages or shorter hours, of obliging the masters to employ certain men to the exclusion of others, or of introducing any regulation whatsoever: this under a minimum penalty of three months' imprisonment or two months' hard labour. Those who tried to induce men not to work in certain workshops or refused to work with them, who took part in illicit meetings and received or gave money for the organization of such meetings, were threatened with the same penalty.[1] To the items of accusation which had been thus specified should be added those which might, in the mind of an unfriendly magistrate, be included in that vague and formidable word combination. 'No one journeyman would be safe in holding any conversation with any other on the subject of his trade or employment.'[2] What gave the Act a special note of partisanship was that, as had been pointed out by Hobhouse and Lord Holland, the accused were denied the guarantee of trial by jury and placed at the mercy of a Justice of the Peace who, according to the prevailing notions of that period, must be a representative of the cause of order as understood by the ruling classes.[3]

Feeling ran very high when the men realized the blow which had been dealt to their budding organizations. Petitions of protest were sent from all trades and all parts of the country,[4] and it was found difficult to ignore them completely. An amending Bill was therefore brought in and passed in July 1800.[5] But it did not touch the principle and the main provisions of the Combination Act. No change was made

[1] Later on these penalties were thought to be insufficient. Use was then made against the men of an Act passed in 1797 (17 Geo. III, c. 123), which dealt with seditious conspiracies and had been enacted during the mutiny of the fleet at the Nore. In 1834, it was this Act which was applied in the famous judgment which sentenced six Dorchester day labourers to transportation, ten years after the 1799 Act had been repealed.

[2] Petition from day labourers, workmen and artisans of Liverpool. *Journals of the House of Commons*, LV, 646.

[3] 'The petitioners and others are, by the said law, deprived of a trial by a jury of their country, and to be tried by one Justice of the Peace who, for the most part, is engaged in trade, and whom in all cases it is competent for the master to select.' Ibid.

[4] Ibid., LV, 648, 665, 672, 706, 712, etc.

[5] 39 & 40 Geo. III, c. 106.

of journeymen manufacturers and workmen in various parts of this Kingdom have by unlawful meetings and combinations endeavoured to obtain advance of their wages, and to effectuate other illegal purposes, and the laws at present in force against such unlawful conduct have been found to be inadequate to the suppression thereof, whereby it is become necessary that more effectual provision should be made against such unlawful combinations and for preventing such unlawful practices in the future, and for bringing offenders to more speedy and exemplary justice ... ' A similar Act was passed for Ireland in 1803 (43 Geo. III, c. 86).

in the jurisdiction, but the sentence was to be passed by two magistrates instead of one, neither of whom should be a master in the particular trade affected. The most important amendment consisted in certain arbitration clauses: questions concerning wages or hours of labour were allowed to be examined by two arbitrators respectively nominated by employers and men, and if they did not agree a Justice of the Peace was to decide, at the request of either party. But these provisions were in fact made inoperative by the ill-will of the employers.[1] Sheridan, in the course of the debate, had called for the total repeal of the Combination Act, than which 'a more intolerable mass of injustice had never been entered on the Statute Book'.

The following twenty-five years of the history of trade unionism have left behind them the memory of an age of persecution. It was the semi-legendary time of secret societies and midnight meetings, the records of whose proceedings were for reasons of safety buried in places known only to the initiated.[2] As a matter of fact sentences were frequent and severe: 'The Combination Laws were considered as absolutely necessary to prevent ruinous extortions of workmen, which, if not thus restrained, would destroy the whole of the trade, manufactures, commerce and agriculture of the nation ... So thoroughly was this false notion entertained, that whenever men were prosecuted to conviction for having combined to regulate their wages or the hours of working, however heavy the sentence passed on them was, and however rigorously it was inflicted, not the slightest feeling of compassion was manifested by anybody for the unfortunate sufferers. Justice was entirely out of the question: they could seldom obtain a hearing before a magistrate, never without impatience or insult ... Could an accurate account be given of proceedings, of hearings before magistrates, trials at sessions and in the Court of King's Bench, the gross injustice, the foul invective, and terrible punishments inflicted, would not, after a few years have passed away, be credited on any but the best evidence.'[3]

---

[1] J. L. and L. B. Hammond, *The Town Labourer*, p. 126.

[2] S. and B. Webb, *History of Trade Unionism*, pp. 64 ff., and Webb MSS., General History, II (Laws relating to trade unions).

[3] Francis Place, *On Combination Laws*, in Webb, op. cit., pp. 73 ff. As early as 1804 we find this iniquitous system criticized in a parliamentary report: 'The wisdom and humanity of Parliament would shrink from sanctioning the Combination Law, if it appeared to them, at the time of its enactment, likely to operate only in favour of the strong and against the weak, if it had any apparent tendency to secure impunity to oppressors, and to give an undue advantage to the masters, who can combine with little danger of detection, and who can carry their projects with little fear of opposition. The legislature could never mean to injure the man whose only desire is to derive a subsistence from his labour ... ' *Report on the Petition presented by the Journeymen Calico Printers* (1804), p. 7.

Nevertheless combinations, even those permanent ones from which trade unions sprang, could not be entirely prevented or suppressed. Persecution, very unequal in its treatment, spared many. For in order that a case might be brought before the Justices a formal complaint had to be lodged, and this was not always done. Some societies even had open and peaceable relations with the employers.[1] If threatened, some were able to call on the law for protection: they confined themselves, in principle at any rate, to petitions to Parliament or to recourse to a court of law, both of which were the right of every British subject.[2] Others, forced to a greater degree of dissimulation, disguised themselves as Friendly Societies or Benefit Clubs.[3] It was thus that the Cotton Spinners' Associations managed to exist or develop. The earliest, those of Oldham and Stockport founded in 1792, had always been Benefit Clubs, giving unemployment and sickness benefits.[4] Their real strength

[1] See examples given by S. and B. Webb, pp. 74 ff.

[2] The Cotton Weavers' Association which has been mentioned above belonged to this class.

[3] These societies, encouraged by an Act of 1793 (33 Geo. III, c. 54) were already numerous, many of them being formed by men of the same trade. See F. M. Eden, *State of the Poor*, I, 600 ff. On the relations between Friendly Societies and Trade Unions, see W. Bowden, *Industrial Society towards the end of the Eighteenth Century*, pp. 295 ff.

[4] Webb MSS., Textiles, III ('Oldham Spinners'), and *Fifth Report from the Select Committee on Artizans and Machinery*, p. 410. We do not know why S. and B. Webb mention 1786 as the date of the foundation of the Stockport Society (*History of Trade Unionism*, p. 35). Some of these societies, at least to begin with, must have devoted themselves exclusively to the duties of a Friendly Society. See the Statutes of the Friendly Associated Cotton Spinners of Manchester (1795), article 25: 'If one person or persons belonging to the said Society shall assault or abuse any master or person employed as foreman, or manager in the business of cotton-spinning, or shall do any wilful or voluntary damage to their houses, buildings or property, on any pretence whatsoever, or shall combine together to raise the price of their wages, contrary to law, or shall make any riot or disturbance against the public peace, or shall disobey any summons or orders of any of His Majesty's Justices of the said county … each person or persons shall be immediately expelled from this Society, and not partake of the advantages thereby intended for the encouragement of sobriety, industry, and peaceful behaviour.' *Articles, Rules and Regulations made to be observed by and between the Members of the Friendly Associated Cotton Spinners*, p. 15.

The suspicions very soon directed against such Friendly Societies were clearly stated in *Observations on the Cotton Weavers' Act* (1804), pp. 15-16:

'I cannot forbear taking occasion here to observe upon the baneful effects which the increase of Friendly Societies has had in the manufacturing districts since the countenance given them by Mr Rose's Act. The circumstance shows how the best intentions can be perverted … In lieu of adding to the comforts or improving the morals of the members, these clubs have become the very focus of cabals and dissatisfaction … Under the mask of the name and exhibition of nominal rules, the workmen unite together in classes according to their trades and hold communications with their brethren at home and at remote distances. Their contributions in many instances have been so great as to have afforded subsistence to such a number of them as it was agreed should turn out against their masters. When one master proved obstinate and would not give way, his men returned to work, and another set fell

was shown in the great 1810 strike in Manchester in which several thousand men took part, and strike pay was distributed amounting to as much as £1,500 a week.[1]

The Lancashire cotton-spinners were factory hands. They had the same difficulty in organizing themselves as agricultural and unskilled labourers have today. They were mostly new to their trade, had no cohesion or common tradition, and their technical skill was not sufficient to make them indispensable or to prevent the disastrous competition of women and children. They thus found themselves less and less able to hold their own against the capitalist manufacturer: 'Their ephemeral combinations and frequent strikes were, as a rule, only passionate struggles to maintain a bare subsistence wage ... outbursts of machine-breaking and outrages, with intervals of abject submission and reckless competition.'[2] They had, however, begun to forge the weapon for future struggles.

II

One of the objects which the workers who combined most consistently pursued, and which they thought was one of the best means to better their condition, was the maintenance and extension of old regulations.[3] All the more, therefore, when they were forbidden to combine for the purpose of protecting their common interests did they appeal to the protection, real or illusory, which these regulations afforded them against economic oppression.

These regulations had a double origin. On the one hand there were legal regulations under the Statute of Artificers of 1563 – a regular code of all the ancient municipal and guild regulations, the continued existence of which brought the economic system of the Middle Ages up to the threshold of our own times.[4] On the other hand, there were guild regulations peculiar to certain towns or certain

[1] Webb MSS., Textiles, I.

[2] S. and B. Webb, *History of Trade Unionism*, p. 87.

[3] According to Brentano most eighteenth-century workers' associations were founded with the sole object of keeping up the existing trade regulations, both legal and customary. Where the Government's action stopped, their action began. *On the History and Development of Gilds and the Origin of Trade-Unions*, p. clxxvii.

[4] Excellent pages on the Statute of Artificers (5 Eliz. c. 4) will be found in W. Cunningham's *Growth of English Industry and Commerce*, II, 27-43.

---

out, and so on in succession till their objects were accomplished. These conspiracies have existed, with slight intermissions, for several years, one part or other of the trade having been seldom free from them, and they have nearly always succeeded. Yet so difficult is the proof, although many attempts have been made at punishment, very few convictions have taken place under the Combination Act.'

trades in which they held the force of law. Both these sets of regulations, together with the rules dealing with industrial technique and with the provisions of the Poor Laws, were part and parcel of one whole, a characteristic monument of traditional legislation. In the middle of the eighteenth century this edifice was still standing, though much decayed and battered. But it was to be soon shattered, more by new interests than by new ideas, and the workers tried in vain to prop up its crumbling ruins.[1]

The two main points on which they were most anxious to insist were the apprenticeship regulations and the legal settlement of wages.[2] Under the Act of 1563 no person could exercise a trade in Great Britain unless he had first served a seven years' apprenticeship under an indenture which defined the mutual obligations of master and apprentice.[3] Moreover, the number of apprentices was limited, or at any

[1] On the gradual abandonment of the Statute of Artificers, and particularly of its provisions on apprenticeship, see O. J. Dunlop, *English Apprenticeship and Child Labour*, pp. 118, 121, 228-30. The town authorities no longer cared to enforce the old guild regulations, and the Bench showed much indulgence to transgressors.

[2] We shall not refer again to the efforts made to revive sixteenth-century prohibitions against machinery. See above, chap. III.

[3] 5 Eliz., c. 4, art. 31. Here for instance is the indenture of apprenticeship of J. Wedgwood (which, be it noted, was for five and not seven years): 'This indenture made the eleventh day of November in the seventeenth year of the reign of our Sovereign Lord George the Second by the grace of God King of Great Britain and so forth, and in the year of our Lord one thousand seven hundred forty and four, between Josiah Wedgwood son of Mary Wedgwood of the Churchyard in the County of Stafford of the one part, and Thomas Wedgwood of the Churchyard in the County of Stafford potter of the other part, witnesseth that the said Josiah Wedgwood of his own free will and consent to and with the consent and direction of his said mother hath seal and doth hereby bind himself apprentice unto the said Thomas Wedgwood ... and with him as an apprentice to dwell continue and serve from the day of the date hereof unto the full end and term of five years from thence next ensuing and fully to be complete and ended; during which said term the said apprentice do his said masters will and faithfully shall serve, his secrets keep, his lawful commands everywhere gladly do.

'Hurt to his said master he shall not do or wilfully suffer to be done by others, but the same to his power shall let or forthwith give notice thereof to his said master; the goods of his said master he shall not embezzle or waste, nor them lend without his consent to any; at cards, dice and other unlawful games he shall not play, taverns or ale houses he shall not haunt or frequent, fornication he shall not commit, matrimony he shall not contract. From the service of his said master he shall not at any time depart, or absent himself without his said master's leave, but in all things as a good and faithful apprentice shall and will demean and behave himself towards his said master and all his during the said term;

'And the said master do learn his apprentice the said art of throwing and handling which he now useth with all things thereunto, shall and will teach and instruct or cause to be well and sufficiently taught and instructed after the best way and manner he can, and shall and will also find and allow unto the said apprentice meat, drink, washing and lodging and apparel of all kinds, both linen and woollen, and all other necessaries, both in sickness and in health, meet and convenient for such an apprentice

rate it bore some relationship to the number of adult workers.[1] These regulations were suited to the traditions of men who were proud of their technical skill, and who regarded their trade as their exclusive property. Anxious as they were to erect barriers round their privilege they were careful to make their guild regulations stricter than the law. The Cutlers of Hallamshire did not allow of more than one apprentice to each master, except in the case of the master's son.[2] Almost everywhere, if the apprentice's parents were not in the trade themselves they had to pay entrance fees, which were often fairly high.[3] This was not so much in order to keep a high standard in the trade as to reserve for its members a sort of hereditary monopoly.

It is obvious that the employers' interest, as soon as they ceased to belong themselves to the class of artisans, was to do away with these regulations. Had these really been strictly enforced they would have opposed serious obstacles to the progress of industry. For this reason they were constantly broken, and complaints of their evasion were heard at a very early stage. In 1716 the Colchester weavers accused the manufacturers of taking on too many apprentices. In 1728 those of Gloucester protested against men being engaged who had not served their legal term of apprenticeship.[4] In order to put an end to all these claims, employers sometimes took the line of asking for the formal repeal of regulations which limited their freedom of action. This was the course taken by the hatters, the dyers and the calico-printers. The latter acknowledged that in their workshops hardly one-tenth had been apprentices, and they gave the reason: 'The trade does not require that all the men they employ should be brought up to it; common labourers are sufficient.'[5] This was an argument to which the introduction of machinery was soon to give additional strength.

The attitude of Parliament, when faced with such contradictory requests, is interesting. Parliament had no intentions of surrendering

[1] 5 Eliz., c. 4, art. 33, fixed the minimum proportion of one workman to three apprentices in the following trades: cloth manufacturers, fullers, weavers, tailors, shoemakers. The margin was a very broad one.

[2] Charter of the 'Cutlers of Hallamshire', 21 James I, c. 31.

[3] From £5 to £20, according to S. and B. Webb, *History of Trade Unionism*, p. 83, note 1.

[4] *Journals of the House of Commons*, XVIII, 171, and XXI, 153. See also petitions of 1742, XXIV, 117 and 124.

[5] Ibid., XXXVI, 194. Workers' counter-petition, p. 283. The employers won their case by the Acts 17 Geo. III, c. 33, and 17 Geo. III, c. 55 (1777).

during the term aforesaid, and for the true performance of all and every the said Covenants and agreement either of the said parties bindeth himself unto each other by these presents: in witness whereof they have interchanged and set their hands and seals the day and year as before mentioned.' Published by Eliza Meteyard, *Josiah Wedgwood*, I, 222-3.

its right of regulating industry, as is shown by the Act of 1768 dealing with the wages and the hours of work of journeymen tailors,[1] and by the Spitalfields Act of 1773.[2] It had not yet been influenced by the new economic doctrines. Its members had not read Adam Smith, and that for a very good reason,[3] for it was in 1753, twenty-three years before the publication of the *Essay on the Nature and Causes of the Wealth of Nations*, that the Statutes of the Company of Stocking Frame Knitters were declared to have become obsolete as 'contrary to reason and derogatory to the liberty of English subjects'.[4] The spirit of *laissez-faire* showed itself only gradually and on special occasions, before it came out into the open and based its claims on a general theory which was in harmony not only with the employers' interests but with the equally obvious interest of the growing industrial system.

The industrial revolution was to strike a fatal blow at the apprenticeship regulations, while giving the workers fresh reasons for desiring to have them maintained. With the improvement in equipment and the increasing division of labour a long technical training was becoming more and more unnecessary. Yet the number of apprentices in the textile trades kept on growing, particularly in the cotton manufacture. The spinning mills were full of them. In calico-printing there were often as many apprentices as workmen, and sometimes many more. About 1800 a certain factory was said to have fifty-five or sixty apprentices to two workmen.[5] But did they really deserve the name of apprentices? They were in fact nothing but non-adult workers, whose age was an excuse for paying them the lowest possible wages and subjecting them to a stern discipline. They were often engaged without any indenture. Sometimes the employer, while regarding them as bound to his service, claimed for himself the right to send them away at a moment's notice. Sometimes, on the other hand, he kept them for eight or ten years instead of seven,[6] and during all that time they earned from 3s. 6d. to 7s. a week, while a man's wage amounted to 25s. or more. Thus naturally the men regarded this as one of the reasons, and perhaps the chief one, for their own frequent

---

[1] 8 Geo. III, c. 17. This renewed and amended the clauses of an Act of 1721 (7 Geo. I, st. I, c. 13). See texts in F. W. Galton, *The Tailoring Trade*, pp. xliii, 16-22, 60-3.

[2] 13 Geo. III, c. 68. See Part I, chap. I.

[3] See the criticism of the traditional system of apprenticeship in the *Inquiry into the Nature and Causes of the Wealth of Nations*, p. 55 (MacCulloch edit.).

[4] *Journals of the House of Commons*, XXVI, 593, 764, 779, 788. See W. Felkin, *A History of the Machine-wrought Hosiery and Lace Manufactures*, pp. 80 ff.; A. Held, *Zwei Bücher zur socialen Geschichte Englands*, pp. 486-8; *Victoria History of the County of Nottingham*, II, 353-4, and *Victoria History of the County of Derby*, II, 367.

[5] *Report from the Committee to whom the Petition of several Journeymen Calico Printers, etc., was referred* (1804), p. 3.

[6] Ibid., p. 4.

unemployment, adult workers being driven out by the surplus numbers of apprentices.[1] As for the apprentices themselves, when they grew up their position became most difficult. In their turn they had no work unless they agreed to renew their contract for a fresh period of five or seven years, on any terms which the employers saw fit to lay down.[2]

It was, therefore, not without reason that in 1803 and 1804 the calico-printers agitated for an Act to reintroduce the apprenticeship system into their industry, together with a limitation of the number of apprentices. They succeeded in obtaining an inquiry, and spent over £1,000, collected in pennies throughout the Kingdom, to enable their witnesses to appear before the Committee.[3] Sheridan spoke eloquently for the men who had incurred such heavy expenses in order to lay their case before Parliament, and against their opponents, 'a number of very wealthy men, who derived that wealth from their labour'.[4] After many delays a Bill was drafted, the enactment of which would have met the men's claims. But in spite of another strong appeal from Sheridan[5] the Bill did not go beyond the second reading. The House of Commons followed Sir Robert Peel's lead (and who more fitted than he to put the case for the manufacturers?) and felt that they were serving the cause of industrial progress against ignorance and blind prejudice.

The wool-weavers met with no more success in their attempts to obtain, not fresh legislation on their behalf, but simply the enforcement of the Statute of Artificers of 1563. They began by prosecuting the 'illegal' weavers and those who employed them. The cloth-makers retorted by claiming the repeal of antiquated rules, which 'operated as positive impediments to the increase of hands and to the maintenance of that subordination which is the life of all manufactures, and at present so much wanted in this important branch of commerce'.[6] Several of them gave evidence. They agreed in stating that since the invention of the fly shuttle, weaving could be learned in a year or even in a few months, and that in any case men who had had a

---

[1] 'The petitioners and other journeymen calico printers have been at times, for a series of years past, greatly distressed for want of work which has arisen not from any deficiency in the trade of calico-printing, but from an overstock of hands brought up and employed therein.' 'Petition of the Calico Printers', *Journals of the House of Commons*, LVIII, 180.

[2] See Lord King's speech in the House of Lords, May 27th, 1805, *Parliamentary Debates*, V, 118, and that of P. Moore in the House of Commons on May 30th, ibid., pp. 147-8.

[3] See *Minutes of the Evidence taken before the Committee to whom the Petition of several Journeymen Calico Printers ... was referred* (1804).

[4] June 27th, 1804, *Parliamentary Debates*, II, 858-9.

[5] April 23rd, 1807, ibid., IX, 535-8.

[6] Petition from Halifax Manufacturers, *Journals of the House of Commons*, LVIII, 380.

seven years' apprenticeship were now in a minority. A Bradford manu-facturer, being asked whether there was much difference between those who had served their regular term and those who had not, answered that 'he could not speak to that, because he did not know of any who had served a regular apprenticeship'.[1] Such statements induced Parliament to suspend the operation of the Statute of Artificers,[2] a measure which was renewed annually until the Statute was finally repealed.[3]

Nevertheless, and in spite of its failure, the movement was taking hold of the whole working class. Even employers in small-scale indus-tries joined in, moved by their strong feeling against capitalist under-takings. In 1813 and 1814, when a final effort was made to save the old apprenticeship system, over three hundred thousand signatures were collected for petitions representing every district and every trade.[4] The Committee appointed to report on the question (Huskisson and Can-ning being among its members) found it difficult to arrive at a conclu-sion, so great was the change in their former opinions caused by the facts thus brought to their notice. The chairman, Mr Rose, declared himself converted to the workmen's views. But the interest of the manufacturers was now allied to the idea of economic freedom, which had by this time become a dogma. The provisions of the Act of 1563 relating to apprenticeship were repealed in the name of 'the true principles of trade', which were unknown in the reign, 'glorious though it was', of Queen Elizabeth.[5]

III

The previous year another clause of the Elizabethan Act had dis-appeared, namely the clause which empowered Justices of the Peace to fix rates of wages.[6]

---

[1] *Journals of the House of Commons*, LVIII, p. 392. John Lees of Halifax declared that 'legal' weavers were not short of work. On the contrary there was a shortage of labour which caused women to be employed as weavers and wool-sorters. Cf. Sir Robert Peel's evidence before the 1806 Committee, *Report from the Committee on the State of the Woollen Manufacture*, p. 440.

[2] By 43 Geo. III, c. 136.

[3] The repeal had effect in the woollen industry in 1809 (49 Geo. III, c. 109).

[4] *Parliamentary Debates*, XXVII, 574.

[5] See the debate in the House of Commons, *Parliamentary Debates*, XXVII, 503 ff., and the repealing Act, 54 Geo. III, c. 96.

[6] 5 Eliz., c. 4, art. 15. This power had been first given them in 1389 (13 Rich. II, c. 8): 'Forasmuch as a man cannot put the price of corn and other victuals in certain, the Justices should at Michaelmas and Easter, according to the price of provisions, make proclamation how much every mason, carpenter and other workmen and labourers should receive by the day as well in harvest as in other times of the year with or without meat or drink.' Thus instead of fixing wages once and for all as had formerly been done, the Act set up an authority with the power to regulate the

Among the many duties of the Justices of the Peace, who were the chief agents of the old interventionist system, this is not the least interesting, and it has been the subject of repeated studies.[1] Shall we accept Dean Cunningham's opinion, that by the beginning of the nineteenth century the system had in fact ceased to exist and was no more than a legal curiosity?[2] It is a fact that the assessment of wages under the Act of Elizabeth had been discontinued for many years.[3] But more recent Acts were still in force in connection with specially regulated industries, and thus kept the interventionist tradition alive. For instance, under the Spitalfields Act renewed by an Act of 1792,[4] the silk-weavers' wages continued to be fixed by the Middlesex Justices of the Peace and the authorities of the City of London. Those of the London and Westminster tailors were fixed by the City authorities alone, but this was only a formal difference which did not alter the principle. When the Speenhamland magistrates passed their famous resolution they began by stating that they had no desire to revive the assessment of wages. In this they were true to their class interests and the ideas of their day, but what, after all, was the scale established by them but the basis for an indirect regulation of wages? Instead of regulating wages they fixed the minimum amount which was to be allowed a day labourer, and the obligation which it was desired not to put on the employers was put on the parishes instead. But this implied the very principle which it was sought to rule out.

Such a principle, when the population suffered, found many adherents. Its past blessings were probably over-estimated, for it had no doubt been used against the men more frequently than in their interest.[5] Those who asked for a legal fixation of wages meant that

[1] On its origins see Miss MacArthur's articles, 'The Boke longyng to a Justice of the Peace and the Assessment of Wages', *English Historical Review*, IX, 1894, 'A Fifteenth-century Assessment of Wages' (ibid., XIII, 1898), 'The Regulation of Wages in the Sixteenth Century' (ibid., XVI, 1900). For the later period see W. Cunningham, 'The Shropshire Wages Assessment at Easter 1732', *Economic Journal*, IV, 1894, 51; W. A. S. Hewins, 'English Trade and Finance, chiefly in the Seventeenth Century'; and 'The Regulation of Wages by the Justices of the Peace', *Economic Journal*, VIII, 1898, 340-6).

[2] W. Cunningham, *Growth of English Industry and Commerce*, II, 43. In 1776 Adam Smith already noted its disuse.

[3] One of the last examples known is the 'assessment' made by the Shropshire Justices of the Peace in 1782. See *Economic Journal*, IV, 516.

[4] 32 Geo. III, c. 44.

[5] 'I contend that from 1563 to 1824 a conspiracy, concocted by the law and carried out by parties interested in its success, was entered into to cheat the English workman of his wages, to tie him to the soil, to deprive him of hope, and to degrade

rates at certain fixed times and according to circumstances. We must remember that the Justices of the Peace also fixed the price of bread. See A. Held, op. cit., and S. and B. Webb, 'The Assize of Bread', *Economic Journal*, XIV, 196-218 (1904).

there should be a minimum wage guaranteed by law, and varying with the price of food. This idea was welcome particularly in the country districts, severely tried by the crisis through which England was passing,[1] and, as we have already noted, it led to a first attempt at organization on the part of agricultural labourers. In his *Annals of Agriculture*, Arthur Young opened a discussion on the subject. His correspondents, landlords or farmers, were as might have been expected generally opposed to a measure which they considered to be directed against their freedom of action.[2] The question was brought before Parliament in a Bill introduced in November 1795 by Samuel Whitbread and seconded by Fox, but it met with determined opposition. The mover himself seemed to be quite apologetic for his apostasy from the true faith, which could only be justified by the peculiar circumstances of the case.[3] In vain Fox asked that the poor should be given means of earning their living without recourse to public charity. Pitt, in the name of the Government, spoke against the Bill, which was thrown out. Whitbread returned to the attack a few years later, but met with no greater success.[4] To all the other reasons which the ruling classes had against an artificial raising of wages, was added the fear that it would result in a rise in prices, and that a real evil would thus only be treated by an illusory remedy.[5]

But all was not yet over. By an odd turn of the wheel of fortune, the system thus abandoned and condemned in the name of a doctrine which was daily becoming more assured was about to be applied once more in a particular case. The cotton-weavers, constantly wrangling with their employers over their rates of pay which had been steadily

[1] D. Davies, *The Case of Labourers in Husbandry* (1795), pp. 105-6.

[2] See *Annals of Agriculture*, vol. XXV.

[3] 'I feel as much as any man how greatly it is to be desired that there should be no legislative interference in matters of this nature, and that the price of labour, like every other commodity, should be left to find its own level.' *Parliamentary History*, XXXII, 703.

[4] In 1800, ibid., XXXIV, 1426-36. This was just after the Combination Act, which gave Whitbread a good case for arguing plausibly in favour of a minimum wage.

[5] It was also argued that a compulsory minimum wage would mean that inferior workers would not be able to obtain work. See petition of Cheshire magistrates, *Journals of the House of Commons*, LI, 383.

---

him into irremediable poverty. The English law and those who administered the law were engaged in grinding the English workman down to the lowest pittance, in stamping out every expression or act indicating any organized discontent.' Thorold Rogers, *Six Centuries of Work and Wages*, p. 398. This is probably exaggerated. Later research has shown that the decisions of the Justices of the Peace were not always taken against the men. See Leonard, 'The Relief of the Poor by the State Regulation of Wages', *English Historical Review*, XIII (1898).

falling since 1792, and deprived of means of resistance by the Combination Act, appealed to Parliament for help. They asked for a rapid and inexpensive method of arbitration to remove the difficulties which were constantly arising between masters and men, 'and for the settling of the wages, pay and price of labour, from time to time, as occasion shall require'.[1] Some employers, anxious to prevent the constant renewal of disputes, supported the men's request, and this is perhaps why in spite of all precedents that request was taken into consideration.

The men had two objects in view, although the first one only was openly pursued: the settlement of individual disputes over the execution of contracts of service, and a more decisive intervention which might modify the very terms of a contract. The witnesses produced by the cotton-weavers in support of their petition set forth the abuses of which they complained: 'It frequently happens that the master will give out a web of a certain length, containing perhaps four or five pieces; he will agree, when you take this web out, that you shall have a certain price. He may, perhaps, give it you for the first piece and for the remainder will abate you a certain proportion.'[2] In such a case, the men always had the right to appeal to a Justice of the Peace without any necessity for a special Act.[3] But they complained of the incompetence of the Justices in dealing with the sometimes highly technical matters submitted to them, and of the delay involved in appealing to Quarter Sessions,[4] which meant a great trial of patience and often exhausted the resources of poor plaintiffs. The men asked that the magistrates before whom they appeared should not only investigate individual grievances but also settle collective claims, and be empowered to raise insufficient wages; in short, that they should be invested with the powers which the law gave the Justices of the Peace and of which they refused to make use.

The moment was not favourable for presenting such requests. Whitbread's Bill had just been thrown out a second time. Pitt, tending

[1] 'Petition from the Cotton Weavers in the Counties of Chester, York, Lancaster and Derby', *Journals of the House of Commons*, LV, 262 (March 5th, 1800). This and similar petitions collected over 23,000 signatures. Webb MSS., Textiles, IV, 1.

[2] 'Inquiry into the Cotton Weavers' Petition', *Journals of the House of Commons*, LV, 487. See also pp. 489 and 493 (deductions for cost of equipment, arbitrary increase in the length of pieces, etc.).

[3] 20 Geo. II, c. 19 (1747), authorized the Justices to enforce payment of wages owed up to £10 and, if necessary, to distrain. This seems fair, but the same Act contained other and less liberal clauses. Any workman or apprentice, accused by his master of 'miscarriage or ill-behaviour', could be sentenced by the Justice of the Peace to a month's hard labour. If on the other hand he complained of bad treatment or of lack of food, then all the Justice could do was to release him from his contract, and the employer was in no way penalized.

[4] *Journals of the House of Commons*, LV, 488 and 492, and *Report on the Cotton Weavers' Petition*, pp. 9 ff.

more and more to follow the economists, was in principle opposed
to all State interference. Nevertheless, he realized that something
had to be done to meet these well-founded complaints, which did
not come from the men alone. The Arbitration Act of 1800 marked
the limit beyond which he was determined not to go.[1] It enacted
that all disputes about wages, payments for accessory equipment, and
the delivery or quality of goods, must go before two arbitrators
appointed by the two parties respectively. If within three days the
arbitrators were unable to come to any decision the matter was to be
settled by a Justice of the Peace, who was in no circumstances to be
a manufacturer or in any way interested in the industry concerned.
Arbitration was compulsory, and if either party refused to appoint
an arbitrator he was liable to a penalty of £10, to be paid to the other
party. If we judge by appearances alone, this enactment recalls our
most recent and boldest legislative experiments. The word arbitration
makes the illusion more complete. But there should be no misunderstanding about it: arbitration under the Act of 1800 was a very
different thing from arbitration as understood for instance in Australia
and New Zealand. It rather resembled, in a narrower and more modest
sphere, the working of the French 'Conseils de Prud'hommes'. It
was not the beginning of a new era of legislation, but rather the
partial and temporary revival of a system which had fallen into
disuse and which there was no question of restoring to its former
existence.

Even though the cotton-weavers were not completely satisfied with
the new Act, yet they gave it a good reception as providing at any rate
some protection against economic oppression. Its popularity may be
gauged by the efforts made by the Paisley and Glasgow workmen in
order to obtain a similar law for Scotland,[2] which was granted in 1803.[3]
Many cases were submitted to arbitration and were quickly and
cheaply settled,[4] usually in favour of the workers, who were the victims

---

[1] On this subject see the evidence of a manufacturer, R. Needham of Bolton:
'In 1800 we applied to Parliament for a regulation of wages on the principles of the
Spitalfields Act. Mr Pitt at that time, being Chancellor of the Exchequer, sent our
solicitor down to Lancashire to propose that, if we would give up the regulation of
wages, he would grant us a law that would answer our purpose as well or better than
the regulation. We unanimously agreed at a meeting of delegates to fall in with the
offer of Mr Pitt, and he granted the Arbitration Law, 39 & 40 Geo. III, c. 90.' *Fifth
Report of the Select Committee on Artisans and Machinery* (1824), p. 544.

[2] See the petitions from the Scotch Workmen in the *Journals of the House of Commons*,
LVII, 174; LVIII, 216. Counter petitions from employers, ibid., LVIII, 236, 278.

[3] 43 Geo. III, c. 151. The text is slightly different from that of the English Act.
Instead of the arbitrators being appointed by the parties concerned, they were
appointed by the magistrate who heard the complaint.

[4] The expenses were hardly more than 1s. *Minutes of Evidence on the Cotton Weavers'
Petition* (1803), p. 11.

of unjustifiable frauds and abuses.[1] The manufacturers were less satisfied, for an Act which in any way limited their absolute power was obnoxious to them, and they stopped at nothing to get rid of it. They did all they could to hinder its operation: when they had to appoint an arbitrator they delayed the formation of the tribunal by appointing a man who was bound to excuse himself, or one who lived three hundred miles away.[2] At other times they took it upon themselves to alter the effect of judgments given against them by taking back from the men what they had been forced to allow them the day before.[3] But as, in spite of everything, they could not completely evade the Arbitration Act, they started a campaign to secure its repeal.[4]

Their feelings are exactly reflected in a pamphlet which was published in Manchester in 1804, with the title of 'Observations on the Cotton Weavers' Act'. Every argument which has been used since against labour legislation is there propounded and vehemently upheld. Here for instance are the familiar phrases about leaders who artificially promote agitation among the men: 'The plan was originally contrived by a factious few of notorious character, who began meetings, formed resolutions and entered into subscriptions in private ... A great similarity to the principles of Jacobinism guided their measures ... The weavers at large would have remained (as they really were) happy and contented but for the machinations of the turbulent few, who gained an influence over the quiet many.'[5] Here too is the classic theory of freedom of contract: 'It certainly is not very consistent with our ordinary ideas that there should be any interposition between master and man in making a bargain. If they agree upon the price, the work is undertaken; if not, the man is as much at liberty to seek another master, as the master is to get another workman; or if the man can earn more by one sort of labour than by another, he will

---

[1] *Minutes of Evidence on the Cotton Weavers' Petition*, pp. 3 and 91.

[2] *Parliamentary Debates*, I, 1081.

[3] 'Have you any instances fallen within your knowledge where, in consequence of disputes under the Arbitration Act, the weaver having been redressed, the master has signified a resolution to indemnify himself out of the work subsequently to be done? – Yes, I know an instance ... Mr Joshua Crook of Bolton would reduce the man, contrary to his contract, 3s. for 25 yards; the weaver would not sit down with it, but would arbitrate his master for his wages. It was brought to a reference, and the referees did not agree. It was then referred to Colonel Fletcher, the magistrate. The master told Colonel Fletcher that he would pay what he liked for his work: he would have it in his power to give anything or nothing, as he liked, to his workmen, and if he insisted that he should pay the wages he would reduce them so much tomorrow.' *Minutes of Evidence on the Cotton Weavers' Petition*, p. 23.

[4] See petitions from Manchester, Bolton, Preston and Stockport manufacturers, *Journals of the House of Commons*, LVIII, 275-6, 316, 351.

[5] *Observations on the Cotton Weavers' Act*, pp. 9-10.

change his employ.'[1] The author does not mention the case when the employer did not feel bound to keep his promises. But what shocks him even more than the principle of arbitration is the recognition of the men's right to appoint their own representative as arbitrator. For this 'places the master within the power and under the control of his servant[2] ... There can be nothing more repugnant to the feelings of a master, or contrary to the spirit of the old law of the land, than to see tribunals of this description set up ... which must necessarily be exclusively filled by the most artful from among the body of weavers, who would, as experience has already shown, lay themselves out to make a livelihood of their new profession. It is not to be expected that men of character and respectability will be induced to become arbitrators on the part of the masters, as they must meet and place themselves on a level with the low fellows that would be opposed to them.'[3] This attack has at any rate the merit of candour.

Such decided hostility to the Arbitration Act, shared even by the magistrates responsible for its execution,[4] rapidly made it inoperative. The 1804 amendments, the object of which was to prevent systematic violation of the Act,[5] had no effect. The agitation therefore continued, the discontented weavers now endeavouring to secure a minimum wage by means of a regulation 'on the principle of the Spitalfields Act'. A petition which was circulated among the cotton-weavers of Lancashire, Cheshire and York, and presented to Parlia-

[1] *Observations on the Cotton Weavers' Act*, p. 21. A more valid argument dealt with the evil effects which the regulation of industry might have on the men themselves. In the silk industry, where wages were regulated, the only way in which employers could reduce their expenses in bad times was by dismissing some of their men: 'So the master saves himself for the time, but the workmen lose their bread.'

[2] It was only in 1875 (38 & 39 Vic. c. 90) that the words master and servant were replaced in law by those of employer and workman.

[3] *Observations on the Cotton Weavers' Act*, p. 6. The author wonders what would happen if this system were extended to other trades: 'It has not appeared by any statement I have yet seen upon what superior ground the cotton-weavers rest their pretensions ... nor why carpenters, shoemakers, smiths, mechanics and everyday labourers, have not an equal claim to legislative regulation: indeed, why the principle, if proper for them, should not become general to all; why the man who weaves a piece of fustian or calico shall have a privilege which they who spin, bleach, dye, print it, or make it into garments, do not possess; or why is he better entitled than the maker of a chair or of an earthenware basin, nor why our footmen and cooks shall be denied the power of calling the umpires to determine their wages and conditions of service.'

[4] Very often, at the employer's request, the Justices of the Peace would agree to act in cases which should first of all have gone before the arbitrators. Ibid., p. 8.

[5] 44 Geo. III, c. 87. 'The Act empowered the magistrate to choose a panel (not less than four or more than six, half to be masters or their agents, the other half to be weavers) from which the two sides should each choose an arbitrator.' J. L. and L. B. Hammond, *The Skilled Labourer*, p. 68. This amendment, which made it impossible to nominate arbitrators who could or would not sit, was strongly opposed by the manufacturers. *Parliamentary Debates*, I, 1172-3, and II, 943.

ment in February 1807, received no less than 130,000 signatures. A remarkable fact is the support given to that movement by manufacturers and merchants, who were concerned with the undesirable effects which constant fluctuations in wages might have on the price of goods and therefore on the conditions of trade.[1] A Bill was actually brought in by the Government, but in a perfunctory manner, Perceval, then Prime Minister, explaining 'that it was better that the cotton weavers should be disappointed after a discussion of the merits of their application by the House of Commons than by a refusal to submit it for consideration'. The principle of the minimum wage was attacked on all sides as indefensible and no voice was heard for it, so that the Bill was promptly withdrawn. This conclusion caused much dissatisfaction and some agitation, particularly in Lancashire.[2] Being thus left without any hope of securing the guarantee they wanted through new legislation – at a moment when both the high price of necessaries and repeated crises in their industry inflicted on them additional hardship the men sought protection in the Statute of Artificers, and asked for the enforcement of its time-honoured provisions.

But this was a hopeless move, for Parliament was only waiting for an opportunity to repeal the Elizabethan Act. It was in vain that the men implored Parliament not to take away their last means of defence: 'The present Bill to repeal the aforesaid law has sunk the petitioners beyond description, having no hope left; the former laws made for their security being unavailing, there is no protection for their sole property, which is their labour.'[3] The step they dreaded was taken without encountering any but their own opposition.[4] Thus disappeared one of the most typical examples of the old social legislation. In Scotland its abolition gave rise to a memorable dispute. After long and expensive negotiations the weavers had obtained a piecework scale of wages, sanctioned by the Edinburgh Court of Sessions. But the magistrates declared that this scale was not compulsory, and the employers refused to abide by it. The textile workers thereupon all went on strike, and thousands of men stopped work at the same time. But a strike

---

[1] The most prominent among them was Ainsworth, who was paying some £40,000 in wages. J. L. and L. B. Hammond, *The Skilled Labourer*, p. 76.

[2] Ibid., pp. 72–80; *Reports of the Cotton Weavers' Petitions*, 1808 and 1809, and *Parliamentary Debates*, XI, 426 ff.

[3] Petition from the Bolton weavers, *Journals of the House of Commons*, LXVIII, 229. Compare with the expressions used in 1799 in the second manifesto of the cotton weavers: 'The opulent expect that Government should guarantee to them the peaceable enjoyment of their property; the poor have the same claims upon it and expect the same, which property is the full value of their labour.' W. Radcliffe, *Origin of the New System of Manufacture commonly called 'Power Loom Weaving'*, p. 77.

[4] 53 Geo. III, c. 40 (1813).

was one of those occurrences in which the public authorities did not feel their usual scruples at intervening between masters and men. The leaders were arrested and sentenced, and resistance was completely broken.[1] This was the last attempt to restore the traditional system of wage regulation.

The policy of *laissez-faire* was supreme, and went unchallenged in the courts as well as in Parliament. While that policy at first had been purely empirical, and had not been followed in all cases, it was now supported by the peremptory formulas of political economy: there it found its theoretical justification, while its actual *raison d'être* and its practical power were derived from the interests of the capitalist class. Theory and interest, walking hand in hand, proved irresistible, and when they happened to conflict with each other we need hardly ask which prevailed over the other. The Combination Act gives the meaning of economic freedom as understood by the ruling classes at that time. But, at the same time, motives other than mere interest and principles not to be found in books on political economy had begun to work, and, while the old structure of medieval regulations was crumbling away, were laying the foundations of labour legislation.

IV

The development of humanitarian ideas is a subject quite different from those which form the subject-matter of this book. But however independent from one another they may be, both in kind and in origin, the broad movements which determine the material, moral and intellectual life in the same period of history are always to some extent interconnected, or at any rate they touch and meet, and thus act and react on one another. A few dates will recall to us what was taking place in the world during the lifetime of the founders of the modern factory system, and in what general atmosphere their lives were spent. While Hargreaves and Highs were inventing spinning machinery and while Watt was mastering the hidden forces of steam, Jean-Jacques Rousseau was David Hume's guest at Wootton Hall. Between the time when Arkwright settled in Nottingham and the time when he died, rich and titled, leaving a princely fortune to his children, the American and the French revolutions broke out. And a few months before Arkwright another pioneer died, full of years and good works: John Wesley, the apostle of Methodism, whose powerful preaching also brought about a great silent revolution.

This spirit of progress, awakened in England by philosophical

---

[1] *Second Report from the Committee on Artizans and Machinery* (1824), p. 59. The story of this struggle is shortly related in S. and B. Webb's *History of Trade Unionism*, pp. 58 ff.

discussion and religious propaganda, found expression both in writing and in action. In the realms of theory it ventured far and wide. Paine was the advocate of democratic equality, whilst Godwin and Spence went as far as communism and anarchy. In practice this spirit restrained its daring flights, and curbed its ambitions to conform to the conservative tendencies of English society, and, being above all moral and sentimental, it became identified with philanthropy. Howard's charitable efforts to improve the condition of prisoners, Burke's impassioned speeches against the tyranny and the extortions of Warren Hastings, Wilberforce's motion for the abolition of Negro slavery, all date from these very years, which saw the first modern factories set up in the Midlands and the north of England. The same period also witnessed the establishment of philanthropical societies, such as the Society for the Prevention of Crime, and the Society for the Improvement of the Poorer Classes, though these were more concerned with education than with charity. And their ideas were already influencing legislation. Parish relief became less inhuman through the abolition of the hateful law of settlement. This influence was most clearly seen in the Act of 1788, passed to protect the little chimney-sweeps from the dangers of their calling and the brutality of their masters.[1] This was indeed the sort of case that would touch all 'sensitive souls', whose emotions and effusions, in France as in England, re-echoed throughout the second half of the eighteenth century.

There is no doubt that the best type of manufacturers felt this influence, for there were many open minds and fine characters among them. In politics and religion some, like Boulton, Wedgwood and Wilkinson, professed advanced opinions. Many were dissenters, including a noticeable proportion of members of the Society of Friends, whose strong puritan upbringing left upon them an ineradicable stamp. Naturally they belonged to their class and time. They knew nothing of what has been expressively termed social compunction, and they never for a moment doubted that they had a right to wealth and power. But in a world of coarse hard upstarts they were exceptional in that they acknowledged a duty towards their fellow-men in general, and their own workmen in particular. Sometimes even, they rose to the notion of some special duty, the accomplishment of which satisfied their pride as much as their conscience: the duty of the master to his servant, or of the medieval baron to his vassal. We have seen how Boulton at Soho, and Wedgwood at Etruria, founded sick clubs for their workmen and opened dispensaries and schools.[2] At Coalbrookdale Richard Reynolds, who during the famine of 1795 sent the handsome sum of £20,000 to

---

[1] 28 Geo. III, c. 48. As a matter of fact this Act was quite inoperative, as was shown by several subsequent inquiries.

[2] See preceding chapter.

help the London poor, looked after the welfare of his men and him-self conducted 'Working Class Rambles'.[1] These obviously were no more than isolated acts without extensive consequences, which showed kindliness rather than any definite views as to how the condition of the working class could be improved. But they proved to be the starting points for more systematic efforts; from David Dale's philanthropy sprang Robert Owen's socialism.

David Dale was a nonconformist, a member of that austere sect the Independents, and a most zealous member, who every Sunday preached to his co-religionists in Glasgow.[2] But he was also a most active and capable business man who founded and ran one of the most important industrial undertakings in Great Britain. His religion and his practical ability did not conflict in the least, for with him philan-thropy often went hand in hand with business. In 1784, when with the help of Arkwright (who was most impressed with the advantages of the position, and saw New Lanark as a future Scottish Manchester)[3] he set up a spinning mill by the falls of the Clyde, the great difficulty was the scarcity of labour. The district was sparsely populated and the country people detested the discipline of the factory even more than the English did, and obstinately refused to work there.[4] In order to attract them David Dale built a model village near the factory, with houses laid out on a regular plan, and offered to let for very low rents. The scheme was successful, and a number of families, chiefly drawn from the barren Highland districts, settled in New Lanark. Meanwhile, following the example of other millowners, David Dale asked the parishes of Edinburgh and Glasgow to send him several hundred pauper children as apprentices. By 1792 the village had a population of 2,000 inhabitants.[5] The privileges which they enjoyed did even more honour to the owner's generosity than to his cleverness. They not only had cheap houses, but by a tacit understanding they were guaranteed constant employment: when one of the factory buildings was burnt down the two hundred and fifty men employed

[1] See S. Smiles, *Industrial Biography*, p. 98.

[2] R. Dale Owen, *Threading my Way*, p. 15.

[3] F. Espinasse, *Lancashire Worthies*. I, 450. Arkwright's and Dale's partnership came to an end after the lawsuit in 1785.

[4] 'It was necessary to collect a new population to supply the infant establishment with labourers. This, however, was no light task, for all the regularly trained Scotch peasantry disdained the idea of working early and late, day after day, within cotton mills.' Robert Owen, *Second Essay on the Formation of Character*, 1857 ed., p. 276. 'Two modes then only remained of obtaining these labourers, the one, to procure children from the various public charities of the country, and the other, to induce families to settle around the works.' *The Life of Robert Owen, written by Himself*, p. 58.

[5] *Annual Register*, 1792 (*Chronicle*, p. 27); R. Dale Owen, op. cit., pp. 12-13; David Bremner, *The Industries of Scotland*, p. 281.

there still drew their wages throughout the whole period of their enforced idleness.[1] The management of the apprentices, who were usually so brutally treated, deserved even higher commendation. Dale had strictly forbidden the foremen to keep them in the workshops after seven o'clock in the evening. Their food and clothing was carefully looked after, and they slept in spacious and well-kept dormitories, while they were given out-of-door exercise in the neighbouring countryside. Ten schoolmasters were responsible for their education, and we need scarcely say that religion played a large part in the teaching. The New Lanark factories, though not yet famous, were soon known and visited by persons who were interested in education and relief work: David Dale's humanitarian work was praised by them in terms which may sometimes have been too lyrical, but such praise was justified by the novelty of his ideas and the generosity of his intentions.[2]

Unfortunately he did not himself live at New Lanark, and, taken up as he was with his many undertakings, he only went there from Glasgow three or four times a year.[3] This was not enough for effective supervision and a true judgment of results. In 1797 Robert Owen was made manager, and looking into matters more closely was dissatisfied with what he saw. Although the children were much better treated than anywhere else they were still badly overworked. Children of six worked eleven and a half to twelve hours a day, and their physical and intellectual development suffered from it.[4] As for the adult workers, drawn as they were from the most unstable and least respectable elements of the rural population, their morality left much to be desired. Owen writes that 'the great majority of them were idle, intemperate, dishonest, devoid of truth'.[5] In undertaking their improvement

[1] Robert Owen did the same during the American embargo of 1806. R. Dale Owen, op. cit., p. 15.

[2] Evidence of a visitor in 1796: 'Four hundred children are entirely fed, clothed and instructed at the expense of this venerable philanthropist. The rest live with their parents in neat comfortable habitations, receiving wages for their labour. The health and happiness depicted on the countenance of these children show that the proprietor of the Lanark mills has remembered mercy in the midst of gain. The regulations here to preserve health of body and mind present a striking contrast to those of most large manufactories in this kingdom, the very hotbeds of contagion and disease. It is a truth that ought to be engraved in letters of gold, to the eternal honour of the founder of New Lanark, that out of nearly three thousand children who have been at work in these mills throughout a period of twelve years, only fourteen have died, and not one has suffered criminal punishment.' *Gentleman's Magazine*, LXXIV, 493-4.

[3] *Report on the State of the Children employed in the Manufactories of the United Kingdom* (1816), p. 25 (Robert Owen's evidence).

[4] Ibid., p. 20. It must be remembered that Samuel Oldknow a few years before was considered as an exceptionally humane employer because his apprentices worked *only* twelve hours a day.

[5] *The Life of Robert Owen, written by Himself*, p. 57. There is some difference between

Owen felt that he was carrying on the work of David Dale, whose successor he became soon after. In his own eyes and in those of his contemporaries, he was still merely a philanthropic manufacturer. When he reorganized the schools at New Lanark and applied in his factory the same system of reports on work and conduct, or when he bought provisions wholesale and resold them at cost price,[1] he did not do it because of any new doctrine. He was only applying to immediate social problems the moral teachings which, like Dale, he had received from his religious education. But his philanthropical experiments were gradually leading him to believe in one idea, which was later to develop into his theory of the formation of character and to become the cornerstone of his whole system. He believed that men were no more responsible for their vices or crimes than they were for their ignorance or their poverty; that they were merely the products of a social system, and that it was therefore the social system which must be changed, if men were to be made better and happier.[2] This is very near the doctrine which prepared the French Revolution — Rousseau's doctrine — and we are approaching the critical moment when theory joined hands with practice and became embodied in action and facts. When, later on, Owen developed his scheme for a regenerated society, he was guided by the work in which at first he had only taken part but which he had finally made his own. The industrial and agricultural communities which were to serve as nuclei to regenerated mankind were idealized New Lanarks, and the real New Lanark, which Owen only thought of as an imperfect copy of them, had in fact provided him with his original model.

V

The same feelings which inspired the individual efforts of David Dale and Robert Owen, struck the first blow at the inhuman sophistry of *laissez-faire*. As early as 1784 the condition of the apprentices in the

---

[1] *The Life of Robert Owen*, pp. 80-4.

[2] See the two dialogues which form the introduction to the *Life of Robert Owen*, particularly pages iv, v and xii. The same idea was clearly expressed, as early as 1815, in 'Observations on the Effect of the Manufacturing System': 'The inhabitants of every country are trained and formed by its great leading existing circumstances, and the character of the lower orders in Britain is now formed chiefly by circumstances arising from trade, manufactures, and commerce.' Ibid., Appendix H, p. 39.

---

the tone of this passage, written in the latter part of his life, and his evidence given in 1816. Possibly he made the picture rather more gloomy than it really was, the better to show up his own part, and this in all good faith, because he thought of himself as the real founder of New Lanark.

spinning mills was the subject of a medical report to the Lancashire magistrates. After studying that report the magistrates decided to forbid the parishes placing children in factories where there was night work.[1] But this resolution does not seem to have had any effect, or at any rate was quickly forgotten. Manufacturers, who were every day becoming more numerous, wealthy and powerful, continued to find as many apprentices as they needed and to use them as they chose. On January 25th, 1796, a new and emphatic report was published. It had been drawn up by Dr Percival of Manchester, for a new committee called the Manchester Board of Health which had just been formed to investigate the sanitary condition of the city. The conclusions of this report have often been quoted and deserve to be quoted once more, for they were the preface to all later factory legislation:

'(1) It appears that the children and others who work in the large cotton factories are peculiarly disposed to be affected by the contagion of fever, and that where such infection is received it is rapidly propagated, not only among those who are crowded together in the same apartments, but in the families and neighbourhoods to which they belong. (2) The large factories are generally injurious to the constitution of those employed in them, even where no particular diseases prevail, from the close confinement which is enjoined, from the debilitating effects of hot and impure air, and from the want of the active exercises which nature points out as essential in childhood and youth, to invigorate the system and to fit our species for the employments and for the duties of manhood. (3) The untimely labour of the night, and the protracted labour of the day, with respect to children, not only tends to diminish future expectations as to the general sum of life and industry, by impairing the strength and destroying the vital stamina of the rising generation, but it too often gives encouragement to idleness, extravagance and profligacy in the parents, who, contrary to the order of nature, subsist by the oppression of their offspring. (4) It appears that the children employed in factories are generally debarred from all opportunities of education, and from moral and religious instruction. (5) From the excellent regulations which subsist in several cotton factories, it appears that many of these evils may in a considerable degree be obviated. We are therefore warranted by experience, and are assured we shall have the support of the liberal proprietors of those factories, in proposing an application for Parliamentary aid (if other methods appear not likely to effect the purpose) to establish a general system of laws for the wise, humane and equal government of all such works.'[2]

[1] See Hutchins and Harrison, *History of Factory Legislation*, p. 8.
[2] 1816 *Report*, pp. 139-40.

The last paragraph gave this document its historical importance, for it quite definitely demanded State intervention. It recognized that private philanthropy was unequal to the task of suppressing the abuses which followed on the development of the factory system. And it suggested that the State should compel all manufacturers to adopt the standard which had been set, out of pure humanity, by a few of them. The Manchester Board of Health had only expressed a wish and a hope, the need for action remained. This action was taken by a manufacturer. When Sir Robert Peel walked through the work-shops in his own factories he was struck by the pale and sickly look of the apprentices. He was shocked by the unhealthy conditions under which they lived and by their ignorance.[1] Knowing that other factories were even worse, he realized that some general measure was the only remedy. As he was a member of Parliament, he felt it was his duty to induce the House of Commons to accept such a Bill by intro-ducing it himself, which he did on April 6th, 1802.

A few days before,[2] the attention of the House had been directed to the scandalous bargains concluded between manufacturers and parishes. Once the children had been handed over to their new masters like so many head of cattle they practically disappeared, as it was often impossible to find out where they were. We can imagine how many criminal abuses could be carried on under this deliberately created cloak of darkness. A motion insisting that the Poor Law authorities should keep a register of the names and domiciles of all apprenticed children was unanimously carried, and thus the ground was cleared for the Bill introduced by Sir Robert Peel, who was both an

---

[1] 'The house in which I have a concern gave employment at one time to nearly one thousand children of this description. Having other pursuits, it was not often in my power to visit the factories, but, whenever such visits were made, I was struck with the uniform appearance of bad health, and in many cases, stunted growth of the children. The hours of labour were regulated by the interest of the overseer, whose remuneration depending on the quantity of work done: he was often induced to make the poor children work excessive hours, and to stop their complaints by trifling bribes ... Finding our own factories under such management, and learning that the like practices prevailed in other parts of the Kingdom where similar machines were in use, the children being much overworked, and often little or no regard paid to cleanliness and ventilation in the buildings, having the assistance of Dr Percival and other eminent medical gentlemen of Manchester, together with some distinguished characters both in and out of Parliament, I brought in a Bill ... ' 1816 *Report*, p. 132 (Sir Robert Peel's evidence).

[2] March 13th, 1802. See *Parliamentary Register*, New Series, XVII, 199 (Wilbraham Bootle's motion). The question of the treatment of parish apprentices in factories had just been brought to the attention of the public by various incidents. In 1801 a Lancashire manufacturer called Jouvaux had been sentenced to one year hard labour for maltreating his apprentices. It had been also noticed that the Birmingham magis-trates had refused to send pauper children to the factories. Hutchins and Harrison, *History of Factory Legislation*, p. 15.

influential member of the party in power and a qualified representative of industry. In any other country but England it would be surprising to find that so little discussion took place on a subject which involved such an important principle, namely the right of the State to interfere in the direction of private undertakings. As a matter of fact the principle was lost sight of and the question was dealt with as a special case. The motive was humanity, rather than any theoretical considerations.

In introducing his Bill, Peel laid special stress on the moral degradation of the young people employed in the factories: 'It would easily be believed that, where a large number of persons were crowded together, impurity would arise, and that impurity would be followed by disease.' The first object of the Act was to do away with the material conditions which had created such a lamentable state of things, the second being to destroy their effects by 'instruction, the want of which had given rise to much immorality'.[1] This was an argument which touched even the least sensitive, because it appealed to the national sense of morality which in 1802 was at least as much offended by indecency as by cruelty. Lord Belgrave, who seconded the motion, enlarged the scope of the debate by denouncing all the abuses of the factory system: 'The cruelties and hardships under which these poor children laboured were enormous.' And the Act should not apply to apprentices only, or those of one industry: 'It should be extended to the woollen as well as to the cotton manufacture, and relaxation should be stipulated for the children as well as cleanliness and instruction. Wealth was pursued in this country with an eagerness to which every other consideration was sacrificed, and with excesses calculated to call down the vengeance of Heaven.'[2] This aristocratic voice, raised in protest against the sins of industrial capitalism, seems to foreshadow that generous movement which in the following generation was led by Lord Shaftesbury. Wilberforce also spoke, asking that the title given to the new Act should clearly indicate its extension to all factories and workshops.[3] Peel was congratulated by everyone on his 'humanity and public spirit',[4] and the Act, having passed through all its stages in both Houses without difficulty, received the royal assent on June 22nd, 1802.[5]

It contained first sanitary provisions. The walls and ceilings of all workshops had to be whitewashed twice a year. Every factory had to be

[1] Later on he declared that he wanted to make the factories 'correct and moral'. Ibid., p. 447.

[2] Ibid., p. 448.

[3] The final title was: *An Act for the Preservation of the Health and Morals of Apprentices and Others, employed in Cotton and other Mills and Cotton and other Factories* (42 Geo. III c. 73).

[4] See *Morning Chronicle* of April 7th, 1802.

[5] *Parliamentary Register*, New Series, XVIII, 63, 183, 457, 591.

provided with a sufficient number of windows, and with sufficiently large ones, to allow of the room being properly ventilated. Each apprentice had to be supplied with two complete suits of clothes, one to be renewed at least every year. Girls and boys were to have separate dormitories, with enough beds for not more than two children to have to share a bed. Then followed clauses dealing with hours of work. These were never to exceed twelve hours a day, exclusive of mealtimes. Work was not to continue after nine o'clock at night or to begin before six o'clock in the morning. Education became compulsory during the first four years of apprenticeship. All apprentices had to be taught reading, writing and arithmetic, and the time had to be taken out of work hours. Religious instruction was also compulsory, and had to be given every Sunday, the children going to church either within or without the factory.

In order to see that the provisions of the Act were observed the Justices of the Peace for the county were every year to appoint two inspectors, the one a local magistrate and the other a clergyman of the Church of England. These inspectors had the right of entry to all factories at all times, and they could also summon a doctor if they detected any infectious illness. They were to report to the Quarter Sessions of the Justices of the Peace. Then followed a list of penalties. Every offence was punishable with a fine of from £2 to £5. Refusal to admit the inspectors or to afford them facilities was punishable by a fine of from £5 to £10. A printed copy of the Act was to be posted in every factory or workshop governed by its provisions, so that all those whom it concerned could read it, and if necessary insist on its being enforced.

This Act, which slipped almost unobserved through Parliament,[1] deserves the attention of history. It established the principle of factory inspection, which throughout the nineteenth century has occupied such an important place in British social legislation and which has been adopted by all civilized countries. It obliged employers to conform to certain rules concerning workshop hygiene, education for apprentices and hours of labour. By restricting, in however slight a degree, the manufacturer's arbitrary power, it marked the first step on the road which begins at complete *laissez-faire* and ends at State Socialism.

It must be acknowledged that the practical results of the Act were unfortunately very limited. To begin with it only applied to the large factories, and especially to the spinning mills. The small and middle-sized factories, where the apprentices were often hardly better

[1] Cobbett's *Parliamentary History* does not even mention it. 'The Act was regarded exclusively as a bit of Poor Law legislation.' Hutchins and Harrison, *History of Factory Legislation*, p. 17.

treated,[1] escaped all supervision. Even where actual inspection took place the employers, after complaining about this so-called attack on their liberty and on the interests of industry,[2] soon managed to render it quite illusory. The terms of the Act were too vague, and the penalties too light. The simplest method of evading it was to engage young workpeople without any apprenticeship indentures: as, legally speaking, they were not apprentices, they could be forced to work night and day with impunity.[3] As soon as the steam engine took the place of the water-wheel this practice became almost universal, because, as the manufacturers could now build their factories within reach of large towns, they were no longer obliged to rely for their labour on the parishes.[4] The Act had appointed inspectors, but these showed no great zeal in carrying out their duties. For they were above all most anxious not to quarrel with the employers, who were often their friends and neighbours. In fact in some districts, after a few years inspectors were no longer appointed. And lastly, no printed copy of the Act was ever posted in any workshop. Robert Blincoe, whose sufferings have been related above, read the text for the first time eleven or twelve years after its publication.[5] Even if it had been scrupulously enforced this Act would have been but an inadequate remedy for abuses which went on for many years. Even after the inquiry of 1816, which revealed them in all their gravity, no definite action was taken.[6] No serious attack on such abuses could be made until public opinion had been stirred by the vigorous and passionate appeals of a few generous men like Richard Oastler and Michael Sadler.

The Act of 1802 was not meant, by those who voted for it, to create a precedent. They regarded it as an exceptional measure, dictated by purely sentimental considerations. Even Sir Robert Peel, its author, was and remained till his death one of the most convinced advocates of *laissez-faire*. Both before and after 1802 he strongly opposed the

---

[1] A. Held, *Zwei Bücher zur socialen Geschichte Englands*, p. 420.

[2] Petition from the Manchester, Stockport, Preston, Bolton and Glasgow spinners on Feb. 11th, 1803. *Journals of the House of Commons*, LVIII, 149. Petition from the Leeds spinners, ibid., p. 161.

[3] Dr Lettsom, 'Remarks on Cotton Mills', *Gentleman's Magazine*, LXXIV, 492 ff. (1804). At Holywell in Flintshire, a mill employed about seven hundred children who worked in shifts, and without interruption, from midnight on Sunday to midnight on Saturday.

[4] 1816 *Report*, p. 137. See ibid., pp. 183, 282, 317, 321. In 1815 some factories in Stockport were still working eighteen hours a day (p. 89, Robert Owen's evidence). The hours of work had increased since 1802 (N. Gould's evidence, pp. 98-9).

[5] 'Memoir of Robert Blincoe', in *The Lion*, I, 156.

[6] The Act of 1819 (59 Geo. III, c. 66) did no more than forbid the employment of children under nine years of age, and extend to all non-adult workers the (theoretical) benefit of a twelve-hour day.

maintenance or the renewal of the old apprenticeship regulations, or in fact any measures which tended to bind industry in any way.[1] He had been careful to limit the scope of the Act in order to emphasize its exceptional character: 'I remember very well that in passing that Bill I had a great deal of care upon my hands to prevent the manufacturer suffering as well as the apprentices; many gentlemen would have urged me in the most earnest manner to shorten the hours of labour much below what I thought it proper to shorten them. I was desired to let that Bill operate through every cottage in the country. I deemed that so unreasonable, that I was determined to give up all management of the measure if it was not left to me.'[2] But whether he meant to or not, he did lay the foundation for all modern labour legislation. The tendency, which he had followed and resisted at the same time, was to grow side by side with the opposite tendency. Both drew their strength from the industrial revolution, which on the one hand, by its economic consequences, hastened the breaking up of the old regulations, while on the other hand its social consequences entailed the necessity or the duty of creating a new branch of legislation.

CONCLUSION

In the first decade of the nineteenth century, which closes the period we set out to study, the industrial revolution was far from being completed. The use of machinery was still limited to certain industries, and in these industries to certain specialities or certain districts. Side by side with great metal works such as Soho and Coalbrookdale the small workshops of the Birmingham toyman and of the Sheffield cutlers continued to exist, and survived for many decades. Side by side with

---

[1] See the part he played in 1808, in the debates over the calico-printers' petition, while Sheridan supported the men, *Parliamentary Debates*, IX, 538 ff. See also his evidence in 1806, before the Commission of Inquiry on the State of the Woollen Manufacture: 'With respect to the apprenticing, I am almost inclined to think that the good sense of those who appear here would hardly wish that any restrictions should be imposed upon the trade in that respect; I have that feeling for all those who are employed in it, that if I conceived any Act of Parliament or any Act now on our Statute book had a tendency to throw an advantage in favour of the few at the expense of the many of the lower orders of the people, I should be one of the foremost to get these alterations, that the lower orders of the people might have every opportunity of advancing their own interests. On the other hand, if any were so blind to their own interest as to wish to expose their own trade to inconveniences, though I may not be classed as one of their friends, I should oppose their wishes, lest they should do themselves an injury.' *Report from the Committee on the State of the Woollen Manufacture* (1806), p. 441.

[2] Alfred, *History of the Factory Movement*, I, 31.

the Lancashire cotton mills and the West Riding woollen mills, thousands of weavers went on working at home on their old hand looms. Steam, which was to multiply and generalize the results of all other mechanical inventions, had hardly begun its triumphant progress. Nevertheless the modern industrial system did already exist with all its essential features, and it is possible to detect in the developments which had taken place at that time the main characteristics of the great change.

From the technical point of view the industrial revolution consists in the invention and use of processes which made it possible to speed up and constantly to increase production: some are mechanical processes, as in the textile industries, others chemical as in the metalworking industries; they help either to prepare the raw material or to determine the form of the finished product, and the phrase machine industry is inadequate to the variety and to the possibilities offered by such developments. The invention of such processes (at least in the beginning) owed little to conclusions drawn from purely scientific discoveries. It is an established fact that most of the first inventors were anything but scientists. They were technical men who, being faced with a practical problem, used their natural faculties and their expert knowledge of the habits and needs of the industry to solve it. Highs, Crompton, Hargreaves, Dudley, Darby and Cort were men of this type. A few others, such as Wyatt and Cartwright, undertook their researches instinctively and out of pure curiosity, without either scientific or professional training. Under the pressure of necessity and on purely concrete data they set to work without a definite plan, and only reached their goal after much groping in the dark. They represent economic necessity, silently and powerfully moulding men to its will, overcoming obstacles and forging its own instruments. Science came later and brought its immense reserves of power to bear on the development which had already begun, thus giving at once to partial developments in different industries a common direction and a common speed. This is specially noticeable in the case of Watt and the steam engine. Thus two streams from different sources met, and though it was to their combined power that the industrial revolution owed its actual size and strength, yet the change had already begun and its first results were conspicuous.

From the economic point of view the industrial revolution is characterized by the concentration of capital and the growth of large undertakings, the existence and working of which from being only exceptional came to be the normal conditions of industry. Though, not without reason, this concentration is often considered as the result of technical inventions, yet to a certain extent it preceded such inventions. It was essentially a commercial phenomenon and was connected with the gradual hold obtained by merchants over industry. Not only was it accompanied, but it was also prepared by the expansion of trade and credit. Its necessary conditions were internal security, the development of communications and of maritime trade. The historical transition between the master craftsman of the Middle Ages and the modern industrialist was provided by the merchant manufacturer. We find him at first, so to speak, on the margin of industry, with the sole function of linking up producers with markets which were becoming too large and too distant for them. Later on, as his capital grew and the manufacturer came to rely on him more and more, he became the master of production and finally the owner of all raw material, buildings and equipment, while independent workmen were degraded to the rank of mere wage-earners. This concentration of the means of production in the hands of capitalists who were more concerned with trade than with industry is a fact of paramount importance. No doubt 'manufacture', with the great number of men it employed, the highly specialized division of its labour and its many likenesses to the factory system, was a more striking fact, but it played a much smaller part in the evolution of industry. It marked a stage on the road, but a stage no sooner reached than passed. Economists, studying this evolution, have conceived and described it as a simple development, one phase following another like the different parts of a geometrical curve. But to the eyes of the historian a movement of such complexity is more like a river, which does not always flow at the same pace but sometimes slackens its course, sometimes rushes on, now running through narrow gorges and now spreading out over the plain, now breaking up into many divergent branches and now winding about, so that it seems to curve back on itself. Merely to enumerate the different points it passes by is not to describe it. To do this we must follow, step by step, its varied winding course, which in spite of its changes of direction remains continuous like the slope which bears it to its end.

From the social point of view the industrial revolution had such extensive and profound results that it would be presumptuous for us to attempt to summarize them in a short formula. Even though, unlike political revolutions, it did not actually alter the legal form of society, yet it modified its very substance. It gave birth to social classes whose progress and mutual opposition fill the history of our times. It would be easy, by quoting some of the facts mentioned in this very book, to try and show that in this respect there has been no revolution, that the same social classes were already in existence, that their opposition had begun long before, its nature and cause always remaining the same. One of the objects we have always kept in mind was precisely to show the continuity of the historical process underlying even the most rapid changes. None of these changes took place suddenly, as by a miracle, but each of them had been expected, prepared and outlined before it actually took place. It would be an equal error either to undervalue those preliminaries or to take them for what they only foreshadowed. We know that there were machines before the era of machinery, 'manufacture' before factories, combinations and strikes before the formation of industrial capitalism and of the 'factory proletariat'. But in the slow-moving mass of society a new element does not make itself felt immediately. And we have not only to note its presence but its relation to its environment and, as it were, the space it occupies in history. The industrial revolution is precisely the expansion of undeveloped forces, the sudden growth and blossoming of seeds which had for many years lain hidden or asleep.

After the beginning of the nineteenth century the growth of the factory system was visible to all. It was already influencing the distribution as well as the material condition of the population. To the factory system were due the importance and sudden prosperity of districts such as Lancashire, South Wales and part of the Lowlands of Scotland, which until then had been considered as being among the least prosperous parts of the country. It was the factory system which, following on the redistribution of landed property, quickened the migration of the rural population towards the factories. When the census of 1811 was taken, sixty or seventy per cent of the inhabitants in the counties of Middlesex, Warwickshire, Yorkshire and Lancashire were employed in trade or industry, and at least fifty per cent of those of Cheshire, Leicestershire, Nottinghamshire and Staffordshire.[1] In these new centres, full of such intense activity, with their contrasting extremes of wealth and poverty, the data of the social problem, much as we know them today, could already be descried. The moment was not far off when that problem was to be defined for the first time by Robert Owen in his *Letter to the Manufacturers of England* and his *Observations on the Consequences of the Factory System.* And he spoke not for England alone but for all the nations of the West, for while the factory system continued to develop in the country of its birth it had already begun to spread to other countries. It had made its appearance on the Continent, and from that time onward its history was no longer English but European – until it extended to the whole world.

[1] The information supplied by the 1801 census on the occupations and professions of the inhabitants is very vague and unreliable. See *Abstract of the Answers and Returns to the Population Act*, 41 *Geo. III*, I, 497.

BIBLIOGRAPHY

I. DOCUMENTS

A. Unpublished documents. B. Printed documents. (1) Statistical documents and compilations. (2) Documents relating to the technique (patents, descriptions of machines, lawsuits on patent rights, etc.). (3) Official documents: Journals of the House of Lords and of the House of Commons, Parliamentary debates, Reports of Committees, Statutes of the Realm, etc. (4) Selections illustrating economic or social history.

II. CONTEMPORANEOUS INFORMATION

A. Descriptive books. B. Travels. C. Technical treatises and memoirs. D. Newspapers and periodicals.

III. CONTEMPORANEOUS LITERATURE ON ECONOMIC SUBJECTS

A. General literature, commerce, communications. B. Agriculture, enclosures, price of provisions. C. Population and pauperism. D. Textile trades. E. Metal trades and pottery.

IV. WORKS ON SPECIAL SUBJECTS

A. Histories of trades and industries. B. Histories of localities. C. Biographies. D. Agriculture, enclosures, etc. E. Economic and social questions.

V. GENERAL

VI. BIBLIOGRAPHIES

A. General. B. Special. (1) Parliamentary Papers. (2) Economic literature. (3) History of trades and agriculture. (4) Biography.

SUPPLEMENT TO THE BIBLIOGRAPHY
A. History of trades and industries. B. Histories of localities. C. Biographies. D. Agriculture, enclosures. E. Economic and social questions. F. General. G. Bibliographies. H. Statistics.

I. DOCUMENTS

A. UNPUBLISHED DOCUMENTS

Manuscript sources are plentiful, in spite of the destruction of many commercial documents which had lost all practical use and were thought not to be of historical interest, but they are much scattered and often difficult of access. Their complete exploration, which can be achieved only by a collective effort, calls for the preparation of numerous monographs.[1] The records of great business firms, when preserved, are of course of exceptional interest. Town records, as well as Quarter Session Books, documents in solicitors' offices and other legal papers, can supply valuable information. Some aspects of the social conditions can be studied in the Home Office Papers. England offers no equivalent to the quantity of documents produced by the centralized bureaucracy of the old French monarchy, but possesses instead a wealth of parliamentary documents (petitions, reports, etc.), which we list in a subsequent section of the bibliography.

BIENCOURT, MARQUIS DE: Mémoire sur l'état agricole, industriel et commercial de l'Angleterre (1784) – In Archives des Affaires Etrangères, Mémoires et Documents, Angleterre, LXXIV, fol. 24 ff.

Census of the Townships of Manchester and Salford (1773) – Census taken in 1773 by a group of private persons. 3 vols. Chetham's Library, Manchester, No. 6710.

CLARKE, L. W.: History of Birmingham – Many copies of documents relating to the history of Birmingham; 7 vols. of manuscripts. Birmingham Central Library (reference section), No. 122040.

Considérations sur les Manufactures de Mousseline de Callico dans la Grande-Bretagne (1788) – In Archives des Affaires Etrangères, Mémoires et Documents, Angleterre, LXXIV, fol. 182 ff.

Correspondence and papers of Josiah Wedgwood and his partner, Thomas Bentley – 'Liverpool' and 'Etruria' Collections (about 64,000 items), Josiah Wedgwood Museum, Stoke-on-Trent. The John Rylands Library, Manchester, also contains some letters by Wedgwood.

---

[1] Considerable progress has been made already in this direction: on documents concerning the woollen trade, consult H. Heaton, *Yorkshire Woollen and Worsted Industries* (Preface); on Samuel Crompton's letters, see G. W. Daniels, *Early English Cotton Industry*, pp. 166 ff.; on the Oldknow records at Mellor, G. Unwin, A. Hulme and G. Taylor, *Samuel Oldknow and the Arkwrights*, pp. v-xvi; the Coalbrookdale, Horsehay and Huntsman MSS. (still in the possession of those firms) and other original documents concerning the iron and steel trades have been used and described by T. S. Ashton, *Iron and Steel in the Industrial Revolution*, pp. v-viii; J. Lord (*Capital and Steam Power*) had access to the Tew MSS. (kept at the Assay Office, Birmingham) containing part of the private correspondence between Boulton and Watt. J. L. and L. B. Hammond's books (see below, IV, D, and Supplement to the Bibliography) show the use that can be made of Home Office records.

LA ROCHEFOUCAULD-LIANCOURT, F. AND A.: Voyage en Suffolk et Norfolk (1784); Voyage aux Montagnes (1786) – Manuscripts communicated by M. Ferdinand Dreyfus. 4 vols.

Owen MSS. – 89 vols. of notes and documents on the history of Lancashire. See particularly vol. LXXX. Manchester Central Library (reference section).

Patents and Specifications – Patent Office, London.

Place MSS. – Francis Place's papers, full of information on social conditions at the end of the eighteenth and the beginning of the nineteenth century. British Museum, Add. MSS. 27789-27859.

Soho MSS. – Records and papers of the firm of Boulton and Watt from 1795; 50 vols. of copies and 7-8,000 original letters. Birmingham Central Library (reference section).

Timmins MSS. – Notes and documents relating to the history of the city and industries of Birmingham, collected by Samuel Timmins. Birmingham Central Library (reference section).

Webb MSS. – Notes and documents gathered by Sidney and Beatrice Webb for the preparation of their works on economic history. British Library of Political and Economic Science, London School of Economics (Webb Trade Union Collection, Collection E, Section A).

Wyatt MSS. – Papers of the inventor John Wyatt, of Lewis Paul, etc. (1732-1813). 2 vols. Birmingham Central Library (reference section), No. 93189.

B. PRINTED DOCUMENTS

1. Statistical documents and compilations

Abstract of the Answers and Returns to the Population Act, 41 Geo. III. 2 vols. London, 1802.

Abstract of the Answers and Returns to the Population Act, 11 Geo. IV. 3 vols. London, 1833. [See the preface by J. Rickman, which contains a critical study of the preceding censuses and of the estimates made before the nineteenth century.]

ROGERS, J. E. THOROLD. *A History of Agriculture and Prices in England,* vol. VII (1703-93). Oxford, 1902.

TOOKE, T. *A History of Prices and of the State of the Circulation from 1793 to 1837.* 2 vols. London, 1838. [Tables of the price of corn from the Eton College Records.]

2. Documents relating to the technique (patents, descriptions of machines, lawsuits on patent rights, etc.)

Abridgments of Specifications relating to the Manufacture of Iron and Steel, part I, A.D. 1620-1866. Second edition. London, 1883. [Published by the Patent Office.]

Abridgments of Specifications relating to Pottery. London, 1863.

Abridgments of Specifications relating to Spinning, part I, A.D. 1664-1865. London, 1866.

Abridgments of Specifications relating to Weaving, part I, A.D. 1620-1859. London, 1861.

Abridgments of Specifications relating to Bleaching, Dyeing and Printing Calico and other Fabrics and Yarns, part I, A.D. 1617-1857 (vol. I). London, 1859.

WOODCROFT, BENNET. *Subject-matter Index of Patents of Invention from March 2, 1617 (14 James I) to October 1, 1852 (16 Victoriae).* 2 vols. London, 1854, 1857.

Chronological Index of Patents of Invention. 2 vols. London, 1860.

Richard Arkwright versus Peter Nightingale (Court of Common Pleas, February 17th, 1785). London, 1785.

The Trial of a Cause instituted by R. P. Arden esq., His Majesty's Attorney General, by Writ of Scire facias, to repeal a Patent granted on the 16 December 1775 to Mr Richard Arkwright (Court of King's Bench, June 25th, 1785). London, 1785.

3. Official documents: Journals of the House of Lords and of the House of Commons, Parliamentary debates, Reports of Committees, Statutes of the Realm, etc.

Calendar of Home Office Papers of the Reign of King George III (1760-75). 4 vols. London, 1873-99.

Journals of the House of Commons. Containing summary reports of proceedings, petitions, reports from Committees, documents laid before the House, etc. Vols. XX-LXX (1714-1815).

Journals of the House of Lords. Proceedings of the House of Lords and annexed documents. Vols. XX-XLIX (1714-1815).

General Index to the Journals of the House of Commons. In four parts: first part, vols. I to XVII (1547-1714), published 1852; second part, vols. XVIII to XXXIV (1714-73), published 1778; third part, vols. XXXV to LV (1774-1800), published 1798-1803; fourth part, vols. LVI to LXXV (1801-20), published 1825. [Not unreservedly reliable.]

General Index to the Journals of the House of Lords. In four parts: first part, vols. I to X (1509-1649), published 1836; second part, vols. XI to XIX (1660-1714), published 1834; third part, vols. XX to XXXV (1714-79), published 1817; fourth part, vols. XXXVI to LIII, published 1832. [Same observation.]

Parliamentary Register (1743-1802). 88 vols. London, 1775-1803. Reports of Parliamentary debates, taken from newspapers and periodicals. [More complete than the following collection.]

COBBETT, W. (ed.). *Parliamentary History of England from the Norman Conquest to the Year 1803.* 36 vols. London, 1806-20.

HANSARD (ed.). *Parliamentary Debates.* First series (1803-12). 22 vols. London, 1804-13.

Reports from the Committees of the House of Commons from 1715 to 1801. 16 vols. London, 1803.

General Index to the Reports from the Committees of the House of Commons (1715-1801). London, 1803.

General Index to the Reports from Select Committees of the House of Commons from 1801 to 1852. London, 1852.

Among the Committee Reports published separately the following must be mentioned:

Report from the Committee to whom the Petition of the Cotton Spinners in and adjoining to the County of Lancaster ... was referred. 1780.

Report from the Committee to whom the Petitions from the Woolcombers complaining of certain Machines constructed for the Combing of Wool were referred. 1794.

Report from the Select Committee appointed to take into consideration the Means of promoting the Cultivation and Improvement of the Waste, Uninclosed, and Unproductive Lands of the Kingdom. 1795.

Second Report from the Committee, etc. 1797.

Report from the Select Committee appointed to consider of the most effectual Means of facilitating under the Authority of Parliament the Inclosure and Improvement of the Waste, Uninclosed and Unproductive Lands. 1800. [This report prepared the General Inclosure Act.]

Reports from the Committee appointed to consider of the present high Price of Provisions. 1800. [Six reports.]

Report from the Committee to whom the Petitions from several Master and Journeyman Weavers ... were referred. 1800.

Report on the Improvement of the Port of London. 1801.

Reports from the Select Committee appointed to consider of the Standing Orders relating to Bills of Inclosure, so far as regards the setting out or the altering of Public Roads. 1801.

Reports from the Committee appointed to consider of the present high Prices of Provisions. 1801. [Seven reports.]

Report from the Select Committee on the Petitions of Persons concerned in the Woollen Trade and Manufactures in the Counties of Somerset, Wilts and Gloucester. 1803.

Report from the Select Committee on the Petition of Merchants and Manufacturers concerned in the Woollen Manufacture in the County of York and Town of Halifax. 1803.

Report from the Select Committee on the Petitions of the Manufacturers of Woollen Cloth in the County of York. 1803.

Minutes of the Evidence taken before the Committee to whom the several Petitions presented to the House in this Session relating to the Act of the 39th and 40th Year of His present Majesty 'for settling Disputes between Masters and Workmen engaged in the Cotton Manufacture' were referred. 1803.

Minutes of the Evidence taken before the Select Committee to whom the Petitions of the Journeymen Callico Printers and other working in that Trade ... were referred. 1804.

Report from the Committee to whom it was referred to examine into the Matter of the Minutes of Evidence respecting the Callico Printers. 1806.

Report from the Select Committee appointed to consider the State of the Woollen Manufacture in England. 1806. [Very important; presents a complete picture of the state of the wool industry from the social and economic point of view in the first years of the nineteenth century.]

Report from the Select Committee to whom the Petition of Edmund Cartwright, Clerk, D.D., respecting a Machine for Weaving, was referred. 1808.

Report from the Select Committee to whom the Petition of Richard Ainsworth, of Bolton, Manufacturer, and also the Petition of several Journeymen Cotton Weavers, resident in England, were severally referred. 1808.

Report from the Select Committee to whom the Petition of several Journeymen Cotton Weavers resident in England, and also the Petition of the Cotton Manufacturers and Operative Cotton Weavers in Scotland were severally referred. 1809.

Report from the Committee of Secrecy on the Disturbances in the Northern Counties. 1812.

Report from the Committee to whom the several Petitions presented to this House, respecting the Apprentice Laws of the Kingdom, were referred. 1813.

Report of the Minutes of Evidence taken before the Select Committee appointed to inquire into the State of the Children employed in the Manufactory of the United Kingdom. 1816. [Very important for the history of factory legislation, as are the three following reports.]

Reports from the Select Committee on Artizans and Machinery. 1824.

Report from the Select Committee to whom the Bill to regulate the Labour of Children in Mills and Factories of the United Kingdom was referred. 1831-2.

Report from the Committee appointed to inquire into the present State of Agriculture. 1833.

Reports from the Central Board of His Majesty's Commissioners ... as to the Employment of Children in Factories. 1833.

Report from the Central Board of His Majesty's Commissioners appointed to Inquire into the Administration and Practical Operation of the Poor Laws. 1834.

Reports from the Select Committee on Hand Loom Weavers' petitions. 1835.

Reports of Commissioners and Assistant-Commissioners on the Condition of the Hand-Loom Weavers. 1839-41.

Statutes at large from Magna Charta to 41 Geo. III. Edited by Runnington. 14 vols. London, 1786-1801.

Statutes at large of the United Kingdom of Great Britain and Ireland from 41 Geo. III (1801) to 25 Victoria (1862). Edited by Tomlins, Raithby and Simons. 26 vols. London, 1862.

4. Selections illustrating economic or social history

BLAND, A., BROWN, P. AND TAWNEY, R. H. *English Economic History: Select Documents.* London, 1914.

GALTON, F. W. *Select Documents illustrating the History of Trade Unionism. I: The Tailoring Trade.* London, 1896.

RAND, B. *Selections illustrating Economic History since the Seven Years War.* London, 1903.

II. CONTEMPORANEOUS INFORMATION

A. DESCRIPTIVE BOOKS

AIKIN, JOHN. *A Description of the Country from thirty to forty miles round Manchester.* London, 1795. [Important.]

ASTON, JOSEPH. *A Picture of Manchester.* Manchester [1816].

CAMPBELL, JOHN. *A Political Survey of Britain: being a series of reflections on the situation, lands, inhabitants, revenues, colonies and commerce of this island.* 2 vols. London, 1774.

CHAMBERLAYNE, JOHN. *Magnae Britanniae Notitia, or the Present State of Great Britain.* London. 1708. [Many editions from 1708 to 1750.]

DEFOE, DANIEL. *A Tour thro' the Whole Island of Great Britain, divided into circuits or journies.* 3 vols. London, 1724-7. [A classic work which abounds in information of all kinds on the state of England between 1720 and 1727.] Revised by S. Richardson. 4 vols. London, 1742.

The Manchester Guide. A Brief Historical Description of the Towns of Manchester and Salford ... Manchester, 1804.

MARSHALL, WILLIAM. *Rural Economy of Yorkshire.* 2 vols. London, 1788.

MAWE, JOHN. *The Mineralogy of Derbyshire, with a Description of the most interesting Mines in the North of England, in Scotland, and in Wales.* London, 1801.

A New and Accurate Description of the present Great Roads and the Principal Cross Roads of England and Wales. London, 1756. [With map of the roads.]

[OGDEN, JAMES]. *A description of Manchester* ... *with a Succinct History of its former original Manufactories* ... *By a Native of the Town.* Manchester, 1783. Republished as *Manchester a Hundred Years Ago.* Manchester, 1887.

PILKINGTON, JAMES. *A View of the present State of Derbyshire.* 2 vols. Derby, 1789.

To such descriptive books should be added the *Agricultural Surveys* written by the correspondents of the Board of Agriculture. They were published in two series (1793-5 and 1802-16). The title of each survey is *A General View of the Agriculture in the County of* ... Together the surveys constitute a source of great value. A shorter edition was compiled by William Marshall from 1808 to 1817:

MARSHALL, WILLIAM. *A Review and Complete Abstract of the Reports to the Board of Agriculture from the Northern Department.* York, 1808.

... *from the Western Department.* York, 1810.

... *from the Eastern Department.* York, 1811.

... *from the Midland Department.* York, 1815.

... *from the Southern and Peninsular Departments.* York, 1817.

B. TRAVELS

FAUJAS DE SAINT-FOND, BENJAMIN. *Voyage en Angleterre, en Ecosse et aux Iles Hébrides.* 2 vols. Paris, 1797. English translation: *Travels in England, Scotland and the Hebrides.* 2 vols. London, 1799.

FORSTER, J. G. A. *Voyage philosophique et pittoresque en Angleterre et en France fait en 1790 ... par George Forster, un des compagnons de Cook.* Paris, an IV (1796).

NEMNICH, P. A. *Beschreibung einer im Sommer 1799 von Hamburg nach und durch England geschehenen Reise.* Tübingen, 1800.

SVEDENSTJERNA, E. T. *Resa igenom en del af England och Skottland, åren 1802 och 1803.* Stockholm, 1804. German translation by J. G. L. Blumhof: *Reise durch einen Theil von England und Schottland, in den Jahren 1802 und 1803, besonders in berg- und hüttenmännischer, technologischer und mineralogischer Absicht.* Marburg, 1811.

Tournée faite en 1788 dans la Grande-Bretagne par un Français parlant la langue anglaise. Paris, 1790.

WENDEBORN, G. F. A. *Beyträge zur Kenntniss Grossbritanniens vom Jahr 1779.* 2 vols. Lemgo, 1780. English translation by the author: *A view of England towards the Close of the Eighteenth Century.* 2 vols. London, 1791.

YOUNG, ARTHUR. *A Six Weeks Tour through the Southern Counties of England and Wales.* London, 1768.
A Six Months Tour through the North of England. 4 vols. London, 1770.
The Farmer's tour through the East of England. 4 vols. London, 1771.
A Tour in Ireland, with General Observations on the Present State of that Kingdom. 2 vols. London, 1780.
Travels in France, Italy and Spain during the years 1787, 1788 and 1789. 2 vols. London, 1790-1.

C. TECHNICAL TREATISES AND MEMOIRS

BECKMANN, JOHANN. *Beyträge zur Geschichte der Erfindungen.* 5 vols. Leipzig, 1780-1805.

BONNARD, R. 'Mémoire sur les procédés employés en Angleterre pour le traitement du fer par le moyen de la houille'. *Journal des Mines*, XVII, 245-96. Paris, Nivôse an XIII (1805).

The Callico Printers' Assistant. London, 1789.

DESAGULIERS, J. T. *A Course of Mechanical and Experimental Philosophy.* 2 vols. London, 1729-44.

HARRIS, JOHN. *Lexicon Technicum, or an Universal English Dictionary of Arts and Sciences.* 2 vols. London, 1704; second edition, London, 1708-10.

HUNTSMAN, BENJAMIN. *Historique de l'Invention de l'Acier fondu en 1750 par B. Huntsman à Attercliffe.* Paris, 1888.

JARS, GABRIEL. *Voyages Métallurgiques, ou Recherches et Observations sur les Mines et Forges de Fer, la Fabrication de l'Acier, etc.* 3 vols. Lyons, 1774-81.

ROBISON, JOHN. *The Articles Steam and Steam-Engines written for the Encyclopædia Britannica, with notes and additions by James Watt, and a letter on some properties of steam by the late J. Southern.* Edinburgh, 1818.

[SHARPE, WILLIAM]. *A Treatise upon Coal Mines.* London, 1769.

SWEDENBORG, EMANUEL. *Regnum Subterraneum sive Minerale: de Ferro.* Dresden and Leipzig, 1734.

SWITZER, STEPHEN. *An Introduction to a General System of Hydrostaticks and Hydraulicks, Philosophical and Practical.* 2 vols. London, 1729. [Contains descriptions, with plates, of Savery's and Newcomen's engines.]

Interesting information on the technique of trades before and during the industrial revolution can be found in the encyclopedias published in England and France between 1760 and 1815:

Encyclopædia Britannica. First edition, Edinburgh, 1768, and fourth edition, 1805. [See in the fourth edition the articles on 'Cotton', 'Iron', 'Steam', etc.]

Encyclopédie méthodique, par une société de gens de lettres. 301 vols. Paris, 1782-1832. [See the volumes on 'Manufactures', by Roland de la Platière, 1785.]

Encyclopédie, ou dictionnaire raisonné des sciences, des arts et des métiers. 28 vols. Paris, 1762-72. [The volumes of plates deserve a particular study: see art. 'Draperie', 'Forge', 'Laines', 'Mines', 'Soie', etc].

Societies' publications also can supply much useful information on the inventions, and the state of agriculture or of industry in different periods:

Annals of Agriculture and other Useful Arts. Edited by the Board of Agriculture. 40 vols. Bury St Edmunds, 1790-1804.

Memoirs of the Literary and Philosophical Society of Manchester. First series, 5 vols., Warrington, 1785-1802; second series, Manchester, 1805 ff.

Philosophical Transactions of the Royal Society. London, 1665 ff. [Containing many papers on mechanical inventions.]

Transactions of the Society for the Encouragement of Arts, Manufactures and Commerce. First series, London, 1761 ff.; second series, 1783 ff.

D. NEWSPAPERS AND PERIODICALS

Annual Register (from 1758).

Birmingham Gazette (from 1741).

Derby Mercury (from 1754).

Gentleman's Magazine (from 1731).

Historical Register (1714-38).

Leeds Mercury. First series 1718-55; second series from 1767.

Manchester Gazette, 1730-60.

Manchester Mercury, 1753-1830.

III. CONTEMPORANEOUS LITERATURE ON ECONOMIC SUBJECTS

(Entries are in chronological order in each section.)

The most important collections of pamphlets on economic subjects are in the library of the British Museum. Besides those pamphlets the collection formed by Professor Foxwell, of Cambridge and London, which was purchased at the beginning of this century by the Goldsmiths Company of the City of London and presented to the University of London, should also be mentioned. It is now known as the Goldsmiths Library of Economic Literature and is kept at the University of London Library, Senate House, London, wc1.

A. GENERAL LITERATURE, COMMERCE, COMMUNICATIONS

YARRANTON, ANDREW. *England's Improvement by Sea and Land*. 2 parts. London, 1677, 1681.

Considerations upon the East-India Trade. London, 1701. [By Sir Dudley North?]

A Short Essay upon Trade in general ... by a lover of his country and the constitution of Great Britain [*i.e.* Thomas Cowper]. London, 1741.

POSTLETHWAYT, MALACY. *The Universal Dictionary of Trade and Commerce, translated from the French of Monsieur Savary with large additions ... and the laws, customs and usages to which all traders are subject*. 2 vols. London, 1751-5; second edition, 1766.

Considerations on taxes, as they are supposed to affect the price of labour in our manufactories. London, 1765.

WHITWORTH, RICHARD. *The Advantages of Inland Navigation*. London, 1766.

[BRINDLEY, J.]. *The History of Inland Navigations, especially those of the Duke of Bridgewater in Lancashire and Cheshire; and the intended one promoted by Earl Gower and other Persons of Distinction in Staffordshire, Cheshire and Derbyshire*. London, 1766.

HOMER, H. S. *An Enquiry into the Means of preserving and improving the Publick Roads of this Kingdom*. Oxford, 1767.

[ACCARIAS DE SÉRIONNE, JACQUES]. *La Richesse de l'Angleterre*. Vienna, 1771.

SMITH, ADAM. *An Inquiry into the Nature and Causes of the Wealth of Nations*. 2 vols. London, 1776. [Our quotations are from MacCulloch's edition, Edinburgh, 1870.]

YOUNG, ARTHUR. *Political Arithmetic, containing Observations on the Present State of Great Britain and the Principles of her Policy in the Encouragement of Agriculture*. Part I, London, 1774; Part II, 1779.

ANDERSON, JAMES. *Observations on the Means of exciting a Spirit of National Industry*. Edinburgh, 1777.

BENTLEY, THOMAS. *A Short View of the General Advantages of Inland Navigations, with a Plan of a Navigable Canal intended for a Communication between the Ports of Liverpool and Hull*. Newcastle-under-Lyme, 1781-94.

The Outlines of a Plan for establishing a United Company of British Manu-facturers. London, 1798.

[PUBLICOLA]. *Reflections on the General Utility of Inland Navigation to the Commercial and Landed Interests of England. With Observations on the intended Canal from Birmingham to Worcester, and some strictures upon the opposition given to it. By the Proprietors of the Staffordshire Canal* [Signed, Publicola]. London [1798].

TATHAM, WILLIAM. *The Political Economy of Inland Navigation, Irrigation and Drainage.* London, 1799.

CHALMERS, GEORGE. *An Estimate of the Comparative Strength of Britain during the Present and Four Preceding Reigns.* London, 1804.

Some rare brochures have been reprinted in *A Select Collection of Early English Tracts on Commerce,* edited by J. R. MacCulloch (London, 1856).

B. AGRICULTURE, ENCLOSURES, PRICE OF PROVISIONS

LAURENCE, EDWARD. *The Duty of a Steward to his Lord.* London, 1727.

TULL, JETHRO. *The New Horse-Houghing Husbandry, or an Essay on the Principles of Tillage and Vegetation.* London, 1731.

COWPER, JOHN. *An Essay proving that inclosing Commons and Commonfield-lands is contrary to the interest of the nation.* London, 1732.

A Method humbly Proposed to the Consideration of the Honourable the Members of both Houses of Parliament, by an English Woollen Manufacturer. London, 1744.

HOMER, H. S. *An Essay on the Nature and Method of ascertaining the Specifick Shares of Proprietors upon the Inclosure of Common Fields.* Oxford, 1766; second edition, 1769.

FORSTER, NATHANIEL. *An Enquiry into the causes of the present high prices of provisions.* London, 1767.

YOUNG, ARTHUR. *The Farmer's Letters to the People of England.* London, 1767.

Rural Economy. London, 1770.

ADDINGTON, STEPHEN. *An Inquiry into the Reasons for and against Inclosing Open-Fields.* Coventry, 1772.

The Advantages and Disadvantages of inclosing waste lands and open fields impartially stated and considered. By a Country Gentleman. London, 1772.

[ARBUTHNOT, JOHN OF MITCHAM]. *An Inquiry into the Connection between the Present Price of Provisions and the Size of Farms. By a Farmer.* London, 1773.

YOUNG, ARTHUR. *Observations on the present state of the Waste Lands of Great Britain.* London, 1773.

An Enquiry into the advantages and disadvantages resulting from Bills of Inclosure. London, 1780.

Observations on a Pamphlet entitled 'An Enquiry into the Advantages, etc.' London, 1781.

A Political Inquiry into the Consequences of inclosing Waste Lands and the Causes of the present high Price of Butcher's Meat. London, 1785.

HOWLETT, JOHN. *An Enquiry into the Influence which Enclosures have had upon the Population of England.* London, 1786.

Cursory Remarks on Inclosures, showing the pernicious and destructive consequences of inclosing common fields, by a country farmer. London, 1786.

STONE, THOMAS. *Suggestions for rendering the Inclosure of Common Fields and Waste Lands a Source of Population and Riches.* London, 1787.

HOWLETT, JOHN. *Enclosures a Cause of Improved Agriculture, of Plenty and Cheapness of Provisions, of Population, and of both Private and National Wealth.* London, 1787.

DAVIES, DAVID. *The Case of Labourers in Husbandry, stated and considered in three Parts.* London, 1795.

WRIGHT, THOMAS. *A Short Address to the Public on the Monopoly of Small Farms, a great cause of the present scarcity.* London, 1795.

PAUL, G. O. *Observations on the General Enclosure Bill.* London, 1800.

GIRDLER, J. S. *Observations on the pernicious consequences of forestalling, regrating and ingrossing.* London, 1800.

YOUNG, ARTHUR. *An Inquiry into the Propriety of applying wastes to the better Maintenance and Support of the Poor.* London, 1802.

'On the Size of Farms'. Essay XXVII in vol. IV of *Georgical Essays,* edited by Alexander Hunter. York, 1803.

SINCLAIR, JOHN (ed.). *General Report on Inclosures, drawn up by Order of the Board of Agriculture.* London, 1808. [Important: reliable descriptions.]

C. POPULATION AND PAUPERISM

KING, GREGORY. *Natural and Political Observations and Conclusions upon the State and Condition of England, 1696.* Published by George Chalmers. An Estimate of the Comparative Strength of Britain during the Present and Four Preceding Reigns. London, 1804.

DEFOE, DANIEL. *Giving Alms no Charity, and employing the Poor a Grievance to the Nation.* London, 1704.

FIELDING, HENRY. *An Enquiry into the Causes of the late Increase of Robbers.* London, 1751.

A Proposal for making an Effectual Provision for the Poor. London, 1753.

PERCIVAL, THOMAS. *Observations on the State of Population in Manchester and other adjacent places.* 2 parts. Manchester, 1773, 1774.

Reasons for the late increase of the poor rates or a comparative view of the prices of labour and provisions. London, 1777.

EDEN, WILLIAM, Baron Auckland. *Four Letters to the Earl of Carlisle.* Third edition, to which is added a fifth letter on Population. London, 1780.

PRICE, RICHARD. *An Essay on the Population of England from the Revolution to the present Time.* London, 1780.

HOWLETT, JOHN. *An Examination of Dr Price's Essay on the Population of England and Wales; and the doctrine of an increased population in this Kingdom established by facts, etc.* Maidstone, 1781.

WALES, WILLIAM. *An Inquiry into the present state of Population in England and Wales ...* London, 1781.

Uncertainty of the Present Population of this Kingdom. London, 1781.

GILBERT, THOMAS. *Considerations on the Bills for the Better Relief and Employment of the poor.* London, 1787.

HOWLETT, JOHN. *The Insufficiency of the Causes to which the Increase of the Poor and of the Poor Rates have been commonly ascribed.* London, 1788.

A Letter to Sir T. C. Bunbury, Bart ... on the poorrates and the high price of provisions with some proposals for removing both. By a Suffolk Gentleman. Ipswich, 1795.

EDEN, F. M. *The State of the Poor, or a History of the Labouring Classes in England from the Conquest to the Present Period.* 3 vols. London, 1797. [Good documentary evidence on the second half of the eighteenth century.]

An Estimate of the Number of Inhabitants in Great Britain and Ireland. London, 1800.

MALTHUS, T. R. *An Essay on the Principle of Population as it affects the future Improvement of Society.* London, 1798.

An Investigation of the Cause of the present high Price of Provisions. London, 1800.

D. TEXTILE TRADES

ROBERTS, LEWES. *The Treasure of Traffike, or A Discourse of Forraigne Trade.* London, 1641.

HAYNES, JOHN. *A View of the present State of the Clothing Trade in England, with remarks on the causes of its Decay and a scheme of proper Remedies for the recovery of it.* London, 1706.

Provision for the poor, or a View of the decayed State of the Woollen Manufacture. London, 1715.

A Brief State of the Printed Callicoes, Woollen and Silk Manufactures. London, 1719. [By Daniel Defoe?]

A Brief State of the Question between the Printed and Painted Callicoes, and the Woollen and Silk Manufactures. London, 1719.

[ASGILL, JOHN]. *A Brief Answer to a Brief State of the Question between the Printed and Painted Callicoes and the Woollen and Silk Manufactures.* London, 1719.

The Just Complaint of the Poor Weavers truly represented. London, 1719.

The Weavers' Pretences examined. London, 1719.

The Weavers' True Case. London, 1720.

The Case of the Journeymen Callico-Printers. London, 1720.

Observations on Wool and the Woollen Manufacture, by a Manufacturer of Northamptonshire. London, 1739.

An Essay on Riots. London, 1739. [On the weavers' riots in Wiltshire.]

Remarks on the Essay on the Weavers' Riots. London, 1739.

The Case between the Clothiers and the Weavers. London, 1739.

SMITH, JOHN. *Chronicon rusticum-commerciale; or, Memoirs of Wool ... 2* vols. London, 1747. [Contains extracts from rare pamphlets on the woollen manufacture.]
Memoirs of Wool, Woolen Manufacture, and Trade (Particularly in England) From the Earliest to the Present Times. 2 vols. Second edition, revised and enlarged. London, 1757.

SHUTTLE, TIMOTHY. *The Worsted Small-Ware Weavers' Apology, Together with all their Articles which either concern their Society or Trade.* Manchester, 1756. [The only copy in existence is kept in the Manchester Central Library. No. 677. S18.]

DYER, JOHN. *The Fleece, a Poem in four Books.* London, 1757.

The Petitions and Memorial of the Manufacturers and Printers of Silks, Linens, Callicoes, Fustians and Stuffs, in and near Manchester in the County of Lancaster. Manchester, 1778.

MARCH, R. *A Treatise on Silk, Wool, Worsted, Cotton and Thread.* London, 1779.

Thoughts on the Use of Machines in the Cotton Manufacture, addressed to the Working People in that Manufacture and to the Poor in General, by a Friend of the Poor. Manchester, 1780. [According to W. Radcliffe the author was a county magistrate named Dorning Rasbotham.]

DALRYMPLE, JOHN. *The Question considered, Whether wool should be allowed to be exported, when the price is low at home, on paying a duty to the public?* London, 1781.

Considerations upon the present State of the Wool Trade, by a Gentleman resident on his Estate in Lincolnshire. London, 1781.

[CHALMERS, GEORGE]. *The Propriety of allowing a Qualified Exportation of Wool discussed historically.* London, 1782.

FORSTER, NATHANIEL. *An Answer to Sir John Dalrymple's Pamphlet upon the Exportation of Wool.* Colchester, 1782.

The Contrast; or a Comparison between our Woollen, Linen, Cotton and Silk Manufactures. London, 1782.

Plain Reasons addressed to the people of Great Britain against the intended Petition to Parliament for leave to export Wool. Leeds, 1782.

A Letter to the landed Gentlemen and Graziers of Lincolnshire by a Friend and a Neighbour. Cambridge, 1782.

A Short View of the Proceedings of the several Committees and Meetings held in consequence of the intended Petition to Parliament from the County of Lincoln for a limited Exportation of Wool. London, 1782.

The Case of Richard Arkwright and Co., in relation to Mr Arkwright's Invention of an Engine for Spinning Cotton etc. into Yarn, stating his Reasons for applying to Parliament for an Act to secure his Right in such Invention. London, 1782.

A Short Essay written for the Service of the Proprietors of Cotton Mills and the Persons employed in them. London, 1784.

WRIGHT, JOHN. *An Address to the Members of both Houses of Parliament on the late Tax laid on Fustian and other Cotton Goods.* Warrington, 1785.

Manufactures improper Subjects of Taxation. London, 1785.

COLQUHOUN, PATRICK. *The Case of the Cotton Printers of Great Britain.* London, 1785.

A Report of the Receipts and Disbursements of the Committee of the Fustian Trade. Manchester, 1786.

A Letter showing the Necessity to amend the Laws concerning the Woollen Manufacture. Ipswich, 1787.

The Humble Petition of the poor Spinners of the Town and County of Leicester. Leicester, 1787.

An important Crisis, in the Callico and Muslin Manufactory in Great Britain, explained. London, 1788. [Very scarce; Manchester Central Library. No. M30/6.]

The Question of Wool Truly stated. London, 1788.

COLQUHOUN, PATRICK. *An Account of Facts relating to the Rise and Progress of the Cotton Manufacture in Great Britain.* London, 1789.

Wool Encouraged without Exportation; or Practical Observations on Wool and the Woollen Manufacture by a Wiltshire Clothier. London, 1791.

EDERSON, W. *A Letter to the Spinners and Manufacturers of Cotton Wool upon the present Situation of the Market.* London, 1792.

DUNDAS, H. *The Cotton Manufacture of this Country.* London, 1793.

Articles, Rules, Orders and Regulations made, and to be observed, by and between the members of the Friendly Associated Cotton Spinners within the township of Manchester. Manchester, 1795.

[MERCATOR]. *A Letter to the Inhabitants of Manchester on the Exportation of Cotton Twist.* Manchester, 1800.

A Second Letter to the Inhabitants of Manchester on the Exportation of Cotton Twist. Manchester, 1800.

Observations founded on Facts upon the Propriety or Impropriety of exporting Cotton Twist for the Purpose of being manufactured into Cloth by Foreigners. London, 1803.

A View of the Cotton Manufactories of France. Manchester, 1803.

ANSTIE, JOHN. *Observations on the Importance and Necessity of introducing improved machinery into the woollen manufactory more particularly as it affects the counties of Wilts, Gloucester and Somerset.* London, 1803.

Observations on the Cotton Weavers' Act. Manchester, 1804.

OWEN, ROBERT. *Observations on the Effect of the Manufacturing System, with Hints for the Improvement of those Parts of it which are most injurious to Health and Morals.* London, 1815.

E. METAL TRADES AND POTTERY

STURTEVANT, SIMON. *Metallica, or, the Treatise of Metallica, briefly comprehending the Doctrine of diverse new Metallicall Inventions.* London, 1612.

ROVENZON, JOHN. *A Treatise of Metallica, but not that which was published by Mr Simon Sturtevant upon his Patent.* London, 1613.

DUDLEY, DUD. *D.D.'s Metallum Martis: or, iron made with pit-coale, sea-coale, etc. and with the same fuell to melt and fire imperfect mettals, and refine perfect mettals.* London, 1665.

POVEY, CHARLES. *A Discovery of indirect Practices in the Coal Trade.* London, 1700.

SAVERY, THOMAS. *The Miner's Friend, or, an Engine to raise Water by Fire described, and of the Manner of fixing it in Mines.* London, 1702.

The present State of Mr Wood's Mine Partnership. London, 1729.

To all Lovers of Art and Ingenuity. London, 1729. [Wood's prospectus.]

A Letter from a Merchant at Whitehaven to his Friend in London. London, 1730.

A Letter from a Merchant at Whitehaven to an Ironmaster in the South of England. London, 1730.

An Account of Mr Wood's Iron made with pulverized Ore and Pit-coal. London, 1731.

Beware of Bubbles. London, 1731.

POSTLETHWAYT, MALACY. *Considerations on the Making of Bar Iron with pitt or sea coal fire.* London, 1747.

The State of the Trade and Manufactory of Iron Considered. London, 1750.

WEDGWOOD, JOSIAH. *An Address to the Young Inhabitants of the Pottery.* Newcastle-under-Lyme, 1783.

An Address to the Workmen in the Pottery, on the subject of entering into the Service of foreign Manufacturers. Newcastle-under-Lyme, 1783.

DALRYMPLE, JOHN. *Address and Proposals from Sir J. D. on the subject of the Coal, Tar, and Iron Branches of the Trade.* London, 1784.

WATT, JAMES. *An Answer to the Treasury Paper on the Iron Trade of England and Ireland.* London, 1785.

BRAMAH, JOSEPH. *A Letter to the Right Hon. Sir James Eyre, Lord Chief Justice of the Common Pleas, on the subject of the cause Boulton & Watt v. Hornblower & Maberly.* London, 1797.

BOULTON, MATTHEW, AND WATT, JAMES. *Proposals to the Adventurers.* Birmingham, 1800. [Prospectus addressed to mineowners.]

IV. WORKS ON SPECIAL SUBJECTS

A. HISTORIES OF TRADES AND INDUSTRIES

ANDREADES, A. M. *Essai sur la fondation et l'histoire de la Banque d'Angleterre, 1694-1844.* Paris, 1901. English translation by Christabel Meredith: *History of the Bank of England.* London, 1909; second edition, 1924.

ARCHER, MARK. *A Sketch of the History of the Coal Trade of Northumberland and Durham. Part I, being to the year A.D. 1700.* [No other parts published.] London, 1897.

ASHTON, T. S. *Iron and Steel in the Industrial Revolution.* Manchester, 1924. [Important; fresh material from original sources.]

BAINES, EDWARD. *History of the Cotton Manufacture in Great Britain.* London, 1835. [Still useful; the author was able to collect evidence from direct witnesses.]

BARLOW, ALFRED. *The History and Principles of Weaving by Hand and by Power*. London, 1878.

BECK, LUDWIG. *Die Geschichte des Eisens in technischer und kulturges-chichtlicher Beziehung*. 5 vols. Brunswick, 1884-1903.

BISCHOFF, J. *A Comprehensive History of the Woollen and Worsted Manufac-tures*. 2 vols. London, 1842. [An indifferent compilation, but useful from the bibliographical point of view.]

BOCH, ROGER VON. *Geschichte der Töpferarbeiter von Staffordshire im neunzehnten Jahrhundert*. Vol. XXXI of the *Münchener volkswirt-schaftliche Studien*. Stuttgart, 1899.

BOYD, R. N. *Coal Pits and Pitmen. A short history of the coal trade, and the legislation affecting it*. London, 1892.

BURNLEY, JAMES. *The History of Wool and Woolcombing*. London, 1889. [Now partly superseded by more recent and better books.]

CHAPMAN, S. H. *The Lancashire Cotton Industry. A Study in economic development*. [Very reliable, and particularly interesting on the organization of the industry and the conditions of labour.]

CLAPHAM, J. H. 'The Transference of the Worsted Industry from Norfolk to the West Riding'. *Economic Journal*, XX, 195-210. London, 1910.

A Complete History of the Cotton Trade including also that of the silk, calico-printing and hat manufactories. By a person concerned in trade. Manchester, 1823. [Contains much that is of the nature of direct evidence.]

'Cotton-spinning Machines and their Inventors'. *Quarterly Review*, CVII, 1860. [Original researches and interesting discussions.]

DANIELS, G. W. *The Early English Cotton Industry. With some unpublished letters of Samuel Crompton*. Publications of the University of Man-chester, Historical Series, No. 36. Manchester, 1920. [Very scholarly work.]

DECHESNE, LAURENT. *L'évolution économique et sociale de l'industrie de la laine en Angleterre*. Paris, 1900.

DOBSON, B. A. *Humidity in Cotton Spinning*. Revised and supplemented by W. W. Midgley. Manchester, 1901.

DOBSON, B. P. *The Story of the Evolution of the Spinning Machine*. Man-chester, 1910. [A useful compendium of technical history.]

ELLISON, THOMAS. *The Cotton Trade of Great Britain, including a history of the Liverpool Cotton Market*. London and Liverpool, 1886.

FAIRBAIRN, WILLIAM. *Iron: its history, properties and processes of manufac-ture*. Third edition, revised and enlarged. Edinburgh, 1869.
Treatise on Mills and Millwork. London, 1861-3. [Contains informa-tion on millwrights and the setting up of the first factories with mechanical equipment.]

FAREY, JOHN. *A treatise on the Steam Engine, historical, practical and descrip-tive*. London, 1827.

FELKIN, WILLIAM. *A History of the Machine-wrought Hosiery and Lace Manufactures*. Cambridge, 1867. [Still valuable.]

FRANCIS, J. H. *History of the Bank of England*. Chicago, 1888.

GALLOWAY, R. L. *The Steam Engine and its inventors*. London, 1881.
    A History of Coal Mining in Great Britain. London, 1882.
GUEST, RICHARD. *A compendious history of the cotton-manufacture; with a
    disproval of the claim of Sir Richard Arkwright to the invention of its
    ingenious machinery*. Manchester, 1823. [Very interesting and fairly
    conclusive.]
    The British cotton manufactures. Manchester, 1828.
HEATON, HERBERT. *The Yorkshire Woollen and Worsted Industries from
    the Earliest Times up to the Industrial Revolution*. Vol. X of the Oxford
    Historical and Literary Studies. Oxford, 1920. [Thorough and
    reliable, particularly as concerns the first half of the eighteenth
    century.]
HENSON, G. *The Civil, Political and Mechanical History of the Framework
    Knitters in Europe and America*. London, 1831. [Used by W. Felkin.]
HERTZ, G. B. 'The English Silk Industry in the Eighteenth Century'.
    English Historical Review, XXIV, 710-27, 1909.
HIRST, WILLIAM. *History of the Woollen Trade for the last Sixty Years*.
    Leeds, 1844.
JAMES, JOHN. *History of the Worsted Manufacture in England from the
    Earliest Times*. London, 1857.
JEWITT, L. F. W. *The Ceramic Art of Great Britain from Prehistoric Times
    down to the Present Day*. 2 vols. London, 1878. [Important especially
    for the study of styles and marks.]
JOYCE, HERBERT. *The History of the Post Office from its establishment down
    to 1836*. London, 1893.
KENNEDY, JOHN. 'On the Rise and Progress of the Cotton Trade'.
    Memoirs of the Literary and Philosophical Society of Manchester, Second
    Series, vol. III. Manchester, 1819.
LIPSON, EPHRAIM. *The History of the Woollen and Worsted Industries*.
    London, 1921. [Popular, but interesting.]
LISTER, J. 'Coal Mining in Halifax'. *Old Yorkshire*, Second Series.
    London, 1885.
LOHMANN, FRIEDRICH. *Die staatliche Regelung der englischen Wollindustrie
    vom fünfzehnten bis zum achtzehnten Jahrhundert*. (Staats- und sozial-
    wissenschaftliche Forschungen, edited by G. Schmoller, No.
    XVIII.) Leipzig, 1900. [Painstaking and useful work.]
LORD, JOHN. *Capital and Steam-Power, 1750-1800*. London, 1923. [From
    original sources; shows how the penetration of industry by steam
    began owing to the efforts of Boulton and Watt.]
LOWER, M. A. 'Historical and Archaeological Memoir on the Iron-
    works of the South-East of England (particularly of Sussex)'.
    Contributions to Literature, Historical, Antiquarian and Metrical, pp.
    85-138. London, 1854. [Mostly anecdotal.]
MACADAM, W. I. *Notes on the Ancient Iron Industry of Scotland*. London,
    1887.
MARWICK, W. H. 'The cotton industry and the industrial revolution
    in Scotland.' *Scottish Historical Review*, XXI, 207-18. Glasgow,
    1924.

MATSCHOSS, CONRAD. *Die Entwicklung der Dampfmaschine.* Second edition. 2 vols. Berlin, 1908. [Technical. Useful plates.]

MUSHET, DAVID. *Papers on Iron and Steel, practical and experimental.* London, 1840. [Mostly technical; two or three articles are of historical interest.]

NICHOLLS, H. G. *Iron Making in the Olden Times.* London, 1866. [On the mines and forges in the Forest of Dean.]

PERCY, J. *Metallurgy of Iron and Steel.* London, 1864. [Historical notes in the last part.]

PROTHERO, R. E., Baron Ernle. *The Pioneers and Progress of English Farming.* London, 1888. Revised edition, with new title: *English Farming, Past and Present.* London, 1912, etc. [Very clear and comprehensive.]

RADCLIFFE, WILLIAM. *Origin of the New System of Manufacture, commonly called 'Power Loom Weaving'.* Stockport, 1828. [Mixed history and polemics; criticized in G. W. Daniels's *Early English Cotton Industry.*]

RIGBY, EDWARD. *Holkham, its Agriculture.* Norwich, 1817.

'Rise, Progress, present State and Prospects of the British Cotton Manufacture.' *Edinburgh Review,* XLVI. Edinburgh, 1827. [A critical study of R. Guest's *Compendious History.*]

ROGERS, J. E. T. *The First Nine Years of the Bank of England.* Oxford, 1887.

SCRIVENOR, HARRY. *History of the Iron Trade from the Earliest Records to the Present Period.* Second edition. London, 1854. [Interesting statistical tables.]

SHOLL, SAMUEL. *A Short Historical Account of the Silk Manufacture in England.* London, 1811. [History of early working-men's combination in the silk trade.]

THURSTON, R. H. *A History of the Growth of the Steam-Engine.* London, 1878.

UNWIN, GEORGE. 'Transition to the Factory System'. *English Historical Review,* XXXVI, 206-18, 383-97, 1922.

WARDEN, A. J. *The Linen Trade, ancient and modern.* London, 1864.

B. HISTORIES OF LOCALITIES

Many books on local history, although sometimes of little scientific value, contain useful information and documents on economic facts.

ABRAM, W. A. *Parish of Blackburn, County of Lancaster. A History of Blackburn. Town and Parish.* Blackburn, 1877.

AXON, W. E. A. (ed.). *The Annals of Manchester: a chronological record from the earliest times to the end of 1885.* Manchester, 1886.

BAINES, EDWARD. *History of the County Palatine and Duchy of Lancaster, Vol. II.* London, 1836.

BAINES, THOMAS. *History of the Commerce and Town of Liverpool, and of the*

rise of manufacturing industry in the adjoining counties. London, 1852.
Yorkshire, past and present. 2 vols. London, 1871, 1877.

BAINES, THOMAS AND FAIRBAIRN, WILLIAM. *Lancashire and Cheshire, past and present. With an account of the rise and progress of manufactures and commerce* ... 2 vols. London, 1868, 1869.

BRAND, JOHN. *The History and Antiquities of the Town and County* ... *of Newcastle upon Tyne, including an account of the coal trade of that place.* 2 vols. London, 1789. [Important for the history of coal mines.]

BREMNER, DAVID. *The Industries of Scotland; their rise, progress, and present condition.* Edinburgh, 1869.

BROWN, ANDREW. *History of Glasgow; and of Paisley, Greenock and Port Glasgow.* 2 vols. Glasgow, 1795, 1797.

BUTTERWORTH, EDWIN. *An Historical Account of the Towns of Ashton-under-Lyne, Stalybridge and Dukinfield.* Ashton, 1842.
Historical Sketches of Oldham. Oldham, 1856. [Information on the origins of the great industrial families of the district.]

CLEGG, JAMES. *Annals of Bolton.* Bolton, 1888.

DUMBELL, S. 'Early Liverpool Cotton Imports and the Organization of the Cotton Market in the Eighteenth Century'. *Economic Journal,* XXXIII, 363 ff., 1924.

DUNSFORD, MARTIN. *Historical Memoirs of the Town and Parish of Tiverton.* Exeter, 1790. [Interesting for the history of labour in the woollen trade in Devonshire.]

ENFIELD, WILLIAM. *An Essay towards the history of Liverpool.* Warrington, 1773.

HARDING, WILLIAM. *The History of Tiverton in the County of Devon.* 2 vols. Tiverton, 1845-7.

HARDWICK, CHARLES. *History of the Borough of Preston and its Environs, in the County of Lancaster.* Preston, 1857.

HELM, ELIJAH. *Chapters in the History of the Manchester Chamber of Commerce.* London and Manchester, 1902.

HOLLINGWORTH, RICHARD. *Mancuniensis.* Manchester, 1839. [Written in the first half of the seventeenth century.]

HUNTER, JOSEPH. *Hallamshire: the History and Topography of the Parish of Sheffield.* A new and enlarged edition by A. Gatty. Sheffield, 1869. [Interesting information on the steel industry.]

HUTTON, WILLIAM. *An History of Birmingham.* Third edition. Birmingham, 1795. [Of little value except for the period corresponding to the author's own lifetime.]
The History of Derby from the remote Ages of Antiquity to the year 1791. Derby and London, 1791.

JAMES, JOHN. *The History and Topography of Bradford in the County of York.* London and Bradford, 1841.
Continuation and Additions to the History of Bradford and its Parish. Bradford, 1866. [Much information concerning the worsted industry.]

LANGFORD, J. A. *A Century of Birmingham Life; or, a chronicle of local events from 1741 to 1841.* 2 vols. Birmingham, 1868.

LEADER, R. E. *Sheffield in the Eighteenth Century*. Sheffield, 1901.

LLOYD, JOHN. *The Early History of the Old South Wales Iron Works, 1760-1840*. From original documents. London, 1906.

Local Notes and Queries. 15 vols. Birmingham, 1856-1914. [Collection of documents concerning the history of Birmingham. Kept in the Birmingham Central Library.]

MACGREGOR, GEORGE. *The History of Glasgow, from the earliest period to the present time*. Glasgow, 1881.

MAYHALL, J. *The Annals of Yorkshire from the Earliest Period to the Present Time*. 3 vols. London, 1874.

MUIR, J. R. B. *A History of Liverpool*. London, 1907.

OGDEN, JAMES. *Manchester a hundred years ago*. Manchester, 1887.

SHAW, SIMEON. *History of the Staffordshire Potteries and the Rise and Progress of the Manufacture of Pottery and Porcelain*. Hanley, 1829. [Much information collected from direct witnesses.]

SHAW, W. A. *Manchester Old and New*. 3 vols. London, 1896.

TIMMINS, SAMUEL (ed.). *The Resources, Products and Industrial History of Birmingham and the Midland Hardware District*. London, 1866. [The historical aspect is not stressed.]

Victoria History of the Counties of England: Derbyshire. London, 1905. *Nottinghamshire*. London, 1906. *Lancaster*. London, 1906-14. *Yorkshire*. London, 1907. *Staffordshire*. London, 1908. *Warwickshire*. London, 1908.

WARD, JOHN. *The Borough of Stoke-upon-Trent*. London, 1843.

WELFORD, RICHARD (ed.). *History of Newcastle and Gateshead*. London, 1884, etc.

WHEELER, JAMES. *Manchester: its Political, Social and Commercial History, Ancient and Modern*. London, 1836.

WHITTLE, PETER. *A topographical, statistical and historical account of the Borough of Preston*. 2 vols. Preston, 1821-37.

C. BIOGRAPHIES

BROWN, JOHN. 'A Memoir of Robert Blincoe'. *The Lion*, vol. I. London, 1828. [History of an apprentice in the cotton industry at the end of the eighteenth century.]

CARTER, THOMAS. *Memoirs of a Working Man*. London, 1845. [Variously attributed to John and Thomas Carter.]

DICKINSON, H. W. *John Wilkinson, Ironmaster*. Ulverston, 1914.

ESPINASSE, FRANCIS. *Lancashire Worthies*. 2 vols. London, 1874-7.

FARRER, K. E. (ed.). *Correspondence of Josiah Wedgwood*. London, 1906.

Fortunes made in Business. A series of original sketches ... by various writers. 3 vols. London, 1884-7. [Interesting data from private papers. Not much about the eighteenth century.]

FRENCH, G. J. *The Life and Times of Samuel Crompton, inventor of the spinning machine called the Mule*. London and Manchester, 1859. [Contains R. Cole's 'Account of Lewis Paul and his Invention of the Machine for Spinning Cotton Wool by Rollers'.]

JARDINE, R. 'An Account of John Roebuck, M.D., F.R.S.'. *Transactions of the Royal Society of Edinburgh*, IV, 1796.

JEWITT, L. F. W. *The Wedgwoods, being a Life of Josiah Wedgwood with notices of his Works and their Productions, Memoirs of the Wedgwood and other Families, and a history of the early Potteries of Staffordshire.* London, 1865. [Interesting documents, used without much method.]

KENNEDY, JOHN. 'A Brief Memoir of Samuel Crompton, with a Description of his Machine called the Mule'. *Memoirs of the Literary and Philosophical Society of Manchester*, Second Series, vol. V. Manchester, 1831.

Memoir of Edmund Cartwright, D.D. London, 1825.

Memoir of Matthew Boulton esq., late of Soho. Birmingham, 1809.

METCALF, JOHN. *The Life of John Metcalfe, commonly called Blind Jack of Knaresborough.* York, 1795.

METEYARD, ELIZA. *The Life of Josiah Wedgwood. From his private Correspondence and Family Papers.* 2 vols. London, 1865, 1866.
A Group of Englishmen ... being records of the younger Wedgwoods and their friends. London, 1871.

MUIRHEAD, J. P. *The Origin and Progress of the Mechanical Inventions of James Watt.* 3 vols. London and Glasgow, 1854.

NICHOLSON, F. *Notes on the Wilkinsons, Ironmasters.* Manchester, 1905.

OWEN, ROBERT. *The Life of Robert Owen, written by Himself (with selections from his writings and correspondence).* London, 1857-8. [Interesting for the history of Owen's ideas and because Owen was the first to mark the bearing of the industrial revolution on the structure of society.]

OWEN, ROBERT DALE. *Threading my Way.* London, 1874. [Some interesting pages on David Dale and the organization of the New Lanark establishment.]

PALMER, A. N. *John Wilkinson and the old Bersham Iron Works.* Transactions of the Hon. Society of Cymmrodorion. London, 1899.

PARKER, C. S. *Sir Robert Peel, from his private papers.* Second edition. 3 vols. London, 1899. [See first volume.]

'The Peel Family, its Rise and Fortunes'. *Manchester Examiner and Times*, October and November, 1850.

PEEL, LAWRENCE. *A Sketch of the Life and Character of Sir Robert Peel.* London, 1860. [The author made use of family papers.]

SMILES, SAMUEL. *Lives of the Engineers.* 3 vols. London, 1861-2.
Industrial Biography: Iron Workers and Tool Makers. London, 1863.
Lives of Boulton and Watt. London, 1865.
Josiah Wedgwood, F.R.S.: his personal History. London, 1894.
[Smiles had access to many original documents, from which he frequently quotes; this makes his popular books still useful, although not scientific.]

TAYLOR, W. COOKE. *Life and Times of Sir Robert Peel.* 3 vols. London, 1846. Vol. IV by Charles Mackay, 1851.

TIMMINS, SAMUEL. *Matthew Boulton.* From the Transactions of the Archaeological Section of the Birmingham and Midland Institute.

Birmingham, 1872. [A short notice, but one which, like the following two works, shows the evidence of original researches.] *James Watt*, 1872. *William Murdock*, 1894.

UNWIN, GEORGE. *Samuel Oldknow and the Arkwrights: the Industrial Revolution at Stockport and Marple.* With chapters by Arthur Hulme and George Taylor. Publications of the University of Manchester, Economic History Series, vol. I. Manchester, 1924. [A very thorough monograph.]

WEBSTER, THOMAS. 'The Case of Henry Cort, and his Inventions in the Manufacture of British Iron'. *Mechanics' Magazine*, New Series, I and II. London, 1859.

WEDGWOOD, F. J. *The Personal life of Josiah Wedgwood the Potter ...* Revised and edited by C. H. Herford. London, 1915.

WILLIAMSON, GEORGE. *Memorials of the Lineage, Early Life, Education and Development of the Genius of James Watt.* Greenock, 1856.

WOODCROFT, BENNET. *Brief Biographies of Inventors of Machines for the Manufacture of Textile Fabrics.* London, 1863.

John Wyatt, Master Carpenter & Inventor, A.D. 1700-1766. Compiled from original manuscripts. London, 1885.

WYATT, CHARLES. 'On the Origin of spinning Cotton &c. by Machinery'. *Repertory of Arts, Manufactures and Agriculture*, Second Series, XXXII, 79-83. London, 1818.

D. AGRICULTURE, ENCLOSURES, ETC.

COOKE, G. W. *The Act for the Enclosure of Commons in England and Wales: with a Treatise On the Law of Rights of Common.* London, 1846.

CURTLER, W. H. R. *The Enclosure and Redistribution of our Land.* Oxford, 1920. [A very thorough study.]

DUNLOP, O. J. *The Farm Labourer. The history of a modern problem.* London, Leipzig, 1913.

ELIASCHEWITSCH, ALEXANDER. *Die Bewegung zugunsten der kleinen landwirtschaftlichen Güter in England.* Munich and Leipzig, 1914. [The first ninety pages deal with the eighteenth century.]

GAY, E. F. 'The Inquisition of Depopulation in 1517 and the Domesday of Inclosures'. *Transactions of the Royal Historical Society*, New Series, XIV, 1900. [A critical examination of Leadam's *Domesday of Inclosures.*]
Zur Geschichte der Einhegungen in England. Staats- und sozial-wissenschaftliche Forschungen. Leipzig, 1902.
'Inclosures in England in the Sixteenth Century'. *Quarterly Journal of Economics*, XVII, 576-97, 1903.
'The Midland Revolt and the Inquisition of Depopulation in 1607'. *Transactions of the Royal Historical Society*, New Series, XVIII, 1904.

GONNER, E. C. K. *Common Land and Inclosure.* London, 1912. [Important; effort to collect and compare statistical data.]

GRAY, H. L. 'Yeoman Farming in Oxfordshire from the Sixteenth Century to the Nineteenth'. *Quarterly Journal of Economics*, XXIV, 293.

HAMMOND, J. L. AND L. B. *The Village Labourer, 1760-1832*. London, 1911. [Not unbiased, but based on serious research work.]

HASBACH, WILHELM. *Die englischen Landarbeiter in den letzten hundert Jahren und die Einhegungen*. Leipzig, 1894. English translation: *A History of the English Agricultural Labourer*, edited by author, translated by Ruth Kenyon. London, 1908.
'Der Untergang des englischen Bauernstandes in neuer Beleuchtung'. *Archiv. für Sozialwissenschaft und Sozialpolitik*, XXIV, 1-29. Tübingen, 1907.

JENKS, EDWARD. *Modern Land Law*. Oxford, 1899.

JOHNSON, A. H. *The Disappearance of the Small Landowner*. Ford Lectures, 1909. Oxford, 1909. [The author made use of the Land Tax Assessments kept by the Clerks of the Peace.]

LEADAM, I. S. *The Domesday of Inclosures*. 2 vols. London, 1897.

LEONARD, E. M. 'The Inclosure of Common Fields in the Seventeenth Century'. *Transactions of the Royal Historical Society*, New Series, XIX, 101-46, 1905.

LEVY, HERMANN. 'Der Untergang kleinbaüerlicher Betriebe in England'. *Jahrbücher für Nationalökonomie und Statistik*, LXXXI, 145-67. Jena, 1903.
Entstehung und Rückgang des landwirtschaftlichen Grossbetriebes in England. Berlin, 1904. English translation: *Large and Small Holdings*. Cambridge, 1911.

NASSE, ERWIN. *Ueber die mittelalterliche Feldgemeinschaft und die Einhegungen des sechszehnten Jahrhunderts in England*. Bonn, 1869.

RAE, JOHN. 'Why have the Yeomanry perished?' *Contemporary Review*, XLIV, 546-65, October 1883.

SCRUTTON, T. E. *Commons and Common Fields*. Cambridge, 1887. [A legal study.]

SEEBOHM, FREDERIC. *The English Village Community*. London, 1883.

SLATER, GILBERT. *The English Peasantry and the Enclosure of the Common Fields*. London, 1907.

TAWNEY, R. H. *The Agrarian Problem in the Sixteenth Century*. London, 1912.

TAYLOR, H. C. *The Decline of Landowning Farmers in England*. Madison, Wisconsin, 1904.

E. ECONOMIC AND SOCIAL QUESTIONS

ALFRED [i.e. SAMUEL KYDD]. *The History of the Factory Movement from the Year 1802 to the Enactment of the Ten Hours' Bill in 1847*. 2 vols. London, 1857. [Careful analysis of Parliamentary inquiries into work in the factories.]

ASCHROTT, P. F. *The English Poor Law System, past and present*. Translated from the German by H. Preston-Thomas. Second edition. London, 1902.

BOUNIATIAN, MENTOR. *Studien zur Theorie und Geschichte der Wirtschafts-krisen. Vol. 2: Geschichte der Handelskrisen in England im Zusammen-hang mit der Entwicklung des englischen Wirtschaftsleben, 1640-1840.* Münich, 1908.

BOWLEY, A. L. *Wages in the United Kingdom in the Nineteenth Century.* Cambridge, 1900. [A good example of statistical method.]

BRENTANO, LUJO. *On the History and Development of Gilds, and the Origin of Trade-Unions.* London, 1870.
Die Arbeitergilden den Gegenwart. 2 vols. Leipzig, 1871, 1872.

BUSCHING, PAUL. *Die Entwickelung der handelspolitischen Beziehungen zwischen England und seinen Kolonien bis zum Jahre 1860.* Münchener volkswirtschaftliche Studien, No. 48. Stuttgart and Berlin, 1902.

DUMAS, F. *Etude sur le traité de commerce de 1786 entre la France et l'Angle-terre.* Toulouse, 1904.

DUNLOP, O. J. *English Apprenticeship and Child Labour.* London, Leipzig, 1912.

GASKELL, P. *The Manufacturing Population of England; its Moral, Social and Physical Conditions, and the Changes which have arisen from the Use of Steam Machinery.* London, 1833.
Artisans and Machinery. London, 1836.

GONNER, E. C. K. 'The Population of England in the Eighteenth Century'. *Journal of the Royal Statistical Society,* LXXVI, 261-303, 1913. [With valuable maps.]

HAMMOND, J. L. AND L. B. *The Town Labourer, 1760-1832.* London, 1917.
The Skilled Labourer, 1760-1832. London, 1919.
[Both these books are comparable in style and value to *The Village Labourer,* which has been mentioned above. The authors have made an extensive use of Home Office Papers.]

HARPER, C. G. *The Great North Road, the old Mail Road to Scotland.* 2 vols. London, 1900.

HELD, ADOLF. *Zwei Bücher zur socialen Geschichte Englands.* Leipzig, 1881.

HEWINS, W. A. S. *English Trade and Finance, chiefly in the Seventeenth Century.* London, 1892. [Documented studies; good critical method.]
'The Regulation of Wages by the Justices of the Peace'. *Economic Journal,* VIII. London, 1898.

HOWELL, GEORGE. *The Conflicts of Capital and Labour Historically and Economically Considered.* Second and revised edition. London, 1890.

HULME, E. W. 'On the History of Patent Law in the Seventeenth and Eighteenth Centuries'. *Law Quarterly Review,* XVIII, 280 ff. London, 1902.

HUTCHINS, B. L. AND HARRISON, AMY. *A History of Factory Legislation.* Second edition. London, 1911. [An excellent monograph.]

LA ROCHEFOUCAULD-LIANCOURT. *Notes sur la Législation Anglaise des Chemins.* Paris, 1801.

LEONARD, E. M. *The early History of English Poor Relief.* Cambridge, 1900.

NICHOLLS, GEORGE. *A History of the English Poor Law, in connection with*

the State of the Country and the Condition of the People. 3 vols. London,
1898, 1899. [Not very satisfactory, but contains useful information
and documents.]

PHILLIPS, JOHN. *A General History of Inland Navigation, Foreign and
Domestic.* London, 1792. Supplements published in 1793 and 1794.
[Presents accurately the state of navigable routes at the time of
publication.]

PRIESTLEY, JOSEPH. *Historical Account of the Navigable Rivers, Canals and
Railways throughout Great Britain.* London, 1831. [Gives an alpha-
betical list of the works, with reference to the Acts of Parliament
authorizing them.]

ROSE, J. H. 'The Franco-British Commercial Treaty of 1786'. *English
Historical Review*, XXIII, 709-24, 1908.

WAGNER, C. A. *Ueber die wirthschaftliche Lage der Binnenschifffahrtsunternehmungen in Grossbritannien und Irland.* Archiv für Eisenbahnwesen.
Berlin, 1901, 1902.

WALFORD, CORNELIUS. *Fairs, past and present: a chapter in the history of
Commerce.* London, 1883.

WEBB, SIDNEY AND BEATRICE. *The History of Trade Unionism.* Revised
edition. London, 1920. [A classic.]
'The Assize of Bread'. *Economic Journal*, June, 1904.
The Story of the King's Highway. London, 1913. [Chiefly from the
administrative point of view.]

WELLS, L. B. 'A Sketch of the History of the Canal and River Navigations of England and Wales'. *Memoirs and Proceedings of the Literary
Society of Manchester*, New Series, VIII. Manchester, 1894. [With
map.]

WESTERFIELD, R. B. *Middlemen in English Business, particularly between
1660 and 1760.* New Haven, Conn., 1915.

WEYER, O. W. *Die englische Fabrikinspektion. Ein Beitrag zur Geschichte
der Fabrikgesetzgebung in England.* Tübingen, 1888.

V. GENERAL

ANDERSON, ADAM. *An Historical and Chronological Deduction of the Origin
of Commerce.* 2 vols. London, 1764. Second edition, 4 vols., 1787-9.
[An old compilation, still useful for the eighteenth century.]

ASHLEY, W. J. *An Introduction to English Economic History and Theory.
Part II: The End of the Middle Ages.* London, 1893. [A standard
work.]
The Economic Organization of England. London, 1914.

BOWDEN, WITT. *Industrial Society in England towards the end of the
Eighteenth Century.* New York, 1925. [Full of interest; an excellent
historical work.]

CUNNINGHAM, WILLIAM. *Modern Civilisation in some of its economic aspects.*
London, 1896. [General views on economic evolution.]
The Growth of English Industry and Commerce. Part II. Fourth edition.

Cambridge, 1912. [Indispensable for a general study of the economic history of England.]

CUNNINGHAM, WILLIAM AND MACARTHUR, ELLEN. *Outlines of English Industrial History.* Cambridge, 1895.

GASKELL, P. *The Manufacturing Population of England; its Moral, Social and Physical Conditions, and the Changes which have arisen from the Use of Steam Machinery.* London, 1833.
Artisans and Machinery. London, 1836. [A revised edition of the preceding work.]

GIBBINS, H. DE B. *Industrial History of England.* London, 1890.
Industry in England — its historical outlines. London, 1896.

HAMMOND, J. L. AND L. B. *The Rise of Modern Industry.* London, 1925.

HASBACH, WILHELM. 'Zur Charakteristik der Englischen Industrie'. *Jahrbuch für Gesetzgebung, Verwaltung und Volkswirtschaft im Deutschen Reich,* XXVI, 455-504, 1015-62. Leipzig, 1902.

HOBSON, J. A. *The Evolution of Modern Capitalism. A Study of Machine Production.* London, 1894. [Mainly theoretical.]

HOWELL, GEORGE. *The Conflicts of Capital and Labour Historically and Economically Considered.* Second and revised edition. London, 1890. [On nineteenth-century trade unions.]

KNOWLES, L. C. A. *The Industrial and Commercial Revolutions in Great Britain during the Nineteenth Century.* Third edition. London, 1924.

KULISCHER, JOSEF. 'Die Ursachen des Übergangs von der Handarbeit zur maschinellen Betriebsweise um die Wende des 18 und in der ersten Hälfte des 19. Jahrhunderts'. *Jahrbuch für Gesetzgebung, Verwaltung und Volkswirtschaft im Deutschen Reich,* XXX, 31-79. Leipzig, 1906.

LEVI, LEONE. *The History of British Commerce and of the Economic Progress of the British Nation, 1763-1878.* Second edition. London, 1880. [Superficial.]

LEVY, H. J. *Monopole, Kartelle und Trusts in ihrer Beziehungen zur Organization der kapitalistischen Industrie.* Jena, 1909.
Monopoly and Competition: a Study in English Industrial Organization. London, 1911. [See chapters on seventeenth- and eighteenth-century monopolies.]
Die Grundlagen des ökonomischen Liberalismus in der Geschichte der englischen Volkswirtschaft. Jena, 1912.

MACPHERSON, DAVID. *Annals of Commerce, Manufactures, Fisheries and Navigation.* 4 vols. London, 1805. [Continuation of A. Anderson's book on the origin of commerce; shows chiefly the movement of external commerce until 1801.]

MARX, KARL. *Das Kapital: Kritik der politischen Œkonomie.* Vol. I. Third edition. Hamburg, 1883. [Chapters VIII, XI, XII, XIII, XIX, XXIII contain many references to the economic history of England.]

MOFFIT, L. W. *England on the Eve of the Industrial Revolution: a Study of Economic and Social Conditions from 1740 to 1760, with special Reference to Lancashire.* London, 1925.

PORTER, G. R. *The Progress of the Nation in its various Social and Economical Relations.* New edition. London, 1851. [Statistical information.]

ROGERS, J. E. THOROLD. *Six Centuries of Work and Wages.* 2 vols. London, 1884.
A History of Agriculture and Prices in England. Vol. VII: 1703-93. Oxford, 1902.

SCHMOLLER, G. F. VON. 'Die geschichtliche Entwickelung der Unternehmung'. *Jahrbuch für Gesetzgebung, Verwaltung und Volkswirtschaft im Deutschen Reich,* XVII, 359-91, 959-1018. Leipzig, 1893. [Important for the history of banking.]

SCHULZE-GAEVERNITZ, GERHART VON. *Der Grossbetrieb, ein wirtschaftlicher und socialer Fortschritt.* Leipzig, 1892. [On the cotton industry.] French translation by Guéroult: *La Grande Industrie.* Paris, 1896. English translation: *The Cotton Trade in England & on the Continent.* London, 1895.

SOMBART, W. 'Der Kapitalistische Unternehmer'. *Archiv für Sozialwissenschaft und Sozialpolitik,* XXIX, 689-758, 1909.

TAYLOR, R. W. COOKE. *Introduction to a History of the Factory System.* London, 1886. [Superficial, but clear and interesting.]
The Modern Factory System. London, 1891.
The Factory System and the Factory Acts. London, 1894.

TOYNBEE, ARNOLD. *Lectures on the Industrial Revolution in England.* London, 1884.

TRAILL, H. D. AND MANN, J. S. (eds.). *Social England.* 6 vols. London, 1901-4. [Collective work; good chapters on agriculture and industry in the eighteenth century by T. Warner and R. E. Prothero (Baron Ernle)].

UNWIN, GEORGE. *Industrial Organization in the Sixteenth and Seventeenth Centuries.* Oxford, 1904.

URE, ANDREW. *The Cotton Manufacture of Great Britain systematically investigated.* 2 vols. London, 1836. [The first volume contains a long historical study, based in part on verbal testimony (the author knew James Watt).]

USHER, A. P. *An Introduction to the Industrial History of England.* Cornell University, Ithaca, 1920; London, 1921.

WARNER, G. T. *Landmarks in English Industrial History.* London, 1899.

VI. BIBLIOGRAPHIES

Bibliographies appear in the following:

A. GENERAL

BOWDEN, WITT. *Industrial Society in England towards the end of the Eighteenth Century.* New York, 1925.

HELD, ADOLF. *Zwei Bücher zur socialen Geschichte Englands.* Leipzig, 1881.

MOFFIT, L. W. *England on the Eve of the Industrial Revolution.* London, 1925.

TRAILL, H. D. AND MANN, J. S. (eds.). *Social England.* 6 vols. London, 1904.

WEBB, SIDNEY AND BEATRICE. *History of Trade Unionism.* Second edition. London, 1902.

B. SPECIAL

1. Parliamentary Papers

Catalogue of the Parliamentary Reports and a Breviate of their Contents, 1696-1834. London, 1837.

JONES, H. V. *Catalogue of Parliamentary Papers 1801-1900, with a few of earlier date.* London, 1904.

2. Economic literature

EDEN, F. M. 'Catalogue of Pamphlets on the Poor Laws', in *The State of the Poor,* vol. III. London, 1797.

HALKETT, SAMUEL AND LAING, JOHN. *A Dictionary of the Anonymous and Pseudonymous Literature of Great Britain.* 4 vols. Edinburgh, 1882-8. [Useful for the attribution of anonymous works.]

MACCULLOCH, J. R. *The Literature of Political Economy.* London, 1845. [Critical bibliography.]

MASSIE, JOSEPH. *Bibliography of the Collection of Books and Tracts on Commerce, Currency, and Poor Law, 1557 to 1763, formed by Joseph Massie.* Transcribed from Lansdowne Manuscript MXLIX with historical and bibliographical introduction by William A. Shaw. London, 1937. [Done with care.]

3. History of trades and agriculture

BISCHOFF, J. *A Comprehensive History of the Woollen and Worsted Manufactures.* London, 1842.

CHAPMAN, S. *The Lancashire Cotton Industry.* Manchester, 1904.

ELIASCHEWITSCH, ALEXANDER. *Die Bewegung zugunsten der kleinen landwirtschaftlichen Güter in England.* Münich and Leipzig, 1914.

HEATON, H. *The Yorkshire Woollen and Worsted Industries.* Oxford, 1920.

4. Biography

Valuable bibliographical notices in the *Dictionary of National Biography.*

SUPPLEMENT TO THE BIBLIOGRAPHY

compiled in 1958 by

A. J. BOURDE, Ph.D.

Lecturer ('Maître de Conférences') at the University of Aix-Marseilles

The masterly bibliography which completed the present work in its original form was enlarged by the author himself to accompany the revised English edition of 1928. For the present edition it was necessary to acquire additional material of a standard of scholarship comparable in every way with that of its predecessors.

It was not enough to refer solely to the works published by the more eminent specialists, notwithstanding their wealth of information and the wisdom of their conclusions. One of them, Professor T. S. Ashton, published in 1937 a study of the bibliography of the industrial revolution, a knowledge of which is essential for any correct approach to this complex subject, since the true significance of these historic developments is becoming apparent not only in the content of the works devoted to them, but in their very number and diversity.

Any bibliography of the industrial revolution is necessarily at the same time a sketch of that stage of civilization — and a sketch that becomes more distinct and more elaborate as the years go by; for, since 1928, a vast number of works on economic history have appeared, accompanying and, one might say, escorting the successive editions of Paul Mantoux's book.

The present bibliography does not claim to give a full account of thirty years of research. It is intended only as an accessory to a classic of economic history, supplying a guide for further exploration of the field opened up more than fifty years ago.

It is for this purpose that the principal works published since 1928 are indicated below. Further up-to-date information is, of course, available to readers in the book-lists and reviews appearing regularly in scientific periodicals, as well as in the outstanding bibliographical studies which have been published recently. The author of the present supplement, who was kindly permitted to pursue his work at the Cambridge University Library and at the Bodleian Library, ventures to hope that this contribution will also be of service.

He owes a further debt of gratitude and appreciation to Dr W. H. Chaloner of the University of Manchester, whose experience and scholarship are never called upon in vain by his friends and colleagues.

A. J. B.

The publishers would particularly like to express their gratitude to Professor T. S. Ashton, Professor W. Röpke and Professor P. Vaucher, who were kind enough to bring their great knowledge to bear on the selection of works for inclusion in this bibliography.

A. HISTORY OF TRADES AND INDUSTRIES

ABERCONWAY, Lord. *The basic industries of Great Britain: coal, iron, steel, engineering, ships: an historic and economic survey.* London, 1927.

ASHTON, T. S. *Iron and steel in the Industrial Revolution.* Second edition. Manchester, 1951.

ASHTON, T. S. AND SYKES, J. *The Coal Industry of the Eighteenth Century.* Manchester, 1929.

BARKER, T. C., DICKINSON, R., AND HARDIE, D. W. F. 'The origins of the synthetic alkali industry in Britain'. *Economica,* XXIII, May 1956.

CHALONER, W. H. 'Further light on the invention of the process for smelting iron ore with coke'. *Economic History Review,* Second Series, II, No. 2, 1949.

CLOW, A. AND N. L. *The Chemical Revolution. A contribution to social technology.* London, 1952.

COLEMAN, D. C. *The British paper industry, 1495-1860.* Oxford, 1958.

CULE, J. E. 'Finance and Industry in the Eighteenth Century: the Firm of Boulton and Watt'. *Economic History,* IV, No. 15.

DICKINSON, H. W. *A Short History of the Steam Engine.* Cambridge, 1939.

FRÉMONT, CHARLES. *Monographies sur les outils et les mécanismes,* published by the Soc. d'Encour. à l'Industr. Nat. (6 vols. Bibliothèque du Conservatoire National des Arts et Métiers).

GOUGH, J. W. *The Mines of Mendip.* Oxford, 1930.

GUILLET, L. *La Métallurgie.* Paris, 1941.

HADFIELD, CHARLES. *British Canals: An illustrated history.* London, 1950.

HAMILTON, HENRY. *The English Brass and Copper Industries to 1800.* London, 1926.

JOHNSON, B. L. C. 'The charcoal iron industry in the early eighteenth century'. *Geographical Journal,* CXVII, 1951.

LIPSON, EPHRAIM. *A Short History of Wool and its Manufacture — mainly in England.* London, 1953.

MATHIAS, PETER. 'Agriculture, and the Brewing and Distilling Industries in the Eighteenth Century'. *Economic History Review,* Second Series, V, No. 2, 1952.

MINCHINTON, W. E. *The British tinplate industry.* Oxford, 1957.

MOTT, R. A. *The History of Coke Making and of the Coke Oven Managers' Association.* 1936.
  'Dud Dudley and the early cast iron industry'. *Trans. Newcomen Soc.,* XV.

PARTINGTON, J. R. *Origins and Development of Applied Chemistry.* London, 1935.

ROLL, ERICH. *An Early Experiment in Industrial Organisation: being a history of the firm of Boulton and Watt, 1775-1805.* London, 1930.

SCHUBERT, H. R. *History of the British iron and steel industry from c. 450 B.C. to A.D. 1775.* London, 1957.

TURNBULL, GEOFFREY (ed.). *A history of the Calico-Printing Industry of Great Britain*. Altrincham, 1951.

USHER, A. P. *A History of Mechanical Inventions*. Revised edition. Cambridge, Mass., 1954.

B. HISTORIES OF LOCALITIES

BARKER, T. C. AND HARRIS, J. R. *A Merseyside Town in the Industrial Revolution: St Helens 1750-1900*. Liverpool, 1954.

BECKWITH, F. 'The population of Leeds during the Industrial Revolution', *Sotheby Soc. Misc.*, XII, No. 2, 1948.

CHALONER, W. H. *The Social and Economic Development of Crewe, 1780-1923*. (Publications of the University of Manchester. Economic History Series, No. 14.) Manchester, 1950.

CHAMBERS, J. D. *Nottinghamshire in the Eighteenth Century. A study of life and labour under the squirearchy*. London, 1932.
   The Vale of Trent 1670-1800: a regional study of economic change. Economic History Review Supplements, No. 3. Cambridge, 1957.

CHAPPELL, E. L. *History of the Port of Cardiff*. Cardiff, 1939.

COURT, W. H. B. 'Industrial organization and economic progress in the eighteenth-century Midlands'. *Trans. Roy. Hist. Soc.*, Fourth Series, XXVIII, 1946.
   The Rise of the Midland Industries, 1600-1838. London, 1938.

CRUMP, W. B. (ed.). *The Leeds Woollen Industry, 1780-1820*. (Publications of the Thoresby Society, vol. 32.) Leeds, 1931.

DAVIES, D. J. *The Economic History of South Wales prior to 1800*. Cardiff, 1933.

DODD, A. H. *The Industrial Revolution in North Wales*. Second edition enlarged. Cardiff, 1951.

GEORGE, M. D. *London Life in the XVIIIth Century*. London, 1925. Reissued by the London School of Economics, 1951.

GILL, CONRAD AND BRIGGS, ASA. *History of Birmingham*. 2 vols. London, 1952.

HADFIELD, E. C. R. 'The Thames Navigation and the Canals, 1770-1830'. *Economic History Review*, XIV, No. 2, 1944.

HAMILTON, HENRY. *The Industrial Revolution in Scotland*. Oxford, 1932.

HARRIS, T. R. 'Engineering in Cornwall before 1775'. *Trans. Newcomen Soc.* XXV, 1950.

HEATON, HERBERT. 'Benjamin Gott and the Industrial Revolution in Yorkshire'. *Economic History Review*, III, No. 1, 1931.

HOSKINS, W. G. *Industry, Trade and People in Exeter, 1688-1800. With special reference to the serge industry*. (History of Exeter Research Group. Monograph No. 6.) Manchester, 1935.

HUGHES, EDWARD. *North Country Life in the Eighteenth Century*. London, 1952.

JENKINS, R. 'Early engineering and iron-founding in Cornwall'. *Trans. Newcomen Soc.*, XXIII, 1948.

JOHN, A. H. *The Industrial Development of South Wales, 1750-1850.* Cardiff, 1950.

JONES, H. G. 'The Merioneth woollen industry from 1750 to 1820'. *Trans. Hon. Soc. Cymmrodorion*, 1939.

MacCUTCHEON, K. L. *Yorkshire Fairs and Markets to the end of the eighteenth century.* (Publications of the Thoresby Society, vol. 39.) Leeds, 1940.

MINCHINTON, W. E. 'Bristol, metropolis of the West in the eighteenth century'. *Trans. Roy. Hist. Soc.*, Fifth Series, IV.

PARKINSON, C. N. *The Rise of the Port of Liverpool.* Liverpool, 1952.

PELHAM, R. A. 'The West Midland iron industry and the American market in the eighteenth century'. *University of Birmingham Hist. Journal*, II, No. 2, 1950.

POUNDS, N. J. G. 'Population movement in Cornwall and the rise of mining in the eighteenth century'. *Geography*, XXVIII, No. 2.

RAISTRICK, A. AND ALLEN, E. 'The South Yorkshire ironmasters'. *Economic History Review*, IX, No. 2, 1939.

RAWSON, R. R. 'The coalmining industry of the Hawarden district on the eve of the Industrial Revolution'. *Arch. Camb.*, XCVI, No. 2.

BEDFORD, ARTHUR. 'The emergence of Manchester'. *History*, XXIV, No. 93.

ROWE, W. J. *Cornwall in the age of the Industrial Revolution.* Liverpool, 1953.

SPATE, O. H. K. 'Geographical aspects of the industrial evolution of London till 1850'. *Geographical Journal*, XCII, No. 5.

TUPLING, G. H. *The Economic History of Rossendale.* (Publications of the University of Manchester. Economic History Series, No. 4.) Manchester, 1927.

WADSWORTH, A. P. AND MANN, J. DE LACY. *The Cotton Trade and Industrial Lancashire 1600-1780.* (Publications of the University of Manchester. Economic History Series, No. 7.) Manchester, 1931.

WARBURTON, W. H. *The History of Trade Union Organization in the North Staffordshire potteries.* London, 1931.

WILLAN, T. S. *The Navigation of the River Weaver in the Eighteenth Century.* Manchester, 1951.

WILLIAMS, J. E. 'Whitehaven in the Eighteenth Century'. *Economic History Review*, Second Series, VIII, April 1956.

See also: AGRICULTURE, ENCLOSURES.

C. BIOGRAPHIES

ASHTON, T. S. *An Eighteenth-Century Industrialist: Peter Stubs of Warrington, 1756-1806.* Manchester, 1939.

BARRETT, A. L. *George Stephenson, Father of Railways.* New York, 1948.

BIRCH, A. 'The Haigh ironworks: a nobleman's enterprise during the Industrial Revolution'. *Bulletin John Rylands Library*, XXXV, 1952-3.

CHALONER, W. H. 'Charles Roe of Macclesfield (1715-81) an eighteenth-century industrialist'. *Trans. Lancs. and Ches. Antiq. Soc.*, LXII, 1950-1.
'The Canal Duke'. *History Today*, 1951.
John Wilkinson, ironmaster, 1952.
'The Cartwright brothers. Their contribution to the wool industry'. *Wool Knowledge, the Journal of Wool Education*, Summer 1953.

DEVEREUX, R. [i.e. M. R. ROY PEMBER-DEVEREUX]. *John Loudon McAdam. Chapters in the history of highways*. London, 1936.

DICKINSON, H. W. AND JENKINS, RHYS. *James Watt and the Steam Engine*. Oxford, 1927.

DICKINSON, H. W. *James Watt, Craftsman and Engineer*. Cambridge, 1936. *Matthew Boulton*. Cambridge, 1937.

FAY, C. R. *Adam Smith and the Scotland of his Day*. (Social and Economic Studies, No. 3.) Cambridge, 1956.

HARRIS, T. R. 'John Edwards (1731-1807) Cornish industrialist'. *Trans. Newcomen Soc.*, XXIII, 1948.

HART, I. B. *James Watt and the History of Steam Power*. New York, 1949.

JOHN, A. H. *The Walker family, ironfounders and manufacturers*, 1741-1893. Council for the Preservation of Business Archives, 1951.

NORRIS, J. M. 'Samuel Garbett and the early development of industrial lobbying in Great Britain'. *Economic History Review*, X, No. 3, April, 1958.

RAISTRICK, A. *Dynasty of Iron Founders: the Darbys of Coalbrookdale*. London, 1953.

RÉMOND, ANDRÉ. *John Holker, manufacturier et grand fonctionnaire en France au XVIIIe siècle, 1719-1786*. Paris, 1946.

SUTHERLAND, L. S. *A London Merchant 1695-1774*. (A study of the business activities of William Braund.) London, 1933.

D. AGRICULTURE, ENCLOSURES

BERESFORD, M. W. 'Commissioners of Enclosure'. *Economic History Review*, XVI, No. 2, 1946.

CHAMBERS, J. D. 'Enclosure and the small landowner'. *Economic History Review*, X, No. 2.
'Enclosure and labour supply in the Industrial Revolution'. *Economic History Review*, V, No. 3, 1935.

DAVIES, E. 'The small landowner, 1780-1832, in the light of his land tax assessments'. *Economic History Review*, I, No. 1, 1927.

FUSSELL, G. E. *The English Rural Labourer. His house, furniture, clothing and food from Tudor to Victorian times*. London, 1949.
The Farmer's Tools, 1500-1900. The history of British farm implements, tools and machinery before the tractor came. London, 1952.

HARVEY, N. 'Sir Richard Weston and the new farming'. *Agriculture*, LIX, 1952-3.

HUNT, H. 'The chronology of Parliamentary enclosure in Leicestershire'. *Economic History Review*, X, No. 2, December 1957.

LAVROVSKY, V. M. *Parliamentary Enclosure of the Common Fields in England at the end of the Eighteenth and the beginning of the Nineteenth Centuries.* (In Russian.) Moscow-Leningrad, 1940. See review in the *Economic History Review*, XII, 1942.

MINGAY, G. E. 'The Agricultural Depression 1730-1750'. *Economic History Review*, Second Series, VIII, No. 3, April 1956.

ORWIN, C. S. *A History of English Farming.* (Nelson's Agriculture Series.) London, 1949.
The Open Fields. Oxford, 1938.

PARKER, R. A. C. 'Coke of Norfolk and the Agrarian Revolution'. *Economic History Review*, Second Series, VIII, No. 2, December 1955.

PLUMB, J. H. 'Sir Robert Walpole and Norfolk Husbandry'. *Economic History Review*, Second Series, V, No. 1, 1952.

PROTHERO, R. E., Baron Ernle. *English Farming* ... New edition, edited by A. D. Hall. 1936.

RICHES, NAOMI. *The Agricultural Revolution in Norfolk.* University of North Carolina Press, Chapel Hill, 1937.

TATE, W. E. 'Parliamentary counter-petitions during the enclosures of the eighteenth and nineteenth centuries'. *English Historical Review*, LIX, September, 1944.
'Opposition to Parliamentary enclosure in eighteenth-century England'. *Agricultural History*, July, 1945.
'Members of Parliament and the proceedings upon enclosure bills'. *Economic History Review*, XII, Nos. 1 and 2, 1942.
'Members of Parliament and their personal relation to enclosure: a study with special reference to Oxfordshire enclosures, 1757-1843'. *Agricultural History*, XXIII, No. 3, 1949.
'The cost of Parliamentary enclosure in England (with special reference to the county of Oxford)'. *Economic History Review*, Second Series, V, No. 2, 1952.

E. ECONOMIC AND SOCIAL QUESTIONS

ASHTON, T. S. 'The standard of life of the workers in England, 1790-1830'. *Journal of Economic History*, Supplement IX, 1949, 'The task of Economic Hist.'
'Changes in the standard of comfort in eighteenth-century England'. *Proceedings of the British Academy*, XLI, 1955.

BEBB, E. D. *Nonconformity and Social Life, 1660-1800. Some problems of the present as they appeared in the past.* London, 1935.

BENNETT, F. N. C. *The Food of the People, being the history of industrial feeding.* London, 1949.

BUER, M. C. *Health, Wealth and Population in the Early Days of the Industrial Revolution.* London, 1926.

CLAPHAM, J. H. *The Bank of England: a History.* 2 vols. Cambridge, 1944.

COLE, G. D. H. *A Short History of the British Working Class Movement, 1789-1925.* Vol. I (1789-1848). London, 1925.

COLEMAN, D. C. 'Industrial growth and Industrial Revolution'. *Economica*, XXIII, No. 89, 1956.

DAVIS, R. 'Seamen's sixpences: an index of commercial activity (1697-1828)'. *Economica*, XXIII, November 1956.

DUBOIS, A. B. *The English Business Company after the Bubble Act, 1720-1800*. New York, 1938.

FOSSATI, A. 'Lavoro e tecnica, prezzi e costi nella Rivoluzione Industriale inglese come fattori di espanzione commerciale'. *Raccolta di studie in onore del sen. Prof. Pietro Sitta*. Ferrare, 1937.
'Note informative sui costi di produzione nell'industria inglese ai tempi della Rivoluzione Industriale'. *Rivista di Politica Economica*, XXVIII, No. 3, March 1938.
'Capitale fisso e capitale salario nelle industrie tessili e minerarie inglesi di un secolo fà.' *Rivista di Politica Economica*, XXVIII, No. 5, May 1938.

GEORGE, M. D. 'The combination laws reconsidered'. *Econ. Journ.*, Econ. Ser., May 1927.

GILBOY, E. W. 'Demand as a factor in the Industrial Revolution'. *Articles by former students of E. F. Gay*, 1932.
Wages in Eighteenth-Century England. (Harvard Economic Studies, vol. 45.) Cambridge, Mass., 1934.

GLASS, D. W. 'The population controversy in eighteenth-century England'. First Part, I, *Population Studies*, VI, 1952-3.

GRIEVE, A. M. *The Last Years of the English Slave Trade, Liverpool 1750-1807*. London, 1941.

GRIFFITH, G. T. *Population Problems of the Age of Malthus*. Cambridge, 1926.

GRUBB, ISABEL. *Quakerism and Industry before 1800*. London, 1930.

HABAKKUK, H. J. 'English Population in the Eighteenth Century'. *Economic History Review*, Second Series, VI, No. 2, December 1953.

HAMMOND, J. L. 'The Industrial Revolution and discontent'. *Economic History Review*, II, No. 2, January 1930.

HENDERSON, W. O. 'The Anglo-French commercial treaty of 1786'. *Economic History Review*, X, No. 1, August 1957.

HOBSBAWM, E. J. 'The British standard of living, 1790-1850'. *Economic History Review*, X, No. 1, August 1957.

HUGHES, EDWARD. *Studies in Administration and Finance 1558-1825*. (Publications of the University of Manchester. Economic History Series, No. 10.) Manchester, 1934.

JOHN, A. H. *Aspects of the growth of industrial capital in the eighteenth and early nineteenth centuries*. See Meeting of the Economic History Society in 1953, in the French periodical, *Annales*, No. 3, 1954.
'Investment insurance and the London money market of the eighteenth century'. *Economica*, XX, May 1953.
'War and the English economy, 1700-1763'. *Economic History Review*, VII, No. 3, 1955.

JOSLIN, D. M. 'London Private Bankers, 1720-1785'. *Economic History Review*, Second Series, VII, No. 2, December 1954.

McKEOWN, T. AND BROWN, R. G. 'Medical evidence related to English population changes in the eighteenth century'. *Population Studies*, IX, 1955.

MARSHALL, D. *The English Poor in the Eighteenth Century*. A study in social and administrative history. London, 1926.
English People in the Eighteenth Century. London, 1956.

MARSHALL, T. 'Population problem during the Industrial Revolution'. *Economic History Review*, 1929.

MATHIAS, P. 'The social structure in the eighteenth century: a calculation by Joseph Massie'. *Economic History Review*, X, No. 1, August 1957.

PARES, RICHARD. *War and Trade in the West Indies 1739-1763*. Oxford, 1936.
A West-India Fortune. London, 1950.

PARKINSON, C. N. *Trade in the Eastern Seas 1793-1813*. Cambridge, 1937.

PARKINSON, C. N. (ed.). *The Trade Winds. A study of British overseas trade during the French Wars 1793-1815*. London, 1948.

PRESSNELL, L. S. *Country Banking in the Industrial Revolution*. 1956.

SCHLOTE, WERNER. *Entwicklung und Strukturwandlungen des englischen Aussenhandels von 1700 bis zur Gegenwart, etc.* (Probleme der Weltwirtschaft, No. 62.) Jena, 1938.

SCHUYLER, R. L. *The Fall of the Old Colonial System. A study in British free trade, 1770-1870*. New York, 1945.

WARNER, W. J. *The Wesleyan Movement in the Industrial Revolution*. London, 1930.

WEBB, SIDNEY AND BEATRICE. *English Local Government. English Poor Law History*. Part I: *The Old Poor Law*. London, 1927.

WILLAN, T. S. *River Navigation in England, 1600-1750*. London, 1936.

WILLIAMS, E. E. *Capitalism and Slavery*. University of North Carolina Press, Chapel Hill, 1944.

WILSON, C. H. *Anglo-Dutch Commerce and Finance in the Eighteenth Century*. (Cambridge Studies in Economic History.) Cambridge, 1941.

F. GENERAL WORKS

ASHTON, T. S. *An Economic History of England: the 18th Century*. London, 1955.
The Industrial Revolution 1760-1830. London, 1948.

BOWDEN, WITT. *The Industrial History of the United States*. New York [1930].

BRUGMANS, I. J. *Aanteekeningen over de Industrielle Revolution in England*. (Mélanges Byvanck), Varia historica, Assen, 1954.

CLAPHAM, J. H. *An Economic History of Modern Britain: The Early Railway Age 1820-1850*. Second edition. Cambridge, 1930.
A Concise Economic History of Britain. From the earliest times to 1750. Cambridge, 1949.

CLARK, G. N. *The Wealth of England from 1496 to 1760*. London, 1946.
The Idea of the Industrial Revolution. Being the twentieth lecture of

the David Murray Foundation, in the University of Glasgow, delivered on October 15th, 1952. Glasgow, 1953.

COURT, W. H. B. *A Concise Economic History of Britain from 1750 to recent times.* Cambridge, 1954.

FAY, C. R. *English Economic History, mainly since 1700.* Cambridge, 1940.

FEAVEARYEAR, A. E. *The Pound Sterling. A History of English money.* Oxford, 1931.

FRIEDMANN, G. 'Révolution Industrielle et crise du progrès.' *Annales,* 1948.

HENDERSON, W. O. *Britain and Industrial Europe 1750-1870. Studies in British Influence on the Industrial Revolution in Western Europe.* Liverpool, 1954.

HOFFMANN, W. G. *Wachstum und Wachstumsformen der Englischen Industriewirtschaft von 1700 bis zur Gegenwart* (Probleme der Weltwirtschaft, No. 63.) Jena, 1940. English translation by W. O. Henderson and W. H. Chaloner: *British Industry 1700-1950.* Oxford, 1955.

NEF, J. U. 'The Industrial Revolution reconsidered'. *Journal of Economic History,* III, May 1943.
'Wars and the Rise of Industrial Civilisation 1640-1740'. *Canadian Journal of Economic and Political Science,* X, No. 1.

PLUMB, J. H. *England in the Eighteenth Century.* (Pelican Books, No. 231, Pelican History of England, vol. 7.) Harmondsworth, 1950.

REDFORD, ARTHUR. *The Economic History of England, 1760-1860.* London, 1931.

RÖPKE, W. *Jenseits von Angebot und Nachfrage.* Zürich-Stuttgart, 1958.

RUESTOW, ALEXANDER. *Ortsbestimmung der Gegenwart. Eine universalgeschichtliche Kulturkritik.* Vol. 3. Zürich, 1957.

SALIN, E. 'Industrielle Revolution', *Kyklos,* IX, 1956.

TREVELYAN, G. M. *English Social History. A survey of six centuries, Chaucer to Queen Victoria.* Third edition. London, 1946.

WEBER, MAX. *Wirtschaftsgeschichte … Abriss der universalen Sozial- und Wirtschaftsgeschichte.* Munich, 1923.

The following eight entries are taken from notes prepared by the author in 1932 for a proposed new edition of this book – a work which other commitments prevented him from carrying out.

DICKINSON, H. W. AND JENKINS, R. *James Watt and the Steam Engine.* Oxford, Clarendon Press, 1927. [Exhaustive work, compiled from original sources. Large bibliography.]

HAMILTON, HENRY. *The English brass and copper industries to 1800.* London, 1926. [Extensive bibliography.]

LIPSON, EPHRAIM. *The Economic History of England. The Age of Mercantilism.* 2 vols. London, 1931.

PINCHBECK, IVY. *Women Workers and the Industrial Revolution, 1750-1850.* (Studies in Economic and Social History.) London, 1930. [Extensive work. Bibliography.]

RICHARDS, R. D. *The Early History of Banking in England.* London, 1929. [Exhaustive bibliography, indicating manuscript sources.]

SOMBART, W. *Der Moderne Kapitalismus*, vol. II (*Das Europäische Wirt-schaftsleben im Zeitalter des Fruhkapitalismus*). Munich and Leipzig, 1924. [Copious bibliographies.]

USHER, A. P. *A History of Mechanical Inventions*. New York, 1929. [Classified bibliography.]

WARNER, W. J. *The Wesleyan Movement in the Industrial Revolution*. London, 1930. [Bibliography of contemporary sources.]

G. BIBLIOGRAPHIES

ASHTON, T. S. *The Industrial Revolution. A Study in bibliography*. (Economic History Society, Bibliographies and Pamphlets, No. 3.) London, 1937.

CHALONER, W. H. 'Bibliography of recent works on enclosure, open fields, etc.' *Agricultural History Review*, II, 1954.

POWER, EILEEN. *The Industrial Revolution 1750-1850. A select bibliography*. (Economic History Society, Bibliographies, No. 1.) London [1929].

H. STATISTICS

ASHTON, T. S. 'Some Statistics of the Industrial Revolution in Britain'. *Trans. Manchester Statist. Soc. for 1947-8*.

CLARK, G. N. *A Guide to English Commercial Statistics 1696-1782*. With a catalogue of material by Barbara M. Franks. (Royal Historical Society Guides and Handbooks, No. 1.) London, 1938.

HULME, E. W. 'Statistical History of the Iron Trade of England and Wales 1717-1750'. *Trans. Newcomen Soc.*, IX.

SCHUMPETER, E. 'English Prices and Public Finance 1660-1822'. *Review of Economics and Statistics*, XX, No. 1.

SILBERLING, N. J. 'British prices and business cycles, 1779-1850'. *Review of Economics and Statistics*, Prelim., V, Supplement 2.

WRIGHT, J. F. 'An Index of the Output of British Industry since 1700'. *Journal of Economic History*, 1956.

INDEX

AGRICULTURE: and industry, 60, 63, 138, 182-5, 204, 263n.; reform of, 156-63, 185, 348n.; reform as vindication of enclosures, 177, 178; changes due to engrossing of farms, 173; Board of, 162, 179, 419; agricultural labourers, 181, 182, 419n., 421, 422, 423-4, 429, 439, 445

Albion flour mills, 309, 333

alcoholism, 430 and note

alienation, process of, 64-5

American colonies, trade with, 62; iron from, 272, 280; cotton-growing, 201

American war, and mercantilism, 99; crisis caused by, 263, 389, 401n.

apprentices, 71-2, 81, 193, 410, 412, 425, 453, 454-5, 470, 473; education of, 465, 467, 472; medical report on, 469;

apprenticeship: laws, 393, 452-6; system, cotton trade free of, 261; in woollen industry, 269; importance diminished by industrial revolution, 454; agitation regarding, 455-6; indenture of, 452n.

arbitration, 449, 459-63; Arbitration Act (1800), 460, 461, 462

aristocracy: and canals, 128, 395; and trade, 134-5; and agriculture, 158-60, 167-9; and mining, 276, 277; and Boulton, 327, 328; Wedgwood, 396

Arkwright, Sir Richard, 203, 206, 212, 213, 214, 216, 219, 220-34, 235, 236, 246, 248, 249, 264, 295, 301, 334, 367, 368, 370, 371, 373 and note, 374, 376, 397n., 402, 464, 466

asiento, 99, 107

'atmospheric engine', 315, 320, 336

BACON, ANTHONY, 302

Bakewell (stockbreeder), 161

Baltic Company, 93

Bank of England, 96-7, 98

bankruptcy, 214, 253, 254, 303, 324

Banks, Sir Joseph, 379

banks and banking, 95-7, 254, 255; provincial, 223, 254, 255; bankers, 365, 367

beer, 69, 96n., 181n., 429

Beighton, Henry, 317

Belgrave, Lord, 471

Bell, Thomas, 244

bellows, 287; strengthened, 291, 298; hydraulic, 303; iron sides for, 306

Bentley, Thomas, 128, 384

Berthollet (chemist), 245

'Big Ben' (combing machine), 268-9

Birmingham, 104, 105, 129, 130, 182, 213, 274-5, 279, 280, 297, 325, 326, 336, 349n., 355, 362, 411, 422, 426n.; goods, 274, 326

Black, Joseph, 295, 319, 322

'black book', 393

Black Country, the, 105, 275, 337, 363

'Black Indies', the, 283

blacksmiths, 241, 273n., 315, 372

Blackburn, 216, 218, 248, 349n., 360n., 401

Blauenstein, 288, 293

bleaching, 245

Blincoe, Robert, 414, 473

blockade, continental, 405

Bloomfield collieries, 329

Bolton, 202, 235, 236, 238-9, 248, 359-60, 392, 422, 423, 442

Boulton, Matthew, 104, 129, 279, 322, 324-7, 329, 331, 335, 368, 372, 378-81, 389, 390, 465

Boulton and Watt, 301, 324, 329-32, 374, 377, 422

Bourne, Daniel, 323

Bowling foundries, 304

Bradford, 55, 66, 70, 103, 110, 262, 263, 269, 335, 349n., 361n., 367

brewers and breweries, 283, 289, 307, 333

bridges, iron, 307-8

Bridgewater, Duke of, 123-5, 276, 360n., 395

Brindley, James, 124, 125, 129, 318

Bristol, 52, 54, 104, 105, 115, 275, 287, 300, 349n., 354, 361

Broadwater collieries, 314

bronzes, ornamental, 279, 326, 378

Brook, of Pudsey, 265

'Brummagem' ware, 104

Bryan, of Manchester, 33

Buck, Captain, 287

Burke, Edmund, 328, 432n., 465

Burslem (potteries), 383, 385, 386

Bury, 51, 207, 208, 227, 248, 360n., 397, 422, 442

CALICO, 224, 238, 242, 244; printing works, 245; printers, 217, 422, 447, 453, 454, 455

Calley (Cawley), John, 316

canals, 121-32, 317, 395; and transport of coal, 123; and exports, 129-30; Caledonian, 323, 325; Forth & Clyde, 126; Grand Trunk, 125, 126; Grand Junction, 126; Mersey, 123, 125, 128,

canals—cont.
129, 357, 366, 387; Trent, 122, 123, 125, 128, 129; Worsley, 123-4, 357, 366
capital: mainspring of industrial activity, 26-8; and machinery, 38; commercial to industrial, 62, 67; concentration of, 57, 73, 248, 279, 475; circulation of, 96; raising of, 213, 223, 226, 233, 242, 264, 289, 295, 303, 304, 323, 374; sums invested in undertakings, 248, 249, 303, 304, 326, 328, 329n.; and mines, 275; owners of, before 18th c., 365; supremacy of commercial, 369
capital and labour: separation of, 36, 69, 74, 82; opposition of, 392-3, 418, 440, 441; disputes between, 74, 441-51, 459-64
capitalism: early forms of, 32, 35-6, 64n.; industrial: and machinery, 195; individual character of early, 250; origins of, 365; and Poor Law, 439
capitalists, 32n., 33, 62, 65, 66, 82, 90, 103, 192, 417, 418, 476; and Bank of England, 96; in agriculture, 185 (see also manufacturers)
carding, 58, 66, 67, 206, 267; machines, 214, 217, 225, 232, 236
Carlyle, Thomas, 27, 220
carpenters, 175, 209, 216, 241
'carronades', 303, 306
carrying trade, 90
Cartwright, Edmund, 234, 240-3, 244, 268, 335, 368, 425, 475
cattle, 112, 148, 150, 157, 158, 163; breeding, 152, 157, 160, 161, 163
Caus, Salomon de, 312
Cave, Edward, 210, 214
Cavendish, Henry, 319
Chacewater mines, 329
'Chaillot fire-pump', 330
Chamber of Manufacturers, 390-2
charcoal, 281, 284, 289, 290, 291, 292, 300, 302n.
Chatham, William Pitt, Earl of, 99, 342
chemistry, industrial, 303, 379, 383
Cheshire, 108, 129, 173, 274, 462, 477
Chester, typical town of the past, 47
Child, Sir Josiah, 97
children, employment of, 58, 70, 81, 204, 208, 238, 268, 371, 410-12, 414, 425, 454, 466-7, 469, 470-2; as chimney sweeps, 465; sufferings of, 414, 416; accidents to, 413 (see also apprentices)
China, trade with, 67, 98, 199, 201, 205
classes, social, 27, 28, 367, 441; contest between, 441; manners of living of, 67, 69, 181, 239, 366 and note, 426, 429-30 (see also aristocracy, capitalists, manufacturers, middle classes, workers; and capital and labour)

climate, and the cotton industry, 202, 204, 247
clockmakers, 222, 216, 229, 231, 296
Cloth Halls, 59, 110, 262n., 361
cloth manufacturers, 453n.; merchants, 33-4, 265, 366; shearers, 425
clothiers, merchant, 59-61, 62, 63-7, 68-9, 75, 110, 123; 'The Clothiers' Delight', 75-7; clothing trade, 66n., 73
Clyde valley, 50, 247
coal: in industry, 43, 123, 283-4, 299, 300, 301; for smelting, 284-92, 298; for refining, 292-6, 298; and the steam engine, 337; transport of, 123, 129, 283n., 337; tax on, 389; gas from, 332; early use of, 282-3; trade, 94, 108, 112, 283; trade disputes, 82; peat coal, 284n.; pit coal, 123n., 284n.; sea coal, 123, 283, 284n., 292; stone coal, 284n. (see also mines)
coasting trade, 112
coins: counterfeit, 274n., 336, 380; Monnerons, 336n.; Wilkinson's, 301
coining press (Boulton's), 336, 378-9
coke, 285-92, 300n., 301, 362
Coke of Holkham (Earl of Leicester), 160-1
Colbert and Colbertism, 29-30, 31, 32, 35, 83
Colchester, 50, 51, 206, 207, 262, 453
Coldbrook valley, ironworking centre, 290
colliers, 74, 82, 402
combinations: of workers, 74, 82, 393, 441; prosecution and persecution of, 449-50; of employers, 447; Combination Act (1799), 445-9, 464
combing, 50, 66, 67; machines, 268-9, 425; combs for looms, 206, 207 (see also wool-combers)
commerce and industry, reciprocal influence of, 91 et seq., 104 et seq., 203, 279
commercial: travelling, 104, 110-11, 119, 326; treaties: Anglo-French (1786), 257, 391, Anglo-Irish (1785), 390; expansion and large-scale production, 391-2
'common fields', used synonymously with 'open fields', 142-3
common lands and commons, 142-51, 170-1; enclosure of, 73; division of, 172, 173; for terms used in land legislation, see 142, 148-50
communications, 56, 109, 112, 302 (see also canals, roads)
companies: joint stock, 95, 126; mining, 275-6; ironworks, 304; for selling Newcomen's engine, 317
competition, 26, 172, 202, 224, 261, 264, 266, 280, 331, 334, 361, 385; between

cotton and woollen trades, 252;
foreign, 87, 91, 196, 199-200, 203, 256,
257; foreign, fear of, 239, 256; between men and machines, 184, 244,
400, 423 (see also machinery, workers'
hostility to); in the labour market,
262, 423

contracts, 418, 422n., 446, 459, 461-2;
freedom of contract, 461-2

Considerations upon the East-India Trade
(1701), 37, 132-4

Copley (ironworker), 287

co-operation, 36n.; of firms, 331

copper, 129, 279, 305, 389; coins, 289,
336; tax on, 389 (see also mines)

copyholders, 137, 140, 143

copying press, 329

corn, 122n., 129, 130, 152, 153, 173;
Corn Laws, 42

Cornwall, 276, 300, 301, 313, 314, 329,
330, 332, 377

Cort, Henry, 294-5, 298, 304, 374, 475

cottage industry, see industry, domestic
system; cottagers, 151, 170-1

cotton and cotton goods, 107, 120, 197-8,
199, 224, 242, 251; —— cloth, demand
for, 239n.; —— gin, the, 245n.; proposed tax on, 259

cotton industry: and the advent of
machinery, 43; Antwerp first northern
European centre of, 198; beginnings of
in England, 104, 108, 197-204;
centres of, 108, 201-2, 247-8; classic
example of modern large-scale industry, 191; leads way for other textile
industries, 209; crises in, 241, 252-6,
401n.; and foreign competition, 199-
201; and the woollen industry, 202,
203-4, 252; protection and freedom,
200, 203, 256-60; unfettered by regulations, 204, 260-1; domestic system in,
204, 219, 238, 246, 250-1; fustian
masters, 204-5; transformation and
development, 206-19, 234, 238, 246,
250-2

Cotton Spinners' Associations, 450

Cotton Weavers' Society, 442-3

Cranage, Thomas and George, 293

crank and comb, 225, 232

Crawshay, Richard, 295, 302, 372

crises, industrial and financial, 239, 252-
6, 347, 423, 437

Crompton, Samuel, 234, 235-7, 359, 368,
374, 475

crops, rotation of, 144-5, 147, 157, 158,
163

Cuthbert of Kendal, 33

cutlers and cutlery, 66n., 274, 278, 297,
444 (see also Hallamshire)

cylinders, 315, 316, 318, 320, 331, 332;
air, 298

DAGNEY, EDWARD, 287

Dale, David, 232, 371, 409n., 466-7

Darby, Abraham, and sons, 290-2, 297,
299-300, 304, 307, 368, 372

Darwin, Erasmus, 324, 379

Defoe, Daniel, 33n., 50 et seq., 106, 157,
273, 356

deforestation, and iron industry, 281-2,
285, 287, 299

Derby, 116, 194, 196, 214, 219, 223,
349n., 371

Derbyshire, 157, 173, 196, 232, 247, 248,
262, 324, 391

Derwent river, 194, 195, 197, 223, 226

Devonshire, 52, 54, 79, 264, 269, 315,
364, 369

distillers and distilleries, 283, 307, 427

Dobson, Isaac, 371-2

'doffers', 425

Doncaster, 242, 268, 296

dressing machine, 374

Drinkwater, Peter, 334

drop box, invention of, 208

druggets and drugget weavers, 50, 51,
421

Dudley, Dud, 281n., 286-8, 475

Dudley, Edward, Earl of, 286

Dumbarton, power looms at, 243

Dyer, John, 49, 214-15

dyers and dyeing, 58, 245, 248, 264-5,
283, 374, 453

EARNSHAW, LAWRENCE, 400

earthenware pipes, 386

East India Company, 72, 93, 97-8, 104,
256, 336

Eden, William, 345, 419

Elers, Paul, 386

emigration, 27

employers and workers, relations between, 69, 70, 75, 192, 366, 381, 384-5
(see also capital and labour)

enclosures, 73, 141, 151; in the 16th and
17th c., 152-6, 165; in the 18th c.,
165-9; and pasture land, 154, 171,
173-4; complaints against, 152-3, 174;
lack of formal protest, 174; riots
against, 154, 175; consequence of, 169-
73, 183-5; and depopulation of rural
districts, 176, 178, 182; arguments for,
176-9, 184; wrongs suffered, 152 and
note, 169-72, 179-80; Commissioners
of, 168-9, 179

epidemics, decline in, 348n.

Etruria (Wedgwood's factory), 129, 379,
382n., 383, 385, 465

excise duty on cotton goods, 249, 259;
agitation against, 259

Exeter, 52, 65, 361

exports: woollens, 52, 62, 67, 263n.; cotton goods, 198, 205, 239, 252; spun yarns, campaign against, 257-8; toys, 274-5; cast steel, 296; and Boulton, 327, 377; Wedgwood, 385; export bounties, 257

FABRICS, painted or printed, 199, 200, 202, 203, 244
factories: the first: silk, 194-6; cotton, 246-51; wool, 264-5, 360; location of, 247, 337, 355; workers' hatred of, 408-9; unhealthy conditions of, 415, 469, 470; immorality in, 416-17, 467, 471; inspection of, 472-3 (see also mills)
factory, definition of, 38-9, 246; the modern, created by Arkwright, 233; legislation, 42, 469 (for factory system, see industry)
fairs, 109
Fallowfield, William, 290
farms, engrossing of, 172-3, 183
farmers, gentlemen, 160; a new social class of, 160, 181; affected by enclosures, 169-70
Feeder, the, 225, 226, 232
Fielden, Joshua, 371
'fire-engines', 312, 317, 318, 327, 328n.
Fitzgerald (steam power), 318, 321
fly shuttle, 206-8, 244, 261-2, 359; in woollen industry, 267, 455
fly-wheels, 309
Forest of Dean, ironworking, 273-4, 287
Fothergill (Boulton's partner), 326-7, 329
Fox, C. J., 259, 390, 458
France: industry during reign of Louis XIV, 29-33; villenage abolished, 73; canals, 121; travels of Young in, 161, 429; factory system and rural population, 184; gives refuge to Lee, 192, and Kay, 208; competition with, 196, 239; war with, 255, 427; commercial treaty with, 257, 391; ironworks in, 301; reimportation of buckles from, 325; comparison with England, 429
Franklin, Benjamin, 324
freeholders, 139, 143
free trade, 391 (see also laissez-faire)
Friendly Societies, 78, 450-1
Frome, 52, 66, 262, 361-2
fuel, lack of, and the scarcity of iron, 280-1, 282, 287, 299
furnaces, blast, 272, 273, 274, 277, 281, 282, 286, 289, 298, 299, 300, 301, 303, 305, 306n., 329, 363; reverberatory, 288
fustian and fustian masters, 198n., 199, 203, 204, 250; fustian tax, 390, 392

GARBETT, SAMUEL, 129, 303, 372
Garnett (cotton manufacturer), 269
gas lighting, 332
Gennes, de, 240
Germany, trade with, 205; metal-working in, 272; Watt's engine in, 330
gig mills, 84, 403, 405, 407, 408
Gilbert's Act (1782), 435
gin, 430
Glasgow, 50, 238, 243, 248, 441-2
glaziers, 287, 316
Gloucester, county of, 52, 71, 264, 282, 453
Godwin, Thomas, 465
Goldsmith, Oliver (quoted), 176
Gott, Benjamin, 264-5
Greenock, 50, 318
Grimshaw, the brothers, 243

HALES, JOHN, 155
Halifax, 51, 54, 55, 66, 68, 110, 262, 265, 349n., 361, 444; Halifax valley, domestic system in, 57-62, 89, 361
Hallamshire, 274; —— Cutlers' Company, 278, 296, 444
Hamilton, Sir William, 383
hammers, forge, 190; hydraulic, 277, 298, 309; steam, 298
Hancock, Joseph, 279
Hargreaves, James, 212, 213, 216-19, 223, 230, 231, 232, 297, 374, 401, 464, 475
hatters, 446, 453
Hawkes, William, 372
'headland', 144
Heeley, Richard, 210
Herschel, Sir William, 379
Heslop, Adam, 336
Highs, Thomas, 228, 229-32, 235, 464, 475
Hirst, William, 265
Hitchin, open fields in, 143
Hobhouse, Benjamin, 447
Hodgkins of Halifax, 33
Holkham, Norfolk, 160, 180
Holland, trade with, 62; commercial supremacy of, envied, 92; and the idea of a national bank, 95
home industries, see industry, domestic system
Homfray, Francis, 307n.; Samuel, 302, 305
Hooke, Robert, 316
Hornblower, Jonathan, 331, 335
Horrocks, John, 243, 249
Horsehay furnace, 300, 421
horses, pack, 119; horsebreeding, 158n.
housing problem in industrial towns, 430-1
Howard, John, 465

Huddersfield, 55, 110, 262, 408n.
Hudson Bay Company, 94
Hull, 104, 274, 349n.
Hume, David, 464
Huntsman, Benjamin, 296-7, 299, 303, 368, 372, 419n.

IMPORTS, 84, 98, 101-4, 252; raw cotton, 201, 203, 252, 253; cotton goods, 98, 199, 252, 253; tea, 98; iron ore, 272, 274, 280; raw silk, 193; cereals, 426; restrictions on, 200, 203; import duty, 257n.; bounties, 257, 427n.
India, trade with, 67, 98, 132-4, 198, 199, 200-1, 238, 256
industrial revolution: origin of the expression, 25; limits of the present investigation, 42-3; as defined by Toynbee, 83; fostered by the growth of trade, 90; the yeomanry and the, 141; machinery and the, 189; social consequences of, 28, 341; the working class and the, 399 et seq.; cannot be summed up in a simple formula, 297; not the cause of sufferings of the poor, 430; social problems of the, 440; conclusion, 474-7
industry: stages in the development of, 29 et seq., 66, 68, 73-4, 89, 216, 223, 250-1, 279, 327, 369, 476
'domestic system': 57-62, 68-9, 141, 183, 264, 265-6, 278, 387, 409
system dominated by merchant manufacturer, 62-6, 192, 204
dispersion characteristic of early, 49, 52-4, 55, 272
(see also 'manufacture', and manufacturers, merchant)
factory system: 25-32, 35, 36, 38-40, 73, 213; its characteristics, 365; due to commercial expansion, 91, 103-5, 108, 203, 279; beginnings of, 196, 234, 246-7; main lines laid down, 251; role of Arkwright, 220, of Boulton, 326; incessant progress of, 245, 251, 261; need for internal freedom, 261; development in Yorkshire, 369; concentration of, 49-50, 55, 195, 248-50, 275, 279; government attitudes and policies towards, 258-9, 280, 453-4; principle of State intervention, 470, 472
textile, and metal-working, compared, 297; lack of balance in, due to uneven technical advance: between spinning and weaving, 208-9, 215, 217, 238-9, smelting and refining, 292, 296 (see also the various textile and metal-working industries)
inland navigation, 120-32

inventions, 204, 205-6, 216, 245, 290, 292, 299, 311, 321, 322, 368, 400, 475
in the textile industry: the stocking frame, 191; silk-throwing machine, 194; fly shuttle, 206-8; carding process (Kay's), 206; carding machines, 214 (Paul's), 217 (Hargreaves's), 225 (Arkwright's), 236 (Crompton's); steel combs for looms, 207; spinning machines, 210-13 (Wyatt's), 400 (Earnshaw's); jenny, 217; water frame, 222-3; mule, 234-5; crank and comb, roving frame, feeder, 225-6; the cotton gin, 245n.; power loom, 241-2; combing machine, 268
metallurgy: coke, 290-1; puddling, 294; cast steel, 296
mechanics: steam engine, 313-14 (Savery's), 315 (Newcomen's), 319-21 (Watt's); rotary motion, 333
(see also under separate headings)
inventors, hostility to, 207, 208, 218, 297, 400; misfortunes of, 207, 211, 213, 214, 236, 242, 295; did not become manufacturers, 368
(for textile industry, see Arkwright, Bell, Bourne, Cartwright, Crompton, Earnshaw, Hargreaves, Highs, Kay, Kelly, Lee, Paul, Wyatt; for metallurgy, see Blauenstein, Cort, Darby, Dudley, Huntsman, Smeaton, Sturtevant, Wood; for mechanics, see Hornblower, Newcomen, Savery, Watt)
Ireland, trade with, 52, 79, 108, 199, 280, 282, 391; commercial treaty with, 390; Irish in Lancashire, 359
iron: bar, 191, 280, 289, 291, 292, 295, 296; cast, 291; pig, 129, 191, 272, 280, 288, 289, 292, 296, 300, 305, 306n.; worked, 129; new uses for, 300, 306-9; ore, 272, 274, 277, 280, 284, 292; proposed tax on, 389, 390; industry, 43, 271 et seq., 305 et seq.; and scarcity of fuel owing to deforestation, 281-2; and machinery, 190-1; conservative tendency of, before mid-18th c., 280; later ascendancy of, 296, 305; ironworks, 299-306, 362; distribution of in 1720, 272n.; names mentioned: Bersham, 301, 306, 362; Bradley, 301, 309, 333; Broseley, 301, 329; Carron, 293, 298, 302-3, 323, 362; Coalbrookdale, 290, 291, 299, 300, 306, 333, 362, 419n., 465, 474; Creusot (France), 301; Cyfarthfa, 295, 302, 305; Fontley, 293, 295; Indret (Wilkinson's in France), 301; Merthyr Tydvil, 293, 305; Pen-y-Darran, 302; Sedgeley, 286; ironmasters, 277, 286, 290, 292, 295, 301, 302, 308, 333, 366, 372, 374, 377

Italy, and idea of a national bank, 95; trade with, 205; and silk industry, 193-4, 196

Jacquart, J. M., 240, 399
Jellicoe, Adam, 295, 304
jenny, the, 212, 216-19, 234, 235, 237, 238, 246, 252, 367, 371, 401; for wool, 263-4, 267; double, 230
Johnson, Thomas, 374
Justices of the Peace, 82, 85, 114, 26on., 403, 432, 433n., 447, 448, 449, 456-7, 459, 460, 462n., 472

Kay, John, 206-8, 218, 240n.
Kay, John, of Warrington, 222, 229, 231
Kay, Robert, 208n.
Kelly, William, 237
'Kendal cottons', 51n., 198n.
Kett, Robert, 154-5
King, Gregory, 341, 342, 343, 347
Kinloch, Andrew, 243n.
Kinneil engine, 323, 325

Labour, division of, 36, 37, 89n., 476; increased by use of machinery, 56; in domestic industry, 57, 205; and the exchange of commodities, 41; and the extent of the market, 90, 132; in *Considerations upon the East-India Trade*, 133; in agriculture, 177; in the metal industry, 277-9, 280; and technical training, 454
labour force: movement of, from country to town, 181-4, 439; size of, in various factories, 195, 213, 214, 224, 226, 247, 249, 305; recruitment of, 322, 375, 409, 410; discipline over, 375-6; difficulty in obtaining, 409, 466; mobility of, 434 (*see also* children, workers, and capital and labour)
lace industry, 66n., 73
laissez-faire and economic freedom, 42, 256, 257-61, 393-4, 407n., 454, 456, 459-60, 464, 468, 472, 434
Lancashire, 51, 105, 107, 108, 173, 217, 355, 367, 401-2, 442, 462, 469, 477; cotton industry, 196, 201, 204, 218, 226, 243, 245, 247, 252, 262, 269; woollen trade ended, 218; climate, 202; home of textile inventions, 290
land, division of, *see* enclosures, and common lands; parcelling, 143-6; purchase of encouraged, 164n.; sale of 172; tenure, 136-7, 158; arable, 146-7, 155, 163; pasture, extension of, 152, 153-5, 173; England a country of pasture, 47, 136, 163

landlords and tenants, 158, 161
landowners: and canals, 128; and enclosures, 165-8, 171, 177, 185n.; small, 169-70, 175, 181; as owners of capital, 365; manufacturers become, 373; in favour of protectionist system, 392
lathes, metal, 190, 309; metal-turning, 299
Lavoisier, 293
Laxton estate, 143n.
leases and leaseholders, 137, 158, 161
Lebon, Philippe, 332
Lee, William, and family of, 191-2
Leeds, 51, 54, 55, 60, 115-16, 207, 262, 264, 265, 267, 335, 349n., 360-1, 408; market, 59; cloth halls, 59n.
Lees, John, 232; Lees family, 372
legislation: in early industry, 34-5, 63, 73, 79-80, 83-6; payment in kind, 73n.; emancipation of serfs in mines, 74; enclosures, 141-2, 153-4, 165, 167, 169, 171, 174, 428; canals, 129n.; turnpike and other road acts, 114, 115, 116; silk industry, 82n., 196n., 457; woollen industry, 48n., 266; cotton industry, 200, 203, 224, 258; iron industry, 28on., 281; damage committed by workmen, 392, 401; 'frauds and embezzlements', 393n., 409n.; use of machinery, 403; apprenticeship, 398, 410n., 456; Poor Law, 431n., 432, 434, 435, 437; combination acts, 445-8; wages, 454, 457, 458, 463; Arbitration Act, 460-3; chimneysweeps, 465; Factory Act, 470-4 (*see also* Gilbert's Act, Speenhamland Law, Spitalfields Act, Statute of Artificers)
Leicester, 81, 264, 426n.
Levant, trade with, 62;—— Company, 94
Lincolnshire, 50, 157, 355
linen industry, 265n.; linen and cotton mixed, 202
Liverpool, 47, 105-8, 129-30, 201, 300, 349n., 354, 358
locksmiths, 216, 315, 322
locomotive, Murdock's, 332
Lombe, John and Thomas, 194, 195-6, 197, 224, 233, 414n.
London, 65, 73, 81-2, 94, 96, 130, 135, 193, 196, 199, 201, 300, 308, 314-15, 317, 349, 354; City of, 95
loom, hand, 57-8, 64; power, 240-4; Dutch, 207n., 240; of de Gennes, 240
lord of the manor, rights of, 149; and enclosures, 166
Low Moor Company, 304
Luddite riots, 405-6
Lunar Society, the, 379

McAdam (roadbuilder), 118
Macclesfield, 192n., 196

'machine industry', 39-40, 190, 191

machinery, use of: ancient and early, 190; and the factory systems, 25-6, 27, 38, 39, 40, 41, 42, 55, 189, 190, 297-8, 474; leading fact in the industrial revolution, 189; division of labour increased by, 56; its effect compared with that of enclosures, 185; in the textile industries, 104 et seq., 220 et seq.; in metal-working industries, 298-9, 309, 336; and reign of iron and steel, 309; and need for factory discipline, 375-6; and labour of women and children, 425, 453; and reduction of labour, 430; prohibitions against, 403, 452n.; effect on weavers, 424-5; workers' hostility to, 192, 207, 218, 242, 286, 399-401, 408 (see also riots, anti-machine); changed attitude in cotton and woollen industries, 404; and new Poor Law, 438

machines, definition of, 190; textile, prohibition against export of, 258; made of wood, 237, 309; of metal, 309, 243; for forging nails and turning screws, 299; for making other machines, 299; drills for boring cannon, 299 (see also inventions)

Malthus, T. R., 346-8

Manchester, 27, 47, 50, 51, 105-6, 107, 108, 205, 257, 349n., 422, 430, 451; cotton trade, 198, 199, 202, 226, 248, 251, 269; history of, 355-9; Board of Health, 469-70

'manufacture', 35-7, 366, 476; distinguished from factory system, 37-40, and from workshop of master craftsman, 57; never prevalent in England, 89, 246; relation of to factory system, 65; 223, 279, 280, 327 (see also under industry); examples of survival of, 66n.

manufacturers: meanings of the word, 60, 366
in old type of industry; 33-4; merchant 62n., 75, 138, 184, 204, 223, 264, 265, 266-7, 268, 279; and the factory system, 250, 369, 476 (see also clothiers, merchant; and fustian master)
in the factory system: 250, 469; mutual spying among, 260; disagreements among, 391; hostile to protectionist system, 392; as a class, 367; recruitment, 369-73; characteristics, 233, 367-8, 373-5, 377, 388; exceptions, 378-88; class consciousness, 388-92; class interests, 392-4; official attitude to, 392; social position of, 394-5, 396-7; power, 395-6, and political influence, 397-8; and Arbitration Act, 461-2; and minimum wage, 463; and Poor Law, 463

(see also capitalists; and Arkwright, Bacon, Boulton, Crawshay, Darby, Fielden, Gott, Homfray, Lombe, Oldknow, Peel, Radcliffe, Reynolds, Roebuck, Walker, Watt, Wedgwood, Wilkinson)

manufactures royales and manufactures privilégiées, 30-1

Mare clausum, 93

markets: for industry, 29, 91; local, 52, 59, 108, 109-10, 275; home, 62, 129, 254, 256; foreign, 129, 257, 392; extension of, 156, 261, 275, 476; problem of, 376-7; free, 391

Marx, Karl, 25n., 35, 37n., 89, 139, 152n., 165, 170n., 346, 366

Maudsley, Henry, 299

meat-eating, 72, 163, 348n., 429, 430

medicine, progress of, and its consequences, 348n.

mercantile system, 84, 85-6, 99; theory of mercantilism, 256; mercantile marine, 94

Merchant Adventurers, Company of, 93n.

merchants, 95, 279, 365, 367; travelling, 110-11 (see also clothiers and manufacturers)

metal-working, 272, 284; beginning of large-scale, 299 (see also iron, refining, small wares, smelting, steel); metalworkers, 422

Metcalf, John, 117

methods and materials for research in economic history, 418-21, 428-9

middle classes: political role in 1688, 95; social importance of, 134-5; envied by aristocracy, 158; buy landed property, 172, 373; hostility to machines, 403 (see also manufacturers)

middlemen, 62, 67, 110

mill, use of the word, 38, 224
mills: public, 58; water, 190, 321; rolling, 191, 294, 298, 309; slitting, 191; for silk, 195, 415n.; for flour, malt, flint, sugar-cane, 333; steam, 334-5; spinning, 213, 214, 219, 224, 226, 232, 242, 244, 247, 248n., 265n., 309, 358, 413
spinning mills mentioned: Altham, 227, 402; Bakewell, 232, 233; Belper, 219, 226; Birkacre, 226; Burton, 227; Chorley, 219, 264; Cromford, 219, 223, 224, 247, 358; Wirksworth, 232

Miller, Robert, 243n.

millowner, typical, 195

millwrights, 216-17, 290, 322, 332, 445, 446

mines and mining, 43, 82, 275-6, 283; coal, 74, 123, 129, 276, 303, 323; copper, 276, 313, 314; iron, 276; tin, 301; miners, 273

Mint, the London, 336n.; in Russia (Boulton's), 336

monopolies, industrial: in the 17th c., 32; Young's comments on, 88; of cotton in the home market, 256; capitalist, 265; of Boulton and Watt, 328, 331; commercial, 97

Monteith, John, 243

More, Sir Thomas, 152

mule, spinning, 234-5, 237-8, 246n., 250-1; for wool, 267, 269

Müller, Anton, 240n.

Murdock, William, 321n., 332, 335, 377

Muscovy Company, 93

muslin, 238, 242, 256, 422

NANTES, EDICT OF, and silk weavers, 104, 193

Navigation Act, 93-4

Need (Arkwright's partner), 223, 224, 226, 250n.

New Lanark mills, 232, 466, 468

New River Company, 329

Newcastle, 82, 94, 129, 275, 283, 303, 317, 349n., 421

Newcomen's engine, 299, 315-18, 320, 323, 329, 330

Newton, George, 372

night work, 265, 413, 417, 469, 473

Nightingale, Peter, 228

Nonconformists, 290, 343, 394, 465, 466

Norfolk, 50, 54, 67, 71, 159-60, 269, 369, 445

North, Roger, 139

Northumberland, 157, 283, 303

Norwich, 50, 54, 67, 70, 89, 103, 160, 262, 263, 269, 349n., 361

Nottingham, 65, 81, 192, 218, 219, 223, 232, 240, 269, 349n.

OASTLER, RICHARD, 473

Oldham, 51, 236, 248, 349n., 359, 372, 450

Oldknow, Samuel, 249, 335, 415n., 467n.

Onions, Peter, 293

'open fields', 142, 143-6, 163, 172; open field system, 143, 146-8, 164

out-relief, 437, 445

Owen, Robert, 120, 377, 466, 467-8, 477

'oxgang', 143

PAINE, TOM, 465

Paisley, 50, 238

pamphlets: on export of raw wool, 87n.; on East India Co., 97n.; inland navigation, 122n.; enclosures, 155n., 175n.;

imported calicoes, 200n.; cotton industry, 248n., 251n., 252n., 254n., 259n., 264n.; export of cotton twist, 258n.; iron industry, 299n.; population, 345n.; food prices, 387n.; alcoholism, 430n.; Fielding's, on sufferings of the poor, 435n.; workers' association, 441n.

papermakers, 444-5, 446

Papin, Denys, 312, 316, 319, 399

Papplewick, first steam mill at, 334

Paris, Treaty of, 99; water supply: pipes for, 308, steam pump for, 330; Wedgwood's visit to, 396

parish, the: and upkeep of roads, 115; distribution of property in, 143; and enclosures, 167; and paupers, 181, 182, 432-9, 465; and apprentices, 193, 410-11, 413, 469, 470, 473

Parker, John, 372

pasture, rights of, 149-51 (for pasture land, see land)

patents and patent rights, 194, 201n., 210n., 211, 216, 218, 222, 225-6, 242, 286, 287n., 288n., 290, 293n., 294n., 295, 298n., 301n., 306n., 309n., 313n., 320, 321n., 324, 327, 328, 331, 333, 336n., 385; suspensions, lapsing, 196, 227, 285, 286, 295; court cases, 227, 228-32, 243

Paterson, Nathaniel, 195

Paul, Lewis, 209-11, 213-14, 215, 217, 222, 233

pedlars, 111

Peel, Sir Robert (I), 233n., 236, 249, 258, 260, 334, 370, 373n., 397-8, 402, 410, 455, 470, 473-4

Peel, Sir Robert (II), 248, 370, 398

Peel family, 217, 227, 370

Peeters, Maurice, 198

Percival, Dr, 469

Périer, the brothers, 330

petitions: weavers', 79, 424; journeymen tailors', 71-2; inland navigation, 123n., 124n.; enclosures, 150n., 151n., 166n., 167n., 173-4n., 174 and note; cotton industry, 200 and note, 256, 259, 392n.; for grants, 237, 243; for patent rights, 227, 328; for establishing a joint stock company, 250n.; woolcombers', 268n.; iron imports, 282n.; coal prices, 283; woollen trade, 265-6; use of machinery, 403, 406, 408n.; food prices, 426n., 427; combination law, 440n., 446, 447, 448; apprenticeship, 455, 456; arbitration, 459n., 460n., 461n., 462-3

philanthropy, 384, 465-8

piece work, 64n., 463

'piecers', 425

pipes, cast iron, 307, 308

Pitt, William, *see* Chatham, Earl of

Pitt, William (the younger), 255, 259, 260, 295, 389, 390, 392, 393, 397, 412, 434, 447, 458, 459-60

Place, Francis (quoted), 111n., 449n.

plating, gold and silver, 279, 326

Poor Law, 182, 431-4, 440, 452; reform of, 347, 434, 437-8

Poor Rate, 181, 437-9, 443n.

population: growth of, 27, 355-60; theories regarding, 342-8; pre-census lack of statistics, 342-3; first official census, 342, 347; various figures given, 54, 343, 344, 347, 348, 349, 354, 360; average density of, 349, 354; movement of centre of gravity, 182, 349, 354; distribution of, 354 (*see also* maps, 350-3); depopulation of villages after enclosures, 176, 178

porcelain, 386; Chinese, 98

Porto Bello, 'permission ship' of, 99

ports, 92, 100, 104, 105, 107, 274, 283

postal service, 119-20

potatoes, 120, 428, 429, 430

Potter, Humphrey, 317

Potteries, the, 40, 105, 128, 386, 387; potters, 387; pottery, 129, 378, 385, 386n.; export of, 385-6

power, motive: and the factory system, 26, 39, 189, 216n., 246, 338; and definition of a machine, 189-90; and Wyatt's machine, 212; provided by animals, 190, 212, 213, 223, 242, 243; by men, 217, 287; hydraulic, 39, 58, 190, 214, 232, 237, 247, 263, 268, 269, 277, 291, 299-300, 302, 305, 311-12; hydraulic, aided by steam engine, 232, 242, 243, 251, 263, 265, 268, 305, 321, 329; wind, 212, 312n.; steam, 243, 333, 334, 338, 358; steam supersedes hydraulic, 333, 335

Preston, 220, 222, 249, 360n.

prices: foodstuffs, 68, 72, 109n., 163, 347, 426-8; raw silk, 196; cotton goods, 239n., 244; cotton thread, 208, 215, 253; coal, 283; pig iron, 288; bar iron, 289, 293; reduction of, 27; rise in, 173; in relation to wages, 426, 428-9; fixation of, 256

Priestley, William, 293, 379, 380, 383

printing, 191

production, 25-6; controlled by artisan, 59; by merchants, 66, 279, 476; action of foreign trade on, 103; increased by technical processes, 38, 251, 475; freedom of, 260-1; output figures, 61, 238, 296n., 300, 304, 306n.; and free circulation of labour, 434; no statistics for early cotton industry, 252; agricultural, and enclosures, 185

overproduction, 253, 254, 255

means of: ownership of the, 57, 58, 64, 82-3, 90, 192, 193, 279, 441; concentration of the, 25, 250, 476; improvement in the, 368

profit and profits, 27, 90, 185, 214, 233, 234, 238, 253, 295, 323, 329, 330, 370, 400

progress, spirit of, 464-5

protection and protectionism, 84-7, 99, 256-60, 266, 269, 391

puddling, 293-6, 302

pumps and pumping engines, 312-13, 321, 323, 329-30 (*see also* steam engine)

QUARTER SESSIONS, 169, 447, 459, 472

RADCLIFFE, WILLIAM, 63, 239n., 257, 370-1, 374, 442

rails, iron, to replace wooden, 300

railways, 130-1

Rainham estate, 159

Rasbotham, Dorning, 404

Réamur, 296

refining, open hearth, 292 (*see also* puddling)

Rennie, John, 309, 333

rent, farm, 177; for knitting frames, 65

reports and enquiries: agriculture, 138n., 139-40, 162n., 164n.; apprenticeship, 456; canal-building, 126, 129; combinations, 449n.; commercial credit, 255n.; cotton, 225; deforestation, 281; enclosures, 144, 148, 149, 155, 163n., 166n., 179, 185n., 427n.; food prices, 159, 427n., 428n.; hand-loom weavers (1839), 243; iron industry, 272n.; of Manchester Board of Health, 469; Poor Law, 435n.; silk industry, 195; waste lands, 166; woollen industry, 65n., 197n., 262, 266, 267n., 408

revolution, fear of, 437, 438, 445; American, 464; French, 384, 398, 437, 464, 468

Reynolds, Richard, 300, 304, 306, 333, 372, 465

'riders out', 119n.

Riot Act (1769), 401; riots: in old type of industry, 79, 80; turnpike, 115; enclosure, 154, 175; anti-machine, 226, 264, 401, 404-5, 444; Luddite, 405-6; foodstuff prices, 426n., 427; not actuated by revolutionary ideas, 440n.

rivers, deepening and canalization of, 106, 122-3

roads, 112-20, 302, 386, 387

Robertson, J. L., 243

Robinson (of Papplewick), 334

Robison, Sir J., 316n., 319

Roebuck, John, 293, 302-3, 304, 322, 323-4, 325, 328, 329, 372, 374
rotary motion, 321, 332, 333
Rotherham foundries, 304
'roundsmen', 181n., 435n.
Rousseau, J. J., 464, 468
Rovenzon, John, 285, 286
roving frame, 225-6, 232
Royal African Company, 94
Royal Company of Mines, 276, 289
royalties, 207, 227, 276, 295, 330
'run-rig' system, 145n.
Rupert, Prince, 94, 286
Russia, iron from, 280, 293

SADLER, MICHAEL, 473
salt, and salt pans, 74, 129, 303; —— glaze, 386
Savile, Sir George, 296-7
Savery, Thomas, 313
science, first application of to technology, 311, 475
Scotland, Lowlands of: ironworks in, 302-3; strikes in, 463-4
Séguin, Marc, 379
Selden, John, 93
serfs, 74
shearing, mechanical, 407, 425
Sheffield, 274, 275, 279, 280, 296, 297, 303, 349n., 363, 422, 444
sheep, 47, 52n., 87, 154, 155, 163; breeding, 87, 152, 160
Shelburne, Lord, 327, 342
Shepton Mallet, 52, 264
Sheridan, R. B., 259, 390, 449, 455, 474n.
Sherrard, John, 195
ships and shipping, 100, 101, 106-7, 271; and coal trade, 283n.; iron ships, 308
sick clubs, 77n., 385
silk: industry, 104, 193-7; weavers, 81-2, 192n.
Sinclair, Sir John, 162
slave trade, 99, 107
Slavery, Society for the Abolition of, 384
small wares, metal, 104, 274, 325, 326
Smalley, John, 222, 223
Smeaton, John, 298, 303, 318
smelting, 272, 277, 281, 284-92, 296
Smith, Adam, 36-7, 86, 90, 130, 132, 249, 433, 454
smuggling, 87, 99, 193, 196n., 260
Socialism, 472
Society: for the Abolition of Slavery, 384; for the Encouragement of Arts and Manufactures, 215; for the Improvement of the Poorer Classes, 465; for the Prevention of Crime, 465; of Friends, 465; Lunar ——, 379

Soho works, 294, 324, 325-7, 329, 332, 333, 336, 363, 376, 377, 379, 419n., 465
Somerset, 52, 79, 262, 264, 369
South Sea Company, 96, 159
specialization, 56, 58-9, 70 (see also labour, division of)
speculations, 96, 159, 254, 255
Speenhamland Law, 436-7, 457
Spence, Thomas, 440n., 465
spinning, hand, 58, 63-4, 70; mechanical: cotton, 209, 211-12, 221, 224, 234-5, 238; wool, 215, 263-4, 267; and employment of women and children, 410; machines, 40, 210-13, 400; wheel, 58, 63, 217, 218, 219, 321n., 438
Spitalfields, 81, 193, 197; —— Act, 82, 454, 457
squires, 137, 181; and enclosures, 167
Staffordshire, 129, 324, 355, 427
'staple trade', 48, 199, 202
starch factories, 427
'Statesmen' of Cumberland and Westmorland, 140, 141n.
Statute of Artificers, 260, 451-2, 455-6; repeal of, 463
steam, condensation of, 316, 320; engine, 43, 309, 311 et seq.; traction, 332; and population, 355 (see also power)
steel, 274; cast, 296, 303-4; industry, 271, 296; first steelworks, 297
stockings and stocking industry, 50, 223, 224, 374; stocking frame, 191-2; frame knitters, 65, 80-1, 421
Stockport, 196, 249, 360n., 450
strikes, 74, 78-9, 80, 81, 82, 451, 463-4
Strutt, Jedediah, 223, 224, 226, 250n., 371, 374
Stubs, Peter, 372
Stump of Malmesbury, 33
Sturtevant, Simon, 284-5, 286
Sussex, ironworking in, 273, 277, 281
sulphuric acid factory, 303
Svedenstjerna, Erick, 305-6, 319n., 335, 363
sweating system, 73, 244
Sweden, ores from, 272n., 274, 280; metal-working in, 272
Swedenborg, Emanuel, 289
Swift, Jonathan, 289

TAILORS, 71-2
Talbot, Lord, 302
Tamworth, 397
tariffs, 256
taxation, 259, 389; colonial, 99
Taylor, Charles, 245
Taylor, John, 279n.

tea and tea-drinking, 72, 429
teaseling, 58, 84n.
Telford, John, 118
Thames Water Supply Company, 317
Thomas, John, 290
Tiverton, 65, 66, 78, 262, 264, 361
towns, 27, 47, 364; growth of, 355-63;
  woollen industry, of East Anglia,
  Midlands, and south-west, 50-2, 361-2
Townshend, Lord, 159-60
toy industry, 104, 274-5, 325, 326
trade, growth of, and industrial expansion, 35, 62, 90, 91-2; foreign, 67, 98,
  99-108, 132-4, 364, 377, 385, 404n.;
  home, transformation of, 108-12;
  colonial, 199; maritime, 49, 354, 426
  (see also commerce, exports, imports,
  market)
trade regulations, 42, 83-7, 256, 451-6;
  in the woollen industry, 48, 269; cotton industry unhampered by, 204,
  260-1; in metal industry, 278, 444
Trade, Board of, 257
trade unions, origins of, 75, 77 et seq.
  (see also Part III, chap. IV, 440-51, and
  combinations and workers' associations)
transport, 116, 123, 275; rates, 120, 125
treadle wheel, 321 and note
truck system, 73, 76
tubular boilers, 379
Tull, Jethro, 158, 160, 164
Turnpike Act, 114; roads, 115-18; riots,
  115-16

UNEMPLOYMENT: in domestic industry,
  71; owing to enclosures, 175; agricultural, 181; weavers, 200, 215, 217,
  238, 392, 424; cotton industry, 252,
  404, 422, 423; and machinery, 401n.,
  406n., 408 (see also machinery, workers' hostility to); and apprentices,
  455; and Poor Law, 439
Utrecht, Treaty of, 99, 100

VAGRANCY, 432
valves, safety, 317; slide, 321
Vaucansen, 240
villenage, 73-4
'virgate', 145n.
Voltaire, 134

WAGES, 285, 263, 332n., 410n., 418-26,
  440, 447, 456n., 463; in domestic
  industry, 64, 69 et seq., 78; in kind, 73;
  forced down by supply of cheap labour,
  193, 423-4; by industrial crisis, 239,
  404; lack of statistics on, 419-20;
  figures, 421-2; high rates of, 238-9,

268, 422-3; industrial higher than
  agricultural, 421-2; and prices, 419,
  420, 426; and the factory system, 423;
  women's, 425; children's, 410, 425,
  454; and poor rate, 438; fixing rates of,
  456; minimum, principle of, 457-8, 463
Wakefield, 51, 55; market, 110
Wales, 274, 293, 302, 305, 377
Walker, Aaron, 372; Samuel, 297n.,
  303-4
Walpole, Horace, 159, 327
war, effects of on trade, 61, 99, 100, 255,
  257, 263, 401n., 404, 427-8, 438
Warwickshire, 47, 52, 255, 272, 282, 324,
  355
water: frame, 216, 221-3, 224, 227, 230,
  234, 235, 236, 238, 247, 251; power,
  sources of, and distribution of large-
  scale industry, 337; supply, by steam
  pumps, 333; wheel, see power, hydraulic; ways, see inland navigation
Watt, James, 228, 232, 245, 294-5, 298,
  303, 309, 318-35, 368, 374, 377, 378,
  379, 390, 464, 475; 'Watt's governor',
  321; 'Watt's parallelogram', 322
weavers, hand-loom, 34-5, 58-9, 63, 64,
  65, 70-1, 79-80, 110, 204-5, 238-9, 243,
  411, 446, 453, 455-6; cotton, 442-3,
  458-9, 460-4; and unemployment,
  200, 215, 217, 238, 392, 424; wages,
  421, 423, 424, 443n., 458-9
weaving, 224, 238; power-loom, 240,
  243, 244; hand and power-loom side
  by side, 250
Wedgwood, Josiah, 40, 125n., 128, 252n.,
  265, 326, 376, 379, 382-8, 390, 391,
  396, 401-2, 427, 452n., 465
Wesley, John, 387, 464
West Indies, 93, 99, 108, 401n.
West Riding, 51, 56, 61, 262-3, 267, 443
Weston, Sir Richard, 156n.
Whig party, alliance with large-scale
  industry, 259-60
Whitaker, John, 358
Whitbread, Samuel, 458
Whitney, Eli, 245n.
Wigan, 108, 123, 129, 306
Wilberforce, William, 447, 465, 471
Wilkinson, Isaac, 301, 306
Wilkinson, John, 298, 301, 304, 306-7,
  308, 309, 329, 333, 335, 372, 380n.,
  465
Wilson, John, 245, 374
Wiltshire, 262, 264, 354, 369, 424
Winchcombe, John, 33-4, 36
Wolverhampton, 129, 275, 422
women, employment of, 58, 70, 204, 213,
  214, 238, 388, 410, 456n.
wood, replaced by iron in machinery,
  309
Wood, William, 289-90

Woodward, Robert, 414
wool-combers, 78-9, 267, 406, 424-5, 446
wool workers, 'Institution' or 'Community' of, 443-4
woollen industry, 33-5, 43, 47-56, 57-68, 78-80, 199-200, 261-70, 369; crisis in, 436; slower development of, 424
Worcester, Marquess of, 312
Worcestershire, 282, 286
work, hours of, 72, 80, 376, 413, 416-17, 467, 472
workers: associations, 77-82, 441-51; corporation, 80, 192-3; condition of, 57-60, 68-74, 177, 179, 244, 399 et seq., 418 et seq., 440; condition compared with France, 429, to serfdom, 432n.; status of, 416
workhouse, 432, 434
worsted industry, 50n., 71, 263, 267-8; first worsted mill, 265n.

Wyatt, Charles, 209n., 210; John, 209-16, 222, 223, 230n., 231n., 233, 297, 475

'YARDLAND', 145n.
Yarranton, Andrew, 121-2, 273, 282, 411
yeomanry, decline of the, 136-41, 180-1, 184; yeomen, 170, 172, 183, 235, 403; capitalists recruited from, 370, 372-3
Yorkshire, 157, 349, 367, 369, 443, 477; woollen industry, 51, 54, 55, 61-2, 68, 262-9, 335; coal, 263; iron and steel, 272, 276, 303
Young, Arthur, 48, 70, 87, 107, 117, 159n., 161-3, 168, 169, 173, 181, 344, 345, 346, 419, 429, 433n.